BLACK FLIES
Ecology, Population Management,
and Annotated World List

Sponsors

The Pennsylvania State University College of Agriculture
NE–118 Technical Committee
U.S. Department of Agriculture, Cooperative State Research Service
U.S. National Science Foundation
U.S. Public Health Service
World Health Organization
Sandoz/Zoecon, Inc.
Abbott Laboratories
Biochem Products
D. M. Wood

BLACK FLIES

Ecology, Population Management, and Annotated World List

Edited by

KE CHUNG KIM

The Frost Entomological Museum
Department of Entomology
The Pennsylvania State University
University Park, Pennsylvania

and

RICHARD W. MERRITT

Department of Entomology
Michigan State University
East Lansing, Michigan

THE PENNSYLVANIA STATE UNIVERSITY
UNIVERSITY PARK AND LONDON

Library of Congress Cataloging-in-Publication Data

Black flies.

Includes index.
1. Simuliidae. I. Kim, Ke Chung. II. Merritt,
Richard W.
QL537.S55B58   1986   595.77′1   85–43562
ISBN 0-271-00417-7

CONTENTS

IV Ecology of Adults

V Population Management

VI Epidemiology and Control of Simuliid-Borne Diseases

VII Industrial Perspectives

VIII Black Fly Species of the World

CONTRIBUTORS

Peter H. ADLER, Department of Entomology, 114 Long Hall, Clemson University, Clemson, SC 29631

John R. ANDERSON, Division of Entomology and Parasitology, University of California, Berkeley, CA 94720

D. A. T. BALDRY, WHO Onchocerciasis Control Programme, B. P. 549, Ouagadougou, Burkina Faso (Upper Volta), West Africa

William R. BECK, Zoecon Corporation, A Sandoz Company, Palo Alto, CA 94343

John F. BURGER, Department of Entomology, University of New Hampshire, Durham, NH 03824

Robert J. CIBULSKY, Chemical and Agricultural Products Division, Field Research and Development, Abbott Laboratories, North Chicago, IL 60064

M. H. COLBO, Department of Biology, Memorial University of Newfoundland, St. Johns, Newfoundland, Canada A1B 3X9

Douglas A. CRAIG, Department of Entomology, University of Alberta, Edmonton, Alberta, Canada T6G 2E3

Roger W. CROSSKEY, Department of Entomology, British Museum (Natural History), Cromwell Road, London SW7 5BD, United Kingdom

Ken W. CUMMINS, Appalachian Environmental Laboratory, University of Maryland, Frostburg, MD 21532

E. W. CUPP, Department of Entomology, Cornell University, Comstock Hall, Ithaca, NY 14850

Douglas C. CURRIE, Department of Entomology, University of Alberta, Edmonton, Alberta, Canada T6G 2E3

Douglas M. DAVIES, Department of Biology, McMaster University, Hamilton, Ontario, Canada L8S 3K1

J. B. DAVIES, Department of Medical Entomology, Liverpool School of Tropical Medicine, Pembroke Place, Liverpool L3 5QA, United Kingdom

John D. EDMAN, Department of Entomology, Fernald Hall, University of Massachusetts, Amherst, MA 01003

F. J. H. FREDEEN, Research Station, Research Branch, Agriculture Canada, 107 Science Crescent, Saskatoon, Saskatchewan, Canada S7N 0X2

Robert A. FUSCO, Chemical and Agricultural Products Division, Field Research and Development, Abbott Laboratories, North Chicago, IL 60064

Mary M. GALLOWAY, Department of Entomology, University of Manitoba, Winnipeg, Manitoba, Canada R3T 2N2

Rolf GARMS, Bernhard-Nocht-Institut für Schiffs-und-Tropenkrankheiten, Bernhard-Nocht-Strasse 74, D-2000 Hamburg 4, Federal Republic of Germany

Victor I. GOLINI, Department of Biology, McMaster University, Hamilton, Ontario, Canada L8S 4K1

Jorg GRUNEWALD, Tropenmedizinisches Institut, Eberhard-Karls-Universität, D 7400 Tübingen Wilhelmstrasse 31, Federal Republic of Germany

D. G. HAILE, Insects Affecting Man and Animals Research Laboratory, U.S. Department of Agriculture, *Agricultural Research Service,* P.O. Box 14565, Gainesville, FL 32604

David D. HART, Academy of Natural Sciences, 19th and Parkway, Philadelphia, PA 19103, U.S.A.

Ke Chung KIM, The Frost Entomological Museum, Department of Entomology, The Pennsylvania State University, University Park, PA 16802

H. J. KNUTTI, Sandoz, Ltd., Agro Division/Development, CH-4002, Basel, Switzerland

Daniel C. KURTAK, WHO Onchocerciasis Control Programme, B.P. 549, Ouagadougou, Burkina Faso (Upper Volta), West Africa

Lawrence A. LACEY, Vector Biology and Control Project (USAID/MSCI), 1611 North Kenton St., Suite 503, Arlington, VA 22209

Susan B. McIVER, Department of Environmental Biology, University of Guelph, Guelph, Ontario, Canada, N1G 2W1

Stefanie E. O. MEREDITH, Program of Tropical Medicine and International Health, Department of Tropical Public Health, Harvard School of Public Health, 665 Huntington Avenue, Boston, MA 02115

Richard W. MERRITT, Department of Entomology, Michigan State University, East Lansing, MI 48824

Daniel P. MOLLOY, Biological Survey, New York State Museum, The State Education Department, Albany, NY 12230

Bernard PHILIPPON, Chief, Vector Control Unit, WHO Onchocerciasis Control Programme in the Volta River Basin Area (OCP), B.P. 549, Ouagadougou, Burkina Faso (Upper Volta), West Africa

Angela PHILLIPS, Department of Medical Entomology, Liverpool School of Tropical Medicine, Liverpool L3 5QA, United Kingdom

Rory J. POST, Department of Biological Sciences, University of Salford, Salford M5 4WT, United Kingdom

Douglas H. ROSS, Professional Pest Management Division, Zoecon Industries, 12200 Denton Drive, Dallas, TX 75234

Klaus H. ROTHFELS, Department of Botany, University of Toronto, Toronto, Ontario, Canada M5S 1A1

M. W. SERVICE, Department of Medical Entomology, Liverpool School of Tropical Medicine, Pembroke Place, Liverpool L3 5QA, United Kingdom

J. A. SHEMANCHUK, Animal Parasitology Section, Research Station, Agriculture Canada, Lethbridge, Alberta, Canada T1J 4B1

Kenneth R. SIMMONS, Massachusetts Division of Fisheries and Wildlife, Field Headquarters, Westboro, MA 01581

James F. SUTCLIFFE, Department of Biology, University of Waterloo, Waterloo, Ontario, Canada N2L 3G1

Takeshi SUZUKI, Formerly Guatemala-Japan Cooperative Project on Onchocerciasis Research and Control, 1–4–5 Tamatsutsumi, Setagaya-ku, Tokyo, Japan 158

Hiroyuki TAKAOKA, Division of Medical Zoology, Medical College of Oita, Hazama, Oita, Japan

Harold TOWNSON, Department of Medical Entomology, Liverpool School of Tropical Medicine, Liverpool L3 5QA, United Kingdom

Albert H. UNDEEN, Insects Affecting Man and Animals Research Laboratory, U.S. Department of Agriculture, Agricultural Research Service, P.O. Box 14565, Gainesville, FL 32604

James Frank WALSH, Department of Biology, University of Salford, Salford M5 4WT, United Kingdom

D. E. WEIDHAAS, Insects Affecting Man and Animals Research Laboratory, SEA-ARS, P. O. Box 14565, Gainesville, FL 32604

Peter WENK, Tropenmedizinisches Institut Eberhard-Karls-Universität, D 7400 Tübingen Wilhelmstrasse 31, Federal Republic of Germany

Roger S. WOTTON, Department of Life Sciences, University of London, Goldsmiths' College, Rachel McMillan Building, Creek Road, London SE8 3BU, United Kingdom

PREFACE

Black flies (Diptera: Simuliidae) are among the most notorious worldwide pests of man, animals, and birds. Adult females of most species feed on blood, resulting in painful, often allergic reactions by the host. They may cause enormous distress to humans and livestock and thus their abundance causes considerable reduction in outdoor recreational activities and annual economic losses in production and control costs for beef and dairy cattle. Black flies also are serious vectors of disease agents, second only to mosquitoes and ticks. More than 20 million people in tropical Africa and South America are inflicted with onchocerciasis (river blindness) caused by a filarial worm transmitted by black flies.

Because of their economic and medical importance, black flies have been intensively studied on all aspects: ecological, taxonomic, biochemical, cytogenetic, and control. Tremendous progress has been made in many areas of black fly research during the last ten years, particularly in North America through the Northeast Regional Project on Black Flies (NE–118) and in tropical Africa and America through the Onchocerciasis program of the World Health Organization.

Although a large body of knowledge exists about black flies, these diverse data have not been subjected to a vigorous synthesis. Lack of synthesis also owes to the rapidity at which new and existing discoveries are independently generated in the many laboratories throughout the world. Accordingly, it is timely that the opportunity in which isolated studies in diverse fields can be integrated into an overall, cohesive understanding of the black flies is provided for researchers in the black fly community.

An international conference was organized to bring together a significant number of black fly researchers to exchange ideas and recent developments toward an overall synthesis, with emphasis on systematics, biology, ecology, and control of both immatures and adults. The *International Conference on Ecology and Population Management of Black Flies (Diptera: Simuliidae)* was convened 28–31 May 1985 at The Pennsylvania State University. The world's leading biologists working with black flies and simuliid-related problems were assembled to address the ecology and population management of black flies, as well as the epidemiology and control of onchocerciasis. The goals of this conference were to: (1) exchange information and ideas, (2) summarize and synthesize recent advances, (3) present new information, methodologies, and approaches, and (4) identify data gaps and future research needs and prospects for population management of simuliids.

The conference was attended by 48 invited speakers and more than 100 participants. Participants represented 12 countries: Canada, Central African Republic, Federal Republic of Germany, France, Iceland, Japan, Malawi, New Zealand, Switzerland, United Kingdom, United States of America, and West Africa.

The conference was carefully structured to avoid overlap with material in the 1981 book published by Academic Press entitled *Blackflies: The Future for Biological Methods in Integrated Control*, edited by Marshall Laird. Participants of the conference specifically concentrated on post-1978 developments and their efforts directed toward a synthesis of ideas and future research needs, rather than a review of literature.

The last recent conference on North American black flies was held 30 January–2 February 1977 at Dixville Notch, New Hampshire, with participants primarily from Canada and the northeastern United States. Prior to the Dixville Notch conference, there were three international (primarily North American) conferences on black flies. The first conference was held 1 November 1958 at the Entomology Laboratory, Canada Department of Agriculture, Guelph, Ontario, with fourteen scientists participating, one from the United States and thirteen from Canada. The second conference was convened 23–24 September 1960 at Queen's University Biological Station, Chaffey's Locks, Ontario, in which twenty-five scientists participated, all from Canada and the United States. Two years later, the third conference on black flies was convened 14–15 September 1962 at the Wildlife Research Station, Ontario Department of Lands and Forests, Algonquin Park, Ontario, Canada. This conference was attended by thirty-two scientists, including twenty-five from Canada, six from the United States, three from the United Kingdom, and two from Upper Volta.

After a relatively inactive period in the 1960s and the early 1970s, the Northeast Regional Project on Black Flies, entitled "Black Fly Damage Threshold, Biology and Control" (NE–118), was launched in 1977 with nine Northeastern states participating: Delaware, Maine, Maryland, Massachusetts, Michigan, New Hampshire, New York, Pennsylvania (joined 1978), and West Virginia.

Every annual meeting of the NE–118 Technical Committee has attracted many black fly researchers from other organizations and regions throughout North America and sometimes from Europe. Enthusiasm and scientific interests of the NE–118 Technical Committee have led to the International Conference on Ecology and Population Management of Black Flies. This book is the direct result of this conference. All manuscripts were revised from the conference drafts and reviewed through a rigorous referee process. Titles of many chapters were changed and three papers were added: Chapters 30 and 31 on industrial perspectives, and Chapter 32, An Annotated Checklist of the World Black Flies (Diptera: Simuliidae).

The book is divided into eight parts. In the first two sections, the functional role of black flies in stream ecosystems and the aspects of black fly systematics are discussed, respectively. The third section deals with questions on ecology of immatures. This is followed by the fourth section on behavior and ecology of adult black flies. In the fifth, sixth, and seventh sections, the principles and various strategies of population management of black flies and control of simuliid-borne diseases are presented. Finally, the last section presents, for the first time, an annotated checklist of the world black flies.

The conference and the publication of this book could not have been possible without the financial support of the following organizations and individuals: The Pennsylvania State University (College of Agriculture), NE–118 Technical Committee, U.S. Department of Agriculture, Cooperative State Research Service, U.S. National Science Foundation, U.S. Public Health Service, World Health Organization, Sandoz/Zoecon, Inc., Abbott Laboratories, Biochem Products, and D. M. Wood. Their contributions are duly acknowledged. We are indebted to members of NE–118 Technical Committee and the Organizing Committee (P. H. Adler, J. D. Edman, K. C. Kim, D. Leonard, and R. W. Merritt) for their encouragement and support. Our special thanks for their personal interest and support go to: Robert C. Riley, Principal Entomologist, Cooperative State Research Service, U.S. Department of Agriculture; Charles R. Krueger, Associate Dean, College of Agriculture, The Pennsylvania State University; and Charles W. Pitts, Head, and his office staff, Department of Entomology, The Pennsylvania State University.

We acknowledge the following publishers for permission to use the figures indicated: Elsevier Publications (Cambridge) for Figure 25.6 and Springer-Verlag (Heidelberg) for Figures 16.1, 16.2, and 16.4.

We are deeply indebted to Mrs. June Bloom for her excellent assistance in developing and coordinating the conference and copyediting the manuscripts, and also to Allen L. Norrbom, Thomas A. Miller, and others in the Department of Entomology, The Pennsylvania State University, for their kind assistance in the conference operation. Our appreciation is owed to the authors of this book for their congeniality and kind efforts in prompt revision of their chapters and in reviewing other chapters. Finally, we thank the staff of The Pennsylvania State University Press for their efforts in the publication of this book.

KE CHUNG KIM
University Park, PA

RICHARD W. MERRITT
East Lansing, MI

Part I Introduction

1 THE FUNCTIONAL ROLE OF BLACK FLIES IN STREAM ECOSYSTEMS

Kenneth W. Cummins

I have spent a significant portion of the last twenty years investigating the functional roles played by organisms in running-water ecosystems. At the outset it should be made clear that here running-water ecosystems are defined as the wetted channel together with the inseparably linked riparian zone—the upper bank of small streams to the gallery forest and floodplain of larger rivers (Cummins et al. 1984).

In considering the ecological role of simuliids, it is useful to adopt a functional perspective. The taxonomic view (i.e., the species is the basic unit of ecology) is not incompatible with the functional approach. If groups of species are viewed as operating in the same mode with regard to resource utilization, habitat exploitation, etc., then processes at the population level dictate such things as the overall turnover rate of given components such as fine particulate organic matter (FPOM). An example illustrating that invertebrate taxonomy is generally based on functional morphology is the fact that *An Introduction to the Aquatic Insects of North America* (Merritt and Cummins 1984) can be used to "key out" Australian, West African, or South American aquatic insects even though the resulting taxa are incorrect. For example, the leptophlebeid mayflies and leptocerid caddisflies have undergone significant radiation, assuming body forms represented by other families in North America and Europe. Also, clearly, a uniformly applied species concept for microbes through fish is not tractable. Microbiologists have long used a functional approach in their "species" separations.

Food found in the digestive tract is not a reliable indicator of functional feeding group. The acquisition system (Fig. 1.1) can result in a wide range of materials being ingested. For example, the food of filtering collectors is essentially the entire spectrum of resource material in the system (detritus plus microbes, algae, microinvertebrates). Further, the particle sizes observed may or may not reflect those actually ingested because of aggregation or dissociation.

As larvae, black flies (Simuliidae) fit into the resource-utilization functional groups termed filtering collectors or suspension feeders (e.g., *Simulium, Prosimulium, Cnephia*) and scrapers (e.g., *Twinnia, Gymnopais, Crozetia*) (Wallace et al. 1977, Wal-

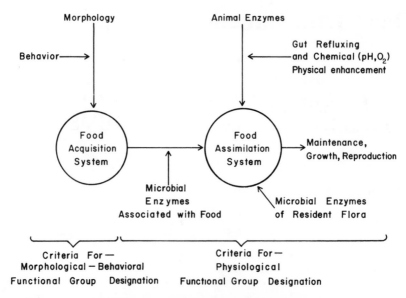

FIG. 1.1 Simuliid functional groups: acquisition and assimilation systems.

lace and Merritt 1980, Merritt et al. 1984). Simuliids are categorized with the habit group termed clingers, which are essentially restricted to the more rapidly flowing portions of running waters. A system-level functional view of filtering-collector black flies is shown in Figure 1.2, whereby their role in resource turnover (energy flux and material cycling) is emphasized. A functional view of resource relationships for scraping black flies is given in Figure 1.3. Although much more difficult, a classification

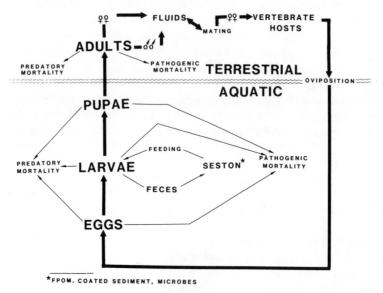

FIG. 1.2 Summary of roles of black flies in running-water ecosystems. Larvae-filtering collectors and associated terrestrial habitats (adults).

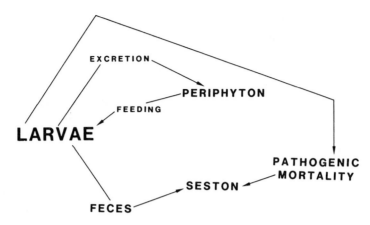

F<small>IG</small>. 1.3 Modification of Figure 1.2 for black fly larvae belonging to the scraper functional group.

into functional groups based on the assimilation system (Fig. 1.1) would be of greater resolution and rather analogous to the functional view of microbial "species," which is based on organic substrate utilization (e.g., cellulose degraders).

Eggs and pupae of black flies enter the general nonfeeding portion of the interactive system depicted in Figure 1.2, the pharate-feeding pupae being an exception (Cupp 1981). The adults, being terrestrial, enter the terrestrial (and secondarily the aquatic) predator and pathogenic mortality fluxes. Because the adult females of many species are pests or vectors of disease for man and domestic animals, they have received special attention.

The treatment that follows will concentrate on the quantitative and qualitative importance of black flies to stream ecosystems as components of the filtering-collector and scraper functional groups. The role of black flies in lotic (eggs, larvae, pupae) and terrestrial (adults) ecosystems can be broadly categorized as their participation in food webs—that is, utilization of and contribution to organic-matter fluxes, and serving as prey for invertebrate and vertebrate predators. The sources and fates of the organic matter and some of the predators differ for the eggs, larvae, pupae, and adults. In addition, the life cycle of some black fly species involves the transfer of disease agents, for example, to mammals, such as man. Thus the adults of certain species are considered a nuisance pest (e.g., in Canada, Alaska, and the northeastern United States), or they are the vectors of disease agents, such as the filarial parasite *Onchocerca volvulus*.

LARVAL UTILIZATION OF ORGANIC MATTER

In all considerations of the ecological role of black flies, which is taken here to mean function within the ecosystems of which various black fly species are components, it is necessary to consider both quantitative and qualitative terms of reference.

Studies of stream ecosystems that have measured particulate organic matter in storage (benthic) and in transport (sestonic) have shown that physical conditions influence annual budgets more than does biological processing (Fisher and Likens

1973, Cummins et al. 1983). In a broad, comparative investigation of streams, known as the "River Continuum" study (Sedell et al. 1978, Vannote et al. 1980, Minshall et al. 1983) and in subsequent studies (e.g., Wallace et al. 1982), the dominance of ultrafine transported (sestonic) organic matter (UTOM: 0.45 μm up to 50 μm) has been demonstrated for a wide range of running-water types. UTOM constitutes 50% or more of the organic particulates in transport and a quarter of the total organic matter, including dissolved, which is typically approximately 50% of the total. It should be noted that the percent estimate includes organics adsorbed to mineral surfaces in the UTOM size category as well as detrital fragments, free microbes, and microalgal cells.

Quantitative Role

Many investigators have concluded that black fly larvae filter-feed primarily on particles in the UTOM size range (e.g., Williams et al. 1961, Chance 1970, Wotton 1977) and can efficiently ingest particles < 2 μm (e.g., Fredeen 1964; Wotton 1976, 1977, 1978a, 1978b). There is evidence that larger particles (100–150 μm) can be preferentially filtered (Kurtak 1978, Merritt et al. 1978), which may be important in driving the smaller particles through the gut (Colbo and Wotton 1981). Thus black fly larvae draw their food resource from the dominant particle-size category of the seston. Filtering (and gathering) collectors that feed on ultrafine particulates are not likely to have a significant effect on this most abundant size category.

Particle filtering efficiencies of 1–10% (Kurtak 1978) by black flies at local microsites also provide for little quantitative impact. Wallace et al. (1983) demonstrated that total invertebrate removal with methoxychlor resulted in a significant increase in seston release from a study reach of a small stream during a stable flow period. Although black fly larvae, as a portion of the collector functional group, undoubtedly contribute to such whole system effects, their role is still minor (Merritt et al. 1984).

Voshell (1985) has attempted to estimate the effect of the black fly *S. jenningsi* on the production of other invertebrates below an impoundment. The estimated effect, excluding midges, was about 11% (about 15% on Cheumatopsyche). Such estimates are extremely difficult to make and are based on a large number of measurements, all of which have their own error terms.

For those black fly species that are obligate scrapers (grazers), analysis of their quantitative role in running-water ecosystems is subject to the myriad problems attendant to the scraper functional group in general (e.g., see review by Gregory 1983). Scrapers may have a quantitatively significant effect on algal periphyton community structure, but not on production. That is, scrapers often shift the algal community to small, rapid turnover cells and colonies from larger, slower-growing forms (Gregory 1983).

For some species, the importance of scraping (grazing) has not been evaluated. It must be remembered that: (1) the presence of algae in the gut does not prove scraping, as there are all types of cells in all sorts of conditions in the seston; and (2) release of a viable cell in the feces does not prove nonutilization of algae or bacteria, because extracellular release (exudates, enzymes) may be significant and be utilized very efficiently (Lawson et al. 1984). Filtering collector black fly larvae may function as facultative scrapers under certain conditions (see Currie and Craig, this volume). The significance of this can only be judged when accompanied by growth measurement expressed as efficiencies, that is, the proportion of ingestion converted to growth. Possibly at very low seston densities, facultative scraping may provide for maintenance or some short-term survival level of weight loss that could be adaptive. However, behavioral drifting would seem a more likely first response to such conditions. At very high periphyton densities, feeding by brushing away loosely attached algae may require less energy than filtering, but current and/or oxygen depletion (at night) may preclude long-term residence at such microsites. As Chance (1978) has suggested, scraping (browsing) may actually function to clean surfaces for better silk attachment.

Qualitative Role

As Short and Maslin (1977) showed, there may be a growth-stimulating effect of a shredder on a collector; the presence of one collector species may have a significant qualitative effect on another. Thus perhaps the most important qualitative role played by black fly larvae is to change detrital particle size—from the UTOM (ultrafine) to the fine particulate organic matter category (FPOM: 50 μm–1 mm) and to change its quality. As shown in Figure 1.1, resident gut microflora (and fauna) potentially can be highly significant in the process of qualitative change. Such change would not only be biochemical in nature but would also involve an alteration in the microbial components from those associated with the food particle to those sloughed from the digestive system and incorporated into the feces. Coprophagy may be important (Wotton 1980), as it seems most likely that material passed through the digestive tracts of one species will be maximally useful to another, assuming gut enzyme and microbial systems to be different. An example of this sort of mechanism was found in the mayfly *Paraleptophlebia* and phantom cranefly *Ptychoptera*, which occur in the same reach of a western Oregon stream. Each produces fecal pellets outside the range of particles they ingest (*Ptychoptera*, larger; *Paraleptophlebia*, smaller), and in the laboratory they readily consume each other's feces (Cummins, unpublished observations).

In order to evaluate adequately the qualitative and quantitative role of black fly larvae in any running-water system, experimental manipulation is required. If a truly selective toxin for Simuliidae were developed, for example, *Bacillus thuringiensis* serotype H–14, it would constitute the ideal experimental tool for evaluating the role of black flies in stream seston dynamics. Field experiments of the type conducted by Wallace et al. (1983) with methoxychlor would allow comparisons between control streams (reaches) and treated ones as to changes in the quantity, size distribution, and quality of seston and changes in periphyton, invertebrate community structure, etc., when black flies are removed. Although perhaps beyond the resolution of field measurement, it is the approach most likely to detect any qualitative changes.

It is important to note that criticism has often been leveled at basic research that the questions addressed and the answers obtained are not relevant, at least in the short term, to important management and/or control problems. The historical record is clear, however, that most significant advances in the solution of problems as

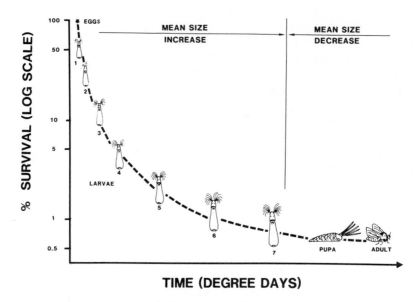

FIG. 1.4 Generalized survivorship curve for Simuliidae.

perceived by man have been founded on an understanding provided by basic research, although, with time lags, frequently in the range of a decade. The other side
of the coin is that an enormous amount of application has yielded little or no useful
information for basic science. A case in point is the extensive use of pesticides to
eradicate black flies; although nontarget effects may be assessed, no information is
gathered on system function, for example, seston dynamics.

Mortality

As shown in Figure 1.4, the data on black flies indicate that they exhibit the negative
exponential survivorship (mortality) curve typical of insects. That is, probability of
dying is greatest in the early stages and decreases with age. Mortality at the beginning (egg and first instar) and survivorship at the end (adults) of the life cycle
approach 100%. The major numerical mortality is in the first stages, while the major
biomass mortality might be in the later stages (Fredeen 1959, Reisen 1975). May
(1983) has argued convincingly that animal mortality, including insects, may largely
be due to pathogenic causes. In this view, prey are important to predators, but not
the reverse. Predation is merely an alternate source of mortality, which would still
occur in its absence. The importance of this relationship is that, from a system
perspective, the contribution of simuliids to the seston as a result of pathogenic
death may be greater than their impact on the seston during the period of preimaginal feeding (Figs. 1.2 and 1.3). Also, the role of black flies as carriers and dispersing
agents of pathogens (Weiser and Undeen 1981) is potentially of considerable intra-
and interspecific importance.

As potential prey for invertebrate and vertebrate predators in running waters,
black flies are but one component of the prey base (e.g., see review by Davies

1981). Although their location in rapid-flowing microhabitats may restrict potential benthic predators, their frequent occurrence in the drift makes them available to many. Again, the contribution by black flies alone is probably not of primary quantitative importance. However, Voshell (1985) has estimated that black flies could account directly (21%) and indirectly (7%, i.e., as an intermediate prey) for a total of approximately 28% of the production of the helmgrammite *Corydalus cornutus.*

The details of stream drift bear significantly on the ecological role of larval simuliids inasmuch as their dispersal is important in making them available to predators and, through location at the most efficient filtering sites, maximizing their impact on the FPOM food resource. The role of drift, and the mechanism by which the response is elicited, has long been of interest in aquatic entomology and is presently an area of major controversy. The distinction between accidental and behavioral drift is of particular interest. Black flies have been considered behavioral drifters (Colbo and Wotton 1981), but the level at which the behavior operates has not been shown. If animals become more active in accordance with some light schedule (for example, night active), they may be more susceptible to accidental dislodgment into the drift.

The exact role played by the diurnal light cycle in the drift phenomenon is not clear. There may be analogies with recent studies with zooplankton that have raised significant questions concerning the role of light in controlling vertical migration (e.g., Forward et al. 1984). Haney et al. (1984) have shown that both absolute light intensity and rate of change in intensity are involved in the drift response of stream insects. If black fly drift is primarily behavioral, is it in response to food quantity or quality, intra- and/or interspecific crowding, insufficient current and/or low oxygen conditions, predator avoidance, some pathogenically induced change in photo-, rheo-, or geotactic response, or some complex combination of some or all of these factors? Disney (1972) observed increased night drift of simuliids in experimental channels when night-active mayflies were introduced, suggesting dislodgment or avoidance through interspecific interaction. Colbo and Moorhouse (1979) reported that drift of first-instar black fly larvae reached peak levels at midday and declined at night, when older larvae predominated. In such studies of size-specific drift, it is important to relate the population density of the various ages available to drift.

ENVIRONMENTAL PROTECTION AND DEGRADATION

In a general way, the initial role of black flies was essentially to protect the environment from the vastly accelerated alteration of environmental systems in space and time by man. Because of the massive application of pesticides used in attempts at black fly eradication, they have played a role in subsequent wide-scale environmental deterioration resulting from effects on nontarget organisms and the opening of heretofore undeveloped regions for exploitation. Many long-term effects certainly have yet to be realized. The area of pest and disease vector control will be treated in detail in other chapters. One observation, however, is relevant here. Despite very extensive attempts, neither eradication nor culturing under controlled conditions has been completely successful—"we can't kill them and we can't grow them" (an exception is *S. decorum;* Simmonds and Edman 1978).

SUMMARY

Thus the role of larval simuliids in aquatic ecosystems is largely qualitative, representing only small components of system energy flux and material cycling. The qualitative roles concern feeding (impact on seston and periphyton), being fed upon (food of predators or their feces and corpses as part of the seston), and as habitats (resident gut organisms) and substrates (pathogens) for a variety of microorganisms. Inasmuch as many species belong to the filtering collectors that can remove ultrafine (< 50 μm > 0.45 μm) particles from the passing water column, they may constitute a critical conversion from this excessively abundant size fraction, which is likely high in quality, to a larger dimension, represented by their feces, which is in a size range available to a greater number of collector species. Adult simuliids have played roles both as protectors of and the stimulus for degradation of running water and associated riparian environments by man.

Epilogue

Today I salute the clever simuliid
though not as robust as your average tipulid

By circlet of hooks they are firmly attached
a feat many lesser bugs never have matched

They feed in the current on tiny debris
known fondly as F-POM by you and by me.

It's hard to believe that this filtering collector
is the juvenile precursor of a dread gnat spector

For once they emerge from their "antlered" cocoon
to buzz 'round about' some swampy lagoon

They're the scourge of fishermen, and aboriginal native
so, control of the fly has become quite creative

After spraying chem poisons we've come to our senses
and dealt them a blow with *B. thuringiensis*

But this wonderful paradox persists all the same
We can't kill them in nature—nor grow them as tame!

Acknowledgments

This paper was prepared with the support of the U.S. Department of Energy, Grant No. DE–FG05–85ER60301. However, any opinions, findings, conclusions, or recommendations expressed herein are those of the author and do not necessarily reflect the views of DOE. Many important suggestions and criticisms in preparing this manuscript were made by Dr. Margaret A. Wilzbach.

LITERATURE CITED

Chance, M. M. 1978. The functional morphology of the mouthparts of black fly larvae (Diptera: Simuliidae). *Quaest. Entomol.* 6:245–284.

Colbo, M. H., and D. E. Moorhouse. 1979. The ecology of preimaginal Simuliidae (Diptera) in South-Eastern Queensland, Australia. *Hydrobiologia* 63:63–79.

Colbo, M. H., and R. S. Wotton. 1981. Preimaginal black fly bionomics. Pp. 209–226 in M. Laird Ed., *Blackflies: the future for biological methods in integrated control.* Academic Press, New York and London. 399 pp.

Cummins, K. W., J. R. Sedell, F. J. Swanson, G. W. Minshall, S. G. Fisher, C. E. Cushing, R. C. Petersen, and R. L. Vannote. 1983. *Organic matter budgets for stream ecosystems: problems in their evaluation.* Pp. 299–353 in J. R. Barnes and G. W. Minshall, Eds., *Stream ecology, application and testing of general ecological theory.* Plenum, New York. 399 pp.

Cummins, K. W., G. W. Minshall, J. R. Sedell, C. E. Cushing, and R. C. Petersen. 1984. Stream ecosystem theory. *Verh. Int. Verein. Limnol.* 22:1818–27.

Cupp, W. E. 1981. Black fly physiology. Pp. 199–206 in M. Laird, Ed., *Black flies: the future for biological methods in integrated control.* Academic Press, New York and London. 399 pp.

Davies, D. M. 1981. Predators on black flies. Pp. 139–158 in M. Laird, Ed., *Blackflies: the future for biological methods in integrated control.* Academic Press, New York and London. 399 pp.

Disney, R. H. L. 1972. Observations on chicken-biting black flies in Cameroon with a discussion of parous rates of *Simulium damnosum. Ann. Trop. Med. Parasitol.* 66:149–158.

Fisher, S. G., and G. E. Likens. 1973. Stream ecosystem: organic energy budget. *BioScience* 22:33–35.

Forward, R. B., T. W. Cronin, and D. E. Stearns. 1984. Control of diel vertical migration: photoresponses of a larval crustacean. *Limnol. Oceanogr.* 29:146–154.

Fredeen, F. J. H. 1959. Rearing black fly larvae in the laboratory (Diptera: Simuliidae). *Can. Entomol.* 91:73–83.

———. 1964. Bacteria as food for black fly larvae (Diptera: Simuliidae) in laboratory cultures and in natural streams. *Can. J. Zool.* 42:527–548.

Gregory, S. V. 1983. Plant-herbivore interactions in stream ecosystems. Pp. 157–189 in J. R. Barnes and G. W. Minshall, Eds., *Stream ecology, application and testing of general ecological theory.* Plenum, New York. 399 pp.

Haney, J. F., T. R. Beaulieu, R. P. Berry, D. P. Mason, C. R. Miner, E. S. McLean, K. L. Price, M. A. Trout, R. A. Vinton, and S. J. Weiss. 1983. Light intensity and relative light change as factors regulating stream drift. *Arch. Hydrobiol.* 97:73–88.

Kurtak, D. C. 1978. Efficiency of filter feeding of black fly larvae (Diptera: Simuliidae). *Can. J. Zool.* 56:1608–23.

May, R. M. 1983. Parasitic infections as regulators of animal populations. *Am. Scientist* 71:36–45.

Merritt, R. W., M. M. Mortland, E. E. Gersabeck, and D. H. Ross. 1978. X-ray diffraction analysis of particles ingested by filter-feeding animals. *Entomol. Exp. Appl.* 24:27–34.

Merritt, R. W., K. W. Cummins, T. M. Burton. 1984. The role of aquatic insects in the processing and cycling of nutrients. Pp. 134–163 in V. H. Resh and D. M. Rosenbert, Eds., *The ecology of aquatic insects.* Praeger, New York. 625 pp.

Minshall, G. W., R. C. Petersen, K. W. Cummins, T. L. Bott, J. R. Sedell, C. E. Cushing, and R. L. Vannote. 1983. Interbiome comparison of stream ecosystem dynamics. *Ecol. Monogr.* 53:1–25.

Reisen, W. K. 1975. Quantitative aspects of *Simulium virgatum* Cog. and S. species life history in a southern Oklahoma stream. *Ann. Entomol. Soc. Am.* 68:949–954.

Sedell, J. R., R. J. Naiman, K. W. Cummins, G. W. Minshall, and R. L. Vannote. 1978. Transport of particulate organic matter in streams as a function of physical processes. *Verh. Int. Verein. Limnol.* 20:1366–75.

Short, R. A., and P. E. Maslin. 1977. Processing of litter by a stream detritivore: effect on nutrient availability to collectors. *Ecology* 58:935–938.

Simmons, K. R., and J. D. Edman. 1978. Successful mating, oviposition, and complete generation rearing of the multivoltine black fly *Simulium decorum* (Diptera: Simuliidae). *Can. J. Zool.* 56:1223–25.

Vannote, R. L., G. W. Minshall, K. W. Cummins, J. R. Sedell, and C. E. Cushing. 1980. The river continuum concept. *Can. J. Fish. Aquat. Sci.* 37:130–137.

Voshell, J. R., Jr. 1985. Trophic basis of production for macroinvertebrates in the New River below Bluestone Dam. Rept. West Virginia Dept. Natural Resources. 83 pp.

Wallace, J. B., J. R. Webster, and W. R. Woodall. 1977. The role of filter feeders in flowing waters. *Arch. Hydrobiol.* 79:506–532.

Wallace, J. B., and R. W. Merritt. 1980. Filter-feeding ecology of aquatic insects. *Ann. Rev. Entomol.* 25:103–132.

Wallace, J. B., J. R. Webster, and T. Cuffney. 1982. Stream detritus dynamics: regulation of invertebrate consumers. *Oecologia* 53:197–200.

Weiser, J., and A. H. Undeen. 1981. Diseases of black flies. Pp. 181–196 in M. Laird, Ed., *Blackflies: the future for biological methods in integrated control*. Academic Press, New York and London. 399 pp.

Williams, T. R., R. C. Connolly, H. B. N. Hynes, and W. E. Kershaw. 1961. Size of particles ingested by Simulium larvae. *Ann. Trop. Med. Parasitol.* 55:125–127.

Wotton, R. S. 1976. Evidence that black fly larvae can feed on particles of colloidal size. *Nature* (London) 261–697.

———. 1977. The size of particles ingested by moorland stream black fly larvae (Simuliidae). *Oikos* 29:332–335.

———. 1978a. The feeding rate of *Metacnephia tredecimatum* larvae (Diptera: Simuliidae) in a Swedish lake outlet. *Oikos* 30:121–125.

———. 1978b. Growth, respiration, and assimilation of black larvae (Diptera: Simuliidae) in a lake outlet in Finland. *Oecologica* 33:279–290.

———. 1980. Coprophagy as an economic feeding tactic in black fly larvae. *Oikos* 34:282–286.

Part II Systematics

2   THE FUTURE OF BLACK FLY TAXONOMY

Roger W. Crosskey

The taxonomist who works on insects, especially on what Americans call a high-visibility group, is not often given to contemplating the future or adopting the guise of a prophet. For the museum taxonomist the classical requirements of the job (identification, classification, curation) leave little time for crystal gazing, and taxonomists as much as others must publish if they are not to perish. Now and again, however, it is as well for any taxonomist to pause awhile and reflect on how the taxonomy of his chosen group stands today, and where, with good fortune, it might stand tomorrow. In these few pages I shall attempt a little forecasting of where we appear to be headed, based upon a stock-taking of the status quo and the potential of the varied strands in our current black fly taxonomy.

Does black fly taxonomy have a future at all? To this, at least, we can on the evidence of the present answer yes with conviction. Interest in the Simuliidae has grown dramatically in the last decade or two, and it seems unlikely to abate in the near future. The literature swells prodigiously, and "black fly" and "onchocerciasis" are becoming household words. Taxonomy has shared significantly in the spreading concern over black flies as pests and vectors: it has moved from the wings to center stage as the problem of species complexes has made it increasingly obvious that a more perfected system is a *sine qua non* if biological data are to be rightly interpreted. In West Africa the preplanning of onchocerciasis vector-control schemes is enmeshed with the fundamentals of *Simulium damnosum* complex taxonomy—and to such an extent that sibling species identifications are prime determinants of control-area limits. An appraisal of today's taxonomy and the directions it is taking is therefore wholly germane to any review of black fly ecology and population management.

THE FAUNAL AND GEOGRAPHICAL BACKGROUND

Faunal studies have traditionally been the province of the taxonomist, supplemented once in a while by the ecologist with a taxonomic bent, and the future will no doubt still expect the taxonomist to be the prime generator of faunistic works—the provider of keys and treatises. These staples of the taxonomist's trade should not, in the current enthusiasm for new taxonomic techniques, be demeaned or forgotten. For as far ahead as we can see we shall need good local taxonomically-based publications—the provincial identification key or the regional monograph. These are the works that give faunal perspective and provide practical working tools for the nontaxonomist (especially the field ecologist); the burgeoning interest in black flies can only swell the demand for them.

There are too few monographs at present, a fact reflecting the dearth of taxonomists working on simuliids, inadequate material, and the tediously slow nature of careful morphotaxonomy. Only the Palaearctic and Afrotropical regions have monographic coverage, and the work for the latter (Freeman and de Meillon 1953) is now over thirty years old. Lack of a comprehensive Nearctic monograph is surprising in view of the attention that black flies have otherwise received in North America because of their socioeconomic importance.

Black flies are nearly cosmopolitan, and about 1,450 described and named species are valid on available evidence (to 1984). Faunal knowledge, though, is very uneven, with parts of the globe (e.g., high Himalayas, Bolivia, Solomon Islands) largely terra incognita. The central fact to be recognized is that there is no such thing as a well-known fauna; there are only some faunas better known than others. Reference to England (a country with a history of study) demonstrates this point: within 200 kilometers of London in the last ten years have been found (a) a highly distinctive morphospecies of *Metacnephia* new to science, (b) a distinctive and mainly Mediterranean morphospecies breeding in several larger rivers, (c) four sibling species in the morphospecies *Simulium vernum,* and (d) several siblings in other morphospecies so far investigated. Similar findings could be cited for the larger geographical scale of North America or West Africa, other areas where taxonomists have been especially active. The conclusion is that we have only scratched the surface, even for the areas we know best, and there is no foreseeable end to the work still needed if we are to acquire a more profound knowledge of world forms or even local faunas. Routine faunistics is slow work, and it could occupy an army of taxonomists merely at the morphological level of study.

REFERENCE COLLECTIONS

An obvious yet neglected fact, insufficiently attended even by the taxonomists, is that taxonomy depends on its raw material. Without new influx of simuliid specimens there is little prospect of future taxonomic advance. Useful morphotaxonomic work can still be done on material already existing in institutional collections, especially by pooling specimens through loan and exchange, but the best simuliid collections are soon found wanting when the taxonomist attempts critical revisionary/comparative work. Few collections hold material that adequately covers the black fly taxa in their geographical area of interest—or if all species are present, then only some are represented by larvae, pupae, and reared-associated adults.

Major collections are few. The most comprehensive is at the British Museum (Natural History), which has a worldwide collection (1985) of 685 species; this is nearly half of the world species, but many are represented by very few specimens. The main collections in North America (U.S. National Museum, American Museum of Natural History, Canadian National Collection) are primarily New World, and that of the Academy of Sciences in Leningrad is preponderantly Palaearctic. Much smaller collections in many other centers have mainly local or historical importance.

Investigators in countries where black flies have until lately been almost unknown (e.g., China, Ecuador, Portugal) are beginning to form new local collections. These have great potential as repositories of material for future taxonomic studies. The old-established museums cannot go as far as might be thought to help in the formation of new collections, because even the largest have little disposable material (i.e., specimens of the same sex or life stage with identical data). The "return" of specimens to their countries of origin, an appealing idea to less-developed countries, would weaken the major resource museums, where material has been assembled and cared for over a century and more, and thus be detrimental to the future development of the morphotaxonomy at the places where it can best be done on a global or regional basis. New local collections should be formed *ab initio* from freshly collected material.

Most simuliid taxonomists are experienced collectors, but for financial or other reasons they cannot always reach the places from which material is needed. Nontaxonomists are helping nowadays to build up reference collections by depositing "voucher" specimens related to fieldwork in museums, but this is not yet routine practice. Such voucher specimens are valuable for future taxonomic research and to verify former identifications. (When a field study or control scheme is over, any accumulated material should go to a taxonomic center rather than be abandoned on the dusty ledges of the field laboratory.)

Apart from the need for material, there is the matter of its quality. The taxonomist is sometimes expected to perform miracles of identification on indifferent material. Black flies are not hard to preserve well (recommended methods in Crosskey, in press), and voucher specimen collections should emphasize quality. A modicum of material well preserved has more value for future studies than a jarful of rubbed and fragmenting specimens.

TRENDS IN TAXA DESCRIPTION

An interesting question is whether descriptive morphotaxonomy and its associated formal naming of new taxa is on the decline. Is there any sign of a slackening in the rate of description of new species or of new genera/subgenera? What does the future hold in this regard?

A review of the present situation and of recent trends is illuminating, and it can form the basis on which to forecast how things are likely to stand in, for convenience, the year 2000. Prediction beyond that date is more hazardous.

To the end of 1984 the literature contained 1,990 names for species-level taxa (forms and subspecies subsumed in "species"). Of these, 1,947 are "available" in the technical meaning of the *International Code of Zoological Nomenclature* and can be legitimately used for recognized species. On current evidence the world fauna contains 1,450 named valid species, with 497 names treated as synonyms. This total

Table 2.1 Numbers of black fly species currently recognized (end of 1984) in each zoogeographical region in contrast with last estimate (1976). *Note:* (a) world totals do not correspond with sum of regional figures because some species occur in more than one region; (b) 8-year increase figures (last column) do not coincide with the differences between the figures in the other columns because of new synonymies and reestablished validities in this interim, and the fact that only approximated figures were available for the earlier date prevent useful direct comparison.

Region	1976[a]	1984[b]	Species described 1977–84 and listed as valid[b]
Afrotropical	166	193	35
Australasian	102	104	2
Nearctic[c]	147	152	9
Neotropical[c]	300	319	37
Oriental	110	159	53
Palaearctic	485	547	44
Total world	1,270	1,450	180

[a]Figures as given in Crosskey (1981).
[b]Figures to end of 1984.
[c]Mexico is both Nearctic and Neotropical but has been covered as Neotropical for the purpose of tabulation.

represents a 14% increase in the eight years since the last assessed figure of 1,270 species at the end of 1976 (Crosskey 1981). There are now 2.4 times as many valid species as forty years ago (a 135% increase) in the last published catalogue (Smart 1945). Table 2.1 shows how the species increase has affected faunal size in each zoogeographical region in these past eight years.

Some 200 to 300 new morphospecies have been described each decade since 1920, and this descriptive rate continues (278 in the 1970s and already 107 in the four years 1981–84). Figure 2.1 shows the numbers per decade and the cumulative trend. It is likely that, barring some unexpected factor such as reduced funding for fieldwork, there could be perhaps 1,950 named morphospecies considered valid by the year 2000. (To this total must be added the formally unnamed sibling species, for which the total number presently recognized is uncertain. A guess of 150 is indicated in Figure 2.1.)

What about new genera or subgenera? Figure 2.2 shows the cumulative number of erected genera/subgenera since *Simulium* (the only genus until 1906) was first divided. The pattern does not suggest that the description rate for new genera/subgenera is declining. There are now (1984) 115 available generic/subgeneric names for the Simuliidae, a figure that could be considered grossly top-heavy for the size and exceptional homogeneity of the family. No fewer than 48 of the 115 have been proposed since 1960, and of these there have been 10 new genera/subgenera in the last four years. At this rate we can expect a total of about 130 available genus-group names by the year 2000, but predicting how many might be in use for valid genera is impossible because of contrasting attitudes toward classification by different taxonomists. Insufficient sources are available from which to derive "validity trends" in different classifications. Only Rubtsov's works on Palaearctic simuliids permit a chronological trend to be seen, i.e., that for the "restricted-genera" policy that he has increasingly adopted (inset, Figure 2.2): two genera in 1940, 17 in 1956, 20 by 1964, and 40 in 1984 (Rubtsov 1940, 1956, 1959-64; Rubtsov and Yankovsky 1984). Except for a few instances of the actual discovery in the fauna of distinctive new taxa "unfittable" to preexisting genera, this increase has been due to ever-tighter refinement of supraspecific groupings ("split-and-promote classification"). Future taxonomists must beware of making today's species group into tomorrow's genus as an action barren of any new insight.

APPROACHES TO TAXONOMY

A generation ago the taxonomy of Simuliidae, like that of most insects, was still locked in the morphological straitjacket. Since then the taxonomist has found at his disposal an almost bewildering array of techniques, each with its individual capabilities, but all with an exciting potential for future advance. The common ground of all these newer methods has been to show unequivocally how little we know when only "hard-parts" anatomy is available to us, and to show us that almost any conventionally recognized species we care to examine closely is biologically a "species complex."

The nonmorphological approaches to simuliid taxonomy include chromosomal cytology (chromosomes are conventionally treated as outside morphology), the new field of gas liquid chromatography, and the techniques collectively known (e.g., Berlocher 1984) as molecular systematics, which for black flies currently embrace the practices of enzyme electrophoresis and DNA sequencing. These methods can be reviewed only superficially in this short, general panorama, but fuller specialist treatment is given in the chapters on cytological and biochemical taxonomy elsewhere in this book.

Morphotaxonomy

Careful taxonomy of whatever kind is slow work, and nonmorphological approaches are only gradually having an impact on the taxonomic scene. Morphology still provides nearly the entire simuliid discriminatory and classificatory system. As shown above, there is no abatement in description of morphologically-based taxa, and (taking simuliids at large) there is now scarcely a morphological attribute of any life stage or either sex that has not been well scrutinized, either to discover characters (a "character" is an attribute that has taxonomic value) or to discern probable function. Peterson and Dang (1981) have listed the morpho-characters of Simuliidae.

The SEM (scanning electron microscope) has improved our visual perception but has done little to further the discovery of characters. The morphological lemon appears to have been sucked nearly dry for characters of practical use. This is not to say that new kinds of character should not be sought, but the "character-future" appears to lie more in the morphometric study of old ones rather than in the discovery of new ones.

Morphometrics is the most neglected aspect of simuliid morphotaxonomy, despite

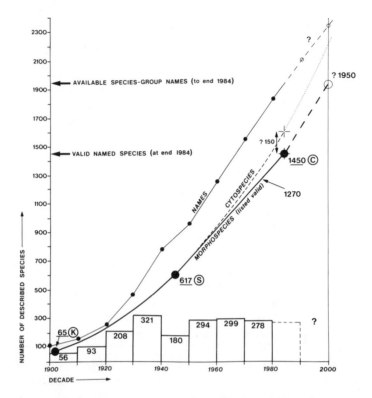

FIG. 2.1 The history of simuliid species description and the anticipated future trend to the year 2000, shown cumulatively for proposed names and for species considered valid, and by individual numbers per decade since 1900.

Notes: (a) The dashed line gives an arbitrary indication of the approximate number of unnamed sibling species (cytospecies), additional to the named morphospecies, since siblings were first chromosomally differentiated in the early 1950s. This number is now (end of 1984) about 150 (it excludes named members of the *Simulium damnosum* complex, which are treated as separate morphospecies). (b) The few subspecies and forms with Latin names available in nomenclature are subsumed as "species" (their names are "species-group" names potentially usable at species rank, and most are now so used). (c) The underlined numbers of species considered valid at different times are from the following sources: K = Kertész (1902); S = Smart (1945); C = Crosskey (Chapter 32, this volume). The figure of 1,270 species is that given by Crosskey (1981) and based on an unpublished figure for 1976.

the fact that many characters cited in taxonomic descriptions or used as identifying criteria are proportional (e.g., dilation of the front tarsus or the length of Lutz's organ in its maxillary pulp segment), or meristic (e.g., number of larval head-fan rays). Can such characters be relied upon? Few critical studies exist by which to judge the limits of intraspecific proportional and meristic variation and to differentiate it from interspecific variation. Morphometric literature and data are almost nonexistent, and the first morphological priority should be to remedy this deficiency, whenever possible in association with nonmorphological, identity-confirming criteria. Pending such studies, taxonomists should be wary of quick, superficial judgments on the specific value of observed proportional/meristic differences shown by small groups of specimens (too often purporting to differentiate species in keys and diagnoses).

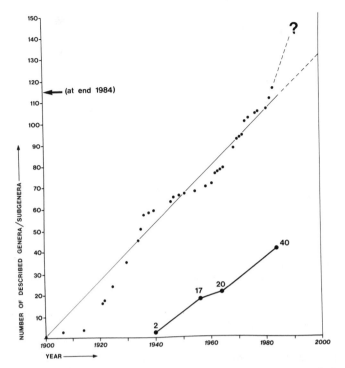

FIG. 2.2 The cumulative history of the number of described simuliid genera/subgenera, and (thick numbered inset line) the increase in the number of Palaearctic full genera treated as valid by Rubtsov in successive classifications (see text).

Note: Generic and subgeneric names together constitute coordinate "genus-group" names in the meaning of the *International Code of Zoological Nomenclature*. Most proposals of subgenera are treated as genera by some authors. The rank is therefore not distinguishable for the purpose of the graph.

Cytotaxonomy

Thirty years of larval cytotyping has shown the most skeptical morphotaxonomist that nearly every black fly morphospecies is actually a sibling species complex. The number of cytotypes shown to be discrete sibling species, on the basis of their co-occurrence and nonpatency of genetic introgression, is growing fast. The number of these "cytospecies" is probably now at least 150, but a vast increase in the number of recognized species complexes and included sibling species can be anticipated as more and more morphospecies are cytologically investigated. At present fewer than 10% of the world total of named morphospecies have been studied chromosomally; there are no chromosomal data for the fauna of the Orient and scarcely any for South America, and even for Africa (nearly 200 morphospecies) only *Simulium damnosum* s.l. has been significantly investigated.

The future for cytotaxonomy, then, can be perceived essentially as a continuation and expansion of established procedure—"more of the same." The taxonomic value of chromosomes (especially at specific and infraspecific levels) is universally appreciated, yet the cytologists have been somewhat conservative, confined for a whole generation to the polytene chromosomes of the larval silkglands. An excellent review has been provided by Rothfels (1979). Adult chromosomes are only now beginning to play a part in taxonomy, with the realization that they can sometimes be successfully processed from the flies with the right techniques, the right tissues, and the right physiological stages. This may open the chance to establish for the unknown faunas an imago-based cytotaxonomy that could make possible the direct identification of wild flies in the field, eliminating the troublesome process of inferential identification via the cytotyping of associated larvae. Larval polytene chromosomes are likely, however, to remain the most important diagnostic basis for new cytotaxa.

Chemotaxonomy

Of the three processes now in use, the one most exciting in its future potential for "classical" taxonomy is gas liquid chromatography (GLC). The museum taxonomist has for long envisaged—with small hope of its realization—a future in which by some magical nonmorphological means it would be possible to screen preserved specimens and "read" their identities. The ideal would be a system so sensitive that identification would be possible without damage to specimens of any age, condition, or life stage. The new technique of cuticle hydrocarbon (CH) analysis by gas liquid chromatography comes closer to this taxonomic nirvana than anything yet seen, and it holds great promise in insect taxonomy. One of its allures is that it does not require specimen destruction, yet at the same time it can, if required, be used on an isolated cuticular structure (e.g., a wing). It would, for instance, leave old museum type-specimens unscathed after their CHs had been analyzed to determine identity and any consequential synonymy. (This even suggests advantages over the recovery of DNA from ancient museum specimens, soon perhaps to be possible.)

Current work on CHs in the *Simulium damnosum* complex indicates the existence of intersibling differences in CH biochemistry (Phillips et al. 1985), detectable both in larval and adult stages and in parts of specimens as well as whole ones. If further work confirms the validity of these first findings, CH chemotaxonomy could become a driving force in simuliid taxonomy.

The taxonomic use of enzyme electrophoresis in black flies has made only modest progress since its birth a decade ago. Apart from some studies in North America (on the *Prosimulium fuscum/mixtum, Simulium jenningsi,* and *S. venustum* complexes), and on a few Central American morphospecies, enzyme taxonomy has concentrated on *Simulium damnosum* s.l. The findings on the *S. damnosum* complex indicate that isoenzymes do not necessarily unlock all the secrets of a species complex, and enzyme electrophoresis may not advance simuliid taxonomy as rapidly as at first seemed possible. Experience with the *damnosum* complex is cautionary because to date only two out of 44 tested enzyme systems have shown sibling-diagnostic characters—and these distinguish only two of the six widespread West African cytospecies (Meredith and Townson 1981). When a diagnostic isoenzyme is found, however, it is taxonomically potent because it then provides a known criterion of specificity against which to evaluate other attributes for their worth as taxonomic characters. The reliability of morphological characters for differentiating two members of the *damnosum* complex has been shown by "preidentifying" adult flies morphologically and then identifying the same specimens by their enzymes (Garms and Zillmann 1984). The verifying role of enzyme electrophoresis could be one of its best contributions to future taxonomy.

The taxonomic potential of DNA analysis in black flies so far has not received much attention. A DNA hybridization technique for estimating sequence divergences was applied to black flies in the early 1970s (Teshima 1972, Sohn et al. 1975) but not pursued. Under a new initiative, studies are in progress (R. J. Post, personal communication) on the taxonomic use of DNA in the *Simulium damnosum* complex. This involves the mass extraction of DNA from the flies, its enzymatic fragmentation with a restriction endonuclease, the formation of "genomic libraries" against which DNA extracted from pairs of known species can be screened comparatively, and assessment of the degree of between-species hybridization by autoradiography. The aim is to find reliable diagnostic cloned sequences that can be used for the identification of individual adult flies belonging to the various sibling species (cytospecies), either because they are present in one but absent from another or have differential copy numbers when jointly present. This approach is showing great promise, but its full taxonomic potential cannot yet be assessed.

NOMENCLATURE OF SIBLING SPECIES

A problem for taxonomists is the nomenclature to be adopted for the fast-increasing number of sibling species revealed by the gamma-taxonomic methods just discussed. Many of the sibling species first recognized by chromosomal criteria ("cytospecies") have been described and given Latin or Latinized names that enter into formal zoological nomenclature, particularly when taxa first diagnosed only on cytological characters have subsequently shown themselves to be identifiable also on their external ("hard parts") morphology. In the interim, such sibling species have nearly always been given an informal vernacular nomenclature that lies outside the formalized Latin system and is not subject to regulation and control by the *International Code of Zoological Nomenclature*. Sooner or later the need arises to collate the cytotaxonomic and morphotaxonomic data and to bring the nomenclature of sibling species into line with the classical system.

This raises some important questions when a former "morphospecies" proves to be a complex of several sibling species: should these "cytospecies" be formally named in future? If so, should old names that have stood in junior synonymy with that of the morphospecies be resurrected and applied to them, or should the old synonyms be disregarded and the siblings baptized with completely new names? Should a uniform system of vernacular nomenclature be used until the vernacular names are superseded by formal nomenclature?

These questions are especially relevant to the future of black fly taxonomy, which is increasingly concerned with sibling complexes as its first priority. My answers to them, venturing a personal viewpoint, are: (1) sibling species should be formally named, once their status has been established beyond reasonable doubt; (2) old synonyms should be recovered and used for sibling species whenever there is proof, or strong circumstantial evidence, for their correct assignment ("founder" species of complexes such as *Simulium aureum, S. ornatum, S. tuberosum, S. venustum,* and *S. vittatum* all have synonymic names that could be restored to valid use for particular siblings); (3) a unified vernacular system for chromosomal taxa, as a precursor terminology to formal nomenclature, is much needed (at present there is no consistent vernacular system in use in cytotaxonomy, and taxa are given "handles" such as letters, collection-site names, or inversion sequence numbers). There is little to be said for newly recognized siblings being named in an unmemorable way by their interdiagnostic chromosomal inversions, which is still common practice.

A common policy among cytotaxonomists on how to designate cytotaxa with a vernacular terminology would be a helpful step toward a better-integrated taxonomic system. Some of the "handles" currently used are complicated except for a specialist (virtually using diagnostic criteria as names), and consistency in the same work is often disregarded. The discussion of the question by Rothfels (this volume) is a most welcome start toward unification and will, one hopes, bear fruit for the future.

CLASSIFICATION AND PHYLOGENY

Species-level taxonomy is the main thread of this chapter because it is the aspect of taxonomy most pertinent to black fly ecology and control. Classification and phylogeny, nevertheless, should not be wholly disregarded in an appraisal of the future, especially in view of the uneasy relationship between them in black fly taxonomy today.

Classification is still based on morphological characters, and an alternative has not yet been seriously considered. Cytologists, however, are nearing the point at which a cyto-classification based on chromosomal criteria for supraspecific groups could be proposed. It would be illuminating to find how far such a classification, divorced from morphological "prethinking," would coincide with existing morphological concepts for black fly classification.

Speciation in Simuliidae is, so to speak, a pianissimo process that produces little phenotypic "noise." Structural homogeneity is an outstanding family trait, one black fly looking much like another. Similarities and differences used to define taxa are often not sharply defined and can be incongruently related between life stages. The main difficulty comes from trying to make classification fit ideas about black fly phylogeny when we often do not know if a character is antecedent or derivative. Morpho-evolution cannot be "seen" in the absence of a fossil record (although it may be variously inferred by applying cladistic methodology): we have only two palaeontological "knowns," viz., that black flies with the larval morphotype of cascade inhabitants (like those of subgenera *Shewellomyia, Anasolen,* and *Obuchovia*) existed by lower Cretaceous times (the age of early Pangeal breakup and initiation of the Atlantic Ocean), and that adult flies exactly like modern forms occur in Oligocene amber and Pleistocene interglacial deposits.

Now that the weakness of morphological data for inferring phylogeny is inescapably obvious, taxonomists are turning an interested eye on the phylogenetic potential of chromosomal and molecular data. The risk here lies in confusing the purposes of classification and phylogeny. There is a tacit assumption running through the black fly literature that classification should be subservient to phylogeny and changed in response to phylogenetic findings. One quote is indicative: Sohn et al. (1975) state, about an aspect of their DNA hybridization study, that "this finding indicates that the present generic limits in black flies bear re-examination." The implication is clear: if phylogeny demands, reconstruct the classification.

Evidence is accumulating that morphological differences between taxa are often not matched by equivalent differences in their chromosomes (and conventional wisdom assumes that the latter are superior indicators of relationship). Craig (1983), for example, found that morphology and cytology of Polynesian simuliids yielded discrepant phylogenies. The many small cytophylogenies already demonstrated, based on well-known pivotal morphospecies such as *Simulium aureum, S. damnosum, S. ornatum,* and *S. venustum,* are gradually coalescing into a family-wide cytophylogenetic "continuum" in which the main character breaks do not always coincide with the morphological gaps used in conventional morphotaxonomic classification. The black fly phylogeneticist will soon have to take more account of the disharmonies between genetic distance and morpho-phenotypic distance.

Classifications are needed for practical ends (taxa definition, identification), but phylogenies are not essential for day-to-day purposes. The fact that black fly classification and phylogeny could become blatantly antagonistic if the prevailing taxonomic rationale—that classification must change to suit phylogenetic data—is not modified seems as yet largely unrecognized. Wood (1978) has faced a practical consequence of such discordance and has wisely upheld two genera (*Gymnopais* and *Twinnia*) as valid despite their now almost certain phyletic subordinacy to *Prosimulium* (writing that "workers at the present time will find such an arrangement most acceptable"). Acceptability is the criterion of useful classification, and the "service industry" face of taxonomy is important. Phylogeny potentially destabilizes the current *compromise* classification—which in future should either be preserved from too much phylogenetic disruption or abandoned altogether in favor of new alternative classifications, each eclectic for its own special aims.

FUNDING AND THE SUPPLY OF TAXONOMISTS

Black flies became a high-visibility group only recently, with the consequence that the supply of taxonomists falls short of taxonomic demand, especially in conventional ("museum") taxonomy that offers the assured long-term opportunities for significant morphotaxonomic advances to be made. There are some half-dozen such specialists today (no more than fifty years ago), and most of these work perforce on geographically limited faunas (i.e., without developed expertise on a global basis). Undiminishing interest in the Simuliidae suggests that taxonomists could be found as replacements for today's specialists when these become "time-expired," but whether money will be found is an unpredictable matter dependent on future budgeting priorities.

Short-term grant-aided research directly relevant to discriminating and identifying black fly pests and vectors will probably attract future funding, especially as the potential of chromosomal and molecular taxonomy becomes still more apparent. This will be welcome to all taxonomists, but it will (it should be kept in mind) result in taxonomic development mainly on those few groups of Simuliidae that have reached the gamma-taxonomic stage. It will be haphazard progress by individuals working on ad hoc grant projects, rather than the much needed long-term and comprehensive taxonomic progress that the "institutional" specialists are best able to make.

CONCLUSION

This review has looked at the taxonomic background and tried to show where, with old and new methods, there are opportunities to be exploited for future advancement in black fly taxonomy. Some simuliids are in the van of taxonomic progress and subjected to the latest gamma-taxonomic methods of study, while others are still in the horse-and-buggy era of crude descriptive alpha-taxonomy. For the one group, looking at chromosomes is already old-fashioned; for the other it will be sophisticated taxonomy when it comes.

The future of black fly taxonomy depends on which black flies we mean, for a uniform level of taxonomy cannot be simultaneously attained for each systematic group in the whole world fauna in the foreseeable future. In fact, it is possible that the gap between the taxonomic "haves" and "have-nots" will widen as pest and vector species inevitably and rightly attract more attention than the harmless simuliids of more academic interest. Even a generation or more from now we are unlikely therefore to have a perfect taxonomy that satisfies all taxonomists. We can reasonably assume, however, that by then we shall have a more fully described world fauna, a more exactly traced phylogeny, and more reliable criteria for the diagnosis and identification of taxa. Some neglected fields of research, such as experimental and behavioral genetics, should have contributed some of their taxonomic potential (how sympatric black fly sibling species originate and maintain their genetic integrity is not a question of interest only to population geneticists).

The future needs better taxonomic standards, as some tendencies—such as description of putatively new species on inadequate evidence, a too-typological approach to variation, and an excessive propensity to description of unnecessary supraspecific taxa—retard progress. Taxonomy alters slowly, by careful evaluation of new data, and a dramatically rapid advance cannot be expected; a forecast made thirty years ago, when chromosomes were the new frontier, would certainly have predicted more radical changes in simuliid taxonomy than have actually happened. Premature claims must not be made for the taxonomic usefulness of any new line of research. I conclude with a reminder: that the new taxonomic wizardries coming into use have far to go to prove their real worth as practical weapons in the taxonomist's armory.

LITERATURE CITED

Berlocher, S. H. 1984. Insect molecular systematics. *Ann. Rev. Entomol.* 29:403–433.

Craig, D. A. 1983. Phylogenetic problems in Polynesian Simuliidae (Diptera: Culicomorpha): a progress report. *GeoJournal* 7:533–541.

Crosskey, R. W. 1981. Geographical distribution of Simuliidae. Pp. 57–68 in M. Laird, Ed., *Blackflies: the future for biological methods in integrated control.* Academic Press, New York and London. 399 pp.

——. (In press). The vectors of human onchocerciasis and their biology. In G. S. Nelson and C. D. Mackenzie, Eds., *Human onchocerciasis*. Academic Press, London.

Freeman, P., and B. de Meillon. 1953. *Simuliidae of the Ethiopian region*. British Museum (Natural History), London. 224 pp.

Garms, R., and U. Zillmann. 1984. Morphological identification of *Simulium sanctipauli* and *S. yahense* in Liberia and comparison of results with those of enzyme electrophoresis. *Tropenmed. Parasitol.* 35:217–220.

Kertész, C. 1902. *Catalogus dipterorum hucusque descriptorum*. I. Budapest. 338 pp.

Meredith, S. E. O., and H. Townson. 1981. Enzymes for species identification in the *Simulium damnosum* complex from West Africa. *Tropenmed. Parasitol.* 32:123–129.

Peterson, B. V., and P. T. Dang. 1981. Morphological means of separating siblings of the *Simulium damnosum* complex (Diptera: Simuliidae). Pp. 45–56 in M. Laird, Ed., *Blackflies: the future for biological methods in integrated control*. Academic Press, New York and London. 399 pp.

Phillips, A., J. F. Walsh, R. Garms, D. H. Molyneux, P. Milligan, and G. Ibrahim. 1985. Identification of adults of *Simulium damnosum* complex using hydrocarbon analysis. *Tropenmed. Parasitol.* 36:97–101.

Rothfels, K. H. 1979. Cytotaxonomy of black flies (Simuliidae). *Ann. Rev. Entomol.* 24:507–539.

Rubtsov, I. A. 1940. *Fauna of the USSR*. No. 23, Insects. Diptera 6 (6) Simuliidae. Akademiya "Nauk" SSSR, Moscow and Leningrad (in Russian with English summary and keys). 532 pp.

——. 1956. *Fauna of the USSR*. No. 23, Insects. Diptera 6 (6) Simuliidae. 2nd ed. Akademiya "Nauk" SSSR, Moscow and Leningrad (in Russian). 859 pp.

——. 1959–1964. Simuliidae (Melusinidae). Die Fliegen der Palaearktischen Region. 14. Stuttgart (in German). 689 pp.

——, and A. V. Yankovsky. 1984. *Keys to the genera of Palaearctic blackflies*. "Nauka," Leningrad (in Russian). 175 pp.

Smart, J. 1945. The classification of the Simuliidae (Diptera). *Trans. R. Entomol. Soc. London* 95:463–532.

Sohn, U., K. H. Rothfels, and N. A. Straus. 1975. DNA:DNA hybridization studies in black flies. *J. Mol. Evol.* 5:75–85.

Teshima, I. 1972. DNA-DNA hybridization in blackflies (Diptera: Simuliidae). *Can. J. Zool.* 50:931–940.

Wood, D. M. 1978. Taxonomy of the Nearctic species of *Twinnia* and *Gymnopais* (Diptera: Simuliidae) and a discussion of the ancestry of the Simuliidae. *Can. Entomol.* 110:1297–1337.

3 BIOCHEMICAL APPROACHES TO BLACK FLY TAXONOMY

Harold Townson, Rory J. Post, and Angela Phillips

The use of biochemical characters in taxonomy has a long history, and there are a number of excellent reviews of the field (Hawkes 1968, Wright 1974, Bisby et al. 1980, Ferguson 1980, Oxford and Rollinson 1983, Berlocher 1984). If we accept that the most useful taxonomic characters should be those that are relatively free of environmental and other nongenetic influences, then it follows that among biochemical compounds, those that are most closely linked to the genome should show the greatest value. This implies a biochemical hierarchy with a close correspondence with taxonomic usefulness. In practice, however, knowledge of this hierarchy has had relatively little impact on the way in which biochemical characters are chosen and used in taxonomy, the decisions usually being made on empirical grounds.

Despite the special pleading of biochemists and geneticists, traditional systematists seem long ago to have decided that biochemical data as taxonomic criteria should be evaluated no differently than other characters (Cain 1968, Heslop-Harrison 1968). To quote Cronquist (1980): "Chemical characters are like other characters: they work when they work, and they don't when they don't work."

Systematists have applied biochemical techniques not only to the differentiation of taxa but also to produce far-reaching conclusions concerning evolutionary processes, biological clocks, and phylogenetic trees (see Cain 1983 for a criticism of this approach). In this chapter, however, we focus on a much narrower taxonomic problem: that of the assignment of individuals to one or another species within a species complex. Indeed, the biochemical approach in taxonomy seems of greatest value where speciation has occurred in the absence of much morphological differentiation.

In view of the special problems of the taxonomy of simuliids and their relevance to control, it is perhaps surprising that so little attention has been devoted to potential biochemical characters. In this chapter we shall briefly discuss the particular problems and importance of species identification in simuliids and then examine three different biochemical approaches that appear to hold particular promise in providing taxonomic characters. The advantages and disadvantages of these approaches will be discussed and we shall attempt to identify the likely future developments in this field.

SPECIAL PROBLEMS OF SIMULIID TAXONOMY AND THEIR RELEVANCE TO CONTROL

Cytological studies of the polytene chromosomes from the salivary glands of simuliid larvae have shown that the family comprises a large number of species complexes (Rothfels 1979). While some progress has been made in the identification of adult females by the preparation of polytene chromosomes from the Malpighian tubules and ovarian nurse cells (Bedo 1976; Procunier, pesonal communication), the cytological technique has been extensively applied only to larvae, and it seems unlikely that examination of adult polytene chromosomes, requiring as it does females in a particular physiological condition, can be used on a large scale for practical identification.

The importance of a reliable means of identification of adult females in studies of the epidemiology of onchocerciasis vectors and in the planning and execution of control measures has been repeatedly emphasized (WHO 1978, Townson and Meredith 1979, Garms and Zillman 1984). Thus there may be marked differences between individual species in macro- and microgeographical distribution (Crosskey 1981), in larval habitat (Garms and Vajime 1975, Quillévéré et al. 1977), in host preference and vectorial capacity (Quillévéré 1979, Garms 1983), in migration and dispersal behavior (Garms et al. 1979), and susceptibility to larvicides (Guillet et al. 1980). It seems likely that other biological features of importance to disease transmission, such as biting cycle and population age structure, will also differ between species.

Difficulties have been encountered in the use of morphological characters for adult identification, whether they be metrical or qualitative (Garms 1978, Townson and Meredith 1979, Meredith et al. 1983, Garms and Zillman 1984). In the light of such studies, the value of alternative methods of adult identification is self-evident, and the search for biochemical characters by which species can be differentiated has received its impetus almost wholly as a result of the practical problems of control of pest species and onchocerciasis vectors.

BIOCHEMICAL METHODS

A considerable variety of biochemical methods has been applied to problems of insect identification, although relatively few of these have proved reliable enough to be used in a routine manner. The only techniques of significant value in identification of simuliids have been those of enzyme electrophoresis, gas liquid chromatography of cuticular hydrocarbons, and DNA-DNA hybridization using cloned DNA sequences. The latter two techniques have only been applied to diagnostic problems in the Simuliidae relatively recently, and a full evaluation of their potential and their limitations has yet to be achieved. Nevertheless, they have already shown considerable potential and an ability to differentiate adults of species for which no other diagnostic characters exist.

ENZYME ELECTROPHORESIS

The value of enzymes as taxonomic characters has been extensively reviewed in the literature (Avise 1974, Ferguson 1980, Ayala 1983, Bullini 1983). Similarly, methods and principles of enzyme electrophoresis have been widely documented (see, for example, Harris and Hopkinson 1976, Ferguson 1980) and the limitations of the approach discussed (Ferguson 1980).

It would seem that the allelic variants of enzymes or allozymes are particularly useful in the identification of incipient or sibling species (Ayala 1975). Their usefulness arises from the fact that species are often considerably differentiated, whereas local populations are not; that enzyme variants are often immediate expressions of the genotype and little subject to phenotypic modification; and that several loci may be diagnostic and can be used to provide a joint estimate of the probability of incorrect diagnosis (Ayala 1983). In addition, allozymes can be used to identify naturally occurring hybrids and hence are very sensitive measures of the degree of reproductive isolation of incipient species (Bullini 1983).

However, the extent of enzyme divergence during speciation is often highly variable between different groups. For example, for pairs of sibling species of *Drosophila* the proportion of enzyme loci that are diagnostic varies from 12% to 52% (Lewontin 1974). There are few guiding principles as to what level of allozyme divergence to expect. For the practical biologist faced with a taxonomic problem, there is little alternative other than the empirical approach of examining as many enzymes as possible in the hope of finding one or two of diagnostic value.

A major disadvantage of the technique of enzyme electrophoresis is that it requires the use of either live organisms or ones that have been preserved by refrigeration at low temperatures; sometimes storage at −20°C is inadequate and material has to be kept at −70°C or in liquid nitrogen. A further disadvantage is that it requires the destruction of the specimen, although in our studies we have found it convenient to remove head, legs, and wings for morphometric studies before homogenizing specimens for electrophoresis. While less destructive methods have proved possible with some larger diptera, these have not yet been applied to simuliids.

Only a limited number of studies have been carried out with black flies. Townson and Meredith (1979) and Meredith and Townson (1981) reviewed the literature up to 1981.

S. jenningsi group.   May et al. (1977) examined 11 enzyme systems in three closely related species of the *S. jenningsi* group but found only 4 enzymes showing interspecific differences. The man-biting species in the area of study could be identified by means of allozymes of malic dehydrogenase and lactic dehydrogenase. This study illustrated the potential of enzyme techniques for providing taxonomic characters that are sufficiently reliable to permit identification of the principal man-biting species in an area.

S. venustum-verecundum species complexes.   *S. venustum* s.l. appears to differ from *S. verecundum* s.l. by its complement of lactic dehydrogenase electromorphs. There were no clear-cut differences between siblings within either group, but there were considerable differences between some siblings in frequencies of electromorphs of a number of enzymes (Snyder 1982).

Prosimulium fuscum-mixtum group.   A unique complement of electromorphs of 6-phosphogluconate dehydrogenase enabled individual larvae and adults of *P. fuscum* and *P. mixtum* to be separated, whereas conventional morphological characters from existing keys were found to be of limited value (Snyder and Linton 1983).

S. metallicum.   It has long been recognized that *S. metallicum* shows important biological variation over its range, and it has been suggested that it may constitute a species complex.

In a study carried out in Panama, Petersen (1981, 1982) examined 22 enzyme loci using cellulose acetate electrophoresis. There was a significant deviation for Hardy-Weinberg equilibrium in phosphoglucomutase (PGM) allele frequencies, a finding that suggested the existence of two or more reproductively isolated populations correlated with differences in pupal morphology. The results are sufficiently encouraging to warrant a more comprehensive survey of enzyme systems in these groups. This study illustrates the principle that morphological and enzyme data taken together may throw more light on a problem than if each is used separately.

Simulium damnosum complex.   In an electrophoretic study of *S. damnosum* populations in West Africa, 44 enzyme systems were examined, of which 15 were found to give consistently well-stained and well-defined bands. Six of these appeared to be monomorphic among the six species examined, while a further seven enzymes were polymorphic and showed differences in allele frequencies, but it was not possible to use them for unequivocal identification (Meredith and Townson 1981). Two enzymes, PGM and trehalase, had allozymes that were species-diagnostic, the PGM B_1 allele being a highly reliable character for identifying *S. yahense*. The trehalase allozyme TRE A was almost fixed in populations of *S. yahense* and *S. squamosum* so that the two enzymes together served to identify *S. squamosum* with a very high degree of accuracy. Meredith (1982) was able to use these characters to identify *S. yahense* and *S. squamosum* in flies caught biting man.

In a more comprehensive series of studies carried out for the Onchocerciasis Control Programme (Townson and Meredith, unpublished reports to WHO/OCP), more than 6,000 specimens were examined from Ivory Coast, Togo, and Benin and a smaller series from Ghana and Sierra Leone. The validity of enzyme characters for differentiating *S. yahense* and *S. squamosum* throughout this range was confirmed, although there were differences in allozyme frequencies between populations of *S. squamosum* in Ivory Coast and those in Togo. The allozyme characters were used to examine the diagnostic value of certain morphological characters. This illustrates the principle that once allozyme characters have been validated they may be used as the basis for a more intensive investigation of morphological characters. Recently this principle has been extended by Garms and Zillman (1984) to the examination of a number of morphological characters in populations of *S. sanctipauli* and *S. yahense* in Liberia. *S. yahense* individuals were positively identified by the distinctive PGM allozyme described by Meredith and Townson (1981). This study was able to validate the use of the color of the setae on the ninth abdominal tergite to separate these species, with a precise estimate of the risk of misclassification when using this character.

So far, little has been done to examine the use of allozymes as diagnostic characters for East African populations of *S. damnosum*. Meredith and Townson (1981 and unpublished) examined a small number of specimens from Tanzania. An allozyme of xanthine dehydrogenase was found that appeared to be diagnostic for the Sanje form of *S. damnosum* (Meredith 1980), but further work would be necessary to confirm this. Recently Mebrahtu (1984, and Mebrahtu et al., 1986) has examined allozymes in *S. damnosum* s.l. populations from Kenya. There were differences in the allozymes between populations from the Mount Kenya area and those from western Kenya, but in the absence of cytotaxonomic identification of the species in these populations it was not possible to say which variants were present in which species. Clearly this is an area of considerable interest that should be further investigated.

In conclusion, despite the limitations imposed by the need to use specimens in which enzyme activity is retained, enzyme electrophoresis has considerable potential for resolving some of the taxonomic problems with species complexes in the Simuliidae. It is perfectly feasible to examine more than a hundred specimens per day for both morphological and allozyme characters, and hence the methods are suitable for processing large numbers of specimens derived from sampling over extensive areas.

THE TAXONOMIC USE OF DNA SEQUENCES

The analysis of DNA represents the most direct analysis of genetic variation that is possible and as such is obviously attractive for taxonomic and evolutionary studies. Flavell (1982) and Dover (1980) have reviewed the use of DNA for the study of species relationships.

Early studies were limited by the technology then available to analyses of reassociation kinetics for denatured genomic DNA from different species. The only previously reported studies of black fly DNA (Teshima 1972, Sohn et al. 1975) used this approach to compare the phylogenetic relationships between a number of North American black fly species from several genera. The results indicated a clustering of species within genera and hence largely confirmed classical taxonomic opinion.

While these techniques are suitable for phylogenetic inference, they are slow, laborious, and require large amounts of DNA. They are therefore unsuitable for routine taxonomy of individual flies. However, with the advent of modern cloning techniques it has become possible to isolate and replicate large quantities of individual specified sequences that may be used as taxonomic probes for individual specimens. One of the attractions of DNA sequences for taxonomic research is that they are highly unlikely to show any environmentally mediated variation (although see Cullis 1977 for an exception).

DNA sequences can vary in three basic ways (Flavell 1981). The copy number per genome can be altered by deletion or amplification, the chromosomal position of a sequence can be altered by several different translocation mechanisms, and the exact base sequence can be altered by point mutations or small additions or deletions. All three types of change could yield species-diagnostic variability, but change in copy number is probably the most promising class of variability for taxonomic use in *Simulium*. This is because such changes can be detected by dot-blot hybridization, a simple technique that can be adapted for field use (Massamba and Williams 1984). Furthermore, the DNA sequences that change in copy number are by definition repetitive and as such will give greater sensitivity than

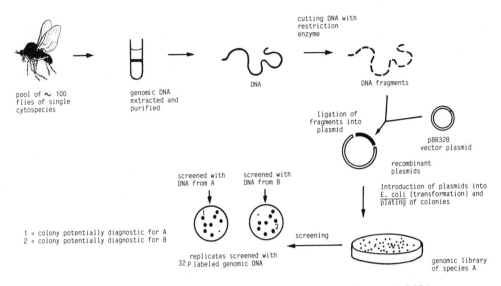

FIG. 3.1 Schematic representation of the procedures used to clone diagnostic DNA sequences that differ in copy number between species.

single-copy sequences when used as diagnostic probes. As a class, repetitive sequences are known to undergo rapid evolutionary change (Flavell 1982) and are thus more likely to show interspecific differences.

Taxonomic Use of DNA Sequences with Variable-Copy Number in the *Simulium damnosum* Complex

Post and Crampton (unpublished) have isolated three cloned DNA sequences that can be used, in combination, to separate individual adult flies into one of three groups: *S. squamosum/yahense*, *S. sanctipauli/soubrense* "B", and *S. sirbanum* (other species have yet to be examined). The basic procedures are illustrated schematically in Figure 3.1. DNA was extracted *en masse* from adults reared from pupae collected at natural breeding sites of known single cytospecies. Genomic libraries were constructed for *S. soubrense* "B" and *S. squamosum* using standard procedures with the plasmid pBR328 as vector and *Escherichia coli* MC1061 as host (Maniatis et al. 1982). The bacterial colonies containing the recombinant plasmids constitute the individual "volumes" in the genomic library, each colony containing a single random black fly DNA sequence; the total library contains an almost complete representation of all the DNA sequences of the genome.

To identify those colonies containing DNA sequences of taxonomic interest, replicates of the libraries were screened with ^{32}P-labeled genomic DNA from pairs of sibling species using the colony hybridization technique of Grunstein and Hogness (1975). This technique identifies individual clones homologous to DNA sequences that are repeated more than 50 to 100 times per genome (Crampton et al. 1981) and reveals differences in the copy number of sequences between species. Colonies that hybridized differentially were further characterized to see if they contained diagnostic sequences. The genetic function of these repetitive sequences is not known, but it can be argued that this is unimportant to their use as taxonomic characters.

Three cloned sequences were isolated (pSO3, pSO11, and pSQ1) and used to identify by dot-hybridization (Kafatos et al. 1981) single adult flies collected from the wild. Adult flies were reared from pupae collected at breeding sites of known cytospecies, principally in Sierra Leone, and preserved in either 95% propanol (Rake 1972) or liquid nitrogen. DNA was extracted from single flies (Coen et al. 1982), denatured, and one-third absorbed onto a nitrocellulose filter to provide these replicate filters (Kafatos et al. 1981). Each replicate was then hybridized to one of the radio-labeled probes (Fig. 3.2). The comparative amount of hybridization, as revealed by autoradiography, allowed identification of each individual fly according to the key shown in Figure 3.2. The technique has also been used by Post and Crampton (unpublished) to identify individual adult females caught at human bait.

Other DNA Sequences of Use in Studies of Simuliids

DNA sequences that show species-specific variation in copy number are probably the most appropriate for taxonomic studies of the *S. damnosum* complex because of the simple technology and the small amounts of genomic DNA required. However, sequences can show other sorts of species-specific variation, for example, in the size of restriction fragments. A range of restriction enzymes are available that cut DNA at highly specific sites according to exact base sequence (see Malcolm 1981). The resultant DNA restriction fragments can be fractionated, according to size, by electrophoresis through an agarose gel. Following denaturation, the DNA may be transferred to nitrocellulose filters and hybridized to radio-labeled cloned DNA (Southern 1975). Subsequent autoradiography reveals the position of homologous sequences. A

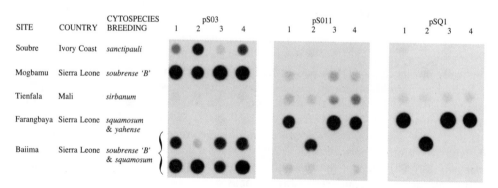

FIG. 3.2 Autoradiograph of three replicate dot blots of genomic DNA of individual flies hybridized to ^{32}P-labeled pSO3, pSO11, and pSQ1, respectively. Flies were reared from pupae collected together with larvae that were cytotaxonomically identified. The intensity of each dot is related to the degree of hybridization, and hence adults can be identified directly by reciprocal comparisons of the dot intensities between probes. KEY: If hybridization to pSO3 is much stronger than to pSO11 or pSQ1, then the specimen is *S. soubrense* "B"/*sanctipauli*. Of remaining individuals, if hybridization to pSO11 is stronger than to pSQ1, then the specimen is *S. sirbanum;* otherwise it is *squamosum/yahense*.

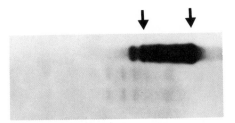

Fig. 3.3 Autoradiograph of a Southern blot of genomic DNA from *S. squamosum* ♀♀ (lane 1) and *S. soubrense* "B" ♂♂ and ♀♀ (lanes 2 and 3, respectively) probed with ^{32}P-labeled pSQ1. There are equal amounts of DNA in the three lanes. Not only does *S. squamosum* hybridize more strongly to pSQ1, but it also shows two restriction fragments (arrowed) that appear to be absent from the specimens of *S. soubrense* "B".

Southern blot of genomic DNA from *S. soubrense* "B" and *S. squamosum* restricted with the enzyme Eco R1 and probed with pSQ1 is shown in Figure 3.3. Restriction fragments that appear to be species-specific are indicated by arrows.

The main obstacle to the application of DNA probes in field situations may well be the general difficulties of handling radioactive reagents and particularly the short life (< 3 weeks) of ^{32}P-labeled DNA probes. Because of the tremendous interest in DNA probes for clinical diagnosis, it is highly probable that the next two years could see the development of nonradioactive methods of labeling DNA that yield probes as sensitive as those labeled with [32]P.

CUTICULAR HYDROCARBONS

The cuticular waxes of insects are thought to protect the insect against dessication and abrasion by dust as well as having a role in chemical communication in some species (Carlson et al. 1971, Jones et al. 1971). The chemistry of these waxes has been reviewed by Jackson and Blomquist (1976) and their composition in many insects investigated (Bursell and Clements 1967; Armold et al. 1969; Cavill et al., 1969; Blomquist et al. 1976; Lockey 1976, 1978; Hadley and Jackson 1977). Predominant components of insect cuticular waxes include fatty acids, sterols, esters, and hydrocarbons. Lockey (1978) brought together the detailed analysis of the hydrocarbons of 30 species of adult insects, representing seven orders. He concluded that insect orders could not be characterized by their cuticular hydrocarbons alone, as their constituent species varied too greatly in their hydrocarbon profiles. However, the very fact that the cuticular waxes of closely related species vary forms the basis of the use of cuticular hydrocarbons in taxonomy.

With the advent of new instrumentation and techniques, quantitation and identification of cuticular waxes has become a relatively simple analysis. Extraction of these waxes involves immersion of the insect in an organic solvent (e.g., hexane) for a short period of time, c. 10 minutes, to prevent penetration of hexane and the extraction of internal lipids (Jackson and Blomquist 1976; Phillips et al. 1985). Gas liquid chromatography (GLC) is next used to separate and quantitate the components in the sample; the recent developments of fused silica capillary columns and

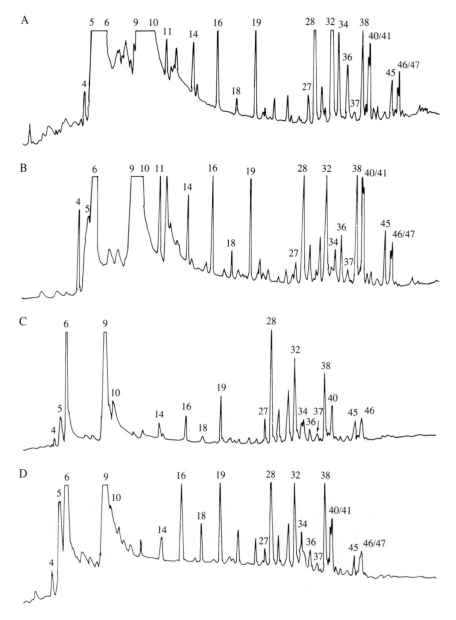

Fig. 3.4 Gas liquid chromatograms of hexane-extracted cuticular waxes from individual females: A. *Simulium damnosum* s.s., B. *S. sirbanum*, C. *S. sanctipauli*, D. *S. yahense*. The peaks are numbered in the order in which they come off the column. Peaks 4–10 are fatty acids and their esters; peaks 11 onward are hydrocarbons. Each chromatographic run began at 120°C for 2 minutes, followed by 7°C min^{-1} rise to 310°C for 20 minutes. The column was a 10M CPSil5 CB with 0.32 mm O.D and 0.15 μm phase thickness. The GLC apparatus was a Hewlett-Packard HP 5790 A linked to a HP 3390 A recording integrator.

on-column injection have greatly improved the accuracy and sensitivity of GLC, enabling samples from individual adults and larvae to give profiles containing up to 50 peaks. Components emerging from the column are best detected by a flame ionization detector and recorded as peaks in the resulting chromatogram. The area under each peak is proportional to the concentration of that component in the sample and is usually calculated by a recording integrator. Tentative identification of hydrocarbons can be made by calculation of the Kovats Index (Kovats 1965) based on retention time, which assigns a carbon number to each peak. However, gas liquid chromatography/mass spectrometry (GLC/MS) is usually employed, allowing both separation of components and their subsequent analysis by mass spectrometry. Hydrocarbons are difficult to identify absolutely when using electron impact (EI) mass spectrometry, but chemical ionization methods (CI) improve their characterization.

The first application of GLC techniques to simuliids enabled the separation of individual females of *S. squamosum* and *S. sirbanum* (Carlson and Walsh 1981). Recent work with GLC techniques has shown that individual adults of four species of the *S. damnosum* complex can be successfully distinguished (Phillips et al. 1985). Figure 3.4 illustrates the profiles obtained from individual female *S. damnosum* s.s., *S. sirbanum, S. sanctipauli,* and *S. yahense.* Identification of all peaks was possible with GLC/MS; peaks 4 to 10 represent fatty acids and their esters, while peaks 11 onward are hydrocarbons. Figure 3.5 shows the electron impact and chemical ioniza-

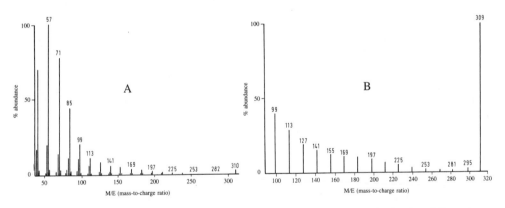

FIG. 3.5 The mass spectra based on electron impact (A) and chemical ionization (B) methods for peak 11 of the gas liquid chromatogram. The spectra show the fragmentation pattern of the component in the peak and hence allow deduction of its chemical structure (peak 11 is a C_{22} straight-chain hydrocarbon). The mass spectra are used to confirm the identity of individual peaks within and between species. Chemical ionization methods allow identification of the pseudomolecular ion and its molecular weight, thus providing more precise identification of compounds within peaks than is possible by electron-impact methods.

tion spectra for peak 11. Peak identification is necessary to enable subsequent comparison of identical peaks between individuals. Analysis of data was based on comparison of the areas of chromatographic peaks both within and between species. Using multivariate statistics, the importance of all peaks could be considered simultaneously in order to determine whether cytospecies could be distinguished on the basis of their hydrocarbons and also which peaks were the most useful in discriminating between groups. Discriminant analysis was used to separate cytospecies on *a priori* grounds and also to produce a characterization of these groups in terms of the data. Each chromatographic peak was weighted to indicate its relative usefulness in discriminating between cytospecies. Scatter diagrams were plotted using scores on discriminant functions as rectangular coordinates. Figure 3.6 shows the scatter dia-

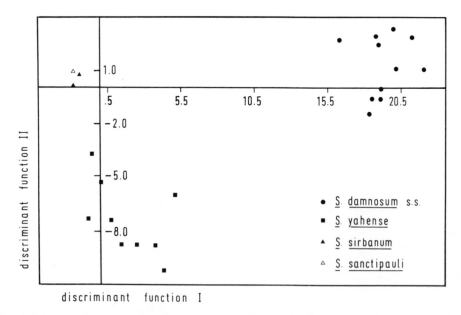

FIG. 3.6 Scatter diagram for discriminant functions based upon the relative abundance of the various peaks in the gas liquid chromatogram. For *S. damnosum* s.s. and *S. yahense,* values for individual specimens are shown. For *S. sirbanum* and *S. sanctipauli,* 111 individuals were examined, and because the data points are highly clustered for these specimens, the group centroid values are shown. (Two populations of *S. sirbanum* and one population of *S. sanctipauli;* for further details, see Phillips et al. 1985.)

gram for 131 females of the *S. damnosum* complex that have been analyzed in this way. So far, it has not been possible to examine species from a wide geographical range to determine the consistency of the differences observed.

The analysis of cuticular hydrocarbons of sibling species complexes by gas chromatography shows great potential as a tool in identification. The many advantages of this technique include the ease of collection and preparation of samples. Dead, dried specimens are best used, with care being taken to avoid handling and unnecessary contact with plastic. Specimens may be stored dry in glass containers for many years without loss of their lipid quality. Collection procedures do not involve the need for liquid nitrogen or dry ice and the consequent difficulty of transporting these compounds in tropical and subtropical areas. The limitations of this technique include the high initial cost of GLC equipment and the need for linked data systems and automatic sampling for increased speed of analysis. At present, the system also relies on prior identification of the insects by other methods, although this will not be necessary once a data bank of information has been acquired.

CONCLUSIONS

There is clearly considerable scope for the future application of each of the bio-chemical techniques discussed in this chapter. Allozymes have proven valuable in the identification of incipient or sibling species. DNA probes are likely to play an increasing role in the identification of sibling species within insect vector popula-tions; similar work is in progress with the *Anopheles gambiae* complex (Gale and Crampton, personal communication) and *An. balabacensis* complex (Panyim et al. 1984). The recent improvements in techniques for GLC/MS analysis of cuticular hydrocarbons with their increased sensitivity have enabled identification of individu-als from their wings only. Such advantages may well outweigh any other disadvant-ages of this technique.

LITERATURE CITED

Armold, M. T., C. J. Blomquist, and L. L. Jackson. 1969. Cuticular lipids of insects. III. The surface lipids of the aquatic and terrestrial life forms of the big stonefly *Pteronarcys californica* Newport. *Comp. Biochem. Physiol.* 31:685–692.

Avise, J. C. 1974. Systematic value of electrophoretic data. *Syst. Zool.* 23:465–481.

Ayala, F. J. 1975. Genetic differentiation during the speciation process. *Evol. Biol.* 8:1–78.

———. 1983. Enzymes as taxonomic characters. Pp. 3–26 in G. S. Oxford and D. Rollinson, Eds., *Protein polymorphism: adaptive and taxonomic significance.* Academic Press, New York and London.

Bedo, D. G. 1976. Polytene chromosomes in pupal and adult blackflies (Diptera: Simuliidae). *Chromosoma* (Berlin) 57:387–396.

Berlocher, S. H. 1984. Insect molecular systematics. *Ann. Rev. Entomol.* 29:403–433.

Bisby, F. A., J. G. Vaughan, and C. A. Wright, Eds. 1980. *Chemosystematics: principles and practice.* Academic Press, New York and London.

Blomquist, G. J., T. T. Blailock, R. W. Scheetz, and L. L. Jackson. 1976. Cuticular lipids of insects. VII. Cuticular hydrocarbons of the crickets *Acheta domesticus, Gryllus penn-sylvanicus* and *Nemobius fasciatus. Comp. Biochem. Physiol.* 54B:381–386.

Bullini, L. 1983. Taxonomic and evolutionary inferences from electrophoretic studies of vari-ous animal groups. Pp. 179–192 in G. S. Oxford and D. Rollinson, Eds., *Protein polymorphism: adaptive and taxonomic significance.* Academic Press, New York and London.

Bursell, E., and A. N. Clements. 1967. The cuticular lipids of the larva of *Tenebrio molitor* L (Coleoptera). *J. Insect Physiol.* 13:1671–78.

Cain, A. J. 1968. The assessment of new types of character in taxonomy. Pp. 229–234 in J. G. Hawkes, Ed., *Chemotaxonomy and serotaxonomy.* Academic Press, New York and London.

———. 1983. Concluding remarks. Pp. 391–397 in G. S. Oxford and D. Rollinson, Eds., *Protein polymorphism: adaptive and taxonomic significance.* Academic Press, New York and London.

Carlson, D. A., M. S. Mayer, D. L. Silhacek, J. D. James, M. Beroza, and B. A. Bierl. 1971. Sex attractant pheromone of the housefly: Isolation, identification, and synthesis. *Science* 174:76–78.

Carlson, D. A., and J. F. Walsh. 1981. Identification of two West African blackflies (Diptera: Simuliidae) of the *Simulium damnosum* species complex by analysis of cuticular paraffins. *Acta tropica* 38:235–239.

Cavill, G. W. K., D. V. Clark, M. E. H. Howden, and S. G. Wyllie. 1970. Hydrocarbon and other lipid constituents of the bull ant *Myrmecia gulosa*. *J. Insect Physiol.* 16:1721–28.

Coen, E., J. M. Thoday, and G. Dover. 1982. Rate of turnover of structural variants in the rDNA gene family of *Drosophila melanogaster*. *Nature* (London) 295:564–568.

Crampton, J. M., K. E. Davies, and T. F. Knapp. 1981. The occurrence of families of repetitive sequences in a library of cloned cDNA from human lymphocytes. *Nucl. Acids Res.* 9:3821–33.

Cronquist, A. 1980. Chemistry in plant taxonomy: an assessment of where we stand. Pp. 1–27 in F. A. Bisby, J. G. Vaughan, and C. A. Wright, Eds., *Chemosystematics: principles and practice*. Academic Press, New York and London.

Crosskey, R. W. 1981. Simuliid taxonomy—the contemporary scene. Pp. 3–18 in M. Laird, Ed., *Blackflies: the future for biological methods in integrated control*. Academic Press, New York and London.

Cullis, C. A. 1977. Molecular aspects of the environmental induction of heritable changes in flax. *Heredity* 38:129–154.

Dover, G. 1980. Problems in the use of DNA for the study of species relationship and the evolutionary significance of genomic differences. Pp. 241–68 in F. A. Bisby, J. G. Vaughan, and C. A. Wright, Eds., *Chemosystematics: principles and practice*. Academic Press, New York and London.

Ferguson, A. 1980. *Biochemical systematics and evolution*. Blackie, Glasgow and London.

Flavell, R. B. 1981. Molecular changes in chromosomal DNA organisation and origins of phenotypic variation. *Chromosomes Today* 7:42–54.

———. 1982. Sequence amplification, deletion and rearrangement: major sources of variation during species divergence. Pp. 301–323 in C. A. Dover and R. B. Flavell, Eds., *Genome evolution*. Academic Press, New York and London.

Garms, R. 1978. Use of morphological characters in the study of *Simulium damnosum* s.l. populations in West Africa. *Tropenmed. Parasitol.* 29:483–491.

———. 1983. Studies of the transmission of *Onchocerca volvulus* by species of the *Simulium damnosum* complex occurring in Liberia. *Z. Ang. Zool.* 70:101–117.

Garms, R., J. F. Walsh, and J. B. Davies. 1979. Studies on the reinvasion of the Onchocerciasis Control Programme in the Volta River Basin by *Simulium damnosum* s.l. with emphasis on the south-western areas. *Tropenmed. Parasitol.* 30:345–362.

Garms, R., and C. G. Vajime. 1975. On the ecology and distribution of the species of the *Simulium damnosum* complex in different bioclimatic zones of Liberia and Guinea. *Tropenmed. Parasitol.* 26:375–380.

Garms, R., and U. Zillman. 1984. Morphological identification of *Simulium sanctipauli* and *S. yahense* in Liberia and comparison of results with those of enzyme electrophoresis. *Tropenmed. Parasitol.* 35:217–220.

Grunstein, M., and D. Hogness. 1975. Colony hybridisation: a method for the isolation of cloned DNAs that contain a specific gene. *Proc. Natl. Acad. Sci. USA.* 72:3961–65.

Guillet, P., H. Escaffre, M. Ouedraogo, and D. Quillévéré. 1980. Mise en evidence d'une resistance au temephos dans le complexe *Simulium damnosum* (*S. sanctipauli* et *S. soubrense*) en Côte d'Ivoire. *Cah. ORSTOM sér. Entomol. Méd Parasitol.* 18:291–299.

Hadley, N. F., and L. L. Jackson. 1977. Chemical composition of the epicuticular lipids of the scorpion *Paruroctonus mesaensis*. *Insect Biochem.* 7:85–89.

Harris, H., and D. A. Hopkinson. 1976. *Handbook of enzyme electrophoresis in human genetics*. North-Holland, Amsterdam.

Hawkes, J. G., Ed. 1968. *Chemotaxonomy and serotaxonomy*. Academic Press, New York and London.

Heslop-Harrison, J. 1968. Chairman's summing up. Pp. 279–284 in J. G. Hawkes, Ed., *Chemotaxonomy and serotaxonomy*. Academic Press, New York and London.

Jackson, L. L., and G. J. Blomquist. 1976. Insect waxes. Pp. 201–233 in P. E. Kolattukudy, Ed., *The chemistry and biochemistry of natural waxes*. Elsevier, Amsterdam.

Jones, R. L., W. J. Lewis, M. C. Bowman, M. Berosa, and B. A. Bierl. 1971. Host-seeking stimulant for parasite of corn earworm: isolation, identification and synthesis. *Science* 173:842–843.

Kafatos, F. C., G. Thireos, C. Weldon Jones, S. G. Tsitilou, and K. Iatrou. 1981. Dot hybridization and hybrid-selected translation: methods for determining nucleic acid concentrations and sequence homologies. Pp. 537–50 in J. G. Chirikjian and T. P. Papas, Eds., *Gene amplification and analysis: 2. Structural analysis of nucleic acids*. Elsevier–North Holland, Amsterdam.

Kovats, K. 1965. Gas chromatographic characterisation of organic substances in the Retention Index system. *Adv. Chromatogr.* 1:229–247.

Lewontin, R. C. 1974. *The genetic basis of evolutionary change*. Columbia Univ. Press, New York and London.

Lockey, K. H. 1976. Cuticular hydrocarbons of *Locusta*, *Schistocerca* and *Periplaneta*, and their role in water-proofing. *Insect Biochem.* 6:457–472.

———. 1978. The adult cuticular hydrocarbons of *Tenebrio molitor* L. and *Tenebrio obscurrus*. F. *Insect Biochem.* 8:237–250.

Malcolm, A. D. B. 1981. The use of restriction enyzmes in genetic engineering. Pp. 129–173 in R. Williamson, Ed., *Genetic engineering*, vol. 2. Academic Press, New York and London.

Maniatis, T., E. F. Fritsch, and J. Sambrook. 1982. *Molecular cloning: a laboratory manual*. Cold Spring Harbor Laboratory, Long Island, New York.

Massamba, N. N., and R. O. Williams. 1984. Distinction of African trypanosome species using nucleic acid hybridization. *Parasitology* 88:55–65.

May, B., L. S. Bauer, R. L. Vadas, and J. Granett. 1977. Biochemical genetic variation in the Family Simuliidae: electrophoretic identification of the human biter in the isomorphic *Simulium jenningsi* group. *Ann. Entomol. Soc. Am.* 54:637–640.

Mebrahtu, Y. 1984. Characterization of *Simulium damnosum* s.l. from six river-systems in Kenya using ecological parameters and cellulose acetate electrophoresis. M.Sc. Thesis, University of Nairobi.

Mebrahtu, Y., R. F. Beach, C. P. M. Khamala, and L. D. Hendricks. 1986. Characterization of *Simulium* (*Edwardsellum*) *damnosum* s.l. populations from six river systems in Kenya by cellulose acetate electrophoresis. *Trans. R. Soc. Trop. Med. Hyg.* 80:914–922.

Meredith, S. E. O. 1980. A study of methods for the identification of members of the *Simulium* (*Edwardsellum*) *damnosum* complex. Ph.D. Thesis, University of Liverpool.

———. 1982. Enzyme identification of *Simulium damnosum* s.l. caught biting man. *Ann. Trop. Med. Parasitol.* 76:375–376.

Meredith, S. E. O., R. A. Cheke, and R. Garms. 1983. Variation and distribution of forms of *Simulium soubrense* and *S. sanctipauli* in West Africa. *Ann. Trop. Med. Parasitol.* 77:627–640.

Meredith, S. E. O., and H. Townson. 1981. Enzymes for species identification in the *Simulium damnosum* complex from West Africa. *Tropenmed. Parasitol.* 32:123–129.

Oxford, G. S., and D. Rollinson, Eds. 1983. *Protein polymorphism: adaptive and taxonomic significance*. Academic Press, New York and London.

Panyim, S., R. Rosenberg, R. Andre, V. Baimai, C. Green, and N. Tirawanchai. 1984. DNA probes for differentiating mosquito sibling species. *Abstracts of the Joint Meeting of the Royal and American Societies of Tropical Medicine and Hygiene. 2–6 December 1984*. P. 183.

Petersen, J. L. 1981. *Simulium metallicum:* un complejo de especies? Pp. 64–66 in *Proc. Guatemala-Japan Joint Conference on Onchocerciasis Research and Control.* Japan International Cooperation Agency.

———. 1982. Population genetics of some new world Simuliidae. In W. W. M. Steiner, W. J. Tabachnick, K. S. Rai, and S. Narang, Eds., *Recent developments in the genetics of insect disease vectors.* Stipes Publishing Co., Illinois.

Phillips, A., J. F. Walsh, R. Garms, D. H. Molyneux, P. Milligan, and G. Ibrahim. 1985. Identification of adults of the *Simulium damnosum* complex using hydrocarbon analysis. *Tropenmed. Parasitol.* 36:97–101.

Quillévéré, D. 1979. Contribution à l'étude des caractéristiques taxonomiques, bioécologique et vectrices des membres du complexe *Simulium damnosum* présents en Côte d'Ivoire. *Trav. Doc. ORSTOM.* 109:304pp.

Quillévéré, D., M. Gouzy, Y. Séchan, and B. Pendriez. 1977. Etude du complexe *Simulium damnosum* en Afrique de l'Ouest. VI. Analyse de l'eau des gîtes larvaires en saison des pluies; comparaison avec la saison sêche. *Cah. ORSTOM. sér. Entomol. Méd. Parasitol.* 15:195–207.

Rake, A. V. 1972. Isopropanol preservation of biological samples for subsequent DNA extraction and reassociation studies. *Anal. Biochem.* 48:365–368.

Rothfels, K. H. 1979. Cytotaxonomy of black flies (Simuliidae). *Ann. Rev. Entomol.* 24:507–539.

Snyder, T. P. 1982. Electrophoretic characterizations of blackflies in the *Simulium venestum* and *verecundum* species complexes (Diptera: Simuliidae). *Can. Entomol.* 114:503–507.

Snyder, T. P., and M. C. Linton. 1983. Electrophoresis and morphological separation of *Prosimulium fuscum* and *P. mixtum* larvae (Diptera: Simuliidae). *Can. Entomol.* 115:81–87.

Sohn, U.-I. K., K. Rothfels, and N. A. Straus. 1975. DNA:DNA hybridization studies in black flies. *J. Mol. Evol.* 5:75–85.

Southern, E. M. 1975. Detection of specific sequences among DNA fragments separated by gel electrophoresis. *J. Mol. Biol.* 98:503–517.

Teshima, I. 1972. DNA-DNA hybridization in blackflies (Diptera: Simuliidae). *Can. J. Zool.* 50:931–940.

Townson, H., and S. E. O. Meredith. 1979. Identification of Simuliidae in relation to onchocerciasis. Pp. 145–174 in A. E. R. Taylor and R. Muller, Eds., *Problems in the identification of parasites and their vectors.* 17th Symposium of the British Society of Parasitology. Blackwell, Oxford.

World Health Organization. 1978. Onchocerciasis Control Programme in the Volta River Basin area. Evaluation report. Part I. WHO mimeo. doc. WHO/VBC/78.2. 111 pp.

Wright, C. A., Ed. 1974. *Biochemical and immunological taxonomy of animals.* Academic Press, New York and London.

4 CYTOLOGICAL APPROACHES TO BLACK FLY TAXONOMY

Klaus H. Rothfels

Black flies are a favorable group for cytotaxonomic studies because of their large and clear larval salivary-gland chromosomes and low chromosome number (n=3, rarely 2). Early studies have been reviewed by Rothfels (1979a, 1981a,b). Chubareva and Petrova (1979) presented summaries of the cytotaxonomic literature with strong emphasis on contributions from the USSR.

The objective of this chapter is to update the cytotaxonomic literature. The subject matter falls logically into two sections: (1) identification of species (including sibling species) on the basis of polytene chromosomes, with a section on attempts to obtain workable polytene chromosomes from adults; and (2) the construction of phylogenies based on sequential chromosome rearrangements, including attempts to root these. In addition, some suggestions for a standard nomenclature for simuliid cytology are given in the Appendix at the end of the chapter.

CYTOLOGICAL SPECIES DEFINITIONS

It is now generally accepted that many morphospecies in Simuliidae are complexes of sibling species. These sibling species commonly differ in fixed rearrangements (mainly inversions), floating or polymorphic rearrangements, details of sex chromosomes, absence/presence of B-chromosomes, chiasmate/achiasmate meiosis, chiasma pattern, etc., apart from aspects of their biology. One criterion that has come to be employed recently, namely, the stage of gonadal development in mature larvae (Shields and Procunier 1982), may not be reliable, there being considerable evidence (Procunier 1984) that it varies with the season, at least in multivoltine species. Likewise, the diagnostic value of B-chromosomes is limited by the frequent variation in frequency among populations.

Larval Chromosomes

Virtually all cytotaxonomic studies of late instar larvae continue to reveal sibling species or previously undetected taxa, as in *Prosimulium onychodactylum* (Newman 1983; Henderson, 1985a, 1986b), in which approximately 12 sibling species have been recognized, and in the case of *P. transbrachium* (Adler and Kim 1985), which was first recognized cytologically by Rothfels and Freeman (1983).

Sibling speciation is particularly striking in many common *Simulium* morphospecies. Thus sibling species continue to be discovered in *S. articum* (Shields and Procunier 1982, 1987; Procunier 1984), in *S. tuberosum* (Mason 1982, 1984), in *S. (Hellichiella) congareenarum* group (Rothfels and Golini 1983), in the *S. canonicolum* group (Golini and Rothfels 1984), in the *S. vernum* group (Brockhouse 1985, Hunter and Connolly 1986), in the *S. aureum* group (Leonhardt 1985), in *S. virgatum* in Arizona (Conn and Rothfels, unpublished), and in *S. neornatipes* from New Caledonia (Bedo 1984).

Of special practical interest is the mounting evidence for sibling speciation in vectors of *Onchocerca volvulus* and *Mansonella ozzardi*. The already large number of species in *S. damnosum* s.l. (Dunbar and Vajime 1981) is still being added to (Dunbar and Vajime 1987, Vajime and Dunbar 1987). Post (1986) distinguishes *S. soubrense* and *S. soubrense* "B", and there may be other related siblings (Beffa and "form konkoure"). Procunier and Barbiero (1984) consider a monomorphic XoYo form from the Sudan to be specifically distinct from *S. sirbanum*. Indications are of similar situations in Central American *Onchocerca* vectors. In *S. ochraceum* in Guatemala, Hirai and Uemoto (1983) and Hirai (personal communication) chromosomally distinguish three sibling species (A–C). More recently, Hirai et al. (1987) further distinguished three cytotypes within "A." Likewise, for *S. metallicum* in Central America, it has been known for some time (Hirai 1983) that there are two sibling species differing in position of the nucleolar organizer (terminal in IS of "B" vs. basal in IIS of "A"), as well as in fixed rearrangements in chromosome arms IIIL and IIIL (Conn, personal communication). Procunier, Arzube, and Shelley (1986) in Ecuador find three siblings of *S. exiguum* (provisionally designated IIL–std., IIL–3.4, IIL–5+6). Cytological studies of the taxonomically confused *S. amazonicum* complex are just beginning, but there are already indications of the existence of sibling species (Shelley et al. 1987).

Adler (1987) has pointed out that sibling speciation may be suspected wherever a morphospecies occupies very different niches in a stream continuum. Presumably the same applies to forms occupying very different allopatric habitats. To these heuristic guides may be added heterogenous traits with respect to transmission of parasites, incongruence of onchocerciasis foci and the distribution of putative simuliid vectors being a recurrent phenomenon.

All recent studies indicate that the number of biological species yet to be discovered in Simuliidae is large even in relatively well-studied faunas. The synonymizing on the basis of cytological data of some Holarctic forms (*S. venustum* EFG/C-*S. truncatum*, *S. verecundum* ACD-*S. sublacustre* [Rothfels et al. 1978] and *S. corbis-S. rostratum* [Procunier, unpublished]) will not come anywhere near compensating for the increase to be expected in the number of recognized species. Crosskey (1987) has presented a linear extrapolation; the increase may well be exponential.

In a strict sense, assignment of sibling-species status can only be made in sympatric situations, where hybrids are absent. In allopatry, if samples are few and far be-tween, assertion of species status is often impossible because polymorphism frequen-cies may vary locally, may be distributed along clines, or, in extremes, may be fixed for alternative sequences in different parts of the range. Thus as Teshima (unpub-lished) has shown, *Prosimulium pleurale* from the Canadian East (Lake Superior to Labrador) differ from *P. pleurale* in Alaska by two "fixed" inversions in IIIL. Yet, because of the wide gap between eastern and western samples, it would be prema-ture to suggest distinct species.

A similar situation exists, for example, in *Simulium corbis*. Populations from Labra-dor, Quebec, and Ontario have no overt sex chromosomes (Xo,Yo), while samples from Alberta, Alaska, and the Yukon have differentiated Y chromosomes (Shields and Procunier 1987). All these populations share some floating inversions and are endemic for others. In such situations, it is best to proceed conservatively and desig-nate distinctive entities as "cytotypes," or even more noncommittally as "forms," pending further study. Otherwise one may be forced into a reversal, as in the case of *Simulium congareenarum,* for which Dunbar (1967) proposed a southern form (*S. congareenarum*) and a northern form "B," whereas a subsequent study (Rothfels and Golini 1983) demonstrated cytological intermediacy of a geographically intervening population and suggested a panmictic continuum, although with autosomal and sex inversion gradients.

Notwithstanding this caveat, when studies are done on an adequate geographical scale, species status of allopatric populations may be substantiated. A case in point is *S. pugetense,* as studied by Hunter and Connolly (1986) and Choate (1984). A number of cytotypes exist (Fig. 4.1). There are populations ("A") that lack both differentiated sex chromosomes and (numerically) significant autosomal polymorph-isms. Such populations are known from Quebec, Ontario, Alberta, British Colum-bia, and Alaska. Other populations from Alaska and British Columbia have differ-entiated sex chromosomes (IL–1=Y1), but they fall into two categories in Alaska, a southern one with extreme autosomal polymorphism ("B") and a northern one ("B′"), which is strictly monomorphic. These two kinds of populations highlight the allopatric problem. Because of the wide gap between southern and northern samples, species status should not be assumed without studying geographically inter-mediate samples. Populations from Quebec and New Hampshire ("C") also lack autosomal polymorphism, but their males are consistently heterozygous for IL–2+3. Distinctive populations exist in Cypress Hills and the Queen Charlotte Islands (for details, see Fig. 4.1). It is the wide distribution of some cytotypes ("A") and the more restricted but overlapping one of others ("C") that suggest separate species.

Similar but rather more extensive studies exist for *Prosimulium onychodactylum* (Newman 1983; Henderson 1986a, 1986b), where siblings are sympatric in various combinations, and for *S. arcticum* (Shields and Procunier 1982, 1987; Procunier 1984), where perhaps as many as eight distinct siblings exist that are sympatric or widely overlapping in distribution. Likewise, from the studies of Landau (1962) and Mason (1982, 1984, and unpublished), patterns of sibling-species distribution of Holarctic *S. tuberosum* are beginning to emerge. Even entities that are established on the basis of single collections, or from populations of a single locality, as, for example, *S. venustum* A/C (Rothfels et al. 1978), may become validated on further study, pure populations having recently been found in northern Michigan by T. P. Snyder (unpublished) and in Alaska by G. Shields (unpublished).

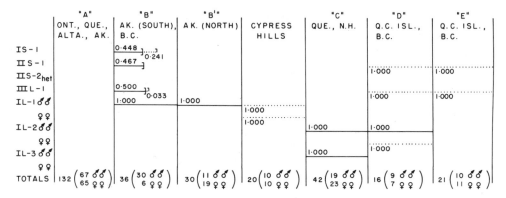

FIG. 4.1 Cytotypes of *Simulium pugetense*. Solid lines indicate heterozygotes, dotted lines indicate inverted homozygotes, and no lines indicate standard homozygotes for the inversions shown on the left. (Data of Hunter and Connolly 1985 and Choate 1984; the method of showing polymorphism data is that of F. Hunter)

Pedestrian though it may appear, it is worthwhile to run the cytotaxonomic studies into the ground geographically, for only this procedure will yield valid conclusions about taxonomic status. It will as well contribute to emerging generalizations on aspects of evolutionary diversification in Simuliidae.

Adult Chromosomes

One of the persistent problems in black fly taxonomy is the linking up of adults with larvae of known cytotype. A number of indirect approaches are available (Rothfels et al. 1978: 1126), primarily the exploitation of pure (monosibling) populations. In some Nematocera, notably anopheline mosquitoes, ovarian nurse cells provide workable polytene chromosomes. This is not the case with simuliids. Fortunately, as Bedo (1976) showed for a number of Australian species, readable polytene chromosomes can be obtained from Malpighian tubules. Using this technique we (unpublished) were able to distinguish adult females of *Cnephia dacotensis* and *C. ornithophilia*. Similarly, Adler (personal communication) could differentiate IS–7 and IIIL–1 wild-caught females of the first (autogenous) generation of *S. vittatum*.

Once diagnostic sibling characteristics are established from larval polytenes, even less-than-perfect preparations from adults may suffice to identify siblings. Thus Procunier (1984) was able to identify the Athabascan cattle pest (IIS–10.11) within the *S. arcticum* complex simply because, among the seven sibling species recognized as larvae in the Athabasca drainage system, IIS–10.11 is the only one that does not have a chromocenter. Procunier (1985) has shown recently that in order to obtain readable adult chromosomes the developmental and nutritional state is critical; the right stage can be judged from the correlated degree of polyteny of ovarian nurse cells. Procunier and Post (1986) were able to obtain chromosomes of adult *S. damnosum* s.l. (sibling soubrense "B") in which the diagnostic interspecific inversions could be identified. These studies are worth pursuing in the hope of obtaining better yields of readable preparations routinely. Certainly all other available approaches, including the biochemical ones, discussed by Townson et al. (1987), allozyme electrophoresis (Snyder 1982; Snyder and Linton 1983, 1984), cuticular hydrocarbons, and DNA probes, should be pursued with vigor.

In concluding this section, it should be iterated (Rothfels et al. 1978: 1126) that in relation to conventional taxonomy the sibling-species concept is provisional. Especially in the usage of taxonomically untrained cytologists, it simply means that the siblings in available larval keys appear to be the same morphospecies or that samples have tentatively been identified by collectors or taxonomists. Subsequent detailed morphological study may well reveal differences, at least in some stages of the life cycle, and permit proper description and naming. This has proven true for some western North American members of the *S. vernum* complex (Adler and Currie 1986). On the other hand, in extensive multivariate analyses, Snyder and Linton (1983) still had difficulty separating the larvae of *P. fuscum* and *P. mixtum*. As proposed by Adler and Kim (1985), taxonomic description should include wherever possible references to cytology and be supported by voucher slides and photographs of polytene chromosomes. This procedure proved decisive in the naming of species in the *sanctipauli* subgroup of *S. damnosum* by Post (1986) based on holotype chromosome preparations deposited by Vajime and Dunbar in the British Museum (Natural History) in 1975.

Cytophylogenies

The principles of the construction of cytophylogenies date back to the early work on *Drosophila pseudoobscura*. Seriation of species is based on sequential rearrangements, commonly inversions and occasionally interchanges, on the assumption that complex rearrangements are compounded of successive two-break steps of unique origin.

In a strict sense, such cytophylogenies are unrooted. Rothfels (1979a: 509) has argued that on the basis of cytology alone the most rational choice of the origin or reference standard for a group of related species is the composite of the central arrangement in each chromosome arm. *Central* here means being present as such in a number of taxa (preferably including different genera) and having given rise to the largest number of independent derivative lines or "phylads" in *Drosophila* jargon. On this basis, a chromosome phylogeny was presented that interrelates *Gymnopais, Twinnia,* and *Prosimulium,* with the prospect of adding *Parasimulium* following chromosome analysis of the recently discovered larvae (Wood; Courtney and Craig, personal communications).

This procedure is in essence equivalent to an application of the principle of parsimony (Farris 1983) and the "outgroup" comparison of Watrous and Wheeler (1981). Gordon (1982) has explicitly applied both outgroup comparison and the L' test (Farris 1978) in attempting to relate three species in the *S. jenningsi* group to the *Simulium* subgeneric standard proposed by Rothfels et al. (1978). Clearly as discussed in relation to IL–1 and the IIIS sequences of the Prosimuliinae (Rothfels 1979a: 533) centrality of a sequence in a number of genera does not *prove* ancestrality; a peripheral type may represent the origin even though it may persist in only one or two taxa. Where the number of taxa examined is small and no outgroup comparisons suggest themselves, the choice of standard must be entirely arbitrary and is usually based on the species represented by the best available slides and photographs.

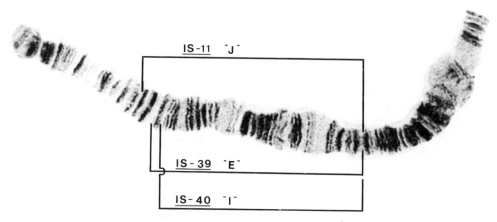

F<small>IG</small>. 4.2 Coincidence and near-coincidence of inversion breakpoints in the *IS–11* region of *S. aureum* (plotted on the "J" sequence). *IS–11* is the inversion by which "J" differs from standard in this region. *IS–39* ("E") and *IS–40* ("I") each largely invert *IS–11* to simulate standard. This led to the erroneous placement of "E" and "F" in the phylogeny of Dunbar (1959). (Data of Leonhardt 1985)

From this standard, however chosen, taxa are arranged, generally dichotomously, on the basis of shared rearrangements. In arranging phylad sequences there are a number of pitfalls. The first of these is the occurrence of "mimic" inversions (Fig. 4.2), i.e., independent inversions that have very similar breakpoints. Such inversions occur much more frequently than expected on the basis of randomness of breakpoints, either because there are hotspots of breakage or more likely because there is induction of breakage and/or failure of restitution in rearrangement heterozygotes (Rothfels and Fairlie 1957, Thompson 1962), leading to derivative mimic inversions. Unfortunately the result is that a two-step derivative of standard (inverted plus reinverted mimic) bears greater resemblance to the standard itself than does the single-step intermediate.

Confusion with the standard will lead to erroneous phylogenies, as in the case of the *S. aureum* complex (see Fig. 4.2). Similarly, Rothfels initially interpreted the IIIL sequence of the Alaskan *Prosimulium* "*hirtipes*" group as standard until Basrur (1962) showed that it is doubly inverted, IIIL–2 being followed by its mimic IIIL–3. The IIIL sequences of *S. venustum* and *S. verecundum* provide another example where two inversions (IIIL–3 and IIIL–4) with one coincident breakpoint effectively transpose a very small chromosome section to a new site (Rothfels et al. 1978). It must also be understood that in banding comparisons small (fixed) differences may simply be overlooked or read through—presumption of identity is always provisional—and misinterpretations may be detected on subsequent, more careful reexamination. A recent example is the reanalysis by Post (1986) of the *sanctipauli* subgroup of *S. damnosum* s.l., which revealed two previously overlooked inversions (IL–A and 2L–A) and resolved a muddled situation. The only safeguard against these pitfalls is a very precise comparison of banding patterns and determination of breakpoints.

Another confounding feature is the appearance, following its apparent initial ab-

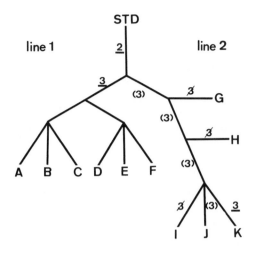

FIG 4.3 Seeming convergent (or independent) origin of an inversion in two separate lines. In line 1 of the *Prosimulium* (IIIL)–*2* group (IIIL)–*3* is fixed in all 6 species (A–F). In line 2 it is absent in the first 2 species (G, H) but "surfaces" in the more distal J and K. It is postulated that *IIIL–3* is monophyletic, was carried floating, (3), in line 2, was lost in G, H, and I, remained floating in J and became fixed, *3*, in K. (Simplified from Rothfels 1979a, fig. 4)

sence, of an arrangement fixed in a related lineage, i.e., an apparent convergence or homoplasy. Such arrangements are best interpreted as unique in origin, being fixed in one lineage and carried polymorphically in the other, with loss in "early" derivative species but survival (floating or fixed) in "later" ones (Fig. 4.3). This interpretation may apply to the sporadic surfacing of IIIL–3 in the IIIL–2 lineage of Alaskan *Prosimulium* (R. Nambiar, unpublished; Rothfels 1979a; fig. 4) or to the emergence of IIIS–2 in members of the *Helodon* IIIS–3 series (Rothfels, unpublished). Single origin is supported by the fact that for inversions such homoplasy occurs only in closely related lines. This is not true for interchanges that when fixed are universally whole-arm (Rothfels 1979b: 216) and therefore can occur only in limited number. Thus we would argue that the interchange of the related *Prosimulium magnum* and *P. multidentatum* is monophyletic, as is that common to all *Metacnephia,* but that the interchanges shared between *P. vernale* and *Metacnephia* and between *Twinnia hirticornis* and *Paraustrosimulium* (Rothfels, unpublished) are convergent.

While it is desirable to resolve completely chromosome rearrangements throughout the members of a group, even a partial resolution may yield useful indications of relationships. The principle of "uniqueness of rearrangements" (Rothfels 1956) implies that if two taxa share continuity over at least one inversion breakpoint relative to a third (or group of others) they are related at least in that segment. We stipulate continuity over *one* breakpoint, since each breakpoint specifies the inversion, but one transition may be disrupted by a subsequent rearrangement. Such a comparison extended to a number of chromosome regions may enable the construction of a cladogram—on a Hennigian basis, as recently attempted by Green et al. (1985) for a group of anopheline mosquitoes. The same approach is being applied in attempts to generate a cohesive flow sheet combining the disjunct chromosomal analyses of various groups of *Simulium* (e.g., Rothfels and Golini 1983, Golini and Rothfels 1984, Leonhardt 1985, Hunter and Connolly 1986), each at present with its own individual group standard.

A number of unrooted cytophylogenies were compiled for the previous review (Rothfels 1979a). Since then, Henderson (1986a), using her own and Newman's (1983) data, provided a chromosome phylogeny for *Prosimulium onychodactylum* siblings. Procunier (1982b) published an extended phylogeny for *Metacnephia* confounded by the uncertain taxonomic relationship (and possible identity) of Palaearctic *M. pallipes* and Nearctic *M. saileri*. Another phylogeny interrelates species in *Cnephia* s. str. (Procunier 1982a), of particular interest in the derivation of the n=2 *C. lapponica*. For *Simulium* (*Gnus* or *malyshevi* group), Shields and Procunier (1987) have a cytophylogeny relating a considerable number of *S. arcticum* siblings (Shields and Procunier 1982) to *S. corbis*, *S. defoliarti*, *S. malyshevi*, and *S. nigricoxum*. Brockhouse (1985), Hunter and Connolly (1986), and Hunter (unpublished) give a cytophylogeny of the Holarctic *S. vernum* group. Publications by Landau (1962) and Mason (1982, 1984) may be used to generate a cytophylogeny of *S. tuberosum*. Feraday (1980) presents a phylogeny of the *S. decorum-ornatum* group. Leonhardt (1985) revised and extended Dunbar's (1959) cytophylogeny of *S. aureum*, and Bedo (1984) updated the chromosome phylogeny of the *S. ornatipes/neornatipes* assemblage.

Even though they are unrooted, cytophylogenies may make possible cytogeographic conclusions of some value. In this context, it is reassuring to find that the geographical distribution of groupings recognized on the basis of cytology (but not morphology) makes sense, as, for example, in the array of the main lineages of *Prosimulium* (Rothfels 1979a: 516) and the east-west distribution of siblings of *S. damnosum* s.l. in Africa (Dunbar and Vajime 1981). Interfaunal connections may be suggested or made plausible. Thus Brockhouse (1985) in his study of the Holarctic *S. vernum* complex found that the only member common to the Old and New World (Alaska) is the "Knebworth" type, and that in North America the farther east and south the *S. vernum* siblings are in distribution, the more remote they are from Knebworth—the standard. Thus the connection between the Old and New World members of the complex appears to be via "Beringia." The same appears to be true for *S. tuberosum*, sibling FGI being common to Norway and Alaska but not occurring in the Nearctic East (Mason 1982, 1984). In contrast, for *S. verecundum* (ACD) the connection between the New World and the Old World (as *sublacustre*) may have been via Greenland (as *groenlandicum*), and *S. vittatum* appears to be extending its range from North America via Greenland, Iceland, and the Faroes. Its absence in Siberia is perhaps explained by its confinement south of the Brooks Range in Alaska.

In very special cases partial or complete directionality of a cytophylogeny can be established. Species such as *S. aureum* and *C. lapponica* with n=2 must clearly be derived from trichromosomic ancestors. For *C. lapponica*, Procunier (1982a) could demonstrate the chromosomal constitution of the ancestral *Cnephia*. For *S. aureum*, Leonhardt (1985) carried out a comparison with possible antecedents suggested by Crosskey (personal communication) on morphological grounds in the *S. vernum* and *S. ruficorne* (*nigritarse* subgroup) groups. Her comparisons suggest that the origin of *S. aureum*, whether from the *S. vernum* or *S. ruficorne* group, is Old World. The very recent discovery (Leonhardt, unpublished) that the African *Simulium* (*Freemanellum*) *manense* is n=2, male-achiasmate, and in banding sequence intermediate between *S. vernum* and *S. aureum* lends additional support to an Old World origin of the *S. aureum* complex. These findings give directionality to the chromosome phylogeny and show that sibling "A" is the most derived member of the complex in the New World.

Utopian though it may appear at present, the linking up of the various partial phylogenies using shared transitions over breakpoints and proceeding stepwise may ultimately permit construction of a rough chromosomal flow sheet extending through the entire family Simuliidae. Fixation of the origin then becomes a matter of controversy among morphologists, zoogeographers, etc., but will ultimately be settled by DNA (nucleotide) sequence outgroup comparisons to chironomids, mosquitoes, and sandflies.

APPENDIX

Nomenclature

It is desirable to achieve a degree of uniformity in the nomenclature of chromosomes, rearrangements, and taxonomic entities. We are saddled with a considerable load of published usages that are not easy to reconcile. It should be recalled that it took several international meetings before a nomenclatural system for the human chromosome complement was agree on at the Paris conference, and human cytogeneticists are concerned with *one* species and ordinary somatic chromosomes. Initial proposals for chromosome and inversion nomenclature were published by Basrur (1959: 532) and elaborated by Bedo (1977: 39). The following notes do not offer definitive proposals but merely some suggestions.

Most black fly species have n=3 more or less metacentric chromosomes, and there is some agreement, for example, between the Leningrad and Toronto laboratories, to use I, II, and III in decreasing order of size. However, 1, 2, and 3, as used by some authors (Landau 1962, Post 1986), will be readily understood.

Centromeres (CI–CIII) in most species are expanded and distinctive and frequently morphologically similar in two or all three chromosomes. Where they are not immediately self-evident, they can sometimes be identified by recurrent ectopic pairing or by comparison of banding pattern to related species in which they are distinctive or in which they are joined in a chromocenter. For the designation of chromosome arms, *S* and *L* for short and long appears preferable to the "right" and "left" of *Drosophila* heritage. In early studies the usage prevailed of measuring polytene chromosomes and chromosome arms, often accompanied by appropriate statistics. This now appears rather pointless; in fact, probably no one uses measurements provided in the literature for identification of chromosomes. Identification of chromosome arms has to be by "landmarks," since arm association may change through whole-arm interchanges. To the list of interchanges already published should be added *S. nigricoxum* (IS+IIIL; Shields and Procunier 1987) and *Paraustrosimulium* (IIS+IIIS; Rothfels, unpublished).

The best available guide to the identification of landmarks is probably in the maps proposed for *Simulium* (*Simulium*) by Rothfels et al. (1978). Unfortunately, for IS and IL there are no universal landmarks, but the banding pattern of the IS end is highly conserved, and in *Simulium* s.l. the basal "3" and the "cup and saucer" (sections 11 and 12) may serve. Landmarks of wide applicability in IL are the major "marker" (section 26) and the subterminal "3" (40 distal), in addition to the end pattern. IIS, the second shortest arm, is readily recognized by the Ring of Balbiani (RB), the "shoestring" usually central in the "double bubble" or "bulges" and in many forms by the basal "trapezoid(al)." IIL is universally characterized by "3 sharp" bands adjacent to the centromere and interstitially by a characteristic puff termed Parabalbiani (PB) with one sharp and one flared profile. IIIS, the shortest arm, has a conspicuous "heavy" band group bounded on one side by two more or less distinct light bands and on the other side by a puffed alveolar region ("blister"). The end is frequently "frazzled" and the arm carries a conspicuous "sawtooth" or "capsule," usually basally.

For IIIL, again there are no universal markers, though there is a tendency for a single, heavy basal band (section 54), a compound "basal marker" (BM), and the subterminal (section 99) "three heavy groups" to be preserved. The nucleolar organizer (NO), because of its "mobility," is of no general use in identifying chromosome arms, though its position frequently is preserved in related species. Unfortunately, in addition to the landmark designations given above, many others loosely and descriptively used have become "immortalized" in the literature. Like our own, many of these are not particularly apropos and not consistently used, and their usage should be discouraged.

Regarding band designation, the practice of partitioning the complement into 100 sections (IS–IIL) is gaining ground, with subdivisions in letters (commonly A–C), and with individual bands enumerated in a ternary system as 1A1, 1A2, . . . This practice will eventually lead to some difficulties as band resolution is increased. Regardless of measured length of chromosome arms, it may be useful to adopt total section numbers per arm as in Rothfels et al. (1978).

As to inversion designations, a number of systems are in use. The early studies numbered inversions consecutively by arms IS–1, IS–2 . . . in order of discovery within species groups. This became unwieldy, and in some publications, beginning with Basrur (1962), a distinction was made between fixed inversions (underlined), which were given consecutive numbers by arms (IS–1), and intraspecific (floating-polymorphic) inversions, which were identified by an abbreviated specific epithet (IS–1tr [for *travisi*]). Both systems run into trouble. First, for groups that are studied in several laboratories (e.g., *S. damnosum*), coordination becomes difficult and subsidiary systems, for example, based alphabetically (IS–A), come into use that are of limited availability and uncertain synonymy. The specific epithet system becomes clumsy where a floating inversion is shared among several species (e.g., a IIIL inversion among four species in the *S. canonicolum* group [Rothfels and Golini 1983]). It is also awkward where an inversion fixed between two species is floating in a third.

As regards designation of complex inversions, following Basrur (1959) a period is frequently used to separate included inversions (IS–1.2) and a comma to separate overlapping ones (IS–1,2). Graphically, inversions are best shown by brackets (exact or approximate ⌐⌐ ⋯) on chromosome maps. This alleviates problems with the ternary breakpoint designations. Again following Basrur (1959), dotted brackets are sometimes used for X-linked inversions and broken ones for Y-linked sequences. This usage runs into trouble when an inversion is sex-linked in one species and autosomal in another, or where sex-linkage is partial. In the textual description of sex-chromosome systems, XoYo is frequently used to denote undifferentiated sex chromosomes, and X1X2 . . . and Y1Y2 . . . for sex chromosomes of (generally) increasing complexity (Post 1982). For complex inversions, limits of the second inversion (when overlapping) are generally shown by a dotted-line extension to standard, the order of brackets being arbitrary for included inversions.

Regarding the naming of siblings species, a number of systems are in use. The simplest are alphabetical A, B, C . . . (e.g., Dunbar 1959 for *S. aureum*) or numerical 1, 2 . . . (e.g., Newman 1983 for *P. onychodactylum*). A second system uses inversion numbers of sex-linked arrangements (e.g., Rothfels and Featherston 1981 for *S. vittatum*) of autosomal ones (e.g., Shields and Procunier 1982 for some *S. arcticum*). A letter system describing sex-chromosome constitution (IIS) in *S. tuberosum* was introduced by Landau (1962) and perpetuated by Mason (1982, 1984) and Rothfels et al. (1978). This last system becomes awkward when sex arm switches occur. Finally, geographic designations have been used (e.g., Brockhouse 1985 for *S. vernum*). What is definitely to be discouraged is the use of collection numbers, which are frequently uninterpretable unless one has access to the collector's "black book." As for the rest, the advantages of mnemonic usefulness of inversion designations have to be weighed against the simplicity of the alphabetical (or numerical) system. The upshot of all this is that not too many conventions should be "prescribed" and authors should use whatever system best fits their material. Taxonomists (e.g., R. W. Crosskey, personal communication) urge strongly and reasonably the adoption of the A,B, . . . system to facilitate citation and communication with noncytologists.

Finally, there is the matter of designation of entities as cytotypes/cytospecies, zymotypes/zymospecies, forms/sibling (species), species (morphospecies), species complexes, and species groups. The first point to be made is that species are species as long as the evidence for reproductive isolation (real or potential) is good, regardless of whether this evidence comes from morphology, cytology, or biochemistry. Use of the prefixes morpho-, cyto-, zymo-, etc., is of value only in indicating the nature of the evidence. Cytotype is a provisional designation to indicate that regional (or temporal) collections are cohesive *inter se* and differ in significant respects from collections taken elsewhere or at other times. Usage of zymotypes is analogous. A "complex," as proposed by Crosskey (1981), is an assemblage of sibling species within a morphospecies. A species "group" includes a number of related morphospecies with their siblings. There are large gray areas in all these concepts. Cytotypes may become cytospecies and eventually morphospecies. They may also evaporate entirely. Regarding complexes and groups, the usual situation is that a number of names are available, some of which may collapse into synonymy, and others may prove to designate valid morphospecies or even a group of morphospecies once the requisite taxonomic revisions are carried out. In practice, what is important is to produce well-documented descriptions of the forms under study and all else will follow. One need not worry unduly about limits of complexes or other provisional designations.

ACKNOWLEDGMENTS

I acknowledge constructive comments on the manuscript by R. W. Crosskey and P. H. Adler. Studies from our laboratory were financially supported by the NSERC (Canada).

EDITOR'S NOTE: Because of Dr. Rothfel's untimely death, the page proofs of this chapter were kindly checked by R. M. Feraday, whose efforts are duly acknowledged.

LITERATURE CITED

Adler, P. H. 1987 (this volume). Ecology of black fly sibling species.

Adler, P. H., and D. C. Currie. 1986. Taxonomic resolution of three new species near *Simulium vernum* Macquart (Diptera: Simuliidae). *Can. Entomol.* 118:1207–1220.

Adler, P. H., and K. C. Kim. 1985. Taxonomy of black fly sibling species: two new species in the *Prosimulium mixtum* group (Diptera: Simuliidae). *Ann. Entomol. Soc. Am.* 78:41–49.

Basrur, P. K. 1959. The salivary gland chromosomes of seven segregates of *Prosimulium* (Diptera: Simuliidae) with a transformed centromere. *Can. J. Zool.* 37:527–570.

———. 1962. The salivary gland chromosomes of seven species of *Prosimulium* (Diptera: Simuliidae) from Alaska and British Columbia. *Can. J. Zool.* 40:1019–33.

Bedo, D. G. 1976. Polytene chromosomes in pupal and adult blackflies. *Chromosoma* 57:387–396.

———. 1977. Cytogenetics and evolution of *Simulium ornatipes* Skuse (Diptera: Simuliidae). I. Sibling speciation. *Chromosoma* 64:37–65.

———. 1984. Sibling speciation and sex chromosome differentiation in *Simulium neornatipes* (Diptera: Simuliidae). *Can. J. Genet. Cytol.* 26:318–325.

Brockhouse, C. 1985. Sibling species and sex chromosomes in *Eusimulium vernum* (Diptera: Simuliidae). *Can. J. Zool.* 63:2145–61.

Choate, L. A. 1984. A cytological description of *Eusimulium vernum*, *E. X*, and the *E. pugetense* complex (Diptera: Simuliidae) in Alaska. M.Sc. Thesis, University of Alaska, Fairbanks.

Chubareva, L. A., and N. A. Petrova. 1979. Basic characteristics of blackflies (Diptera, Simuliidae) of the world fauna. (In Russian.) Pp. 58–95 in *Karyosystematics of the invertebrate animals.* Academy of Sciences of the USSR.

Crosskey, R. W. 1981. Simuliid taxonomy—the contemporary scene. Pp. 3–18 in M. Laird, ed., *Blackflies: the future for biological methods in integrated control.* Academic Press, New York and London.

———. 1987 (this volume). The future of black fly taxonomy.

Dunbar, R. W. 1959. The salivary gland chromosomes of seven forms of black flies included in *Eusimulium aureum* Fries. *Can. J. Zool.* 37:495–525.

———. 1967. The salivary gland chromosomes of six closely related nearctic blackflies near *Eusimulium congareenarum* (Diptera: Simuliidae). *Can. J. Zool.* 45:377–396.

Dunbar, R. W., and C. G. Vajime. 1981. Cytotaxonomy of the *Simulium damnosum* complex. Pp. 31–43 in M. Laird, Ed., *Blackflies: the future for biological methods in integrated control.* Academic Press, New York and London.

———. 1987. Cytotaxonomic identification of *Simulium* (*Edwardsellum*) *oceepeense* new species and *S.* (*E.*) *damnosum* (Theobald) (Diptera: Simuliidae). (in preparation)

Farris, J. S. 1978. Inferring phylogenetic trees from chromosomal inversion data. *Syst. Zool.* 27:275–284.

———. 1983. The logical basis of phylogenetic analysis. *Adv. Cladistics* 2:7–36.

Feraday, R. M. 1980. The polytene chromosomes of members of the *Simulium ornatum-decorum* lineage. M.Sc. Thesis, University of Toronto, Ontario.

Golini, V. I., and K. Rothfels. 1984. The polytene chromosomes of North American blackflies in the *Eusimulium canonicolum* group (Diptera: Simuliidae). *Can. J. Zool.* 62:2097–2109.

Gordon, A. E. 1982. The cytotaxonomy of three species in the *jenningsi*-group of the subgenus *Simulium* (Diptera: Simuliidae) in New York State. *Can. J. Zool.* 62:347–354.

Green, C. A., B. A. Harrison, T. Klein, and V. Baimai. 1985. Cladistic analysis of polytene chromosome rearrangements in anopheline mosquitoes, subgenus *Cellia*, series *Neocellia*. *Can. J. Genet. Cytol.* 27:123–133.

Henderson, C. A. P. 1986a. A cytological study of the *Prosimulium onychodactylum* complex (Diptera: Simuliidae). *Can. J. Zool.* 64:32–44.

———. 1986b. Homosequential species 2a and 2b within the *Prosimulium onychodactylum* complex (Diptera): temporal heterogeneity, linkage disequilibrium and Wahlund effect. *Can. J. Zool.* 64:859–866.

Hirai, H. 1983. A cytogenetic study of *Simulium metallicum* obtained from Guatemala and Venezuela. In I. Tada, Ed., *A comparative study on onchocerciasis between south and central Americas*. Shimoda Printing and Co., Ltd., Matsubase, Shimomashiki-jun, Kumamoto.

Hirai, H., and K. Uemoto. 1983. The analysis of salivary gland chromosomes of *Simulium ochraceum* from Guatemala and Mexico. *Jpn. J. Sanit. Zool.* 34:120.

Hirai, H., K. Uemoto and J. O. Ochoa. 1987. Polytene chromosome polymorphisms of *Simulium ochraceum* Walker (Diptera: Simuliidae): the main vector for Central American onchocerciasis. *Am. J. Trop. Med. Hys.* (submitted).

Hunter, F. F., and V. Connolly. 1986. A cytotaxonomic investigation of seven species in the *Eusimulium vernum* group. *Can. J. Zool.* 64:296–311.

Landau, R. 1962. Four forms of *Simulium tuberosum* (Lundstr.) in southern Ontario: a salivary gland chromosome study. *Can. J. Zool.* 40:921–939.

Leonhardt, K. G. 1985. A cytological study of species in the *Eusimulium aureum* group. *Can. J. Zool.* 63:2043–61.

Mason, G. F. 1982. Cytological studies of sibling species of *Simulium tuberosum* (Lundstroem) (Diptera: Simuliidae). *Can. J. Zool.* 60:292–303.

———. 1984. Sex chromosome polymorphism in the *Simulium tuberosum* complex (Lundstroem) (Diptera: Simuliidae). *Can. J. Zool.* 62:647–658.

Newman, L. J. 1983. Sibling species of the blackfly *Prosimulium onychodactylum* (Simuliidae, Diptera): a salivary gland chromosome study. *Can. J. Zool.* 61:2816–35.

Post, R. J. 1982. Sex-linked inversions in blackflies (Diptera: Simuliidae). *J. Hered.* 48:85–93.

———. 1986. The cytotaxonomy of *Simulium sanctipauli* and *Simulium soubrense* (Diptera: Simuliidae). *Genetica* 69:191–208.

Procunier, W. S. 1982a. A cytological study of species in *Cnephia* s. str. (Diptera: Simuliidae). *Can. J. Zool.* 60:2866–78.

———. 1982b. A cytological description of ten taxa in *Metacnephia* (Diptera: Simuliidae). *Can. J. Zool.* 60:2852–65.

———. 1984. Cytological identification of pest species of the *Simulium arcticum* complex present in the Athabasca River and associated tributaries. *Alberta Agric. Farming for the Future Tech. Rept.* (82–0101). 44 pp.

———. 1985. Adult identification in *Simulium:* apparent dependence of polyteny on food source in Malpighian tubule and nurse cell nuclei during oogenesis. *Final report to the OCP/OMS program*, Ouagadougou, Burkino Faso.

Procunier, W. S., M. Arzube, and A. J. Shelley. 1986. Sibling species of *Simulium exiguum* (Diptera): the primary vector of onchocerciasis in Ecuador. *Rev. Ecuat. Hig. Med. Trop.* (in press).

Procunier, W. S., and V. K. Barbiero. 1984. Identification of a new form of *Simulium sirbanum* from the Abu Hamed oncho focus in Sudan. (Paper presented to the American and Royal Societies of Tropical Medicine, Baltimore, Md., December 1984).

Procunier, W. S., and R. J. Post. 1986. Development of a method for the cytological identification of man-biting sibling species within the *Simulium damnosum* complex. *Tropenmed. Parasitol.* 37:49–53.

Rothfels, K. 1956. Blackflies: siblings, sex and species grouping. *J. Hered.* 47:113–122.

———. 1979a. Cytotaxonomy of black flies (Simuliidae). *Ann. Rev. Entomol.* 24:507–539.

———. 1979b. Chromosomal variability and speciation in blackflies. Pp. 207–224 in *R. Entomol. Soc. London Symp. No. 10*, Oxford, Blackwell Scientific Publications.

————. 1981a. Cytotaxonomy: principles and their application to some northern species-complexes in *Simulium*. Pp. 19–29 in M. Laird, ed., *Blackflies: the future for biological methods in integrated control*. Academic Press, New York and London.

————. 1981b. Cytological approaches to the study of blackfly systematics and evolution. Pp. 67–83 in M. W. Stock, Ed., *Application of genetics and cytology in insect systematics and evolution*. Forest Wildlife Range Exp. Stn., University of Idaho, Moscow, Idaho.

Rothfels, K., and T. W. Fairlie. 1957. The non-random distribution of inversion breaks in the midge *Tendipes decorus*. *Can. J. Zool.* 35:221–263.

Rothfels, K., and D. W. Featherston. 1981. The population structure of *Simulium vittatum* (Diptera: Simuliidae): the IIIL–1 and IS–7 sibling species. *Can. J. Zool.* 59:1857–83.

Rothfels, K., R. Feraday, and A. Kaneps. 1978. A cytological description of sibling species of *Simulium venustum* and *S. verecundum* with standard maps for the subgenus *Simulium* Davies (Diptera). *Can. J. Zool.* 55:482–507.

Rothfels, K., and M. Freeman. 1983. A new species of *Prosimulium* (Diptera: Simuliidae): an interchange as a primary reproductive isolating mechanism? *Can. J. Zool.* 61:2612–17.

Rothfels, K., and V. I. Golini. 1983. The polytene chromosomes of species of *Eusimulium* (*Hellichiella*) (Diptera: Simuliidae). *Can. J. Zool.* 61:1220–31.

Shelley, A. J., A. P. A. Luna Dias, M. A. P. Moraes, and W. S. Procunier. 1987. The status of *Simulium oyapockense* s.l./*roraimense* and *Simulium limbatum* of the *S. amazonicum* group as vectors of human onchocerciasis in lowland tropical forest and savannah areas of northern Brazil. *Ann. Trop. Med. Hyg.* (in press).

Shields, G. F., and W. S. Procunier. 1982. A cytological description of sibling species of *Simulium* (*Gnus*) *arcticum* (Diptera: Simuliidae). *Polar Biol.* 1:181–192.

————. 1987. Cytological descriptions of North American black flies in the group *Gnus* (Simuliidae). (In preparation).

Snyder, T. P. 1982. Electrophoretic characterizations of black flies in the *Simulium venustum* and *verecundum* species complexes (Diptera: Simuliidae). *Can. Entomol.* 114:503–507.

Snyder, T. P., and M. C. Linton. 1983. Electrophoretic and morphological separation of *Prosimulium fuscum* and *P. mixtum* larvae (Diptera: Simuliidae). *Can. Entomol.* 115:81–87.

————. 1984. Population structure in black flies: allozymic and morphological estimates for *Prosimulium mixtum* and *P. fuscum* (Diptera: Simuliidae). *Evolution* 38:942–956.

Thompson, P. E. 1962. Asynapsis and mutability in *Drosophila melanogaster*. *Genetics* 51:23–40.

Townson, H., R. J. Post, and A. Phillips. 1987 (this volume). Biochemical approaches to black fly taxonomy.

Vajime, C. G., and R. W. Dunbar. 1987. Distribution and sex in the black flies *Simulium* (*Edwardsellum*) *sirbanum* and *S.* (*E.*) *sudanense* in West Africa (Diptera: Simuliidae). (in preparation).

Watrous, L. E., and Q. D. Wheeler. 1981. The out-group comparison method of character analysis. *Syst. Zool.* 30:1–11.

5 THE ROLE OF SYSTEMATICS IN BLACK FLY POPULATION MANAGEMENT

Stefanie E. O. Meredith

In order to assess the role of systematics in population management, I will briefly discuss the interpretation of systematics and approaches to systematics, population management, and finally the application of systematics in field situations and its problems.

Systematics is a rather nebulous term that has different connotations to different authors. Some regard the term as synonymous with taxonomy or classification (Mason 1950, Ross 1974). Others, such as Blackwelder (1967), Mayr (1969), and Fergusson (1980), use it in a comprehensive sense, as the study and description of the diversity of organisms and their relationships. Simpson (1961) defined systematics as the science of diversity, but even with a concise definition the term still remains a somewhat vague concept that may be adapted to different requirements.

In my opinion, systematics is indeed a broader field of biology than taxonomy or classification. The term "systematics" has evolved to include continually increasing knowledge about the ecology, behavior, physiology, genetics, biochemistry, and biogeography in the system of classification. The organisms are not only placed in an evolutionary context, as they are in modern taxonomy, but also in the context of their relationships with each other and the physical environment.

If we define taxonomy as classification, determination of phylogenetic relationships, and nomenclature of species, then taxonomy provides the backbone and basis of the science of systematics. Knowledge about an organism's taxonomic classification already provides a great deal of information about it. Indeed, no intelligible biological studies of any kind can be conducted outside such a classificatory framework. Broadly speaking, however, the end goal for a taxonomist lies in the identification and determination of phylogenetic relationships. The more complex an organism's life cycle and relationships to other species, in cases, for example, of vector and parasite species, the more multifaceted its classification. Different criteria, perhaps classical, morphological, biochemical, cytological, or numerical criteria, may be applied, yielding different but not always entirely coinciding descriptions of how the organisms are related to each other. Behavior and ecology become significant classificatory criteria in programs of pest control and management. It is systematics that attempts to reconcile the various criteria into an accurate, understandable, and practically useful framework for the pursuit of further biological studies.

APPROACHES TO SYSTEMATICS (WITH PARTICULAR REGARD TO SIMULIIDAE)

Clearly, the first step is the collection of material for taxonomic identification, and subsequently the storage of the collections as permanent reference material and records. The role and importance of setting up and maintaining good systematic collections has been cogently argued by Kosztarab (1975), Kim (1978), and Hardy (1982). Until fairly recently, museum collections were composed of preserved specimens identified on the basis of their morphological "hard parts." In general, the conventional taxonomic techniques based on structural features will allow identification to species group of at least one of the life stages of simuliids, and morphological characters still provide the framework for other criteria. However, in the light of the recent discovery that black flies, like many other organisms, often consist of sibling species or species complexes, which by definition are "morphologically similar or identical species which are reproductively isolated" (Mayr 1942), other methods and criteria are required in order to distinguish the sibling species.

Grjebine et al. (1973) consider that the enormous progress in the evolution of systematics of vector species is largely due to the development of vector control programs and the need for greater understanding of the vector species. The resulting application of combined morphological, genetical, cytological, and biochemical studies has revealed the existence of numerous species complexes and sibling species. The unmasking of these extra species and subspecies may complicate matters, however, rather than elucidate them. In many vector control programs (malaria in particular), a great deal of disagreement and confusion arises because of the misunderstanding of what is meant by a species or subspecies. The concept of what is a species, or when is a species a species, has always been a controversial matter. Workers on different groups of organisms frequently employ different criteria in determining the specific status of a population. The biological attributes of various groups may be interpreted in quite different ways; for example, what may seem like demic variation to an ichthyologist may indicate distinct species to an entomologist. At this level, the differences in opinion provide interesting academic discussions; but when workers in the same field hold different criteria, the confusion and complications become serious. We risk reaching this stage with the integrated approach to systematics when an entomologist may be a biochemist/morphologist/cytologist or geneticist and may emphasize or even rely on different criteria for species differentiation.

I will briefly discuss some of the current techniques used in the identification of sibling groups. The method that has probably contributed most to our knowledge of the existence of sibling species of black flies is the study of polytene chromosomes. In fact, many species have recently been described on the basis of their chromosome arrangements. Despite some hesitation in the beginning, chromosome morphology is now widely accepted as a bona fide criterion for species description. Type specimens of chromosome preparations are also legitimate and should be included in systematic collections to allow specific identification of sibling species. However, chromosome descriptions should be accompanied by morphological descriptions of the larvae, pupae, and adults (and, of course, the converse).

Biochemical studies of isoenzymes have proven useful in the differentiation of many vector species, particularly in mosquito groups and less so in black flies. Isoenzymes, however, can provide a useful tool for identification rather than a means of describing a species (Townson et al. 1987). Newer, biochemical and molecular techniques also show considerable promise as tools for the specific identification of members of species complexes. Other criteria that are of value in the identification of insect vectors include genetic information, e.g., hybridization and mating compatibilities, behavioral differences of feeding, resting, etc., and biogeographical data. In some groups of Simuliidae these kinds of data can be obtained, but unfortunately many groups are extremely difficult to maintain in laboratory colonies and thus preclude such studies.

POPULATION MANAGEMENT AND CONTROL

Both man and animals can be directly affected by black flies; certain species are merely biting nuisances, while others are significant disease vectors. Even as biting nuisances, black flies can cause economic losses: diminished dairy and meat production (Edgar 1953, Anderson and Voskuil 1963, Charnetoski and Haufe 1981) and disrupted tourist industries (Jamnback 1976, La Scala and Burger 1981). Their major medical importance is due to their role as vectors of onchocerciasis in the tropical Americas, Africa, and Yemen. (See Crosskey 1973 and Jamnback 1976 for details of pathogens other than *Onchocerca volvulus* transmitted by simuliid species.)

Control programs against black flies, then, are instituted either to control biting pests or to interrupt disease transmission. The control of biting nuisances generally requires no more than the reduction of the pest population. But the vector population must be reduced far lower in the case of disease control to assure the interruption of transmission.

Once the nature and the extent of the control program has been determined, the pest species has to be identified. In some cases, this may be fairly straightforward. La Scala and Burger (1981), for example, describe an instance in which *Simulium decorum,* a source of annoyance to tourists vacationing in New Hampshire, was easily distinguished from the small number of other simuliid species present. Similarly, the differentiation between *S. arcticum, S. venustum,* and *S. vittatum* in control programs in northern Alberta is also straightforward. Often, though, the identification of the problem species is more challenging. For example, one of the first published descriptions of the application of enzyme electrophoresis to the determination of biting species of black fly resulted from an investigation of biting species in an area of Maine (Snoddy and Bauer 1977). Here, three closely related species, morphologically indistinguishable in the adult stage, coexisted. Only electrophoretic analysis of the emerged adults of known species and comparison of flies caught in the act of biting permitted the differentiation and identification of the new species *S. penobscotensis* from the *S. jenningsi* group (May et al. 1977).

Control programs aimed at disease vectors (in the case of simuliids, primarily vectors of onchocerciasis) are presented with more complications, even with such basic problems as vector determination. In Central and South America, onchocerciasis occurs in relatively localized foci from Mexico and Guatemala to Venezuela, Colombia, Equador, and northern Brazil. Several simuliid species are incriminated as vectors. The main vectors are thought to be members of the *S. ochraceum* complex, *S. metallicum* complex, and *S. oyapockense* (Shelley and Procunier, in press).

In each of the various foci and endemic areas, the disease may be associated with a different species of black flies. A vector species in one locality may exist in another but be of relatively little vectorial importance. Our understanding of the relative medical importance of the species and of their special biological characteristics, however, remains somewhat vague. Prerequisite to any proposed vector control program in these areas will be careful studies of the incidence and prevalence of onchocerciasis in the human population, of seasonal transmission and vector activity, and of behavior and ecology.

In Africa, our knowledge of the disease and its vectors is much more detailed. The situation is slightly simpler in that the principal vectors in West, central, and East Africa are known to be members of the *S. damnosum* complex, with the *S. neavei* complex acting as vectors in localized areas in East Africa. In central Africa, there may also be other species capable of transmitting onchocerciasis.

Because considerable research has been done on it, the *S. damnosum* complex provides a good illustration of the significance of systematics in population control. Early in the *S. damnosum* studies, differences in biting behavior, eclosion time, and vectorial capacity of morphologically similar, if not indistinguishable, populations were noted. This led to the discovery, by means of a series of cytological studies that *S. damnosum* represents a complex rather than a single species (Dunbar and Vajime 1981, Quillévéré 1975). To date, no less than 34 forms have been described. Eight of these have been formally named on the basis of chromosome morphology (Vajime and Dunbar 1975) and eight on morphological grounds (Gouteux 1977a,b: Elsen et al. 1984). The fact that there is some question about the relationship between certain cytologically delineated forms and some of the morphologically described ones indicates some of the difficulties encountered at this level of classification. It also illustrates the importance of communication between workers. With our present knowledge of the different approaches to systematics, the naming of conspecific morphospecies arising through the use of different criteria need not occur. Many of the members of the *damnosum* complex coexist sympatrically, although each form probably has slightly distinct ecological requirements.

For vector control, the differences in biting behavior, emergence time, and vectorial capacity must be qualified as well as quantified. In this way, the role of each species, form, or perhaps even population in disease transmission may be assessed. In the case of a large-scale operation like the Onchocerciasis Control Programme (OCP) of the World Health Organization in West Africa, which spreads out over seven countries and some 654,000 square kilometers (Walsh et al. 1981), this information must be gathered for each species throughout the range of its distribution. Because control measures tend to be directed at larvae rather than at the biting adults, accurate identification of all the life stages of each species is very important, but as suggested before, it is rather difficult to achieve. Specific identification of the larval stages provides the basis for studies on spatial and temporal distribution, duration of life stage, and, ultimately, susceptibility to control methods. At the adult stage, specific identification is needed for investigation of emergence times, flight range, longevity, and disease transmission.

This kind of information should be collected for at least one full year before a control program is instituted; in the tropics, two or three years' data are really needed to account for variations in climatic conditions. Such changes can influence species distribution, flight ranges, and therefore, to some extent, the epidemiology of the disease.

With these baseline data, the control strategy can be planned and implemented. Despite an apparent reluctance among biologists to rely on and expand the use of insecticides (Pant et al. 1977), the most common control measure in the OCP, as elsewhere, remains the application of larvicides to the rivers in which black fly larvae breed; with the occasional adjunctive use of adulticides.

Alternative methods of black fly control have been successfully carried out on a small scale, for example, the environmental approach described by La Scala and Burger (1981). Other biological control methods involving parasitic nematodes, fungi, and bacteria are being intensively researched at present.

Biological and integrated control methods are more fashionable and philosophically pleasing (Metcalf 1980, Hardy 1982). Unfortunately, they are not really applicable to vector control because of the unacceptability of "equilibrium levels" of the pest in the context of human disease. Service (1983) discusses the limitations of biological control as applied to mosquito species, and most of his arguments hold true for the Simuliidae. Besides the high control criteria required for vector species, unstable ecosystems, high fecundity, and vagility and difficulties in large-scale colonization are discouraging factors.

During a large-scale vector control campaign, constant evaluation and surveillance must be carried out. This allows the assessment of the effectiveness of the control, as well as monitoring changes in susceptibility of the organism to the insecticide, and any changes instigated in the behavior, distribution, or colonizing abilities of the target populations.

Occasionally, I am asked to justify the necessity of identifying the various members of the *S. damnosum* complex as part of OCP's routine evaluation procedures, since the larvae of all species present are to be sprayed anyway. In answer, I can give the example of the *S. soubrense* group, part of the *damnosum* complex. This species became resistant to the larvicide temephos in Ivory Coast (Guillet et al. 1981, Kurtak et al. 1982). Because of its notable vagility, its movements have had to be monitored rigorously with a combination of cytological (in larval stages) and morphological (in adults) identification as well as insecticide susceptibility tests. It was also observed that the various sibling species had differential susceptibilities to insecticides (Kurtak, personal communication). Not only has the control strategy for the species and area in question had to be modified, but, when the OCP extends its operations West, as it plans to do, into an area where this resistant species also occurs, strategic decisions must also be based on this information. Thus these seemingly minor morphological or cytological differences among these closely related species can reflect functional characteristics of great significance, ultimately, to the human being bitten by these black flies. Thus the importance of specific identification, knowledge of species distribution, and bionomics, that is, of systematics, becomes even more evident in the planning and subsequent monitoring of control strategies.

THE APPLICATION OF SYSTEMATICS IN THE FIELD AND ASSOCIATED PROBLEMS

In taxonomy and systematics problems regarding nomenclature have always arisen. Morphospecies with specific names that are conspecific but described by various groups working in different areas are not uncommon. However, now there is the additional problem of the use of divergent criteria and the interpretation of variation in these criteria; this is particularly so in analysis of allopatric populations. As an example, I will take a member of the *damnosum* complex, *Simulium squamosum*.

S. squamosum, like the other members of the *damnosum* complex in West Africa, was described on the basis of its chromosome arrangements (Vajime and Dunbar 1975). In Ivory Coast, this is typically a species of heavily forested, small, fast-flowing rivers or streams. The adult is of an overall dark appearance with primarily dark basal wing tufts.

In Togo, some 1,000 kilometers further east, the larval morphology is similar, but the species is found in a more open environment of gallery forest in Guinean savanna. The adults are generally golden in aspect with primarily pale basal wing tufts. The phosphoglucomutase enzyme variant, which can be used to differentiate *squamosum* from other members of the *damnosum* complex (Meredith and Townson 1982), has a different mobility in this population from the Ivory Coast population, and the vectorial capacity appears to be somewhat different.

Squamosum in Cameroon and central Africa, 3,000 kilometers further east, is chromosomally similar, but the habitat is large rivers in open savanna and gallery forest. The larval morphology is slightly different in that the tubercles are less pronounced and the setae are most filiform. The adult morphology is also generally paler than in the west. I cannot comment on the vectorial capacity with any authority, but I believe that it is greater in central Africa than in West Africa. In addition, *squamosum* in Cameroon has been reported as resistant to temephos. It would also be interesting to analyze the enzyme banding pattern.

Thus on morphological and ecological grounds, these three populations could be considered as different subspecies or species even, yet on chromosomal criteria the populations are conservative. Chromosomal features are not infallible and homosequential speciation is known to occur, notably among the Drosophilidae (Carson et al. 1970), but also between *Simulium tahitiense* and *Simulium oviceps* (Crosskey 1981).

Biological systems are flexible; they change constantly. The biosystematics of a species in one part of its range may not be the same as in another part, particularly at the fringes of its distribution. The vectorial capacity of, for example, the *S. soubrense* group at the northern limit of its range is negligible in comparison to elsewhere. A very important point is that what is known about a species in one locality cannot be assumed to be true in another. Such a situation is confusing for the field biologist as it would appear logical on some grounds to assign groups of insects that behave or perform differently in geographically separated areas to different species or subspecies. In this kind of situation it is therefore important to define not only the chromosomal identification but additional factors, e.g., morphology, environment, vectorial capacity, insecticide susceptibility, and also the disease epidemiology.

Problems in control and control strategies arise when several cytospecies occur sympatrically as each of the species has a differential role in disease transmission, varying ecological requirements, and possibly differing susceptibility to insecticides. Misidentification of a species can lead to confusion in the interpretation of results, e.g., of insecticide tests, flight range studies, etc. This occurred recently in the *S. soubrense* group, which was described by Vajime and Dunbar (1975). The sympatric species *S. soubrense* and *S. sanctipauli* were differentiated on the basis of a single inversion (IIL–7). The data indicated the presence of two species, although there were some anomalies, notably the presence of heterozygotes for the diagnostic inversion in some localities. The diagnostic inversion is easy to see and therefore to use. However, as the OCP progressed, temephos resistance occurred simultaneously in these two "species," and further doubt was thrown on the validity of the species. The resistant populations of both species were found to possess a small, fixed inversion that was absent in the susceptible populations of the two species. This inversion was useful as a marker for the resistant population (Meredith et al. 1986). Post reanalyzed the chromosome arrangements and as a result it seems that, although two species do indeed occur, the wrong inversion has been used to differentiate them (Post 1986). Thus the biological information was in fact correct.

Clearly, systematics provides the initial, crucial identification of the subject and its environment. It then incorporates relevant biological information for pest-control strategies. However, I have had to justify the need for specific identification of vector species during a control program. Indeed, it has been argued that detailed systematics studies are of purely academic interest since they are unlikely to influence the method of attack or the results on the target species. In fact, the successful control of the *S. neavei* group in Kenya occurred through application of an insecticide (DDT), although little was known of the systematics of the group. However, despite this argument, there is a constant need for systematics. This may be at the taxonomic level of vector (or pest) identification, or at the systematics level of vector identification, determination of vector potential (or biting nuisance), origin of the flies through knowledge of its ecology and flight range (this may be anything from a few to several hundred kilometers), and finally, control by virtue of knowledge of its biology.

There are certainly problems in the application of systematics. These arise partly from the fact that the criteria held by workers in various domains may result in different interpretations of information. In addition, there are difficulties in applying criteria that may seem quite clear to a laboratory worker but less clear in a field situation, which has many more extrinsic factors and is less concise than in a laboratory or museum. An important role of the systematist is to bridge the two domains.

ACKNOWLEDGMENTS

I would like to thank Ms. A. Von Hoffman and Mr. F. Van Eysinga for reviewing and editing the manuscript, and the secretarial assistance of Mrs. Dugas-Rosenberg, Miss L. Ikoli-Fatou, and Mrs. O. Maurette.

LITERATURE CITED

Anderson, I., and G. A. Voskuil. 1963. Reduction in milk production caused by the feeding of blackflies (Diptera: Simuliidae) on dairy cattle in California, with notes on the feeding activities on other animals. *Mosquito News* 23:126–131.

Blackwelder, R. E. 1967. *Taxonomy.* Wiley, New York.

Carson, H. L., D. E. Hardy, H. T. Spieth, and W. S. Stone. 1970. The evolutionary biology of the Hawaiian Drosophilidae. Pp. 437–543 in M. K. Hecht and W. C. Steere, Eds., *Essays in evolution and genetics in honour of Theodosius Dobzhansky.* Appleton-Century-Crofts, New York.

Charnetski, W. A., and W. O. Haufe. 1981. Control of *Simulium arcticum* Malloch in northern Alberta, Canada. Pp. 47–132 in M. Laird, Ed., *Blackflies: the future for biological methods in integrated control.* Academic Press, New York and London.

Crosskey, R. W. 1973. Simuliidae. Pp. 109–153 in K. G. V. Smith, Ed., *Insects and other arthropods of medical importance.* British Museum (Natural History), London.

———. 1981. Simuliid taxonomy—The contemporary scene. Pp. 3–18 in M. Laird, Ed., *Blackflies: the future for biological methods in integrated control.* Academi Press, New York and London.

Dunbar, R. W., and C. G. Vajime. 1981. Cytotaxonomy of the *Simulium damnosum* complex. Pp. 31–43 in M. Laird, Ed., *Blackflies: the future for biological methods in integrated control.* Academic Press, New York and London.

Edgar, S. 1953. A field study of the effect of blackfly bites on egg production of laying hens. *Poultry Sci.* 32:779–780.

Elsen, P., A. Fain, M. C. Henry, and M. De Boeck. 1983. Description morphologique de divers membres du complexe *Simulium damnosum* provenant du Zaire occidental. *Rev. Zool. Afr.* 97:653–673.

Fergusson, A. 1980. *Biochemical systematics and evolution.* Blackie, Glasgow and London.

Gouteux, J. P. 1977a. Description d'une simulie nouvelle de Kivu Zaire: *Simulium (Edwardsellum) juxtadamnosum* n. sp. (Diptera: Simuliidae). *Cah. ORSTOM sér. Entomol. Méd. Parasitol.* 25:347–352.

———. 1977b. Description de *Simulium (Edwardsellum) kilibanum* sp. nov. et position de cette espèce dans le complexe *S. damnosum. Tropenmed. Parasitol.* 28:456–460.

Grjebine, A., I. Coz, J. M. Elouard, J. Mouchet, and I. Ragean. 1973. La notion d'espèces chez les moustiques: étude de quatre complexes les problemes de l'espèce dans le regne animal, vol. 1. *Mém. Soc. Zool. France* 38:249–305.

Guillet, P., H. Escaffre, M. Ouedraogo, and D. Quillévéré. 1981. Mise en évidence d'une resistance au temephos dans le complexe *Simulium damnosum (S. sanctipauli* and *S. soubrense*) en Côte d'Ivoire. (Zone du programme de lutte contre l'onchocercose dans la region du bassin de la Volta). *Cah. ORSTOM sér. Entomol. Méd. Parasitol.* 18:291–299.

Hardy, D. E. 1982. The role of taxonomy and systematics in integrated pet management programmes. *Prot. Ecol.* 4:231–238.

Jamback, H. 1976. Simuliidae (blackflies) and their control. IV. WHO mimes. doc., WHO/VBC/76.653.

Kim, K. C. 1978. The changing nature of entomological collections: uses, functions, growth and management. *Entomol. Scand.* 9:146–177.

Kosztarab, M. 1975. Role of systematics collections in pest management. *Bull. Entomol. Soc. Am.* 21:95–98.

Kurtak, D., M. Ouedraogo, M. Ocran, B. Télé, and P. Guillet. 1982. Preliminary note on the appearance in Ivory Coast of resistance to chlorphoxim in *Simulium soubrense/sanctipauli* larvae already resistant to temephos (Abate®). WHO mimeo. doc., WHO/VBC/82.850.

LaScala, P. A., and J. F. Burger. 1981. A small-scale environmental approach to blackfly control in the USA. Pp. 133–138 in M. Laird, Ed., *Blackflies: the future for biological methods in integrated control.* Academic Press, New York and London.

Mason, H. L. 1950. Taxonomy, systematics, botany and biosystematics. *Madrono* 10:1983–2008.

May, B., L. S. Bauer, R. L. Vadas, and I. Garnett. 1977. Biochemical genetic variation in the family Simuliidae: electrophoretic identification of the human biter in the isomorphic *Simulium jenningsi* group. *Ann. Entomol. Soc. Am.* 70:637–640.

Mayr, E. 1942. *Systematics and the origin of the species.* Columbia Univ. Press, New York.

———. 1969. *Principles of systematics zoology.* McGraw-Hill, London.

Meredith, S. E. O., and H. Townson. 1981. Phosphoglucomutase and trehalase variants in the *S. damnosum* complex. *Trop. Med. Parasitol.* 31:123–129.

Meredith, S. E. O., D. Kurtak, and J. Adiamah. 1986. Following movements of resistant populations of *Simulium soubrense-sanctipauli* (Diptera: Simuliidae) by means of chromosome inversions. *Tropenmed. Parasitol.* 37:290–294.

Metcalf, R. L. 1980. Changing role of insecticides in crop production. *Ann. Rev. Entomol.* 25:219–256.

Pant, C. P., R. E. Fontaine, and N. Y. Gratz. 1977. A review of the World Health Vector Biology and Control Programme. *Mosquito News* 37:595–603.

Post, R. J. P. 1986. The cytotaxonomy of *Simulium sanctipauli* and *Simulium soubrense* (Diptera: Simuliidae). *Genetica* 69:191–207.

Quillévéré, D. 1975. Etude du complexe *Simulium damnosum* en Afrique de l'Ouest. I. Techniques d'étude. Identification des cytotypes. *Cah. ORSTOM sér. Entomol. Méd. Parasitol.* 13:87–100.

Ross. 1974. *Biological Systematics.* Addison-Wesley, Reading, Mass., London, and Ontario.

Service, M. W. 1983. Biological control of mosquitoes, has it a future? *Mosquito News* 43:113–120.

Shelley, A. J., and W. F. Procunier. Taxonomic studies on onchocerciasis vectors in Ecuador and Brazil. *Proc. 11th Int. Congr. of Malaria. Calgary, Canada.* Academic Press, New York. (In press).

Simpson, G. G. 1961. *Principles of animal taxonomy.* Columbia Univ. Press, New York.

Snoddy, E. L., and L. S. Bauer. 1977. *Simulium (Phosterodos) penobscotensis,* a new species of blackfly (Diptera: Simuliidae) from Maine, U.S.A. *J. Med. Entomol.* 14:579–581.

Townson, H., R. J. Post, and A. Phillips. 1987 (this volume). Biochemical approaches to black fly taxonomy.

Vajime, C. G., and R. W. Dunbar. 1975. Chromosomal identification of eight species of the subgenus *Edwardsellum* near and including *Simulium (Edwardsellum) damnosum* Theobald (Diptera: Simuliidae), *Tropenmed. Parasitol.* 26:111–138.

Walsh, J. F., J. B. Davies, and B. Cliff. 1981. World Health Organization Onchocerciasis Control Programme in the Volta River Basin. Pp. 85–104 in M. Laird, Ed., *Blackflies: the future for biological methods in integrated control.* Academic Press, New York and London.

Part III Ecology of Immatures

6 ECOLOGY OF BLACK FLY SIBLING SPECIES

Peter H. Adler

Among the major advances in simuliid research has been the discovery of reproductively isolated but morphologically similar populations (sibling species) within previously established morphospecies. Most sibling species within the Simuliidae have been revealed by cytological analyses of larval polytene chromosomes (Rothfels 1979). Precisely how many sibling species exist within the Simuliidae is unknown. In southern Ontario (Algonquin Park southward), an area relatively well sampled by black fly taxonomists and cytogeneticists, about 62 species occur (Davies et al. 1962; Rothfels 1979, unpublished; Mason 1984). Twenty-one of these were first revealed chromosomally and therefore qualify as sibling species. The state of Pennsylvania has 45 recorded species, of which 19 were first recognized chromosomally (Adler and Kim 1986). The number of sibling species in Pennsylvania is undoubtedly higher; about seven of the state's nominal species have not been examined adequately for sibling species. The preceding figures suggest approximately one or two sibling species, on average, per nominal species in a given area. Cytological studies in other zoogeographical regions (Rothfels 1979) substantiate this estimate.

The ecology of many black fly sibling species is poorly known. In large part, this is because most studies have addressed only the morphospecies without regard to potential syntopic and synchronic sibling species. In addition, some early ecological studies of sibling species were conducted under the assumption that a site supported a single sibling, because previously cytotyped collections yielded one or a majority of one species. This assumption is still sometimes made, but it does not account for compositional changes in the black fly community over time, or for additional sibling species that might be present in low densities, in unsampled microhabitats, or as early instars.

In this chapter the ecological literature on black fly sibling species is examined, a case study of coexistence among members of the *Prosimulium mixtum* group in eastern North America is presented, and overall conclusions regarding ecology of sibling species are drawn.

PREIMAGINAL ECOLOGY

Macrohabitat

Ecological information first appeared for three sibling species of the genus *Prosimulium* (Davies and Syme 1958). Interspecific differences were related largely to physical factors of streams in which the immatures occurred. Over the next twenty years, little ecological work was conducted at the level of the sibling species, although cytological studies provided preliminary information on macrohabitat (collection sites).

The need for laboratory colonization of disease vectors rejuvenated ecological studies of sibling species, particularly in Africa. A number of physical and chemical factors were quantified for preimaginal habitats of sibling species in the African *S. damnosum* complex (Dunbar and Grunewald 1974; Grunewald 1974, 1976a,b; Quillévéré et al. 1976, 1977). Grunewald (1981) concluded that the four most important abiotic factors influencing preimaginal distributions of the *S. damnosum* siblings were pH, conductivity, water temperature, and velocity. In laboratory experiments, Grunewald and Grunewald (1978) demonstrated that pH and conductivity values less than those in typical breeding areas adversely affected survival of the "Kibwezi" and "Kisiwani" cytospecies.

Other studies have also examined the potential for ecologically characterizing sibling species on the basis of abiotic variables of preimaginal habitats. In New York State, 21 chemical and physical factors were analyzed for larval habitats of *S. venustum* CC, *S. verecundum* AA–AC and ACD (Gordon and Cupp 1980), and three species with isomorphic preultimate instars in the *S. jenningsi* group (Gordon 1984). In both studies, species were divided into groups on the basis of pH and ionic content of the water. Brockhouse (1985) noted that some siblings of the *S. vernum* complex in England and Norway apparently occur in streams of different pH.

Partitioning of habitat along watercourses occurs within a number of species complexes. Sibling species, IIIL–1 and IS–7, in the *S. vittatum* complex partition habitat largely according to factors affecting respiration, *viz.*, water temperature, velocity, and oxygen content (Adler and Kim 1984). These factors change in a rather continuous fashion along many watercourses and produce sibling gradients. Three siblings of the *S. tuberosum* complex in Alberta partition habitat along a gradient of physical and chemical factors: FGH is restricted to small, cool streams; AB is found in wide, warm rivers; and FG occurs most frequently in streams of intermediate character, although it overlaps with both AB and FGH (Adler 1986). Within the *Stegopterna mutata* complex, the diploid sibling is restricted to the headwaters, whereas the triploid occurs for a considerable distance from headwaters toward the mouth (Adler and Kim 1986). Some siblings in the *S. arcticum* complex (e.g., IIS–10.11) occur at downstream sites in major rivers, whereas others (e.g., IIL–3) are restricted to the tributaries (Procunier 1984). Other species complexes (e.g., *P. magnum*) that occupy a wide variety of habitats from headwaters to mouth also include siblings that appear to partition macrohabitat.

Preliminary ecological information is available for sibling species in a number of additional complexes. Adler and Kim (1986) provided data for siblings in nine complexes in Pennsylvania, including *S. aureum* A and B; *S. vernum* "Caledon"; *S. pictipes* A and B; *S. tuberosum* A, AB, CDE, CDEM, CKL, FG, and FGH; *S. venustum* CC and CC2; and *S. verecundum* AA and A/C. Lake and Burger (1983) presented information on preimaginal habitats of *S. venustum* CC, A/C, and AC(gB), and *S. verecundum* A/C and ACD in New Hampshire. Currie and Adler (1986) described preimaginal habitats of *Prosimulium onychodactylum* 10, *Stegopterna* "X", *Simulium aureum* B, *S. pugetense* D and E, *S. vittatum* IS–7, *S. arcticum* IIL–2, *S. venustum* CC, and *S. verecundum* ACD on the Queen Charlotte Islands, British Columbia. Vajime and Dunbar (1975) provided notes on larval ecology of eight isomorphic species (*S. squamosum, S. yahense, S. soubrense, S. sanctipauli, S. dieguerense, S. damnosum, S. sirbanum, S. sudanense*) in the *S. damnosum* complex. Craig (1983) briefly mentioned larval macrohabitats of a few Tahitian sibling species. Petersen (1982), using electrophoresis and pupal chaetotaxy, characterized two subgroups in the Central American *Simulium metallicum* complex that apparently differ ecologically.

Seasonality

Probably more information is available on seasonal occurrence than any other biological aspect of black fly sibling species, in part because cytological studies usually provide collection dates for each sibling. Of 11 major species complexes in eastern North America, six are univoltine (*P. hirtipes sensu* pre-1956, *P. magnum*, St. *mutata, S. pugetense, S. vernum,* and *S. venustum*) and five are multivoltine (*S. aureum, S. vittatum, S. pictipes, S. tuberosum,* and *S. verecundum*). These figures indicate that voltinism is not a reliable predictor of the potential for sibling species within a morphospecies.

Most sibling species within a complex overlap broadly in time. However, staggered preimaginal development within the same stream is common for many morphologically similar species: siblings in the *P. onychodactylum* complex (Newman 1983); *P. fontanum* and *P. mixtum* (Davies and Syme 1958); *C. ornithophilia* and *C. dacotensis* (Procunier 1975); *S. tuberosum* FGH, FG, and CDE (Mason 1984); *S. venustum* CC1 and CC (Species status of CC1 apart from CC was argued principally on the basis that larvae of CC1 were found earlier than those of CC [Rothfels et al. 1978]); *S. venustum* CC, A/C, and AC(gB) (Lake and Burger 1983); *S. arcticum* IIL–St, IIL–1, and IIL–2 (Shields and Procunier 1982); and *P. magnum* 3 and *P. multidentatum* (Rothfels and Nambiar 1981).

In cases of staggered development, all sibling species within a complex are generally univoltine. Occasionally only the earliest sibling in the succession is univoltine (e.g., *S. tuberosum* FGH and *S. arcticum* IIL–St). However, some siblings may be univoltine in one system and multivoltine in another, for example, *S. tuberosum* FGH (Mason 1984), *S. venustum* CC (Adler and Kim 1986), and *S. vernum* "Caledon" (Brockhouse 1985). Temporal patterns of *P. onychodactylum* siblings are consistent from year to year within streams but differ among streams during a single year (Newman 1983). In multivoltine complexes, syntopic siblings show various degrees of asynchrony. Population peaks of *S. vittatum* IIIL–1 and IS–7 usually do not coincide (Adler and Kim 1984), nor do those of *S. ornatipes* A1 and A2 (Bedo 1979) or of *S. damnosum* "Ketaketa" and "Nkusi" (Dunbar and Vajime 1981). Many of the above patterns may be driven by water temperature, which influences hatching times and developmental rates (Ross and Merritt 1978).

Completely allochronic siblings are as yet unconfirmed. Siblings of the *P. onycho-*

dactylum complex, such as 4a and 7b, with final instars appearing five months apart, probably do not overlap in time (Newman 1983). However, if some a/b sibling pairs in the complex are actually single species, then temporal overlap could occur. Populations of near-homosequential siblings 4a and 4b were given tentative species status based primarily on nonoverlapping larval maturation periods.

Microhabitat

Very little is known of preferences among sibling species for substrate, spacing, water velocity, or water depth. Some data have been presented for substrate usage by siblings in the *S. vittatum* complex (Adler and Kim 1984). At sites where both sibling species occur, the proportion of larvae on rocks relative to those on grasses is generally greater for IIIL–1 than for IS–7. Larvae of IIIL–1 are found on the undersurface of rocks more frequently than are larvae of IS–7. These microdistribution patterns may be related to preferences in velocity, substrate texture, or other factors.

Biotic Interactions

Competition and predation have not been investigated directly for sibling species. However, drift patterns, which are influenced by biotic interactions (Wiley and Kohler 1981; K. Simmons, personal communication), have been presented for several sibling species in Pennsylvania (Adler et al. 1983b).

Host specificity of parasites and pathogens of preimaginal simuliids has not been found at the sibling-species level. At least three species of microsporidian protozoans, a cytoplasmic polyhedrosis virus, and a nematode are shared between siblings of the *S. vittatum* complex (Adler and Kim 1984; Adler 1986). The fungus, *Coelomycidium simulii,* has a wide host range within the Simuliidae and often occurs in several siblings of the same complex (Adler and Kim 1986). Interpretations of host specificity depend on the accuracy of specific identification not only of the host but of the pathogen or parasite as well. Currently, we do not know if isomorphic species exist among microsporidia, fungi, or nematodes of simuliids.

Feeding

Little is known of differences in feeding strategies among sibling species. For instance, we do not know if some siblings preferentially browse food from the substrate while others within the complex primarily filter their food from the water column. There are no documented cases of closely related species filtering quantitatively or qualitatively different particulate matter. However, larvae of *P. transbrachium* have significantly fewer primary fan rays than those of *P. mixtum* from the same stream (Adler and Kim 1985). The difference was interpreted to be an adaptation to differing particulate loads in upstream (*P. mixtum*) versus downstream (*P. transbrachium*) habitats.

If food resources are partitioned among larval size classes, then temporally staggered, syntopic siblings might use different food sources or size classes of particles. Within *S. vittatum* s.l., first and second instars retain more coarse particles relative to fine particles than do third through final instars (Meritt et al. 1978). In most instances we do not know if food is a limiting resource for simuliid larvae. Attachment sites are likely to become limiting (Harding and Colbo 1981) before food in many cases.

ADULT ECOLOGY

Ecological studies of the imagines of sibling species have lagged behind those of the larvae mainly because of technical limitations to identification. Polytene chromosomes generally have not provided the potent identification tool for adults that they have for larvae. Nonetheless, Bedo (1976) obtained good chromosome preparations from adults of six Australian species. Through modification of Bedo's technique, females of some sibling species in the *S. damnosum* complex were identified (Procunier and Post, in preparation) and pest species in the *S. arcticum* complex were determined (Procunier 1984).

Some information is available on reproductive aspects of morphologically similar species. In sympatry, *P. mixtum* is anautogenous and *P. fuscum* is autogenous, but in Newfoundland, where *P. fuscum* is not known to occur, *P. mixtum* is autogenous (Larson and Colbo 1983). By collecting eggs of ovipositing females and rearing the larvae for cytological analysis, M. Colbo determined that *S. venustum* EFG/C (= *S. truncatum*) deposits eggs singly, whereas *S. verecundum* AA oviposits in masses on trailing vegetation (Rothfels et al. 1978). Similar procedures established the oviposition habits of *S. vittatum* IIIL–1 (Adler et al. 1983a; Adler and Kim 1986). Data on mating, blood feeding, fecundity, and related parameters have been obtained through rearing studies of several members of the *S. damnosum* complex (Raybould 1981; Simmons and Edman 1982).

Larval polytene chromosomes often provide indirect evidence of adult ecology. By evaluating inversion polymorphisms in larval chromosomes, Rothfels (1981) discovered evidence for site-specific mating and oviposition in *P. fuscum;* populations separated by only several kilometers differed markedly in the frequency of particular rearrangements. Polymorphisms of the closely related *P. mixtum* showed no discontinuities and therefore little evidence of site specificity. However, analyses of allozymic polymorphisms indicated greater departures from panmixia for *P. mixtum* than *P. fuscum;* the data suggest that *P. mixtum* may consist of two or more biological species (Snyder and Linton 1984). Landau (1962) provided evidence that *S. tuberosum* AB is site-specific in some areas, again based on inversion spectra. Abrupt changes in inversion polymorphisms of *Austrosimulium australense* also suggest site specificity, although homosequential siblings could be involved (McLea and Lambert 1983). Chromosomal analyses of larvae of *S. pictipes* B revealed near-identical inversion profiles between populations 25 kilometers apart on the same river, but markedly different profiles between populations in different streams only 14 kilometers apart (Bedo 1975). The ecological inference in this case is that mating and oviposition occur primarily within natal watercourses rather than between neighboring systems.

Scant ecological information on adults of isomorphic species has come from other than cytological means. May et al. (1977) successfully used electrophoresis to identify a human-biting pest (later described as *S. penobscotensis*) from among three species isomorphic as females. Townson (1976) used electrophoresis to demonstrate anthropophily in *S. yahense,* a sibling of the *S. damnosum* complex. Unfortunately, simple starch gel electrophoresis often does not provide resolution of species that are isomorphic in all stages (Snyder 1982; but see Townson and Meredith 1979).

Much of the remaining information on adult ecology of sibling species comes from the assumption that only one species occurs or predominates in a given area. These data should be viewed in light of the dispersal capabilities of black fly adults (Wenk 1981) and the changeable nature of lotic systems and constituent siblings.

CASE STUDY: COEXISTENCE IN THE *PROSIMULIUM MIXTUM* GROUP

The *Prosimulium mixtum* group in eastern North America includes eight (or nine) described species, all morphologically similar and cytologically unified by chromosomal inversion IIIL–1. Prior to 1955, the name *P. hirtipes* subsumed the as-yet-unknown species in the *P. mixtum* group. In 1955 Stone and Jamnback recognized *P. rhizophorum* and *P. saltus* from New York, principally on the basis of unique pupal gills. Rothfels in 1956 cytologically demonstrated the specific integrity of three taxa within *P. hirtipes* and designated them *P.* "*hirtipes* 1", *P.* "*hirtipes* 2", and *P.* "16". Syme and Davies (1958) described these species as *P. fuscum, P. mixtum,* and *P. fontanum,* respectively. The name *P. hirtipes* was restricted to a Palearctic species (Rothfels and Basrur 1960). In 1970 Peterson described a sixth eastern Nearctic species, *P. mysticum,* based on earlier cytological evidence (Rothfels, unpublished) and morphological characters. A seventh species, tentatively designated *P. approximatum,* was discovered in a chromosomal study of the previous six Nearctic species (Rothfels and Freeman 1977). In 1983 Rothfels and Freeman revealed an eighth member of the *P. mixtum* group. Adler and Kim (1985) subsequently described it as *P. transbrachium* and established that the tentatively designated *P. approximatum* was a new species, *P. arvum.* Peterson (1970) placed true *P. approximatum* in the *P. mixtum* group but also recognized that it shared characters of both the *P. mixtum* and *P. magnum* groups. Its group affinity remains unresolved and its ecology unknown.

The preceding historical recapitulation of the eastern *P. mixtum* group illustrates the tentative nature of sibling-species status. All species in the group are now recognized morphologically, although each is indistinguishable from at least one other species in one or more life stages. This morphological uniformity has impeded biological and ecological studies. The following is an account of the preimaginal ecology, emphasizing strategies of coexistence, of the group members. All information, unless otherwise indicated, is drawn from Adler and Kim (1986) and the author's unpublished data and is based on chromosomal identifications of individual larvae.

Seasonality

All members of the eastern *P. mixtum* group are univoltine. Egg hatch of *P. mixtum* and *P. fuscum* begins in October and continues into the spring. The life history of *P. arvum* is similar; third or fourth instars have been found in late November in northern Virginia and fifth instars have been found from early January through April in Pennsylvania. *Prosimulium mysticum* might behave similarly (Mansingh et al. 1972; Merritt et al. 1978), but the data are based on morphological, not chromosomal, identifications. Eggs of *P. rhizophorum* probably begin hatching in January in Pennsylvania, based on the presence of early instars during the first week of February. However, in the mountains of eastern West Virginia, fifth instars have been found in early January. Fifth instars of *P. transbrachium* have been found as early as February, indicating that some eggs may hatch in December or January. Hatching times for *P. saltus* are poorly known, but final instars have been found from April to May in New York (Stone and Jamnback 1955) and West Virginia. In Pennsylvania, eggs of *P. fontanum* probably begin to hatch in March, since third instars are found during the first week of April. This pattern is also true of *P. fontanum* in Ontario (Davies and Syme 1958). Vernal flooding of eggs in sediments above stream level can produce second cohorts of some *Prosimulium* species (Ross and Merritt 1978).

Terminal dates of larval occurrence are generally related to the date of egg hatch. Larvae of *Prosimulium mixtum, P. fuscum,* and *P. arvum,* which hatch from eggs in late fall or early winter, attain final instar from early February to mid-May in Pennsylvania. *Prosimulium transbrachium,* though probably hatching later than these species, also completes larval development by mid-May, since it occurs in waters that warm rapidly. Larvae of *P. rhizophorum* are found into mid-June; those of *P. fontanum* occur into late August, although numbers become attenuated.

Macrohabitat

Habitat studies of mixed-species populations, in conjunction with those of single-species populations, have been particularly helpful in resolving coexistence strategies of members of the eastern *P. mixtum* group. Five species (occasionally six) in the group occur in one stream, Slab Cabin Run, in central Pennsylvania. Physical and chemical characteristics for 10 sites along this stream form a gradient from shaded, rocky, cold, and acidic upstream to unshaded, silted, warm, and alkaline downstream (Table 6.1).

Species distributions in Slab Cabin Run are consistent over time (1981–84) and reflect the patterns of change in abiotic factors along the stream. Consequently, habitat is partitioned along the continuum (Table 6.2). An upstream (headwaters) group of species includes *P. fontanum, P. mixtum,* and *P. rhizophorum. Prosimulium mixtum* occupies the broadest range of habitats, but it is poorly represented in downstream areas. No larvae of *P. mixtum* have been found in four years of qualitative sampling along an 8-kilometer stretch of Slab Cabin Run immediately downstream from site 10. A downstream species group includes *P. arvum* and *P. transbrachium.* In some years, these species experience temperatures of nearly 20°C, high enough to cause mortality in certain species of *Prosimulium* (Mansingh et al. 1972). *Prosimulium arvum* and *P. transbrachium* consistently occur for an additional 6.5 kilometers downstream from site 10. *Prosimulium fuscum,* when present (February), occurs in downstream reaches (sites 8 and 9).

Species-habitat relationships throughout much of eastern North America are consistent with those in Slab Cabin Run. *Prosimulium fontanum* is generally restricted to flows arising from springs and bogs, as originally discovered in Ontario by Davies

Table 6.1 Selected characteristics for 10 sites on Slab Cabin Run, Centre County, Pennsylvania. Chemical and physical factors were measured 18 and 26 April and 7 May 1984.

site	elevation (m)	distance from site 1 (km)	vegetative cover (%)	substrate (rocks:grasses) (%)	temperature[c] (°C)	pH[c]	alkalinity[c] (mg CaCO₃/l)
1[a]	472	0	100	100: 0	5.5–9.0	5.23–5.28	0–0.9
2	469	0.2	100	100: 0	6.0–9.5	6.44–6.58	2.5–3.7
3	412	1.2	100	100: 0	6.5–9.0	6.28–7.06	4.5–6.9
4[a]	390	1.5	0	100: 0	6.5–10.0	7.03–7.28	8.1–10.8
5[a]	384	1.6	0	90:10	7.0–12.0	7.28–7.55	8.2–11.7
6[ab]	381	1.8	100	100: 0	7.0–13.0	7.18–7.55	8.7–12.0
7[a]	360	2.7	10	80:20	7.0–10.5	7.83–7.95	59.5–68.2
8	354	3.3	0	70:30	7.0–10.0	7.79–7.88	64.0–73.9
9	341	4.6	10	60:40	8.0–13.0	8.16–8.43	100.0–117.9
10	326	7.4	0	20:80	9.0–15.0	8.20–8.77	134.0–146.0

[a]Intermittent flow.
[b]Stream is subterranean between sites 6 and 7.
[c]Minimum-maximum.

Table 6.2 Relative percent abundance within each of five species in the *P. mixtum* group at ten sites along Slab Cabin Run, Centre County, Pennsylvania, 12 April 1984. Samples are based on total middle through final instars collected in five 0.1-m² stratified random benthic samples (strata:rocks, vegetation) per site. All larvae were identified chromosomally.

		Site									
	n	1	2	3	4	5	6	7	8	9	10
fontanum	10	40.0	20.0	40.0	0	0	0	0	0	0	0
rhizophorum	166	94.6	2.4	3.0	0	0	0	0	0	0	0
mixtum	430	3.0	2.3	75.6	4.4	6.3	1.9	1.6	4.4	0.5	0
arvum	36	0	0	0	0	0	0	0	50.0	16.7	33.3
transbrachium	88	0	0	0	0	0	0	5.7	55.6	27.3	11.4

and Syme (1958). *Prosimulium rhizophorum* is most common in small, low-alkalinity flows that usually dry up for about half the year. *Prosimulium mixtum* occurs in the widest range of habitats, from small seepages to rivers over 250 meters wide (e.g., New River, below Bluestone Dam, West Virginia). *Prosimulium arvum* is found most frequently in productive lowland streams issuing from limestone or dolomite and coursing under an open canopy. *Prosimulium transbrachium* has been found in streams comparable to those occupied by *P. arvum,* but it is known from only five streams in central Pennsylvania. *Prosimulium fuscum* occurs in streams more than 1.5 meters wide, especially at lake outlets (Davies and Syme 1958) and in lowland areas.

Little information on habitat is available for *P. saltus* and *P. mysticum. Prosimulium saltus* is an upstream species found in steep mountainside streams and streams, like the type locality (Stone and Jamnback 1955), with cascades. Limited records of

P. mysticum from rivers in Ontario, Quebec, Newfoundland, and Wisconsin (Roth-fels and Freeman 1977) indicate that it is a downstream species.

Habitat fidelity is reflected in species associations within the *P. mixtum* group (Table 6.3). Downstream species (*P. fuscum, P. arvum, P. transbrachium*) are rarely, if ever, collected with upstream species (*P. fontanum, P. rhizophorum, P. saltus*). *Prosimulium mixtum* is less restricted in habitat and therefore is the only species likely to be found with all other *Prosimulium* species (see Table 6.3), includ-ing *P. saltus*, with which it has been collected at Brooktondale, New York (Rothfels, personal communication), and in West Virginia.

Although six species of the *P. mixtum* group can occur in the same stream, rarely do more than three species occur synchronously at a given site. In 337 collections of the group from Georgia, Kentucky, Pennsylvania, South Carolina, Virginia, and West Virginia (1981–86), only one contained more than three group members. Site 9 on Slab Cabin Run (February 1984) supported *P. arvum, P. fuscum, P. mixtum,* and *P. transbrachium*, each in densities of less than 15 larvae/m^2. In more northern areas (southern Ontario and Quebec), *P. arvum, P. fuscum, P. mixtum,* and *P. mysticum* occasionally might occur together.

Summary

Coexistence of species within the eastern *P. mixtum* group is facilitated by partition-ing of habitat along the stream continuum and, to a lesser degree, by temporal shifts. The group can be divided into an upstream and a downstream component, each with four species. However, *P. mixtum* can occur in both upstream and downstream habitats, depending on the particular site and perhaps geographic loca-tion. The tendency to avoid ecological overlap is best illustrated by species that are most similar morphologically and chromosomally, such as *P. mixtum* and *P. trans-brachium*. *Prosimulium saltus*, which is closely related to *P. mixtum* (Rothfels 1979), apparently subdivides the upstream habitat by occupying the steepest areas. *Prosi-mulium fontanum* minimizes overlap with *P. mixtum* and perhaps *P. rhizophorum* by matching earlier instars with later instars. Overlaps of species in the group might be minimized further by differences in microhabitat.

CONCLUSIONS

The frequency with which sibling species occur within the Simuliidae serves as a caveat that any study involving simuliids should consider their impact. Bearing in mind that the species is the ecological unit of investigation, the potential for undis-covered siblings, as well as known sibling species, must be considered. However, identification or detection of sibling species often requires a specialist. Voucher collections play an essential role in this regard. Properly retained specimens can be evaluated at a later date if morphological criteria become available. In studies of larval simuliids, preparations of chromosomes from salivary glands involve routine procedure (Rothfels and Dunbar 1953) and should be a requisite part of the voucher collection.

Studies that address the ecology of sibling species must consider the possibility of

Table 6.3 Associations of species in the *P. mixtum* group, based on chromosomal identifications of middle through final instars collected from 204 streams in Pennsylvania, 1981–84. Values given are percent probabilities of collecting a species in the left-hand column given a species in the top row.

	arvum (n^a=98)	fontanum (n=25)	fuscum (n=18)	mixtum (n=114)	rhizophorum (n=23)	transbrachium (n=90)
arvum	—	0	22.2	28.1	0	60.0
fontanum	0	—	0	4.4	13.0	0
fuscum	4.1	0	—	8.8	0	1.1
mixtum	32.6	20.0	61.1	—	43.5	4.4
rhizophorum	0	12.0	0	8.8	—	0
transbrachium	55.1	0	5.6	3.5	0	—

^{a}Number of collections.

co-occurrence. Rigorous sampling is necessary in order that ecological interpretations be valid. Sampling programs aimed at ecological study of sibling species ideally should ensure that (1) samples are taken randomly, (2) densities are quantified, (3) a wide variety of habitats is sampled, (4) sampling is conducted over all seasons, (5) sampling is long-term, (6) a fair portion of the geographic range is sampled, (7) samples are fixed cytologically, and (8) chromosomal, morphological, and other characters are integrated to provide accurate identifications.

Ecological studies of black fly sibling species are still primarily in a descriptive phase, although some patterns are emerging: (1) Sibling species are common within univoltine and multivoltine morphospecies. (2) Species within a given complex generally overlap in time but have staggered developmental periods. (3) A morphospecies that is considered a habitat generalist, such as *S. vittatum, S. damnosum,* and *S. tuberosum,* is commonly a composite of sibling species, each essentially a habitat specialist. (4) Because habitats are not strictly compartmentalized along the stream continuum, spatial distributions of sibling species are expected to, and in most cases do, overlap. (5) Morphospecies occupying a restricted portion (e.g., headwaters) of the stream continuum are not composed of sibling species. Cytological analyses of *Twinnia tibblesi, S. impar, S. parnassum,* and others (Rothfels and Freeman 1966; Hunter and Connolly 1986; Rothfels, unpublished) substantiate this prediction.

Watercourses, as systems of more or less continuous physical and chemical variables, foster the occurrence of sibling species. These continua provide a variety of habitats without necessitating overt morphological differentiation of the resident simuliids. Structural similarity between closely related species appears greatest when overlap in space and time is most complete (Snyder and Linton 1983). Perhaps differentiation has been more physiological than morphological. Physiological aspects of sibling species deserve more experimental exploration.

Occurrence of syntopic and synchronic sibling species implies that efficient prezygotic isolating mechanisms are operating. Data on these isolating mechanisms are central to an understanding of speciation processes in black flies. Difficulties with adult identification have permitted only speculation as to the mechanisms and ecological correlates. Mating swarms of different siblings might be separated in space or time. If preimaginal habitats differ between closely related species, adults often should emerge in different habitats because vegetation and terrestrial habitat also change along watercourses. Consequently, different mating behaviors, including choice of swarm markers, would be adaptive in different habitats.

Control programs are particularly dependent on a sound working knowledge of black fly ecology. Within several species complexes (e.g., *S. damnosum* and *S. arcticum*), only certain siblings have been implicated as pests or disease vectors. Precise targeting of the specific pests will provide more economical, effective, and environmentally sound management programs. As part of this scenario, biological control programs must assess the suitability and host specificity of control organisms.

The past thirty years have witnessed a tremendous advance in our understanding of the species concept in simuliid biology. Future advances rely on understanding the interaction of the species with its environment.

ACKNOWLEDGMENTS

I thank K. C. Kim and D. A. Craig for the opportunity to work in their laboratories, R. Barrera for field assistance (Tables 6.1 and 6.2), and K. Rothfels and C. R. L. Adler for thoughtful reviews of the manuscript.

LITERATURE CITED

Adler, P. H. 1986. Ecology and cytology of some Alberta black flies (Diptera: Simuliidae). *Quaest. Entomol.* 22:1–18.

Adler, P. H., and K. C. Kim. 1984. Ecological characterization of two sibling species, IIIL–1 and IS–7, in the *Simulium vittatum* complex (Diptera: Simuliidae). *Can. J. Zool.* 62:1308–15.

———. 1985. Taxonomy of black fly sibling species: two new species in the *Prosimulium mixtum* group (Diptera: Simuliidae). *Ann. Entomol. Soc. Am.* 78:41–49.

———. 1986. The black flies (Diptera: Simuliidae) of Pennsylvania: bionomics, taxonomy, and distribution. *Penn State Agric. Exp. Stn. Bull.* 856. 87 pp.

Adler, P. H., K. C. Kim, and R. W. Light. 1983a. Flight patterns of the *Simulium vittatum* (Diptera: Simuliidae) complex over a stream. *Environ. Entomol.* 12:232–236.

Adler, P. H., R. W. Light, and K. C. Kim. 1983b. The aquatic drift patterns of black flies (Diptera: Simuliidae). *Hydrobiologia* 107:183–191.

Bedo, D. G. 1975. Polytene chromosomes of three species of blackflies in the *Simulium pictipes* group. *Can. J. Zool.* 53:1147–64.

———. 1976. Polytene chromosomes in pupal and adult blackflies (Diptera: Simuliidae). *Chromosoma* 57:387–396.

———. 1979. Cytogenetics and evolution of *Simulium ornatipes* Skuse. II. Temporal variation in chromosomal polymorphism and homosequential sibling species. *Evolution* 33:296–308.

Brockhouse, C. L. 1985. Sibling species and sex chromosomes in *Eusimulium vernum* (Diptera: Simuliidae). *Can. J. Zool.* 63:2145–61.

Craig, D. A. 1983. Phylogenetic problems in Polynesian Simuliidae (Diptera: Culicomorpha): a progress report. *GeoJournal* 7.6:533–541.

Currie, D. C., and P. H. Adler. 1986. Black flies (Diptera: Simuliidae) of the Queen Charlotte Islands, British Columbia, with discussion of their origin and description of *Simulium (Hellichiella) nebulosum* n. sp. *Can. J. Zool.* 64:218–227.

Davies, D. M., B. V. Peterson, and D. M. Wood. 1962. The black flies (Diptera: Simuliidae) of Ontario. Part I. Adult identification and distributions of six new species. *Proc. Entomol. Soc. Ont.* 92:70–154.

Davies, D. M., and P. D. Syme. 1958. Three new black flies of the genus *Prosimulium* (Diptera: Simuliidae). Part II. Ecological observations and experiments. *Can. Entomol.* 90:744–759.

Dunbar, R. W., and J. Grunewald. 1974. Distribution of four species near *Simulium damnosum* along a mountain river. *Proc. III Int. Congr. Parasitol.* 2:922–923.

Dunbar, R. W., and C. G. Vajime. 1981. Cytotaxonomy of the *Simulium damnosum* complex. Pp. 31–43 in M. Laird, Ed., *Blackflies: the future for biological methods in integrated control.* Academic Press, New York and London.

Gordon, A. E. 1984. Observations on the limnological factors associated with three species of the *Simulium jenningsi* group (Diptera: Simuliidae) in New York state. *Freshwater Invertebr. Biol.* 3:48–51.

Gordon, A. E., and E. W. Cupp. 1980. The limnological factors associated with cytotypes of the *Simulium (Simulium) venustum/verecundum* complex (Diptera: Simuliidae) in New York state. *Can. J. Zool.* 58:973–981.

Grunewald, J. 1974. The hydro-chemical living conditions of the immature stages of some forms of the *Simulium damnosum* complex with regard to their laboratory colonization. *Proc. III Int. Congr. Parasitol.* 2:914–915.

———. 1976a. The hydro-chemical and physical conditions of the environment of the immature stages of some species of the *Simulium (Edwardsellum) damnosum* complex (Diptera). *Tropenmed. Parasitol.* 27:438–454.

———. 1976b. The hydro-chemical and physical conditions of the environment of the aquatic stages of some West African cytotypes of the *Simulium damnosum* complex, and studies on the water quality at some potential locations for a rearing laboratory. WHO Rept. (1976). Pp. 1–27.

———. 1981. Hydro-chemical and physical characteristics of the larval sites of species of the *Simulium damnosum* complex. Pp. 227–235 in M. Laird, Ed., *Blackflies: the future for biological methods in integrated control.* Academic Press, New York and London.

Grunewald, J., and E. B. Grunewald. 1978. The influence of pH, conductivity and ionic composition on the aquatic stages of two cytospecies of the *Simulium damnosum* complex (Diptera, Simuliidae) of East Africa. *Arch. Hydrobiol.* 82:419–431 (in German).

Harding, J., and M. H. Colbo. 1981. Competition for attachment sites between larvae of Simuliidae (Diptera). *Can. Entomol.* 113:761–763.

Hunter, F. F., and V. Connolly. 1986. A cytotaxonomic investigation of seven species in the *Eusimulium vernum* group. *Can. J. Zool.* 64:296–311.

Lake, D. J., and J. F. Burger. 1983. Larval distribution and succession of outlet-breeding blackflies (Diptera: Simuliidae) in New Hampshire. *Can. J. Zool.* 61:2519–33.

Landau, R. 1962. Four forms of *Simulium tuberosum* (Lundstr.) in southern Ontario: a salivary gland chromosome study. *Can. J. Zool.* 40:921–939.

Larson, D. J., and M. H. Colbo. 1983. Chapter 15. The aquatic insects: biogeographic considerations. Pp. 593–677 in G. R. South, Ed., *Biogeography and ecology of the island of Newfoundland.* Junk Publishers, The Hague.

Mansingh, A., R. W. Steele, and B. V. Helson. 1972. Hibernation in the blackfly *Prosimulium mysticum:* quiescence or oligopause? *Can. J. Zool.* 50:31–34.

Mason, G. F. 1984. Sex chromosome polymorphism in the *Simulium tuberosum* complex (Lundström) (Diptera: Simuliidae). *Can. J. Zool.* 62:647–658.

May, B., L. S. Bauer, R. L. Vadas, and J. Granett. 1977. Biochemical genetic variation in the family Simuliidae: electrophoretic identification of the human biter in the isomorphic *Simulium jenningsi* group. *Ann. Entomol. Soc. Am.* 70:637–640.

McLea, M. C., and D. M. Lambert. 1983. Cytogenetics of New Zealand blackflies of the genus *Austrosimulium* (Diptera: Simuliidae). 1. The cytogenetics of *Austrosimulium australense*. *New Zealand J. Zool.* 10:271–280.

Merritt, R. W., M. M. Mortland, E. F. Gersabeck, and D. H. Ross. 1978. X-ray diffraction analysis of particles ingested by filter-feeding animals. *Entomol. Exp. Appl.* 24:27–34.

Newman, L. J. 1983. Sibling species of the blackfly *Prosimulium onychodactylum* (Simuliidae, Diptera): a salivary gland chromosome study. *Can. J. Zool.* 61:2816–35.

Petersen, J. L. 1982. Population genetics of some New World Simuliidae. Pp. 628–642 in W. W. M. Steiner, W. J. Tabachnick, K. S. Rai, and S. Narang, Eds., *Recent developments in the genetics of insect disease vectors*. Stipes Publishing Co., Champaign, Illinois.

Peterson, B. V. 1970. The *Prosimulium* of Canada and Alaska. *Mem. Entomol. Soc. Can.* 69:1–216.

Procunier, W. S. 1975. A cytological study of two closely related blackfly species: *Cnephia dacotensis* and *Cnephia ornithophilia* (Diptera: Simuliidae). *Can. J. Zool.* 53:1622–37.

———. 1984. Cytological identification of pest species of the *Simulium arcticum* complex present in the Athabasca River and associated tributaries. *Farming for the Future Final Report, Agriculture Canada* (82–0101), Lethbridge, Alberta. 44 pp.

Procunier, W. S., and R. J. Post. 1985. Adult identification of *Simulium damnosum s.l.* (In preparation).

Quillévéré, D., M. Gouzy, Y. Sechan, and B. Pedriez. 1976. Etude du complexe *Simulium damnosum* en Afrique de l'Ouest. IV. Analyse de l'eau des gites larvaires en saison seche. *Cah. ORSTOM sér. Entomol. Méd. Parasitol.* 14:315–330.

———. 1977. Etude du complexe *Simulium damnosum* en Afrique de l'Ouest. VI. Analyse de l'eau des gites larvaires en saison pluies; comparaison avec la saison seche. *Cah. ORSTOM sér. Entomol. Méd. Parasitol.* 15:195–207.

Raybould, J. N. 1981. Present progress towards the laboratory colonization of members of the *Simulium damnosum* complex. Pp. 307–315 in M. Laird, Ed., *Blackflies: the future for biological methods in integrated control*. Academic Press, New York and London.

Ross, D. H., and R. W. Merritt. 1978. The larval instars and population dynamics of five species of black flies (Diptera: Simuliidae) and their responses to selected environmental factors. *Can. J. Zool.* 56:1633–42.

Rothfels, K. H. 1956. Blackflies: siblings, sex, and species grouping. *J. Hered.* 47:113–122.

———. 1979. Cytotaxonomy of black flies (Simuliidae). *Ann. Rev. Entomol.* 24:507–539.

———. 1981. Cytological approaches to the study of blackfly systematics and evolution. Pp. 67–83 in M. W. Stock, Ed., *Application of Genetics and Cytology in Insect Systematics and Evolution*. Forest Wildlife Range Exp. Stn., Univ. Idaho, Moscow, Idaho.

Rothfels, K. H., and P. K. Basrur. 1960. The interrelations of *Prosimulium hirtipes* (Fries) and allied European and North American species (Diptera: Simuliidae). A salivary gland chromosome study. XI. *Int. Congr. Entomol.*

Rothfels, K. H., and R. W. Dunbar. 1953. The salivary gland chromosomes of the black fly *Simulium vittatum* Zett. *Can. J. Zool.* 31:226–241.

Rothfels, K. H., and D. M. Freeman. 1966. The salivary gland chromosomes of three North American species of *Twinnia* (Diptera: Simuliidae). *Can. J. Zool.* 44:937–945.

———. 1977. The salivary gland chromosomes of seven species of *Prosimulium* (Diptera, Simuliidae) in the *mixtum* (IIIL–1) group. *Can. J. Zool.* 55:482–507.

———. 1983. A new species of *Prosimulium* (Diptera: Simuliidae): an interchange as a primary reproductive isolating mechanism? *Can. J. Zool.* 61:2612–17.

Rothfels, K., R. Feraday, and A. Kaneps. 1978. A cytological description of sibling species of *Simulium venustum* and *S. verecundum* with standard maps for the subgenus *Simulium* Davies (Diptera). *Can. J. Zool.* 56:1110–28.

Rothfels, K., and R. Nambiar. 1981. A cytological study of natural hybrids between *Prosimulium multidentatum* and *P. magnum* with notes on sex determination in the Simuliidae (Diptera). *Chromosoma* 82:673–691.

Shields, G. F., and W. S. Procunier. 1982. A cytological description of sibling species of *Simulium (Gnus) arcticum* (Diptera: Simuliidae). *Polar Biol.* 1:181–192.

Simmons, K. R., and J. D. Edman. 1982. Laboratory colonization of the human onchocerciasis vector *Simulium damnosum* complex (Diptera: Simuliidae), using an enclosed, gravity-trough rearing system. *J. Med. Entomol.* 19:117–126.

Snyder, T. P. 1982. Electrophoretic characterizations of black flies in the *Simulium venustum* and *verecundum* species complexes (Diptera: Simuliidae). *Can. Entomol.* 114:503–507.

Snyder, T. P., and M. C. Linton. 1983. Electrophoretic and morphological separation of *Prosimulium fuscum* and *P. mixtum* larvae (Diptera: Simuliidae). *Can. Entomol.* 115:81–87.

———. 1984. Population structure in black flies: allozymic and morphological estimates for *Prosimulium mixtum* and *P. fuscum* (Diptera: Simuliidae). *Evolution* 38:942–956.

Stone, A., and H. Jamnback. 1955. The black flies of New York state (Diptera: Simuliidae). *N.Y. State Mus. Bull.* 349. 44 pp.

Syme, P. D., and D. M. Davies. 1958. Three new Ontario black flies of the genus *Prosimulium* (Diptera: Simuliidae). Part I. Descriptions, morphological comparisons with related species, and distribution. *Can. Entomol.* 90:697–719.

Townson, H. 1976. Enzyme polymorphism in vectors of disease—its study and interpretation of results: studies of enzymes in the *Simulium damnosum* complex and *Aedes scutellaris* group. WHO mimeo. doc., VBC/SC/76.21.

Townson, H., and S. E. O. Meredith. 1979. Identification of the Simuliidae in relation to onchocerciasis. Pp. 145–174 in A. E. R. Taylor and R. Muller, Eds., *Problems in the identification of parasites and their vectors.* 17th Symp. Br. Soc. Parasitol. Blackwell Scientific, Oxford.

Wenk, P. 1981. Bionomics of adult blackflies. Pp. 259–279 in M. Laird, Ed., *Blackflies: the future for biological methods in integrated control.* Academic Press, New York and London.

Wiley, M. J., and S. L. Kohler. 1981. An assessment of biological interactions in an epilithic stream community using time-lapse photography. *Hydrobiologia* 78:183–188.

Vajime, C. G., and R. W. Dunbar. 1975. Chromosomal identification of eight species of the subgenus *Edwardsellum* near and including *Simulium (Edwardsellum) damnosum* Theobald (Diptera: Simuliidae). *Tropenmed. Parasitol.* 26:111–138.

7 PROBLEMS IN ESTIMATING BLACK FLY POPULATIONS IN THEIR AQUATIC STAGES

M. H. Colbo

The problems involved in estimating benthic populations in lotic systems have appeared in an enormous array of papers. Some recent reviews covering aspects of the problems of choosing sampling methods, determining the number of samples required, and then interpreting the data are Elliott 1977; Elliott and Tullett 1978; Flannagan and Rosenberg 1982; Merritt et al. 1984; Resh 1979; and Rosenberg and Resh 1982. If a more restricted scope is taken, namely, the simuliid fauna, the literature is still extensive because black flies are frequently studied, being pests of man and animals, disease vectors, and important members of many stream benthic communities (see Cummins, this volume). The approaches to sampling immature simuliid populations have been reviewed by Carlsson et al. (1981), Fredeen and Spurr (1978), and, although not directly specified, Flannagan and Rosenberg (1982) and Rosenberg and Resh (1982).

The present approach will not be to review the literature comprehensively, but to examine some aspects of immature simuliid biology in relation to sampling and how the aims of a study will determine the problems involved in obtaining the appropriate data, given normal time and economic constraints.

Biological and Ecological Considerations

To design and execute a sampling program that will provide data on a set of questions about any given species, current understanding is necessary of the known biology and ecology of the stages to be sampled. Some parameters that influence the distribution of the stages, many being discussed in detail by Colbo and Wotton (1981) and elsewhere in this volume, are provided in Table 7.1. I will now examine in more detail aspects of sampling the various immature stages.

Table 7.1 Some examples of biological and ecological parameters affecting immature simuliids that will influence sampling procedures

Stage	Habitat Preferences with Regard to:	Biological and Ecological Considerations
All immature stages	size of stream substrate makeup, both mineral and nonmineral current velocity water chemistry proximity to lentic outflows terrestrial vegetation cover (forest, canopy, open forest, barrens, etc.)	seasonality of stage development rates physiological constraints (temperature, pH tolerance, etc.)
Eggs	substrate preference if adhered to a substrate ponds and pools or obviously flowing channels eggs lying in surface deposits or buried	oviposition onto water or substrate diapausing or not potential survival time
Larvae		inter- and intraspecific competition for space diurnal activity patterns number of instars phoretic or not phoretic
Pupae		inter- and intraspecific competition for space diurnal rhythms phoretic or not phoretic

Eggs

Eggs have been surprisingly little studied. Possible explanations are the difficulty of aiming a control measure at this stage and the minor role eggs play in stream system biotic processes. To compound this, eggs are impossible or difficult to identify and may be equally hard even to collect. This also makes them unlikely targets for faunistic surveys. Eggs are in fact for the most part ignored. This is unfortunate, for the maximal population of a cohort occurs in this stage, and for a number of species the longest period of the life cycle and perhaps the greatest immature-stage mortality occurs in the egg. It is apparent, then, that this lack of knowledge hampers the understanding of the population dynamics of most species. For example, Colbo and Moorhouse (1974) showed that eggs of *Austrosimulium pestilens* MacKerras and MacKerras could survive for at least two years and perhaps several more, while the larval through adult stages may be completed in a few days. Reports of Rühm (1972, 1975) have indicated the importance of understanding the survival of the eggs in predicting the adult populations of *Simulium* (*Boophthora*) *erythrocephalum* De Geer and other species in Germany. This species and several others oviposit on a substrate, so the population of eggs can be monitored by sampling these substrates.

Sampling difficulties in species ovipositing on surface substrates are primarily in defining the oviposition cues for habitat selection so as to define the sampling area.

Golini and Davies (this volume), Imhof and Smith (1979), and Rühm (1972, 1975) have reviewed our current understanding of these oviposition cues. As eggs on any one substrate may range from newly oviposited to hatched (Imhof and Smith 1979, Rühm and Schlepper 1979), a knowledge of development time and aging is needed to design a sampling protocol for some studies such as temporal egg production and mortality. Rühm and Schlepper (1979) have outlined an approach to this type of study for species ovipositing on a substrate. For those species that oviposit on substrates below the water surface, the problem for a researcher is compounded. The major initial problem is locating and defining the oviposition sites and then identifying the eggs. A general benthic sampling program to obtain population and survival estimates of these eggs appear to be a formidable task because of the potential difficulty of sorting benthic samples for attached eggs and obtaining samples of some substrates (boulders, bedrock, large logs).

Many species, perhaps the majority, oviposit eggs into the water. These eggs have a sticky outer coating and have been seen to attach to substrates and particles in the water and on the streambed (Colbo and Moorhouse 1974). In rapid-flowing sections eggs can be collected at the time of oviposition by fine plankton nets, but because of the small mesh size required, rapid clogging is a problem. These eggs can also be recovered from stream substrates by a variety of methods (Tarshis 1968). In some alluvial streambeds, where considerable bed erosion and deposition occur, these eggs can be buried deep into streambeds and banks (Colbo and Moorhouse 1974). In these cases core sampling and flotation techniques would appear to be applicable. Again, problems of identification and determining age and development time may all have to be dealt with to answer certain questions needed to develop an effective sampling program.

Larvae

The larval stage is by far the most often sampled and studied by researchers interested in faunistics, stream biology, and vector and/or pest control. All but a few species of simuliids have passive filter-feeding larvae with two expandable cephalic fans that extend into the current, where they filter small particulate matter from the water column (Currie and Craig, Craig and Galloway, this volume). Since they are passive filter feeders, larvae must locate on substrates exposed to the appropriate current velocity, the optimal velocity being different for different species (Philipson 1956, Kurtak 1978, Gersabeck and Merritt 1979). Craig and Galloway (this volume) review many of the clear relationships between parameters describing the nature of the stream flow, which in turn reflect the current velocity, depth, and substrate roughness. Given this, one would expect larvae of a given species to locate on a substrate suitable for attachment with optimal current velocities and characteristics for that species.

Nevertheless, flow characteristics in a stream channel are influenced by gradient, channel morphology, and the substrates. Although the mean current can be estimated knowing certain parameters, the pattern of microcurrents is very complex and dynamic, making prediction of current velocities over all the substrate surface in a natural stream impossible. Furthermore, these patterns of flow and velocities can change with discharge. Thus, even given the larval requirement for a certain range of flow characteristics, the dynamic variability of these characteristics over stream substrates makes predicting the pattern of simuliid larval distribution over a streambed difficult at best and in most cases still impossible. However, what these studies do show is that larval distributions will be contagious and dynamic even if all substrate surfaces were equally suited for attachment, which is true for many stream organisms.

A considerable effort has been expended to develop methods for predicting the size (area) and number of substrate samples required to obtain a population estimate of a given accuracy for such contagious distributions (Elliott 1977, Southwood 1978, Resh 1979, Downing 1979, Morin 1985). The number of samples required is related to the mean density and whether the sampling can be stratified (Elliott 1977, Resh 1979). However, in planning a sampling program, costs must also be considered and related to the desired accuracy. Two recent papers by Sheldon (1984) and Morin (1985) address this question. Morin (1985), using a black fly example, showed that by combining precision, density, sampler size, and cost per sample (which depends on density and sampler size) one could optimize the number of samples in relation to organism density. Thus, the sampling program must be tailored to the simuliid species, its density, distribution, and to the financial and human resources available.

The techniques for obtaining larval samples has been very varied. One approach has been the use of artificial substrates such as plastic strips, tree fronds, or leaves, rope, wood, blocks, bricks, tiles, and cones (Fredeen and Spurr 1978, Nakamura et al. 1978, Gersbeck and Merritt 1979, Carlsson et al. 1981) and more recently plastic balls (Walsh et al. 1981). Two aims have led to these developments. The first is to have a substrate in the stream that can be easily sampled. This is particularly necessary in large, deep streams, streams with bedrock, and large boulder and/or coarse cobble beds, where it is difficult or impossible to sample the natural substrates (Figs. 7.1 and 7.2). The second aim was to have each substrate with a uniform surface area and texture in order to reduce between sample variability.

Although artificial substrates simplify sampling, there are still many problems, especially in data interpretation. Certain samplers, such as tiles (Lewis and Bennett 1974), were suggested as good sampling devices because they have the same texture, color, and surface area and are easy to collect, thus making temporal and spatial comparisons easier. This is true in the physical sense of the tiles themselves, but rarely do tiles have a uniformity in the water velocity over their surface; yet this parameter is one of the most important in controlling larval and pupal distributions. This lack of uniformity in current velocity over the surface is a problem for most artificial samplers. The reason is the complex, turbulent nature of fluid flow in a channel, especially one with the lack of uniformity of a stream (see Craig and Galloway, this volume). This can be demonstrated by putting a handful of mud in a small clear stream and watching it shoot past some area of the substrate, flow smoothly over some, and eddy around others. Larvae seek out those clean substrate surfaces that have the flow patterns suitable for their filtering requirements (Figs. 7.3 and 7.4) (Currie and Craig, this volume). An example of the contagious distribution of *Prosimulium mixtum* larvae on a uniform substrate (glass windows) due to current variation in a stream was illustrated by Colbo (1979). Thus if we could easily see current patterns, which occasionally larval distribution permits us to do, the patchiness would become very evident (Figs. 7.3–7). What is more, the larval distribution itself alters the current patterns (Fig. 7.5). Furthermore, Morin (1985) has

FIG. 7.1 Walsh River, near Labrador City, Labrador. Example of a wide, deep section of a river not easily sampled because of its depth.

FIG. 7.2 Bauline Brook, near St. John's, Newfoundland, illustrating a stream that is difficult to sample because the streambed consists of bedrock and large boulders.

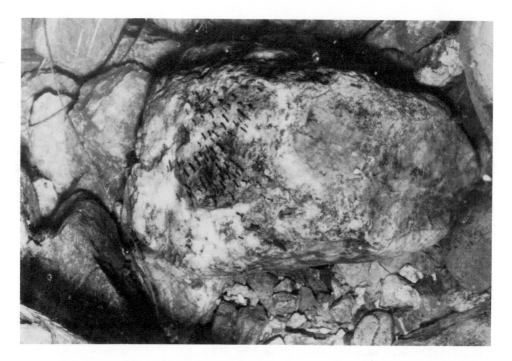

FIG. 7.3 Example of the contagious distribution of a simuliid, *Simuliid clathrinum*, Cabbage Tree Creek, near Ipswich, Queensland.

FIG. 7.4 Example of a patchy microdistribution on a limited area of substrate. (Same species and site as Figure 7.3.)

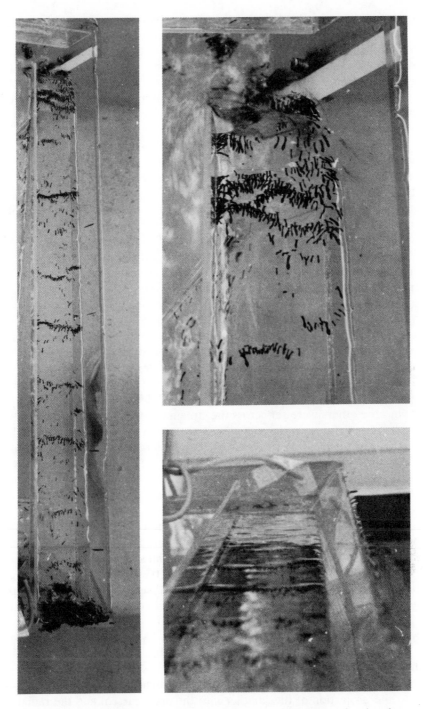

FIGS. 7.5–7.7 *Cnephia ornithophilia* larvae in a Plexiglas trough system showing the very contagious distribution of these larvae on a uniform substrate (*left*). Figure 7.6 Detail (*top right*). Figure 7.7 shows how their presence modifies the pattern of flow (*bottom right*).

shown that in fact varying the size of the tile in relation to larval densities would optimize the sampling effort for a given sample accuracy.

The conical sampling devices can overcome some of the heterogeneity of current flow over a known surface if they can be sited to face directly into the current. Since complex current patterns rarely flow parallel to either the banks or the bottom, siting the sampler into the current is difficult. Recently a ball was suggested as a sampling unit because, small enough, no matter which way the cell of water strikes the ball, the same surface area and configuration would be exposed (Walsh et al. 1981). However, the nature of the flow over the ball is not uniform, and what occurs is a band of suitable velocities usually found only around the perimeter of the surface facing into the flow. The width of this band will in part depend on the water velocity and tolerance range of the larvae.

A problem with all samplers placed in a stream is to keep them stable. Sampler movement will continuously alter the currents on the surface, a situation that is unsuitable for a filtering organism. For example, floating strips and natural vegetation do very poorly in turbulent waters because they are constantly twirling, although high densities occur on them when stable. The same can be true for floating or suspended samplers placed between an anchor and a buoy in large rivers (Fredeen and Spurr 1978) if care is not taken in placement.

In order to demonstrate the variation between the same artificial substrate and between different artificial substrates, data from a two-week trial are provided (Tables 7.2 and 7.3). Artificial substrates were placed in a 5-meter-wide riffle with natural substrates consisting primarily of cobble, a few small boulders, and a small bar of finer gravel. The samplers were set in two ways within a 20-meter stretch of riffle. One set was grouped in three clusters of mixed samplers, two of each type per cluster, and the others were set across the stream in rows consisting of five sites, one on each bank and three in the channel, with two samplers at each site. The data obtained are shown in Tables 7.2 and 7.3. Considerable variation was evident between the same substrate at each paired site and between types of substrates. Although the substrate's physical size and texture can be defined, the proportion of that surface with the appropriate current is not easily controlled, and high variance results.

The small trial with thick monofilament line (1.7 mm d × 20–25 cm long) projecting into the current from a streambed anchor was of interest because it collected very high densities of larvae. Nakamura et al. (1978) had similar success with small PVC tubing. Small tubes and filaments may be effective because they project into the main current and their small size causes minimal resistance to the flow. Their flexibility permits them to bend down when hit by floating debris, unlike stiff rods, stretched lines, or tapes. Nakamura et al. (1978) showed that the small PVC tubes had the highest larval density and less variation than scrub brushes, tiles, PVC strips, bricks, and 5-minute hand collections. Thus small-diameter tube, flexible plastic-coated wire, or heavy monofilaments clamped in an anchor appear to be easily replicable samplers readily colonized by several species of black flies. The higher density observed probably relates to the projection of the sampler into the main current and the radial attachment of larvae. Thus, although their attachment organs are in close proximity, their heads are more widely spaced, which is not possible on a flat substrate. It is of interest also that sticks and branches protruding into the water column in natural rivers can have very high larval densities (Benke et al. 1984).

Table 7.2 The example of the variation between paired samples of *Simulium venustum* taken in a 5-meter wide boulder-cobble riffle in Broad Cove River near St. John's, Newfoundland, over two weeks in May 1984. Numbers are larvae/100 cm^2 of substrate.

	Tiles	Balls	Ribbons	Stones	Filaments
Cluster 1	15	235	23	23	3120
	104	220	90	8	2240
Cluster 2	19	28	75	81	3568
	42	88	53	20	—
Cluster 3	60	84	23	44	736
	13	16	64	7	—
Row 1 bank	1	72	2	—	—
	11	135	3	—	—
Row 1	12	38	8	—	—
	30	22	12	—	—
Row 3	31	3	72	—	—
	46	44	14	—	—
Row 4	54	279	39	—	—
	139	—	42	—	—
Row 5 bank	188	1130	353	—	—
	216	975	109	—	—

Table 7.3 The mean, range, and 20% confidence-interval estimates of a population of *Simulium venustum* larvae collected by different methods in a riffle near St. John's, Newfoundland. (Data from Table 7.2.)

Cluster Sites	n	Range	$X \pm Ci$
Natural stones	6	7–81	31 ± 28
Tiles	6	13–104	42 ± 37
Balls	5	16–235	112 ± 102
Ribbons	6	23–90	55 ± 27
Filaments	4	736–3568	2466 ± 1728
Rows			
Tiles	10	1–216	73 ± 55
Balls	9	3–1130	300 ± 328
Ribbons	10	2–353	65 ± 75
Total			
Tiles	16	1–216	61 ± 35
Balls	15	3–1130	224 ± 191
Ribbons	16	2–353	61 ± 45

Do we want high density and uniformity between samplers? If our goal is only replication, such as in testing efficacy of a control agent, then efficient artificial sampling devices may meet our needs. However, severe problems remain if micro-distribution, life-history data, productivity, natural mortality rates, etc., are the goals of the studies using these samples. These problems have been recognized by others and reviewed by Rosenberg and Resh (1982). Some of the problems can be illustrated by examining the data in Tables 7.2 and 7.3. It is evident that certain types of samplers yield much higher density estimates of *Simulium venustum* than others, even considering the variation between samples and locations.

Sampling programs could be designed even with the variation between sites to provide a given accuracy of density estimates based on the populations on that type of sampler. This, however, could not be extrapolated as a density estimate for the total streambed even at the site sampled. In the present case there are two obvious reasons. The first is that the density per unit area is not constant between substrates (Table 7.2 and 7.3). Second, in most streams it is very difficult to estimate the area of natural substrate available to simuliids and to judge the relative suitability of those that may appear to be suitable. This is in part due to current variation over the substrates, which in the present case was from 0.18 to 1.24 ms^{-1}. Futhermore, the current velocities can vary considerably over a given point with changes in discharge. Thus there is a historical element, e.g., discharges in the immediate past, influencing distributions at sampling time.

If we examine another aspect, species interactions—e.g., those between simuliid-*Drunella* spp. or simuliid-*Rhyacophila* spp.—they will not be the same on all substrates. For in the above example it is unlikely that either *Drunella* spp. or *Rhyacophila* spp. would colonize small filaments. Wiley and Kohler (1981) used photographic sampling of natural substrates to show the interaction between *Rhyacophila acropedes* Banks and simuliids, and how with time the former altered the distribution and density of the latter. It is quite possible that if certain artificial substrates had been photographed this interaction would not have been observed. On the other hand, some substrates like monofilaments may make larvae more exposed to fish predation. Thus predation studies using different artificial substrates may yield quite different results. In fact, the overall relevance of data from artificial samplers, with respect to ecology of simuliids in the natural stream, creates considerable difficulties in interpretation.

In summary, the state of the art in sampling design provides the mathematical methodology for determining the number of samples, given the mean density, the population distribution, confidence limits desired, and a knowledge of certain flow characteristics (Craig and Galloway, this volume). In addition, several artificial samplers will collect large numbers of black fly larvae, and with proper placement, perhaps with low variance. The data obtained will be adequate for testing the efficacy of pesticides. However, in studies where the goal is to understand the population dynamics of a natural stream population, artificial substrates can provide very misleading data. Natural substrate sampling may be required, yet it is often difficult or impossible to accomplish. Certain aspects such as seasonality, species present, estimates of development time, etc., can be obtained as well as estimates of overall productivity. The most difficult is determining effects of natural predation and disease and in what instar or stage these have an impact on the population in question.

Pupae

The factors influencing larvae and the problems of sampling such populations also hold true for pupae. The pharate pupa moves, but once it selects the site for the cocoon and spins one, no further movement occurs despite velocity changes. The pupal habitat in most species differs from that of the larvae (Colbo and Wotton

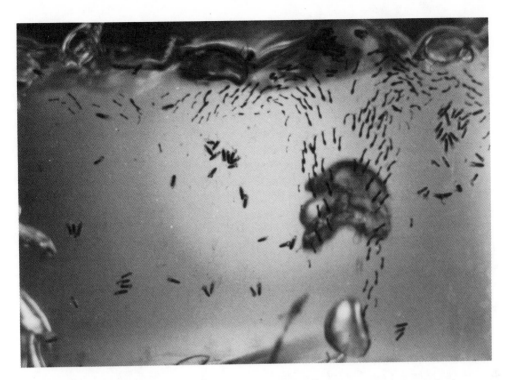

FIG. 7.8 The distribution of *Simulium ornatipes* larvae and pupae on the glass wall of an aquarium illustrating their different current preferences. Current produced by compressed air.

1981), as illustrated in Figure 7.8. Consequently, it is possible that several artificial samplers, such as small tubes, filaments, or thin, smooth tiles, may not be suitable substrates for pupation. This unsuitability could lead to severe underestimates of pupation rates due to the pharate pupae migrating off the samplers.

CONCLUSION

1. There appears to be a definite need for the development of sampling techniques that would make the study of the biology and ecology of the egg stages more practical, particularly those found in the bottom substrates. These techniques need to cover oviposition, aging, separating from substrate, identification, etc.
2. Sampling design techniques and artificial samplers are available for effectively studying pesticide efficacy, seasonal distribution of larvae and pupae, and development rates.
3. Artificial samplers will provide indications of a species' preferences for a general current velocity, depth, distribution along a channel, and the general distribution in a range of streams.
4. Artificial samplers, however, do not necessarily indicate the true population density or its age structure in a stream, and thus they may not permit the

development of realistic life tables, etc. But sampling natural substrates does not necessarily make this task easier. The contagious nature of natural population, resulting from a combination of many factors (current velocities, suitability of substrate for attachment, competition with other species, bed movement, and changing discharge), still makes sampling difficult.

5. Despite sampling problems for some species, more complete autecological studies of many other species are possible using a combination of photography, artificial substrates, and natural substrate sampling planned by available statistical techniques of sample design and analysis. However, since they are still laborious, more imaginative and innovative approaches are needed to make studies rigorous scientifically yet feasible with the resources available.

LITERATURE CITED

Benke, A. C., T. C. Van Arsdall, Jr., D. M. Gillespie, and F. K. Parrish. 1984. Invertebrate productivity in a subtropical blackwater river: the importance of habitat and life history. *Ecol. Monogr.* 54:25–63.

Carlsson, G., P. Elsen, and K. Muller, 1981. Trapping technology-larval blackflies. Pp. 283–286 in M. Laird, Ed., *Blackflies: the future for biological methods in integrated control.* Academic Press, New York and London.

Colbo, M. H. 1979. Distribution of winter-developing simuliidae (Diptera), in Eastern Newfoundland. *Can. J. Zool.* 57:2143–52.

Colbo, M. H., and D. E. Moorhouse. 1974. The survival of the eggs of *Austrosimulium pestilens.* Mack & Mack (Diptera, Simuliidae). *Bull. Entomol. Res.* 64:629–632.

Colbo, M. H., and R. S. Wotton. 1981. Preimaginal blackfly bionomics. Pp. 209–226 in M. Laird, Ed., *Blackflies: the future for biological methods in integrated controls.* Academic Press, New York and London.

Downing, J. A. 1979. Aggregation, transformation and design of benthos sampling programs. *J. Fish. Res. Board Can.* 36:1454–63.

Elliott, J. M. 1977. Some methods for the statistical analysis of samples of benthic invertebrates, 2nd ed. *Freshwater Biol. Assoc. Sci. Publ.* 25. 160 pp.

Elliott, J. M., and P. A. Tullett. 1979. A bibliography of samplers for benthic invertebrates. *Freshwater Biol. Assoc. Occ. Publ.* 4. 61 pp.

Flannagan, J. F., and D. M. Rosenberg. 1982. Types of artificial substrates used for sampling freshwater benthic macroinvertebrates. Pp. 237–266 in J. Cairns, Jr., Ed., *Artificial substrates.* Ann Arbor Science, Ann Arbor, Michigan.

Fredeen, F. J. H., and D. T. Spurr. 1978. Collecting semi-quantitative samples of black fly larvae (Diptera: Simuliidae) and other aquatic insects from large rivers with the aid of artificial substrates. *Quaest. Entomol.* 14:411–431.

Gersabeck, E. F., and R. W. Merritt. 1979. Effects of physical factors on the colonization and relocation behaviour of immature blackflies. (Simuliidae: Diptera). *Environ. Entomol.* 8:34–39.

Imhof, J. E., and S. M. Smith. 1979. Oviposition behaviour, egg masses and hatching response of eggs of five nearctic species of *Simulium* (Diptera: Simuliidae). *Bull. Entomol. Res.* 69:405–425.

Kurtak, D. C. 1978. Efficiency of filter feeding of blackfly larvae (Diptera: Simuliidae). *Can. J. Zool.* 56:1608–23.

Lewis, D. J., and G. F. Bennett. 1974. An artificial substrate for quantitative comparison of densities of larval simuliid (Diptera) populations. *Can. J. Zool.* 52:773–775.

Merritt, R. W., K. W. Cummins, and V. H. Resh. 1984. Collecting sampling and rearing methods for aquatic insects. Pp. 12–26 in R. W. Merritt and K. W. Cummins, Eds., *An introduction to the aquatic insects of North America.* Kendall/Hunt, Dubuque, Iowa.

Morin, A. 1985. Variability of density estimates and optimization of sampling programs for stream benthos. *Can. J. Fish. Aquat. Sci.* 42:1530–34.

Nakamura, Y., K. Saito, and M. Takahashi (1978). Studies on ecology of black flies (Simuliidae: Diptera) (1) Comparison of some quantitative sampling methods for larvae. *Jpn. J. Sanit. Zool.* 29:209–212.

Phillipson, J. 1956. A study of factors determining the distribution of the larvae of the blackfly *Simulium ornatum* Mg. *Bull. Entomol. Res.* 47:227–238.

Resh, V. H. 1979. Sampling variability and life history factors: basic considerations in the design of aquatic insect studies. *J. Fish. Res. Board Can.* 36:290–311.

Rosenberg, D. M., and V. H. Resh. 1982. The use of artificial substrates in the study of freshwater benthic macroinvertebrates. Pp. 175–235 in J. Cairns, Jr., Ed., *Artificial substrates.* Ann Arbor Science, Ann Arbor, Michigan.

Rühm, W. 1972. Zur populations dynamik von *Boophthora erythrocephala* de Geer. *Z. Ang. Entomol.* 71:35–44.

———. 1975. Freilandbeobachtungen zum Funktionskries de Eiablage verschiedener Simuliidenarten unter besonderer Berucksichtigung von *Simulum argyeatum* Meig. (Simuliidae, Diptera). *Z. Ang. Entomol.* 78:321–334.

Rühm, W., and R. Schlepper. 1979. Versuche zur guanitativen Erfassung der Eiablageintensitat von Simuliiden. *Z. Ang. Entomol.* 88:204–216.

Sheldon, A. L. 1984. Cost and precision in a stream sampling program. *Hydrobiologia* 111:147–152.

Southwood, T. R. E. 1978. *Ecological methods with particular reference to the study of insect populations,* 2nd ed. Chapman & Hall, London. 524 pp.

Tarshis, I. B. 1968. Collecting and rearing black flies. *Ann. Entomol. Soc. Am.* 61:1072–83.

Walsh, D. J., D. Y. Yeboah, and M. H. Colbo. 1981. A spherical sampling device for black fly larvae. *Mosquito News* 41:18–21.

Wiley, J. W., and S. L. Kohler (1981). An assessment of biological interactions in an epilithic stream community using time-lapse cinematography. *Hydrobiologia* 78:183–188.

8 FACTORS AFFECTING LARVAL BLACK FLY DISTRIBUTIONS AND POPULATION DYNAMICS

Douglas H. Ross and Richard W. Merritt

Understanding aquatic invertebrate annual dynamics and distributions is a central aim of freshwater ecology. Knowledge of the nature and causes of natural fluctuations is necessary for empirical testing of hypotheses relating to community structure and function. It is also a prerequisite for assessing the impact of man's activities on freshwater ecosystems. Larval black flies are often dominant members of lotic systems, reaching densities as high as 10^6 individuals/m^2 (Wotton 1984). Many factors have been associated with the numerical changes occurring in larval populations over an annual period, and in the number of species present or absent in a system. The main objective of this chapter is to try and identify some of the major environmental factors influencing larval black fly distributions and population dynamics. Biotic factors will not be treated here since they have recently been dealt with elsewhere (Davies 1981), or included here in the chapters by Hart, Molloy, and Lacey and Undeen.

A review of the major environmental factors associated with larval black fly distributions and/or population dynamics is presented in Table 8.1. Those investigations attributing numerical changes or a species' presence/absence to more than one factor are listed after each factor. On examination of these papers we found that: (1) A multitude of factors affect the same genus and often the same black fly species. Very few studies identify only one factor as being responsible for population or species changes; and (2) Investigators were hesitant to identify the causal mechanisms underlying observed distributional patterns. It became clear to us that most studies have associated a particular environmental factor or set of factors with the presence/absence of a species using correlation analysis rather than cause-and-effect relationships. Since the former is inherently weak, it is possible that the observed relationship is only indirect. A given species' distribution or abundance may actually be controlled by a factor such as food quantity or quality that may be related to the physicochemical parameter under study (cf. Hynes 1970, Cummins 1975). It was also evident that many of the environmental factors considered are so closely associated with or dependent on each other that it has been difficult to isolate their individual effects.

Table 8.1 Major environmental factors associated with larval black fly growth, distribution, and population dynamics

Factor	Genus	Selected References
Limnological factors	*Boophthora*	Grunewald (1972)
(pH, ionic concentration, conductivity, etc.)	*Prosimulium*	I. B. Tarshis (unpublished data)
	Simulium	Grunewald (1974, 1976)
		Quillévéré et al. (1976, 1977)
		Glatthaar (1978)
		Grunewald and Grunewald (1978)
		Grunewald et al. (1979)
		Gordon and Cupp (1980)
		Townsend et al. (1983)
		Gordon (1984)
		I. B. Tarshis (unpublished data)
	Stegopterna	I. B. Tarshis (unpublished data)
Depth	*Eusimulium*	Carlsson (1962)
	Odagmia	Ulfstrand (1967)
		Carlsson (1962)
	Prosimulium	Lewis and Bennet (1975)
	Simulium	Carlsson (1962)
		Lewis and Bennet (1975)
	Stegopterna	Lewis and Bennet (1975)
Substrate	*Boothphora*	Pegel and Rühm (1976)
	Eusimulium	Carlsson (1962)
	Odagmia	Ulfstrand (1967)
		Carlsson (1962)
	Prosimulium	Lewis and Bennet (1975)
	Simulium	Zahar (1951)
		Freeden and Shemanchuk (1960)
		Carlsson (1962)
		Maitland and Penny (1967)
		Lewis and Bennet (1975)
		Colbo and Moorhouse (1979)
		Niesiolowski (1980)
		Boobar and Granett (1980)
	Stegopterna	Lewis and Bennet (1975)
Current velocity and flow	*Austrosimulium*	Colbo and Moorhouse (1979)
	Cnephia	Colbo (1979)
	Eusimulium	Carlsson (1962)
		Maitland and Penny (1967)
	Odagmia	Carlsson (1962)
		Ulfstrand (1967)

Table 8.1 (continued)

Factor	Genus	Selected References
	Prosimulium	Lewis and Bennet (1975) Colbo (1979) Lake and Burger (1983)
	Stegopterna	Lewis and Bennet (1975)
	Simulium	Wu (1931) Zahar (1951) Phillipson (1956, 1957) Carlsson (1962) Maitland and Penny (1967) Chutter (1968) Lewis and Bennet (1975) Colbo (1979) Colbo and Moorhouse (1979) Lake and Burger (1983) Adler and Kim (1984)
Discharge	*Prosimulium*	Ross and Merritt (1978)
	Simulium	Wotton (1978) Lake and Burger (1983)
Daylength	*Simulium*	Post (1983)
Food supply	*Cnephia*	Anderson and Dicke (1960)
	Eusimulium	Thorup (1974)
	Gnus	Carlsson (1962)
	Metacnephia	Carlsson et al. (1977)
	Odagmia	Carlsson (1962) Glötzel (1973) Thorup (1974)
	Prosimulium	Glötzel (1973) Merritt et al. (1982)
	Schonbaueria	Carlsson et al. (1977)
	Simulium	Zahar (1951) Anderson and Dicke (1960) Fredeen and Shemanchuk (1960) Carlsson (1962) Chutter (1968) Thorup (1974) Carlsson et al. (1977) Ladle et al. (1977) Elsen (1979) Reisen (1977) Colbo and Porter (1981) Ladle and Hansford (1981)
Temperature	*Cnephia*	Ross and Merritt (1978)
	Eusimulium	Carlsson (1962) Thorup (1974)
	Odagmia	Carlsson (1962) Thorup (1974)

Table 8.1 (continued)

Factor	Genus	Selected References
	Prosimulium	Davies and Smith (1958)
		Davies and Syme (1958)
		Ross and Merritt (1978)
		Colbo (1979)
		Merritt et al. (1982)
		Lake and Burger (1983)
	Simulium	Zahar (1951)
		Carlsson (1962)
		Becker (1973)
		Thorup (1974)
		Mokry (1976)
		Quillévéré (1976)
		Ladle et al. (1977)
		Reisen (1977)
		Wotton (1978)
		Colbo and Porter (1981)
		Lake and Burger (1983)
		Post (1983)
		Adler and Kim (1984)
	Stegopterna	Ross and Merritt (1978)
		Colbo (1979)
		Merritt et al. (1982)
	Wilhelmia	Glatthaar (1978)
		Neveu and Lapchin (1979)

Although several authors have noted specific environmental factors that affect black fly distributions (e.g., Grenier 1949, Ulfstrand 1967, Chutter 1968, Colbo and Wotton 1981, and others), to our knowledge the only studies that actually addressed the entire range of factors are those of Carlsson (1962, 1967) on Scandinavian black flies and Glatthaar (1978) on Swiss species. These authors listed the following major factors as influencing larval simuliids: food supply, substratum, current velocity, depth, light, physical and chemical conditions (i.e., temperature, gas pressure, pH, etc.), and pollution. Before we examine individual factors, we will make some generalizations about life-history strategies of Simuliidae.

LIFE HISTORIES

Our specific life-history examples will be biased toward temperate North American species because: (1) they have received most of our own research effort; and (2) a great deal of information about these species exists in the literature (e.g., Davies and Syme 1958, Anderson and Dicke 1960, Lewis and Bennett 1974, Ross and Merritt 1978, Adler and Kim 1984, Lake and Burger 1984, and others). However, as Colbo and Wotton (1981) note, the general strategies discussed below are commonly seen in many Simuliidae.

The life histories of temperate North American black flies fall into three general categories (Fig. 8.1). The first group includes some univoltine *Prosimulium* spp. and *Stegopterna mutata* (Malloch) (and perhaps a *Simulium vittatum* Zetterstedt sibling).

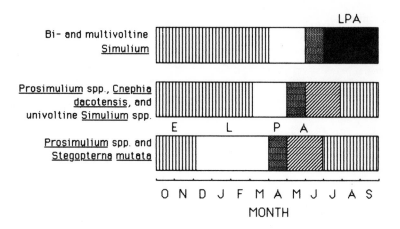

F<small>IG</small>. 8.1 Generalized life-history strategies of temperate North American Simuliidae.

Eggs hatch in late fall and early winter. Larval growth is slow at low water temperatures prevailing in January and February. Following snowmelt, growth increases and pupation occurs in late March or April. Emergence follows and adults are present for 1–2 months. Females lay eggs that settle to the sediment and undergo obligate diapause until the following fall.

The second group also contains some univoltine *Prosimulium* spp., some univoltine *Simulium* spp., and others such as *Cnephia dacotensis* (Dyar and Shannon). Eggs hatch in early spring after stream temperatures begin to rise. Larval growth is more rapid than the "winter" species. Pupation begins in late April or early May, and emergence and oviposition follow. Eggs of these species also undergo obligate diapause lasting until the following spring.

The third group includes bi- and multivoltine *Simulium* spp. Some "species" may actually be temporally separated sibling species (see Adler, this volume). Eggs hatch later than the previous group, and larval growth is similar. Females lay eggs that hatch to produce a second generation. Some species have three or more generations, and larvae, pupae, and adults can be found all summer. Eggs laid by females of the last summer or fall generation diapause until the next spring (see Fig. 8.1).

These strategies evolved as adaptations to environmental conditions (e.g., photoperiod, temperature, discharge, food sources, etc.) in lotic ecosystems that change on a diel, seasonal, and annual basis. The remainder of this chapter examines some of these factors and their specific effects on larval black flies.

WATER TEMPERATURE

Thermal regimes of lotic systems are complex but predictable. Diurnal changes in water temperature vary seasonally, and the difference between annual maximum and minimum temperatures can be quite large. Rates of increase and decrease in temperature and its diurnal change also vary seasonally (Sweeney 1984). Accumulated degree days (°D) vary inversely with latitude, but they can be similar for different order streams in the same drainage basin (Vannote and Sweeney 1980).

Ide (1935) observed that downstream increases in water temperature and its diel fluctuation were associated with the number of mayfly species. He states that a species' distribution is determined by the interaction of growth and developmental thresholds with a stream's thermal regime. He concludes that water temperature sets limits to mayfly distribution, within which are other limits determined by flow, substrate, and vegetation. Recent research provides insight into the mechanisms by which thermal regime actually influences aquatic insect growth, development, fecundity, and ultimately their distribution.

Vannote and Sweeney (1980) propose that an "optimum" thermal regime exists for each species. This regime maximizes adult size and fecundity. Regimes warmer or cooler than "optimum" produce smaller, less fecund adults. For stream mayflies, variation of the thermal regime from the "optimum" influences the equilibrium between two temperature-dependent developmental processes: (1) rate and duration of larval growth; and (2) the time during larval development when adult tissues begin to mature and the rate at which they mature (Vannote and Sweeney 1980). In regimes warmer than "optimum": (1) energy assimilation increases; (2) relatively less of this energy is available for growth due to a disproportional increase in maintenance metabolism; (3) adult tissue maturation begins earlier and proceeds rapidly, shortening time for larval growth; and (4) the short growth period and increased maintenance requirements result in decreased adult body size and fecundity. Conversely, in a cooler regime: (1) energy assimilation will decrease; (2) energy expenditure for growth and metabolism will be similar; (3) duration of the larval stage will be increased due to the slow maturation of adult tissue; (4) adult size is reduced due to low temperatures favoring adult tissue maturation over larval tissue growth; and (5) fecundity is reduced because of reduced size and low temperature, slowing conversion of stored materials into eggs (Vannote and Sweeney 1980).

Reduced size and fecundity resulting from nonoptimal thermal regimes ultimately limit, in part, a species' distribution both within drainage systems and over geographical areas. Decreased adult size and fecundity at the limits of a species' range place it at a competitive disadvantage compared to other species living "closer" to their optimum regime.

Taylor (1981) studied the developmental rates of 54 insect species (including four Culicidae) and their relationship to thermal regimes on elevational and longitudinal gradients. Development rate as a function of temperature follows a normal distribution truncated to the right of the mean (due to lethal effects of high temperatures). For each insect there exists a temperature, T_m, at which development is maximized, and a T_δ, the rate at which the development rate falls away from T_m. (T_δ is analogous to the standard deviation of a normal distribution and influences the "shape" of the curve.)

Aquatic insect species with low values of T_m and T_o should find "optimum" thermal conditions: (1) in cooler upstream reaches, where groundwater input reduces diel temperature fluctuation; and (2) during winter months, when temperatures are low and fluctuate little. On the other hand, species with higher T_m and larger T_δ should find "optimum" conditions: (1) in warmer, higher-order streams, where diel fluctuation is greater; and (2) during spring and summer months, when stream temperature and its diel fluctuation are higher. Species possessing high T_m and low T_δ would be expected to occur in habitats such as tropical streams, where temperatures are generally high but fluctuate minimally. There are also species with low T_m

and high T_o, such as *P. mixtum* and *P. fuscum*. These simuliid species spend most of their larval life at temperatures below 4°C, but they tolerate diel fluctuations as great as 10°C (Ross and Merritt 1978).

A number of studies support the notion of an "optimum" thermal regime and its influence on larval simuliid distributions. Laboratory studies show that increased rearing temperatures generally shorten developmental time (e.g., Becker 1973, Mokry 1976, Colbo and Porter 1981). The latter authors also observed that: (1) *S. vittatum* fecundity decreased as temperature increased above 15–20°C; and (2) the quantity of food required for maximum growth increased exponentially with increasing temperature. Increased maintenance metabolism at the higher temperatures is probably responsible for the increased need for food (Vannote and Sweeney 1980).

Field studies of simuliids with more than one generation or cohort/year show that winter generations frequently contain larger larvae (e.g., Thorup 1974, Ladle et al. 1977, Ross and Merritt 1978) and produce larger and more fecund females than summer generations (Post 1983). Summer generation development times are also shorter (e.g., Wotton 1978). Ross and Merritt (1978) and Post (1983) report that a reduction in instar number occurs at temperatures above "optimum." In the former study, development time, instar number, and larval size were all reduced at the higher temperature regime, but the number of °D necessary for development of the two cohorts was identical.

Larval insect growth and the onset and rate of adult tissue development are mediated by the neuro-endocrine system (Ratte 1984) and quantitative and qualitative changes in enzymes involved in assimilation and digestion (Sweeney 1984). Little is known about the mechanism(s) by which temperature influences endocrine systems, and this should be an area of future research.

LIMNOLOGICAL FACTORS

Attempts to explain freshwater species' distributions in terms of chemical differences have had little success except where conditions are extreme (Macan 1961, 1974). Although different limnological factors have been associated with larval black fly distributions and abundance (see Table 8.1), our knowledge of these factors and how they operate is limited. For as many papers that show a relationship between species distributions and limnological factors, equally as many show no correlations (Ali et al. 1974; Chutter 1963, 1968; Glötzel 1973; Lewis and Bennett 1975; Maitland and Penny 1967; Reisen 1977). Grunewald and colleagues have conducted the most complete analyses of chemical and physical factors affecting larval black flies (Grunewald 1972, 1973, 1974, 1976; Grunewald and Grunewald 1978; Grunewald et al. 1979). Those factors most often associated with larval distributions are dissolved oxygen (DO), pH, conductivity, ionic composition, alkalinity, and hardness.

Although cited regularly in earlier papers (see Table 8.1), DO is usually not limiting in running waters except where it is depleted by biological activity. Most watercourses containing black flies are saturated with DO; however, *Simulium adersi* (Pomeroy) can undergo development with DO saturation at 50%, and larval *S. damnosum* s. l. Theobald have been found in natural habitats with DO saturation as low as 75% (Grunewald 1976). Stream DO concentration varies diurnally, and this variation has been used to reflect net primary productivity (Odum 1956). Consequently, no reliable estimate of a stream segment's DO content can be made from a few spot samples.

Calcium (Ca) is probably more variable than any other ion in freshwater. There is hardly a group of freshwater animals whose distribution has not been related to Ca concentration (Armitage 1961; Macan 1961, 1974; Wetzel 1975). Several black fly studies have monitored Ca concentrations (Grunewald 1976, Grunewald et al. 1979, Gordon and Cupp 1980, Gordon 1984), but significant effects were not detected. Usually the amount of Ca utilized by the biota is so small compared to existing levels that effects cannot be seen in normal analyses (Wetzel 1975). Merritt et al. (1982) found that black fly production in a hardwater stream ($CaCO_3$ alkalinity > 200 mg/L and total hardness averaging 150–300 mg/L) was generally higher than simuliid production reported for softwater streams with low concentrations of other ions. They suggested that more rapid microbial processing of allochthonous detritus may occur with high alkalinity. This would increase the food available to shredder and collector organisms. However, as Hynes (1970) pointed out, the mechanism(s) by which these agents operate are poorly understood, and effects attributed to them may be indirect (cf. Lock and Hynes 1975).

Of all the limnological factors reported to affect larval black fly distributions, pH appears to be one of the most significant (Grunewald 1976, 1978; Quillévéré et al. 1977, Grunewald and Grunewald 1978; Townsend et al. 1983). Levels of pH vary widely in running waters, and they are greatly influenced by the buffering capacity of the stream and free CO_2 concentration (Talling 1976). Grunewald and Grunewald (1978) studied the influence of electrolyte concentration, ionic composition, and pH on two cytospecies of the *S. damnosum* complex. Both species breed in alkaline streams with high conductivity but showed poor laboratory survivorship in water of neutral pH and low conductivity. This paper was significant because it recommended that for successful larval rearing, pH, conductivity, and ionic composition of laboratory culture water be adjusted to and maintained at levels similar to those found in natural habitats. Grunewald et al. (1979) also found that the hydrochemical and physical environments of two *S. neavei* Roubaud complex species in Africa differed with respect to their conductivity, pH, concentrations of ammonium and nitrite ions, and silicate content. Each species appears to be restricted to habitats containing specific physiochemical characteristics. More recently, Gordon and Cupp (1980) and Gordon (1984) found that pH and ionic concentration of some North American streams are the factors most closely associated with observed distributions of the black fly species they studied.

Despite the strong correlation between a limnological factor (e.g., pH) and the abundance and/or distribution of aquatic invertebrates, it is not always clear whether the correlation is direct, indirect, or fortuitous. Studies in the English River Duddon (Minshall and Kuehne 1969, Sutcliffe and Carick 1973a,b, Macan 1974, Minshall and Minshall 1978) show that chemical factors (i.e., K, Na, Mg, Ca, etc.) operated directly to restrict the benthic invertebrate community, including *Simulium,* rather than indirectly through the food chain. These studies conclude that although pH differs markedly in the upper and lower Duddon, and there is a high correlation between pH and macroinvertebrate abundance, pH is not the primary factor responsible for their distribution. Nor is it the cause of the paucity of bacterial and fungal populations in the river. This conclusion was reached through corroborative laboratory experiments aimed at isolating the effects of specific factors on the fauna (Minshall and Minshall 1978).

It is difficult to duplicate conditions prevailing in a headwater stream in the laboratory. Thus, there are bound to be discrepancies between experimental results and field observations. A major problem is that the best correlations come from studying one or two factors in the laboratory. However, these same factors may operate very differently in the field under the influence of numerous other parameters. It is well known that diel cycles in limnological factors (DO, pH, P, N, dissolved organic carbon, and others) occur in the field (Hynes 1970, Wetzel 1975, Cole 1983). Most laboratory studies involving aquatic insects have maintained constant conditions for chemical parameters. This may be because of technical difficulties in producing appropriate test environments or due to interpretation problems (cf. Sweeney 1984). This concern is equally true for constant temperature rearing to evaluate thermal effects (Sweeney 1984). Taking into account the time period for which a particular factor prevails at a given level is also important. Grunewald (1976) cites one instance of a breeding site for three *Simulium* species that had ammonium concentrations as high as 1.21 mg NH_4-N/L recorded immediately after cattle had crossed the river. A few minutes later the concentration had dropped to its normal level. In the laboratory, the larvae could tolerate a temporary increase of ammonium concentration, but they would have died within a few hours if the level remained above the maximum measured in their natural breeding areas.

Most studies investigating limnological factors affecting aquatic insects have been field surveys with some corroborative laboratory experiments. Few have actually involved experimental manipulations in the field. A notable exception is a study by Hall et al. (1980) on the effects of acid precipitation. These authors experimentally acidified a small northeastern U.S. stream for six months by continuous addition of dilute sulfuric acid. Benthic invertebrate densities and emergence of adult collectors decreased in the treatment area. Immature black flies, chironomids, and mayflies increased in drift samples during the first week after acidification. The acidified section of the stream released greater concentrations of Al, Ca, Mg, and probably other cations that may have resulted from their replacement by H^+ ions, presumably via cation-exchange reactions with the sediments (Hall et al. 1980). Thus the physiological response to increased acidity, either directly through ion-exchange mechanisms or indirectly through heavy metal toxicity or a synergistic combination appeared to be the cause for observed changes rather than a diminished food supply. Experimental studies such as this, which attempt to examine the cause-and-effect relationships of pH, community dynamics, trophic interactions, metabolism, and biogeochemistry of a freshwater ecosystem, are sorely needed to understand better the influence of environmental factors on the fauna.

CURRENT, VELOCITY, DEPTH, DISCHARGE, AND SUBSTRATE

The velocity and depth of flowing water greatly influence the substrate size and composition of a given stream reach (Krumbein and Pettijohn 1938). Although these environmental factors are listed separately in Table 8.1, they are difficult to separate and are most easily discussed together.

The association between current velocity and larval simuliid distribution was established long ago (e.g., Wu 1931). Individual species inhabit a wide range of flows, but each apparently has a limited optimum velocity range (Phillipson 1956, 1957). Turbulence also influences larval distribution (e.g., Colbo 1979) and may affect feeding efficiency (Kurtak 1978).

Larval black flies occur on a variety of substrates, including bedrock, boulders, smaller stones, vegetation, snags, and "artificial" substrates introduced into streams. As mentioned above, substrate size and composition are influenced by current velocity. However, different substrates also affect flow patterns over their surfaces (Vogel 1981). Consequently, it can be difficult to determine whether substrate or current velocity is directly responsible for observed patterns of larval black fly distribution. Most published observations noting a simuliid species' "preferred" a substrate or current velocity are good examples of "correlation" rather than "cause and effect." The insect's association with the observed velocity-substrate combination certainly exists, but mere observation provides no insight to the actual factors involved. In addition, if the organism is affected by a given factor, then the level of that factor at which the organism most frequently occurs in nature is most likely to be optimal. The extreme levels at which ecological factors become limiting are unlikely to be detected if only a few habitats are sampled (cf. Macan 1974).

Larval black fly microdistribution across ranges of current velocity and substrate appears ultimately to be determined by hydrodynamics. Several authors (Rubenstein and Koehl 1977, Vogel 1981, Newbury 1984, Nowell and Jumars 1984) point out the general interrelationships between benthic invertebrate ecology and fluid dynamics, substrate size and orientation, boundary-layer dynamics, particle size and motion, drag, the morphology and distribution of organisms, and other hydrodynamic factors. Craig and Chance (1982) and Craig and Galloway (this volume) discuss hydrodynamic principles associated with larval simuliids. Identification and quantification of the hydrodynamic forces associated with larval black flies and their habitats clearly deserves further study.

FOOD

Larval black flies are important components of the "collector" functional feeding group in lotic systems (see Cummins, this volume; Merritt and Cummins 1984). Although larvae of some genera possess either reduced fans or modified structures that serve as efficient raking or scraping organs (Craig 1974, 1977; Davies 1974), most feed by filtering with cephalic fans and rely on water flow to transport suspended particulate food, called seston. Different aspects of simuliid feeding behavior are covered elsewhere in this book (see Currie and Craig, Craig and Galloway, this volume), and a general review was presented by Wallace and Merritt (1980).

The "food" of larval black flies may come from autochthonous (produced within the ecosystem) or allochthonous (transported into the system from elsewhere) sources. It consists largely of fine particulate organic matter (0.5 μm < FPOM < 1 mm) and is derived from several different sources, including: (1) the feeding activities of macroinvertebrates (e.g., "shredders" of leaf material) on coarse particulate organic matter (CPOM > 1 mm) and subsequent release of feces; (2) abrasion of

CPOM by sediments in transport; (3) decaying macrophytes; (4) scouring of algal cells from the substrate; and (5) flocculation of dissolved organic matter (DOM) by physical-chemical processes (Ladle et al. 1972, Anderson and Sedell 1979, Cummins and Klug 1979, Wallace and Merritt 1980, Merritt et al. 1984). At lake outlets, FPOM utilized by larval black flies will consist of bacterioplankton, small phytoplankton, zooplankton, and detritus, some of which will be generated as water passes from the lake to the river (Wotton 1984, see also chap. 11). FPOM can also enter the stream from adjacent terrestrial areas through windblow, surface runoff, bank erosion (Winterbourn et al. 1981), or from rain dripping through the forest canopy, which leaches particles into the stream (Fisher and Likens 1973). Events in the riparian ecosystem largely determine the quantity, quality, timing, and retention of allochthonous material received by streams (Nelson 1969, Sedell et al. 1974, Hynes 1975, Cummins 1980).

Simuliid larvae ingest organic and inorganic particles ranging in diameter from 0.091 μm (colloidal) to 350 μm. The majority of studies report sizes < 200 μm (Williams et al. 1961; Chance 1970; Merritt et al. 1978a; Wotton 1976, 1977; Elsen 1979). There is also ample evidence from lotic studies that concentration of particulate organic seston in most streams is skewed toward the smallest size fractions (< 50 μm) (Lush and Hynes 1978, Sedell et al. 1978, Naiman and Sedell 1979). Larval food includes bacteria, algae and diatoms, other insects, and detritus (Anderson and Dicke 1960; Carlsson 1962, 1967; Baker and Bradnam 1976; Wallace and Merritt 1980). Larvae have been reared successfully on a suspension of bacteria alone (Fredeen 1964) and may also ingest algal filaments ≥ 1 mm in length (Burton 1973). Simuliid gut-retention times are generally short, with most values falling between 20–30 minutes (Ladle et al. 1972, Kurtak 1978, Wotton 1978). Since gut-retention times for macroinvertebrates grazing on periphyton ("scrapers") or those feeding on CPOM colonized by microorganisms ("shredders") are longer (2–12 hours; Cummins 1973, 1975), it has been suggested that the collector strategy might be to pass a comparatively low-quality food (i.e., detritus) through the gut rapidly (Cummins and Klug 1979). However, feeding rates and retention times are dependent on several factors, including the species, larval age, filtering efficiency, water temperature and velocity, and seston size, concentration, and quality (Wallace and Merritt 1980).

The studies cited in Table 8.1 suggest that larval black fly densities and/or distributions are strongly influenced by the quality and/or quantity of seston present in the habitat. Food quality can be defined as the nutritive content per unit food intake and the quantity as the density per unit of environment (Cummins 1974, Anderson and Cummins 1979). Colbo and Porter (1979) demonstrate in the laboratory that reduced food supply to back fly larvae resulted in longer developmental times, declining survival, and decreased adult size and fecundity, indicating the importance of nutrition in life-history events. This finding is particularly relevant to field studies, since these results are often attributed to other environmental factors.

The high abundance of filter-feeding simuliids and net-spinning caddisflies in lake-outlet streams and below impoundments, followed by a precipitous downstream decrease, has been associated with declining seston quantity and/or quality (Chutter 1963, Ulfstrand 1968, Glötzel 1973, Carlsson et al. 1977, Sheldon and Oswood 1977, Merritt et al. 1978b, Wotton 1978, Oswood 1979). However, Carlsson et al. (1977) studied black fly assemblages inhabiting Swedish lake outlets, and they could detect no major differences in the type and abundance of seston (i.e., large particles of phytoplankton and coarse detritus) along the watercourse. There did not seem to be any direct relationship between this potential resource and black fly abundance. Instead, they attributed the huge aggregations immediately below lake outlets to minute particles, 2 μm in size, presumably rich in microflora (Wotton 1978), produced on the lake bottom by decomposition processes during winter and washed into the river at ice melt. Naiman (1982) also found that seston concentrations in a boreal forest with abundant filter feeders did not change between the lake outlet and the sea ($\approx$ 7 km). Other studies fail to document declining seston concentrations downstream (Wallace and Merritt 1980), which would indicate that filter-feeder abundance may be associated more with food quality than quantity (e.g., Wotton 1979, Richardson 1984). These findings also suggest that filter-feeding insects such as black flies may influence their own densities and the life histories of other organisms downstream by their own feeding activities, that is, ingesting seston and producing fragments as feces, which may then be recycled to provide renewed surfaces for microbial colonization and growth (Hargrave 1976; Wotton 1978, 1980; Cummins and Klug 1979).

Food quality and/or quantity appear to influence the distribution of larval black flies as well as their densities. Wotton (this volume) surveyed the literature and concluded that there are black fly species that definitely colonize lake outlets, although they also may be found at lower population densities in similar types of habitats. Carlsson et al. (1977) propose the following three main factors to account for the distribution and abundance of simuliids at lake outlets: (1) available substrates are stable and function as natural spillways, providing broad areas of shallow running water for attachment; (2) substrate stability, lower water depth, and marked visual and sensory cues at the site, which facilitate adult oviposition; and (3) the food quality, which may only be available a short distance downstream from the lake (see also Wotton, this volume).

The interactions between food quantity and quality and stream temperature are complex (Anderson and Cummins 1979, Colbo and Wotton 1981, Sweeney 1984). Temperature can influence the growth of microbial populations on detrital particles (FPOM). This type of indirect control on macroinvertebrate growth and survivorship is difficult to separate from the direct effects of temperature on macroinvertebrate metabolism (Cummins and Klug 1979). Seasonal changes in simuliid adult size and fecundity, which may affect succeeding larval generations, have been related to temperature (Neveu 1973, Hechler and Rühm 1976, Ladle et al. 1977); however, food supply may also play a role in these changes (Colbo and Wotton 1981). Merritt et al. (1982) investigated the influence of stream temperature and seston on the growth and production of overwintering black flies. They report that increases in seston organic content coincide with periods of rising stream temperature and increases in larval growth. They conclude that temperature and seston organic content contribute significantly to this rapid growth and development; however, since food availability did not appear to be limiting to the larvae, temperature is probably the driving force behind their rapid growth and production during late winter.

It is clear that we know very little about the complex interactions of temperature and food and how they affect larval simuliids. Colbo and Porter (1979, 1981) have attempted to clarify these interactions and show that the size and fecundity of black fly species is influenced by the temperature and quantity of food provided. How-ever, it remains difficult to determine the relative contributions of each factor on life-history events (Merritt et al. 1982). Experimental studies, similar to those men-tioned above, on a variety of species in which growth or developmental response is measured over a broad range of temperatures and food types are needed. Only then will the relative importance of each variable be evident (cf. Sweeney 1984).

CONCLUSION

We began writing this chapter with some prejudices about which factors exert the greatest influence on larval black fly distributions and population dynamics, namely, food and temperature (Ross and Merritt 1978, Merritt et al. 1982). All heterotrophic organisms require a food source to successfully complete their life histories, and the significance of temperature to the life histories of ectothermic organisms, including larval simuliids, is indisputable. Temperature and food quantity and quality have significant interactions with aquatic insect growth rates (Anderson and Cummins 1979), however, other factors are certainly involved.

The biological strategies and dynamics of river systems are greatly influenced by a gradient of physical factors formed by the drainage network. Fluvial geomorphic processes appear to be primary regulators of energy input and organic-matter trans-port, storage, and use by lotic macroinvertebrates (Vannote et al. 1980). Stream width, depth, current velocity, sediment load, etc., all interact with stream insect communities (Newbury 1984). Hydrodynamics have recently been recognized as having significant impact on larval simuliids (Craig and Chance 1982, Craig and Galloway, this volume).

The presence or absence of a species in a particular habitat may be due to the complex interaction of several biotic and/or abiotic factors, or it may be due to the species in question having failed to reach the stretch of water being studied. This simple possibility must be examined before more involved ones are investigated. Limiting factors are generally considered one by one, which seems illogical, although more practical, in view of the fact that the distribution of any one species depends on the interactions of several factors (cf. Macan 1974). To achieve an adequate understanding of this chapter's topic, future research must move away from tradi-tional studies emphasizing simple observation and correlation. Experimental studies (field and laboratory) testing specific hypotheses about cause-and-effect relation-ships are needed to elucidate the specific role(s) each factor plays and how different factors interact.

ACKNOWLEDGMENTS

We extend special thanks to Dr. I. Barry Tarshis. His infectious enthusiasm for black fly research stimulated our initial interest in these insects over a decade ago, and his continued interest never ceases to amaze us. We also thank Mary Schlesinger for typing parts of the manuscript.

LITERATURE CITED

Adler, P. H., and K. C. Kim. 1984. Ecological charcterization of two sibling species, IIIL–1 and IS–7, in the *Simulium vittatum* complex (Diptera: Simuliidae). *Can. J. Zool.* 62:1308–15.

Ali, S. H., P. P. Barburtis, W. F. Ritter, and R. W. Lake. 1974. Black fly (*Simulium vittatum*) densities and water quality conditions in Red Clay Creek, Pennsylvania-Delaware. *Environ. Entomol.* 3:879–881.

Anderson, J. R., and R. J. Dicke. 1960. Ecology of the immature stages of some Wisconsin black flies. *Ann. Entomol. Soc. Am.* 53:386–404.

Anderson, N. H., and K. W. Cummins. 1979. Influences of diet on the life histories of aquatic insects. *J. Fish. Res. Board Can.* 36:355–342.

Anderson, N. H., and J. R. Sedell. 1979. Detritus processing by macroinvertebrates in stream ecosystems. *Ann. Rev. Entomol.* 24:351–377.

Armitage, K. B. 1961. Distribution of riffle insects of the Firehole River, Wyoming. *Hydrobiologia* 17:152–174.

Baker, J. H., and L. A. Bradnam. 1976. The role of bacteria in the nutrition of aquatic detritivores. *Oecologia* 24:95–104.

Becker, C. D. 1973. Development of *Simulium* (*Psilozia*) *vittatum* Zett. (Diptera: Simuliidae) from larvae to adult at thermal increments from 17.0 to 27.0°C. *Am. Mid. Nat.* 89:246–251.

Boobar, L. R., and J. Granett. 1980. *Simulium penobscotensis* (Diptera: Simuliidae) habitat characteristics in the Penobscot River, Maine. *Environ. Entomol.* 9:412–415.

Burton, G. J. 1973. Feeding of *Simulium hargreavesi* Gibbins larvae on *Oedogonium* algal filaments in Ghana. *J. Med. Entomol.* 10:101–106.

Carlsson, G. F. 1962. Studies on Scandinavian black flies. *Opusc. Entomol. Suppl.* 21:1–280.

———. 1967. Environmental factors influencing black fly populations. *WHO Bull.* 37:139–150.

Carlsson, M., L. M. Nilsson, B. J. Svensson, S. Ulfstrand, and R. S. Wotton. 1977. Lacustrine seston and other factors influencing the blackflies inhabiting lake outlets in Swedish Lapland. *Oikos* 29:229–238.

Chance, M. M. 1970. The functional morphology of the mouthparts of black fly larvae. *Quaest. Entomol.* 6:245–284.

Chutter, F. M. 1963. Hydrobiological studies on the Vaal River in the Vereeninging area. Part I. Introduction, water chemistry and biological studies of the fauna of habitats other than muddy bottom sediments *Hydrobiologia* 21:1–65.

———. 1968. On the ecology of the fauna of stones in the current in a South African river supporting a very large *Simulium* population. *J. Appl. Ecol.* 5:531–561.

Colbo, M. H. 1979. Distribution of winter-developing Simuliidae (Diptera) in Eastern Newfoundland. *Can. J. Zool.* 57:2143–52.

Colbo, M. H., and D. E. Moorhouse. 1979. The ecology of pre-imaginal Simuliidae (Diptera) in south-east Queensland, Australia. *Hydrobiologia* 63:63–79.

Colbo, M. H., and G. N. Porter. 1979. Effects of the food supply on the life history of Simuliidae. *Can. J. Zool.* 57:301–306.

———. 1981. The interaction of rearing temperature and food supply on the life history of two species of Simuliidae (Diptera). *Can J. Zool.* 59:158–163.

Colbo, M. H., and R. S. Wotton. 1981. Preimaginal black fly bionomics. Pp. 209–226 in M. Laird, Ed., *Blackflies: the future of biological methods in integrated control*. Academic Press, New York and London.

Cole G. A. 1983. *Textbook of limnology,* 3rd ed. C. V. Mosby Co., St. Louis. 401 pp.

Craig, D. A. 1974. The labrum and cephalic fans of larval Simuliidae. *Can. J. Zool.* 52:133–159.

————. 1977. Mouthparts and feeding behavior of Tahitian larval Simuliidae. *Quaest. Entomol.* 13:195–281.

Craig, D. A., and M. M. Chance. 1982. Filter feeding in larvae in Simuliidae (Diptera: Culicomorpha): aspects of functional morphology and hydrodynamics *Can. J. Zool.* 60:712–724.

Craig, D. A., and M. M. Galloway. 1987 (this volume). Hydrodynamics of larval black flies.

Cummins, K. W. 1973. Trophic relations of aquatic insects. *Ann. Rev. Entomol.* 18:183–206.

————. 1974. Structure and function of stream ecosystems. *BioScience.* 24:631–641.

————. 1975. Macroinvertebrates. Pp. 170–198 in B. A. Whitton, Ed., *River ecology.* Univ. California Press, Berkeley.

————. 1980. The multiple linkages of forests to streams. Pp. 191–198 in R. H. Waring, Ed., *Forests: fresh perspectives from ecosystems analysis.* Proc. 40th Ann. Biol. Colloq., Oregon St. Univ., Corvallis. 198 pp.

Cummins, K. W., and M. J. Klug. 1979. Feeding ecology of stream invertebrates. *Ann Rev. Ecol. Syst.* 10:147–172.

Davies, D. M. 1981. Predators upon blackflies. Pp. 139–158 in M. Laird, Ed., *Blackflies: the future of biological methods in integrated control.* Academic Press, New York and London.

Davies, D. M., and P. D. Syme. 1958. Three new Ontario black flies of the genus *Prosimulium* (Simuliidae). Part II. Ecological observations and experiments. *Can. Entomol.* 90:744–759.

Davies, L. 1974. Evolution of larval head-fans in Simuliidae as inferred from the structure and biology of *Crozetia crozetensis* (Wormersley) compared with other genera. *Zool. J. Linn. Soc.* 55:193–224.

Davies, L., and C. D. Smith. 1958. The distribution and growth of *Prosimulium* larvae (Diptera: Simuliidae) in hill streams in northern England. *J. Anim. Ecol.* 27:335–348.

Elsen, P. 1979. La nature et la taille des particules ingérées par les larves du complexe *Simulium damnosum* dans les rivières de Côte d'Ivoire (Diptera: Simuliidae). *Rev. Zool. Afr.* 93:476–484.

Fisher, S. G., and G. E. Likens. 1973. Energy flow in Bear Brook, New Hampshire: an integrative approach to stream ecosystem metabolism. *Ecol. Monogr.* 43:421–439.

Fredeen, F. J. H. 1964. Bacteria as a source of food for black-fly larvae in laboratory cultures and in natural streams. *Can. J. Zool.* 42:527—548.

Fredeen, F. J. H., and J. A. Shemanchuk. 1960. Black flies of irrigation systems in Saskatchewan and Alberta. *Can. J. Zool.* 38:723–735.

Glatthaar, R. 1978. Verdreitung und Ökologie der Kriebelmucken (Diptera: Simuliidae) in der Schweiz. *Vjschr. Naturf. Ges. Zurich.* 123:71–124.

Glötzel, V. R. 1973. Populations dynamik und Ernährungsbiologie von Simuliidenlarven in einem mit organischen Abwässern verunreinigten Gebirgsbach. *Arch. Hydrobiol. Suppl.* 42:406–451.

Gordon, A. E. 1984. Observations on the limnological factors associated with three species of the *Simulium jenningsi* group (Diptera: Simuliidae) in New York state. *Freshwater Invertebr. Biol.* 3:48–51.

Gordon, A. E., and E. W. Cupp. 1980. The limnological factors associated with cytotypes of the *Simulium* (*Simulium*) *venustum/verecundum* complex (Diptera: Simuliidae) in New York state. *Can. J. Zool.* 58:973–981.

Grenier, P. 1949. Contribution a l'étude biologique des simuliides de France. *Physiol. Comp. Oecol.* 1:165–330.

Grunewald, J. 1972. Die hydrochemischen Lebensbedingungen der praimaginalen Stadien von *Boophthora erythrocephala* De Geer (Diptera: Simuliidae). 1. Freilanduntersuchungen. *Z. Tropenmed. Parasitol.* 23:432–445.

————. 1973. Die hydrochemischen Lebensbedingungen der praimaginalen Stadien von *Boophthora erythrocephala* De Geer (Diptera: Simuliidae). 2. Die Entwicklung einer Zucht unter experimentellen Bedingungen. *Z. Tropenmed. Parasitol.* 24:232–249.

————. 1974. The hydrochemical living conditions of the immature stages of some forms of the *Simulium damnosum* complex with regard to their laboratory colonization. *Proc. II Int. Congr. Parasitol.* 2:914–915.

————. 1976. The hydro-chemical and physical conditions of the environment of the immature stages of some species of the *Simulium* (*Edwardsellum*) *damnosum* complex (Diptera). *Tropenmed. Parasitol.* 27:438–454.

————. 1978. Die Bedentung der Stickstoff-Exkretion und Ammoniak-Empfindeichkeit von Simuliiden-Larven (Diptera) fur den Aufbau von Laboratoriumskulturen. *Z. Ang. Entomol.* 85:52–60.

Grunewald, J. R., and E. B. Grunewald. 1978. Der Einfluss der Wasserstoffionen und Gesamtionenkonzentration sowie der Ionenkomposition aud die aquatischen Stadien zweier Zytoarten des *Simulium damnosum* komplexes (Diptera, Simuliidae). *Arch Hydrobiol.* 82:419–431.

Grunewald, J. R., E. B. Grunewald, J. N. Raybould, and H. K. Mhiddin. 1979. The hydrochemical and physical characteristics of the breeding sites of the *Simulium neavei* Roubaud group and their associated crabs in the Eastern Usambara Mountains in Tanzania. *Int. Revue Gesamten Hydrobiol.* 64:71–88.

Hall, R. J., G. E. Likens, S. B. Fiance, and G. R. Hendry. 1980. Experimental acidification of a stream in the Hubbard Brook Experimental Forest, New Hampshire. *Ecology.* 61:976–989.

Hargrave, B. T. 1976. The central role of invertebrate feces in sediment decomposition. Pp. 301–321 in J. M. Anderson and A. Macfadyen, Eds., *The role of terrestrial and aquatic organisms in decomposition processes.* Blackwell, Oxford. 474 pp.

Hechler, J., and W. R. Rühm. 1976. Ergänzende Untersuchungen zur potentiellen Natalität vershiedener Kriebelmückenarten (Simuliidae, Dipt.). *Z. Ang. Entomol.* 81:208–214.

Hynes, H. B. N. 1970. *The ecology of running waters.* Univ. Toronto Press, Toronto. 555 pp.

————. 1975. The stream and its valley. *Verh. Int. Verein. Limnol.* 19:1–15.

Ide, F. P. 1935. The effect of temperature on the distribution of the mayfly fauna of a stream. *Publs. Ontario Fish. Res. Lab., No. 50.* Univ. Toronto Press, Toronto.

Krumbein, W. D., and F. J. Pettijohn. 1938. Manual of sedimentary petrography. Appleton, Century, New York.

Kurtak, D. C. 1978. Efficiency of filter feeding of black fly larvae. *Can. J. Zool.* 56:1608–23.

Ladle, M., J. A. B. Bass, and W. R. Jenkins. 1972. Studies on production and food consumption by the larval Simuliidae of a chalk stream. *Hydrobiologia 39:429–448.*

Ladle, M., J. A. B. Bass, F. R. Philpott, and A. Jeffrey. 1977. Observations on the ecology of Simuliidae from the River Frome, Dorset. *Ecol. Entomol.* 2:197–204.

Ladle, M., and R. G. Hansford. 1981. The feeding of the larvae of *Simulium austeni* Edward and *Simulium* (*Wilhemia*) spp. *Hydrobiologia* 78:17–24.

Lake, D. J., and J. F. Burger. 1983. Larval distribution and succession of outlet-breeding blackflies (Diptera: Simuliidae) in New Hampshire. *Can. J. Zool.* 61:2519–33.

Lewis, D. J., and G. F. Bennett. 1975. The blackflies (Diptera: Simuliidae) of insular Newfoundland. III. Factors affecting the distribution and migration of larval simuliids in small streams on the Avalon Peninsula. *Can. J. Zool.* 53:114–123.

Lock, M. A., and H. B. N. Hynes. 1975. The disappearance of four leaf leachates in a hard and soft water stream in south western Ontario, Canada. *Int. Revue Gesamten Hydrobiol.* 60:847–855.

Lush, D. L., and H. B. N. Hynes. 1978. Particulate and dissolved organic matter in a small partly forested Ontario stream. *Hydrobiologia* 60:177–185.

Macan, T. T. 1961. Factors that limit the range of freshwater animals. *Biol. Rev.* 367:151–198.

———. 1974. *Freshwater ecology,* 2nd ed. John Wiley & Sons, New York. 343 pp.

Maitland, P. S., and M. M. Penney. 1967. The ecology of the Simuliidae in a Scottish river. *J. Anim. Ecol.* 36:179–206.

Merritt, R. W., M. M. Mortland, E. F. Gersabeck, and D. H. Ross. 1978a. X-ray diffraction analysis of particles ingested by filter-feeding animals. *Entomol. Exp. Appl.* 24:27–34.

Merritt, R. W., D. H. Ross, and B. V. Peterson. 1978b. Larval ecology of some lower Michigan black flies (Diptera: Simuliidae) with keys to the immature stages. *Great Lakes Entomol.* 11:177–208.

Merritt, R. W., D. H. Ross, and G. J. Larson. 1982. Influence of stream temperature and seston on the growth and production of overwintering larval black flies (Diptera: Simuliidae). *Ecology* 63:1322–31.

Merritt, R. W., and K. W. Cummins, Eds. 1984. *An introduction to the aquatic insects of North America,* 2nd ed. Kendall/Hunt, Dubuque, Iowa. 722 pp.

Merritt, R. W., K. W. Cummins, and T. M. Burton. 1984. The role of aquatic insects in the processing and cycling of nutrients. Pp. 134–163 in V. H. Resh and D. M. Rosenberg, Eds., *The ecology of aquatic insects.* Praeger, New York.

Minshall, G. W., and R. A. Kuehne. 1969. An ecological study of invertebrates of the Duddon, an English mountain stream. *Arch. Hydrobiol.* 66:169–191.

Minshall, G. W., and J. N. Minshall. 1978. Further evidence on the role of chemical factors in determining the distribution of benthic invertebrates in the River Duddon. *Arch. Hydrobiol.* 83:324–355.

Mokry, J. E. 1976. Laboratory studies on the larval biology of *Simulium venustum* Say (Diptera: Simuliidae). *Can. J. Zool.* 54:1657–63.

Naiman, R. J. 1982. Characteristics of sediment and organic carbon export from pristine boreal forest watersheds. *Can. J. Fish. Aquat. Sci.* 39:1699–1718.

Naiman, R. J., and J. R. Sedell. 1979. Characterization of particulate organic matter transported by some Cascade Mountain streams. *J. Fish Res. Board Can.* 36:17–31.

Nelson, D. J. 1969. The stream ecosystem: terrestrial-lotic community interactions. Pp. 14–19 in K. W. Cummins, Ed., The stream ecosystem. *Mich. St. Univ. Instit. Wat. Res. Tech. Rept.* 7.42 pp.

Neveu, A. 1973. Estimation de la production de populations larvaires du genre *Simulium. Ann. Hydrobiol.* 4:183–199.

Neveu, A., and L. Lapchin. 1979. Ecologie des principaux invertebrates filtreurs de la basse nivelle (Pyrenees-Atlantiques). I. Simuliidae (Diptera, Nematocera). *Annls. Limnol.* 14:225–244.

Newbury, R. W. 1984. Hydrologic determinants of aquatic insect habitats. Pp. 323–357 in V. H. Resh and D. M. Rosenberg, Eds., *The ecology of aquatic insects.* Praeger, New York.

Niesiolowsku, S. 1980. Studies on the abundance, biomass and vertical distribution of larvae and pupae of black flies (Simuliidae, Diptera) on plants of the Grabia River, Poland. *Hydrobiologia* 75:149–156.

Nowell, A. R. M., and P. A. Junars. 1984. Flow environments of aquatic benthos. *Ann. Rev. Ecol. Syst.* 15:303–328.

Odum, H. T. Primary production in flowing waters. *Limnol. Oceanogr.* 1:102–117.

Oswood, M. W. 1979. Abundance patterns of filter-feeding caddisflies and seston in a Montana (USA) lake outlet. *Hydrobiologia* 63:177–183.

Pegel, M., and W. Ruhm. 1976. Versuche zue Besiedlung kunstlicher Substrate durch praimaginale Stadien von Simuliiden unter besonderer Berucksichtigung von *Boophthora erythrocephala* de Geer (Simuliidae, Diptera). *Z. Ang. Entomol.* 82:65–71.

Phillipson, J. 1956. A study of factors determining the distribution of the larvae of the blackfly, *Simulium ornatum* Mg. *Bull. Entomol. Res.* 47:227–238.

———. 1957. The effect of current speed on the distribution of the larvae of black flies, *Simulium variegatum* (Mg.) and *Simulium monticola* Fried. (Diptera). *Bull. Entomol. Res.* 48:811–819.

Post, R. J. 1983. The annual cycle of *Simulium erythrocephalum* (Diptera: Simuliidae) at a sight in Norfolk. *Freshwater Biol.* 13:379–388.

Quillévéré, D. M. 1977. Etude du complexe *Simulium damnosum* en Afrique de l'Ouest. VI. Analyse de l'eau des gîtes larvaires en saison des pluies: comparaison avec la saison sèche. *Cah. ORSTOM sér.Entomol. Méd. Parasitol.* 15:195–207.

Quillévéré, D., M. Gouzy, Y. Séchan, and B. Pendriez. 1976. Étude du complexe *Simulium damnosum* en Afrique de l'Ouest. IV. Analyse de l'eau des gîtes larvaires en saison sèche. *Cah. ORSTOM sér. Entomol. Méd. Parasitol.* 14:315–330.

Ratte, H. T. 1984. Temperature and insect development. Pp. 33–66 in K. H. Hoffmann, Ed., *Environmental physiology and biochemistry of insects.* Springer Verlag, Berlin.

Reisen, W. K. 1977. The ecology of Honey Creek, Oklahoma: population dynamics and drifting behavior of three species of *Simulium* (Diptera: Simuliidae). *Can. J. Zool.* 55:325–338.

Richardson, J. S. 1984. Effects of seston quality on the growth of a lake-outlet filter-feeder. *Oikos* 43:386–390.

Ross, D. H., and R. W. Merritt. 1978. The larval instars and population dynamics of five species of black flies (Diptera: Simuliidae) and their responses to selected environmental factors. *Can. J. Zool.* 56:1633–42.

Rubenstein, D. I. and M. A. Koehl. 1977. The mechanisms of filter-feeding: some theoretical considerations. *Am. Nat.* 111:981–994.

Sedell, J. R., F. J. Triska, F. S. Hall, N. H. Anderson, and J. H. Lyford. 1978. Sources and fates of organic inputs in coniferous forest streams. Pp. 57–69 in *Integrated research in the coniferous forest biome.* Coniferous Forest Biome Ecosystem Analytical Study, US/IBP Bull. No. 5, Univ. Washington, Seattle.

Sedell, J. R., R. J. Naiman, K. W. Cummins, G. W. Minshall, and R. L. Vannote. 1978. Transport of particulate organic material in streams as a function of physical processes. *Verh. Int. Verein. Limnol.* 20:1366–75.

Sheldon, A. L., and M. W. Oswood. 1977. Blackfly (Diptera: Simuliidae) abundance in a lake outlet: test of a predictive model. *Hydrobiologia* 56:113–120.

Sutcliffe, D. W., and T. R. Carrick. 1973a. Studies on mountain streams in the English Lake District. I. pH, calcium and the distribution of invertebrates in the River Duddon. *Freshwat. Biol.* 3:437–462.

Sutcliffe, D. W., and T. R. Carrick. 1973b. Studies on mountain streams in the English Lake District. II. Aspects of water chemistry in the River Duddon. *Freshwater Biol.* 3:543–560.

Sweeney, B. W. 1984. Factors influencing life-history patterns of aquatic insects. Pp. 56–101 in V. H. Resh and D. M. Rosenberg, Eds., *The ecology of aquatic insects.* Praeger, New York.

Talling, J. F. 1976. The depletion of carbon dioxide from lake water by phytoplankton. *J. Ecol.* 64:79–121.

Taylor, F. 1981. Ecology and evolution of physiological time in insects. *Am. Nat.* 117:1–23.

Thorup, J. 1974. Occurrence and size distribution of Simuliidae (Diptera) in a Danish spring. *Arch. Hydrobiol.* 74:316–335.

Townsend, C. R., A. G. Hildrew, and J. Francis. 1983. Community structure in some southern English streams: the influence of physicochemical factors. *Freshwater Biol.* 13:521–544.

Ulfstrand, S. 1967. Microdistribution of benthic species (Ephemeroptera, Plecoptera, Tri- choptera, Diptera: Simuliidae) in Lapland streams. *Oikos.* 18:293–310.

———. 1968. Benthic animal communities in Lapland streams. A field study with particular reference to Ephemeroptera, Plecoptera, Trichoptera and Diptera: Simuliidae. *Oikos Suppl.* 10:1–116.

Vannote, R. L., and B. W. Sweeney. 1980. Geographic analysis of thermal equilibria: a conceptual model for evaluating the effect of natural and modified thermal regimes on aquatic insect communities. *Am. Nat.* 115:667–695.

Vogel, S. 1981. *Life in moving fluids: The physical biology of flow.* Willard Grant Press, Boston. 353 pp.

Wallace, J. B., and R. W. Merritt. 1980. Filter-feeding ecology of aquatic insects. *Ann. Rev. Entomol. 25:103–132.*

Wetzel, R. G. 1975. *Limnology.* W. B. Saunders Co., Philadelphia. 743 pp.

Williams, T. R., R. Connolly, H. B. N. Hynes, and W. E. Kershaw. 1961. Size of particles ingested by *Simulium* larvae. *Nature* 189:178.

Winterbourn, M. J., J. S. Rounick, and B. Cowrie. 181. Are New Zealand stream ecosystems really different? *New Zealand J. Mar. Freshwater Res.* 15:321–328.

Wotton, R. S. 1976. Evidence that blackfly larvae can feed on particles of colloidal size. *Nature* 261:697.

———. 1977. The size of particles ingested by moorland stream blackfly larvae. *Oikos* 29:332–335.

———. 1978. The feeding rate of *Metacnephia tredecimatum* larvae in a Swedish lake outlet. *Oikos* 30:121–125.

———. 1979. The influence of a lake on the distribution of blackfly species (Diptera: Simulii- dae) along a river. *Oikos* 32:368–372.

———. 1980. Coprophagy as an economic feeding tactic in blackfly larvae. *Oikos* 34:282–286.

———. 1984. The relationship between food particle size and larval size in *Simulium noelleri* Friederichs. *Freshwater Biol.* 14:547–550.

Wu, Y. F. 1931. A contribution to the biology of *Simulium Pap. Mich. Acad. Sci. Arts Lett.* 13:543–599.

Zahar, A. R. 1951. The ecology and distribution of blackflies (Simuliidae) in South-east Scotland. *J. Anim. Ecol.* 20:33–62.

9 PROCESSES AND PATTERNS OF COMPETITION IN LARVAL BLACK FLIES

David D. Hart

In principle, competition can have a pervasive influence on organisms, affecting life-history traits, patterns of resource use, population dynamics, and distributions. However, in spite of an extensive set of theoretical and empirical investigations, the importance of competition in natural populations and communities remains highly controversial (for a range of opinions, see papers in Cody and Diamond 1975, Strong et al. 1984, and Diamond and Case 1986). In contrast to this considerable degree of attention, the subject of competition has seldom been addressed in ecological investigations of larval simuliids, one of the most intensively studied families of insects occurring in running waters.

This paper evaluates the importance of larval competition in the ecology of black fly populations. Given the limited number of investigations related to this subject, my review will of necessity be speculative. First, I summarize some empirical studies providing evidence for competitive interactions among larvae. Second, I examine the relationship between resource availability and competition. Third, I consider how larval competition might influence patterns of resource use. Last, I ask whether insights into the nature of these competitive interactions can aid in the development of programs for the management of black fly populations.

EVIDENCE FOR COMPETITION

Various evidence of competitive interactions among larval black flies can be examined. Competition can be defined as a process in which individuals are negatively affected due to their mutual use (or attempted use) of a limiting resource (cf. Birch 1957). The strongest evidence of competition includes an objective determination of resource limitation and the negative effects that result when consumers interact, but many other kinds of evidence are frequently used to infer competition's existence (cf. Hart 1983). One of these is the spatial dispersion pattern of a population (e.g., Pielou 1977). In black fly larvae, clumps of individuals are often patchily distributed across the stream bottom in an apparent response to heterogeneous physical factors, especially the hydrodynamic environment (e.g., Grenier 1949, Maitland and Penney 1967, Rühm 1970, Décamps et al. 1975, Colbo 1979). However, individuals within these aggregations are sometimes evenly spaced (e.g., Tonnoir 1925, Hocking and Pickering 1954, Elliott 1971, Colbo 1979). For example, I counted the number of individuals in twenty-six 4-cm^2 quadrats within a high-density patch of *Simulium* (*Eusimulium*) *aureum* larvae living in the McCloud River, California. The variance:mean ratio ($s^2 / \bar{x}$ = 1.8/6.8 = 0.26) was significantly less than one ($p < 0.01$), indicating a uniform or even dispersion pattern (Elliott 1971).

In another California stream (Big Sulphur Creek), I photographed a group of larval simuliids that were attached to a large bedrock slab over which water spilled as a thin, uniform sheet. Nearest-neighbor distances were later determined from the photograph, and these were analyzed for deviation from spatial randomness according to the method of Clark and Evans (1955) as corrected by Sinclair (1985). The dispersion index was significantly nonrandom ($c = 6.1$, $p < 0.001$), once again demonstrating even spacing. It is commonly assumed that even dispersion patterns in populations of both plants and animals are the result of negative interactions between neighboring individuals (e.g., Pielou 1977, Davies 1978). However, inferring competition from even dispersion patterns is notoriously difficult (Pielou 1974), and by themselves these patterns would at best provide indirect evidence of competition.

Fortunately, many direct observations indicate that negative interactions between neighboring larvae do occur in some populations (e.g., Tonnoir 1925; Chance 1970, Disney 1972, Kurtak 1973, Colbo 1979, Gersabeck and Merritt 1979, Harding and Colbo 1981, Wiley and Kohler 1981, Hart 1986). Several characteristics of these interactions were described more than sixty years ago by Tonnoir (1925: 216), who indicated that larvae

> are usually very regularly disposed; this arrangement is due to the fact that no larva tolerates one of its congeners in its immediate vicinity, and sweeps away with its head all that come within its reach. When an intruder settles within range of another larva, a fight takes place which may last quite a long time, each larva trying to make its opponent release its hold on the stone, chiefly by pinching it near the extremity of the body until the weaker one retreats.

Aggressive interactions occur between individuals of different black fly species (e.g., Kurtak 1973) as well as between conspecifics. Larvae also attack and displace unrelated taxa, such as mayfly nymphs in the families Heptageniidae (personal observation) and Baetidae (Wiley and Kohler 1981). I have suggested that this behavior can be properly categorized as "territoriality" (Hart 1986). The general controversy surrounding various alternate definitions of territorial behavior notwithstanding (cf. Wittenberger 1981), these larvae occupy a defended area that tends toward exclusive use by the resident with respect to rivals, which is consistent with the definition proposed by Brown and Orians (1970).

It is difficult to determine how widespread such territoriality may be, since behavioral studies of larval black flies have occurred infrequently. Nonetheless, aggressive behavior or the even spacing it can produce have been observed in more than ten species within three genera on four continents (Table 9.1), suggesting that these

Table 9.1 Evidence for territorial behavior in larval black flies

Continent	Location	Taxon	Evidence Even-spacing	Evidence Aggression	Reference
N. America	Newfoundland	*Prosimulium mixtum*	X	X	Colbo 1979
N. America	Newfoundland	*Simulium vittatum*	—	X	Harding and Colbo 1981
N. America	Manitoba	*Simulium venustum*	X	—	Hocking and Pickering 1954
N. America	Alberta	Simuliidae	—	X	Chance 1970
N. America	Newfoundland	*Stegopterna mutata*	X	—	Colbo 1979
N. America	Michigan	*Prosimulium mixtum/fuscum*	—	X	Gersabeck and Merritt 1979
N. America	Michigan	Simuliidae	—	X	Wiley and Kohler 1981
N. America	New York	*Prosimulium* sp.	—	X	Kurtak 1973
N. America	California	*Simulium aureum*	X	X	Hart, this volume
N. America	California	Simuliidae	X	X	Hart, this volume
N. America	California	*Simulium piperi*	—	X	Hart 1986
Europe	England	Simuliidae	X	—	Elliott 1971
Australia	Australia/ New Zealand	*Austrosimulium?*	X	X	Tonnoir 1925
Australia	Queensland	*Simulium ornatipes*	X	—	Colbo and Moorhouse 1979
Africa	West Cameroon	*Simulium damnosum?*	—	X	Disney 1972

Note: — = not reported

interactions are not localized, either taxonomically or geographically. Thus it is likely that a larger number of simuliid taxa will be found to behave aggressively as further studies are conducted.

WHY DO LARVAL BLACK FLIES DEFEND TERRITORIES?

Territoriality should not arise unless resources are: (1) actually or potentially limiting, and (2) economically defendable (Brown 1964). Territorial behavior is used by a wide range of animals to defend such limiting resources as mates, space, and food (cf. Wittenberger 1981). The likelihood that any of these resources are limiting to black fly larvae can be considered in turn.

Many animals defend multipurpose territories that simultaneously provide access to mates and other limiting resources (cf. Wittenberger 1981). However, multipurpose territoriality is unlikely to occur in larval black flies because the immature, aquatic stage is spatially and temporally segregated from the reproductively mature, adult stage. Thus the areas defended by larvae presumably do not serve as mating territories.

It is difficult to distinguish between competition for space versus competition for food in benthic suspension feeders (*sensu* Jørgensen 1966) like larval black flies (cf. Buss 1980, Buss and Jackson 1981, Thorp 1983). Clearly, the only way larvae can gain access to food resources is by occupying a particular attachment site. The hypothesis that animals might compete for space as a means of obtaining food can be evaluated more rigorously by examining how a resident's territorial behavior is related to various components of resource availability.

I examined whether larval aggression was associated with the defense of a feeding territory in *Simulium piperi* (Hart 1986). Because black fly larvae graze periphyton surrounding their attachment sites as well as feed on suspended particles (e.g., Peterson 1956; Anderson and Dicke 1960; Chance 1970; Burton 1973; Mokry 1975; Craig 1977; Currie and Craig, this volume), directional patterns of larval aggression were used to infer which of these two food types was being defended. I predicted that a larva defending periphyton should attack its neighbors with equal frequency regardless of their position relative to that individual, since any of these larvae could potentially remove periphyton from the resident's territory. On the other hand, if the territory is defended to increase access to food particles delivered by the current, the resident should only attempt to displace its upstream neighbors, since particle interception by other larvae would not affect the resident's food supply. Indeed, aggressive behavior was initiated almost exclusively toward upstream neighbors (Fig. 9.1), even though larvae were surrounded by neighbors on all sides. This result strongly supports the hypothesis that territorial behavior in *Simulium piperi* is related to the defense of their suspended food supply. Nearly identical results were obtained in a similar analysis of *Prosimulium mixtum/fuscum* (Hart and Maloney 1984).

I tested the hypothesis that a resident's territorial behavior serves to increase its share of suspended particles by using the labral (or cephalic) fan flick rate as an indirect measure of the ingestion rate (cf. Hart and Latta 1986). This rate increased significantly (by > 35%) after a larva successfully displaced its upstream neighbor

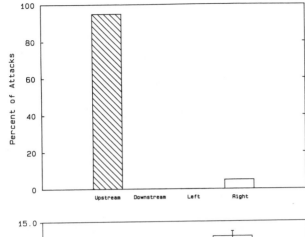

FIG. 9.1 Frequency of larval attacks in four directions (where 180° was defined as the direction of water flow): Upstream = 315°–45°; Right = 45°–135°; Downstream = 135°–225°; Left = 225°–315°. Total number of attacks observed = 20 ($p < 0.001$, x^2 test).

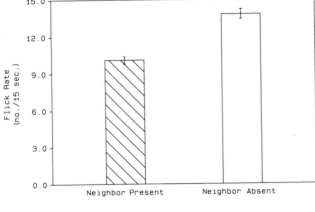

FIG. 9.2 Average number of flicks per 15 seconds (± one standard error) in the presence ($N = 15$) and absence ($N = 20$) of a neighbor ~ 6 mm upstream ($p < 0.001$, t-test).

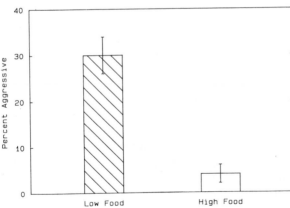

FIG. 9.3 Percent of 15-second time intervals in which one or more larvae within a group (~ 50 individuals in a 14 cm² area) behaved aggresively at low (filtered water) and high (~ 50 mg/l) concentrations of food particles. The number of time intervals sampled was 32 and 33 for the low and high food treatments, respectively ($p < 0.01$, t-test).

(Fig. 9.2). Last, the frequency of territorial defense declined dramatically (by > 80%) as the concentration of suspended particles was experimentally increased (Fig. 9.3), implying that the net benefits of territorial behavior decline as food availability exceeds limiting levels (cf. Carpenter and MacMillen 1976, Wolf 1978).

The previous example suggests that territoriality permits larvae to increase their feeding rate when food abundance is limited. However, considerable controversy surrounds the discussion of whether larval growth rates or population sizes are limited by natural levels of food availability. The total flux rate of seston over a given portion of stream bottom is often high (e.g., Naiman and Sedell 1979, Benke and Wallace 1980), which might suggest that stream suspension feeders are unlikely to be limited by the quantity of food available (e.g., Benke and Wallace 1980, Merritt et al. 1982). Yet it is not the gross abundance of the resource which is important, but that portion which is accessible to the consumer (cf. Wiens 1984). For example, most of this seston is unavailable to benthic suspension feeders because it passes too far above the substrate to be encountered. Even within that thin stratum of the water column in which larvae encounter particles, their suspension-feeding mechanism is so inefficient that only a small fraction of the particles passing by are actually ingested (e.g., Kurtak 1978, Hart and Latta 1986, Schroder 1986a). Furthermore, Hart and Latta (1986) have shown that larval ingestion rates do not plateau until seston concentrations approach levels that are 10 to 100 times greater than those usually present in the field. Thus, if ingestion rate is a good predictor of growth rate, then it is likely that the growth rates of individual larvae in natural populations of black flies are sometimes food-limited.

Various laboratory and field studies have assessed the effect of food availability on either individual or population-level parameters. For example, food availability is often positively correlated with both larval ingestion rates (e.g., Fredeen 1964, Chance 1977, Kurtak 1978, Schröder 1980, Hart and Latta 1986) and larval densities (e.g., Zahar 1951, Sommerman et al. 1955, Phillipson 1956, Hynes 1970, Glötzel 1973, Erman and Chouteau 1979, Gíslason 1985). Indeed, the tendency for larval black flies to occur in extremely high densities below lake outlets is usually thought to stem from the rich planktonic food supply being exported downstream (e.g., Carlsson et al. 1977, Sheldon and Oswood 1977). Peterson et al. (1985) noted increases in the average size of individual simuliid larvae following the experimental fertilization of a tundra stream. They attributed this change to an increased concentration of suspended particulate material that resulted from their phosphorous enrichment. Other studies have shown that such components of fitness as larval growth rate, larval survivorship, pupal mass, adult mass, and fecundity are directly related to food availability (e.g., Chutter 1970; Colbo and Porter 1979, 1981; Mokry 1980; Bernardo et al. 1986; Bernardo et al. 1986; Edman and Simmons, this volume). Conversely, these fitness components are sometimes inversely related to larval densities (e.g., Anderson and Dicke 1960; Colbo 1982; Bernardo et al. 1986; but see Chutter 1970 and Wotton, this volume).

These positive correlations between fitness components and per capita food availability suggest that (when all else is equal) natural selection should favor individuals maintaining high ingestion rates. Territoriality can be viewed as a competitive strategy that permits larvae to increase their share of a limiting food resource. Of course, not all limiting resources are economically defendable (Brown 1964). For example, defendability is influenced by the resource's spatial and temporal variability (e.g., Wittenberger 1981). Because food particles delivered by the current often have high renewal rates, this permits many suspension feeders to occupy small foraging areas that can be more easily defended (Hart 1987; cf. Charnov et al. 1976). The combined effects of high resource renewal rates and the limited availability of feeding sites with suitable hydrodynamic characteristics have probably favored the evolution of territoriality in some larval black flies.

HOW DO UPSTREAM NEIGHBORS AFFECT RESOURCE AVAILABILITY?

Although several forms of evidence suggest that food availability is reduced by upstream neighbors, they do not explain the mechanisms by which this reduction is achieved. The availability of food to these suspension feeders has at least two components (cf. Chance 1977): (1) particle concentration (e.g., particles ml^{-1}), and (2) current velocity through the labral fans. The product of these two components is proportional to the particle encounter rate if larvae feed by sieving and if the mesh size of the filter is less than that of the particles. The effect of current velocity on the particle encounter rate for alternate suspension-feeding mechanisms (e.g., Rubenstein and Koehl 1977, LaBarbera 1984) is more complex. In general, however, larvae can affect food availability by altering either particle concentrations or local hydrodynamic characteristics.

Measures of feeding efficiency provide one estimate of an individual's ability to reduce particle concentrations. The percentage of available particles (i.e., those estimated to flow through the labral fans' projected area) that are actually ingested is low, often < 1% (Kurtak 1978, Hart and Latta 1986, cf. Fuller et al. 1983). These results suggest that particle removal by a single larva should have little effect on the ingestion rate of its downstream neighbor. Indeed, feeding efficiency would have to be > 50-fold higher than indicated by present estimates to account for the increased ingestion rate observed following the displacement of a larva's upstream neighbor (Hart 1986). The above estimates of feeding efficiency should be regarded as tentative, however, since the recent studies of Braimah (1985) indicate that the volumetric flow rate through the fans may be much lower than previously believed. In spite of the likelihood that per capita rates of particle removal are low, some evidence indicates that high densities of larval black flies can collectively reduce particle concentrations as a water mass moves past them (e.g., Maciolek and Tunzi 1968, Reisen 1974). Examples of particle depletion also exist for benthic suspension feeders in marine habitats (e.g., Buss and Jackson 1981, Merz 1984a, Fréchette and Bourget 1985).

The previous points suggest that the reduction in food availability caused by the presence of a single upstream neighbor is due more to altered hydrodynamics than to particle depletion per se. For example, Craig and Chance (1982) have demonstrated that current velocities immediately downstream from the open fans of a filtering larva can be reduced > 80%. Flow patterns in this region may also be more turbulent or more irregular (Chance and Craig 1986). Although these flow alterations occurred at less than 1 mm downstream from the fans, Chance and Craig (1986) have also shown that vortices shed from the larval body can alter flow patterns as far downstream as five body lengths. Similarly, Nowell and Jumars (1984) indicate that flow disruption caused by the presence of a cylindrical object can persist up to 20 cylinder diameters downstream. Even the presence of pupal cocoons is believed to create an unsuitable hydrodynamic environment for early instar larvae (Rühm and Pegel 1986a). Further hydrodynamic studies are clearly needed to understand the potential effects of upstream neighbors on food availability and feeding rates.

If larvae simply avoided areas in which upstream neighbors decreased food availability, territorality should be unnecessary. However, many observations suggest that feeding sites with suitable hydrodynamic characteristics are scarce and patchily distributed on the stream bottom, thereby forcing individuals to aggregate in local areas. Larval distributions are extremely heterogeneous on spatial scales varying from 10^{-2} to 10^2 m, with small-scale variations in hydrodynamics probably accounting for much of this patchiness (see Colbo and Wotton 1981 and references therein). Larvae also readily switch their feeding sites in response to altered hydrodynamic patterns (e.g., Maitland and Penney 1967; Kurtak 1973; Colbo 1979; Gersabeck and Merritt 1979; personal observation). Unfortunately, most attempts to quantify the hydrodynamic characteristics of larval attachment sites have been frustrated by technical difficulties involved in measuring the relevant parameters on appropriate spatial scales. Increased attention toward the effects of microspatial hydrodynamics on larval habitat preferences may reveal that the number of suitable feeding sites available in a typical benthic habitat is quite restricted. Therefore, space may be a limiting factor for high-density larval populations. However, it is important to reemphasize that resource limitation in these consumers most likely involves complex interactions between space *and* food.

An important distinction needs to be stressed here. A population can be limited by a resource without necessarily competing for that resource. For competition to exist, consumers must either lower the resource's availability or impair the ability of other consumers to gain access to the resource. A growing body of direct and indirect evidence suggests that larval simuliids are sometimes limited by either the quantity or quality of their food supply. However, evidence for larval competition is much more tentative. A major challenge facing workers in this area is the need to determine how often black fly populations are food-limited during their larval stage, and whether the degree of resource limitation varies with larval density, thereby indicating competition.

One other spatial resource that may be limiting is suitable pupation sites. Black fly larvae sometimes cover dense pupal aggregations in which individual pupae are stacked on top of each other, forming several layers (e.g., Anderson and Dicke 1960). Pupae at the bottom of these masses may not receive enough oxygenated water to respire, or they may have difficulty emerging from their cocoons. The possibility that larvae preparing to pupate might actively compete for suitable pupation sites deserves attention.

VARIATIONS IN LARVAL SPACING PATTERNS

Spacing patterns and the larval aggression that affects these patterns can vary both within and between species. For example, Hart and Maloney (1984) found that the frequency of territorial defense in *Prosimulium mixtum/fuscum* declined dramatically when either food availability or the local density of conspecifics was high. We suggested that the costs of territorial defense became prohibitive at high competitor densities. These results imply that above some threshold density, the even dispersion pattern maintained by territoriality might condense to a spacing system in which larvae were packed together much more tightly.

Some species of larval black flies typically maintain even spacing patterns, whereas others are clumped with little space between neighboring individuals (e.g., Colbo and Moorhouse 1979; Harding and Colbo 1981; Wotton, this volume). There has been little discussion of the possible adaptive significance of these differences. One hypothesis is that even spacing fails to develop in certain species because they occur where the food supply is regularly unlimited, reducing the benefits of territoriality. Greater insight into these patterns might be gained by examining how larval spacing systems vary across a range of habitats differing in food availability.

However, it would be naive to argue that all variations in larval spacing patterns can be explained by differing intensities of competition. Rather, competition should be viewed as one potentially important factor influencing the costs and benefits an individual experiences in a given spatial arrangement. Other factors related to hydrodynamic alterations and predation risk may also affect larval settlement patterns. For example, Chance and Craig (1986) have proposed that the presence of upstream neighbors may provide a downstream larva with additional food particles that are carried out of the boundary layer by vortices generated as the current flows around the upstream neighbor's body. Although this might allow a potential improvement in feeding rates for a larva and seem to contradict the reduction in feeding rates due to upstream neighbors proposed earlier (Hart 1986), both phenomena could conceivably influence spacing patterns. For example, the relationship between ingestion rate and distance from upstream neighbors might be hump-shaped, with distances too close, producing a reduction similar to that measured by Hart (1986), and distances too far, failing to take advantage of the resuspension effect described by Chance and Craig (1986).

Larvae within dense aggregations may benefit from reductions in drag compared to more solitary individuals. Merz's (1984b) biomechanical analysis of drag forces on suspension-feeding sabellid polychaetes clearly demonstrates that individuals that occur within clusters experience far less drag than solitary individuals. Laboratory investigations are needed to examine whether comparable reductions in drag are experienced by simuliid larvae occurring in clumps, and whether such reductions affect larval growth rates.

To gain a clearer understanding of possible trade-offs between potential hydrodynamic benefits and competitive costs of particular spacing patterns, more detailed analyses of these patterns are required. For example, Chance and Craig (1986) and Craig and Galloway (this volume) have suggested that larvae form distinct rows of individuals oriented perpendicular to the current to take advantage of a mutually induced beneficial flow mechanism resulting from Venturi effects. This rationale suggests that larvae will be tightly spaced along an axis perpendicular to the flow, whereas the upstream interference model (Hart 1986) predicts that larvae will be widely spaced along an axis parallel to the flow. By quantifying the feeding rates and behavioral patterns of larvae in different spacing patterns along with the hydrodynamic characteristics of those patterns, our understanding of these interactions should be significantly enhanced.

An individual's risk of predation (or parasitism) may also depend on larval spacing patterns. Behavioral ecologists have suggested that per capita rates of predator-induced mortality are often higher for solitary individuals than for individuals occurring in a group (e.g., Brown 1975). However, some of the potential mechanisms capable of producing such reductions in predation risk for group-living animals (e.g., Pulliam and Caraco 1984) may be inapplicable to predator-prey interactions involving larval simuliids. For example, in my own field observations of predation by the searching caddisfly *Rhyacophila* on black fly larvae, groups of larvae were not better able to detect an approaching predator than were isolated individuals. Indeed, because larvae rarely attempted to escape until they were touched by the predator, it also seems unlikely that larval groups would benefit from a confusion effect (e.g., Milinski 1979). Furthermore, neither solitary larvae nor larvae in groups made any attempt to defend themselves against these predators, in contrast to observations of mobbing behavior by birds and mammals (e.g., Curio 1978).

Two mechanisms that seem more likely to reduce the predation risk of larval black flies occurring in groups are the dilution effect and the "greater cover due to the presence of conspecifics" effect (Hamilton 1971). The dilution effect simply states that (other things being equal) a larva's chance of being the next meal of a given predator is proportional to the reciprocal of the number of larvae in the group. The increased-cover hypothesis predicts (among other things) that larvae at the core of a group are less likely to be preyed upon than are individuals at the periphery. However, it is presently difficult to evaluate quantitatively the effect of predators and parasites on larval spacing patterns, due in part to the anecdotal nature of most accounts describing these interactions (cf. Davies 1981). Experimental studies are needed to investigate how per capita predation rates vary as a function of the size and density of larval aggregations before it will be possible to understand how predation risk influences the costs and benefits of particular spacing systems.

COMPETITION AND PATTERNS OF RESOURCE USE

The effect of competition on patterns of resource use can be explored from several perspectives. For example, it has been suggested that intra- or interspecific differences in body size might allow individuals to specialize in capturing different particle-size ranges, thereby reducing the intensity of competition (e.g., Wotton 1984; Schröder 1986a, b cf. Wilson 1975, Georgian and Wallace 1981; Polis 1984). Indeed, when Merritt et al. (1982) failed to detect food partitioning by particle size between instars and species, they suggested that food must not be limiting. However, relationships between patterns of particle-size use and competition are likely to be complex for several reasons. First, empirical studies of the relationship between the size range of particles in the gut versus those in the seston are divided, sometimes suggesting selectivity (e.g., Kurtak 1978, Wotton 1984, Schröder 1986a,b) and sometimes not (e.g., Wotton 1977, Merritt et al. 1982; see additional references in Walsh 1985). Second, some mechanistic models of particle capture by simuliids predict that the size range of particles ingested may not correspond closely to either the dimensions of the filtering structures or larval body size (Ross and Craig 1980, Braimah 1985; cf. Nübel 1984). These results imply that differences in larval size may provide little opportunity for reducing niche overlap along resource axes related to food-particle size. Third, even if niche segregation along a particle-size axis could be clearly demonstrated, this pattern might be unrelated to the intensity of competition (e.g., Abrams 1980). This is especially probable if competitors reduce food availability primarily by altering flow rather than depleting particles.

Overall, too little information exists to determine the contribution of larval body-size differences to potential reductions in niche overlap. Before this issue can be rigorously evaluated, we need a better understanding of several important relation-ships (cf. Wilson 1975): (1) how the efficiency of particle capture varies with particle size, and how this depends on larval size; (2) how a larva's energy budget and its encounter rate with particles varies with body size; and (3) how the relative abundance of particles in the seston varies with particle size. Once this information is available, it should be possible to construct and test models predicting the degree of resource overlap and the intensity of competition between larvae of differing body size. At present, however, there is little compelling evidence that exploitative competition in larval black flies is reduced by resource partitioning of particle sizes owing to intra- or interspecific differences in body size (cf. Thorp 1983 and Alstad 1986 for discussion of similar issues regarding net-spinning caddisflies). For example, Schröder (1986b) found that the size and type of food particles consumed by larvae were similar in different instars of the same species as well as in two co-occurring species. He suggested that segregation along spatial and temporal niche axes might be necessary to reduce potential competitive interactions. Nonetheless, such body-size differences may influence the outcome of interference competition.

When the ability to defend a territory differs between individuals (e.g., because of differences in body size), the population may be subdivided into groups of "haves" and "have-nots" in terms of their access to limiting resources (e.g., Brown 1969, Wilson et al. 1978, Riechert 1981). Although there are no studies of larval black flies that specifically focus on the relationship between body size (e.g., instar) and ability to monopolize preferred feeding sites, several authors have suggested that smaller larvae are at a competitive disadvantage in such interactions. For example, Kureck (1969) and Wotton et al. (1979) found that drift rates were higher in earlier instar larvae. Disney (1972: 487) proposed that the "relatively higher drift rate in smaller larvae could be partly due to disturbance by the older larvae" (see also Gersabeck and Merritt 1979). Wotton et al. (1979) also imply that smaller larvae drift at higher rates because of their poorer competitive abilities.

Unfortunately, few workers have directly addressed whether the drift rates of simuliids are influenced by competition. By examining the relationship between benthic densities and drift rates, it is possible to determine whether emigration is density-dependent, which would support the hypothesis that drift results from competitive interactions (cf. Waters 1961). Density dependence was not detected in descriptive studies of simuliid drift rates (e.g., Reisen 1977, Wotton et al. 1979), or in an experimental study examining the relationship between migration rates and manipulated benthic densities (Peckarsky 1981). These results are supported by behavioral studies in which larvae most commonly responded to aggressive interactions by moving short distances (via "looping," *sensu* Smart 1944) rather than drifting downstream (e.g., Colbo 1979; Wiley and Kohler 1981; personal observation).

The local displacement of smaller larvae from preferred feeding sites might be responsible for certain patterns of microdistribution. For example, Colbo and Moorhouse (1979) found that the size composition of a dense patch of *Simulium ornatipes* larvae depended on the location within the patch; peripheral individuals were smaller, whereas individuals at the core of the patch were larger. Current velocity at the center of the larval patch was also nearly twice that at the periphery, raising the possibility that food availability was higher in the former area. Obviously, many processes besides size-structured interference competition could lead to this pattern of microspatial segregation. Therefore, further research is needed to determine

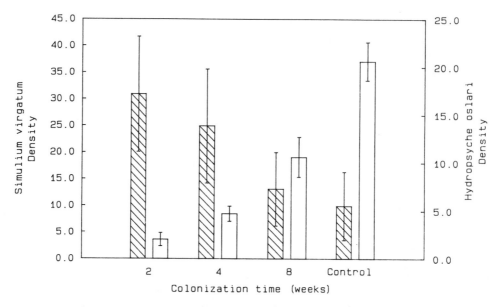

Fɪɢ. 9.4 Changes in the relative abundance of *Simulium* and *Hydropsyche* as a function of time since the substrate was last disturbed. *Simulium* and *Hydropsyche* are represented by hatched and open bars, respectively. Density was defined as the number of 1.7 cm² quadrat spaces occupied by larvae of each species. (*Note:* the control substrate was not disturbed.) (From Hemphill and Cooper (1983)

whether competitive interactions can generate such distributions, and to compare the fitness expectation of individuals living in microhabitats of varying quality (cf. Fretwell and Lucas 1969). Such analyses will require that habitat preferences be compared with observed habitat distributions across a range of larval sizes.

Some larval black flies apparently avoid or are excluded from certain habitats because of the presence of unrelated competitors. For example, the grazing caddis larva *Leucotrichia pictipes* (Trichoptera: Hydroptilidae) defends its feeding territory from a variety of other species (Hart 1985). This aggressive behavior underlies the negative relationship between *Leucotrichia's* abundance and simuliid densities in a Rocky Mountain stream (McAuliffe 1984). There is also sometimes an inverse correlation between the densities of hydropsychid caddisflies and simuliids (e.g., Chutter 1968, Ulfstrand et al. 1974). The exact mechanisms underlying this pattern are unclear, since hydropsychids can potentially prey upon simuliids as well as reduce food availability by particle depletion or flow alteration. As the frequency of substrate disturbance was experimentally increased in a California stream, Hemphill and Cooper (1983) documented an increase in the relative abundance of *Simulium virgatum* and a decrease in the relative abundance of *Hydropsyche oslari* (Fig. 9.4). These results suggest that simuliids are eventually excluded from patches by the more slowly colonizing hydropsychids. From this perspective, simuliids might be viewed as fugitive species (*sensu* Horn and MacArthur 1972) that escape competitive exclusion by dispersing to vacant habitats more rapidly than the competitively superior hydropsychids. These considerations also suggest that larvae are more likely to persist in habitats where space is periodically created by disturbance (Chutter 1968, Hemphill and Cooper 1983).

COMPETITION AND BLACK FLY MANAGEMENT

Insights gained by studying the causes and consequences of larval competition are potentially useful in the management of black fly populations for several reasons. First, a more complete understanding of the population biology of these medically and economically important insects is needed. Colbo (1982) has called for greater attention to the factors regulating adult reproductive potential. In broad terms, we must identify the major factors influencing the mortality and fecundity schedules of black flies. Only then can realistic demographic models be constructed to predict the population dynamics of adult biting flies. In other dipterans that have been more thoroughly studied than simuliids, it is clear that competition during the larval stage can dramatically affect adult population size as well as reproductive and disease-transmission potential (e.g., Gilpin and McClelland 1979, Hawley 1985, Prout and McChesney 1985). For example, two important variables that potentially influence disease transmission (adult longevity and dispersal rate) are correlated to body size (e.g., Roff 1977, Hawley 1985), which may itself be affected by larval competition. Thus the importance of larval competition in determining adult size (and stored energy reserves, cf. Magnarelli and Burger 1984) deserves greater attention. However, even if future investigations obtain compelling evidence that competition occurs in larval black flies and affects adult fitness components, it will still be necessary to evaluate the relative importance of competition compared to other factors (e.g., temperature) that influence the demography of these populations.

Second, understanding the determinants of larval feeding rates and particle-size selection (or lack thereof) is also critical to any control program involving the application of larvicides. Walsh (1985) has recently reviewed how such knowledge can best contribute to the development of improved larvicide formulations and application procedures. The potential effect of competition on larval feeding behavior should also be evaluated in this context.

Last, and in a much more speculative vein, it is possible in theory that competitors could be used as biological-control agents. Although biological control is ordinarily defined as "the action of parasites, predators and pathogens in maintaining another organism's density at a lower average than would occur in their absence" (DeBach 1964), it has also been suggested that competitive displacement of pests by nonpests is a possible control strategy (DeBach 1974). However, little attention has focused on the idea that nonpestiferous black flies or other potential competitors might be manipulated to reduce the abundance of black fly species that are important pests. This is surprising, since DeBach (1974) regarded biting flies as one of the most promising pest groups for the application of control strategies involving competitive displacement. It is much too early to say whether control programs involving the introduction or enhancement of larval competitors are feasible. Yet some of the results presented here suggest that the local distribution and abundance of several larval black flies is greatly affected by interspecific competitors. Further studies are clearly needed to evaluate more fully the causes and consequences of interspecific competitive interactions in these insects (cf. Harding and Colbo 1981, Hemphill and Cooper 1983).

The success of a control program involving the manipulation of interspecific competitors would depend on the strength of their negative effect upon larvae, and the ease with which their abundance could be increased. Particular attention should be paid to the effect of competitors on various fitness components (e.g., adult size and stored energy reserves) of simuliids, since if the principal competitive effect is to lower the stored energy reserves of emerging females, increased competition might actually result in a greater tendency to blood-feed by species that are facultatively anautogenous. Experimental programs in lab and field settings could be designed to assess quantitatively the efficacy of such control strategies, though recent developments in the use of toxins produced by pathogens as control agents may obviate the need for these alternate approaches.

SUMMARY

Locations that allow a sufficient delivery of food to larval black flies are sometimes limiting, and considerable evidence indicates that larvae can aggressively defend these territories. Because larval ingestion rates increase when upstream neighbors are aggressively displaced, and because the frequency of aggression declines as food abundance approaches unlimited levels, this territorial behavior seems closely tied to the defense of a limited food supply.

The effects of competition on larval distribution and abundance have seldom been assessed. Territoriality apparently contributes to the even spacing patterns observed within certain larval aggregations. It may also influence observed patterns of microhabitat segregation between larvae of different size. There is insufficient evidence to support the hypothesis that exploitative competition for food is minimized because of reduced niche overlap in the range of particle sizes used by different larval instars or species. Several kinds of interspecific competitors significantly reduce the local abundance of larval black flies, raising the possibility that the manipulation of such competitors might contribute to the control of these insects. Since competition during the larval stage may affect the fecundity and disease-transmission potential of adult flies, its importance in black fly populations deserves increased attention.

ACKNOWLEDGMENTS

My work on black flies has been generously supported by the National Science Foundation and the National Institutes of Health. Some of the ideas presented here were stimulated by collaborative research with Steve Latta and Lisa Maloney. I was supported by the Ruth Patrick Fund for Research in the Environmental Sciences while writing this chapter. Marcia Brauning helped prepare the text and figures for publication. I thank Jan Ciborowski, Ken Cummins, and Betty Ann Peters for their constructive criticisms of an earlier draft of the manuscript. W. K. Kellogg Biological Station contribution number 576.

LITERATURE CITED

Abrams, P. 1980. Some comments on measuring niche overlap. *Ecology* 61:44–49.
Alstad, D. N. 1986. Dietary overlap and net-spinning caddisfly distributions. *Oikos* 47:251–252.

Anderson, J. R., and R. J. Dicke. 1960. Ecology of the immature stages of some Wisconsin blackflies (Simuliidae: Diptera). *Ann. Entomol. Soc. Am.* 53:386–404.

Bernardo, M. J., E. W. Cupp, and A. E. Kiszewski. 1986. Rearing black flies (Diptera: Simuliidae) in the laboratory: colonization and life table statistics for *Simulium vittatum. Ann. Entomol. Soc. Am.* 79:610–621.

Benke, A. C., and J. B. Wallace. 1980. Trophic basis of production among net-spinning caddisflies in a southern Appalachian stream. *Ecology* 61:108–118.

Birch, L. C. 1957. The meanings of competition. *Am. Nat.* 91:5–18.

Braimah, S. A. 1985. Mechanisms and fluid mechanical aspects of filter-feeding in blackfly larvae (Diptera: Simuliidae) and mayfly nymphs (Ephemeroptera: Oligoneuriidae). Ph.D. Thesis, University of Alberta.

Brown, J. L. 1964. The evolution of diversity in avian territorial systems. *Wilson Bull.* 76:160–169.

———. 1969. Territorial behavior and population regulation in birds: a review and re-evaluation. *Wilson Bull.* 81:293–329.

———. 1975. *The evolution of behavior.* W. W. Norton, New York.

Brown, J. L., and G. H. Orians. 1970. Spacing patterns in mobile animals. *Ann. Rev. Ecol. Syst.* 1:239–262.

Burton, G. J. 1973. Feeding of *Simulium hargreavesi* Gibbins larvae on *Oedogonium* algal filaments in Ghana. *J. Med. Entomol.* 10:101–106.

Buss, L. W. 1980. Bryozoan overgrowth interactions—the interdependence of competition for space and food. *Nature* 281:475–477.

Buss, L. W., and J. B. C. Jackson. 1981. Planktonic food availability and suspension-feeder abundance: evidence of *in situ* depletion. *J. Exp. Mar. Biol. Ecol.* 49:151–161.

Carlsson, M., L. M. Nilsson, B. J. Svensson, S. Ulfstrand, and R. S. Wotton. 1977. Lacustrine seston and other factors influencing the blackflies (Diptera: Simuliidae) inhabiting lake outlets in Swedish Lapland. *Oikos* 29:229–238.

Carpenter, F. L., and R. E. MacMillen. 1976. Threshold model of feeding territoriality and test with a Hawaiian honey-creeper. *Science* 194:639–642.

Chance, M. M. 1970. The functional morphology of the mouthparts of blackfly larvae (Diptera: Simuliidae). *Quaest. Entomol.* 6:245–284.

———. 1977. Influence of water flow and particle concentration on larvae of the blackfly *Simulium vittatum* Zett. (Diptera: Simuliidae) with emphasis on larval filter-feeding. Ph.D. Thesis, University of Alberta.

Chance, M. M., and D. A. Craig. 1986. Hydrodynamics and behavior of Simuliidae larvae (Diptera). *Can. J. Zool.* 64:1295–1309.

Charnov, E. L., G. H. Orians, and K. Hyatt. 1976. Ecological implications of resource depression. *Am. Nat.* 110:247–259.

Chutter, F. M. 1968. On the ecology of the fauna of stones in the current in a South African river supporting a very large *Simulium* (Diptera) population. *J. Appl. Ecol.* 5:531–561.

———. 1970. A preliminary study of factors influencing the number of oocytes present in newly emerged blackflies (Diptera: Simuliidae) in Ontario. *Can. J. Zool.* 48:1389–1400.

Clark, P. J., and F. C. Evans. 1955. On some aspects of spatial pattern in biological populations. *Science* 121:397–398.

Cody, M. L., and J. M. Diamond. 1975. *Ecology and evolution of communities.* Belknap Press, Harvard University, Cambridge, Mass.

Colbo, M. H. 1979. Distribution of winter-developing Simuliidae (Diptera) in eastern Newfoundland. *Can. J. Zool.* 57:2143–52.

———. 1982. Size and fecundity of adult Simuliidae (Diptera) as a function of stream habitat, year, and parasitism. *Can. J. Zool.* 60:2507–13.

Colbo, M. H., and D. E. Moorhouse. 1979. The ecology of pre-imaginal Simuliidae (Diptera) in south-east Queensland, Australia. *Hydrobiologia* 63:63–79.

Colbo, M. H., and G. N. Porter. 1979. Effects of the food supply on the life history of Simuliidae (Diptera). *Can. J. Zool.* 57:301–306.

———. 1981. The interaction of rearing temperature and food supply on the life history of two species of simuliidae (Diptera). *Can. J. Zool.* 59:158–163.

Colbo, M. H., and R. S. Wotton. 1981. Preimaginal blackfly bionomics. Pp. 209–226 in M. Laird, Ed., *Blackflies: the future for biological methods in integrated control.* Academic Press, New York and London.

Craig, D. A. 1977. Mouthparts and feeding behaviour of Tahitian larval Simuliidae (Diptera:Nematocera). *Quaest. Entomol.* 13:195–218.

Craig, D. A., and M. M. Chance. 1982. Filter-feeding in Simuliidae larvae (Diptera: Culicimorpha): aspects of functional morphology and hydrodynamics. *Can. J. Zool.* 60:712–724.

Curio, E. B. 1978. The adaptive significance of avian mobbing. *Z. Tierpsychol.* 48:175–183.

Davies, D. M. 1981. Predators upon blackflies. Pp. 139–158 in M. Laird, Ed., *Blackflies: the future for biological methods in integrated control.* Academic Press, New York and London.

Davies, N. B. 1978. Ecological questions about territorial behavior. Pp. 317–350 in J. R. Krebs and N. B. Davies, Eds., *Behavioral ecology, an evolutionary approach.* Sinauer Associates, Sunderland, Mass.

DeBach, P., Ed. 1964. *Biological control of insect pests and weeds.* Reinhold, New York.

DeBach, P. 1974. *Biological control by natural enemies.* Cambridge University Press, London.

Décamps, H., G. Larrouy, and D. Trivellato. 1975. Approche hydrodynamique de la microdistribution d'invertebres benthiques en eau courante. *Annls. Limnol.* 11:79–100.

Diamond, J., and T. Case. 1986. *Community ecology.* Harper and Row, New York.

Disney, R. H. L. 1972. Observations on sampling pre-imaginal populations of blackflies (Dipt., Simuliidae) in West Cameroon. *Bull. Entomol. Res.* 61:79–100.

Elliott, J. M. 1971. Some methods for the statistical analysis of samples of benthic invertebrates. Publ. no. 25, Freshwater Biol. Assoc., Ambleside, Westmorland.

Erman, D. C., and W. C. Chouteau. 1979. Fine particulate organic carbon output from fens and its effect on benthic macroinvertebrates. *Oikos* 32:409–415.

Fréchette, M., and E. Bourget. 1985. Energy flow between the pelagic and benthic zones: factors controlling particulate organic matter available to an intertidal mussel bed. *Can. J. Fish. Aquat. Sci.* 42:1158–65.

Fredeen, F. J. H. 1964. Bacteria as food for blackfly larvae (Diptera: Simuliidae) in laboratory cultures and in natural streams. *Can. J. Zool.* 42:527–548.

Fretwell, S. D., and H. L. Lucas, Jr. 1969. On territorial behavior and other factors influencing habitat distribution in birds. I. Theoretical development. *Act. Biotheor.* 19:16–36.

Fuller, R. L., R. J. Mackay, and H. B. N. Hynes. 1983. Seston capture by *Hydropsyche betteni* nets (Trichoptera; Hydropsychidae). *Arch. Hydrobiol.* 97:251–261.

Georgian, T. J., Jr., and J. B. Wallace. 1981. A model of seston capture by net-spinning caddisflies. *Oikos* 36:147–157.

Gersabeck, E. F., Jr., and R. W. Merritt. 1979. The effect of physical factors on the colonization and relocation behavior of immature blackflies (Diptera: Simuliidae). *Environ. Entomol.* 8:34–39.

Gilpin, M. E., and G. A. H. McClelland. 1979. Systems analysis of the yellow fever mosquito *Aedes aegypti. Fortschr. Zool.* 25:355–388.

Gíslason, G. M. 1985. The life cycle and production of *Simulium vittatum* Zett. in the River Laxà, north-east Iceland. *Verh. Int. Verein. Limnol.* 22:3281–87.

Glötzel, R. 1973. Populationsdynamik and Ernährungsbiologie von Simuliidenlarven in einem mit organischen Abwässern verunreinigten Gebirgsbach. *Arch. Hydrobiol. Suppl.* 42:406–451.

Grenier, P. 1949. A l'étude biologique des simuliides de France. *Physiol. Comp. Oecol.* 1:165–330.

Hamilton, W. D. 1971. Geometry for the selfish herd. *J. Theoret. Biol.* 31:295–311.

Harding, J., and M. H. Colbo. 1981. Competition for attachment sites between larvae of Simuliidae. *Can. Entomol.* 113:761–763.

Hart, D. D. 1983. The importance of competitive interactions within stream populations and communities. Pp. 99–136 in J. R. Barnes and G. W. Minshall, Eds., *Stream ecology.* Plenum Press, New York.

———. 1985. Causes and consequences of territoriality in a grazing stream insect. *Ecology* 66:404–414.

———. 1986. The adaptive significance of territoriality in filter-feeding larval blackflies (Diptera: Simuliidae). *Oikos* 46:88–92.

———. 1987. Feeding territoriality in aquatic insects: cost-benefit models and experimental tests. *Am. Zool.* 27:371–386.

Hart, D. D., and S. C. Latta. 1986. Determinants of ingestion rates in filter-feeding larval black flies (Diptera: Simuliidae). *Freshwater Biol.* 16:1–12.

Hart, D. D., and L. Maloney. 1984. Allocating time to territorial defense: a test of cost-benefit models with filter-feeding insects. *Bull. Ecol. Soc. Am.* 62:120.

Hawley, W. A. 1985. The effect of larval density on adult longevity of a mosquito, *Aedes sierrensis:* epidemiological consequences. *J. Anim. Ecol.* 54:955–964.

Hemphill, N., and S. D. Cooper. 1983. The effect of physical disturbance on the relative abundances of two filter-feeding insects in a small stream. *Oecologia* 58:378–382.

Hocking, B., and L. R. Pickering. 1954. Observations on the bionomics of some northern species of Simuliidae (Diptera). *Can. J. Zool.* 32:99–119.

Horn, H. S., and R. H. MacArthur. 1972. Competition among fugitive species in a harlequin environment. *Ecology* 53:749–752.

Hynes, H. B. N. 1970. *The ecology of running waters.* Liverpool Univ. Press, Liverpool.

Jørgensen, C. B. 1966. *Biology of suspension feeding.* Pergamon Press, Oxford.

Kureck, A. 1969. Tagesrhythmen lapplandischer Simuliiden (Diptera). *Oecologia* 2:385–410.

Kurtak, D. C. 1973. Observations on filter feeding by the larvae of black flies (Diptera: Simuliidae). Ph.D. Thesis, Cornell University.

———. 1978. Efficiency of filter-feeding of blackfly larvae (Diptera: Simuliidae). *Can. J. Zool.* 56:1608–23.

LaBarbera, M. 1984. Feeding currents and particle capture mechanisms in suspension feeding animals. *Am. Zool.* 24:71–84.

Maciolek, J. A., and M. G. Tunzi. 1968. Microseston dynamics in a simple Sierra Nevada lake-stream system. *Ecology* 49:60–75.

Magnerelli, L. A., and J. F. Burger. 1984. Caloric reserves in natural populations of a blackfly, *Simulium decorum* (Diptera: Simuliidae), and a deerfly, *Chrysops ater* (Diptera: Tabanidae). *Can. J. Zool.* 62:2589–93.

Maitland, P. S., and M. M. Penney. 1967. The ecology of the Simuliidae in a Scottish river. *J. Anim. Ecol.* 36:179–206.

McAuliffe, J. R. 1984. Competition for space, disturbance, and the structure of a benthic stream community. *Ecology* 65:894–908.

Merritt, R. W., D. H. Ross, and G. J. Larson. 1982. Influence of stream temperature and seston on the growth and production of overwintering larval black flies (Diptera: Simuliidae). *Ecology* 63:1322–31.

Merz, R. A. 1984a. Self-generated *versus* environmentally produced feeding currents: a comparison for the sabellid polychaete *Eudistylia vancouveri*. *Biol. Bull.* 167:200–209.

———. 1984b. An experimental field study of the role of flow on feeding behavior, tube structure, and cluster morphology of the sabellid polychaete *Eudistylia rancooreri*. Ph.D. Dissertation, University of Chicago.

Milinski, M. 1979. Can an experienced predator overcome the confusion of swarming prey more easily? *Anim. Behav.* 27:1122–26.

Mokry, J. E. 1975. Studies on the ecology and biology of blackfly larvae utilizing an in situ benthobservatory. *Verh. Int. Verein. Limnol.* 19:1546–49.

———. 1980. Laboratory studies on blood-feeding of blackflies (Diptera: Simuliidae). 2. Factors affecting fecundity. *Tropenmed. Parasitol.* 31:374–380.

Naiman, R. J., and J. R. Sedell. 1979. Characterization of particulate organic matter transmitted by some Cascade mountain streams. *J. Fish. Res. Bd. Can.* 36:17–31.

Nowell, A. R. M., and P. A. Jumars. 1984. Flow environment of aquatic benthos. *Ann. Rev. Ecol. Syst.* 15:303–328.

Nübel, E. 1984. Rasterelektronenmikroskipische Untersuchungen an den Filtrierstrukturen von Kriebelmücken-Larven (Simuliidae, Diptera). *Arch. Hydrobiol. Suppl.* 66:223–253.

Peckarsky, B. L. 1981. Reply to comment by Sell. *Limnol. Oceanogr.* 26:982–987.

Peterson, B. J., J. E. Hobbie, A. E. Hershey, M. A. Lock, T. E. Ford, J. R. Vestal, V. L. McKinley, M. A. J. Hullar, M. C. Miller, R. M. Ventullo, and G. S. Volk. 1985. Transformation of a tundra river from heterotrophy to autotrophy by addition of phosphorous. *Science* 229:1383–86.

Peterson, B. V. 1956. Observations on the biology of Utah black flies (Diptera: Simuliidae). *Can. Entomol.* 92:266–274.

Phillipson, J. 1956. A study of factors determining the distribution of the blackfly, *Simulium ornatum* Mg. *Bull. Entomol. Res.* 47:227–238.

Pielou, E. C. 1974. *Population and community ecology*. Gordon and Breach Science, New York.

———. 1977. *Mathematical ecology*. Wiley-Interscience, New York.

Prout, T., and F. McChesney. 1985. Competition among immatures affects their adult fertility: population dynamics. *Am. Nat.* 126:521–558.

Polis, G. A. 1984. Age structure component of niche width and infra-specific resource partitioning: Can age groups function as ecological species? *Am. Nat.* 123:541–564.

Pulliam, H. R., and T. Caraco. 1984. Living in groups: is there an optimal group size? Pp. 122–147 in J. R. Krebs and N. B. Davies, Eds., *Behavioral ecology, an evolutionary approach,* 2nd ed. Sinauer Associates, Sunderland, Mass.

Reisen, W. K. 1974. The ecology of Honey Creek. A preliminary evaluation of the influence of *Simulium* spp. (Diptera: Simuliidae) larval populations on the concentration of total suspended particles. *Entomol. News* 85:275–278.

———. 1977. The ecology of Honey Creek, Oklahoma: population dynamics and drifting behavior of three species of *Simulium* (Diptera: Simuliidae). *Can. J. Zool.* 55:325–337.

Riechert, S. E. 1981. The consequences of being territorial: spiders, a case study. *Am. Nat.* 117:871–892.

Roff, D. 1977. Dispersal in dipterans: its costs and consequences. *J. Anim. Ecol.* 46:443–456.

Ross, D. H., and D. A. Craig. 1980. Mechanisms of fine particle capture by larval blackflies (Diptera: Simuliidae). *Can. J. Zool.* 58:1186–92.

Rubenstein, D. I., and M. A. R. Koehl. 1977. The mechanisms of filter-feeding: some theoretical considerations. *Am. Nat.* 111:981–994.

Rühm, W. 1970. Zur Dispersion der Larvenstadien und des Puppenstadiums von *Boophlora erythrocephala* de Geer (Simuliidae). *Z. Ang. Entomol.* 6:311–321.

Rühm, W., and M. Pegel. 1986a. Die Substratbesiedlung durch Kriebelmükenlarven und -puppen (Simuliidae, Dipt.). *Arch. Hydrobiol.* 107:75–87.

———. 1986b. Die Alterstructur und die Artenzusammensetzung präimaginaler Populationen von Simuliiden auf Abhängigkeit von der Expositionsdaver (Simuliidae, Dipt.). *Arch. Hydrobiol.* 107:261–268.

Schröder, P. 1980. Zur Ernährungsbiologie der Larven von *Odagmia ornata* Meigen (Diptera: Simuliidae). 2. Morphometrische und physiologische Bezugsgrössen, Darmentleerung und -füllzeit, Ingestion. *Arch. Hydrobiol. Suppl.* 59:53–95.

———. 1986a. Unterschiede in der Partikelselektion der Kieselalgen zwischen Larven der campestrischen Kriebelmückenarten *Simulium reptans* und *Odagmia ornata* (Diptera: Simuliidae). *Arch. Hydrobiol.* 105:531–547.

———. 1986b. Resource partitioning of food particles between associated larvae of *Prosimulium rufipes* and *Eusimulium cryophilum* (Diptera, Simuliidae) in Austrian mountain brooks. *Arch. Hydrobiol.* 107:497–509.

Sheldon, A. L., and M. W. Oswood. 1977. Blackfly (Diptera: Simuliidae) abundance in a lake outlet: test of a predictive mode. *Hydrobiologia* 56:113–120.

Sinclair, D. F. 1985. On tests of spatial randomness using mean nearest neighbor distance. *Ecology* 66:1084–85.

Smart, J. 1944. The British Simuliidae with keys to the species in the adult, pupal, and larval stages. Publ. no. 9, Freshwater Biol. Assoc., Ambleside, Westmorland.

Sommerman, K. M., R. I. Sailer, and C. O. Esselbaugh. 1955. Biology of Alaskan blackflies (Simuliidae: Diptera). *Ecol. Monogr.* 25:345–385.

Strong, D. R., Jr., D. Simberloff, L. G. Abele, and A. B. Thistle. 1984. *Ecological communities: conceptual issues and the evidence.* Princeton Univ. Press. Princeton, N.J.

Thorp, J. H. 1983. An evaluation of hypotheses on the evolutionary differentiation of catch-nets in net-spinning caddisflies (Hydropsychidae). *Oikos* 40:308–312.

Tonnoir, A. L. 1925. Australasian Simuliidae. *Bull. Entomol. Res.* 15:213–255.

Ulfstrand, S., L. M. Nilsson, and A. Stergar. 1974. Composition and diversity of benthic species collectives colonizing implanted substrates in a south Swedish stream. *Entomol. Scand.* 5:115–122.

Walsh, J. F. 1985. The feeding behaviour of *Simulium* larvae, and the development, testing and monitoring of the use of larvicides, with special reference to the control of *Simulium damnosum* Theobald s.l. (Diptera: Simuliidae): a review. *Bull. Entomol. Res.* 75:549–594.

Waters, T. F. 1961. Standing crop and drift of stream invertebrates. *Ecology* 42:532–537.

Wiens, J. A. 1984. Resource systems, populations, and communities. Pp. 397–436 in P. W. Price, C. N. Slobodchikoff, and W. S. Gould, Eds., *A new ecology: novel approaches to interactive systems.* John Wiley and Sons, New York.

Wiley, M. J., and S. L. Kohler. 1981. An assessment of biological interactions in an epilithic stream community using time-lapse cinematography. *Hydrobiologia* 73:183–188.

Wilson, D. S. 1975. The adequacy of body size as a niche difference. *Am. Nat.* 109:769–784.

Wilson, D. S., M. Leighton, and D. R. Leighton. 1978. Interference competition in a tropical ripple bug (Hemiptera: Veliidae). *Biotropica* 10:302–306.

Wittenberger, J. F. 1981. *Animal social behavior.* Duxbury Press, Boston.

Wolf, L. L. 1978. Aggressive social organization in nectarivorous birds. *Am. Zool.* 18:765–778.

Wotton, R. S. 1977. The size of particles ingested by moorland stream blackfly larvae (Simuliidae). *Oikos* 29:332–335.

————. 1984. The relationship between food particle size and larval size in *Simulium noelleri* Friederichs. *Freshwater Biol.* 14:547–550.

————. 1987. The ecology of lake-outlet black flies (this volume).

Wotton, R. S., F. Friberg, J. Hermann, B. Malmqvist, L. M. Nilsson, and P. Sjöström. 1979. Drift and colonization of three coexisting species of blackfly larvae in a lake outlet. *Oikos* 33:290–296.

Zahar, A. R. 1951. The ecology and distribution of blackflies (Simuliidae) in south-east Scotland. *J. Anim. Ecol.* 20:33–62.

10   SPECIALIZED HABITAT SELECTION BY BLACK FLIES

John F. Burger

Immature stages of black flies generally inhabit clean, well-aerated streams with moderate to relatively fast currents. Although different criteria may be used to describe the habitats black fly larvae occupy, most species are found in streams and rivers of variable size that have sustained flow, abundant suspended particulate material for food, and appropriate substrates for attachment.

Black flies may be "specialists," occurring only in a particular kind of stream, or closely associated with other aquatic organisms such as decapod crustaceans and Ephemeroptera in Africa. Others may be "generalists," capable of tolerating a wide range of conditions. These species are widely distributed and can occupy marginal habitats where black flies are rarely found, for example, *Simulium vittatum* Zetterstedt in North America and *S. ruficorne* Macquart in Africa.

Although many factors may influence the ability of black flies to occupy particular habitats, those most commonly identified in studies dealing with black fly larvae are: (1) physiological constraints, (2) trophic considerations, (3) physical constraints, and (4) biotic interactions. These will determine whether a black fly can successfully occupy a particular habitat. If a habitat presents severe constraints to growth and development of larvae, only those species that can adapt to those constraints and successfully develop will occupy it. Such benefits as reduced competition for limited resources (food, space, etc.) may accrue to those species that can adapt to suboptimal conditions.

CRITERIA USED TO DESCRIBE LARVAL BLACK FLY HABITATS

There has been no concerted attempt to classify black fly habitats, except in very general terms. Konurbaev (1977), for example, classified streams in Soviet central Asia by temperature, size, and "alimentation" (categories) and by elevation (type). Each author tends to use certain criteria for characterizing streams inhabited by black flies, depending on what is perceived as important for explaining the presence of particular species.

I have identified eleven criteria used most commonly to characterize black fly stream habitats. A few studies have included some or most of these criteria in their discussion of black fly larval ecology, but most use only a few of them. Criteria most commonly used are: (1) size (width and depth), (2) flow characteristics, (3) temperature, (4) substrates, (5) origin, (6) permanency, (7) gradient, (8) elevation, (9) microhabitat, (10) organic matter, and (11) chemistry. No attempt is made here to determine which of these may be most important in determining what species of black flies occupy a particular habitat, since they would not always be of equal importance. Rather, I shall use these criteria in discussion of particular habitat types to illustrate how they may affect what species of black flies occur there.

SPECIALIZED BLACK FLY LARVAL HABITATS

Thirteen categories are recognized here as being "specialized" or unusual black fly habitats either because relatively few species occur there, because black fly larvae are only occasionally or accidentally found there, or because the species occurring there have specialized morphological, physiological, and behavioral features that allow them to occupy such habitats.

Large Rivers

A large river is defined here as a stream greater than 15 meters wide. They may be quite wide, shallow and turbulent, or deep, with long unbroken stretches, and clear or turbid. Certain groups most commonly found in large rivers are *Ectemnia* species, certain species of the *Simulium jenningsi* group, *Simulium* (*Byssodon*), and some species of *Simulium* formerly placed in the subgenus *Gnus*.

In some parts of the world, large river species are or were severe biting pests of humans, livestock, and other animals. *Simulium arcticum* Malloch and *S. luggeri* Nicholson & Mickel in western North America, *S. jenningsi* Malloch and related species in eastern North America, *S. vittatum* Zetterstedt in the southwestern United States, *S. colombaschense* (Fabricius) in the Danube River Basin in Central Europe, and *Cnephia pecuarum* (Riley), breeding in the Mississippi River and its tributaries, are historically major pest species of livestock and humans, but they are not considered major pests now due to changes in their former breeding habitats. Other species in North America found only in large rivers are *S. johannseni* (Hart), *S. meridionale* Riley, *Ectemnia invenusta* (Walker), and *E. taeniatifrons* (Enderlein). A large number of Eurasian species inhabit large rivers (Usova 1961, Rubtsov 1962, Konurbaev 1977), including *Cnephia znoikoi* Rubtsov, *Metacnephia kirjanovae* Rubtsov, *M. edwardsiana* Rubtsov, *Sulcicnephia jankovskiae* Rubtsov, and numerous species of *Simulium*. Konurbaev (1977) lists eighteen species occurring in large rivers in Soviet central Asia but does not specify the size of streams he considers to be large rivers. In South America, members of the *S. amazonicum* group inhabit large rivers in the Amazon basin (Crosskey, personal communication). Crosskey (1969) listed *Simulium griseicolle* Becker as occurring in large rivers in Africa. In

South America, Dalmat (1955) included *S. jacobsi* Dalmat and *S. haematopotum* Malloch as large river species. Colbo and Moorhouse (1979) listed *S. clathrinum* Mackerras & Mackerras as a river-breeding species in Australia.

Little information is available on how large rivers are colonized by black flies, their life cycles, and their population dynamics. This is likely due to the difficulty of collecting in such habitats, where specialized and expensive equipment is required. Likewise, little is known about why some black fly species occur preferentially in very large rivers. Seston is likely to be abundant seasonally in such streams. Depth at which large river species are found rarely is reported, but the physical requirements and stresses of living in deep rivers must require particular physical and behavioral traits that are presently poorly known. Considering the magnitude of pest problems generated by large river-breeding black flies, more attention should be given to them.

High Mountain Torrents, Cascades, and Waterfalls

Orophilic black flies are characteristically found in high mountain streams and cascades. These species, plus those associated with waterfalls, are always found in turbulent water with fast current. They may be on the lips of waterfalls, in torrents and cascades, or on smooth rock inclines, such as chutes or flumes, where the current is very fast. Relatively few species seem to be restricted to such habitats, although more probably remain to be discovered and described.

Species in the subgenera *Anasolen, Freemanellum,* and some *Metomphalus* of *Simulium* in the Afrotropical region are usually found in very fast torrents, high mountain streams (up to 15,000 feet), and in the fastest cascading streams (Crosskey 1969). *Simulium dentulosum* Roubaud occurs in high mountain torrents. *S. vorax* Pomeroy and *S. colasbelcouri* Grenier & Ovazza were found on the lips of waterfalls and on smooth rock inclines (Crosskey 1960). In North America, species in the subgenus *Shewellomyia* are usually associated with waterfalls. Both *S. pictipes* Hagen and *S. longistylatum* Shewell often occur in dense masses on the lips of waterfalls. In the Neotropical region, *Tlalocomyia revelata* Wygodzinsky & Díaz Najéra has been reported from high mountain streams (Wygodzinsky and Coscarón 1973), and in Guatemala, Dalmat (1955) found *Simulium carolinae* León, *S. ethelae* Dalmat, and *S. larvispinosum* León associated with waterfalls. For the Eurasian fauna, Rubtsov and Yankovsky (1982) reported that *Simulium bukovskii* Rubtsov occurred in cold mountain rivulets. In southern Eurasia, the subgenus *Obuchovia* of *Simulium* occupies habitats similar to those of *Shewellomyia* in North America and may be related to them (Crosskey, personal communication).

Species adapted to high mountain torrents, cascades, waterfalls, and other turbulent water habitats must be able to attach firmly to substrate surfaces. The physical forces of turbulence and current must be dealt with by larvae, although the actual forces that larvae experience may be less than at the water surface. Most larvae inhabiting high mountain cascades have bodies that are enlarged gradually almost to the hind end, then contracting strongly to the circlet of hooks. They also have exceptionally high numbers of hooklet rows, often 200 or more, and more hooks per row than other species (Crosskey, personal communication). These features may contribute to streamlining and anchoring of larvae in strong current or turbulent water.

Crosskey (1969) found that some orophilic species produce microcephalic adults with reduced mouthparts. These features may be the result of isolation of these species in a harsh environment coupled with a switch to autogeny and ground mating in the adult flies, similar to adaptations in the arctic-alpine genus *Gymnopais,* with the ephemeral adult stage less vulnerable to wind and cold.

Konurbaev (1977) suggested that pupae of orophilic species have more respiratory filaments than those found at lower elevations. While this was true for some of the species he investigated, this trend is not consistent, nor did he explain why such species should have more filaments. Currie and Craig (this volume) state that larvae inhabiting fast-flowing water tend to have relatively smaller, robust labral fans. These observations should be investigated further in orophilic species.

Small Streams

Small streams are defined here as those up to 0.3 meters wide. Many black fly species are found in nonpermanent small streams that may or may not be spring-fed. These are treated below under appropriate categories. Exact dimensions of very small streams often are poorly defined in published studies, and terminology is imprecise. Such streams are often called trickles or rivulets, but actual size is rarely given.

Black flies most commonly found in small streams include *Twinnia, Mayacnephia,* and some species of *Prosimulium, Austrosimulium, Boreosimulium,* and *Stegopterna.* In *Simulium,* many representatives of the subgenera *Nevermannia* and *Eusimulium* occupy very tiny streams.

In North America, three species of *Twinnia*—*T. hirticornis* Wood, *T. nova* (Dyar & Shannon), and *T. tibblesi* Stone & Jamnback—are usually found in very small streams (Wood 1978). Eurasian species of *Twinnia* are found in similar habitats. Three species of *Prosimulium*—*P. doveri* Sommerman, *P. fulvum* (Coquillett), and *P. ursinum* (Edwards)—are found in small, cold trickles, often less than 10 cm wide, and very shallow. In arid parts of the southwestern United States, *Simulium tescorum* Stone & Boreham was found in very warm trickles less than 2 cm wide (Lacey and Mulla 1980). Peterson (1959) found *S. bicorne* Dorogostaisky, Rubtsov & Vlasenko in small streams in Utah. This species also occurs in Eurasia. In South America, Wygodzinsky and Coscarón (1973) reported *Mayacnephia pachecolunai* (León) and *M. roblesi* (León) from minute, cold trickles, and Dalmat (1955) found *Simulium ochraceum* Walker in "trickles." In Australia, Tonnoir (1924) reported three species of *Austrosimulium*—*A. australense* Schiner, *A. multicorne* Tonnoir, and *A. longicorne* Tonnoir—from small rivulets. In Eurasia, Rubtsov and Yankovsky (1982) reported *Boreosimulium annulum* (Lundström) from tiny streams and rills.

Relatively few species of black flies appear to be restricted to very small streams. Many found there occur in larger streams as well. Of the species restricted to very small streams, only *Twinnia* are highly specialized anatomically. These have no head fans, and they feed by scraping food from stream substrates. Other species occurring in very small streams have normally developed fans and seem able to live well there. Little is known about the special conditions black flies face in small streams. Flow may not necessarily be limited, but, in fact, larvae must be able to feed successfully when flow is reduced. They may scrape the substrate as well as filter seston from the water, enhancing their feeding capabilities when flow is reduced. Currie and Craig (this volume) suggest that black fly feeding strategies may be more plastic than previously appreciated. This may allow some species to adapt readily to small streams with reduced flow. The conditions faced by larvae in tiny streams need further investigation, especially what physical and trophic conditions may affect the ability of species to live in such habitats.

Glacier-Associated Streams

Streams draining glaciers have large amounts of pulverized material suspended in the water and are sometimes described as "milky." They are cold throughout the year and relatively few black fly species inhabit them.

Some species of *Gymnopais,* particularly *G. dichopticus* Stone and *G. holopticus* Stone, have been reported from glacial streams (Sommerman, Sailer, and Esselbaugh 1955), although small spring-fed streams seem to be the typical habitat (Wood 1978). Two species of *Prosimulium—P. alpestre* Dorogostaisky, Rubtsov & Vlasenko and *P. perspicuum* Sommerman—have also been reported from glacially-fed streams, the former occurring in other streams as well, but the latter apparently restricted to such streams. *Simulium ephemerophilum* Rubtsov, in Tadzhikistan, lives in glacially-fed streams that may remain roofed over with snow and ice for much of the summer (Crosskey, personal communication).

Larvae inhabiting glacially-fed streams must cope with large quantities of inorganic suspended particles in the water column. For scrapers such as *Gymnopais,* this would not be a problem. Perhaps *Prosimulium* species suspend filtering activity periodically, or, if they filter continuously, are able to pass large quantities of material through the gut to obtain sufficient food for sustaining growth. Alternatively, Currie and Craig (this volume) suggest that collecting-gathering and predation may be as important as filtering in allowing certain black flies to develop in such streams and thus compensate for low productivity.

Spring-Fed and Cold, Stenothermal Streams

Spring-fed habitats that support black flies include a diverse assemblage of large and small streams and even some outlet habitats, where streams drain cold bogs or spring-fed lakes. I define such spring-fed/stenothermal waters as those in which the maximum temperature does not exceed 10°C. In this respect, they represent an exceptionally stable thermal environment for black fly development. Some streams may be very small, but they are still permanent, since they draw their flow from underground water sources rather than direct runoff of surface precipitation. Others are intermittent and will be discussed below.

Certain black flies are almost invariably associated with springs. Two such genera are *Twinnia* and *Gymnopais.* Both have representatives in North America and in Eurasia, but the characteristics of habitats they occupy seem to be relatively similar (Bodrova 1975, Wood 1978). *Twinnia* species often occur close to the sources of springs; *Gymnopais* species usually are found in waters where the temperature is 2–6°C (Wood 1978). Many species of *Prosimulium* are found in spring-fed waters, and, in general, species of this genus prefer colder water. *Prosimulium fontanum* Syme &

Davies, for example, occurs in stenothermal tributaries of larger streams, especially in heavily forested regions of eastern North America. Most of these streams probably are spring-fed, although individual studies may not state this explicitly. Other genera with at least some species occurring in spring-fed waters include *Mayacnephia* and *Tlalocomyia* in the Neotropical region (Wygodzinsky and Coscarón 1973), *Greniera* in the Nearctic region (Stone 1964), *Metacnephia* in the Palearctic region (Konurbaev 1977), and *Crozetia* (Davies 1974). At least a few species in several subgenera of *Simulium* usually are found in springs or spring-fed streams. *Simulium pugetense* complex species are invariably found in spring-fed streams, usually close to the source. *Simulium aestivum* Davies, Peterson & Wood usually occurs below spring-fed bogs or small ponds. Streams issuing from spring-fed lakes may promote development of particular species. A sibling species of *Simulium venustum* (ACgB) was very abundant in a stenothermal stream below such a lake, while the more widespread CC sibling was absent (Lake and Burger 1983, Pistrang and Burger 1984). In Europe, *Simulium costatum* Friederichs is probably most characteristic of spring-fed habitats, usually occurring within several hundred meters of the source (Crosskey, personal communication). At least some species in the subgenera *Eusimulium* (other than *costatum*), *Obuchovia*, and *Tetisimulium* may occur in springs (Usova 1961, Rubtsov 1962), but not exclusively. Konurbaev (1977) recorded thirteen species in *Eusimulium* from montane springs in Soviet central Asia and an additional two species from cold tributaries with a temperature range of 4–9°C.

Although spring-fed streams tend to be thermally stable, they also may have low productivity. Perhaps it is not surprising that two genera of black flies whose larvae lack head fans (*Gymnopais* and *Twinnia*) occur in springs. Larvae of these genera are scrapers, collector-gatherers, and even predators (Currie and Craig, this volume) and do not depend on suspended organic seston for food. Those species with normal head fans and feeding modes may switch to scraping, collecting-gathering, or even to predation and thus would be most likely to develop successfully in spring-fed habitats.

Intermittent Streams

Although black flies are most commonly associated with permanent streams, a surprisingly large number of species consistently occur in streams that do not flow during the entire year. Some of these species occur in permanent streams as well but are able to time their development to take advantage of nonpermanent streams; others are particularly adapted to such streams and are found only there. This distinction is not clearly stated in most studies or is unknown.

Descriptions of nonpermanent streams in the literature are often imprecise. Such habitats have been described as semipermanent or temporary, without specifying the length of time that water flows. I suggest employing standard terms to define more closely the length of time that a stream is suitable for black fly breeding: *semipermanent,* for streams that flow for most of the year except for 1–2 months; *seasonal,* for streams that flow for one or more seasons of the year and are suitable for breeding for up to 3–4 months of the year; and *intermittent,* for streams that flow for only a few weeks of the year, or that flow irregularly and depend on periodic rainfall for flow, as often occurs in semiarid or arid regions. Times of flow should be clearly specified.

Several genera of black flies have at least a few species that habitually or occasionally live in nonpermanent streams. These include *Prosimulium, Cnephia, Stegopterna,* and *Twinnia* in the Holarctic, *Araucnephia* and *Araucnephoides* in the Neotropical region (Wygodzinsky and Coscarón 1973), and *Austrosimulium* in the Australian region (Colbo and Moorhouse 1974). In the genus *Simulium,* the subgenera *Hellichiella, Nevermannia,* and *Meillonellum* have some species occurring in nonpermanent streams.

Many species can be found in semipermanent streams where flow ceases for a relatively short time, usually in late summer in temperate regions. Some species of *Prosimulium,* such as *P. decemarticulatum* (Twinn), *P. gibsoni* (Twinn), and *P. rhizophorum* Stone & Jamnback, are often found in such places. In New Hampshire, I have found *P. rhizophorum* only in streams that cease flowing in late summer. *Cnephia dacotense* (Dyar & Shannon) often, but not exclusively, occurs in streams that cease flowing in late summer. Some species of *Simulium,* such as *S. innocens* (Shewell) and *S. croxtoni* Nicholson & Mickel, may be found in semipermanent streams, but they occur in permanent ones as well.

Some species are characteristically found in seasonal streams that, in temperate regions, flow as soon as snow melts in spring and may flow for 2–3 months in spring and early summer. Many of these streams are quite small and may be spring-fed. Some species of *Prosimulium* and *Twinnia* in the Holarctic and *Araucnephia* and *Araucnephoides* in Chile occur in such habitats.

In arid and semiarid regions, some black fly species have adapted to the intermittent or ephemeral flow of rivers or drainage streams that may remain dry for prolonged periods (up to several years) and have flowing water only during sporadic rains or a short, and sometimes uncertain, rainy season. One such species that has been well documented is *Austrosimulium pestilens* Mackerras & Mackerras in Australia (Colbo and Moorhouse 1974, Colbo, Fallis, and Reye 1977). Eggs of *A. pestilens* can survive prolonged periods in riverbeds. Larvae hatch and develop rapidly following sufficient rainfall and flow. Adult life is characteristically short in this hot, dry climate. Another Australian species, *Simulium ornatipes* Skuse, also can occur in intermittent streams. Crosskey and Büttiker (1982) reported *S. yemenense* Crosskey & Garms from foothill wadis of Saudi Arabia, and that *S. arabicum* Crosskey also occasionally occurred there.

Species inhabiting nonpermanent streams must be able to adjust their larval-development period to the flow patterns of particular streams. In general, the shorter the flow time for a particular stream, the more highly adapted the black fly inhabitants of that stream must be to synchronize their aquatic stages with periods of flow. Alternatively, Currie and Craig (this volume) report that larvae of some species of *Gymnopais, Twinnia,* and *Prosimulium* may descend into the stream substrate (hyporheos) and even feed there during periods when stream flow ceases. Species occurring in desert rivers and drainage systems must be able to survive long periods in the egg stage, develop rapidly when flow occurs, emerge, mate, and reproduce before the habitat becomes unsuitable for oviposition. For species inhabiting semipermanent streams, only slight adjustments in timing of aquatic developmental stages is necessary. Univoltine species that develop in spring may be preadapted to live in semipermanent streams, or they may occur there occasionally as well as in permanent streams. Those species that can develop in nonpermanent streams may enjoy less competition for substrate space than in permanent streams, particularly when the stream ceases flowing for prolonged periods. When flow resumes, all submerged substrates are available for attachment and may be able to support larger populations per unit area than permanent streams with substrates already occupied by black flies and other aquatic organisms. There also may be fewer potential predators in such streams, since they usually have longer life cycles or depend on permanent flow.

In general, streams in arid and semiarid environments have received little attention, although their potential for producing disease (onchocerciasis, Arabian peninsula) or pest problems (California-Arizona deserts; Australia) may be greater than appreciated. These areas warrant additional study, such as the excellent review of the black flies of Saudi Arabia by Crosskey and Büttiker (1982).

Outlets of Lakes and Ponds

Of all the habitats considered in this review as specialized or unusual, lacustrine outlet habitats have been most extensively studied, probably because they can produce enormous populations of black flies, some of them severe pests of humans and livestock. Outlet habitats have been most extensively studied in Europe and North America; they are infrequently inhabited by black flies in other parts of the world (Crosskey, personal communication). Considered here are those species consistently reported from outlet habitats. Other species also exploit the favorable thermal and trophic conditions available at or near outlets, but they are not found there consistently. Usova (1961) lists thirteen species in three genera found in or near outlets of lakes, but not all of these are found at outlets exclusively.

At least some species of *Prosimulium*, *Cnephia*, *Metacnephia*, *Austrosimulium*, and *Simulium* (subgenera *Simulium*, *Odagmia*, *Nevermannia*, *Schönbaueria*, and *Psilozia*) have been collected consistently below lake and pond outlets. Those species occurring in large numbers below lake and pond outlets include *Cnephia dacotense*, *C. ornithophilia* Davies, Peterson & Wood, and *Simulium decorum* in North America, *Metacnephia tredecimata* Edwards, *Simulium annulitarsis* Zetterstedt, and *S. noelleri* Friederichs in Europe, and *S. truncatum* Lundström, distributed in a broad Holarctic arc.

Relatively little has been published on the effect of lake or pond size on outlet-species composition. In New Hampshire, for example, *S. truncatum*, *S. aestivum*, and *C. dacotense* occur below small ponds as well as larger lakes. The chemistry of a lake or pond, or its annual temperature regime, may influence the black fly species occurring below its outlet. *S. aestivum*, for example, occurs below very small spring-fed ponds. A particular sibling species of the *S. venustum* complex (ACgB) was invariably found below small stenothermal lakes with relatively high NO_2/NO_3 content (Lake and Burger 1983).

Some species occur in great numbers below "pseudo-outlets," areas of flowing water just below stretches of slack water. I have found large populations of *Prosimulium fuscum* Syme & Davies mixed with *P. mixtum* and *Simulium venustum* (CC sibling) extending 100–200 meters downstream of slack water in canals and streams. Whether these areas mimic outlets in some physical or chemical characteristics is unknown. Possibly adult female black flies prefer to oviposit in streams in or just below quiet water, resulting in very high populations of larvae there.

An excellent study by Wotton (1979) demonstrated that outlet species partitioned the habitat spatially and temporally, with a hatching sequence that allowed three species to develop large populations at the same outlet while minimizing competition for space. This study and others by Wotton and his colleagues have given us an excellent basis for explaining why black flies concentrate at outlets. This topic will be treated more fully in the chapters by Wotton and by Craig and Galloway.

Two factors consistently identified as contributing to the abundance and diversity of outlet-inhabiting species are relatively warm water temperature from warming of lake water and the quality/quantity of seston (productivity) emanating from impounded waters. These can contribute to rapid growth, the large numbers of black flies produced at outlets, and even the expression of autogeny (an indirect result of food quality?) in outlet-breeding species (Magnarelli and Burger 1984). It does not, however, explain why certain species occur at the outlet and others only further downstream. Behavior of ovipositing female flies and subsequent larval behavior must be important factors.

Slow-Moving or Standing Water

Some black flies, for example, species in the subgenera *Eusimulium* and *Pomeroyellum*, seem to adapt readily to streams with little perceptible current. Relatively few species, however, have been reported from standing water, and some of these reports are not well substantiated.

In most biogeographical regions, at least some species of *Eusimulium* can be found in streams with relatively little current. Larvae of these species usually are herbicolous (attached to plants submerged in water). In Africa, the subgenus *Pomeroyellum* seems to be the major slow-water component, with species such as *S. alcocki* Pomeroy occurring in very slow-moving streams.

In North America, Edmunds (1954) reported *S. vittatum* Zetterstedt and *S. griseum* Coquillett living in pools left from irrigation water. He also reported that some of these larvae pupated and produced adults. If the larvae he observed were fully grown, it is possible that some would be able to pupate and produce adult flies. On the other hand, we may not appreciate the extent to which some species, especially highly adaptable ones, may be able to use a range of feeding strategies (scraping, collecting-gathering, and predation) to complete development in standing-water habitats (Currie and Craig, this volume).

In Africa, *S. adersi* Pomeroy has been reported from swamps in Senegal, where there was no flow. Perhaps the most remarkable species reported from slack-water habitats is *S. ruficorne*. Crosskey (1969) listed *S. ruficorne* as being found in very slow, usually small streams where almost no flow existed. It was also reported from the desert fringes of Morocco, Algeria, and Egypt, marshy seeps in very thin films of water, and in marshy "fadamas" in Nigeria. Larvae may even be covered with algae. This species apparently adapts to a wide range of aquatic habitats. If one assumes that larvae depend on at least a slight current for filter feeding, it seems unlikely that larvae could survive in standing water for long, but information presented by Currie and Craig (this volume) on larval-feeding strategies clearly shows that this cannot always be assumed.

In the case of *S. ruficorne*, statements by Cunningham van Someren (1944) have been widely misinterpreted to suggest that it can live and develop in stagnant water, such as animal hoofprints. However, Crosskey and Büttiker (1982) have shown that Cunningham van Someren's statements do not suggest that *S. ruficorne* can develop in puddles, but that its occurrence in muddy hoof holes was the result of stranding of pupae from adjacent running water (Crosskey, personal communication).

Brackish Water

This is one of the most atypical environments for black flies. Pupae of *S. adersi* were found in Man 'O War Bay near Victoria in Cameroon (Crosskey 1960). Pupae were on herbage attached to piles of a wharf in brackish water where a small stream discharged into the sea. Undoubtedly larvae occurred in the stream, but, when washed down to the mouth, they were able to pupate after attaching to herbage on sea piles.

Crosskey (personal communication) has heard of cases in French channel coasts of black fly larvae and pupae found where streams break down the cliffs and fan out over the shingle onto the beach. Although these are freshwater streams, they may receive some salt spray from the sea.

Lacustrine Habitats

Occasionally black flies have been reported from lakes. *Simulium adersi* was reported from the wave-lapped shores of an island in Lake Victoria (Gibbins 1934). The circumstances surrounding this observation are by no means clear, and it has never been repeated. Therefore, it is considered aberrant and of no real importance in defining the unusual habitats of black flies. Wotton (1979) reported that *Metacnephia tredecimata* occurred 10 meters into a lake before the outlet, where there was apparently no current. Such occurrences, however, seem to be unusual.

Anthropogenic Habitats

Human activities, particularly those associated with irrigation projects, hydroelectric, and flood-control acitivities have produced ideal habitats for some black fly species. Places most commonly colonized by black flies are concrete culverts and water channels, concrete aprons below outflow pipes and dam spillways, and sluiceways below natural and artificial lakes and ponds. In some cases, normal seasonal flow can be enhanced by impoundment to produce breeding for as long as climate permits and may create health or pest hazards to humans and livestock nearby.

In North America, two species commonly associated with dams, spillways, and culverts are *S. decorum* and *S. vittatum*. Both seem to flourish in such environments. Another species in western North America, *S. griseum*, commonly occurs in irrigation ditches (Edmunds 1954, Fredeen and Shemanchuk 1960). Other species such as *S. meridionale, S. bivittatum* Malloch, *S. arcticum, S. tuberosum* complex, and the *S. venustum-verecundum* complexes occasionally are found in certain kinds of irrigation ditches, especially if their flow is similar to fast-flowing streams (Fredeen and Shemanchuk 1960). Another species commonly associated with waterfalls, *S. pictipes*, also can be found on concrete spillways (Snow et al. 1958, Stone and Snoddy 1969). In the Palearctic region, Rubtsov (1962) reported *S. paucicuspis* Rubtsov, *S. pseudequinum* Séguy (as *mediterraneum* Puri), and *S. paraequinum* Puri occurring occasionally in irrigation ditches associated with rivers. In Madeira, both native black fly species can be found in small masonry gullies (levadas) that deliver water from the mountains to the valleys (Crosskey, personal communication). In Australia, Colbo and Moorhouse (1979) found very large numbers of *S. clathrinum* and *S. ornatipes* on a concrete apron below an outlet pipe in northwestern Queensland. In Africa, both *S. adersi* and *S. ruficorne* have been reported breeding on dam spillways or in irrigation channels (Burton and McRae 1965).

Some medically important species may also occur in anthropogenic habitats. Burton and McRae (1965) reported *S. damnosum* complex larvae breeding on the side supports of cement culverts in large rivers and on dam spillways in Ghana. Dalmat (1955) found *S. metallicum* larvae in man-made water channels in Guatemala.

The anthropogenic habitats occupied by ecologically tolerant black flies are hydrologically similar to streams normally inhabited by these species. The major differences are in the substrates for attachment, so oviposition behavior by female flies, behavior of the larvae during attachment, and ability to tolerate wide temperature fluctuations would be important determinants of what species colonize such habitats. Some species, such as *S. decorum* and *S. vittatum*, are lake-outlet-inhabiting species. The dams and spillways associated with impounded waters are ideal breeding sites for such species. Indeed, *S. decorum* may produce much larger populations below dams and associated structures than in natural outlet habitats. Thus human activity may enhance the breeding potential of certain species.

Phoretic Associations

Certain groups of black flies, most notably the subgenera *Phoretomyia* and *Lewisellum* of *Simulium* in the Afrotropical region, are always found on other aquatic insects or decapod crustaceans. So far as known, eggs are laid in streams, and larvae attach to the phoretic carrier shortly after hatching. Burton and McRae (1972) summarized what was known of these phoretic associations and provided a table of species and their carriers. Since then, additional information has become available, most notably a series of papers by Disney and by Raybould and colleagues on Afrotropical species, and a review by Rubtsov (1972) on phoretic species in the Soviet Union.

In Africa, twenty-two species of black flies are known to be phoretic on at least seven species of river crabs (Potamidae, *Potamonautes*), two species of river prawns (Atyidae, *Atya*), and three families of Ephemeroptera (Heptageniidae, *Afronurus;* Oligoneuriidae, *Elassoneuria;* Baetidae, *Baetis*). All species of *Lewisellum*, except one, are found on river crabs. All species of *Phoretomyia*, except one, are found on Ephemeroptera. One species in each subgenus is found on river prawns.

Species described from river crabs are:

> *Simulium* (*Lewisellum*) *ethiopiense* Fain & Oomen
> *S.* (*L.*) *goinyi* Lewis & Hanney
> *S.* (*L.*) *hightoni* Lewis
> *S.* (*L.*) *kivuense* Gouteux

S. (*L.*) *neavei* Roubaud
S. (*L.*) *nyasalandicum* de Meillon
S. (*L.*) *ovazzae* Grenier & Mouchet
S. (*L.*) *woodi* de Meillon

Species known from river prawns are:

Simulium (*Lewisellum*) *atyophilum* Lewis & Disney
S. (*Phoretomyia*) *dukei* Lewis, Disney & Crosskey

Species known from Ephemeroptera are:

Simulium (*Phoretomyia*) *afronuri* Lewis & Disney (*Afronurus*)
S. (*P.*) *baetiphilum* Lewis & Disney (Baetidae)
S. (*P.*) *berneri* Freeman (*Elassoneuria*)
S. (*P.*) *copleyi* Gibbins (*Afronurus*)
S. (*P.*) *diceros* Freeman & de Meillon (Baetidae)
S. (*P.*) *kumboense* Grenier, Germain & Mouchet (*Elassoneuria*)
S. (*P.*) *lumbwanum* de Meillon (*Afronurus*)
S. (*P.*) *marlieri* Grenier (*Afronurus*)
S. (*P.*) *melanocephalum* Gouteux (*Afronurus*)
S. (*P.*) *moucheti* Gouteux (*Afronurus*)
S. (*P.*) *rickenbachi* Germain, Grenier & Mouchet (*Afronurus*)
S. (*P.*) *zairense* Gouteux (*Afronurus*)

Larvae of the above species attach to various parts of the phoretic carrier's body. Berner (1954) reported larvae on mayflies behind the labium, between the legs, and between the gills. Pupae were found on the wing pads of nymphs. Although location of larvae may vary, pupae were usually found on the wing pads. Usually relatively few larvae occur on an individual mayfly. Disney (1971) found pupae on the mesonotum as well as the wing covers of mayflies. He also found that pupae of *S. lumbwanum* occurred on medium-sized nymphs, while those of *S. afronuri* were on nearly grown nymphs. Raybould (1969) found larvae associated with crabs to occur on the sides of the body, the chelipeds, basal segments of the walking legs, and in the eye sockets.

Rubtsov (1972) reviewed information on some black fly species living on mayflies of the family Heptageniidae in the Soviet Union. He proposed the genus *Phoretodagmia* to receive *ephemerophilum* Rubtsov, associated with a species of *Iron* in Tadzhikistan (Rubtsov 1948). Crosskey (1981) considers *Phoretodagmia* to be a synonym of the subgenus *Simulium*. Subsequently, Rubtsov described *S. obikumbensis* Rubtsov from *Iron* sp. and *Rhithrogena tjanshanica* Brodsky in the western Pamirs (Tadzhikistan), and *S. alajensis* Rubtsov from *R. tjanshanica* in Kirgizia. Konurbaev (1977) described an additional species, *S. rithrogenophila* Konurbaev. He also found that at least some of the species listed as phoretic by Rubtsov are not invariably so.

Incidental phoresy has been reported for some species of black flies, often in circumstances where severe overcrowding occurs, resulting in a shortage of attachment sites for larvae. In Africa, Corbet (1962) found pupae of *S. adersi*, *S. vorax* Pomeroy, and a possible specimen of the *S. damnosum* complex on nymphs of the libellulid dragonfly, *Zygonyx natalensis* (Martin). This association apparently was the result of overcrowding in normal pupation sites (rootlets of plants) where *Zygonyx* also occurred. Burton and McRae (1972) found two pupae of *S. adersi* and one of *S. medusaeformae hargreavesi* Gibbins on *Zygonyx torrida* Kirby, presumably due to overcrowding. Also incidentally, Ribeiro (1927) found a "simuliid" larva on a mayfly (*Iron* sp.) in India, and Hora (1930) found black fly pupae on Blephariceridae, which was ascribed to "accidental overcrowding." No examples of phoresy have been mentioned from other parts of the world.

Although phoresy for black flies is well documented, there is relatively little information on why some species are phoretic and others not. It is certainly exceptional in black flies as a group. Berner (1954) stated that similarity of feeding habits, high oxygen requirements, and paucity of places in the stream for attachment were possible reasons why some black flies developed phoresy, but he cited no evidence for these suggestions. Crosskey (1969) suggested that if safe pupal attachment sites were at a premium, attachment to other animals in the stream might assure safety for the sessile pupal stage in fast streams. Rubtsov (1972) believed that phoresy improved conditions of aeration and nutrition for larvae, and they were less likely to be killed by rolling stones in fast mountain streams. Burton and McRae (1972) suggested that black fly larvae may get "left overs" (food) from their carriers and that phoretic attachment to a mobile host might protect them from predators such as fish.

Marlier (in Burton and McRae 1972) observed that the guts of phoretic black fly larvae had similar contents to those of its phoretic carrier. Raybould and Mhidden (1978) found that larvae of *S. neavei* could survive on crabs in damp sand under rocks after all water had disappeared from streams for two weeks. These observations suggest that possible enhanced food availability and protection from desiccation may explain why some species have developed obligatory phoresy with other aquatic arthropods. However, the particular circumstances promoting phoresy may not be similar for all species.

Rubtsov (1972) stated that Asiatic phoretic larvae had antennae appreciably shortened, strong development of hairs on the posterior extremity of the body, a conversion of hairs to large scales, strong branching of the rectal appendage, and strengthening of the attaching ring of hooklets. However, it was unclear whether these features were unique to species exhibiting phoresy and, if so, what their functional significance might be. Currie and Craig (this volume) illustrate the head fans of *S. moucheti,* which form short, flat ventral brushes and may be related to unusual feeding habits.

Although one might intuitively cite possible advantages for phoresy, there is little evidence yet to suggest many of the hypothetical advantages. Possible disadvantages, such as loss by molting or predation on the phoretic carrier, have not been investigated thoroughly. Since phoresy is difficult to observe in nature, and because larvae often are not very abundant on their carriers, answers to questions about the functional significance of phoresy might be more easily desired than accomplished.

Other Unusual Habitats

There remain a group of "unusual" habitats difficult to place in a particular category, or where black flies occur only incidentally. These habitats have peculiar physical, chemical, or thermal features.

Perhaps one of the most peculiar is the hyporheic/troglobitic habitat of *Parasimulium crosskeyi* Peterson, recently discovered in Oregon (Courtney and Craig 1985). Larvae occur in spring seepages along the streambed and can only be found with careful searching. The larva of *P. crosskeyi* is unpigmented and is unique among known black fly larvae in being eyeless. Additional information on this unusual black fly will be presented elsewhere. Currie and Craig (this volume) report that larvae of some *Prosimulium* and *Gymnopais* descend into the hyporheos during periods when the small streams they inhabit cease flowing, and that they may also feed there.

Two species have been found in abnormally warm water. Crosskey and Büttiker (1982) reported *S. ruficorne* from water "almost hot to the touch" in Upper Volta (Burkina Faso). The water temperature was 30–31°C, and larvae were exposed to midday sun on exposed rocks where the water was a 2-mm film lapping over rock lips (Crosskey, personal communication). Lacey and Mulla (1980) found *S. tescorum* larvae in a small desert seep where the water temperature was 32°C (90°F). This is the highest recorded temperature of which I am aware for a black fly in a natural habitat. Whether this temperature could be tolerated for the entire life of a larva is unknown.

Dalmat (1955) found *Gigantodax aquamarense* (León) in sulphurous streams of very low pH, stating that this species is characteristically found in such streams. No other black flies have been reported from similar habitats.

Craig (1983), in a detailed study of Polynesian Simuliidae, reported that several species, but, in particular, one from Raratonga, lived inside leaf packs that build up on the upstream sides of rocks and are held in place by water pressure. Larvae and pupae usually were found between the leaves, possibly replacing chironomid larvae, which are poorly represented in the streams.

Craig (1975), in a study of Tahitian Simuliidae, found single larvae of *S. tahitiense* Edwards on the tips of roots where water was seeping down cliff faces and dripping from the roots. However, this species also occurred in almost all running-water habitats, including large streams.

CONCLUSION

Study of specialized and unusual black fly habitats is important for understanding the physical and physiological limits of black flies in aquatic environments. The principal obstacle to characterizing these habitats has been the imprecise definition of habitat features. If future analytical studies are to be useful, habitats must be clearly defined physically, biotically, and (if possible) chemically.

ACKNOWLEDGMENTS

I wish to acknowledge all authors whose published works contributed valuable information to this review. Although many are not specifically cited, their observations were important for compiling data on unusual black fly habitats and attempting to understand where black flies live, and why. I acknowledge especially Richard Merritt, Michigan State University, and Douglas Craig, University of Alberta, for their valuable contributions of information and ideas. I express special thanks to Roger W. Crosskey, British Museum (Natural History), for his suggestions and generous contribution of valuable information to enhance the value of this chapter.

This chapter is Scientific Contribution Number 1407 from the New Hampshire Agricultural Experiment Station.

LITERATURE CITED

Berner, L. 1954. Phoretic association between a species of *Simulium* and a mayfly nymph, with a description of the nymph. *Ann. Mag. Nat. Hist.* (12)7:116–121.

Bodrova, Yu. D. 1975. A new species of black fly (Diptera, Simuliidae) from the Maritime Territory. *Entomol. Obozr.* 54:429–431 (in Russian).

Burton, G. J., and T. M. McRae. 1965. Dam-spillway breeding of *Simulium damnosum* Theobald in northern Ghana. *Ann. Trop. Med. Parisitol.* 59:405–412.

———. 1972. Phoretic attachment of *Simulium* larvae and pupae to mayfly and dragonfly nymphs. *Mosquito News* 32:436–443.

Colbo, M. H., A. M. Fallis, and F. J. Reye. 1977. The distribution and biology of *Austrosimulium pestilens,* a serious biting-fly pest following flooding. *Austral. Vet. J.* 53:135–138.

Colbo, M. H., and D. E. Moorhouse. 1974. The survival of eggs of *Austrosimulium pestilens* Mack. and Mack. (Diptera, Simuliidae). *Bull. Entomol. Res.* 64:629–632.

———. 1979. The ecology of pre-imaginal Simuliidae (Diptera) in south-east Queensland. *Hydrobiologia* 63:63–69.

Corbet, P. S. 1962. Observations on the attachment of *Simulium* pupae to larvae of Odonata. *Ann. Trop. Med. Parasitol.* 56:136–140.

Courtney, G. W., and D. A. Craig. 1985. Discovery of the immature stages of *Parasimulium crosskeyi* (Diptera: Simuliidae) with a discussion of a unique black fly habitat. *Abstract, N. Amer. Benth. Soc., 33rd Ann. Mtg. Corvallis.* p. 96.

Craig, D. A. 1975. The larvae of Tahitian Simuliidae (Diptera: Nematocera). *J. Med. Entomol.* 12:463–476.

———. 1983. Phylogenetic problems in Polynesian Simuliidae (Diptera: Culicimorpha): a progress report. *GeoJournal* 7:533–541.

Crosskey, R. W. 1960. A taxonomic study of the larvae of West African Simuliidae (Diptera: Nematocera) with comments on the morphology of the larval black-fly head. *Bull. Br. Mus. Nat. Hist. (Entomol.)* 10:1–74.

———. 1969. A re-classification of the Simuliidae (Diptera) of Africa and its islands. *Bull. Br. Mus. Nat. Hist. (Entomol.) Suppl.* 14. 195 pp.

———. 1981. Simuliid taxonomy—the contemporary scene. Pp. 3–18 in M. Laird, Ed., *Blackflies: the future for biological methods in integrated control.* Academic Press, New York and London.

Crosskey, R. W., and W. Büttiker. 1982. Insects of Saudi Arabia. Diptera: Fam. Simuliidae. *Fauna of Saudi Arabia* 4:398–446.

Cunningham van Someren, G. R. 1944. Some records of Simuliidae in Abyssinia and British Somaliland. *Bull. Entomol. Res.* 35:113–114.

Dalmat, H. T. 1955. The black flies (Diptera, Simuliidae) of Guatemala and their role as vectors of onchocerciasis. *Smithsonian Misc. Coll.* 125(1):1–425.

Davies, L. 1974. Evolution of larval head-fans in Simuliidae (Diptera) as inferred from the structure and biology of *Crozetia crozetensis* (Womersley) compared with other genera. *Zool. J. Linn. Soc.* 55:193–224.

Disney, R. H. L. 1971. Two phoretic black-flies (Diptera: Simuliidae) and their associated mayfly host (Ephemeroptera: Heptageniidae) in Cameroon. *J. Entomol.* (A) 46:53–61.

Edmunds, L. R. 1954. A note on irrigation drop structures as breeding sites of black flies in western Nebraska (Diptera: Simuliidae). *Mosquito News* 14:65–66.

Fredeen, F. J. H., and J. A. Shemanchuk. 1960. Black flies (Diptera: Simuliidae) of irrigation systems in Saskatchewan and Alberta. *Can. J. Zool.* 38:723–735.

Gibbins, E. G. 1934. Further studies on Ethiopian Simuliidae. *Trans. R. Entomol. Soc. London* 81:37–51.

Hora, S. L. 1930. Ecology, bionomics and evolution of the torrential fauna, with special reference to the organs of attachment. *Phil. Trans. R. Soc. London* (B) 218:171–281.

Konurbaev, E. O. 1977. Ecological classification of running waters in Soviet Central Asia and the distribution pattern of black flies (Diptera, Simuliidae) in watercourses of different types. [In Russian]. *Entomol. Obozr.* 56:736–750.

Lacey, L. A., and M. S. Mulla. 1980. Observations on the biology and distribution of *Simulium tescorum* (Diptera: Simuliidae) in California and adjacent areas. *Pan-Pac. Entomol.* 56:323–331.

Lake, D. J., and J. F. Burger. 1983. Larval distribution and succession of outlet-breeding black flies (Diptera: Simuliidae) in New Hampshire. *Can. J. Zool.* 61:2519–33.

Magnarelli, L. A., and J. F. Burger. 1984. Caloric reserves in natural populations of a blackfly, *Simulium decorum* (Diptera: Simuliidae), and a deerfly, *Chrysops ater* (Diptera: Tabanidae). *Can. J. Zool.* 62:2589–93.

Peterson, B. V. 1959. Notes on the biology of some species of Utah blackflies (Diptera: Simuliidae). *Mosquito News* 19:86–90.

Pistrang, L. A., and J. F. Burger. 1984. Effect of *Bacillus thuringiensis* var. *israelensis* on a genetically-defined population of black flies (Diptera: Simuliidae) and associated insects in a montane New Hampshire stream. *Can. Entomol.* 116:975–981.

Raybould, J. N. 1969. Studies on the immature stages of the *Simulium neavei* Roubaud complex and their associated crabs in eastern Usumbara Mountains in Tanzania. I. Investigations in rivers and large streams. *Ann. Trop. Med. Parasitol.* 63:269–287.

Raybould, J. N., and H. K. Mhidden. 1978. Ibid. III. Investigations on development and survival and their relevance to control. *Ann. Trop. Med. Parasitol.* 72:177–187.

Ribeiro, S. 1927. A note on a simuliid larva found associated with a mayfly nymph. *J. Asiat. Soc. Bengal* (n.s.) 22 (1926): 69–70.

Rubtsov, I. A. 1948. Symbiosis of larvae and nymphs of black flies with Ephemeroptera. *Priroda,* no. 10:77–80.

———. 1962. Short keys to the bloodsucking Simuliidae of the USSR. *Publ. Zool. Inst. Acad. Sci. USSR,* no. 77.

———. 1972. Phoresy in black flies (Diptera, Simuliidae) and new phoretic species from may-fly larvae. *Entomol. Obozr.* 51:403–411 (in Russian).

Rubtsov, I. A., and A. V. Yankovsky. 1982. New genera and subgenera of black flies (Diptera, Simuliidae). *Entomol. Obozr.* 61:183–187 (in Russian).

Snow, W. E., E. Pickard, and J. B. Moore. 1958. Observations on black flies (Simuliidae) in the Tennessee River Basin. *J. Tenn. Acad. Sci.* 33:5–23.

Sommerman, K. M., R. I. Sailer, and C. O. Esselbaugh. 1955. Biology of Alaskan black flies. *Ecol. Monogr.* 25:345–385.

Stone, A. 1964. Guide to the insects of Connecticut. Part IV. The Diptera or true flies of Connecticut. Ninth fascicle. Simuliidae and Thaumaleidae. *State Geological and Natural History Survey of Connecticut Bull.,* No. 97. 126 pp.

Stone, A., and E. L. Snoddy. 1969. The black flies of Alabama (Diptera: Simuliidae). *Auburn Univ. Agr. Exp. Stn. Bull.* 390. 93 pp.

Tonnoir, A. L. 1924. Australasian Simuliidae. *Bull. Entomol. Res.* 15:213–255.

Usova, Z. V. 1961. Flies of Karelia and the Murmansk Region. *Acad. Sci. USSR.* (Trans. by Israel Program for Scientific Translations [1964].)

Wood, D. M. 1978. Taxonomy of the Nearctic species of *Twinnia* and *Gymnopais* (Diptera: Simuliidae) and a discussion of the ancestry of the Simuliidae. *Can. Entomol.* 110:1297–1337.

Wotton, R. S. 1979. The influence of a lake on the distribution of blackfly (Diptera: Simuliidae) species along a river. *Oikos* 32:368–372.

Wygodzinsky, P., and S. Coscarón. 1973. A review of the Mesoamerican and South American black flies of the tribe Prosimuliini (Simuliinae: Simuliidae). *Bull. Am. Mus. Nat. Hist.* 151:129–199.

11   THE ECOLOGY OF LAKE–OUTLET BLACK FLIES

Roger S. Wotton

It has long been recognized that the immature stages of black flies occur in very high population densities at lake outlets, where larvae feed on the abundant particulate material leaving the lake (Knöpp 1952, Müller 1955, Illies 1957, Carlsson 1962, Ulfstrand 1968, Sheldon and Oswood 1977, Lake and Burger 1983, and see Table 11.1 for comparison with other habitats). This material consists of bacterioplankton, small phytoplankton, and zooplankton, plus detritus and other fine particulate organic matter, some of which will be generated as water passes from the lake to the river (Wotton 1984a).

Two kinds of lake outlets can be identified. "Natural" lake outlets result from geological events such as glaciation and its subsequent retreat; "artificial" lake outlets are the result of the recent activity of man (beaver dams are difficult to classify but probably show more features in common with "artificial lake outlets"). Whether outlets are natural or artificial, the black fly fauna that inhabits them will be able to take advantage of the good conditions for growth (providing the release is epilimnetic). Individuals will also need to withstand the adverse effects of resultant high population density, and lake-outlet black flies exhibit strategies that promote coexistence. In this chapter I will discuss a series of studies that illustrate some of these strategies, indicating the potential within the family.

ARE THERE "LAKE-OUTLET BLACK FLIES"?

From surveys (e.g., Carlsson 1962, Davies 1968), it is clear that some black fly species specialize in life at lake outlets, although they can be found at lower population densities in areas of rivers that replicate some of the conditions found at lake outlets (e.g., in thin films of water). This preference for lake outlets is apparent when one considers extensive data sets for large areas, such as those collected by the NE-118 project in the northeastern United States. In Figure 11.1 some data from Cupp and Gordon (1983) have been summarized. The number of recorded sites for

Table 11.1 The maximum population density of black fly immatures recorded in studies from a variety of habitats. Estimates are all given as the number of individuals m^{-2}, and they are placed in ascending order.

Population Density	Type of Water Body	Authority
161	Moorland stream at 580 m	Wotton 1977
456	Moorland stream at 380 m	Wotton 1977
7000	Stream	Carlsson 1962
10900	Stream	Mohsen and Mulla 1982
11474	River	Scullion et al. 1982
19783	Blackwater river	Benke et al. 1984
22000	Natural lake outlet	Wotton 1979
32000	Stream	Olejnicek 1983
35000	Stream 1 km from pond	Colbo 1982
63390	River	Chutter 1968
67655	Natural lake outlet	Ulfstrand 1968
203400	Stream in limestone area	Reisen 1977
312000	River in chalk area	Ladle et al. 1972
483300	River at minimum flow	Colbo and Moorhouse 1979
500000	Stream below waterfall	Kurtak 1974
751479	Artificial lake outlet, SF	Wotton, unpublished
1200000	Artificial lake outlet, GB	Wotton, unpublished

Note: SF = Finland; GB = Great Britain

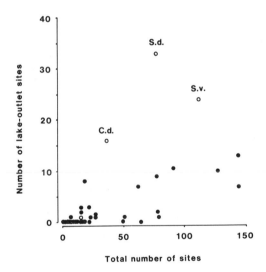

FIG. 11.1 The number of times black flies of each species are recorded at lake-outlet sites plotted against the total number of records (data from Cupp & Gordon 1983). Open circles = populations known to be autogenous. Closed circles = anautogenous populations. *Abbreviations:* C.d., *Cnephia dacotensis;* S.d., *Simulium decorum;* S.v., *Simulium vittatum.*

each species was counted and a note made of the number of times ponds or lakes were included in the description of each site. The number of "lake-outlet" sites was then plotted against the total number of sites where each species was collected. Three species show a higher-percentage occurrence at lake outlets: *Cnephia dacotensis* (Dyar & Shannon), *Simulium decorum* Walker, and *Simulium vittatum* Zett., the second of the three showing the most marked preference for this microhabitat (cf. Imhof and Smith 1979). The advantage of the data presented by Cupp and Gordon (1983) is that there is so much information for one region. Although some sites were probably not classified correctly in my analysis, it is clear that the three species stand out from all the others in the survey, at least of those widely distributed.

WHAT FACTORS PROMOTE THE DEVELOPMENT OF HIGH POPULATION DENSITIES AT LAKE OUTLETS?

In a study of the black flies inhabiting a natural lake outlet in Swedish Lapland, Carlsson et al. (1977) proposed three main factors that caused the concentration of certain simuliid species at lake outlets. Two of these factors will also apply to artificial lake outlets.

1. Natural lake outlets are often formed in regions where the underlying rocks are resistant to erosion. The substratum is therefore stable, with stones tending to be flattened, and the flow over their surface is usually smooth, which may be of advantage to larval feeding. The presence of the lake will also moderate the rate of change of flow, diminishing the effect of sudden spates, which may wash larvae downstream (Yakuba 1959). Artificial lake outlets, in contrast, often consist of concrete or wooden sluices. They can be subject to sudden drying, especially where the volume of water passing from the lake or pond is much less than is usually the case with natural lake outlets.

2. Female adults, having matured eggs, will fly to a river to oviposit and, once a river has been encountered, they will fly upstream. The change in cues provided by the presence of a lake will cause the females to stop this upstream migration and oviposit in the lake outlet.

3. Some food items (probably those < 2 μm in diameter) may be available only a short distance downstream from the lake. If the quality or quantity of available food is reduced, then lower black fly population densities will result.

LIFE-HISTORY STRATEGIES SHOWN BY BLACK FLIES INHABITING THE LAKE OUTLET STUDIED IN SWEDISH LAPLAND

The lake outlet and the first few hundred meters of the river were dominated by three species of black flies, individuals of which were rarely found 5 kilometers downstream.

1. Larvae of *Metacnephia tredecimata* Edw. were able to hatch from eggs at a lower temperature than those of the other two populations. This ensures that larvae of *M. tredecimata* grow considerably by the time that larvae of the other two populations began to appear (Carlsson et al. 1977).

2. and 3. Larvae of *Schoenbaueria annulitarsis* Zett. and *Simulium truncatum* Ldstr. hatched from eggs at about the same time but were separated by differences in habitat preference. Larvae of *Sch. annulitarsis* dominated at the immediate lake outlet; those of *S. truncatum* occurred further downstream in the area inhabited at that time by larger larvae of *M. tredecimata* (Wotton 1979).

The three populations therefore show a temporal separation in the case of *M. tredecimata* and *S. truncatum,* and a spatial separation in the case of the latter population and that of *Sch. annulitarsis.* This difference in realizable niche (Hutchinson 1958) between the three will allow them to coexist in years when population density is very high.

REPRODUCTIVE BIOLOGY OF LAKE OUTLET BLACK FLIES

The reproductive biology of the three populations that dominate the Swedish lake outlet was not studied, although it is known that *S. truncatum* is anautogenous (needing to take a blood meal before eggs can be matured) elsewhere (Davies, Györkös, and Raastad 1977; Wotton 1982a).

A feature of the biology of *C. dacotensis, S. decorum,* and *S. vittatum,* recorded as lake-outlet specialists in the northeastern United States, is that all three are autogenous (able to produce a batch of eggs without needing a blood meal), the latter two in the first gonotrophic cycle only. It is therefore tempting to suggest that the autogenous habit in these populations is something that has been made possible by the conditions existing at lake outlets. Interestingly, of the five autogenous species identified by Davies, Györkös, and Raastad (1977), three are known to inhabit lake outlets in Europe as a whole (Zwick 1978).

There has been discussion in the literature as to whether or not autogeny is under genetic control. Rubtzov (1956) suggests that the environment is the main factor controlling the presence of autogeny in populations. Black flies will be autogenous when larval food supply is good and anautogenous where larval food supply is of lower quality. This was subsequently questioned by Davies (1961), who found two populations of *Prosimulium* coexisting, the one autogenous and the other anautogenous.

Assuming that autogeny in the first gonotrophic cycle developed from anautogeny in *S. decorum,* it is possible to speculate on the events that led up to the development of autogeny. To allow development of the fat body necessary for egg production, larvae of the ancestors of present-day populations had to spend more time in the river than they would should anautogeny be maintained. This longer period of time brings an increased risk of predation, and of being caught in adverse conditions, drying and flooding being unpredictable events. Through evolution there will therefore have been a trade-off between these advantages and disadvantages. In lake outlets, with their abundance of high-quality food, the time taken for the development of a fat body will be reduced. This will make the trade-off more in favor of autogeny, and the strategy will have passed into the whole population, right across its range.

THE ECOLOGY OF *SIMULIUM NOELLERI*—A SPECIALIST AT LIVING IN ARTIFICIAL LAKE OUTLETS

Of the three widespread species of lake-outlet black flies identified from the northeastern United States, *S. decorum* (which has been successfully colonized and reared through several generations in the laboratory by Professor Cupp and co-workers at Cornell University) has a sibling species, *S. noelleri* Fried., in the Palaearctic (Rothfels 1981), and populations of the latter have been investigated in some detail at field sites in Finland, Sweden, and Great Britain (Wotton 1982a,b,c; 1984a,b; 1985).

At the site in Finland, a wooden sluice marks the beginning of the river Teuronjoki, and the surface of this sluice supports large *S. noelleri* populations during the summer. Just downstream, larvae and pupae of *S. noelleri* are not found in such numbers—the immature stages are often confined to the immediate lake outlet (Davies 1968)—and the simuliid fauna here is dominated by larvae of *S. truncatum*, an anautogenous black fly. While being found abundantly just downstream from lake outlets, individuals of this species are also present in the first part of the "normal" river. As no large fat body is produced, there is no advantage to be gained from remaining in the river: adults of *S. truncatum* will emerge, with females going in search of a blood meal, and may disperse to a number of suitable rivers. Individuals of *S. truncatum* thus have a more generalist strategy: those at the lake outlet can benefit from the good food supply there, but those in the main part of the river will have a lower risk of being affected by environmental disturbance, e.g., sudden drying.

At a site in southern Sweden, and at the site in Great Britain, only immatures at the immediate lake outlet were investigated, and in the summer months these were exclusively *S. noelleri*. Larvae and pupae are present in dense aggregations (more than 120 individuals cm^{-2}; Wotton, in preparation), this being very much a "clumping species" (Harding and Colbo 1981). From investigations at these locations, and from the study in Finland, the following conclusions can be made about the biology and life-history strategies of *S. noelleri*.

Factors that Promote Coexistence of Individuals

Combinations of the following characteristics of *S. noelleri* will permit the development of high population density of the immature stages.

1. Larvae of all sizes can filter the range of particles present in the water (up to a certain maximum diameter), though the abundant microfines (Wotton 1984a) will be filtered with lower efficiency. The larger a larva becomes, the greater its ability to capture particles > 52 μm in diameter and the lower its ability to capture particles < 13 μm in diameter (these dimensions relating to the size of particles used in experiments; Wotton 1984b). This intraspecific variation in electivity, which probably results from differences in the feeding apparatus, will promote the coexistence of different-sized individuals, an important factor in creating high population density when development is not synchronous. In the first summer generation of *S. noelleri*, larvae show synchronized early development, since they hatch from eggs laid in masses by females of the winter generation. They therefore colonize the sluice as

small larvae and maintain their position as they grow in size, creating aggregations of high biomass. As adults of the first summer generation emerge from the river for several days, the subsequent generations do not show the same degree of synchrony of larval development, and the difference in electivity could become important in the partitioning of the food resource should this become limiting.

2. There is a marked sexual dimorphism in the size of adults, pharate adults, pupae, pharate pupae, and, presumably, in the size of larvae (Wotton 1982b). Larvae of different size will therefore not only be those of different age but also those of different sex. Such differences should again promote coexistence (Wilson 1975) and the formation of aggregations.

3. The larger a larva becomes, the lower its tolerance of low current velocity. Small larvae have a much higher tolerance of low current velocity, and this will allow their coexistence with larger larvae in dense aggregations where smaller individuals will be occluded (Wotton 1985.)

Effect of Body Size on Energetics and the Advantages of Large Body Size in Adults

Once larvae have achieved a certain body size, the ratio of assimilated energy lost in respiration to that used for growth becomes less than one (Wotton 1978). The result will be that larger larvae are relatively more efficient in growth, and this partly explains their considerable increase in weight in the later life stages. It is known that larger larvae are more likely to ingest surface film (Wotton 1982c), which may provide a high-quality food, and they also have a longer gut-throughput rate, which should increase assimilation efficiency (Wotton 1978). Both factors will be important in maintaining autogeny and the development of large body size, known to be correlated with increased fecundity in female flies.

It is likely that female flies, on emerging from the river, will mate and then fly a short distance to take a meal of nectar and mature their eggs; a process that lasts about five days (extrapolating from laboratory studies; Wotton, unpublished data). Female flies will then search for a suitable lake outlet for oviposition, and this is highly likely to be the outlet from which they recently emerged. There will be a reduced risk of mortality for these female flies as they do not have to fly to, and from, a host and have to run the gauntlet of its antibiting strategy. This is another reason why autogeny is an advantage to the flies in the first gonotrophic cycle. After laying the first batch of eggs, the females will need to go in search of a blood meal, however, before they can lay more eggs.

Females that have just laid eggs will have about 50% of the total body weight they had before oviposition (Wotton, unpublished data), and this considerably reduced body mass will mean that much less induced power is required to overcome the weight of the body. The result will be an altered power curve (Pennycuick 1972), and assuming that parasite power (that needed to overcome the profile drag of the body) is not markedly affected by the decreased size of the abdomen, the result will be an increased ability to disperse; I call them "empty freighters." The dispersal may take female flies over large distances, and this will usually mean that the second batch of eggs, matured after a blood meal, will be laid in a different lake outlet than where the parents spent larval life. This will provide "bet-hedging," the offspring being located at different lake outlets, each with their own risk of drying or flooding. It is not known what proportion of individuals completes more than one gonotrophic cycle.

Dispersal ability will also be increased with increasing size (Roff 1977), and it is known that within one generation females that are late emerging are larger than those that emerge early (Wotton 1982a). The latter will have a lower risk of being affected by environmental catastrophe because they spend a shorter time as immatures. The larger, late-emerging female flies will have been exposed to higher risk, but this will be compensated by higher fecundity (Wotton 1982a).

Another feature of *S. noelleri* is that adults from the densest parts of aggregations are larger than those from areas with lower population density (Wotton, unpublished data). Aggregation could therefore provide a means of achieving higher fecundity without exposure to increased risk: larvae within an aggregation reduce the risk of predation as potential predators will be "swamped," and aggregation will provide a short-term defense against drying, since water is trapped within the mass of immatures.

This section has concentrated on the advantages to females of late emergence, or being part of an aggregation. Male flies will show a similar range of emergence times and are also larger in size when part of dense aggregations. The advantage to male flies is less clear, though late-emerging males will certainly have the opportunity to mate with potentially more fecund females, and larger size may promote increased flying ability and therefore a higher chance of mating successfully.

There is a buildup of detritus and fecal material over the substratum to which larvae and pupae are attached. This allows the development of a community, the animal component of which consists of larval chironomids and oligochaetes. The processing of detritus by these mutualists may be important in providing food for the developing black flies, in addition to that which is obtained by filter-feeding from the water column. A disadvantage is that this detritus also provides a substratum through which larvae of *Limnophora* sp., the only apparent predator at the site in Great Britain, can burrow to attack larvae.

CONCLUSIONS

Lake-outlet black flies provide a means of studying the life-history strategies shown by habitat specialists and of investigating the biology of single-species aggregations. As the community of animals at artificial lake outlets is simple compared to that in the river downstream, there is also good potential for testing theories on interspecific associations.

ACKNOWEDGMENTS

I am grateful to the NSF and Goldsmiths' College for financial assistance and would like to thank Professor K. C. Kim and the organizing committee of the conference for inviting me to attend. An anonymous referee provided many helpful suggestions on an earlier version of this paper.

LITERATURE CITED

Benke, A. C., T. C. van Arsdall, and D. M. Gillespie. 1984. Invertebrate productivity in a subtropical river: the importance of habitat and life history. *Ecol. Monogr.* 54:25–63.

Carlsson, G. 1962. Studies on Scandinavian blackflies. *Opusc. Entomol. Suppl.* 21:1–279.

Carlsson, M., L. M. Nilsson, Bj. Svensson, S. Ulfstrand, and R. S. Wotton. 1977. Lacustrine seston and other factors influencing the blackflies (Diptera: Simuliidae) inhabiting lake outlets in Swedish Lapland. *Oikos* 29:229–238.

Chutter, F. M. 1968. On the ecology of the fauna of stones in the current in a South African river supporting a very large *Simulium* (Diptera) population. *J. Appl. Ecol.* 5:531–561.

Colbo, M. H. 1982. Size and fecundity of adult Simuliidae (Diptera) as a function of stream habitat, year, and parasitism. *Can. J. Zool.* 60:2507–13.

Colbo, M. H., and D. E. Moorhouse. 1979. The ecology of pre-imaginal Simuliidae (Diptera) in south-east Queensland, Australia. *Hydrobiologia* 63:63–79.

Cupp, E. W., and A. E. Gordon. 1983. Notes on the systematics, distribution, and bionomics of Black Flies (Diptera: Simuliidae) in the northeastern United States. *Search Agriculture*, no. 25. 75 pp.

Davies, D. M., H. Györkös, and J. E. Raastad. 1977. Simuliidae (Diptera) of Rendalen, Norway. IV. Autogeny and anautogeny. *Norw. J. Entomol.* 24:19–23.

Davies, L. 1961. Ecology of two *Prosimulium* species (Diptera) with reference to their ovarian cycles. *Can. Entomol.* 93:1113–40.

———. 1968. A key to the British species of Simuliidae (Diptera) in the larval, pupal and adult stages. *Scient. Publs. Freshwater Biol. Assoc.* 24:1–126.

Harding, J., and M. H. Colbo. 1981. Competition for attachment sites between larvae of Simuliidae (Diptera). *Can. Entomol.* 113:761–763.

Hutchinson, G. E. 1958. Concluding remarks. *Cold Spring Harbor Symp. Quant. Biol.* 22:415–427.

Illies, J. 1957. Seeausfluss-Biozönosen lappländischer Waldbächen. *Entomol. Tidskr.* 77:138–153.

Imhof, J. E., and S. M. Smith. 1979. Oviposition behaviour, egg-masses and hatching response of the eggs of five nearctic species of *Simulium* (Diptera: Simuliidae). *Bull. Entomol. Res.* 69:405–425.

Knöpp, H. 1952. Studien zur Statik und zur Dynamik der Biocönose eines Teichenausflusses. *Arch. Hydrobiol.* 46:15–102.

Kurtak, D. C. 1974. Overwintering of *Simulium pictipes* Hagen (Diptera: Simuliidae) as eggs. *J. Med. Entomol.* 11:383–384.

Ladle, M., J. A. B. Bass, and W. R. Jenkins. 1972. Studies on production and food consumption by the larval Simuliidae (Diptera) of a chalk stream. *Hydrobiologia* 39:429–448.

Lake, D. J., and J. F. Burger. 1983. Larval distribution and succession of outlet-breeding blackflies (Diptera: Simuliidae) in New Hampshire. *Can. J. Zool.* 61:2519–33.

Mohsen, Z. H., and M. S. Mulla. 1982. The ecology of blackflies (Diptera: Simuliidae) in some southern California streams. *J. Med. Entomol.* 19:72–85.

Müller, K. 1955. Produktionsbiologische Untersuchungen in nordschwedischen Fliessgewässern. Teil 3: Die Bedeutung der Seen und Stillwasserzonen für die Produktion in Fliessgewässern. *Rep. Freshwater Res. Drottningholm* 36:148–162.

Olejnicek, J. 1983. A contribution to the knowledge of biology of the species *Eusimulium securiforme* Rubzov, 1956. *Folia Parasitol.* (Praha) 30:73–77.

Pennycuick, C. J. 1972. *Animal flight.* Edward Arnold, London. 68 pp.

Reisen, W. K. 1977. The ecology of Honey Creek, Oklahoma: population dynamics and drifting behavior of three species of *Simulium* (Diptera: Simuliidae). *Can. J. Zool.* 55:325–337.

Roff, D. 1977. Dispersal in dipterans: its cost and consequences. *J. Anim. Ecol.* 46:443–456.

Rothfels, K. 1981. Cytotaxonomy: principles and their application to some northern species-complexes. Pp. 19–29 in M. Laird, Ed., *Blackflies: the future for biological methods in integrated control.* Academic Press, New York and London.

Rubtzov, I. A. 1956. Nutrition and facultativity of bloodthirstiness in blackflies. *Entomol. Obozr.* 35:731–751 (in Russian).

Scullion, J., C. A. Parish, N. Morgan, and R. W. Edwards. 1982. Comparison of benthic macroinvertebrate fauna and substratum composition in riffles and pools in the impounded River Elan and the unregulated River Wye, mid-Wales. *Freshwater Biol.* 12:579–595.

Sheldon, A. L., and M. W. Oswood. 1977. Blackfly (Diptera: Simuliidae) abundance in a lake outlet: test of a predictive model. *Hydrobiologia* 56:113–120.

Ulfstrand, S. 1968. Benthic animal communities in Lapland streams. *Oikos Suppl.* 10:1–120.

Wilson, D. S. 1975. The adequacy of body size as a niche difference. *Am. Nat.* 109:769–784.

Wotton, R. S. 1977. Sampling moorland stream blackfly larvae. *Arch. Hydrobiol.* 79:404–412.

———. 1978. Growth, respiration, and assimiliation of blackfly larvae (Diptera: Simuliidae) in a lake-outlet in Finland. *Oecologia* (Berlin) 33:279–290.

———. 1979. The influence of a lake on the distribution of blackfly species (Diptera: Simuliidae) along a river. *Oikos* 32:368–372.

———. 1982a. Different life history strategies in lake-outlet blackflies (Diptera: Simuliidae). *Hydrobiologia* 96:243–251.

———. 1982b. Difference in carbon weight of the immature stages of two co-existing species of blackflies (Diptera: Simuliidae) with contrasting reproductive strategies. *Hydrobiologia* 94:279–283.

———. 1982c. Does the surface film of lakes provide a source of food for animals living in lake outlets? *Limnol. Oceanogr.* 27:959–960.

———. 1984a. The importance of identifying the origins of microfine particles in aquatic systems. *Oikos* 43:217–221.

———. 1984b. The relationship between food particle size and larval size in *Simulium noelleri* Friederichs. *Freshwater Biol.* 14:547–550.

———. 1985. The reaction of larvae of *Simulium noelleri* (Diptera) to different current velocities. *Hydrobiologia* 123:215–218.

Yakuba, V. N. 1959. On the migrations of black-fly larvae (Diptera, Simuliidae). *Entomol. Obozr.* 38:424–434 (in Russian).

Zwick, H. 1978. Simuliidae. Pp. 396–403 in J. Illies, Ed., *Limnofauna Europaea.* Gustav Fischer Verlag, Stuttgart.

12   FEEDING STRATEGIES OF LARVAL BLACK FLIES

Douglas C. Currie and Douglas A. Craig

Simuliid larvae are among the most easily recognized inhabitants of running waters. The character that distinguishes them from most other benthic invertebrates is the elegant pair of labral fans that serve in filter feeding. So conspicuous are these fans that it is seldom deemed necessary to ascribe to these organisms any feeding strategy other than filtering. In the course of this chapter, we will show that filtering is but one of a number of feeding strategies employed by larval simuliids, not only at the family and generic levels but also at that of the species and individual.

Larval feeding strategies of simuliids are of interest to workers in several disciplines. Systematists and functional morphologists rely in part on the feeding strategies (and their attendant adaptations) to help resolve phylogenetic relationships (Dumbleton 1962; Davies 1965, 1974; Wood 1978). This applies to relationships both within the Simuliidae and the suborder Nematocera. The applied entomologist seeks environmentally sound means by which to control pestiferous simuliids. Efforts have been directed toward formulation of particulate larvicides that are selective: i.e., ingested by simuliids, but not by nontarget organisms (Kershaw et al. 1968, Wenk and Dinkel 1981). Stream ecologists attempt to describe the structure and function of communities along river systems—the River Continuum Concept (Vannote et al. 1980). An important component of that type of investigation is resolution of trophic relationships of invertebrates and the role they play in nutrient cycling. All these disciplines require an understanding of feeding strategies of larval simuliids.

Colbo and Wotton (1981) recently provided a review of larval feeding in Simuliidae. Concentrating mainly on filtering species, they briefly discussed aspects of morphology, behavior, size of particles captured, feeding rates, and assimilation efficiencies. Our treatment is oriented more toward the functional morphology and behavioral aspects of larval feeding.

Using the general classification system for aquatic insect trophic relationships (Cummins 1973), we identify four feeding strategies used by larval Simuliidae: collectors-filterers, scrapers, collectors-gatherers, and predators. These feeding groups are dealt with individually, and we present a range of tactics employed within each category. The significance of eclectic feeding strategies of larval simuliids is discussed in relation to systematics, applied entomology, and ecology.

COLLECTORS-FILTERERS

According to Cummins (1973), filter or suspension feeders are a subdivision of the "collectors" functional feeding group. Such organisms remove living and decomposing organic matter suspended in the water column. The particle size that filter feeders ingest is generally less than 1×10^{-3} μm. Simuliid larvae are known to take particles ranging in size from 0.091–350 μm (Wotton 1976, Chance 1977).

Simuliid larvae are particularly well adapted for filter feeding, since most possess a pair of labral fans. Each fan consists of a series of long, curved, primary rays (Fig. 12.1). Each ray has a row of microtrichia that points into the water current (Figs. 12.1, 12.2, and 12.3). Detailed accounts on structure and function of labral fans are given elsewhere (see Colbo and Wotton 1981 for review).

It has long been assumed that particle capture by simuliid larvae was effected by sieving, with larger particles being trapped between the primary rays and smaller particles between microtrichia. However, sieving (= direct interception) is but one of a number of filtration mechanisms suggested for filter-feeding organisms (Rubenstein and Koehl 1977). Ross and Craig (1980) examined filter-feeding mechanisms in simuliids in detail and suggested that the direct interception mechanism, and perhaps that of inertial impaction, working in concert, could be invoked to explain the ability of simuliids to filter such a wide range of particle sizes.

Braimah (1985), using scaled-up models of portions of primary fan rays, concludes that the boundary layer around individual microtrichia is such that water cannot flow appreciably between them. Therefore, the direct interception filtration mechanism is probably not applicable to particles much smaller than 3 μm. This is an important discovery because much of the fine particulate organic matter (FPOM) in flowing water is of this size or smaller (Ross and Craig 1980). Similar results were obtained by Gerritsen and Porter (1982), who studied filtration mechanisms in *Daphnia* Muller. Braimah (1985) obtained better correlation between particle distribution in the gut and that in the water when a diffusion mechanism was invoked. Therefore, as far as water flowing through the fan is concerned, microtrichia probably act as a single, solid structure. Indeed, they probably provide the optimal surface area, with minimum material, upon which sticky mucosubstance can be spread (Ross and Craig 1980).

Yankovsky (1978) suggested that the pattern of michrotrichia on rays might be of taxonomic significance. For some species, the microtrichia are all the same length (Fig. 12.2), but a common pattern is for one long microtrichia to be followed by a number of smaller microtrichia (Fig. 12.3). The small ones may all the same size or may decrease in size toward the next long one. With the possible exception of *Cnephia* Enderlein larvae, which will be discussed later, it is doubtful that the arrangement of microtrichia can be used for resolution of higher taxa, for similar patterns occur independently within many genera of simuliids (personal observation).

If microtrichia serve to increase the surface area of labral fans, then different conformations might be expected in different habitats. Lacey and Lacey (1983) showed that larvae of *Simulium fulvinotum* Cerqueira & Mello, which inhabit fast-flowing, food-poor streams, possess long microtrichia. The converse, shorter microtrichia in water with a high particle load, might also be expected. However, Nübel (1984) examined several morphological parameters of fans of six species of simuliids and did not find evidence that differences had any role in separation of ecological niche.

Fans of larvae of *Cnephia dacotensis* (Dyar & Shannon) and of *C. ornithopilia* Davies, Peterson & Wood have highly modified microtrichia on delicate primary rays. The normal long microtrichia are extremely elongate and alternately extend laterally toward the other rays. The intervening microtrichia are variously reduced but very much shorter. This arrangement forms a true sieve (Fig. 12.4). A consequence of this arrangement must be greater drag on the fan and hence smaller discharge of water through the fan (Vogel 1984). *Cnephia* larvae can live in water of lower velocity and enhanced particulate matter. B. Thompson (personal communication) has clearly shown that *C. ornithopilia* larvae preferentially capture a narrower size range of larger particles than other simuliid larvae. Although *C. dacotensis* larvae have been observed in eutrophic water with velocities greater than 180 cm /s (personal observation) and in cascades from impounded waters (Galloway and Crosskey, personal communication), it appears that these larvae have in part relinquished the ability to deal with faster water with low particle load and have adapted to slower flows and more specific food. In western Canada, larvae of *C. dacotensis* are often the first to hatch in the spring in highly eutrophic, slow-flowing streams, and they usually complete development long before other spring-emerging species of simuliid (personal observation). That is, they are adapted to a very specific, rich food source, which is temporary, but predictable (spring runoff), and thus are able to complete larval development with a minimum of competition from other filterers.

At present our understanding of the relationship of fan structures to hydrodynamic forces exerted upon them is rudimentary. Flowing water produces drag, which is proportional to velocity of flow and to area of structure exposed to flow. Although simuliid body shape and posture help reduce drag (Craig and Chance 1982; Chance and Craig 1986; Craig and Galloway, this volume), fan rays must also be able to resist drag. When the fans cannot resist drag, they collapse and filter feeding is interrupted (personal observation).

Fortner (1937), Grenier (1949), and Carlsson (1962) felt that flow and/or food affected size and strength of the labral fan rays, and we concur. In general, larvae that inhabit fast-flowing water have relatively small fans in proportion to the size of the head. The fan rays also tend to be more robust in such habitats. Relatively large, delicate fans are more characteristic of larvae in slow-flowing water. An interesting example that may relate to this was the replacement of *Simulium arcticum* Malloch complex larvae by those of *S. luggeri* Nicholson & Mickel complex in the South Saskatchewan River (Fredeen 1979). This replacement followed flow-control projects that significantly altered the discharge and turbidity of the river. Fans of *S. luggeri* larvae are more delicate than those of *S. arcticum* and are presumably better adapted to filter optimally in the slower flow and reduced turbidity of the altered habitat.

Although relatively little is known about them, the phoretic larvae of some species of African simuliids are of considerable interest. The labral fans of *S. lumbwanum*

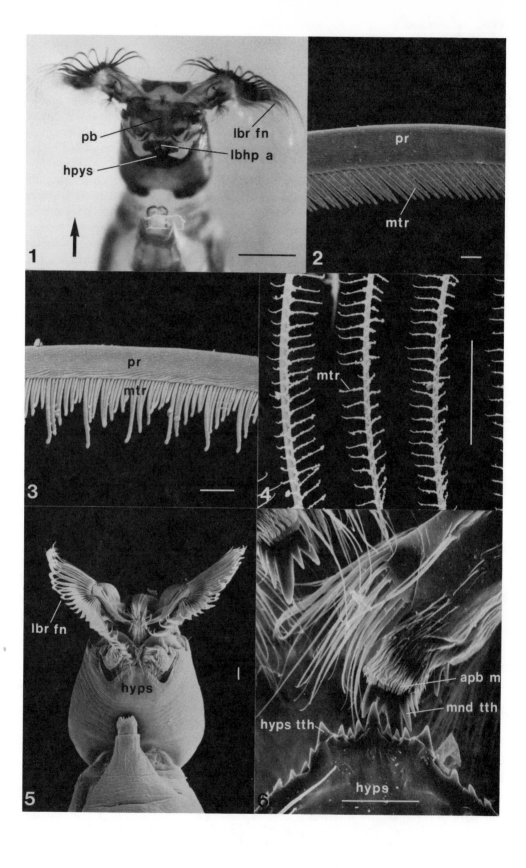

de Meillon larvae are extremely delicate (Crosskey 1969). However, these larvae are found on nymphs of *Afronurus* Lestage (Ephemeroptera), which inhabit clean rocks in fast-flowing water (Disney 1971). How these delicate fans resist the probable high current velocity of the host's habitat is not known. This clearly requires more detailed examination of the microhabitats and behavior of both mayfly host and the *S. lumbwanum* larvae.

Other phoretic larvae have highly aberrant labral fans. Those of *S. moucheti* (Fig. 12.5), instead of being held dorsally and of hemispherical shape, are turned ventrally and form short, flat brushes. The secondary fan is small and probably nonfunctional. Our impression is that the primary fan rays are not used for filtration as such. Marlier (in Burton and McRae 1972) reported that the gut contents of *S. marlieri* Grenier larvae, which have similarly modified fans, have the same type of vegetable fragments in the gut contents as did the host mayfly nymphs. While these highly modified fans may be used for filtration, it is more likely that they are being used for scraping or grazing (see below).

The behavioral component in filter feeding is only now beginning to be understood. Because of the high percentage of time that *S. vittatum* Zetterstedt larvae spend with their fans adducted during filter feeding, Craig and Chance (1982) suggested that a possible strategy for larvae to increase filtering efficiency would be to reduce the time spent cleaning the fans. Concentration of particulate matter in the water is known to affect feeding behavior (Kurtak 1978; Chance 1977; Schröder 1980, 1981; Hart 1985; Hart and Latta 1986). That may be because, for optimal filtration, a filter must remain clean (Rubenstein and Koehl 1977). Indeed, Lacey and Lacey (1983) reported that larvae of *S. fulvinotum* in low-particulate, blackwater streams keep their fans open for up to two minutes! This contrasts with 0.15 second for larvae of *S. vittatum* (Craig and Chance 1982).

SCRAPERS (GRAZERS)

The second most important feeding strategy among larval simuliids is scraping or grazing. Scrapers forage over submerged substrates for algae and associated material

Opposite:
FIGS. 12.1–12.6: (1) Ventral view of head of *Prosimulium travisi* larva. Arrow indicates direction of water flow during filter feeding. Scale = 0.50 mm; (2) middle portion of a primary ray of labral fan of *Simulium tahitiense* larvae, showing microtrichial pattern. Scale = 5.0μm; (3) as for (2), but *Simulium bivittatum*. Scale = 5.0 μm; (4) primary rays and elongated microtrichia of *Cnephia dacotensis* labral fan, showing sievelike arrangement. Scale = 50.0 μm; (5) ventral view of head of phoretic larva of *Simulium moucheti*. Scale = 50.0 μm; and (6) mandibular-hypostomal functional complex of *Simulium vittatum* larva. Scale = 50.0 μm.

KEY

apb m	— apical brush of mandible	mnd tth	— mandibular teeth
hyps	— hypostoma	mtr	— microtrichia
hyps tth	— hypostomal teeth	pb	— palatal brush
lbhp a	— labiohypopharyngeal apparatus	pr	— primary ray of labral fan
lbr fn	— labral fan		

(= periphyton) (Cummins 1973). Although the majority of simuliid larvae are filter feeders and are equipped with well-developed labral fans, many are also known to be capable of scraping (Puri 1925, Peterson 1956, Serra-Tosio 1967, Chance 1970, Craig 1977). Scraping in the typical fanned larva is effected mainly by the mandibles and the labrum (Chance 1970), but the hypostoma may also be involved. The hypostoma arises anteromedially from the ventral wall of the head capsule and has along its anterior margin a series of heavily sclerotized, pointed teeth (Figs. 12.1 and 12.6). When a mandible adducts, the apical mandibular teeth interdigitate with those of the hypostoma, thus forming a functional complex (Craig 1977). Although this complex is thought to function in silk cutting, the co-adaptation of hypostomal and mandibular teeth may also serve as a "pan and broom" arrangement for transfer of food into the cibarium. This action may be aided by the apical brush on the anteroventral surface of the mandible (Fig. 12.6). Hairs of the labiohypopharyngeal apparatus (Fig. 12.1) possibly serve to clean this apical brush. The labrum of typical simuliid larvae is beaklike and variously covered with bristles (= palatal brush) (Fig. 12.1). Bristles on the ventral lobe of the labrum are also thought to be used in grazing (Chance 1970).

As opposed to filter feeding, during which larvae are sedentary, scraping is a very active process, requiring constant movement within and between feeding sites. Loco-motion between feeding sites proceeds in an "inchworm" fashion, the thoracic and anal prolegs being alternately attached and released from the substrate (Barr 1984). Once at a feeding site, a larva attaches both prolegs to the substrate and commences scraping. The process can only occur with the labral fans adducted, except in larvae of *Simulium oviceps* Edwards and others of that complex that possess short fans (Craig 1977, 1983). The thoracic proleg is constantly removed and reapplied to the substrate as the larva browses on either side and in front of itself. Because attached larvae are unable to forage immediately behind themselves, the periphyton is re-moved in a U-shaped pattern (Serra-Tosio 1967). Having depleted the periphyton at one feeding site, the larva must relocate to continue browsing.

It has yet to be determined what proportion of simuliid species actually scrape at some stage during their larval development; or, in species that are known to scrape on occasion, what proportion of their diet is obtained by this strategem. According to Mokry (1975), larval activity of *Simulium venustum* Say s.l. is equally divided between filter feeding, scraping, and resting. Similar results have been found for *S. oviceps,* by Craig (1977). Craig found the guts of *S. oviceps* larvae to contain mainly large inorganic particles and periphyton, indicating that browsing was probably more important nutritionally than filter feeding.

In these instances, browsing constitutes a significant proportion of the larva's activity. Because scraping occurs in a variety of taxa and in diverse geographic regions (Burton 1973), we believe that occasional browsing is a characteristic feeding behavior of Simuliidae larvae.

The foregoing applies to facultative scrapers, those that can feed either by filtering or scraping; but there are some larval simuliids that possess highly modified fans (e.g., *Crozetia crozetensis* [Womersley]), or lack them altogether (*Twinnia* Stone & Jamnback, *Gymnopais* Stone). In these taxa, larvae are unable to filter-feed and obtain most of their food through scraping. We refer to these larvae as obligatory scrapers.

Crozetia Davies is a monotypic genus that occurs only on the remote, subantarctic Crozet Islands. The larva of this simuliid possess labral fans that are short and rakelike (Fig. 12.8). When applied to the substrate, the fans flick 2–3 times a second (Davies 1974). Food captured in that fashion is presumably removed from the "labral rake" by a dense series of hairs on the inner apical margin of the mandible (Fig. 12.7). The general bladelike form of the mandibular and hypostomal teeth, and the excessive wear on them, indicates that the teeth are involved in scraping. Gut analyses of *Crozetia* larvae have shown large blocks of filamentous algae (Dumbleton 1962; personal observation).

Larvae of *Twinnia* and *Gymnopais* are restricted to pristine headwater streams in mountainous regions of Eurasia and North America. The larval heads of these simuliids are similiar in shape, being ovoid in dorsal view, and tapering anteriorly to a conical labrum (Figs. 12.9 and 12.10). This contrasts with the typical larval head, which is more or less parallel-sided (Fig. 12.1), terminating in a rather broad labrum. Without labral fans, larvae of *Twinnia* and *Gymnopais* rely upon flattened, bladelike teeth on the hypostoma and mandibles for scraping. The condition in typical simuliid larvae is for the teeth to be pointed and conical (Fig. 12.6). But in fanless larvae, the hypostomal and mandibular teeth become progressively more worn and chipped toward the end of each larval instar (Wood 1978), thus indicating their importance in scraping (compare Fig. 12.11 with Fig. 12.12, and Fig. 12.13 with Fig. 12.14). *Gymnopais* larvae are further adapted by possessing a dense series of stout, spinelike projections (= apical brush) on the aboral surface of the mandible (Fig. 12.13). These too become worn through use (Fig. 12.14) and presumably serve in transferring periphyton into the cibarium.

The labra of larvae of *Gymnopais* and *Twinnia* differ greatly from those of filtering species (Chance 1970; personal observation). They are elongate and conical and terminate in a pronounced palatal brush (Figs. 12.9 and 12.10). This brush is distinguished by the presence of a dorsal, differentiated region of well-developed bristles. The tips of these are curved and are either simple at their apex (e.g., *Twinnia nova* [Dyar & Shannon] Chance 1970) or pectinate (Fig. 12.15) (e.g., *Twinnia tibblesi* [Stone & Jamnback], Davies 1965; *Gymnopais holopticus* Stone, personal observation). The palatal brush is applied to the substrate during feeding and is observed to be retracted when the mandibles extend (Chance 1970; personal observation).

Not all adaptations for scraping are restricted to the head. The larval abdomens of *Crozetia, Gymnopais,* and *Twinnia* (and that of *S. oviceps*) are all similarly adapted for this feeding strategem. Abdominal segments 1 through 4 are relatively narrow and "corrugated" (fig. 1 in Davies 1974), thus providing the flexibility necessary to bend the body in a tight U-shape. The abdomen expands abruptly at segment 5 and tapers posteriorly to a rather small anal proleg. This arragement permits browsing of a broad C-shaped (rather than a narrow U-shaped) pattern around the larva's point of attachment. Thus at any given feeding site, obligate scrapers are able to feed over a wider area than can facultative scrapers. The fact that similar body forms have evolved independently among obligate scrapers suggests that an advantage is gained through increased flexibility.

COLLECTOR-GATHERERS (DEPOSIT FEEDERS)

According to Cummins (1973), collector-gatherers feed upon decomposing, fine particulate organic matter (FPOM) that is deposited as a loose surface film. For simuliid

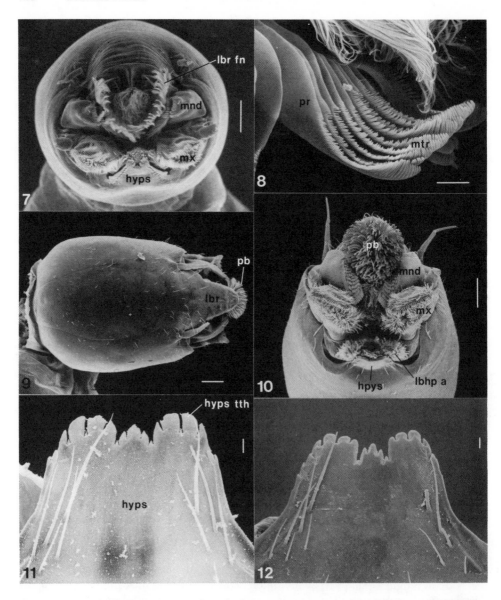

FIG. 12.7–12.12: (7) Frontal view of head of *Crozetia crozetensis* larva. Scale = 100.0 μm; (8) Dorsal view of labral fan of *Crozetia crozetensis* larva, showing rakelike primary rays. Scales= μm; (9) Dorsal view of head of *Gymnopais holopticus* larva, showing tapered labrum. Scale = 100.0 μm; (10) anteroventral view of head of *Gymnopais holopticus* larva. Scale = 100 μm; (11) Hypostoma of teneral last-instar larva of *Gymnopais holopticus,* showing unworn teeth. Scale = 10.0 μm; and (12) as for (13), but of late last instar, showing worn teeth. Scale = 10.0 μm.

KEY

hyps	— hypostoma	mtr	— microtrichia
hyps tth	— hypostomal teeth	mx	— maxilla
lbhp a	— labiohypopharyngeal apparatus	pb	— palatal brush
lbr fn	— labral fan	pr	— primary ray of labral fan
mnd	— mandible		

FIGS. 12.13–12.16: (13) Mandible of teneral last-instar larvae of *Gymnopais holopticus,* showing unworn condition of teeth and apical brush. Scale=10.0 μm; (14) as for (15), but of late last instar, showing worn condition of teeth and apical brush. Scale = 10.0 μm; (15) pectinate bristles of palatal brush of *Gymnopais holopticus* larva. Scale = 10.0 μm; (16) larva of *Prosimulium travisi* preying upon chironomid larva. Scale = 100.0 μm

KEY

apb m   — apical brush of mandible
chir larva — chironomid larva
mnd tth   — mandibular teeth

larvae foraging on the substrate, the distinction between scraping and deposit feeding may not be that useful. This is because periphyton and particulate organic matter often occur together on the substrate, and a browsing larva probably does not distinguish components of its food.

Recent work on simuliid larvae of temporary streams has shown that under certain conditions larvae are capable of descending into the substrate—the hyporheic zone (personal observation). Here periphyton and suspended organic material are replaced by deposited organic matter as the dominant food source (Williams 1984). These conditions often prevail in arctic and subarctic springs, where fanless larvae of *Gymnopais* species coexist with fully fanned larvae of *Prosimulium* Roubaud. This habitat is prone to becoming dry in late summer, and during such periods the larvae of both genera descend into the substrate (personal observation). Depending upon the severity of the drought, larvae can persist and even pupate within the streambed. In instances where surface flow returns (after precipitation), larvae reestablish on the substrate surface. Preliminary observations suggest that larvae may also enter the hyporheic zone during spate conditions (D. Giberson, personal communication; Eymann 1985). Similar results have been found for other invertebrates of intermittent streams (Clifford 1966). In either case, larvae are probably dependent upon interstitial organic deposits during their stay in the hyporheos. Direct observation of hyporheic feeding has not been made, but we presume that particulate organic matter is acquired in the same fashion as periphyton (see section on scrapers).

Fanless larvae (*Gymnopais, Twinnia*) may have an advantage over typical simuliids in the hyporheos because their tapered heads are better suited for movement in interstitial spaces. Organisms with similarly constructed heads are richly represented in hyporheic habitats (e.g., larval chironomids, ceratopogonids), whereas fanned simuliid larvae are more characteristic of surface substrates (Coleman and Hynes 1970). This may in part explain why fanless simuliid larvae, where they occur, outnumber their fanned counterparts in temporary headwater springs.

Simuliid larvae possibly may resort to deposit feeding in drought-stricken streams in Africa. Members of the *Simulium neavei* Roubaud complex possess fully fanned larvae that occur phoretically on crabs. During periods when the stream becomes dry, the crabs (and attached simuliid larvae) descend into the moist mud and sand beneath the surface rocks (Raybould et al. 1978). Here they can remain for several weeks until surface flow returns. Larvae in still water have been observed to browse for food, and they presumably continue to do so beneath the substrate (Raybould et al. 1978). The most likely form of food during the periods of drought is deposited particulate organic matter.

Unlike most larval simuliids, which are facultative inhabitants of the hyporheos, the recently discovered blind, unpigmented larvae of *Parasimulium* Malloch are apparently restricted to life beneath the substrate. Although fully fanned, the presence of coarse particles within the gut suggests that larvae deposit feed, at least occasionally. However, it is likely that there is sufficient current in the hyporheos to make filter feeding possible (Courtney 1986).

Oviposition sites of simuliid adults may determine what food is available for a newly hatched larva. According to Colbo and Wotton (1981), in the original and most common type of oviposition the female drops her eggs into the water as she flies over the stream. These eggs sink to the bottom and often become buried deep in the substrate (e.g., Fredeen et al. 1951, Davies and Syme 1958, Colbo and Moorhouse 1974). Upon hatching, the most readily available food would be deposited particulate organic matter. First-instar larvae of *Prosimulium, Twinnia,* and *Gymnopais* either lack labral fans or possess very simple structures (Craig 1974), so they are probably incapable of filtering. Larvae may instead rely upon rakelike hairs on the anteromedian palatal brush to gather food. First-instar simuliines generally possess well-developed fans, but again it is questionable how effectively they filter, considering the small size of the body and the thickness of the boundary layer on the substrate (Craig and Galloway, this volume). Therefore, deposit feeding may account for a significant proportion of a larva's diet, at least in the early instars. This area requires further study.

PREDATORS

The occurrence of animal matter within the gut of larval simuliids is widely reported. Larval and drowned adult chironomids (Serra-Tosio 1967), early-instar simuliids

(Burton 1971), first-instar mayfly nymphs (Zahar 1951), protozoans and small crustaceans (Puri 1925), and naidid worms (Davies and Syme 1958) are all occasionally represented in the diet of simuliid larvae. Most authors believe that ingestion of these organisms is accidental—that they are captured in the course of other feeding strategies, such as filtering and browsing. This may explain the occurrence of very small organisms within the gut of larval simuliids. Animal remnants in the gut may also be exuviae or corpses.

Investigation of simuliid larvae from arctic and alpine streams has shown that relatively large prey can be taken (personal observation). At one site in north-central Yukon, a larva of *Prosimulium ursinum* (Edwards) was found in the process of ingesting a *Gymnopais holopticus* Stone larva. The latter was fully one-third the size of the predator. Gut analysis of other *P. ursinum* larvae revealed a variety of prey items, including immature conspecifics, chironomid larvae, mayfly (Baetidae) larvae, stonefly (Nemouridae) larvae, and a tipulid larva. Some of the individual prey items comprised up to half of the entire gut contents. In addition to animal matter, larval guts also contained coarse, decomposing plant fragments. This suggests that prey might have been encountered as larvae foraged for deposited organic material. Similar observations were made further south, in the mountainous regions of western North America.

Although predation in simuliids is probably opportunistic, the size and mobility of prey items such as mayflies and stoneflies indicate that *Prosimulium* larvae must actively engage their prey once contacted. The observation that larvae are able to locate and consume dead conspecifics in stagnant water (Wu 1931) suggests some sort of chemoreceptive capability (i.e., prey recognition). In the example of predation shown (Fig. 12.16), the sharp, apical teeth of the larva's mandibles have pierced the prey (a larval chironomid) and are directing it into the cibarium. Simuliids are incapable of dismembering their prey and thus swallow it whole.

That simuliid larvae of arctic and alpine streams resort to predation is hardly surprising if we consider that these habitats are often characterized by low densities of suspended food. Occasional predation is probably a common feature of *Prosimulium* species (and perhaps of other prosimuliine species) that inhabit clear-running, high-altitude, or high-latitude streams.

DISCUSSION AND CONCLUSION

Although the vast majority of larval simuliids are equipped with well-developed labral fans, they are also capable of engaging in other feeding strategies to fulfill their nutritional requirements. This versatility allows them to inhabit widely ranging habitats—from torrential waterfalls to mere trickles, and from food-rich lake outlets to clear-running springs.

What are the implications of such eclectic larval feeding to students of Simuliidae? The phylogenetic significance of labral fans in simuliids has long been debated among systematists (Grenier and Rageau 1960, Dumbleton 1962, Davies 1974). Wood (1978) reviewed this subject and convincingly argued that some form of labral feeding organ is a fundamental (and homologous) feature of the Simuliidae, Culicidae, Dixidae, and Ptychopteridae. This is evidence that these families are derived from a common ancestor, one that fed as a larva with some form of labral brush. If the sister-group relationships proposed by Wood (1978) are accepted, then the primitive simuliid larva would be expected to possess fully functional labral fans. The recent discovery (Courtney 1986) of fully fanned larvae of the supposedly primitive *Parasimulium* corroborates this hypothesis. Absence of fans in larvae of *Gymnopais* and *Twinnia,* and their modification in *Crozetia* and the *S. oviceps* complex, must therefore be the result of loss or reduction.

Larvae of Culicidae, Dixidae, and Ptychopteridae typically use their labral brushes for gathering settled organic deposits from the substrate (= collectors-gatherers). Other mouthparts assist in the transfer of food into the cibarium. Mouthparts of simuliid larvae are fundamentally similar to those mentioned above (Craig 1974, Wood 1978), except that the labral brush is modified for capturing particles suspended in the water column (= collecting-filtering). Despite this modification of the primary food-gathering device, larval simuliids are capable of other feeding strategies, including deposit feeding. Scraping in simuliids appears to be nothing more than a modified form of deposit feeding, except that living (periphyton), rather than decomposing, food is ingested. Predation is probably opportunistic in larval Simuliidae, for there appear to be no morphological adaptations specific to that feeding strategy. This contrasts with major morphological adaptations for predation in some Culicidae.

Studies of larval feeding strategies have already been used to resolve relationships among some nematoceran families (Wood 1978). Such investigations may also lead to a better understanding of relationships within the Simuliidae. Larval mouthparts provide useful characters for defining simuliid genera, and future systematic work will rely heavily upon these structures for phylogenetic reconstructions.

The hydrodynamics of larvae and modeling done of their labral fans (Braimah 1985; Craig and Galloway, this volume) opens a particularly rich area for research, not just in relating structure to the forces inherent in a flowing medium, but perhaps in a more applied manner as well. Adult females of many simuliid species with phoretic larvae are vectors of onchocerciasis, and it might be possible to model the mouthparts of these larvae to gain a better understanding of their feeding strategies. Such investigations might provide more effective means of control. One area of research that will benefit from such basic research will be improvements of formulations of *Bacillus thuringiensis* serovar *israelensis* (*B.t.i.*) and other particulate insecticides. Attention will have to be paid to flow of water through the fans if information on the amount of *B.t.i.* endotoxin necessary to effect the larvae is to be determined.

Research on feeding strategies of Simuliidae larvae must now be of an interdisciplinary nature. Hart and Latta (1986) and Hart (this volume) have shown that larvae can change their territorial behavior and filter-feeding behavior in response to food concentration. Very recent work by Biggs (1981 and personal communication) shows that mouthpart movement of larvae determines transit time of gut contents, and that larvae react differently to various types of suspended particles in the water. Such work shows that filter feeding in simuliid larvae is far from passive.

Anderson and Sedell (1979) indicate that most aquatic insects are opportunistic feeders, and thus noncritical acceptance of categories for functional feeding (as, for example, those given by Merritt and Cummins 1984) can lead to misinterpretation of trophic relationships. This is particularly true of simuliid larvae. The simple ascribing of all fanned larvae to the collector-filterer category does not adequately describe the range of feeding strategies displayed by many simuliids. This applies not only at the generic level but also at the level of species and individual. The typical larva is very well adapted for scraping and has been shown to spend up to one-third of its time so engaged. Newly hatched larvae may feed exclusively upon settled organic deposits, depending on where the eggs were oviposited. Headwater simuliids may resort to predation to supplement their diet. Our understanding of trophic relationships of larval Simuliidae depends on a better understanding of the relationship between food availability and feeding behavior.

ACKNOWLEDGMENTS

We thank R. W. Crosskey for constructive comments and W. B. Barr for Figure 12.6. This work was financially supported by a Natural Sciences and Engineering Research Council of Canada grant, No. A5753, to Douglas A. Craig.

LITERATURE CITED

Anderson, N. H., and J. R. Sedell. 1979. Detritus processing by macroinvertebrates in stream ecosystems. *Ann. Rev. Entomol.* 24:351–377.

Barr, W. B. 1984. Prolegs and attachment of *Simulium vittatum* (sibling IS-7) (Diptera: Simuliidae) larvae. *Can. J. Zool.* 62:1355–62.

Biggs, J. 1981. Analysis of behaviour patterns of *Simulium* larvae. In T. R. Williams, Ed., *British* Simulium *Group Newsletter* 6:4–5.

Braimah, A. S. 1985. Mechanisms and fluid mechanical aspects of filter-feeding in black fly larvae (Diptera: Simuliidae) and mayfly nymphs (Ephemeroptera: Oligoneuridae). Ph.D. Thesis, University of Alberta, Edmonton.

Burton, G. J. 1971. Cannibalism among *Simulium damnosum* (Simuliidae) larvae. *Mosquito News* 31:602–603.

———. 1973. Feeding of *Simulium hargreavesi* Gibbons larvae on *Oedogonium* algal filaments in Ghana. *J. Med. Entomol.* 10:101–106.

Burton, G. J., and T. M. McRae. 1972. Phoretic attachment of *Simulium* larvae and pupae to mayfly and dragonfly nymphs. *Mosquito News* 32:436–443.

Carlsson, G. 1962. Studies on Scandinavian black flies. *Opusc. Entomol. Suppl.* 21:1–280.

Chance, M. M. 1970. The functional morphology of the mouthparts of blackfly larvae (Diptera: Simuliidae). *Quaest. Entomol.* 6:245–284.

———. 1977. Influence of water flow and particle concentration on larvae of the black fly *Simulium vittatum* Zett. Diptera: Simuliidae), with emphasis on larval filter-feeding. Ph.D. Thesis, University of Alberta, Edmonton.

Chance, M. M., and D. A. Craig, 1986. Hydrodynamics and behaviour of Simuliidae larvae (Diptera). *Can. J. Zool.* 64:1295–1309.

Clifford, H. F. 1966. The ecology of invertebrates in an intermittent stream. *Invest. Indiana Lakes Streams* 7:57–98.

Colbo, M. H., and D. E. Moorhouse. 1974. The survival of the eggs of *Austrosimulium pestilens* Mack. and Mack. (Diptera: Simuliidae). *Bull. Entomol. Res.* 64:629–632.

Colbo, M. H., and R. S. Wotton. 1981. Preimaginal blackfly bionomics. Pp. 209–226 in M.

Laird, Ed., *Blackflies: the future for biological methods in integrated control.* Academic Press, New York and London.

Coleman, M. J., and H. B. N. Hynes. 1970. The vertical distribution of the invertebrate fauna in the bed of a stream. *Limmol. Oceanogr.* 15:31–40.

Courtney, G. W. 1986. Discovery of the immature stages of *Parasimulium crosskeyi* Peterson (Diptera: simuliidae), with a discussion of a unique black fly habitat. *Proc. Entomol. Soc. Wash.* 88:280–286.

Craig, D. A. 1974. The labrum and cephalic fans of larval Simuliidae (Diptera: Nematocera). *Can. J. Zool.* 52:133–159.

———. 1977. Mouthparts and feeding behaviour of Tahitian larval Simuliidae (Diptera: Nematocera). *Quaest. Entomol.* 13:195–218.

Craig, D. A., and M. M. Chance. 1982. Filter feeding in larvae of Simuliidae (Diptera: Culicomorpha): aspects of functional morphology and hydrodynamics. *Can. J. Zool.* 60:712–724.

Crosskey, R. W. 1969. A re-classification of the Simuliidae (Diptera) of Africa and its islands. *Bull. Br. Mus. Nat. Hist. (Entomol.) Suppl.* 14:1–95.

Cummins, K. W. 1973. Trophic relations of aquatic insects. *Ann. Rev. Entomol.* 18:183–206.

Davies, D. M., and P. D. Syme. 1958. Three new Ontario black flies of the genus *Prosimulium* (Diptera: Simuliidae). Part II. Ecological observations and experiments. *Can. Entomol.* 90:744–759.

Davies, L. 1965. The structure of certain atypical Simuliidae (Diptera) in relation to evolution within the family, and the erection of a new genus for the Crozet Island black-fly. *Proc. Linn. Soc. London* 176:159–180.

———. 1974. Evolution of larval head-fans in Simuliidae (Diptera) as inferred from structure and biology of *Crozetia crozetensis* (Womersley) compared with other genera. *Zool. J. Linn. Soc.* 55:193–224.

Disney, R. H. L. 1971. Two phoretic black-flies (Diptera: Simuliidae) and their associated mayfly hosts (Ephemeroptera: Heptageniidae) in Cameroon. *J. Entomol. (A)* 46:53–61.

Dumbleton, L. J. 1962. Aberrrant head-structure in larval Simuliidae (Diptera). *Pacific Insects* 4:77–86.

Eymann, M. 1985. The behaviours of the blackfly larvae *Simulium vittatum* and *S. decorum* (Diptera: Simuliidae) associated with establishing and maintaining dispersion patterns on natural and artificial substrate. M.Sc. Thesis, University of Toronto.

Fortner, G. 1937. Zur Ernährungsfrage der Simulium-larve. *Z. Morphol. Ökol. Tiere* 32:360–383.

Fredeen, F. J. H. 1979. Blackfly species adapt to change. *Can. Agric.* 24:15–18.

Fredeen, F. J. H., J. G. Rempel, and A. P. Arnason. 1951. Egg-laying habits, overwintering stages, and life-cycle of *Simulium arcticum* Mall. (Diptera: Simuliidae). *Can. Entomol.* 83:73–76.

Gerritsen, J., and K. G. Porter. 1982. The role of surface chemistry in filter feeding zooplankton. *Science* 216:1225–27.

Grenier, P. 1949. Contribution à l'étude biologique des simuliides de France. *Physiol. Comp. Oecol.* 1:168–325.

Grenier, P., and J. Rageau. 1960. Simulies (Dipt., Simuliidae) de Tahiti. Remarques sur la classification des Simuliidae. *Bull. Soc. Pathol. Exot.* 53:727–742.

Hart, D. D. 1986. The adaptive significance of territoriality in filter-feeding larval blackflies (Diptera: Simuliidae). *Oikos* 46:88–92.

Hart, D. D., and S. T. Latta. 1986. Determinants of ingestion rates in filter-feeding larval black flies (Diptera: Simuliidae). *Freshwater Biol.* 16:1–14.

Kershaw, W. E., T. R. Williams, S. Frost, R. L. Matchett, M. E. Mills, and R. D. Johnson.

1968. The selective control of *Simulium* larvae by particulate insecticides and its significance in river management. *Trans. R. Soc. Trop. Med. Hyg.* 62:35–40.

Kurtak, D. C. 1978. Efficiency of filter-feeding of black-fly larvae (Diptera: Simuliidae). *Can. J. Zool.* 56:1608–23.

Lacey, L. A., and J. M. Lacey. 1983. Filter feeding of *Simulium fulvinotum* (Diptera: Simuliidae) in the Central Amazon Basin. *Quaest. Entomol.* 19:41–51.

Merritt, R. W., and K. W. Cummins, Eds. 1984. *An introduction to the aquatic insects of North America*, 2nd ed. Kendall/Hunt, Dubuque, Iowa.

Mokry, J. E. 1975. Studies on the ecology and biology of blackfly larvae utilizing an *in situ* benthobservatory. *Verh. Int. Verein. Limnol.* 19:1546–49.

Nübel, E. 1984. Rasterelektronenmikroskopische Untersuchungen an den Filtrierstrukturen von Kriebelmücken—Larven (Simuliidae, Diptera). *Arch. Hydrobiol. Suppl.* 66:223–253.

Peterson, B. V. 1956. Observations on the biology of Utah black flies (Diptera: Simuliidae). *Can. Entomol.* 88:496–507.

Puri, I. M. 1925. On the life-history and structure of the early stages of Simuliidae (Diptera: Nematocera). Part I. *Parasitology* 17:295–334.

Raybould, J. N., J. Grunwald, and H. K. Mhiddin. 1978. Studies on the immature stages of the *Simulium neavei* Roubaud complex and their associated crabs in the Eastern Usambara Mountains in Tanzania. IV. Observations on the crabs and their attached larvae under exceptionally dry conditions. *Ann. Trop. Med. Parasitol.* 72:189–194.

Ross, D. H., and D. A. Craig. 1980. Mechanisms of fine particle capture by larval black flies (Diptera: Simuliidae). *Can. J. Zool.* 58:1186–92.

Rubenstein, D. I., and M. A. R. Koehl. 1977. The mechanisms of filter feeding: some theoretical considerations. *Am. Nat.* 111:981–994.

Schröder, P. 1980. Zur Ernährungsbiologie der Larven von *Odagmia ornata* Meigen (Diptera: Simuliidae). 1. Die filtriertatigkeit unter dem Einfluss von Fliessgeschwindigkeit, Wassertemperatur und Futterkonzentration. *Arch. Hydrobiol. Suppl.* 59:43–52.

———. 1981. Zur Ernährungsbiologie der Larven von *Odagmia ornata* Meigen (Diptera: Simuliidae). 3. Ingestion, egestion und assimilation. ^{14}C-markierter algen. *Arch. Hydrobiol. Suppl.* 59:97–133.

———. 1984. Tag-Nacht-Beobachtung der Filtriertatigkeit bei Kriebelmückenlarven (Diptera: Simuliidae). *Arch. Hydrobiol. Suppl.* 66:215–222.

Serra-Tosio, B. 1967. La prise de nourriture chez la larve de *Prosimulium inflatum* Davies, 1957 (Diptera: Simuliidae). *Trav. Lab. Hydrobiol. Piscic. Univ. Grenoble* 57–58:97–103.

Vannote, R. L., G. W. Minshall, K. W. Cummins, J. R. Sedell, and C. E. Cushing. 1980. The river continuum concept. *Can. J. Fish. Aquat. Sci.* 37:130–137.

Vogel, S. 1984. How much air passes through a silkmoth's antenna? *J. Insect Physiol.* 29:597–602.

Wallace, J. B., and R. W. Merritt. 1980. Filter-feeding ecology of aquatic insects. *Ann. Rev. Entomol.* 25:103–132.

Wenk, P., and J. Dinkel. 1981. Die Aufnahme von Latex-Partikeln und mikroenkapsuelierten Larviziden durch verschiedene Larvenstadien Simuliiden (Diptera). *Z. Ang. Entomol.* 19:179–197.

Williams, D. D. 1984. The hyporheic zone as a habitat for aquatic insects and associated arthropods. In V. H. Resh and D. M. Rosenberg, Eds., *The ecology of aquatic insects.* Praeger, New York.

Wood, D. M. 1978. Taxonomy of the Nearctic species of *Twinnia* and *Gymnopais* Diptera: Simuliidae) and a discussion of the ancestry of the Simuliidae. *Can. Entomol.* 110:1297–1337.

Wotton, R. S. 1976. Evidence that blackfly larvae can feed on particles of colloidal size. *Nature* (London) 261:697.

Wu, Y. F. 1931. A contribution to the biology of *Simulium* (Diptera). *Pap. Mich. Acad. Sci. Arts Lett.* 13:543–599.

Yankovsky, A. V. 1978. The taxonomic importance of premandibular structure in black fly larvae (Diptera: Simuliidae). *Entomol. Rev.* 56(2):143–146.

Zahar, A. R. 1951. The ecology and distribution of black-flies (Simuliidae) in south-east Scotland. *J. Anim. Ecol.* 20:33–62.

13   HYDRODYNAMICS OF LARVAL BLACK FLIES

Douglas A. Craig and Mary M. Galloway

Although examples of simuliid larvae completing development in totally stagnant water are known (Crosskey 1973), the majority of species require flowing water for larval development (Colbo and Wotton 1981). The consequences of living in a medium such as flowing water are dealt with well by Vogel (1981), Lugt (1983), and Koehl (1982, 1984). How sessile organisms resist forces produced by flow is described by Koehl (1982, 1984) and Vogel (1984). However, little work has been done on lotic benthic organisms since Ambühl (1959, 1961) showed how such organisms might use the boundary layer to escape from the mainstream velocity. Similar fundamental work was done by Trivellato and Décamps (1968) and later by Décamps et al. (1975), who attempted to relate distribution of simuliid larvae to various flow parameters.

The small amount of work done on hydrodynamics of freshwater benthic organisms is probably caused by the difficulties of dealing with high velocities, and perhaps by the powerful influence of Macan (1962, 1974), who was not convinced that velocity as such determined distribution of benthic organisms. However, there are many works that do correlate velocity alone (or in combination with water depth and physical characteristics of the streambed) with distribution of benthic organisms (e.g., Jaag and Ambühl 1964; Ulfstrand 1967; Trivellato and Décamps 1968; Chutter 1968, 1969). Recently, Gore and Judy (1981), Statzner (1981a,b), and Orth and Maughan (1983) have used combinations of the above parameters of flowing water to construct predictive models of population distribution and densities of macroinvertebrates, including simuliid larvae.

To understand the mutual effects between simuliid larvae and the flow in which they live, some knowledge of the principles governing flowing media is required. Such an understanding is of importance, for as will be shown here, hydrodynamics are fundamental in habitat selection by simuliid larvae and in their feeding behavior. (See Colbo, and Currie and Craig, this volume, and Chance and Craig 1986 for further discussions on this subject.)

We deal briefly here with some hydrodynamics principles, then we relate these to biology of simuliid larvae. More detailed consideration of principles of flow is provided by Vogel (1981), Lugt (1983), and Newbury (1984).

FLOW CHARACTERISTICS

State of flow in a stream can be represented by the ratio of inertial forces to gravitational force, termed the "Froude number," where

$$F = U/\sqrt{g.D}$$

where U = mainstream velocity, D = depth, g = acceleration due to gravity (Chow 1959). When $F = 1$, the flow regime is said to be "critical" and

$$U = \sqrt{g.D}$$

Flow with an $F < 1$ is termed "subcritical" or "tranquil"; flow with $F > 1$ is termed "supercritical," "shooting," or "rapid" (Chow 1959, Streeter and Wiley 1979, Simon 1981). These flow types are illustrated in Figures 13.1 and 13.9.

These types of flow relate directly to "specific energy" of a given flow situation. Specific energy (*SE*) of flowing water is constant between adjacent portions of a stream with uniform flow, and

$$SE = D+(U^2/2g)$$

where D, g, and U are as defined above. If obstacles are encountered by flowing water, velocity and depth of flow change to maintain a constant discharge; i.e., since *SE* is constant, if U increases, then D must decrease. For this reason, the surface of water flowing over a rock, and hence increasing in speed, is lower than that of slower water upstream (Fig. 13.1).

If the obstruction is sufficiently large such that depth of flow is

$$D = 2(U^2/2g)$$

the flow is again "critical" (i.e., where $F = 1$) (Newbury 1984). The water flow will then accelerate down the face of the obstruction as "supercritical" flow (where $F > 1$), then revert to "subcritical" flow ($F < 1$) in a "hydraulic jump," where energy is dissipated as noise and friction in the increased turbulence (Figs. 13.1, 13.9, and 13.10). If the obstruction protrudes above the water surface, critical flow may occur at the sides of the obstacle (Newbury 1984). Critical, subcritical, and supercritical flows are explained in greater detail by Chow (1959), Brater and King (1976), and Newbury (1984).

A point not made in hydraulics texts, but well demonstrated by Newbury (personal communication) and illustrated here in Figures 13.1 and 13.10, is that the turbulent cells of water in subcritical flow are squeezed as flow becomes critical. This is *not* laminar flow, for the cells are only elongated; but it is important because suspended materials in the flow pass through a smaller cross section at higher veloc-

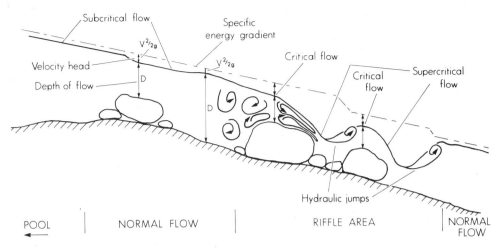

FIG. 13.1 Generalized diagram showing relationship of specific energy gradient to types of flow over obstructions. Arrows indicate direction of water flow.

ity, hence increasing particle flux. This may be important when dams provide ideal habitats for simuliids. Dams are designed so that water flowing over the spillway will achieve critical flow, and dam faces are often designed with a "critical slope" (Brater and King 1976) to produce critical and/or supercritical flow conditions for water flowing away from the spillway.

Types of flow on the substrate depend on the ratio of inertial force to viscous forces and are characterized by Reynolds number:

$$Re = U \cdot L / k$$

where U = velocity, L = a characteristic hydrodynamic linear dimension of the object, and k = kinematic viscosity of the fluid. Like Froude number, Re is a dimensionless number. L can be taken as the length of the object parallel to the flow (Campbell 1977). Kinematic viscosity is temperature-dependent, and for water at 15° C is 1.1 mm^2/sec. It is convenient to measure the other factors in millimeters too, for an approximate Re is then merely the product of the length and velocity.

Flow with Re's lower than 500 is generally laminar; between 500–2,000 transitional; and above that fully turbulent. Water flow in natural streams is almost always fully turbulent (Ambühl 1959, Chow 1959, Hynes 1970, Vogel 1981). Objects of similar shape and Reynolds number have similar flow patterns. This "principle of similitude/similarity" is applied when using scaled-up models (Figs. 13.5–13.7) (Vogel 1981). If the size of an object and its model differ, then either velocity or viscosity needs to be altered to keep Re constant.

At the actual substrate-water interface, velocity of flow is zero because of the effect of viscosity. Velocity increases with distance from the substrate up to the full mainstream velocity (U). The region where the velocity is 90% or less of that of the mainstream can be termed the "boundary layer" (Fig. 13.2) (Vogel 1981). Boundary layers can be laminar, transitional, or turbulent, but the latter do not occur until Re is 20,000–500,000. In natural watercourses, boundary layers are turbulent (Décamps et al. 1975, Jumars and Nowell 1984). However, immediately at the substrate, viscous

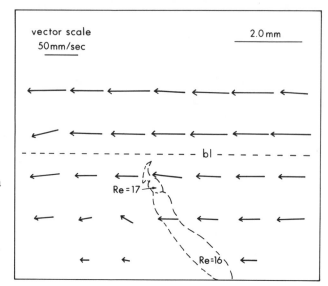

FIG. 13.2 Velocity profile for a simuliid larva (*Simulium vittatum*). Length of vector indicates velocity of flow (see scale). Arrows indicate direction of water flow. bl = boundary layer; Re = Reynolds number.

forces predominate and a laminar sublayer, in which the velocity gradient is steep, is always present.

As water flows around an object or is influenced by the substrate, it gains angular momentum and increases in vorticity. The principles governing vortex formation are dealt with well by Lugt (1983) and in detail for simuliid larvae by Chance and Craig (1986). Briefly, vortex formation is determined by Reynolds number. At Re's < 10, no vortices result; at $10 > Re < 40$, attached vortices occur; and at Re's > 40 the vortices detach with a frequency determined by size of object and velocity of flow (Vogel 1981). Because the boundary layer comprises a velocity gradient, Re for a sessile organism of complex shape will vary with height above the substrate. Therefore, types of flow around an organism may be very complex.

Drag is a critical component of life in flowing water. This may be characterized by the drag coefficient of an object, which is dependent on its surface area. This area may be either the "critical area" (that facing the oncoming flow) or the "wettable" area (that in contact with flowing water). Total drag on an object consists of skin friction and pressure drag from turbulence downstream. Skin friction is more important at low Re's; e.g., at $Re = 100$, skin friction constitutes 30% of total drag on a cylinder, but it becomes relatively less important at higher Re's (Vogel 1981).

Orientation of simuliid larvae has been well described (Fortner 1937, Grenier 1949, Kurtak 1973, Chance and Craig 1986). Larvae attach the posterior end of the body to the substrate with the dorsal surface facing upstream. To present the adoral (ventral) surface of the lateral fans to the water flow, the body is rotated 90–180 degrees longitudinally (Figs. 13.2 and 13.8). Not previously reported is the yaw (lateral deviation from direction of water flow) of the larva. One result of the longitudinal rotation of the body and the yaw is that one fan is positioned close to the substrate and the other higher in the boundary layer (Figs. 13.2 and 13.8). Chance (1977) and Chance and Craig (1986) give more details on the relationship of the boundary layer to simuliid larvae.

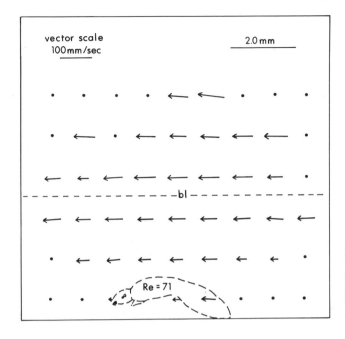

FIG. 13.3 As for Figure 13.1, but with larva exhibiting avoidance behavior. Arrows indicate direction of water flow. bl = boundary layer; Re = Reynolds number.

LARVAL FORM AND STANCE

The effect of the boundary layer on simuliid larvae needs further examination. Décamps et al. (1975) and Jumars and Nowell (1984) showed theoretically that at velocities inhabited by larvae of many simuliid species, a fully formed boundary layer is transitory. Décamps et al. (1975) and Craig and Chance (1982) pointed out that this accounted for the swaying back and forth of attached larvae in turbulent water. Larvae moving in unison are being moved by cells of turbulent water passing over them and reaching down into the boundary layer and to the substrate. Since larvae have a flexible posterior point of attachment, they move with the changing direction of flow so that the head and cephalic fans are always directed downstream and hence flow through the labral fans is presumed to be optimal for the filtering mechanisms involved (Craig and Chance 1982).

The body of a larva is deflected from a vertical stance by the water flow; when faster, larvae lie closer to the substrate. This changing stance is considered to be passive (Grenier 1949, Maitland and Penney 1967), although Kurtak (1973) reported differences in feeding stance between larvae of different species exposed to the same velocity. Chance and Craig (1986) show that for *Simulium vittatum* Zett. larvae the relationship between angle of deflection and velocity is hyperbolic, with deflection increasing rapidly initially (Fig. 13.4). They give a more detailed interpretation of this. However, for a given situation, thickness of boundary layer is influenced by velocity, so the shape of the curve for angle of deflection (Fig. 13.4) probably represents the decrease in boundary-layer thickness with increase in mainstream velocity.

When larvae are disturbed, they interrupt their feeding and exhibit a characteristic behavior of pulling themselves down onto the substrate, thereby bringing their body

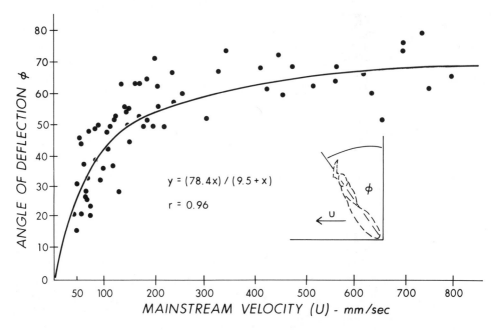

FIG. 13.4 Relationship between angle of deflection of simuliid larva (*Simulium vittatum*) and mainstream velocity. Arrows indicate direction of water flow.

into the reduced velocities of the lower boundary layer. If the disturbance is severe, e.g., a sudden increase in velocity, larvae will sometimes hold onto the substrate with their thoracic proleg (Fig. 13.3). This behavior, by which larvae make use of the sharply reduced velocity in the lower boundary layer, is termed "avoidance behavior" (Chance 1977, Chance and Craig 1986). This was interpreted by Chance as a mechanism for avoiding the full force of the mainstream velocity and hence reducing total drag on the larva.

FEEDING BEHAVIOR AND VORTICES

An underlying assumption of most work on filter-feeding behavior of simuliid larvae, although rarely directly stated, is that behavior of larvae and choice of microhabitat relate directly to their filter feeding. Since efficiencies of particle capture are low, ranging from 0.01–12.0% for the particle sizes investigated (Chance 1977; Kurtak 1978; Wotton 1978; Colbo and Wotton 1981; Schröder 1980, 1981; Hart and Latta 1986), it might be expected that larvae attempt to maximize the difference between benefit and cost of a particular site by achieving water flow around the body and through the fans for maximum filtration efficiency while keeping energetic costs, such as drag, as low as possible.

   Chance and Craig (1986) studied the interaction between flow and the larval body (Figs. 13.5–13.7). The basic phenomena involve paired vortices that are generated when flow passes, for example, a cylindrical object (Vogel 1981, Lugt 1983). Vortices rise up the downstream side of a cylindrical object and detach in a trail of

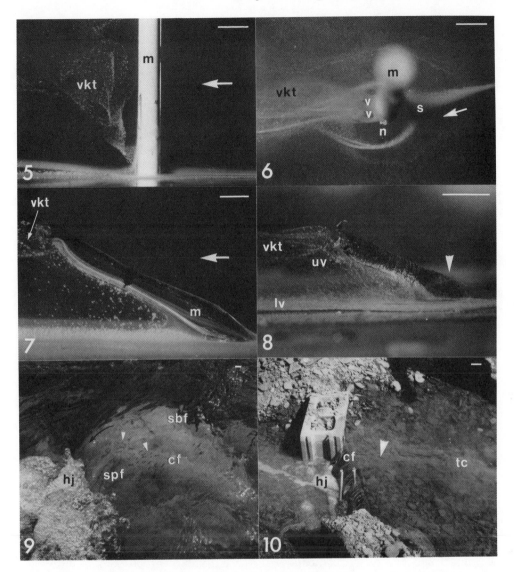

FIGS. 13.5–13.10: (5) Cylindrical glass model (m) showing attached vortices and the von Karman trail (vkt) of detaching vortices; (6) plane view of model in Figure 13.4 showing stagnation point (s), necklace vortex (n), and matched pair of attached vortices (v); (7) glass model of simuliid larva showing upper vortex; (8) simuliid larva showing upper (uv) and lower (lv) vortices in relation to labral fans (partly adducted). Note flow up and over posterior abdomen (arrowhead); (9) rock in stream showing typical flow patterns; sbf = subcritical flow, spf = supercritical flow. Note larvae of *S. arcticum* complex (arrowheads) in region of critical flow (cf); (10) artificial weir showing turbulent cells (tc) of dye in subcritical region, becoming elongate (arrow) as flow approaches critical flow (cf) at the spillway, hj = hydraulic jump.

Unless otherwise specified, larvae are of *Simulium vittatum*. Arrows indicate direction of water flow. Scale bars for Figures 13.5–13.8 = 5 mm; for Figures 13.9 and 13.10 = 5 cm.

regular vortices (= von Karman trail) (Fig. 13.5). A plane view (Fig. 13.6) illustrates the manner in which the flow in the lower boundary layer separates around the stagnation point and necklace (= horseshoe) vortex and then flows into the vortices. When a model shaped like a simuliid larva is positioned (with some yaw) in the flow, only one vortex rises up the downstream side of the model. The other vortex remains low in the boundary layer (Fig. 13.7). Because the *Re*'s of the model and simuliid larva were carefully matched, flow around both is similar (Figs. 13.7 and 13.8). The vortex remaining in the lower boundary layer was termed the "lower vortex" by Chance and Craig (1986) and the other, a more energetic vortex, which rises up the length of the body and discharges through the lower labral fan, the "upper vortex."

The discharge of flow into the upper vortex remains essentially the same at various velocities, but the frontal area of the labral fans decreases as the angle of deflection increases with increased velocity (Chance and Craig 1986). This latter observation probably accounts in part for the decrease in efficiency of ingestion by larvae as velocity increases (Kurtak 1973; Chance 1977; Schröder 1980, 1981). Studies on efficiencies of filtration and ingestion of simuliid larvae must now take into consideration the angle of deflection of the larvae, the concomitant change in the frontal area of the labral fans at different velocities, and different discharges through the two fans.

Since particles in the lower boundary layer are entrained in the upper vortex and pass into the lower labral fan (Chance and Craig 1986), does this provide larvae with any advantage? And since filtration efficiencies of simuliid larvae are low, is the general assumption (Kurtak 1973, 1978; Craig and Chance 1982; Chance and Craig 1986, and others) that much larval feeding behavior is aimed at maximum filtration and ingestion rates valid? This question is addressed in more detail by Currie and Craig (this volume) on feeding strategies. At a very fundamental level, Craig and Chance (1982) showed that water flow around the head and through the fan rays of *S. vittatum* larvae is laminar and hence optimal for known filtration mechanisms (Ross and Craig 1980) at velocities where flow would normally be expected to be turbulent (LaBarbera 1984). Also at this level is the very sophisticated study by Braimah (1985), who examined by way of scaled-up models interaction of suspended particles with the microtrichia of simuliid larval fan rays. He concluded that a "diffusion/deposition" filtration mechanism gave the best explanation of observations on the model fans and of gut contents of larvae fed known proportions of different-sized particles at different velocities (Currie and Craig, this volume).

MICRODISTRIBUTION

Simuliid larvae appear to be sensitive to particle concentration (Kurtak 1973; Chance 1977; Gaugler and Molloy 1980; Schröder 1980, 1981; Hart and Latta 1986). Thus larvae might make advantageous use of particle-enriched vortices from larvae immediately upstream. If so, this may explain in part the clumping and banding of larvae of various species of simuliid (Colbo and Wotton 1981, Craig and Chance 1982). However, Hart (1985) showed that larvae of *Simulium piperi* Dyar & Shannon attempted to dislodge larvae that were within one body length upstream of them and that remaining larvae had enhanced efficiencies of ingestion when upstream larvae were removed. Similar work, involving ingestion efficiencies and dispersion patterns of larvae of other species, has been done by Eymann (1985) and Ciborowski and Craig (1986).

Wotton (1979, 1980) suggested that feces of simuliid larvae were a valuable food source for other larvae and of significance to large aggregations of larvae. Chance and Craig (1986) show that egested fecal pellets roll along the substrate in the necklace vortex and are then entrained into the upper vortex. Because of their mass, these pellets are not entrained high enough to be caught by the larva that egested them. However, Wotton (1980) demonstrated that larvae downstream can capture fecal pellets, and he calculated that one pellet might be nutritionally equivalent to bacteria filtered from 23–100 ml of water. Marine and other filter-feeding organisms go to great lengths to avoid their own feces (Ladle and Griffiths 1980, Nowell et al. 1984) and although microorganisms increase the nutrient content of the older feces, there is evidence that ingestion of feces is disadvantageous (Ladle and Griffiths 1980). The ingestion of feces of larval simuliids by larvae downstream needs to be investigated with respect to possible direct benefits to the larvae and their role in nutrient cycling in lotic systems.

Although Wotton (1980) suggested that aggregations of larvae may be a result of larvae feeding on feces, we suspect that the regular distances observed between bands of larvae are not the result of a single phenomenon, hydrodynamic or other. Fecal pellets of simuliid larvae have a settling velocity of approximately 35 mm/sec in still water (Ladle and Griffiths 1980), and they are entrained to a height of approximately 2 mm by the larva's upper vortex when the mainstream velocity is approximately 150 mm/sec (Chance and Craig 1986). They would then settle out within 9 mm of the head of the larva, assuming no further entrainment. This distance is more than one body length of a mature larva and in general agrees with our observations (unpublished) and those of Tarshis (1968) of distances between bands. Thus feces might sediment out before reaching the upper labral fan of a downstream larva. A pellet rolling along the substrate would not be caught by the lower fan because pellets are too massive to be entrained to the height of the lower fan. Therefore, it seems unlikely that larvae aggregate in bands to enhance feeding on fecal pellets. It is not known if the distance between bands changes with velocity, but that would be relatively easy to investigate.

The distance between bands of larvae may involve the frequency of detaching vortices of the von Karman trail from larvae upstream. The frequency of detaching vortices for a cylindrical object is dependent only on Reynolds number in a relationship termed the "Strouhal number" (Lugt 1983), where

$$St = Hz \cdot L/U$$

where Hz = frequency of detaching vortices, L = diameter of object, and U = velocity. For noncylindrical objects the relationship does not apply directly (Lugt 1983), so for the larva in Figure 13.8, which has a Re of 96 and a frequency of detachment of the upper vortex of 7.0 Hz, the Strouhal number is 0.04. This is approximately one-quarter of that for a similarly sized cylinder (Chance and Craig 1986).

Larvae downstream might detect the presence of upstream larvae by the regular vortices of the von Karman trail. This is a possible explanation for Hart's (1985) observations. Although the habitat must be extremely noisy with random vortices passing, the regular incidence of the vortices in the train would be embedded in the background noise and could possibly be detected by larvae downstream. Further, Brater and King (1976) make the point that critical flow is very unstable and minor disturbances can cause oscillations to build rapidly. Is it possible that critical flow acts as an amplifier for the regular frequency of the detaching von Karman trail of vortices? An advantage for a larva in avoiding water directly downstream from another larva probably lies in its filter-feeding behavior. Wake or eddy flow downstream of an object is of reduced velocity and is more chaotic. Flow through a filtration device should be laminar for optimal operation (Rubenstein and Koehl 1977), and a larva in the wake of a larva upstream would find it more difficult to maintain even discharge of flow through its fans. Distance between bands of larvae then may reflect distance downstream necessary to escape effects on flow generated by larvae upstream.

The shape of larvae probably reduces drag and again, like the ship's bow, determines where the vortices will occur (Chance and Craig 1986). The posterior abdominal shape of larvae of *S. vittatum* (but not of all simuliid larvae) is very similar to the bulbous bow of modern ships. Such bows are designed to reduce bow waves (Saunders 1957) and, importantly, to reduce and position bilge vortices so that they do not interfere with the propellers (Lugt 1983). Water flow up and over the posterior of a larva (Fig. 13.8) is very similar to flow over a bulbous bow (Saunders 1957). Shape and stance of the simuliid larval body modifies the paired vortices, fundamental to flow downstream of a cylindrical object, such that one vortex is positioned to flow through one of the labral fans. This phenomenon applies at all velocities acceptable to larvae (Chance and Craig 1986).

The hydrodynamic phenomena described here apply only to larvae attached to hard, immobile substrates, and not as yet to narrow, flexible substrates such as vegetation. Banding of larvae on grasses, observed by us and others, probably relates to regular vortex formation along the blade of grass. Indeed, we suspect that the hydrodynamic phenomenon observed here may account in part for preferences shown by larvae of some species to particular artificial substrates, and that this has relevance to substrates developed for quantitative sampling (Fredeen and Spurr 1978, Carlsson et al. 1981, Roberts 1983, and others). Relevant here is an aspect of substrates that is virtually ignored—roughness. Décamps et al. (1975) included substrate roughness in their theoretical hydrodynamic calculation but did not relate it to observed distributions of simuliid larvae. Since it is known that such roughness may determine distribution of some lotic benthos (Erman and Erman 1984) and has been observed for some simuliid larvae (Lin-Ki 1975), it might be valuable to determine how extensive the effect on simuliid larvae is.

Non-filter-feeding larvae such as the fanless larvae of *Gymnopais* and *Twinnia*, which scrape periphyton from the substrate (Currie and Craig, this volume), will not be so influenced by hydrodynamic phenomena. However, they are normally found in erosional regions of streams, or in spring outlets where there is no particulate matter for deposition. This choice of habitat no doubt reflects their feeding behaviors, and so their distribution is in part determined by hydrodynamic aspects of the habitat.

Craig and Chance (1982) suggested that larvae of some species, when regularly spaced in rows across the flow, make beneficial use of mutually induced flow patterns between neighbors, because such flow was thought to enhance filter feeding. Chance and Craig (1986) show that enhancement of velocity between larvae is greater than that around single larvae by a factor of between two and four. As stream lines are squeezed closer together, velocity increases and, again as in critical flow, the particle flux increases. Such enhancement of flow might enable larvae to filter more particulate matter per unit time and may be important during periods of low food availability.

In studies on tubular marine organisms and near-bed flow, Eckman et al. (1981) and Eckman (1983) conclude that at some densities massed organisms produce a "skimming" effect, where maximum turbulence and shear stress occur away from the substrate and the organisms themselves become the substrate. Eckman et al. (1981) give critical ratios of minimum densities of tubular elements to produce this effect. Tubes, approximately the same diameter as late-instar simuliid larvae (1.0–1.5 mm), would need a density in the range of 5×10^4 to $10^5 /m^2$ for this effect to occur. The dense aggregations often reported, i.e., 6×10^4 larvae/m^2 (Chutter 1968, Carlsson et al. 1977, Wotton 1982) for simuliid larvae deserve investigation, because it is quite possible that heavier, nutritive particles flow over such aggregations just at the level of the upper labral fans. Likewise, larvae in situations where the boundary layer is thin, either because of high velocity or because it is just beginning to develop (such as on the crest of a spillway), may clump together to reduce drag.

Orth and Maughan (1983) showed that larvae of certain species of *Simulium* have a preference for flow of $F > 0.8$, i.e., approaching critical flow. Statzner (1981a) also demonstrated a similar relationship for simuliid larvae. Kurtak (1973) has a classic illustration of *S. pictipes* Hagen larvae grouped in critical flow, although he did not relate the distribution to flow type. He commented that the larvae changed their location as discharge varied daily. He also showed, and we have observed, that larvae of other species of Simuliidae prefer other types of flow. Therefore, it is most important to determine the species of any simuliids when considering their distribution in relation to Froude number.

Preference of larvae for areas of critical flow is demonstrated by observations of larvae of *S. articum* Malloch complex forming very distinct bands in critical flow over and around boulders (Craig, personal observation; R. W. Newbury, personal communication 1983). Further, on a weir constructed to measure discharge of a creek, and where a whole wide spillway was designed to produce critical flow, larvae were not banded but were more randomly distributed over the available area. Larvae of other sibling species of the *S. arcticum* complex also show this preference for critical flow (Fig. 13.9). Presence of larvae in regions of critical flow may be in part a passive phenomenon. A drifting larva trails behind it a sticky silk thread (Colbo and Wotton 1981). The probability of the thread making contact with the substrate will be greater at positions of critical flow where the cells of turbulence become flattened (Fig. 13.1). Once in such a position, a larva can then move to an optimal position for filter feeding from the enhanced particle flux through the region of critical flow.

Massive concentrations of simuliid larvae at lake outlets have often been reported (Colbo and Wotton 1981). The usual explanation for this is the high concentration of fine particulate organic material (FPOM) available to the larvae (Carlsson et al. 1977, Wotton 1979). The rapid decline in numbers of larvae downstream from lake outlets is usually explained by a decline in available seston or a change in its nutritive quality either by physical processes or by removal by the larvae themselves (Wotton 1979, Colbo and Wotton 1981). Sheldon and Oswood (1977) attempted to model the change in abundance of simuliid larvae downstream from a lake outlet in relation to possible determinants such as sestonic food. They achieved very good correlation between distance downstream and larval density. The major changes in simuliid larval abundance occurred within the first 100m of the stream source. Their data agree with other observations (Carlsson et al. 1977), but not with the usual explanation, since the quantity of seston did not decrease with distance from the stream source.

Almost completely ignored in all studies of this phenomenon is the increase in Froude number as water flows out of a lake. If the larvae are of a species of simuliid sensitive to the factors involved in determination of the Froude number, decrease in abundance may relate to changing Froude number as well as to abundance or quality of seston. Carlsson et al. (1977) commented that lake outlets are often like natural spillways and that their geomorphology might contribute to conditions favorable to concentration of larvae. Indeed, Quélenec et al. (1968) showed that the physical structure (and hence the Froude number) of dam spillways determined population density of *S. damnosum* Theobald complex larvae. If Froude number is important in determining abundance of larvae at lake outlets and man-made structures, it might be possible, with correct attention to hydrodynamic principles, to manipulate such habitats to reduce populations of pestiferous simuliids.

CONCLUSION

Recent investigations of hydrodynamics of simuliid larvae and of their feeding strategies have significantly contributed to our understanding of larval feeding behavior and microdistribution. Larval feeding can no longer be considered a passive affair. Larval anatomy, behavior, and filtering efficiency are all involved in formation of differential vortices and transport, entrainment, and capture of particles. Further investigations of hydrodynamics of preferred habitats of larvae of various species of Simuliidae should provide better information on aggregations and interrelations between larvae, their nutrient use, and flow requirements.

ACKNOWLEDGMENTS

We wish to thank R. B. Aiken, D. C. Currie, and D. D. Hart for constructive comments, and R. W. Newbury for the outline of Figure 13.1. The work was supported by a grant from WHO to the late B. Hocking, and a grant from the Natural Sciences and Engineering Research Council, Canada, grant No. 5753, to Douglas A. Craig.

LITERATURE CITED

Ambühl, H. 1959. Die Bedeutung der Strömung als ökologischer Faktor. *Schwiez. Z. Hydrol.* 21:133–264.

————. 1961. Die Strömung als physiologischer und ökologischer Faktor. *Verh. Int. Verein, Limnol.* 14:390–395.

Bráimah, S. A. 1985. Mechanisms and fluid mechanical aspects of filter-feeding in black fly larvae (Diptera: Simuliidae) and mayfly nymphs (Ephemeroptera: Oligoneuridae). Ph.D. Thesis, University of Alberta, Edmonton.

Brater, E. F., and H. W. King. 1976. *Handbook of hydraulics.* McGraw-Hill, New York.

Burton, G. J., and T. M. McRae, 1965. Dam-spillway breeding of *Simulium damnosum* Theobald in northern Ghana. *Ann. Trop. Med. Parasitol.* 59:405–412.

Campbell, G. S. 1977. *An introduction to environmental biophysics.* Springer-Verlag, New York.

Carlsson, M., L. M. Nilsson, Bj. Svensson, S. Ulfstrand, and R. S. Wotton. 1977. Lacustrine seston and other factors influencing the blackflies (Diptera: Simuliidae) inhabiting lake outlets in Swedish Lapland. *Oikos* 29:229–238.

Carlsson, G., P. Elsen, and K. Muller. 1981. Trapping technology—larval blackflies. Pp. 283–286 in M. Laird, Ed., *Blackflies: The future for biological methods in integrated control.* Academic Press, New York and London.

Chance,* M. M. 1977. Influence of water flow and particle concentration on larvae of the black fly *Simulium vittatum* Zett. (Diptera: Simuliidae), with emphasis on larval filter-feeding. Ph.D. Thesis, University of Alberta, Edmonton. (* = M. M. Galloway).

Chance,* M. M., and D. A. Craig. 1986. Hydrodynamics and behaviour of Simuliidae larvae (Diptera). *Can. J. Zool.* 64:1295–1309. (* = M. M. Galloway).

Chow, V. T. 1959. *Open-Channel Hydrodynamics.* McGraw-Hill, New York and Toronto.

Chutter, F. M. 1968. On the ecology of the fauna of stones in the current in a South African river supporting a very large *Simulium* (Diptera) population. *J. Appl. Ecol.* 5:531–561

————. 1969. The distribution of some stream invertebrates in relation to current speed. *Int. Rev. Gesamten Hydrobiol.* 54:413–422.

Ciborowski, J. J. H., and D. A. Craig. 1986. Influence of current and food concentration on aggregation of *Simulium vittatum* larvae (Diptera: Simuliidae). In *Titles and Abstracts, N. Amer. Benth. Soc., 34th Ann. Mtg.,* Lawrence, Kansas.

Colbo, M. H. 1987. Problems in estimating black fly populations in their acquatic stages (this volume).

Colbo, M. H., and R. S. Wotton. 1981. Preimaginal blackfly bionomics. Pp. 209–226 in M. Laird, Ed., *Blackflies: the future for biological methods in integrated control.* Academic Press, New York and London.

Craig, D. A., and M. M. Chance*. 1982. Filter feeding in larvae of Simuliidae (Diptera: Culicomorpha): aspects of functional morphology and hydrodynamics. *Can. J. Zool.* 60:712–724. (= M. M. Galloway).

Crosskey, R. W. 1973. Simuliidae. Pp. 109–153 in K. G. V. Smith, Ed., *Insects and other arthropods of medical importance.* British Museum (Natural History), London.

Currie, D. C., and D. A. Craig. 1987. Feeding strategies of larval black flies (this volume).

Décamps, H., G. Larrouy, and D. Trivellato. 1975. Approche hydrodynamique de la microdistribution d'invertébrés benthique en eau courante. *Ann. Limnol.* 11:79–100.

Eckman, J. E. 1983. Hydrodynamic processes affecting benthic recruitment. *Limnol. Oceanogr.* 28:241–257.

Eckman, J. E., A. R. M. Nowell, and P. A. Jumars. 1981. Sediment destabilization by animal tubes. *J. Mar. Res.* 39:361–374.

Erman, D. C., and N. A. Erman, 1984. The response of stream macroinvertebrates to substrate size and heterogenity. *Hydrobiologia* 108:75–82.

Eymann, M. 1985. The behaviours of the blackfly larvae *Simulium vittatum* and *S. decorum* (Diptera: Simuliidae) associated with establishing and maintaining dispersion patterns on natural and artificial substrate. M.Sc. Thesis, University of Toronto.

Fortner, G. 1937. Zur Ernährungsfrage der *Simulium*-larva. *Z. Morphol. Ökol. Tiere* 32:360–383.

Fredeen, F. J. H., and D. T. Spurr. 1978. Collecting semi-quantitative samples of black fly larvae (Diptera: Simuliidae) and other aquatic insects from large rivers with the aid of artificial substrates. *Quaest. Entomol.* 14:411–431.

Gaugler, R., and D. Molloy. 1980. Feeding inhibition in black fly larvae (Diptera: Simuliidae) and its effects on the pathogenicity of *Bacillus thuringiensis* var. *israelensis. Environ. Entomol.* 9:704–708.

Gore, J. A., and R. D. Judy, 1981. Predictive models of benthic macroinvertebrate density for use in instream flow studies and regulated flow management. *Can. J. Fish. Aquat. Sci.* 38:1363–70.

Grenier, P. 1949. Contribution à l'étude biologique des simuliides de France. *Physiol. Comp. Oecol.* 1:1–314.

Hart, D. D. 1985. The adaptive significance of territoriality in filter-feeding larval black flies (Diptera: Simuliidae). *Oikos* 46:82–92.

Hart, D. D., and S. C. Latta. 1986. Determinants of ingestion rates in filter-feeding larval black flies (Diptera: Simuliidae). *Freshwater Biol.* 16:1–14.

Hynes, H. B. N. 1970. *The ecology of running waters.* Univ. Toronto Press, Toronto.

Jaag, O., and H. Ambühl. 1964. The effect of the current on the composition of biocoenoses in flowing water streams. *Int. Conf. Wat. Pollut. Res. London* 1:31–49.

Jumars, P. A., and A. R. M. Nowell. 1984. Fluid and sediment dynamics effects on marine community structure. *Am. Zool.* 24:45–55.

Koehl, M. A. R. 1982. The interaction of moving water and sessile organisms. *Sci. Amer.* 247:124–134.

———. 1984. How do benthic organisms withstand moving water? *Am. Zool.* 24:57–70.

Kurtak, D. C. 1973. Observations on filter feeding by the larvae of black flies (Diptera: Simuliidae). Ph.D. Thesis, Cornell University, Ithaca, New York.

———. 1978. Efficiency of filter-feeding of blackfly larvae (Diptera: Simuliidae), *Can. J. Zool.* 56:1608–23.

LaBarbera, M. 1984. Feeding currents and particle capture mechanisms in suspension feeding animals. *Am. Zool.* 24:71–84.

Ladle, M., and B. S. Griffiths. 1980. A study on the faeces of some chalk stream invertebrates. *Hydrobiologia* 74:161–171.

Lin-Ki, C. J. W. 1975. Drift of black-fly larvae and the influence of water velocity, substrate roughness and incident light intensity on their microdistribution (Diptera: Simuliidae). M.Sc. Thesis, McMaster University, Hamilton, Ontario.

Lugt, H. J. 1983. *Vortex flow in nature and technology.* Wiley and Sons, New York and Toronto.

Macan, T. T. 1962. Ecology of aquatic insects. *Ann. Rev. Entomol.* 7:261–288.

———. 1974. *Freshwater ecology.* Longman, London.

Maitland, P. S., and M. M. Penney. 1967. The ecology of the Simuliidae in a Scottish river. *J. Anim. Ecol.* 36:179–206.

Newbury, R. W. 1984. Hydraulic determinants of aquatic insect habitats. Pp. 323–357 in V. H. Resh, and D. M. Rosenberg, Eds., *The ecology of aquatic insects.* Praeger, New York.

Nowell, A. R. M., P. A. Jumars, and K. Fauchild. 1984. The foraging strategy of a subtidal and deep-sea deposit feeder. *Limnol. Oceanogr.* 29:645–649.

Orth, D. J., and O. E. Maughan. 1983. Microhabitat preferences of benthic fauna in a woodland stream. *Hydrobiologia* 106:157–168.

Quélenec, G., E. Simonkovich, and M. Ovazza. 1968. Recherche d'un type de déversior de barrage défavorable à l'implantation de *Simulium damnosum* (Diptera, Simuliidae). *Bull. WHO* 38:943–956.

Roberts, D. M. 1983. The relative abundance of the pupae of three black fly species (*Simulium* spp) on different diameters of strings. *Entomol. Exp. Appl.* 33:125–128.

Ross, D. H., and D. A. Craig. 1980. Mechanisms of fine particle capture by larval black flies (Diptera: Simuliidae). *Can. J. Zool.* 58:1186–92.

Rubenstein, D. I., and M. A. R. Koehl, 1977. The mechanisms of filter feeding: some theoretical considerations. *Am. Nat.* 111:981–994.

Saunders, H. E. 1957. Hydrodynamics in ship design. *Soc. Naval Arch. Mar. Engin.* 1:1–513.

Schröder, P. 1980. Zur Ernährungsbiologie der Larven von *Odagmia ornata* Meigen (Diptera: Simuliidae). 1. Die Filtriertätigkeit unter dem Einfluss von Fliessgeschwindigkeit, Wassertemperatur und Futterkonzentration. *Arch. Hydrobiol. Suppl.* 59:43–52.

———. 1981. Zur Ernährungsbiologie der Larven von *Odagmia ornata* Meigen (Diptera: Simuliidae). 3. Ingestion, Egestion und Assimilation. ^{14}C-markierter Algen. *Arch. Hydrobiol. Suppl.* 59:97–133.

Sheldon, A. L., and M. W. Oswood. 1977. Blackfly (Diptera: Simuliidae) abundance in a lake outlet: test of a predictive model. *Hydrobiologia* 56:113–120.

Simon, A. L. 1981. *Practical hydraulics.* Wiley and Sons, New York and Toronto.

Statzner, B. 1981a. A method to estimate the population of benthic macroinvertebrates in streams. *Oecologia* 51:157–161.

———. 1981b. The relationship between "hydraulic stress" and microdistribution of benthic macroinvertebrates in a lowland running water system, the Schierenseebrooks (North Germany). *Arch. Hydrobiol.* 91:192–218.

Streeter, V. L., and E. P. Wiley. 1979. *Fluid mechanics,* 7th ed. McGraw-Hill, New York.

Tarshis, I. B. 1968. Collecting and rearing black flies. *Ann. Entomol. Soc. Am.* 61:1072–83.

Trivellato, D., and H. Décamps. 1968. Influence de quelques obstacles simples sur l'écoulement dans un "ruisseau" experimental. *Ann. Limnol.* 4:357–386.

Ulfstrand, S. 1967. Microdistribution of benthic species (Ephemeroptera, Plecoptera, Trichoptera, Diptera: Simuliidae) in Lapland streams. *Oikos* 18:293–310.

Vogel, S. 1981. *Life in moving fluids—the physical biology of flow.* Willard Grant Press, Boston.

———. 1984. Drag and flexibility in sessile organisms. *Am. Zool.* 24:37–44.

Wotton, R. S. 1978. Growth, respiration and assimilation of blackfly larvae (Diptera: Simuliidae) in a lake-outlet in Finland. *Oecologia* 33:279–290.

———. 1979. The influence of a lake on the distribution of blackfly species (Diptera: Simuliidae) along a river. *Oikos* 32:368–372.

———. 1980. Coprophagy as an economic feeding tactic in blackfly larvae. *Oikos* 34:282–286.

———. 1982. Different life history strategies in lake-outlet blackflies (Diptera: Simuliidae). *Hydrobiologia* 96:243–251.

Part IV Ecology of Adults

14 MONITORING ADULT SIMULIID POPULATIONS

M. W. Service

Reliable sampling of adult Simuliidae is important in epidemiological studies and for evaluating control programs. Moreover, various nonvectors can be serious pests of man or his livestock, sometimes causing death of animals (Ryan and Hilchie 1982), yet sampling methods are often inadequate to assess the severity of outbreaks. Ecological investigations such as those involving host preferences, oviposition behavior, seasonality, and dispersal also demand appropriate trapping technology.

It has become increasingly fashionable to construct mathematical models in studying disease transmission, but the mathematician is often astounded by the lack of basic information on the vectors, such as feeding frequency, longevity, and dispersal. The science of computing and modeling is relatively new, but in many instances it seems to have outpaced ecology. Before models can be useful in the real world of vector-borne diseases, samples must be obtained that more accurately measure the dynamics of vector populations. For example, Dietz (1982) has recently built models describing onchocerciasis transmission in savanna areas of West Africa that demand reliable estimates of the man-biting and survival rates of the vectors, parameters that can only be obtained from sampling vector populations.

Progress in uniting theory with reality is usually best achieved by scientists who have a sound understanding of mathematics and biology, as exemplified by the works of C. H. N. Jackson during the 1930s and 1940s (see Glasgow 1963) and more recently by Rogers and Randolph (1978) and Hargrove (1980), all of whom have advanced the "art" of tsetse fly sampling. The papers of Vale (1982, 1983) should be read to appreciate the advances made by tsetse workers in trap methodology. In contrast, relatively little progress has been made during the past few decades on quantitative sampling of adult simuliids. In 1966 the World Health Organization stressed the need for alternative methods to human bait collections for sampling vector simuliids, but as yet no reliable substitute has been found.

Techniques for sampling adult simuliids have fairly recently been reviewed (Noblet and Alverson 1978; Service 1977a, 1981), so the present account focuses on some of the more recent and promising developments.

BAIT COLLECTIONS

Despite concern by WHO over ethical considerations, human bait collections (Fig. 14.1) remain the principal method of evaluating the large Onchocerciasis Control Programme (OCP) in the Volta River Basin of West Africa. The procedure involves two people working alternate hours sitting near rivers from 0700–1800 hours and collecting blood-seeking flies. Each hours's catch is placed in an icebox for subsequent identification and dissection. Every week or two weeks more than 200 vector collectors visit 350 catch stations. The catches are expressed as a "fly/man/day density index," that is, the mean number of each species biting a person during an 11-hour day. Both Monthly and Annual Biting Rates (MBR, ABR) and Monthly and Annual Transmission Potentials (MTP, APT) are calculated. While such standardized sampling procedures adequately monitor temporal changes in biting densities and evaluate the efficiency of control operations, it would be naive to believe that the numbers caught represented the number of flies biting an ordinary person going about his normal daily activities.

The Guatemala-Japan Joint Onchocerciasis Research and Control Program in Guatemala also relied on human bait catches. Collections were restricted to three 50-minute periods from 0900–1150 hours and were performed 26 times a year. The numbers of flies caught were multiplied by $660/150 \times 365/26$ to give an estimated Annual Biting Rate (Suzuki 1983). In addition, the "fly round," introduced to simuliid workers by Crosskey (1958), was used as a quick means of monitoring biting densities in many different sites. In studying host preferences in Guatemala, Okazawa et al. (1981) placed a man, cow, horse, dog, and a goat about 5 meters apart in a circle and collected all flies attracted to them. *Simulium ochraceum* Walker was predominantly anthropophagic and when landing on a person soon started biting, whereas those attracted to animals flew around for some time before settling, and even after landing few succeeded in engorging. In contrast, *Simulium metallicum* Bellardi and *Simulium callidum* Dyar & Shannon hovered around a person's legs for some time before settling, and relatively few fed, but those attracted to animals fed more successfully. Such differences in behavior are clearly relevant in sampling biting populations.

In Panama during 148 man-hour comparative collections, almost as many black flies were caught biting people in houses (11.9 flies/man/h) as were caught biting outdoors (14.7 flies/man/h) (Petersen et al. 1983). The degree of endophagy, however, varied among the species. For example, a rather similar number of *Simulium quadrivattatum* Loew bit indoors (1465) and outdoors (1802), and surprisingly more *S. callidum* were collected indoors (291) than outdoors (112). In contrast, only 7 *S. metallicum* were found biting in houses compared to 272 caught on outdoor baits; no *S. ochraceum* were caught indoors, but then only 4 were taken biting outdoors.

In Florida, Pinkovsky et al. (1981) used aspirators to collect flies feeding on uncaged but immobilized turkeys, as well as placing turkeys in a box trap fitted with omnidirectional ramps. *Simulium slossonae* Dyar & Shannon and *Simulium congareenarum* Dyar & Shannon were collected during January and March from immobilized turkeys, but in the summer only *S. slossonae* were caught, and moreover this was the only simuliid collected from the box traps. Unfortunately the numbers of adults caught are not presented in their article.

FIG. 14.1 A human bait collection being undertaken in West Africa. (Courtesy of J. B. Davies)

BAITED TRAPS

Hematophagous insects can be caught by periodically dropping a net over bait animals, but according to McCreadie et al. (1984), suspending a net over a host may deter some bloodsucking insects, especially simuliids. So in trials in Newfoundland they placed a calf in a pen and after 10-minute exposure periods rapidly pulled a collapsible tent of fine-mesh netting over metal hoops to enclose the calf (Fig. 14.2). At least 7 species of simuliids were caught during 337 10-minute exposure periods, including 3,395 *Prosimulium mixtum* Syme & Davies and 6,849 *S. venustum/verecundum* complex.

In Ivory Coast, Bellec and Hébrard (1983a) compared the numbers of *S. damnosum* complex attracted to man with those caught in chicken-, rabbit-, and sheep-baited box traps. Seasonal immigration from the forest of *Simulium soubrense* Vajime and Dunbar, which seems to be more zoophagic than the savanna species (*Simulium damnosum* Theobald and *Simulium sirbanum* Vajime & Dunbar), were believed to account for the observed seasonal shifts in favor of animals.

Many other host-baited traps have been described recently, but I shall mention just two. The first is a CDC trap with the light bulb removed and a bird or small mammal enclosed in a wire-mesh cage fixed near the top of the trap (Emord and Morris 1982). Although intended for sampling mosquitoes, this trap might be worth evaluating for simuliids attracted to small birds or mammals. The other trap is also a modified CDC trap with the bulb removed, but this time replaced with a cassette

FIG. 14.2 The calf-baited trap of McCreadie and colleagues in operation in Canada. (Courtesy of J. W. McCreadie)

recorder broadcasting frog calls. When used in Florida, as many as 566 *Corethrella*—of which frogs are known hosts—and 9 mosquitoes were trapped within 30 minutes (McKeever and Hartberg 1980). It might just be possible to attract ornithophagic black flies to recorded bird songs!

CARBON DIOXIDE TRAPS

Carbon dioxide alone or combined with some other attractant, such as light, has commonly been used to collect many types of hematophagous insects, including black flies. The simplest CO_2-baited trap consists of dry ice housed in a cylinder painted black or dark blue and covered with an adhesive. Recently such traps were used in Guatemala to trap black flies, including *S. ochraceum*. In other traps the dry ice (1 kg) was placed on top, not inside, and a small fan was used to draw the flies into the cylinder (Suzuki 1983).

During evaluation of *Bacillus thuringiensis* var. *israelensis* de Barjac in Newfoundland, Colbo and O'Brien (1984) tied five cloth box-type traps to stakes so that their open bottoms (50 × 50 cm) were 20–30 cm above 500 grams of dry ice placed on the ground. As many as 618 *S. venustum/verecundum* complex and 234 *Eusimulium vernum* Macquart were trapped a day, as well as smaller numbers of *Simulium tuberosum* (Lundstrom), *Stegopterna mutata* (Malloch), and *P. mixtum*.

In Canada, Trueman and McIver (1981) built a 4-foot-high pyramidal trap with radiating baffles over which they released 700 ml CO_2/min (Fig. 14.3). Insects were sucked into the trap by a 12-inch-diameter fan and the catch segregated by a turntable device. As the authors reported that large numbers of black flies were caught, the trap deserves further evaluation. The original model operated from AC electricity, but it should be possible to substitute a smaller suction fan that runs from two 12-V, 25-ampere-h batteries connected in parallel (Wainhouse 1980).

Fig. 14.3 A pyramidal CO_2-baited trap as used by Trueman and McIver in Canada. (Courtesy of S. B. McIver)

Pinkovsky et al. (1981) mentioned that in Florida CO_2-baited Manitoba traps collected *S. congareenarum* and "several other simuliids," but there is no mention of the numbers.

LIGHT TRAPS

Although simuliids were occasionally caught in light traps, they were not considered particularly appropriate until Williams and Davies (1957) caught large numbers of several species in a Rothamsted light trap in Scotland.

In Ghana 720 gravid and 5,800 recently oviposited *Simulium squamosum* Enderlein were caught in one night in a Monks Wood trap that had a flashing ultraviolet tube (Fig. 14.4) sited on a river bank (Service 1979). Three years later, Kyorku (1982) placed a Monks Wood trap, with a white fluorescent nonflashing tube at the same site, but he failed to catch any flies. However, when he moved his trap to the opposite river bank and suspended it over a known oviposition site, 6,981 female *S. squamosum* were caught during the first night. Recently oviposited adults predominated, gravid individuals comprised 10.9–14.9% of the catch, and only three blood-fed individuals were present in a total collection of 10,950 *S. squamosum*. Ovipositing flies started arriving at the river at about 1730 h; by 1830 h egg laying was mostly completed, and 10 minutes later flies were observed flying away. The first female

FIG. 14.4 A Monks Wood light trap with fluorescent tube catching *Simulium squamosum* in Ghana.

entered the trap at about 1845 h, the numbers caught increasing rapidly, so that by 1915 h 76.3–91.2% of the total night's catch had entered the light trap. The trap was removed at 0600 h. These results are in agreement with those of Walsh (1978), who in northern Ghana recorded peak catches of *S. damnosum* s.l. in Monks Wood light traps between 1830–1900 hours. In marked contrast Williams (1964) found that in Scotland a Rothamsted trap had caught only about 21% of the catch within the first quarter of the night, and that black fly activity continued throughout much of the night. The smaller numbers of many simuliid species caught in suction traps compared to Rothamsted light traps showed that light *per se* was attractive (Williams 1964). Somewhat similarly, when Kyorku (1982) substituted a chemical light trap (Service and Highton 1980) in place of the more powerful Monks Wood trap, only 61 *S. squamosum* were caught over three nights.

Kyorku (1982) observed ovipositing *S. squamosum* flying close to the water surface and thought that instead of setting the trap at a height of 1.5 meters (as both he and I had), placing it nearer the water surface might increase the catch.

Kyorku's (1982) collection showed (1) that a flashing ultraviolet light is not necessary; (2) that trap location is critical; (3) that it appears the attraction range is short; (4) that the trap is more attractive to females that have just oviposited than to gravid individuals; (5) that oviposition is restricted to about $1\frac{1}{4}$ hours after sunset, which was about 1800 hours; and finally (6) that flight activity of *S. squamosum* declines rapidly after egg laying.

Light traps cannot at present be routinely used to evaluate adult ovipositing simuliids because they must be placed near mass oviposition sites that are not only difficult to recognize but can change rapidly depending on water flow. Further work is needed to determine if light traps can adequately sample emerging adults, and whether placing them near favored hosts they can catch simuliids orientated to blood-feeding. This latter approach has recently proved useful for catching mosquitoes (Service 1977b).

A series of papers by Bowden describes the factors that influence the numbers of insects caught in light traps and suction traps. The numbers caught is influenced by the light intensity from the trap and natural background illumination; this relationship being formulated as "Insect catch = Constant times W/I," where W is light-trap illumination and I is intensity of background illumination (see Bowden 1982 and earlier papers). Of course the insect's behavior, physiological condition, spectral response, and visual acuity modify its response to light, but once an insect is airborne its capture by a light trap depends on whether or not it enters the region of influence of the trap. Bowden (1984) warns that because of latitudinal and seasonal changes in nocturnal illumination (above 50°N) it may become necessary to use different light sources in traps to maintain comparisons of trap collections.

There have been many descriptions of mechanisms attached to traps to divide catches into hourly samples; one of the more recent designs that might prove useful for simuliid workers is described by Taylor et al. (1982).

VISUAL ATTRACTION TRAPS

Recently Berl (1982) reported that when Challier-Laveissière (1973) biconical tsetse traps were placed by rivers in Cameroon they attracted female *S. damnosum* complex, possibly *S. squamosum;* his maximum catch was 726 females. As with so many traps, their location was critical. The lower half of these tsetse traps were made of dark blue cloth, because this color attracts the largest numbers of tsetse flies, but this is not necessarily the most attractive color for simuliids. For example, *P. mixtum/P. fuscum* complex and *S. mutata* are mostly attracted to black and red silhouettes, while *S. venustum* is attracted more to blue, but *Simulium vittatum* Zetterstedt shows little color preference except that fewest are caught on yellow targets (Bradbury and Bennett 1974, Browne and Bennett 1980). In trials in Assam considerably more *Simulium himalayense* Puri were attracted to men dressed in black and red suits than those wearing green, olive green, or white suits. The least attractive color was yellow, and men dressed in this color caught only 15.8% of the numbers of simuliids caught by men dressed in black (Das et al. 1984).

Manitoba traps have not proved to be of much value in catching simuliids (Service 1977a), but in England Ball (1983) recently experimented with a trap incorporating a black cylinder into which he released carbon dioxide. However, only 96 female simuliids of 6 species (including *Simulium equinum* L., *Simulium ornatum* Meigen, and *Simulium argyreatum* Meigen) were collected from 22 trap-days. Although Ball and Luff (1981) found that heating the cylinder to blood heat increased the catch of female *Hydrotaea irritans* (Fallén) only by 1.8-fold, it might be worthwhile evaluating the effectiveness of a warm target for attracting simuliids in colder climates.

INTERCEPTION TRAPS

In southern England, Hansford and Ladle (1979) wrapped sections (9 cm long, 4 cm diameter) of plastic piping in tree-banding adhesive paper, which were then mounted either on small polystyrene rafts anchored in midstream or on wooden poles staked at the water's edge. These traps were not very successful as they caught only a few nongravid (37) and gravid (6) female *Simulium posticatum* Meigen (= *austeni*), and even less *S. erythrocephalum* (De Geer), *S. aureum* Fries, and unidentified *S.* (*Wilhelmia*). In contrast, Adler et al. (1983) had better success in Pennsylvania when they sprayed a Plexiglas sheet with "Tangle-trap" adhesive and placed it above the water of a stream. From 42 trap-days they caught 5,109 black flies belonging to 10 species, 82.6% of which were *S. vittatum* complex; 78.2% of the females trapped were on the side sampling upstream flights, whereas 60.7% of the males were trapped flying downstream. Female flights mainly occurred within 0.3 meters of the water, and about a quarter of *S. vittatum* were collected within 7.5 cm of the water surface. They also placed a modified Malaise trap across streams, but in 10 days only 593 *S. vittatum* were caught, most of which (94.6–97.2%) were flying upstream.

Malaise traps have not proved very useful in catching black flies. Nevertheless I thought they had potential for sampling newly emerged adults and ovipositing females (Service 1977a). Darsie and Merino (1981) employed a Malaise trap across streams in Guatemala. Four days of trapping yielded 871 *Simulium downsi* Vagas, Martínez Palacios & Díaz Nájera, 85.9% of which were females, and of these 83% were gravid individuals; 93% were caught from 1500–1800 h.

STICKY TRAPS

In West Africa more *S. damnosum* complex have sometimes been caught on 1 m² aluminum sticky plates placed on river banks than from human and animal bait collections or in carbon dioxide traps (Bellec 1976, Bellec and Hébrard 1983b). Although 96.7% were ovipositing females, a very few newly emerged adults (0.5–3%) and males (1–2.5%) were also trapped. These plates, or ones made of shiny corrugated iron, have been employed to study the gonotrophic cycle (Bellec and Hébrard 1980a) and fecundity (Cheke et al. 1982) of *S. damnosum* s.l. Bellec and Hébrard (1983b) have caught as many as 5,950 black flies in one day on a single plate.

A modification consists of suspending plates, made bouyant by fixing empty plastic water bottles underneath, on the end of a rope so they float on the surface of turbulent waters. Another useful modification is to place three bands of self-adhesive plastic on the metal plates and to coat their exposed sides with adhesive, the best being a polybutene compound called "Oecotak." When evaluated in Burkina Faso, these traps proved useful in detecting low-level populations of both newly emerged *S. damnosum* complex and migrant individuals (Bellec et al. 1984).

Bellec and Hébrard (1980b) have also tried to sample *S. damnosum* by spraying resting sites, such as bunches of leaves and branches, with "Tanglefoot," but very few *Simulium* were caught. When they coated various artificial resting sites with adhesive, only 721 simuliids were caught from 8,665 trap-days. Clearly their searches for natural resting places and use of artificial shelters were not very rewarding.

SUCTION TRAPS

Although suction traps have been little used to study simuliids, six 45-cm propeller traps and four 30-cm aerofoil traps with their inlets 3 meters above the ground were operated continuously from April to October 1977 in an attempt to sample the *S. damnosum* complex migrating into the Onchocerciasis Control Programme area in West Africa. A total of 9,002 females, all unfed except for 6 gravid and 5 blood-fed specimens, and 187 male simuliids belonging to at least 10 species were caught (Johnson et al. 1982). However, only a single female of the *S. damnosum* complex was collected! Nevertheless, considerable numbers of *Simulium ruficorne* Macquart and *Simulium adersi* Pomeroy were trapped, and intriguingly also 2,732 adults of *Simulium evillense* Fain, Hallot & Bafort, a species not previously recorded from West Africa. In marked contrast, despite *S. hargreavesi* being abundant in breeding places within the OCP area, only 4 adults were caught. Somewhat similarly, very few *S. vernum* (identified incorrectly at the time as *S. latipes*) were caught in suction traps in Scotland, although larvae were abundant and adults were common in light traps (Davies and Williams 1962, Williams 1965). These instances emphasize the degree of sampling bias that can arise from using traps.

In England, Hansford and Ladle (1979) caught 91 male and 46 female *S. posticatum* (= *austeni*) in a suction trap placed at a swarming site. Finally, from 122 days of trapping, suction traps placed in a field of mixed crops in Pennsylvania caught 374 female and 1 male *S. jenningsi* group (Choe et al. 1984). There was a 99.2% reduction in the numbers caught between traps sited at heights of 2.1 and 7.6 meters.

During the above studies in Pennsylvania, only 4 female *S. jenningsi* group were caught in two tow nets pulled by an airplane making 100 flights (Choe et al. 1984). Previous attempts to sample aerial populations of simuliids have not been very rewarding, but the experiences of Farrow and Dowse (1984) in Australia on migrating insects are worth considering. They used tow nets having a cross-sectional opening of 1 m^2, which they mounted on kites. In winds of 10 km/h or more they were raised to heights of 100–500 meters by a winch or vehicle. When winds were light and variable, kites were kept airborne for up to 30 minutes by a vehicle driven at 5–30 mph. In moderate winds the nets sampled 5×10^4 m^3 air/h. A commercial radio-controlled system sold for model aircraft opened and closed the entrance of the tow nets. This technique should be evaluated for simuliids, and also radio-controlled model planes (which can fly up to heights of 100 meters) might be used to pull tow nets, which could, at least in some instances, sample simuliids. Already such planes are occasionally flown to deliver ultra-low volumes of agricultural pesticides.

VEHICLE-MOUNTED TRAPS

Vehicle-mounted traps have been used for several years for catching mosquitoes, but they have only occasionally been operated to sample simuliids. There are a great variety of vehicle-mounted trap designs (Service 1976), including lightweight portable ones (Holbrook and Wuerthele 1984). In northern Nigeria a car fitted with a roof-mounted trap and driven along a 30-km stretch of road by the River Assob collected 13 simuliid species, the most common being *Simulium hargreavesi* Gibbins, *S. squamosum*, *S. adersi*, *Simulium vorax* Pomeroy, and *Simulium hirsutum* Pomeroy. Most females were unfed (35.1–73.9%), and only a few were blood-fed (1.2–11.6%) (Roberts and Irving-Bell 1984a,b, and personal communication

1985). Parous females of *S. hargreavesi* and *S. squamosum* predominated in early-morning catches, while nulliparous flies were more common in the late afternoons and evenings. Blood-engorged and gravid *S. squamosum* were active only around sunset, whereas host-seeking females exhibited greater activity throughout the day. No flies were caught before 0600 h or between 2000–2200 h, after which trapping ceased.

Barnard (1979) used a lightweight trap for collecting Ceratopogonidae in Colorado, but apart from recording catches of *Simulium bivittatum* Malloch and *S. vittatum,* no other information on simuliids is given.

Truck-trapping has several limitations, the most obvious being that the method is applicable only to terrain over which a vehicle can be driven at the speed required to trap aerial insects. Sampling is supposed to be nonattractive, but it seems likely that at night vehicle headlights may disrupt normal flight behavior, especially when the vehicle is making repeated runs over a road. The trap is often on the roof, with its opening some distance from the front of the vehicle. Because of air turbulence that must be passing over the vehicle, I find it difficult to credit that such traps are sampling insects at that specific height. To try to overcome this problem in their studies on *Culicoides variipennis* (Coquillett) in Colorado, Holbrook and Wuerthele (1984) placed the trap entrance directly above the front of their truck. Nevertheless, I still think this may not completely overcome the problem of air turbulence. As far as I am aware, no studies have been made of air passing over vehicles having traps placed in different positions.

MARK-RECAPTURE STUDIES

There have been several studies involving marking black flies with paints, fluorescent dusts, and radionuclides. For example, in studying the duration of the gonotrophic cycle in *S. damnosum* s.l. in Ivory Coast, Bellec and Hébrard (1980a) anesthetized 4,780 females with carbon dioxide, marked them on the thorax with oil paints, and recaptured them at human bait and on sticky aluminum plates. Recapture rates varied from 1.0–12.5%, with a mean of 5.5%.

Although more insects can usually be marked with powders than paints, dusts are sometimes lost or transferred to other individuals and it is more difficult to use them for multiple marking. The following two chapters will therefore be of special interest to those intending to mark simuliids. Lillie et al. (1981) found that all ten "Day-Glo" micronized fluorescent dusts they tested were unsatisfactory in marking *C. variipennis,* for they failed to adhere to the insects. Furthermore, only three—Green–1953, Green–3206, and Yellow–2267—of the six dusts from U.S. Radium Corporation were retained for sufficiently long periods and were nontransferable. Although these three dusts caused some mortality, they were not considered to reduce survival rates significantly. Bennett et al. (1981) marked insects with "Dayglo" and "Radiant Color" fluorescent powders and used an incident light fluorescent microscope to identify recaptured marked mosquitoes. By using six fluorescent colors applied in combinations of three colors or less, they were able to obtain forty-two unique marking codes.

DISCUSSION AND CONCLUSION

The first consideration in sampling black flies is to decide what information is wanted and the quality and precision required. Only when the objectives have been clearly defined can deliberation be given to selecting the most appropriate methodology. It is also important to recognize the possibility of trap bias when interpreting results from a trapping program.

A review of sampling procedures emphasizes that we are still unable to sample adequately simuliids resting in their natural shelters, and in most instances they are ineffective in monitoring their migration. Although radar is used to study dispersal of large insects (e.g., moths and grasshoppers) (Greenbank et al. 1980), it is unsuitable for smaller insects such as simuliids. Moreover, a serious limitation of radar is that it cannot detect insects within, or immediately above, plant canopies; like aircraft, they fly below the radar-detection zone. Recently, however, a new and relatively inexpensive technique, termed Infra-red Active Determination of Insect Flight Trajectories (IRADIT), has been developed that illuminates insects during the day and night with an intense beam of pulsed infrared radiation. Detection is achieved with a shuttered image intensifier linked with a video camera; flight trajectories and other data can be stored on floppy discs. Insects as small as 1.5 mm^2 can be tracked at midday up to 15 meters; larger insects and those flying at night can be detected at greater distances. This method has considerable potential for studying flight behavior of simuliids; in fact, a simpler device has detected single emerging *Simulium arcticum* Malloch up to 40 meters away (Schaeffer and Bent 1984).

Despite increasing ethical pressure, we have still not found a suitable alternative to human bait collections to monitor anthropophagic black flies. On the other hand, Bellec's sticky plates have proved valuable in measuring population densities of ovipositing *S. damnosum* s.l., while Monks Wood light traps deserve further evaluation in sampling black fly populations.

LITERATURE CITED

Adler, P. H., K. C. Kim, and R. W. Light. 1983. Flight patterns of the *Simulium vittatum* (Diptera:Simuliidae) complex over a stream. *Environ. Entomol.* 12:232–236.

Anderson, J. R., and G. R. DeFoliart. 1981. Feeding behavior and host preferences of some black flies (Diptera:Simuliidae) in Wisconsin. *Ann. Entomol. Soc. Am.* 54:716–729.

Ball, S. G. 1983. A comparison of the Diptera caught in Manitoba traps with those from cattle and other parts of the field ecosystem in northern England. *Bull. Entomol. Res.* 73:527–537.

Ball, S. G., and M. L. Luff. 1981. Attractiveness of Manitoba traps to the headfly, *Hydrotaea irritans* (Fallén) (Diptera:Muscidae): the effects of short-term weather fluctuations, carbon dioxide and target temperature and size. *Bull. Entomol. Res.* 71:599–606.

Barnard, D. R. 1979. A vehicle-mounted insect trap. *Can. Entomol.* 111:851–854.

Bellec, C. 1976. Captures d'adultes de *Simulium damnosum* Theobald, 1903 (Diptera, Simuliidae) à l'aide de plaques d'aluminium, en Afrique de l'Ouest. *Cah. ORSTOM sér. Entomol. Méd. Parasitol.* 14:209–217.

Bellec, C., and G. Hébrard. 1980a. La durée du cycle gonotrophique des femelles du complexe *Simulium damnosum* en zone péforestière de Côte d'Ivoire. *Cah. ORSTOM sér. Entomol. Méd. Parasitol.* 18:347–358.

———. 1980b. Les lieux de repose des adultes du complexe *Simulium damnosum* (Diptera,Simuliidae) 1. Les méthodes d'étude. *Cah. ORSTOM sér. Entomol. Méd. Parasitol.* 18:261–275.

———. 1983a. Les préférences trophiques des vecteurs de l'onchocercose en secteur pré-forestier de Côte d'Ivoire. *Cah. ORSTOM sér. Entomol. Méd. Parasitol.* 21:241–249.

———. 1983b. Les heures d'activité de vol des adultes du complexe *Simulium damnosum* en secteur pré-forestier de Côte d'Ivoire. *Cah. ORSTOM sér. Entomol. Méd. Parasitol.* 21:261–273.

Bellec, C., D. G. Zerbo, J. Nion, G. Hébrard and H. Agoua. 1984. Utilisation expérimentale des plaques d'aluminium pour l'évaluation entomologique du programme de lutte contre l'onchocercose dans le bassin de la Volta. *Cah. ORSTOM sér. Entomol. Méd. Parasitol.* 22:191–205.

Bennett, S. R., G. A. H. McClelland, and J. M. Smilanick. 1981. A versatile system of fluorescent marks for studies of large populations of mosquitoes (Diptera:Culicidae). *J. Med. Entomol.* 18:173–174.

Berl, D. 1982. Note sur l'utilisation de pièges biconiques dans la capture de simulies. *Cah. ORSTOM sér. Entomol. Méd. Parasitol.* 20:172–173.

Bowden, J. 1982. An analysis of factors affecting catches of insects in light-traps. *Bull. Entomol. Res.* 72:535–556.

———. 1984. Latitudinal and seasonal changes of nocturnal illumination with a hypothesis about their effect on catches of insects in light-traps. *Bull. Entomol. Res.* 74:279–298.

Bradbury, W. C., and G. F. Bennett. 1974. Behavior of adult Simuliidae (Diptera). I. Response to color and shape. *Can. J. Zool.* 52:251–259.

Browne, S. M., and G. F. Bennett. 1980. Color and shape as mediators of host seeking responses of simuliids and tabanids (Diptera) in the Tantramar marshes, New Brunswick, Canada. *J. Med. Entomol.* 17:58–62.

Challier, A., and C. Laveissière. 1973. Un nouveau piège pour la capture des glossines (Glossinidae:Diptera,Muscidae): déscription et essais sur le terrain. *Cah. ORSTOM sér. Entomol. Méd. Parasitol.* 11:251–262.

Cheke, R. A., R. Garms, and M. Kerner. 1982. The fecundity of *Simulium damnosum* s.l. in northern Togo and infections with *Onchocerca* spp. *Ann. Trop. Med. Parasitol.* 76:561–568.

Choe, J. C., P. H. Adler, K. C. Kim, and R. A. J. Taylor. 1984. Flight patterns of *Simulium jenningsi* (Diptera:Simuliidae) in central Pennsylvania, USA. *J. Med. Entomol.* 21:474–476.

Colbo, M. H. and H. O'Brien. 1984. A pilot black fly (Diptera:Simuliidae) control program using *Bacillus thuringiensis* var. *israelensis* in Newfoundland. *Can. J. Zool.* 116:1085–96.

Crosskey, R. W. 1958. First results in the control of *Simulium damnosum* Theobald (Diptera,Simuliidae) in Northern Nigeria. *Bull. Entomol. Res.* 49:142–153.

Darsie, R. F., and M. E. Merino. 1981. The oviposition time of *Simulium downsi* trapped over a breeding stream in Guatemala (Diptera, Simuliidae). *Mosquito News* 41:129–132.

Das, S. C., M. Bhuyan, and N. G. Das. 1984. Attraction of Simuliidae to different colors on humans—field trials. *Mosquito News* 44:79–80.

Davies, L., and C. B. Williams. 1962. Studies on black flies (Diptera:Simuliidae) taken in a light trap in Scotland. I. Seasonal distribution, sex ratio and internal condition of catches. *Trans. R. Entomol. Soc. London* 114:1–20.

Dietz, K. 1982. The population dynamics of onchocerciasis. Pp. 209–241 in R. M. Anderson, Ed., *Population dynamics of infectious diseases. Theory and applications*. Chapman & Hall, London. 368 pp.

Emord, D. E., and C. D. Morris. 1982. A host-baited CDC trap. *Mosquito News* 42:220–224.

Farrow, R. A., and J. E. Dowse. 1984. Method of using kites to carry tow nets in the upper air for sampling migrating insects and its application to radar entomology. *Bull. Entomol. Res.* 74:87–95.

Greenbank, D. O., G. W. Schaeffer, and R. C. Rainey. 1980. Spruce budworm (Lepidoptera:Tortricidae) moth and dispersal: new understanding from canopy observations, radar and aircraft. *Mem. Entomol. Soc. Can.*, no. 110. 49 pp.

Hansford, R. G., and M. Ladle. 1979. The medical importance and behaviour of *Simulium austeni* Edwards (Diptera:Simuliidae) in England. *Bull. Entomol. Res.* 69:33–41.

Glasgow, J. P. 1963. *The distribution and abundance of tsetse*. Pergamon Press, Oxford. 241 pp.

Hargrove, J. W. 1980. Improved estimates of the efficiency of traps for *Glossina morsitans morsitans* Westwood and *G. pallidipes* Austen (Diptera: Glossinidae), with a note on the effect of the concentration of accompanying host odours on efficiency. *Bull. Entomol. Res.* 70:777–787.

Holbrook, F. R., and W. Wuerthele. 1984. A lightweight, hand-portable vehicle-mounted insect trap. *Mosquito News* 44:239–242.

Johnson, C. G., R. W. Crosskey, and J. B. Davies. 1982. Species composition and cyclical changes in numbers of savanna blackflies (Diptera:Simuliidae) caught by suction traps in the Onchocerciasis Control Programme area of West Africa. *Bull. Entomol. Res.* 72:39–63.

Kyorku, C. A. 1982. Studies on the egg-stage of some common Ghanaian Simuliidae (Diptera:Nematocera) with particular reference to onchocerciasis vectors. M.Sc. Thesis, University of Ghana.

Lillie, T. H., R. H. Jones, and W. C. Marquardt. 1981. Micronized fluorescent dusts for marking *Culicoides variipennis* adults. *Mosquito News* 41:356–358.

McCreadie, J. W., M. H. Colbo, and G. F. Bennett. 1984. A trap design for the collection of haematophagous Diptera from cattle. *Mosquito News* 44:212–216.

McKeever, S., and W. K. Hartberg. 1980. An effective method for trapping adult female *Corethrella* (Diptera:Chaoboridae). *Mosquito News* 40:111–112.

Noblet, R. and D. R. Alverson. 1978. Sampling methods for black flies (Diptera:Simuliidae). *Tech. Bull. S.C. Agric. Exp. Stn.*, no. 1067. 6 pp.

Okazawa, T., J. O. Ochoa, and K. Matsuo. 1981. Seasonal prevalence, diurnal biting activity and the behaviour of onchocerciasis vectors in Guatemala. Pp. 181–182 in *Proc. Guatemala-Japan Joint Conference on Onchocerciasis Research and Control*. Japan International Cooperation Agency, Tokyo. 230 pp.

Petersen, J. L., A. J. Adames, and L. de León. 1983. Bionomics and control of black flies (Diptera:Simuliidae) at the Fortuna hydroelectric project, Panama. *J. Med. Entomol.* 20:399–408.

Pinkovsky, D. D., D. J. Forrester, and J. F. Butler. 1981. Investigations on black fly vectors (Diptera:Simuliidae) of *Leucocytozoon smithi* (Sporozoa:Leucocytozoidae) in Florida. *J. Med. Entomol.* 18:153–157.

Roberts, D. M., and R. J. Irving-Bell. 1984a. Circadian flight activity of black-flies (Diptera:Culicidae) collected using a vehicle-mounted net in central Nigeria. *Abstract Vol. XVII Int. Congr. Entomol.*, Hamburg. P. 665.

———. 1984b. Circadian activity of blackflies (Diptera:Simuliidae) in the Assob Valley, using vehicle-mounted net. *Nat. Sci. Res. Abstract.* vol. 1. University of Jos, Nigeria. P. 41.

Rogers, D. J., and S. E. Randolph. 1978. A comparison of electric trap and hand-net catches of *Glossina palpalis palpalis* (Robineau-Desvoidy) and *G. tachinoides* Westwood (Diptera:Glossinidae) in the Sudan vegetation zone of northern Nigeria. *Bull. Entomol. Res.* 68:283–297.

Ryan, J. K., and G. J. Hilchie. 1982. Black fly problems in Athabasca county and vicinity, Alberta, Canada. *Mosquito News* 42:614–616.

Schaeffer, G. W., and G. A. Bent. 1984. An infra-red remote sensing system for the active detection and automatic determination of insect flight trajectories (IRADIT). *Bull. Entomol. Res.* 74:261–278.

Service, M. W. 1976. *Mosquito ecology: field sampling methods.* Applied Science, London. 583 pp.

———. 1977a. Methods for sampling adult Simuliidae, with special reference to the *Simulium damnosum* complex. *Trop. Pest Bull.,* no. 5. Centre for Overseas Pest Research, London. 48 pp.

———. 1977b. A critical review of procedures for sampling populations of adult mosquitoes. *Bull. Entomol. Res.* 67:343–382.

———. 1979. Light trap collections of ovipositing *Simulium squamosum* in Ghana. *Ann. Trop. Med. Parasitol.* 73:487–490.

———. 1981. Sampling methods for adults. Pp. 287–296 in M. Laird, Ed., *Blackflies: The future for biological methods in integrated control.* Academic Press, New York and London. 399 pp.

Service, M. W., and R. B. Highton. 1980. A chemical light trap for mosquitoes and other biting insects. *J. Med. Entomol.* 17:183–185.

Suzuki, T. 1983. *A guidebook for Guatemalan onchocerciasis (Robles disease).* The Guatemala-Japan Cooperative Project on Onchocerciasis Research and Control, Guatemala. 155 pp.

Taylor, J., D. E. Padgham, and T. J. Perfect. 1982. A light-trap with upwardly directed illumination and temporal segregation of the catch. *Bull. Entomol. Res.* 72:669–673.

Trueman, D. W., and S. B. McIver. 1981. Detecting fine-scale temporal distributions of biting flies: a new trap design. *Mosquito News* 41:439–443.

Vale, G. A. 1982. The improvement of traps for tsetse flies (Diptera:Glossinidae). *Bull. Entomol. Res.* 72:95–106.

———. 1983. The effects of odour, wind direction and wind speed on the distribution of *Glossina* (Diptera:Glossinidae) and hosts used near stationary targets. *Bull. Entomol. Res.* 73:53–64.

Wainhouse, D. 1980. A portable suction trap for sampling small insects. *Bull. Entomol. Res.* 70:491–494.

Walsh, J. F. 1978. Light trap studies on *Simulium damnosum* s.l. in northern Ghana. *Tropenmed. Parasitol.* 29:492–496.

Williams, C. B. 1964. Nocturnal activity of black flies (Simuliidae). *Nature* (London) 201:105.

———. 1965. Black-flies (Diptera:Simuliidae) in a suction trap in the Central Highlands of Scotland. *Proc. R. Entomol. Soc. London* (A) 40:92–95.

Williams, C. B., and L. Davies. 1957. Simuliidae attracted at night to a trap using ultra-violet light. *Nature* (London) 179:924–925.

15 THE MIGRATION AND DISPERSAL OF BLACK FLIES: *SIMULIUM DAMNOSUM* S.L., THE MAIN VECTOR OF HUMAN ONCHOCERCIASIS

Rolf Garms and James Frank Walsh

Many species of black flies (Diptera: Simuliidae) are well-known biting pests of man and his livestock, and in some parts of the tropics are vectors of *Onchocerca volvulus* (Leuckart, 1893), causative organism of human onchocerciasis. Black flies generally appear to be strong flyers. Long-distance movements away from breeding sites have been reported for many species and have been discussed in the reviews of Hocking (1953), Fallis (1964), and Johnson (1969). Sometimes movements can involve huge numbers of flies. Baranoff (1936) reported that swarms of the Golubatz fly *Simulium colombaschense* were carried downwind from their breeding sites in the Danube and invaded large areas of Yugoslavia. In Canada *S. arcticum* has been reported biting, and even killing, cattle at distances of more than 200 kilometers from its breeding places (Fredeen 1969). Among the vectors of onchocerciasis, *S. damnosum* s.l., in particular, has for many years been considered to travel long distances (Le Berre 1966). Accurate knowledge of this behavior is important for an understanding of the epidemiology of disease and vital for the planning and execution of black fly management programs.

In general, there seem to be two different types of movement made by adult black flies: those that are immediately goal-oriented and those that are not. Goal-oriented flights, sometimes called "appetitive" flights (Johnson 1969), include flights in search of a mate, sugar or blood meal, or oviposition substrate. Flights without an immediate goal provide a means whereby the colonization of new habitats may take place. In practice, non-goal-oriented movements may be wind-assisted or made without the aid of the wind. This usually results in the former being over greater distances than the latter. It should not be assumed that wind-assisted movements are passive, for almost invariably active upward flight is required to take the insect out of the vegetation and above the boundary layer to altitudes permitting displacement downwind. Furthermore, the insect will not remain airborne for long if it ceases to beat its wings. We do not consider that black flies, while on appetitive flights, are accidently "entrained" in meteorological fronts as implied by Wellington (1974).

The meteorological aspects of insect dispersal by wind have recently been considered in detail by Pedgley (1982, 1983).

For convenience, and following earlier authors (Le Berre 1966, Wenk 1981), we refer to long-distance, wind-assisted movement as migration, while short-distance, unaided flights are referred to as dispersal flights. Appetitive flights also may result in the movement of insects away from the natal site, but these will not normally be distinguishable from true dispersal flights. Appetitive flights as such are not considered here.

In this chapter we attempt to present a coherent picture of black fly migration using *S. damnosum* s.l. as an example. Owing to the immense medical and economic importance of this species complex (Le Berre et al. 1978, Walsh 1985), it has recently become one of the most intensively studied of all black flies. We believe that many widespread species that inhabit regions with marked seasonal variations exhibit similar behavior.

TECHNIQUES FOR THE STUDY OF MIGRATION AND DISPERSAL

It is very difficult to obtain conclusive evidence for long-distance movements of small insects. Ideally, data from marking and recapture experiments are required for this. Such studies have been attempted by several workers (Dalmat 1952, Dalmat and Gibson 1952, Fredeen et al. 1953, Crisp 1956, Noamesi 1966, Thompson et al. 1972, Baldwin et al. 1975, Thompson 1976). However, most of these studies only confirmed the views of earlier workers that relatively short-distance movements occurred (but see below for discussion of Thompson's results).

This technique, although giving positive proof of movement, is extremely difficult to apply where the scale of movements may be on the order of hundreds of kilometers. In such cases it may be necessary to mark millions of insects to achieve a single recovery at these extreme distances. Inevitably it requires a very extensive network of trapping or collecting sites.

The first difficulty may be overcome by marking larval populations in their breeding sites, using dyes, radioactive materials, or trace elements. The possibility of working with natural markers should also be considered. Attempts were made, in the OCP, to determine the sources of invading flies by analysis of caught flies for naturally occurring trace elements using X-ray fluorescent spectroscopy (D'Auria and Bennett 1975), with results that showed promise but proved inconclusive. Comparisons of morphological and size differences of flies gave variable information, but in some cases proved of value (Garms 1978, Garms et al. 1982). Genetic markers visible on the polytene chromosomes, e.g., those linked with insecticide resistance (Meredith et al. 1984), may also be of use. Allied to this is the desirability of having adequate sampling devices. Ideally these should be nonattractant, so that flies in nonappetitive flight can be collected. Such devices include suction traps (Johnson et al. 1982) and nets mounted on balloons or aircraft (Rainey and Joyce 1972).

Another valuable procedure is the detection of flies in areas far from active breeding sites, a technique exploited by biogeographers and students of insect migration in general (Williams 1958, Urquhart 1960, Johnson 1969, Rainey 1978). Nor-

mally the requisite absence of *Simulium* breeding over extensive areas, where cog-
nascent entomologists are active, does not occur. However, such a situation can be
created by control operations that eliminate breeding over large areas. An early
example seems to be that of the control of *S. damnosum* s.l. in the Victoria Nile,
Uganda (Prentice 1974), where intermittent eradication of the vector has been
achieved (McCrae 1978). Flies reappeared only after absences of from three to four
and a half years on three occasions. McCrae (1978) considered that the first recolonization must have been from the north, where the nearest focus lies at a distance of
over 120 kilometers.

EVIDENCE FOR MIGRATION IN WEST AFRICAN
SIMULIUM DAMNOSUM S.L.

When control of *S. damnosum* s.l. was attempted in West Africa, results proved
unsatisfactory owing to the regular influx of flies from untreated areas. Ovazza et al.
(1967) explained the recolonization of seasonally flowing rivers in the West African
savanna zone on the basis of a northward migration from permanent breeding sites.
They concluded that this migration was connected with the passage northward of the
Inter-tropical Convergence Zone (ITCZ). As a result of these experiences it was
concluded that female *S. damnosum* s.l. could travel distances on the order of 150
kilometers away from their natal sites (WHO 1973). This greatly influenced the
strategy and tactics planned for the World Health Organization Onchocerciasis Control Programme in the Volta River Basin (OCP).

It was only in 1975, however, when the first phase of the OCP operations, covering an area of 247,000 km^2, was brought into effect (Walsh 1977; Walsh et al. 1979,
1981a) that the full scale of the *S. damnosum* s.l. movement became apparent.
There was an initial spectacular reduction in the numbers of biting flies throughout
the whole area in which breeding sites were treated with the larvicide temephos
applied by aircraft. However, with the passage northward of the ITCZ over the
control area, biting rates rose considerably in those river valleys located in the
southwestern sector, and they stayed high until the end of the rainy season. This
pattern was repeated in the succeeding three years.

Immediately, tremendous efforts, using helicopters, were made to survey the
rivers of the treated area, but they did not reveal failures of treatment, or hitherto
unsuspected breeding sites, which could explain the high numbers of biting flies. It
had to be concluded, albeit reluctantly, that the flies did not originate from within
the treated area but were invaders from sources outside the program.

Although it may be difficult to believe that control could be fully effective over
such a large area, this has been accepted by many distinguished visiting scientists. As
Dr. C. G. Johnson told a meeting of the Royal Society of London: "The intensive
treatment of this vast area of rivers and streams seems to be a daunting prospect,
almost an unbelievable achievement, I think, until one sees for oneself that it is
really practicable" (Le Berre et al. 1979, Johnson in discussion, p. 286). The full
story is given in Garms et al. (1979), Le Berre et al. (1979), and Walsh et al.
(1981b). This account of the events that occurred in the OCP to the end of 1979 will

be drawn mainly from these papers without further citation of the sources. Here we wish to discuss the more important evidence.

The only indisputable facts relate to the flies caught deep inside the control area. However, the circumstantial evidence that these flies are not from local sources but came from outside the original program area, at considerable distances to the southwest, is very strong. Unfortunately, precise information about the flight activities of these flies is lacking. In this chapter, therefore, we attempt to present a hypothesis as to how the movements are achieved on the basis of the direct observations and the circumstantial evidence.

At the main study site, during the months of April through August 1976–78, 12,913 flies were dissected. Only 101 (0.8%) were nulliparous (of these, 75 were from May 1976). This proved that the majority had completed at least one gonotrophic cycle. It came as a surprise because accepted migration theory is that long-distance movements usually occur prior to egg development and reproduction (Johnson 1969, Dingle 1972), and it had therefore been assumed that any migratory movement into the OCP area would be signaled by a high nulliparous rate among the biting flies.

Although it is not possible to distinguish with certainty between *S. damnosum* s.l. in their second and subsequent gonotrophic cycles by ovarian examination, many of these flies appeared to be very old. On dissection, many were found to carry infective (third stage) larvae indistinguishable from those of *O. volvulus*. Flies carrying such larvae must have been a minimum of seven to eight days old. This implies that flies travel after taking a blood meal and continue their migratory activities in later gonotrophic cycles. There was a paucity of flies with developing (first stage) larvae and with double infections (first and third stage larvae in the same fly). In fact, flies with infective larvae were more numerous than those with developing infections, in clear contrast to observations made on uncontrolled *S. damnosum* s.l. populations (Duke 1968, Garms 1973, Philippon 1977).

Mokry (1980) also concluded, from counts of developing eggs, that many flies were in later gonotrophic cycles. In addition, he found that the proportions of older flies in the biting populations increased with increasing distance from the boundary of the control area. The invading flies took blood meals close to their oviposition sites, again in contrast to the situation before control. The vast majority of these biting flies proved to belong to the cytospecies *S. damnosum* s.str. or *S. sirbanum*.

The invasion was not a steady phenomenon. On several occasions it was observed that pronounced peaks, or troughs, occurred simultaneously, or with time shifts of a few days, at different catching sites. Johnson et al. (1985) have analyzed the data relating to the daily biting rates at those sites where fly catches were carried out every day during the early parts of the migration period in 1977 and 1978. They concluded that the migrant flies move in discrete waves in a broad northeasterly direction, averaging 15 to 18 kilometers per day. They also suggested that flies may reach an age of from 31 to 48 days at sites most distant from the source areas.

Our observation that nulliparous flies are rarely caught biting man more than 25 kilometers from their sources suggests that Johnson et al.'s figure actually does relate closely to the daily flight distance, or at any rate to that of the first day's flight.

Although some insects may migrate without the aid of the wind, present evidence suggests that they are the exception (Dingle 1972). In the OCP area at least, *S.*

damnosum s.l. seems to follow the general rule, for the direction of movement of migrant flies is predominantly southwest to northeast, the direction of the prevailing (monsoon) winds behind the ITCZ. This view is supported by experimental larviciding of suspected source areas to the southwest. Such treatments were rapidly followed by a marked decline in the numbers of invading flies, but the invasion did not cease entirely. This strongly suggested that substantial numbers of flies had traveled 400 kilometers and that some flies were probably traveling even greater distances. In retrospect, the phasing in the OCP control operations provided several examples of biting rates falling markedly in areas adjacent to and east of the area brought under control, but never in areas to the west.

It is difficult to associate entomological data concerning peaks of biting activity with particular meteorological events (backtracking), because it has not been possible to determine the exact time of the arrival of the flies. Magor and Rosenberg (1980), however, did have some success with this technique. The day on which flies are caught biting man is not necessarily the day on which they arrived in the vicinity. This is supported by the observations of Dr. C. Bellec (personal communication), who, by means of aluminum plates (Bellec 1976), caught large numbers of gravid flies before peaks of flies occurred on human bait. Furthermore, there is no evidence concerning the time of day at which migrating *S. damnosum* s.l. are undertaking their long-distance flights, or the height at which they travel.

Much of the activity of many species of black flies, including *S. damnosum* s.l., occurs at dawn and dusk. *S. damnosum* s.l. does not take blood meals at night. Several studies, using light traps, have yielded substantial numbers of black flies (Williams and Davies 1957, Walsh 1978, Service 1979). A study in which the light was operated throughout the night, but the catch segregated at regular intervals, provided evidence for movements by *S. damnosum* s.l. throughout the night (Walsh 1978). Among the *S. damnosum* s.l. caught were nulliparous, gravid, and occasional blood-engorged flies (Walsh 1978, Service 1979).

More important are the studies using nonattractant traps. Williams (1965), operating a suction trap in Scotland, caught black flies only at night. Roberts and Irving-Bell (1984) caught thousands of black flies in Nigeria using vehicle-mounted nets. They included many *S. squamosum*. Many blood-engorged and gravid flies were taken after sunset. Cooter (1982), using a flight mill in the laboratory, showed that *S. ornatum* exhibited similar flight activity during day and night. Walsh (1984) found that *S. damnosum* s.l. coming to bite man in the early morning had depleted sugar reserves, a situation unlikely to arise if they had rested overnight. It also indicated that sugar meals were not being obtained at night.

These observations are perhaps of interest in view of the statement of Pedgley (Cheke and Garms 1983, Pedgley in discussion, p. 483): "Winds in the lowest few hundred meters of the atmosphere over the OCP area tend to accelerate during the night, except close to the ground. This is a well recognized character of many land areas subject to both monsoons and trade winds. Long-distance flights above the boundary layer would therefore be favoured at night."

It is known that *S. damnosum* s.l. seeks the upper layers of vegetation. In all physiological states, flies have been trapped at heights above 6 meters in the canopies of trees at six different locations in the West African savanna (Walsh 1980, 1984; Bellec and Hébrard 1980). There are also observations of newly emerged *S. damnosum* s.l. and those that have just completed a blood meal flying upward

(Walsh, unpublished), while engorged *S. ochraceum* fly downward (Garms, unpublished). These observations probably all relate to appetitive behavior in search of temporary resting sites and should not be equated with any attempt to fly above the boundary layer. Nevertheless, it may be that *S. damnosum* s.l. has a strong tendency to upward flight, preadapting it to migratory flight above the boundary layer.

It is clear that flights of long duration will require considerable energy reserves, for even when a fly is transported by the wind it will eventually land if it ceases to beat its wings. It is therefore not surprising that many wild-caught flies have distended crops. By use of the cold anthrone test it has been possible to confirm that the crop contents of large numbers of black fly vectors (Cupp and Collins 1979, Walsh and Garms 1982, Walsh 1984) consist of sugars of plant origin. Cooter (1983), in a valuable series of flight-mill experiments using three species of the *S. damnosum* complex, clearly demonstrated that sugar was essential for sustained flight.

In addition to the work carried out in the OCP area, Thompson (1976), working in the forest zone of Cameroon, provided valuable information about the movement of *S. damnosum* s.l. He succeeded in recapturing marked flies at considerable distances (maximum 79 kilometers) along a large river. This confirmed that even in the forest *S. damnosum* s.l. can make extensive movements in a short time. Two flies traveled 56 and 79 kilometers, respectively, in less than 48 hours. Although linear movements are not considered to be wind-assisted, it is difficult to imagine that these two flights could have been achieved without the aid of the wind.

HOW *SIMULIUM DAMNOSUM* S.L. MIGRATES

From the foregoing observations our impression is that the migrations of female *S. damnosum* s.l. take place in the following manner.

On emergence, the female takes a sugar meal and mates in the vicinity of the site of eclosion. There is evidence to suggest that flies are programmed to make a flight prior to taking their first blood meal. This flight may bring the female to a distance of more than 20 kilometers from the breeding site. Thus even this initial movement may be wind-assisted. It implies that the fly has moved above the boundary layer by active, upward flight and will therefore, of necessity, be traveling downwind. On landing, the fly makes a host-seeking flight that occurs within the vegetation. The blood meal is always taken during daylight.

Sometime after feeding, and having expelled the excess fluid of the meal, the fly continues its migratory flight. In other words, migratory flights (e.g., those taking place downwind, above the boundary layer) take place on more than one occasion post blood meal during each gonotrophic cycle. Otherwise the distances actually observed could not be covered. Each flight period is preceded by a sugar meal. Before the complete maturation of the ovaries the migratory urge wanes. Then, either as a result of visual clues or flight along a humidity gradient, the fly reenters the boundary layer. It again becomes able to control its direction of movement and seeks a suitable breeding site. There it rests in the tree canopy close to its oviposition site for some time before laying its eggs in the late afternoon.

Following oviposition, the fly rests overnight, again in the riverine tree canopy, and then takes a blood meal nearby. This could help to explain the different patterns of "dispersal" of nulliparous and parous flies reported by earlier workers (Le Berre 1966, Duke 1975). Further migratory flights are taken in each succeeding gonotrophic cycle, until the fly dies.

MIGRATORY AND DISPERSAL TENDENCIES OF THE DIFFERENT CYTOSPECIES OF THE *SIMULIUM DAMNOSUM* COMPLEX IN WEST AFRICA

Southwood (1962) has argued that migration is a feature in the life of denizens of temporary habitats. The *S. damnosum* complex in West Africa provides a very clear example of this (Table 15.1). With increasing stability of habitat comes a decreasing tendency for long-distance movement. Really long-range movements have been observed only in the savanna cytospecies *S. damnosum* s.str. and *S. sirbanum*. This strategy enables them to colonize large areas without permanent breeding sites. In the original OCP area of 654,000 km^2, 247,000 km^2 located in the north and northeast are completely without flowing water for at least four months of each year. Furthermore, wind-assisted movements tend to concentrate the insects involved in zones of convergence where rain is likely to fall (Rainey 1978) and consequently where rivers are starting to flow. In such situations nutritional conditions for the filter-feeding simuliid larvae are especially favorable and very few predatory insects are present.

At the southern edge of the range of the *S. damnosum* complex in West Africa, *S. sirbanum* has not been recorded in Liberia. *S. damnosum* s.str. is found there in some perennial sites in the forest only during the dry season, disappearing at the height of the rains (Garms, unpublished). In some areas of dense forest it does not occur, even in the dry season. Presumably the ecological conditions that operate to exclude *S. damnosum* s.str. from this zone are more widespread in the rainy season. They result in a retraction northward of the southern limits of the range of this cytospecies. The factors involved are unknown.

If the migratory strategy employed by these two important vectors is to be successful, it must involve a movement in the reverse direction at the end of the rainy season. Unfortunately, we did not have an opportunity to study this in the OCP area, for there were no potential breeding sites left untreated to the north. Nevertheless, the seasonal oscillation of the southern boundary of the distributional range of *S. damnosum* s.str. in Liberia suggests that such a movement is taking place.

Simulium squamosum is more locally distributed than the other cytospecies. In all probability it consists of a number of isolated populations (Garms 1978, Crosskey 1981) that inhabit the forest and humid savanna zones, especially in mountainous country. In western Ivory Coast this cytospecies lives in well-wooded country and does not appear to travel far from its permanently populated breeding sites. In central Togo, where it inhabits a drier, more open region, there is evidence of considerable migration, sufficient to cause a problem to the OCP. Movements up to 150 kilometers are believed to occur (Garms et al. 1982, Cheke and Garms 1983).

Simulium soubrense (cf. footnote to Table 15.1), an inhabitant of large rivers in the forest and derived savanna zones, shows some tendency to extend its range

Table 15.1 Summary of the migratory and dispersal tendencies of different members of the *Simulium damnosum* complex in West Africa, in relation to habitat stability[a]

Cytospecies	Distribution	Favored Breeding Sites	Permanency of Breeding Sites	Migration	Distance in km Traveled	References
S. sirbanum Vajime & Dunbar	Sudan savanna extending to Guinea savanna	large and small streams	mostly temporary	+	>500	Garms et al. 1979 Walsh et al. 1981
S. damnosum Theobald	dry and humid savannas, extending to forest	rivers and large streams	temporary and permanent	+	>500	Garms et al. 1979 Walsh et al. 1981
S. squamosum Enderlein	forest and wooded savanna in mountainous areas	streams	mostly permanent	+	150 (savanna) 75 (forest)	Cheke and Garms 1983 Walsh et al. 1979
S. soubrense Vajime & Dunbar	forest and humid savanna	rivers	permanent	+ ?	150 ?	Garms et al. 1979
S. sanctipauli Vajime & Dunbar	forest	rivers	permanent	—	> 20	Garms, personal observation
S. yahense Vajime & Dunbar	forest	streams	permanent	—	< 5	Quillévéré 1979; Garms, personal observation

[a]The nomenclature in the table and text of Chapter 15 follows Vajime and Dunbar (1975, *Tropenmed. Parasitol.* 26:111–138). The redefinition of the *Simulium sanctipauli* subcomplex provided by Post (1986, *Genetica* 109:191–207) has not been incorporated.

northward in the rainy season. However, it does not penetrate far into the drier savannas. Evidence for wind-assisted movement is lacking.

*Simulium sanctipauli** is essentially an inhabitant of large rivers in the forest. It does not extend its range into the savanna zone in the rainy season. However, it is known to occur at distances exceeding 20 kilometers from its breeding sites in forest areas (Garms, personal observation). In 1976 areas of the southern Bandama River (Ivory Coast) in which *S. sanctipauli* bred heavily were experimentally treated with temephos larvicide by the OCP. Its population virtually disappeared and took several months to recover (Dr. B. Philippon, personal communication), suggesting little or no movement of flies into the valley from surrounding untreated river basins. Thus while it is extremely unlikely that *S. sanctipauli* is a migrant, dispersal appears to be a normal feature of its behavior.

Simulium yahense is an inhabitant of small rivers in the forest. These are often hydrologically more stable than the large rivers of this zone. *Simulium yahense* seems to have little tendency to travel away from water, being rarely found more than 2 kilometers from its breeding sites (Quillévéré 1979). Of the species so far studied, it seems to have the least tendency to disperse away from watercourses.

It is probable that these observed differences in flight behavior are largely determined by varying sensitivities to changes in microclimate, especially saturation pressure deficit. This helps to explain the well-known differences between wet- and dry-season dispersal patterns. Thus dispersal by savanna flies is largely linear in the dry season, but with increasing humidities at the start of the rainy season flies may lose contact with their natal water courses and disperse radially (Le Berre 1966, Wenk 1981). Even in the forest zone *S. sanctipauli* exhibits marked differences of this type at different seasons (Garms 1973). Clearly flight above the boundary layer, necessary for migration, can only occur when humidity thresholds are exceeded.

Even within savanna cytospecies there appear to be populations that are nonmigratory. It is observed that flies from such populations are larger than normal, a feature that has been noted in other insects (Dingle 1972). Such populations are particularly numerous in the early rainy season, when larval feeding conditions are especially advantageous, and when populations of predators (Mrs. B. Walsh, personal communication) and parasites (Walsh 1984) are at a low ebb. It is clearly adaptive that adults emerging from such favorable environments do not leave their natal streams.

EPIDEMIOLOGICAL IMPLICATIONS OF *SIMULIUM DAMNOSUM* S.L. MOVEMENTS

It is clear that some females of the savanna cytospecies of the *S. damnosum* complex are capable of successive flights during a considerable part of their lives. Therefore, infections acquired in the early life of a fly may be transported over vast distances. This happened in the OCP area, which was consequently not only invaded by the vector but effectively by the disease organism. In consequence, the ultimate success

*Cf. footnote to Table 15.1.

of this important control program was called into question, and it became necessary to extend the area under control to eliminate the sources of the invading flies.

The finding that *S. damnosum* s.l. can fly great distances while infected with *O. volvulus* is in contrast to an earlier hypothesis (Lebied 1950) that infection caused a degeneration of the flight muscles and greatly reduced the flight range. This is a mistaken view that has been repeated in many textbooks. It is perhaps worth pointing out that the mean load of infective larvae found in infective savanna flies varies from about 2.5 in the south to 1.5 in the north, whereas among forest cytospecies mean infective larval loads may exceed 6.0. Nevertheless, in a marking and recapture study using forest *S. damnosum* s.l., Thompson (1976) recovered one experimentally fed fly carrying 10 infective *O. volvulus* larvae at 24 kilometers.

The fact that long-distance migrants tend to bite close to oviposition sites means that they are responsible for significant transmission levels only close to the rivers. It is also clear that as a result of seasonal differences in dispersal behavior many human communities will be subjected to transmission only during the rainy season, even when a perennial breeding river is in the vicinity. Unfortunately, human settlements located on the banks of a river suitable for vector breeding are likely to be subjected to intense transmission. It is these factors that have resulted in the disease, in its worst manifestations, being associated with rivers and called in the English-speaking world "river blindness."

The paucity of first-stage larvae and double infections in migrants caught far from their source areas is difficult to understand. The most plausible explanation seems to be that these flies pay a price in loss of reproductive value (Dingle 1972), in that the gonotrophic cycle becomes extended. This will also have the effect of reducing their vectorial efficiency.

CONCLUSION

We believe that the account of the behavior of *S. damnosum* s.l. presented here fully substantiates the view that some cytospecies of this important vector complex are truly migratory, while others, the inhabitants of more stable environments, are not. However, we are still far from a detailed understanding of this. As Dingle (1972) has said: "Migration in any animal cannot be understood until viewed in its entirety as a physiological, behavioral, and ecological syndrome." It is clear that Simuliidologists themselves have a long way to go.

ACKNOWLEDGMENTS

It will be obvious that without the interest and support of the World Health Organization Onchocerciasis Control Programme this chapter would never have been written. We must again offer our sincere thanks to all our colleagues, past and present, for enabling this work to be carried out. In addition, J.F.W. is grateful to the OCP for supporting a brief visit to Hamburg, during which the chapter was drafted.

LITERATURE CITED

Baldwin, W. F., A. S. West, and J. Gomery. 1975. Dispersal pattern of black flies (Diptera: Simuliidae) tagged with [32]P. *Can. Entomol.* 107:113–118.

Baranoff, N. 1936. *Simulium (Danubiosimulium) columbaczense* Schönb. en Yougoslawie. Studien an pathogenen und parasitischen Insekten IV. Institut für Hygiene und Volksgesundheit in Zagreb. 36 pp.

Bellec, C. 1976. Captures d'adultes *de Simulium damnosum* Theobald, 1903 (Diptera, Simuliidae)

Bellec, C. 1976. Captures d'adultes de *Simulium damnosum* Theobald, 1903 (Diptera, Simuliidae) á l'aide de plaques d'aluminium, en Afrique de l'Ouest. *Cah. ORSTOM sér Entomol. Méd. Parasitol.* 14:209–217.

Bellec, C., and G. Hébrard. 1980. Les lieux de repos des adultes du complexe *Simulium damnosum* (Diptera: Simuliidae) I. Les méthodes d'étude. *Cah. ORSTOM sér. Entomol. Méd. Parasitol.* 18:261–275.

Cheke, R. A., and R. Garms. 1983. Reinfestations of the southeastern flank of the Onchocerciasis Control Programme area by windborne vectors. *Phil. Trans. R. Soc. London* (B) 302:471–484.

Cooter, R. J. 1982. Studies on the flight of black-flies (Diptera: Simuliidae) I. Flight performance of *Simulium ornatum*, Meigen. *Bull. Entomol. Res.* 72:303–317.

———. 1983. Studies on the flight of black-flies (Diptera: Simuliidae). II. Flight performance of three cytospecies in the complex of *Simulium damnosum* Theobald. *Bull. Entomol. Res.* 73:275–288.

Crisp, G. 1956. *Simulium and onchocerciasis in the Northern Territories of the Gold Coast.* H. K. Lewis, London. 171 pp.

Crosskey, R. W. 1981. Geographical distribution of Simuliidae. Pp. 57–68 in M. Laird, Ed., *Blackflies: the future for biological methods in integrated control.* Academic Press, New York and London.

Cupp, E. W., and R. C. Collins. 1979. The gonotrophic cycle in *Simulium ochraceum. Am. J. Trop. Med. Hyg.* 28:422–426.

Dalmat, H. T. 1952. Longevity and further flight range studies on the blackflies (Diptera, Simuliidae), with the use of dye markers. *Ann. Entomol. Soc. Am.* 45:23–37.

Dalmat, H. T., and C. L. Gibson. 1952. A study of flight range and longevity of blackflies (Diptera, Simuliidae) infected with *Onchocerca volvulus. Ann. Entomol. Soc. Am.* 45:605–612.

D'Auria, J. M., and R. Bennet. 1975. X rays and trace elements. *Chemistry* 48:17–19.

Dingle, H. 1972. Migration strategies of insects. *Science* 175:1327–35.

Duke, B. O. L. 1968. Studies on factors influencing the transmission of onchocerciasis. VI. The infective biting potential of *Simulium damnosum* in different bioclimatic zones and its influence on the transmission potential. *Ann. Trop. Med. Parasitol.* 62:164–170.

———. 1975. The differential dispersal of nulliparous and parous *Simulium damnosum. Tropenmed. Parasitol.* 26:88–97.

Fallis, A. M. 1964. Feeding and related behaviour of female Simuliidae (Diptera). *Exp. Parasitol.* 15:439–470.

Fredeen, F. J. H. 1969. Outbreaks of the black fly *Simulium arcticum* Malloch in Alberta. *Quaest. Entomol.* 5:341–372.

Fredeen, F. J. H., J. W. T. Spinks, J. R. Anderson, A. P. Arnason, and J. G. Rempel. 1953. Mass tagging of black flies (Diptera:Simuliidae) with radiophosphorus. *Can. J. Zool.* 31:1–15.

Garms, R. 1973. Quantitative studies on the transmission of *Onchocerca volvulus* by *Simulium damnosum* in the Bong Range, Liberia. *Z. Tropenmed. Parasitol.* 24:358–372.

————. 1978. Use of morphological characters in the study of *Simulium damnosum* s.l. populations in West Africa. *Tropenmed. Parasitol.* 29:483–491.

Garms, R., J. F. Walsh, and J. B. Davies. 1979. Studies on the reinvasion of the Onchocerciasis Control Programme in the Volta River Basin by *Simulium damnosum* s.l. with emphasis on the southwestern areas. *Tropenmed. Parasitol.* 30:345–362.

Garms, R., R. A. Cheke, C. G. Vajime, and S. Sowah. 1982. The occurrence and movements of different members of the *Simulium damnosum* complex in Togo and Benin. *Z. Ang. Zool.* 69:219–236.

Hocking, B. 1953. The intrinsic range and speed of flight of insects. *Trans. R. Entomol. Soc. London* 104:223–345.

Johnson, C. G. 1969. *Migration and dispersal of insects by flight.* Methuen, London. 763 pp.

Johnson, C. G., J. F. Walsh, J. B. Davies, S. J. Clark, and J. N. Perry. 1985. The pattern and speed of displacement of females *Simulium damnosum* Theobald s.l. (Diptera: Simuliidae) across the Onchocerciasis Control Programme area of West Africa for 1977 and 1978. *Bull. Entomol. Res.* 75:73–92.

Johnson, C. G., R. W. Crosskey, and J. B. Davies. 1982. Species composition and cyclical changes in numbers of savanna blackflies (Diptera: Simuliidae) caught by suction traps in the Onchocerciasis Control Programme area of West Africa. *Bull. Entomol. Res.* 72:39–63.

Le Berre, R. 1966. Contribution à l'étude biologique et ecologique de *Simulium damnosum* Theobald, 1903 (Diptera: Simuliidae). *Mém. ORSTOM* 17. 204 pp.

Le Berre, R., R. Garms, J. B. Davies, J. F. Walsh, and B. Philippon. 1979. Displacements of *Simulium damnosum* and strategy of control against onchocerciasis. *Phil. Trans. R. Soc. London* (B) 287:277–288.

Le Berre, R., J. F. Walsh, J. B. Davies, P. Philippon, and R. Garms. 1978. Control of onchocerciasis: Medical entomology—a necessary pre-requisite to socio-economic development. In Medical Entomology Centenary, 23–25 November 1977, Symposium Proceedings. *R. Soc. Trop. Med. Hyg.* (London): 70–75.

Lebied, B. 1950. Une nouvelle théorie endémiologique. Sur le rôle de la fonction du parasitisme x mécanisme de vol du vecteur comme facteur décisif de l'établissement du foyer de l'éndemicité de l'onchocercose et de filarioses en general. *Imp. Darantière,* Dijon. 54 pp.

Magor, J. I., and L. J. Rosenberg. 1980. Studies of winds and weather during migrations of *Simulium damnosum* Theobald (Diptera: Simuliidae), the vector of onchocerciasis in West Africa. *Bull. Entomol. Res.* 70:693–716.

McCrae, A. W. R. 1978. Intermittent eradication of *Simulium damnosum* Theo. on the Nile from Jinja, Uganda: 1951–1977. In Medical Entomology Centenary, 23–25 November 1977, Symposium Proceedings. *R. Soc. Trop. Med. Hyg.* (London): 133–134.

Meredith, S. E. O., D. Kurtak, and J. Grunewald. 1984. Following movements of resistant populations of *Simulium soubrense/sanctipauli* (Diptera: Simuliidae) by means of chromosome inversions. In XVII Int. Congr. Entomol., Hamburg, 20–26 August 1984, abstract vol. (R 15.4, 6), 667.

Mokry, J. E. 1980. A method for estimating the age of field-collected females *Simulium damnosum* s.l. (Diptera: Simuliidae). *Tropenmed. Parasitol.* 31:121–127.

Noamesi, G. K. 1966. Dry season survival and associated longevity and flight range of *Simulium damnosum* Theobald in Northern Ghana. *Ghana Med. J.* 5:95–102.

Ovazza, M., J. Renard, and G. Balay. 1967. Etude des populations de *Simulium damnosum* Theobald, 1903 (Diptera: Simuliidae) en zones des gîtes non permanents. III. Corrélation possible entre certains phénomènes météorologiques et la réapparition des femelles en début de saison des pluies. *Bull. Soc. Path. Exot.* 60:79–95.

Pedgley, D. 1982. *Windborne pests and diseases. Meteorology of airborne organisms.* Ellis Horwood, Chichester, England. 250 pp.

————. 1983. Windborne spread of insect-transmitted diseases of animals and man. *Phil. Trans. R. Soc. London* (B) 302:463–470.

Philippon, B. 1977. Etude de la transmission d'*Onchocerca volvulus* (Leuckart, 1893) (Nematoda, Onchocercidae) par *Simulium damnosum* Theobald, 1903 (Diptera, Simuliidae) en Afrique tropicale. *Trav. Doc. ORSTOM* 63. 308 pp.

Prentice, M. A. 1974. Simulium control program in Uganda. *PAHO Scient. Publ.* no. 298, 87–95.

Quillévéré, D. 1979. Contribution a l'étude des caracteristiques taxonomiques, bioécologiques et vectrices des members du complexe *Simulium damnosum* présents en Côte d'Ivoire. *Trav. Doc. ORSTOM* 109. 304 pp.

Rainey, R. C. 1978. The evolution and ecology of flight: the "Oceanographic" approach. Pp. 33–48 in H. Dingle, Ed., *Evolution of insect migration and diapause.* Springer Verlag, New York.

Rainey, R. C., and R. J. V. Joyce. 1972. The use of airborne Doppler equipment in monitoring wind-fields for airborne insects. 7th Int. Aerospace Instrum. Symp. Cranfield, 8.1.–8.4.

Roberts, D. M., and R. J. Irving-Bell. 1984. Circadian flight activity of black-flies (Diptera: Simuliidae) collected using a vehicle-mounted net in central Nigeria. In XVII Int. Congr. Entomol., Hamburg, 20–26 August 1984, abstract vol. (R 15.4 3), 665.

Service, M. W. 1979. Light trap collections of ovipositing *Simulium squamosum* in Ghana. *Ann. Trop. Med. Parasitol.* 73:487–490.

Southwood, T. R. E. 1962. Migration of terrestrial arthropods in relation to habitat. *Biol. Rev.* 37:171–214.

Thompson, B., J. F. Walsh, and B. Walsh. 1972. A marking and recapture experiment on *Simulium damnosum* and bionomic observations. WHO mimeo. doc., WHO/Oncho/ 72.98. 13 pp., 5 figs.

Thompson, B. H. 1976. Studies on the flight range and dispersal of *Simulium damnosum* (Diptera: Simuliidae) in the rain-forest of Cameroon. *Ann. Trop. Med. Parasitol.* 70:343–354.

Urquhart, F. A. 1960. *The monarch butterfly.* Univ. Toronto Press. 361 pp.

Walsh, J. F. 1977. Problem of migration of vectors of onchocerciasis in control programmes. Proc. 3rd Scient. Mtg. ICIPE, Lagos, 23–26 November 1976 (1977): 70–84.

————. 1978. Light trap studies on *Simulium damnosum* s.l. in northern Ghana. *Tropenmed. Parasitol.* 29:492–496.

————. 1980. Sticky trap studies on *Simulium damnosum* s.l. in northern Ghana. *Tropenmed. Parasitol.* 31:479–486.

————. 1984. Aspects of the biology and control of *Simulium damnosum* s.l. (Diptera: Simuliidae) in West Africa. Ph.D. Thesis, Salford University, England. 432 pp.

————. 1985. Onchocerciasis: river blindness. Pp. 269–294 in A. T. Grove, Ed., *The Niger and its neighbours.* Balkema Press, Rotterdam.

Walsh, J. F., and R. Garms. 1980. The detection of plant sugars in *Simulium damnosum* s.l. by means of the cold anthrone test. *Trans. R. Soc. Trop. Med. Hyg.* 74:811–813.

Walsh, J. F., J. B. Davies, and R. Le Berre. 1979. Entomological aspects of the first five years of the Onchocerciasis Control Programme in the Volta River Basin. *Tropenmed. Parasitol.* 30:328–344.

Walsh, J. F., J. B. Davies, and B. Cliff. 1981a. World Health Organization Onchocerciasis Control Programme in the Volta River Basin. Pp. 85–103 in M. Laird, Ed., *Blackflies: the future for biological methods in integrated control.* Academic Press, New York and London.

Walsh, J. F., J. B. Davies, and R. Garms. 1981b. Further studies on the reinvasion of the Onchocerciasis Control Programme by *Simulium damnosum* s.l.: the effects of an extension of control activities into southern Ivory Coast during 1979. *Tropenmed. Parasitol.* 32:269–273.

Wellington, W. G. 1974. Black-fly activity during cumulus-induced pressure fluctuations. *Environ. Ecol.* 3:351–353.

Wenk, P. 1981. Bionomics of adult blackflies. Pp. 259–279 in M. Laird, Ed., *Blackflies: the future for biological methods in integrated control.* Academic Press, New York and London.

Williams, C. G. 1958. *Insect migration.* Collins, London. 237 pp.

———. 1965. Black-flies (Diptera: Simuliidae) in a suction trap in the Central Highlands of Scotland. *Proc. R. Entomol. Soc. London* (A) 40:92–95.

Williams, C. B., and L. Davies. 1957. Simuliidae attracted at night to a trap using ultra-violet light. *Nature* (London) 179:924–925.

World Health Organization. 1973. Onchocerciasis Control in the Volta River Basin Area. Report of the Preparatory Assistance Mission to the Governments of Dahomey, Ghana, Ivory Coast, Mali, Niger, Togo, and Upper Volta submitted by UNDP, FAO, IBRD, and WHO. WHO doc. OCP/73.1.

16 SWARMING AND MATING BEHAVIOR OF BLACK FLIES

Peter Wenk

Our topic originated in two completely separate research interests, namely, laboratory rearing of black flies to study the biology of the preimaginal stages and the vector biology of the female adult. The former was started in the Nearctic and Palaearctic region and the latter in West Africa in relation to control of onchocerciasis. The author carried out field observations and experiments in the Rhine Valley near Strasbourg and in Burkina Faso (formerly Upper Volta) and Cameroon. In order to establish a self-sustaining colony of any *Simulium* species, mating was believed to be the most difficult condition to fulfill. Swarming seemed to be the behavior where mating occurred under natural conditions. The highly specialized eyes of the male must be involved, since only males form real swarms. However, females of certain species, which were collected in the field as pupae and hatched in the laboratory, were found wearing a spermatophore (up to 90% of all females) even when kept in moderately sized (small) cages. Obviously in these cases mating occurred regularly without swarming. Therefore, under conditions where there is no observable swarming behavior, the spermatophore of wild females could indicate where and at which times a certain species was mating in the field. In this chapter I briefly review the visual conditions for swarming and mating and then describe the spermatophore and its significance in research of mating behavior in black flies.

WHAT IS A SWARM?

Swarming is obviously not a prerequisite for mating in *Simulium*. Black flies are practically ubiquitous, but swarms are rarely observed. There are different kinds of swarms: every aggregation of flies in the air, e.g., around a blood host, may be called a swarm. However, in a typical swarm a fly has to control at least three parameters: (1) its position relative to some feature in the environment, e.g., a tree, a corner of a house, or any bright spot on the ground (marker orientation); (2) its position relative to other members of the swarm (intraswarm or intrasexual orienta-

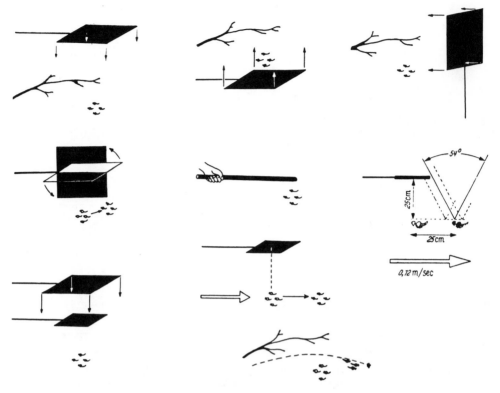

FIG. 16.1 Experiments with swarming *Simulium spec.* males (Wenk 1965b).

tion); and (3) its position relative to a nonmember of the swarm, e.g., a female in a male swarm (intersexual orientation, Zeil 1983b).

In male black fly swarms there exists additionally a hierarchical order in the positions to the optic marker, since males keep a more or less constant distance from each other and compete for the best position within the swarm. Accordingly, swarming is a specialized pattern of behavior. Its conditions may be realized already by a few, perhaps by only two individuals. Even a single male flying at constant height relative to the optic marker can be considered a swarm in extreme reduction. Therefore, the population density and the distribution of suitable markers (swarming sites) in an area determines the size of male swarms.

In the Rhine Valley in July and August male swarms of black flies *Boophthora erythrocephala* and *Wilhelmia equina,* both mammalophilic species, can be regularly observed. They may consist of a few individuals to up to hundreds or even thousands on certain days. The flies orient to an optic marker about 25 cm above the male that keeps the first place in the order. A single prominent tree in an otherwise open area, e.g., of cultivated land, may attract on its downwind side a considerable swarm, stationed at a distance of about 2 meters, as a black cloud. However, the bushes and trees along a small river will disperse males in numerous small swarms of three to five individuals on the downwind side of all the prominent branches. Furthermore, competition between Simuliidae and other swarming Diptera such as Phoridae, Bibionidae, or Syrphidae and hunting insects such as Asilidae or dragonflies restrict the

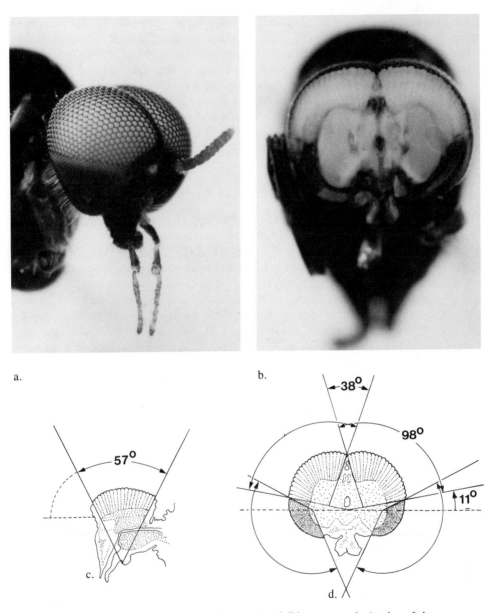

FIG. 16.2 (a) Head of *Simulium spec.* male, total and (b) transversal. Angles of the ommatidial axes sagittal (d) and (c) transversal (Wenk 1965b).

area of scattered swarms to certain sections of the gallery forest. Accordingly, the males of a swarm have to orient continuously to the optic marker, the first male flying closest to it as well as the partners flying alongside. Small moving objects passing above the swarm (a distant bird, for instance) elicit chasing behavior. However, as soon as a dragonfly appears, the swarm scatters immediately in all directions, until the males reappear one by one after half a minute or so. The visual determination of these alternative reactions is obvious and may be demonstrated by black boards as artificial optic markers or small stones thrown above the swarming males (Fig. 16.1). Most probably they recognize females flying to the optic marker for resting. On a paper covered with glue the couples joined in flight and falling down can be caught (Wenk 1965b). Orientation to the optic marker is a rather simple performance. It can be explained by the hypothesis that the optic marker should cover more or less the frontal visual field of the dorsal compound eye when the male is flying against the wind. The distance should not exceed about one meter (Fig. 16.2).

VISUAL DETECTION OF FEMALES BY MALES

The fact that swarming males detect females visually can be demonstrated by moving small lead balls on a nylon thread through the air space between a swarm and an artificial marker. Males chase these dummies when they cross the visual field of their dorsal compound eyes. The dorsal eyes of males are well adapted for this task: facets are much large (25–40 μm diameter) compared with ventral eye facets (10–15 μm), and rhabdomeres are extremely elongated (200–300 μm compared with c. 50 μm in the ventral eye) by passing through the basal membrane and the lamina. This increases the number of quanta absorbed in a rhabdomere according to Lambert-Beers absorption law, and due to a reduction in light quantum noise it allows a better detectability of the small females (Kirschfeld and Wenk 1979). When the light intensity of the open sky falls below 2,000 lux, most males leave the swarm, and no pursuit reactions are observed below 800 lux (Kirschfeld and Wenk, unpublished data). In a few species the upper facets of the male eye are less enlarged and mating occurs mainly while adults crawl on the substrate near the emergence site: *Cnephia dacotensis*, *C. eremites* (Davies and Peterson 1956), and *C. lapponica* (Usova 1961).

A second specialization concerns the visual pigment. Simuliids have a pigment system with maximum sensitivity in ultraviolet at 340 nm. Other flies (*Calliphora, Musca, Drosophila*) have their UV-maximum at 350 nm. Though this difference is small, it improves the simuliid eye, since resolution at the shorter wavelength is higher: the probability of detecting a female is increased by 10% (Kirschfeld and Vogt, in preparation). Recently, recording of flight trajectories by two cameras simultaneously at 50 frames/sec made it possible to analyze flight paths in three dimensions (Dahmen and Zeil 1984). This was carried out with bibionids, the males of which show similarly specialized compound eyes divided into dorsal and ventral parts with large and small ommatidia (Zeil 1983a,b). Similar cinematographic records were made with swarming black flies: the males hunting a ball of 8 mm diameter steer a course to collide with the target (predictive tracking) (Fig. 16.3).

THE RETINAL ORGANIZATION

The similarly constructed bibionid male dorsal compound eyes were studied by neuro-anatomical and micro-optical techniques. The dorsal eye has larger facets and longer rhabdomeres and is a neural superposition eye: groups of six peripheral retinula cells in six next-but-one ommatidia have parallel optical axes and their terminals in the

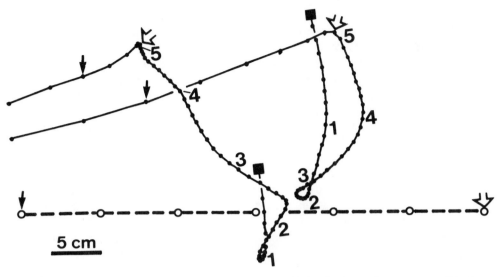

FIG. 16.3 Two independent sequences of Simulium ♂ flight chasing a dummy target (black pea ⌀ 8 mm) seen from below (Zeil, personal communication).

lamina pass to next-but-one cartidges. In comparison to the male ventral and the female eye, the dorsal eyes of males are designed to increase the distance at which a small object can be detected against a homogeneous background (Zeil 1983a). As in bibionids, in the simuliid male dorsal eye, the six rhabdomeres are arranged in a radially symmetrical pattern typical for nematoceran flies, but their optical axes are parallel with rhabdomeres in neighboring ommatidia. In the ventral eye there is additionally a central rhabdomere (Boscheck and Kirschfeld, personal communication).

Finally, in bibionids the projections of the compound eyes to the visual neuropils and the cell types in the lamina and lobula complex were analyzed by means of extracellular cobalt injections and Golgi impregnations. There are separate dorsal and ventral neuropils up to the level of the lobula complex. The dorsal eye lamina is unilayered, while the ventral eye lamina in males and the lamina in females are multilayered. The divided brain of male bibionids enables one to investigate separately the nervous systems involved in the sex-specific visually guided flight behavior and in "general" visually guided flight control (Zeil 1983c). Unfortunately, a similar analysis of the system in simuliids is still lacking.

INTERSEXUAL COMMUNICATION

There is obviously no male-female communication prior to coupling because males are unable to recognize the species or even genus of a female in the absence of wing colorations or other visual signals. Involvement of pheromones seems unlikely, since swarming can occur at remarkably high wind velocities. Equally, acoustic signals do not seem to play a role, considering the clumsy shape of the antenna and the lack of sexual dimorphism. This leaves tactile discrimination upon contact mediated by the highly differentiated male external genital organs. Accordingly, mating is not always followed by insemination of the female. In a laboratory-colonized strain of *S. damnosum* s.l., mating attempts were frequently seen, but the insemination rates were less than one percent (Cupp et al. 1981).

Presumably still in flight, males have to transfer their spermatophore, but most probably it is the female that has the final decision about insemination (female-controlled mating, Borgia 1979). However, species discrimination is very successful: in laboratory-hatched populations there were mixed small numbers of males and females of a cage-mating species (*W. lineata*) with large and equal numbers of *W. equina* (non-cage-mating) and *B. erythrocephala* (cage-mating). Although the density of *W. lineata* was only 2% of the total population, *W. lineata* females were regularly inseminated in the course of one day (Wenk 1965c). The same is true for mosquitoes: in male choice experiments *Aedes aegypti* and *A. a. formosus* males could readily discriminate between their own females and those of *A. mascarensis*. *A. aegypti* males seek out and inseminate their own females even when they are outnumbered by *A. mascarensis* females in a ratio of 19 : 1 (Hartberg and Craig 1968).

BIOLOGICAL SIGNIFICANCE OF SWARMING

Male aggregations at sites without resource-holding potential are called "lek mating systems." In leks, courtship tends to be complex and matings are controlled by females (for example, in acalyptrate flies, Burk 1981). In simuliids swarming of males and localization of females passing overhead needs highly specialized sense organs (the dorsal eye) but a rather simple behavior pattern, since practically no courtship is displayed.

The biological significance of swarming may be contradictory. On the one hand, sibling species have very different hydrochemical requirements during larval development and as larvae are spatially separated even in the same region. As adults, however, they might become completely mixed. Swarming prevents a wide dispersal of the males, improves the chance of encountering females of the same species, and may increase mating attempts between them. On the other hand, orientation of both sexes to the blood host favors intrageneric mating, as is described for Trypetidae, which are attracted to their host plant (Zwölfer 1974).

Without any experimental approach the genetic and evolutionary implications of the presumed female-controlled mating remain completely speculative. Nevertheless, in view of, for example, the capacity of parasite transmission or insecticide resistance of certain cytotaxonomic types in mixed populations, it would be useful to illustrate the fundamental rules reviewed by Spiess (1982): (1) Carefully define discriminatory mating behavior. (2) Ascertain the dimensions (limits) of this behavior as a recognizable trait. (3) Determine its genetic basis so that we may work more intelligently toward (4) the study of how mating recognition and ethological isolation might evolve.

In midges (Ceratopogonidae) the male swarms seem to be mainly assemblages attracted by optic markers on the ground. These markers are formed by contrast between dark areas, such as grass clumps, and light ones, such as barren soil or roadways. Since swarms over large markers are less compact than those on small markers and closely resemble the shape of the marker, intraswarm orientation seems to be less important. Actually the distance between the midges ranges from 2 to 10 cm, decreasing as the number of midges increased. The short-range recognition of the female may be controlled by auditory responses as the antennal setae of the male are erected during coupling. The distance to the optic marker below ranges from 10 to 90 cm (Zimmerman et al. 1982). It is obvious that marker orientation is visually controlled. However, there are no special differentiations seen in the eyes, and swarming may be continued at dusk even 30 minutes after sunset. Mating happens at the edges of the swarm where females enter. The couple falls to the ground and flies remain together for 30 to 120 seconds. It is not clear whether in this time a spermatophore is transferred as it was observed in *Culicoides melleus*, a nonswarming species (Linley and Adams 1972). Every 10 to 15 seconds a couple was observed falling onto a white sheet below the swarm, although in the air the sex ratio ($♀ : ♂$) was only 1:167, as determined by sweep net. A detailed review on the assembly and mating of *Culicoides nubeculosus*, *Aedes hexodontus*, and several other biting Nematocera was given by Downes (1958). More recent reviews of swarming and mating in Diptera and other insects are given by Alexander (1975), Sullivan (1981), and Thornhill and Alcoc (1983). An experimental approach was achieved by cinematographic recording of swarming *Anarete pritchardi*. "The speed of males was not influenced by the size of swarm, but that of females was reduced in swarms of larger size. Turns of 90–120° and 150–180° were more frequent than those of 60–90° and 120–150°. This bimodal distribution was shown in both sexes and various swarm sizes, and was independent of the orientation of the midges in relation to sun, their location over the marker and position in the swarm" (Goldsmith et al. 1980: 526).

MATING WITHOUT SWARMING

Many, if not most, of the sympatric *Simulium* species breeding more or less in the same watercourses of a region are not observed to form any male swarms. Three other possibilities of sex-finding behavior have been reported: (1) males sitting on the stalks of reed grass along riverbanks (*B. erythrocephala*), probably waiting for freshly hatched females to pass by, and (2) males sitting on flowers visited by females for their nectaries, such as parsnip (*Pastinaca sativa*), ivy (*Hedera helix*), knotgrass (*Polygonum aubertii*), hawthorn (*Crataegus monogyna*), and different kinds of willows (*Salix spec.*). The insemination rate of mammalophilic species (*Wilhelmia equina*, *W. salopiense*, *B. erythrocephala*) on flowers was mostly high (85–95%), but in *Eusimulium latipes*, an ornithophilic species, only 33% was observed. In the same region more than 98% of females of mammalophilic species captured from live animals or CO_2-baited traps were inseminated (Lewis 1957, Wenk 1965a, Archipova 1966, Rühm 1970, Pascuzzo 1976). However, only 54% of *E. latipes* females attacking chicken were inseminated (Wenk 1965a). Both *Wilhelmia* species were found to feed exclusively on the ears of horses and cows. Their males were observed to form small swarms close to the moving ears, especially early after sunrise. Therefore, a third (3) possibility of sex-finding behavior is orientation of males to the blood host of the conspecific females. The same behavior was reported for Ceratopogonidae (Wirth 1952), *Aedes varipalpus* (Peyton 1956, Downes 1958), and *Aedes aegypti* (Hartberg 1971). The males of *B. erythrocephala* followed the morning and the evening peak in the host-attacking behavior of the females. The same was true for the males of *W. equina* and *W. salopiense*, except for the final rise of attacking that occurred shortly before sunset. This was observed by catching all the black flies attacking or flying around a person for 10 minutes every hour during the hours of daylight (Wenk 1965a). Fly collectors in the savanna or forest region of West Africa catching females of *S. damnosum* s.l. from their exposed legs are often surprised by some males (up to 1%) that do not feed but obviously land pursuing a female. Since there are no true swarms and even no assemblies of males observed around the collectors, males are probably sitting on grass or flying closely above the grass waiting for passing females. Males can be caught together with many females when a person repeatedly walks in front of a ventilator blowing into a net at grass level. Females carried a spermatophore with increasing rates from 18.2% in the morning up to 48.5% in the evening. At the same time in the immediate vicinity, small male swarms of *S. damnosum* s.l. were observed orienting to optic markers, such as big trees or gallery forests along the same riverbanks as described above for the Palaearctic species. These males are attracted to artificial markers as well (Le Berre and Wenk 1966).

THE SPERMATOPHORE

In Simuliidae, as in several other Diptera, the male transfers a bicavate spermatophore that consists of a hardened secretion (Fig. 16.4). Females of *S. damnosum* s.l. from the forest area of Cameroon that were transported in small cages from field catches to the laboratory retained the spermatophore in equal proportion to females fixed immediately in alcohol or 3 hours later. After 7 to 8 hours this value decreased to two-thirds, and after 18 hours to only 1%. Accordingly, the spermatophore may be held by the female during the rest of the night or during flights over remarkable distances (see below). The sperm is most probably squeezed out by the female's genital plate acting dorsally after the cavity has been opened enzymatically. An extremely thin process (Fig. 16.4, f) can be observed projecting into the genital opening just up to the orifice of the *ductus receptaculi* (Wenk 1965b).

"The mean number of sperm ejaculated into the spermatophore by the male blackfly, *S. decorum* Walker, was 4048 (43 counts). The completeness and rate of sperm transfer were estimated by counts after copulation ended. The beginning of transfer occurred, at the earliest, about 4 minutes after copulation, but it could be delayed until 30 minutes. Transfer rate was interpreted as constant at about 73 sperm/min. and was usually completed by about 55 minutes after copulation. All spermatozoa appeared to be moved to the single spermatheca" (Linley and Simmons 1983: 581). Similar amounts of transferred sperm are recorded from *Drosophila melanogaster* (Kaufmann and Demerec 1942, Gilbert 1981). Besides sperm, there is a concurrent transfer of microtubules, a lipid, peptides, and a variety of enzymes, of which esterase-6 apparently plays a role in the rate of sperm release by the female. The function of these substances and its evolutionary significance are discussed by Gromko et al. (1984). Some similar products are most probably transferred in the content of the spermatophore of *Simulium* males. Females with a spermatophore are always nulliparous, indicating that *Simulium* females are inseminated only once. But

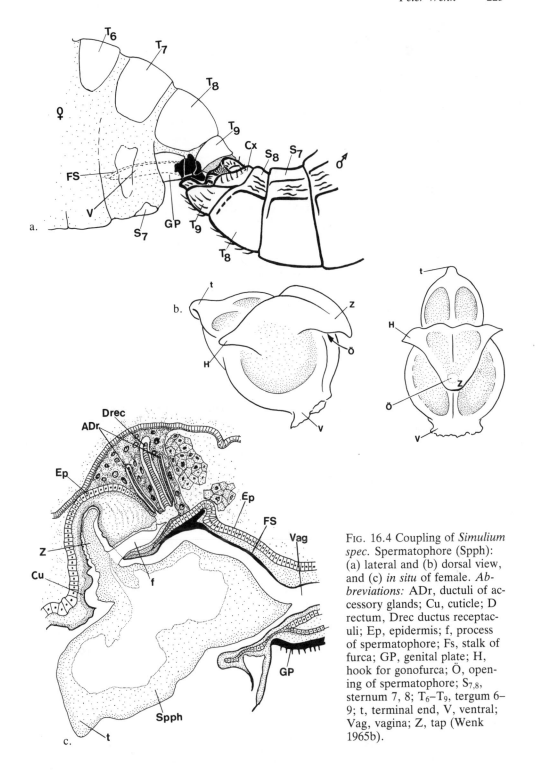

Fig. 16.4 Coupling of *Simulium spec.* Spermatophore (Spph): (a) lateral and (b) dorsal view, and (c) *in situ* of female. *Abbreviations:* ADr, ductuli of accessory glands; Cu, cuticle; D rectum, Drec ductus receptaculi; Ep, epidermis; f, process of spermatophore; Fs, stalk of furca; GP, genital plate; H, hook for gonofurca; Ö, opening of spermatophore; $S_{7,8}$, sternum 7, 8; T_6–T_9, tergum 6–9; t, terminal end, V, ventral; Vag, vagina; Z, tap (Wenk 1965b).

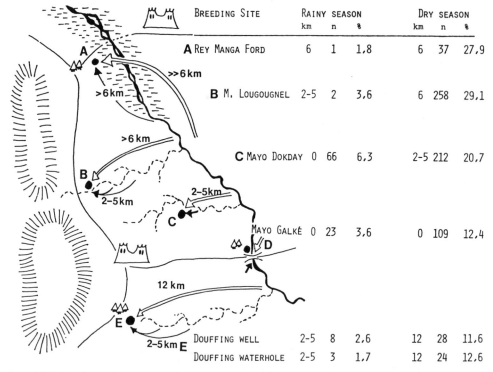

BREEDING SITE	RAINY SEASON			DRY SEASON		
	km	n	%	km	n	%
A REY MANGA FORD	6	1	1,8	6	37	27,9
B M. LOUGOUGNEL	2-5	2	3,6	6	258	29,1
C MAYO DOKDAY	0	66	6,3	2-5	212	20,7
MAYO GALKÉ	0	23	3,6	0	109	12,4
DOUFFING WELL	2-5	8	2,6	12	28	11,6
DOUFFING WATERHOLE	2-5	3	1,7	12	24	12,6

FIG. 16.5 Number of females with spermatophore (*n*) and corresponding rate (%) in relation to nulliparous flies attacking man in various distances (km) from their breeding sites in northern Cameroon. 6 km: Breeding site far distant, probably up to 12 km (Renz, personal communication).

this may differ in different species or cytotaxonomic types. In the mosquito *Aedes aegypti,* a protein "matrone" inhibits multiple insemination. It was isolated by gel-filtration chromatography from whole bodies of males. Injected into virgin females, it renders them sterile for life (Fuchs et al. 1969). In rare cases *Simulium* females with a second spermatophore adherent aside the correctly placed first one can be found, indicating that a (second) male can produce and even transfer its spermatophore without the cooperation of the female. However, there must be a signal preventing them from doing so with parous females.

DAYTIME PATTERN OF THE SPERMATOPHORE RATE

In the rain-forest area (south Cameroon) in females attacking man and fixed immediately, the spermatophore rate increased from 8.3% (7:00 A.M.) to 31.7% (noon). After the midday gap without attacking flies, in the late afternoon the rate was 23.8% (3:30 P.M.), decreasing to 17.2% (5:00 P.M.) (Wenk, unpublished data). In the Sudan savanna region (northern Cameroon), females with a spermatophore showed a similar morning and an evening peak at 10:00 A.M. and 6:30 P.M., respectively, indicating that mating in both cases may occur during the same day during the rainy season. But in the dry season there was an early maximum already after sunrise at 6:00 A.M. and mating must have occurred the day before, probably during the evening. Especially during the dry season, the highest spermatophore rates with pronounced daily rhythmic patterns were observed far away from the breeding sites (Fig. 16.5). Assuming that the flies mated close to the breeding sites, we must conclude that freshly inseminated females prefer to fly large distances to their blood hosts, as has already been shown for nulliparous females (Renz and Wenk 1987).

CONCLUSION

The extremely specialized ommatidium in the dorsal eye of all *Simulium* males is, along with the males of Bibionidae, Ascalaphidae, and Ephemeroptera, unique in the world of insects. There must have been a high selective pressure for its evolutionary development. Swarming as such and orientation to an optic marker are rather simple sensory performances. Accordingly, the visual localization of the small and rapidly moving female must be the decisive point in selection. The fact that species recognition does not seem to occur before coupling means that attempted interspecific couplings between sympatric species may occur at a high rate. This favors the heterozygous offspring of different cytotaxonomic types. Visually controlled mate-finding behavior is an alternative specialization to acoustic recogniton that is favored in dipteran families active during dawn and night. The former requires, especially in the tropics with hot midday hours, the well-known bimodal activity pattern of the daily activity rhythm in both sexes.

LITERATURE CITED

Alexander, R. D. 1975. Natural selection and specialized chorusing behaviour in acoustical insects. Pp. 35–77 in D. Pimental, Ed., *Insects, science and society*. Academic Press, New York.

Archipova, G. A. 1966. Age composition of the population of blood-sucking black-flies in the Upper Kama region. *Med. Parasitol. and Parasit. Diseases* 35:6–11 (in Russian).

Borgia, G. 1979. Sexual selection and the evolution of mating systems. Pp. 19–80 in M. S. and N. A. Blum, Eds., *Sexual selection and reproductive competition in insects*. Academic Press, New York.

Burk, Th. 1981. Signaling and sex in acalyptrate flies. *Florida Entomol.* 64:30–43.

Cupp, E. W., J. B. Lok, M. J. Bernardo, R. J. Brenner, R. J. Pollack, and G. A. Scoles 1981. Complete generation rearing of *Simulium damnosum* (Diptera: Simuliidae) in the laboratory. *Tropenmed. Parasitol.* 32:119–122.

Dahmen, H. J., and J. Zeil. 1984. Recording and reconstructing three-dimensional trajectories. A versatile method for the field biologist. *Proc. R. Soc. London (B)* 222:107–113.

Davies, D. M., and B. V. Peterson. 1956. Observations on the mating, feeding, ovarian development and oviposition of adult black flies (Simuliidae, Diptera). *Can. J. Zool.* 34:615–655.

Downes, J. A. 1958. Assembly and mating in the biting nematocera. *Proc. 10th Int. Congr. Entomol.* 2:425–434.

Fuchs, M. S., G. B. Craig, and D. D. Despommier. 1969. The protective nature of the substance inducing female monogamy in *Aedes aegypti*. *J. Insect Physiol.* 15:701–709.

Gilbert, D. G. 1981. Ejaculate esterase-6 and initial sperm use by female *Drosophila melanogaster*. *J. Insect Physiol.* 27:641–650.

Goldsmith, A., H. C. Chiang, and A. Okubo. 1980. Turning motion of individual midges, *Anarete pritchardi*, in swarms. *Ann. Entomol. Soc. Am.* 73:526–528.

Gromko, M. H., D. G. Gilbert, and R. C. Richmond. 1984. Sperm transfer and use in the multiple mating system of Drosophila. Pp. 371–426 in *Sperm competition and the evolution of animal mating system*. Academic Press, New York.

Hartberg, W. K. 1971. Observations on the mating behaviour of *Aedes aegypti* in nature. *WHO Bull.* 45:847–850.

Hartberg, W. K., and G. B. Craig. 1968. Reproductive isolation in *Stegomyia* mosquitoes. I. Sexual isolation between *Aedes aegypti* and *A. mascarensis*. *Ann. Entomol. Soc. Am.* 61:865–870.

Kaufmann, B. P., and M. Demerec. 1942. Utilization of sperm by the female *Drosophila melanogaster*. *Am. Nat.* 76:445–469.

Kirschfeld, K. 1979. The visual system of the fly: physiological optics and functional anatomy as related to behavior. Pp. 297–310 in F. O. Schmitt and F. G. Worden, Eds., *The neural sciences, fourth study program*. MIT Press, Cambridge, Mass., and London.

Kirschfeld, K., and P. Wenk. 1976. The dorsal compound eye of Simuliid flies: an eye specialized for the detection of small, rapidly moving objects. *Z. Naturforsch.* 31c:764–765.

Lewis, D. J. 1957. Aspects of the structure, biology and study of *Simulium damnosum*. *Ann. Trop. Med Parasitol.* 51:340–358.

Linley, J. R., and G. M. Adams. 1972. A study of the mating behaviour of *Culicoides melleus* (Coquillett) Diptera: Ceratopogonidae). *Trans. R. Entomol. Soc. London* 124:81–121.

Linley, J. R., and K. R. Simmons. 1983. Quantitative aspects of the sperm transfer in *Simulium decorum* (Diptera: Simuliidae) *J. Insect Physiol.* 29:581–584.

Le Berre, R., and P. Wenk. 1966. Beobachtungen über das Schwarmverhalten bei *Simulium damnosum* (Theobald) in Obervolta und Kamerun. *Verh. Dtsch. Zool. Ges. Suppl.* 30:367–372.

Pascuzzoo, M. C. 1976. Fecundity and physiological age in adult black-flies (Simuliidae) with some observations on vertical distribution. M.Sc. Thesis, McMaster University, Hamilton, Ontario.

Peyton, E. L. 1956. Biology of the Pacific Coast tree hole mosquito, *Aedes varipalpus* Coq. *Mosquito News* 16:220–224.

Renz, A. 1985. Studies on the dynamics of transmission of onchocerciasis in a sudan-savannah area of north Cameroon. Ph. D. Thesis, Tübingen.

Renz, A., and P. Wenk. 1987. Studies on the dynamics of transmission of onchocerciasis in a Sudan-savanna area of North Cameroon: I. Prevailing *Simulium* vectors, their biting rates and age-composition at different distances from their breeding sites. *Ann. Trop. Med. Parasitol.* (in press).

Rühm, W. 1970. Untersuchungen über das physiologische Alter der Imagines von *Boophthora erythrocephala* de Geer und einiger anderer Simuliidenarten. *Z. Partasitk.* 34:207–225.

Spiess, E. B. 1982. Do female flies choose their mates? *Amer. Nat.* 199:675–693.

Sullivan, R. T. 1981. Insect swarming and mating. *Florida Entomol.* 64:44–65.

Thornhill, R., and J. Alcock. 1983. *The evolution of insect mating systems.* Harvard Univ. Press, Cambridge, Mass., and London. 547 pp.

Usova, Z. V. 1961. Flies of the Karelia and Murmansk region (Diptera: Simuliidae). *Izdatelstvo Akad. Nauk, SSSR.* [In Russian]. Scient. Transl., 1964.

Wenk, P. 1965a. Über die Biologie blutsaugender Simuliiden (Diptera) I. Besamungsrate der ♀♀ beim Blütenbesuch und Anflug auf den Blutwirt. *Z. Morphol. Ökol. Tiere* 55:656–670.

———. 1965b. Über die Biologie blutsaugender Simuliiden (Diptera) II. Schwarmverhalten, Geschlechterfindung und Kopulation. *Z. Morphol. Ökol. Tiere* 55:671–713.

———. 1965c. Über die Biologie blutsaugender Simuliiden (Diptera) III. Kopulation, Blutsaugen und Eiablage von *Boophthora erythrocephala* de Geer im Laboratorium. *Z. Tropenmed. Parasitol.* 16:207–226.

Wirth, W. W. 1952. The Heleidae of California. *Univ. Calif. Publ. Entomol.* 9:95–266.

Zeil, J. 1983a. Sexual dimorphism in the visual system of flies: the compound eyes and neural superposition in Bibionidae (Diptera). *J. Comp. Physiol.* A 150:379–393.

———. 1983b. Sexual dimorphism in the visual system of flies: the free flight behaviour of male Bibionidae (Diptera). *J. Comp. Physiol.* A 150:395–412.

———. 1983c. Sexual dimorphism in the visual system of flies: the divided brain of male Bibionidae (Diptera). *Cell Tissue Res.* 229:591–610.

Zimmerman, R. H., J. S. Barker, and E. C. Turner, Jr. 1982. Swarming and mating behaviour of a natural population of *Culicoides variipennis* (Diptera: Ceratopogonidae). *J. Med. Entomol.* 19:151–156.

Zwölfer, H. 1974. Das Treffpunkt-Prinzip als Kommunikationsstrategie und Isolationsmechanismus bei Bohrfliegen (Diptera: Trypetidae). *Entomol. Germanica* 1:11–20.

17 SENSORY BASIS OF BEHAVIOR AND STRUCTURAL ADAPTATIONS FOR FEEDING IN BLACK FLIES

Susan B. McIver and James F. Sutcliffe

Four sequential events compose any behavioral pattern elicited by external stimuli: (1) stimulation of appropriate sensilla, (2) integration by the central nervous system of information received, (3) activation of the appropriate efferent systems, and (4) the response of the entire organism. The behavioral and ecological aspects of the various responses of black flies, especially those of the adult female, have been receiving increased attention. Scanning and electron microscopic studies along with careful behavioral investigations have yielded insights into the peripheral sensory system of black flies. The purpose of this chapter is to synthesize the more recent studies on the peripheral sensory systems of larval and adult black flies.

A sense organ or sensillum (pl. sensilla) is a structure within which the energy of a stimulus is transformed into transmittable information, usually in the form of a nervous impulse. The fully differentiated sensillum, which is of ectodermal origin, consists of (a) cuticular components, (b) bipolar sensory neuron(s), and (c) sheath cells. Sensilla are variously modified for detection of visual and thermal stimuli as well as chemical and mechanical cues. Whatever the stimulus, a generator potential in the sensory neuron is produced that leads to the development of action potentials that are conducted along the axon. For additional information on sensilla the reader is referred to McIver (1975), Zacharuk (1980), Altner and Prillinger (1980), Keil and Steinbrecht (1984), and Carlson et al. (1984).

The terminology used in various works on insect sensilla, including those on black flies, lacks uniformity. The Latin terms, e.g., sensillum trichodeum and sensillum coeloconicum, are frequently used, as are the English equivalents of "hair sensillum" and "peg in pit." The terms "hair" and "peg" are commonly used in the literature on sensilla for structures that in systematic works would be called setae. Herein the terms used in the original paper will be retained so as not to introduce additional confusion.

SENSORY COMPLEMENT OF BLACK FLIES

Larvae

The larval head bears a variety of regularly arranged trichoid and a few campaniform sensilla, well described in the taxonomic literature. The other sensilla on the head, namely, ocelli and sensilla associated with the mouthparts and antenna, have been investigated using scanning and/or transmission electron microscopy.

Last instar *Simulium vittatum* possess a lateral ocellus on each side of the head. Each "ocellus" consists of two parts: an anterior and a posterior ocellus, which are connected by a cytoplasmic bridge. Both ocelli lack cuticular and crystalline lenses, meaning they are incapable of image formation. Presumably the ocelli can sense varying degrees of light intensity and in the natural environment of rapidly running water aid in the larva's spatial orientation. Interestingly, the rhabdomeric microvilli of the posterior ocellus are oriented in only one plane, a characteristic of ocelli sensitive to polarized light.

The labial palps bear five sensilla that probably check the food as it is pushed into the cibarium (Craig 1977). The maxillary palps are better endowed with sensilla than the labial ones bearing 12 sensilla of six morphological types with presumed chemo- and/or mechanosensory modalities (Craig and Borkent 1980). On the shaft of the palp are a variety of trichoid sensilla. Craig (1977) showed that the maxillary palps never contact filtered food and suggested that their sensilla may be involved in sensing dissolved substances or perhaps the substrate during browsing. Craig and Borkent (1980) considered in detail the intra- and interfamilial homologies of the maxillary palpal sensilla. On the maxilla and maxillary lobe are basiconic sensilla that probably detect the palatability of food (Craig 1977). Craig and Batz (1982) used light, scanning electron and transmission electron microscopy to investigate the fine structure of the antennal sensilla of larval *S. vittatum, Cnephia dacotensis,* and *Prosimulium mixtum/ fuscum.* Eight morphological types of sensilla innervated by a total of 22 neurons occur on each antenna. At the tip is a uniporous cone with five neurons that probably is involved in chemoreception. Two presumably chemosensitive multiporous pegs, each innervated by two neurons, are located in the mid-region of the antenna. At the base are two uniporous pegs, each with three neurons, two of which have lamellated dendrites. The pegs supposedly function in osmoreception. Also at the antennal base are two types of mechanosensitive trichoid sensilla "1" and "2", each with one neuron, and a presumably chemosensitive multiporous sensillum. The latter is most interesting in that it is covered with probable gram-negative bacteria that apparently thrive on sensillar exudate.

As revealed by scanning electron microscopy, the posterior proleg of larval *S. vittatum* have two groups of short hair sensilla and the thoracic proleg bristles and campaniform sensilla (Barr 1984). The bristles may help larvae to extricate hooks of the thoracic proleg from silk, while the campaniform sensilla probably detect stresses on the apex of the proleg (Barr 1984). Scolopophorous sensilla and stretch receptors, though not detectable externally, are probably present (Barr 1984). Also using scanning electron microscopy, Eymann (personal communication) observed hairs 5–10 μm in length scattered over the body surface of final instar *S. vittatum.* Based on behavioral experiments, the sensilla are apparently mechanosensitive, responding to water currents.

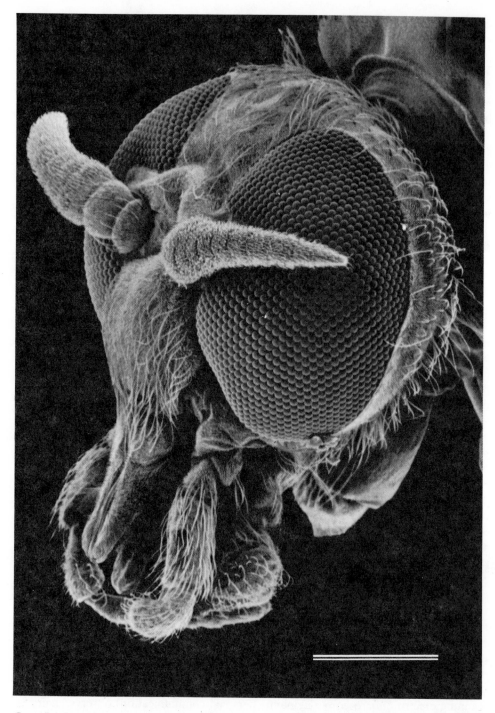

FIG. 17.1 Scanning electron micrograph of antero-lateral aspect of head of female *Simulium vittatum*. Visible are the general head features: compound eyes, antennae, suspended mouthparts. Bar = 200 μm. (Courtesy of D. A. Craig)

Adults

The compound eyes of female simuliids are dioptic (Fig. 17.1), whereas those of the male are holoptic. Each eye of the male is subdivided into a dorsal and a ventral region; the corneal facets in the former are considerably larger (diameter 25–40 μm) than in the latter (diameter 10–15 μm) (Wenk 1965b). Facets of the female eye are similar in size to those in the ventral region of the male. Female *S. vittatum* has approximately 1,200 facets in each eye and males 1,250, with 700 in the dorsal region. All facets in the eyes of both sexes of *S. vittatum* have the same components in identical relative positions. The facets are pseudoconic, have open rhabdomeres, and each possesses eight retinule cells, six of which surround two centrally located ones. Wenk (1965b) reported that the rhabdomeres in the dorsal facets are approximately six times as long as those in the ventral ones.

The combination of large facet lenses and elongated rhabdomeres in the dorsal region of the male eye permits a high angular resolution combined with a high absolute sensitivity (Kirschfeld and Wenk 1976). Both features are important to the function of the dorsal region, which is to detect females against the blue sky as they cross above the swarm of males (Kirschfeld and Wenk 1976). Once detected, the females are pursued by the males and caught for mating. Males of a few species, e.g., *Cnephia dactonesis,* have reduced dorsal facets and mate mainly on the ground near the site of emergence (Davies and Peterson 1956).

Seven types of sensilla occur on the antennae of adult simuliids (Table 17.1). The majority of types (A1, A2, A3 hairs and sensilla styloconica) as well as total numbers (Table 17.2) are probable olfactory sensilla. This indicates that olfactory stimuli play very important roles in simuliid behavior. A case of specific olfactory attraction, unparalleled among blood-feeding flies, occurs with *S. euryadminiculum,* which is attracted to loons chiefly by an extract of the uropygial gland (Fallis and Smith 1964). In view of this specificity, it is interesting that *S. euryadminiculum* does not possess any morphologically distinct type of sensillum (Mercer and McIver 1973a).

The type B sensilla, probable contact chemosensilla, are advantageously located on the outer surfaces and tips of the antennae and tend to curve outward. Both features would facilitate contact with sweat, oils, and other body secretions as the flies crawl through the feathers or fur of the host. The regular arrangement around the pedicel and scape of the sensilla chaetica coupled with their tendency to lie close to the surface of the segment distal to them suggest that they may detect the degree and direction of bending of the pedicel and flagellum.

In view of recent information about sensilla sensitive to hygro- and thermal cues (see McIver and Siemicki 1985 for discussion), the suggestion that sensilla coeloconica may be hygro-/thermosensilla seems more plausible now than when first suggested (Mercer and McIver 1973a).

The characteristics of the three types of scolopidial sensilla found in the Johnston's organs of both sexes of *S. vittatum* are given in Table 17.3. The structure of all types is similar in both sexes, but males have somewhat more types A and B than females (Boo and Davies 1980). The basic structure and location of each type are similar to the corresponding types in the adult mosquito. However, the Johnston's organ in black flies is much less developed than in mosquitoes but similar to that in other insects in which the pedicel is not greatly enlarged. This feature complements previ-

Table 17.1 Characteristics of antennal sensilla

Sensillum	Description	Location	Probable Function
A1	blunt-tipped, untapered, multiporous hairs	distodorsal (segs. 1–8) mediodorsal (seg. 9)	olfaction
A2	blunt-tipped, tapered, multiporous hairs	scattered on flagellum	olfaction
A3	blunt- or pointed-tipped, tapered, multiporous hairs	scattered on flagellum (bare patch at base of seg. 9)	olfaction
Sensilla styloconia	blunt-tipped, cone-shaped peg, slits in distal ⅔	distodorsal (segs. 1–8) mediodorsal (seg. 9)	olfaction
B	blunt-tipped peg; uniporous; thick-grooved walls	medioventral on flagellar segs. 2–4, also at antennal tip	contact chemoreception
Sensilla chaetica	pointed-tipped bristles; nonporous; thick-grooved walls	pedicel, scape	mechanoreception
Sensilla coeloconica	pegs in pits	lateral surface of segs. 1–9	olfaction? hygro-/ thermoreception

Source: Mercer and McIver 1973a.

Table 17.2 Number of antennal sensilla

Species	A1	A2	A3	Styloconica	B	Coeloconica	Sensilla Chaetica	
							Pedicel	Scape
S. baffinense								
male	22	107	620	32	13	11	17	10
female	24	102	660	34	12	12	19	10
S. rugglesi								
male	27	67	663	28	12	16	19	8
female	77	113	1183	64	11	15	19	8
S. euryadminiculum								
female	98	230	1272	121	13	14	22	17
S. venustum								
female	283	119	1030	78	12	16	20	8

Source: Mercer and McIver 1973a.

ous behavioral observations, indicating that sound detection is absent or minimal in simuliids, even in mate-seeking males.

The maxillary palps of adult simuliids bear four types of sensilla, namely, campaniform sensilla, sensilla chaetica, thick-walled, uniporous pegs, and thin-walled, capitate pegs (Mercer and McIver 1973b). Their numbers are given in Table 17.4. Both the campaniform and chaetica sensilla are mechanosensilla; the former respond

Table 17.3 Characteristics of scolopidial sensilla in Johnston's organ in *S. vittatum*

Type	Sensilla/ Johnston's Organ ♂	Sensilla/ Johnston's Organ ♀	No. of Neurons/ Sensillum ♂	No. of Neurons/ Sensillum ♀	Distribution	Suggested Function
A	30	20	2	2	all round pedicel	detect and monitor antennal movements and perceive air currents during flight
B	150	105	3	3	all round pedicel	as above
C	4	5	2	2	medial side of pedicel inside of ring of A and B	joint receptors to perceive changes in the position of the flagellum against the pedicel

Source: Boo and Davies 1980.

Table 17.4 Type and number of palpal sensilla

Species	Sensilla Chaetica	Thick-walled, Uniporous Pegs	Captiate Pegs
S. baffinense			
female	66	52	31
male	75	55	21
S. rugglesi			
female	63	58	76
male	—	—	10
S. euryadminiculum			
female	124	62	74
S. venustum			
female	93	68	56

Source: Mercer and McIver 1973b.

to stresses in the cuticle and the latter likely function as tactile receptors. The uniporous pegs are contact chemosensilla, as demonstrated electrophysiologically by Angioy et al. (1982) on *S. venustum* and Crnjar et al. (1983) on *S. decorum*. In both cases salt- and sucrose-sensitive units are indicated.

Sensilla similar to the capitate pegs on black flies occur on the palps of mosquitoes and other Nematocera and are known to be sensitive to carbon dioxide from electrophysiological studies on female *Aedes aegypti* (Kellogg 1970) and from behavioral studies on male *A. aegypti* (Bassler 1958) and female *Culex pipiens fatigans* (Omer and Gillies 1971). It seems likely that the capitate pegs on simuliids have a similar sensitivity.

The characteristics and numbers of sensilla associated with simuliid mouthparts are summarized in Table 17.5. Twelve morphological types of sensilla occur on the

Table 17.5 Structural characteristics of mouthpart sensilla[a]

Mouthpart	Sensillum	Location on Mouthpart	Form of Cuticular Process	Process Length (μm)	Neurons/ Sensillum	Sensilla/ Individual	Probable Function
Labium	external labial hairs	distally on prementum and first labellar segment	sharp-pointed hair	40–90	1	50	mechanoreception
	aboral labellar bristles	aboral surface of second labellar segment	blunt-tipped bristles with terminal pores	15–120	5–6 4–6[b]	60	chemo-[g,h] /mechanoreception
	oral labellar pegs	oral surfaces of labella	blunt-tipped pegs	15–20	3–4	20–40	chemo- /mechanoreception
	chordotonal organs	within labella	none	NA	2	2	mechanoreception (proprioception)
Labrum	distal labral triplets = apical sensilla[c]	distal tip in prestomal teeth	3 closely associated pegs	3	7[d]	2 triplets	chemo- /mechanoreception
	blindly ending dendrites	inside prestomal teeth	none	NA	3–4	6–8	mechanoreceptions(?)
	subterminal pegs = subapical sensilla[c]	distal labro-palatum					
	a. longer pegs	see above	peglike, no socket	4	2–3	2	chemoreception
	b. smaller pegs	see above	see above	2	1	2 2–6[c,e]	mechanoreception

	lateral labral pegs = lateral sensilla[c,f]	along sides of labro-palatal groove	3	1	peglike, bulbous socket	30	mechanoreception
	medial labral pegs = medial sensilla[c]	within labro-palatal groove	10	3	peglike with smooth walls	2	chemoreception
	basal labral pegs	near base of labro-palatum	5	1	peglike, bulbous sockets	40	mechanoreception
Mandibles	genal hairs	genal processes	unknown	1	hairlike	4	mechanoreception
Cibarium	cibarial pegs	in sides of cibarium	4	2	flattened, triangular pegs; sometimes basally fused[c]	4	chemoreception

[a]Unless otherwise specified, information is from Sutcliffe and McIver 1982.
[b]Elizarov and Chaika 1975.
[c]Colbo et al. 1979.
[d]2 neurons for each of 2 pegs, 3 neurons for third peg.
[e]Faucheux 1978.
[f]Colbo et al. (1979) include lateral and basal labral pegs of Sutcliffe and McIver (1982) in lateral sensilla.
[g]Angioy et al. (1982).
[h]Crnjar et al. (1983).

labium, labrum, and genal processes on which the mandibles articulate (Sutcliffe and McIver 1982). One type of sensillum is found in the cibarium. Ten types have morphological features of mechanosensilla, six of chemosensilla and three of both modalities. The mandibles, hypopharynx, and laciniae lack sensilla.

Using scanning electron microscopy, Colbo et al. (1979) surveyed the labro-cibarial sensilla of both sexes of a number of simuliid species, including autogenous as well as anautogenous ones. They found that all types of sensilla are present on each sex and species irrespective of blood-feeding habit or degree of mouthpart development. This suggests that the full range of sensilla have roles in mediating stimuli involved in both blood and nectar feeding.

The form of cibarial pegs varies; in *S. venustum* they occur as two pairs of discreet pegs (Sutcliffe and McIver 1982), whereas in *S. vittatum* each pair shares a common base and socket but has separate tips (Colbo et al. 1979). Regardless of form, the pegs are presumed chemosensilla and well situated in the cibarium to taste incoming meals. Interestingly, simuliid cibaria do not possess any form of mechanosensilla, a common feature of the cibaria of other insects, and thus lack a clear means of monitoring fluid flow (Sutcliffe and McIver 1982).

Eleven different types of sensilla occur on the legs of black flies (Sutcliffe and McIver 1976). Their characteristics are given in Table 17.6 and their numbers in Table 17.7. The largest number of both types of sensilla and individual sensilla respond to some type of mechanical stimulus. Types 1 and 2 trichodea, types 2 and 3 chaetica, and scalelike hairs are tactile receptors. The hair-plates are also sensitive to touch and owing to their locations detect the relative positions of the legs and body. Campaniform sensilla respond to stress in the cuticle (Pringle 1938). In black flies the campaniform sensilla on the femur, trochanter, tibia, and proximal basitarsus probably monitor stress produced by the weight of the insect on its legs, whereas those on the distal tarsomeres supply the insect with information on the relative positions of the tarsomeres to one another (Sutcliffe and McIver 1976).

Both the peg sensilla and type 1 chaetica are located on the tarsi and have the structural characteristics of contact chemosensilla. Crnjar et al. (1983) demonstrated electrophysiologically that each type 1 sensillum chaeticum of *S. decorum* has at least four chemosensitive neurons. Angioy et al. (1982) showed this for the same sensillar type on *S. venustum*. Salt- and sucrose-sensitive neurons are suggested. The peg sensilla are concentrated on the prothoracic tarsi (Sutcliffe and McIver 1976), a feature relevant to their proposed function. *S. damnosum* (e.g., Lewis 1953) often move over the skin of a prospective host, "patting" it with the prothoracic tarsi before probing. Marr (1962) speculated that some stimulus perceived on contact facilitates probing in black flies. Presumably, then, the peg sensilla perceive this contact stimulus.

The sensilla placodea and bifurcate sensilla may perceive airborne stimuli. The latter are flattened, bilobed short hairs. Each hair has a single pore at the base of the lobes and is innervated by four neurons with unbranched dendrites that terminate just proximal to the pore (McIver et al. 1980). An electron-dense fluid, the sensillum liquor, bathes the ends of the dendrites and extends through the pore and across part of the flattened lobes. This feature probably serves to increase the surface area available for absorption of stimulatory chemicals by the sensillum liquor. The bifurcate sensilla may be contact chemosensilla that have become adapted for olfaction (McIver et al. 1980). The role of these unusual sensilla in black fly behavior is obscure.

Table 17.6 Characteristics of sensilla on the legs

Sensilla	Description	Location	Probable Function
Type 1 trichodea	pointed-tipped hair, thick walled, spiral or straight grooves	general on tarsus, tibia and femur	mechanoreception
Type 2 trichodea	pointed-tipped hair, thick walled, spiral or straight grooves, shorter than type 1	ventral on tarsal segs. 1–4	mechanoreception
Type 1 chaetica	blunt-tipped bristles, thick walled, basal straight grooves, thin cuticle at tip	increasing distally on tarsal segments, distal on tibia	contact chemoreception[b]
Type 2 chaetica	pointed-tipped bristle, thick walled including tip, fluted grooves	increasing distally on tarsal segments,[a] distal on tibia	mechanoreception
Type 3 chaetica	pointed-tipped bristle, thick walled including tip, fluted grooves	medial on first tarsomere, distomedial on pro- and metathoracic tibiae	mechanoreception
Peg sensilla	blunt-tipped peg, thick walled, basal straight grooves, thin cuticle at tip	ventral on tarsomeres 1–4	contact chemoreception
Bifurcate sensilla	thick-walled hair, flattened forked tip, basal straight grooves	ventral on mesothoracic basitarsi	olfaction
Campaniform sensilla	oval domes with ring of raised cuticle	scattered on tarsi, tibia, and femur	mechanoreception (proprioception)
Hair plate sensilla	pointed-tipped, tiny hairs, smooth walls	extreme proximal margins of trochanter and coxa	mechanoreception (proprioception)
Scalelike hairs	compressed-tipped hairs, fine grooves in walls	femur and tibia	mechanoreception
Sensilla placodea	round or oval cuticular plates, indentations along circumference	1 on proximal surface of femur, 1–2 interspersed among campaniform sensilla on proximal region of tibia	olfaction

Source: Sutcliffe and McIver 1976.
[a]No type 2 sensilla chaetica on prothoracic tarsi of *S. articum* and very few on prothoracic tarsi of *S. rugglesi.*
[b]Confirmed in *S. venustum* by Angioy et al. (1982) and in *S. decorum* by Crnjar et al. (1983).

Number of Sensilla and Behavior

Meaningful interpretation of the relationship between the number of sensilla and behavior is fraught with difficulties, as discussed in detail for mosquitoes by McIver (1982). A few general differences, however, seem apparent from the information in Tables 17.2, 17.4, and 17.7. First of all, males have the same morphological types of sensilla as females. In anautogenous species the females have more presumed olfactory sensilla (A1, A2, A3, and styloconic sensilla on the antennae, capitate pegs on the palps, and bifurcate sensilla on the legs) than males. This presumably relates in general to the need of the female to detect olfactory stimuli mediating host and oviposition site location and discrimination.

Female *S. baffinense,* which has reduced mouthparts and is unable to take blood

Table 17.7 Approximate number of leg sensilla[a] per individual

	Type 1 trichodea	Type 2 trichodea	Type 1 chaetica	Type 2 chaetica	Peg sensilla	Bifurcate sensilla	Sensilla placodea	Campaniform sensilla	Hair plates
S. baffinense									
male	10,800	260	280	230	500	50	12	138	42
female	6,100	280	230	160	610	95	12	138	42
S. arcticum									
male	11,700	460	260	190	930	45	12	138	42
female	9,700	500	210	190	920	60	12	138	42
S. euryadminiculum									
male	—	—	—	—	—	—	—	—	—
female	14,000	300	230	340	1100	260	12	138	42
S. rugglesi									
male	8,800	350	260	130	600	25	12	138	42
female	10,100	360	260	130	860	105	12	138	42

Source: Sutcliffe and McIver 1976.
[a]Except type 3 sensilla chaetica and scalelike hairs, for which numerical data were not collected.

(Peterson 1959), has obviously fewer A1, A3, and styloconic sensilla and capitate pegs than any of the anautogenous females examined (Table 17.2). It is tempting to speculate that these sensilla are sensitive to host-associated olfactory cues, whereas A2 and bifurcate sensilla respond to olfactory stimuli, mediating behaviors common to both autogenous and anautogenous females, namely, location of nectar meals and oviposition and resting sites.

Comparisons of the total numbers or densities of the probable antennal olfactory sensilla on ornithophilic (*S. rugglesi* and *S. euryadminiculum*) and mammalophilic (*S. venustum*) species reveal large differences in particular cases, for example, the predominance of A1 sensilla on *S. venustum*. However, no consistent overall pattern is evident. This lack of a general pattern may be due to evolution at the level of the macromolecular receptors in the dendritic membranes, resulting in alterations in sensitivity of the neurons and in observable behavior without any detectable morphological change in sensilla.

ROLE OF SENSILLA IN BEHAVIOR

At any given moment the central nervous system of a black fly receives a complex spatial pattern of information resulting from the activity state of each sensory neuron. Depending on the insect's physiological state, changes in this pattern, such as those brought about by encounter with floral or oviposition-site odors or host-related stimuli, could result in a behavioral response. In Table 17.8 the stimuli that mediate the chief behaviors of adult black flies involving orientation over distance are correlated with the participating sensilla according to the functions that have been tentatively assigned to them in the foregoing discussion. This correlation is incomplete because of limits in our knowledge of the stimuli involved and the spectrum of function of the sensilla. Nonetheless, a synthesis of existing information does provide valuable insights into the role of various sensilla in black fly behavior.

STRUCTURAL MODIFICATIONS FOR FEEDING

Both sexes of black flies feed on sugar sources, while females of most species also blood-feed. The feeding apparatus (mouthparts and food pumps) is adapted to both feeding modes in terms of anatomy and sensory capability.

Mouthpart Structure

Simuliid mouthparts (Fig. 17.2) consist of the syntrophium (a term coined by Jobling 1976 for the functionally unified stylets), which produces and enlarges the wound during blood-feeding. This is ensheathed by the labium. Structure and function of simuliid mouthparts has been addressed in a number of papers. Grenier (1959) reviewed the earlier work in the field. Recent attempts at the functional interpretation of simuliid mouthparts are restricted to three major papers by Wenk (1962), Sutcliffe and McIver (1984), and Sutcliffe (1985).

Table 17.8 Stimuli and sensilla mediating distance orientation

Behavior	Mediating Stimuli	Probable Sensitive Sensilla
Location of host	visual cues[a,b,c,d] (color and shape)	compound eyes
	carbon dioxide[e,f,g]	capitate pegs on palps
	host-associated odors[h,i,j]	A1, A3, and styloconic sensilla on antenna
Location of oviposition site	visual cues[k,l] (color and reflectivity)	compound eyes
	humidity?[o]	?
	oviposition-site-associated odors?[o]	A2 sensilla on antenna bifurcate hairs on basitarsus?
Location of nectar	mainly plant-associated odors[o,p]	A2 sensilla on antenna bifurcate hairs on basitarsus?
	perhaps visual cues?[o]	compound eyes
Location of resting sites	probably a combination of	
	heat	sensilla coeloconica on antenna
	humidity	?
	light intensity	compound eyes
	plant odors	A2 sensilla on antenna bifurcate hairs on basitarsus?
Location of mate	visual cues[m,n] (swarm formation over conspicuous marker, detection of females)	compound eyes
	some spp. orient to hosts or flowers[q]	sensilla involved in host and nectar location

[a]Bradbury and Bennett 1974a;
[b]Browne and Bennett 1980;
[c]Das et al. 1984;
[d]Davies 1972;
[e]Fallis and Raybould 1975;
[f]Fallis et al. 1967;
[g]Thompson 1976a;
[h]Bradbury and Bennett 1974b;
[i]Thompson 1976b;
[j]Fallis and Smith 1964;
[k]Golini 1974;
[l]Golini and Davies 1975;
[m]Kirschfeld and Wenk 1976;
[n]Davies 1978;
[o]Discussed for mosquito behavior, McIver 1982;
[p]Wenk 1965a;
[q]Wenk, this volume.

The syntrophium is the unit formed by the mandibles (M) sandwiched between, and physically linking, the labrum (LR) above and the hypopharynx (H) below (Fig. 17.2). The broad, tapering labrum and hypopharynx both present smooth, thick cuticle on their oral aspects. A semicircular (in cross section) food gutter indents the labropalatum and runs almost to the labral tip. The oral hypopharyngeal surface is notched medio-longitudinally by the salivary gutter (SG), a continuation of the salivary duct. Distally, the mandibles are broad, thin plates that lie one atop the other and separate the food and salivary courses. They have rows of fine teeth on their disto-lateral and disto-medial margins. More proximally, each mandible bears specialized processes; one set inserting against the sides of the labro-palatal food gutter and the other hooking over the edge of the hypopharynx. This unifies the

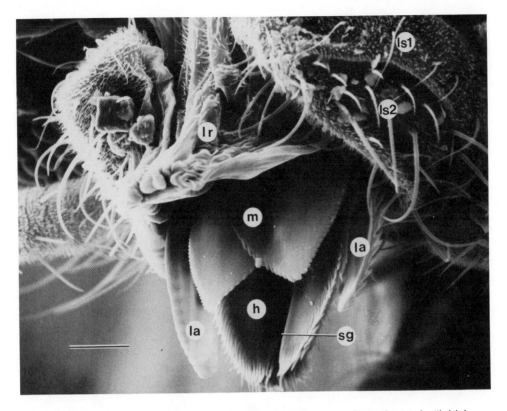

FIG. 17.2 Scanning electron micrograph of antero-lateral aspect of mouthparts in "initial penetration" configuration. *Abbreviations:* H, hypopharynx; LA, lacinia(e); LR, labrum; LS–1, first labellar segment; LS–2, second labellar segment; M, mandibles; SG, salivary gutter. Bar = 100 μm. (Reproduced from Sutcliffe and McIver 1984 with permission)

syntrophium physically and functionally. The laciniae (LA) are also part of the syntrophium. They are lancet-shaped stylets bearing two rows of backward-directed barbs on their front and back distal margins. These rows meet apically to form a sharp tip (Wenk 1962, Sutcliffe and McIver 1984).

The labium consists of the basal prementum, which bears two distal labellar segments (LS-1, LS-2) (Fig. 17.2). The prementum forms a floor and walls that ensheath the basal half of the syntrophium. The labellar segments completely enwrap the more distal parts of the syntrophium. The oral premental and labellar surfaces are composed of thin, flexible cuticle.

Food Pumps

Simuliids have three food-pumping regions along the food canal within the head (Fig. 17.3). The preoral cibarial pump consists of a double rank of muscles (dl cb) inserting into the roof of the U-shaped food canal between the syntrophial base and the level of the antennae. Pharyngeal muscles insert into the anterior pharynx immediately behind the true mouth (dl ant ph) and in the posterior pharynx just forward of the neck foramen (dl p ph-1, dl p ph-2).

Table 17.9 Summary of the actions that compose, and the possible sources of sensory information that control, the biting process in black flies

Action	Result of Action (if applicable)	Possible Sources of Sensory Information	Sensilla Implicated
A. Initial Penetration of the Skin			
1) Proboscis tip (labella) contacts skin		touch and chemical stimuli of the skin	aboral labellar bristles
2) Labella withdrawn	syntrophium end exposed	mechanical stimulation of labellar eversion	aboral labellar bristles, external labial hairs, labellar chordotonal sensilla
3) Syntrophium (labral and hypopharyngeal tips) lowered to skin	skin engaged preparatory to being stretched	touch and chemical stimuli of the skin	distal libral triplet sensilla
4) Labral and hypopharyngeal teeth and hairs grip skin	skin is tautened preparatory to being cut	physical stress in labral pre-stomal teeth and general cuticle	blindly ending dentries; sub-terminal pegs (smaller pair)
5) Mandibles cycle rapidly and repeatedly	initial cut made in skin	tactile stimuli from movement of mandibles along syntrophial "tracks"	lateral labral pegs, genal hairs
B. Wound Enlargement and Mouthpiece Entrenchment			
1) Laciniae driven into wound	syntrophium anchored in place		
2) Lacinial muscles attempt to retract laciniae	syntrophium drawn into wound preparatory to deeper cutting	mechanical pressure stimuli as labella compressed against skin	external labial hairs, aboral labellar bristles, oral labellar pegs, labellar chordotonal sensilla
		tactile and chemical stimuli as blood and tissue fluids released	distal labral triplets, sub-terminal labral pegs, oral labellar pegs
3) Mandibular movement and further lacinial penetration	wound deepened and syntrophium drawn more deeply into it	Similar to A5 and B1	

C. Diet Sampling and Active Feeding		
1) Pooled blood is tasted	if positive, active feeding ensues	blood-borne phagostimulants, especially adenine nucleotides	all mouthpart chemosensilla, except aboral labellar bristles may be involved at different times throughout biting process
2) Salivation into wound	lubrication of mouthparts, prevention of blood coagulation, sealing film around labellar and ligular pads		
3) Active food-pumping	blood drawn/pushed toward mid-gut	tactile stimuli from pumping and from in-rushing blood	basal labral pegs, lateral labral pegs
D. Mouthpart Removal		
1) Laciniae removed from wood tissues	syntrophium released from skin	tactile and other mechanical stimuli associated with general stress release in proboscis	all mouthpart mechanosensilla

Source: Based on information from Wenk (1962); Sutcliffe and McIver (1984) (1985).

Mechanics of Blood-Feeding

Sutcliffe and McIver (1984) divided the blood-feeding process in simuliids into four phases: (1) initial penetration, (2) consolidation of mouthpart position, (3) diet sampling and active feeding, and (4) mouthpart disengagement. Table 17.9 summarizes mouthpart action and sensillar involvement in this process.

After the ensheathing labella are drawn away, exposing the syntrophial tip, the ends of the labrum and hypopharynx contact, and by virtue of their apical spines and hairs engage the skin. Muscle action, supplemented by the fly's own weight, bends the labrum backwards, stretching the skin to allow easier laceration by the mandibles (Fig. 17.2; lr, h, m). The mandibles move along the tracks formed by the labrum and hypopharynx, cutting the skin with a "snipping" action. Recent suggestions that the laciniae are the piercing stylet in simuliids are discussed by Sutcliffe and McIver (1984). These are either based on erroneous interpretations of mouthpart anatomy (Faucheux 1978) or lack evidence (Wenk 1981).

Position consolidation results from a cycle of anchoring lacinial thrusts into the wound followed by mandibular cutting strokes that deepen the wound. Lacinial action draws the syntrophium more deeply into the wound until maximal penetration is achieved (approx. 150–425 μm depending on species; Wenk 1962, 1981). On the basis of specimens frozen in place while feeding through a latex rubber membrane, Sutcliffe and McIver (1984) proposed that the labrum achieves more penetration than described by Wenk (1962). Some question about this conclusion must remain, however, because the structure of the artificial membrane differs in many important ways from that of skin. As the mouthparts cut more deeply, the smooth, flexible oral surfaces of the labella are pressed against the skin surrounding the top and sides of the wound. At the same time, the ligula is everted and pressed up against the skin along the bottom edge of the wound (Sutcliffe 1985).

Work by Sutcliffe and McIver (1975, 1979) and Smith and Friend (1982) suggests that simuliids sample for, and actively feed in response to, adenine nucleotides borne in the blood. In this black flies are similar to other blood-feeders (see reviews by Galun 1975, Friend and Smith 1977). All but one of the six chemosensilla (aboral labellar bristles) associated with the mouthparts probably come into contact with the blood and tissue fluids during biting. Therefore, as Salama (1966) suggested for mosquitoes, meal acceptance in black flies may be based on sensory input from a suite of taste sensilla, each one serving as a "line of defense." The cibarial sensilla would form the last line of defense and may also be involved in directing the meal to the appropriate part of the alimentary canal for storage (midgut for blood, crop for nectar).

Active feeding is accomplished by the cibarial (dl cb) and pharyngeal pumping muscles (Fig. 17.3; dl ant ph, dl p ph-1, dl p ph-2) acting in coordination with the oral and post pharyngeal constrictors. Feeding efficiency is apparently maximized by the sealing properties of the labellar and ligular membranes, which Sutcliffe (1985) concluded help prevent blood leakage out of, and air leakage into, the wound.

Mouthpart disengagement is essentially a problem of freeing the barbed laciniae from the wound. This involves a combination of specialized anatomy (Wenk 1962) and unspecialized tugging and pulling that eventually wrench the mouthparts free.

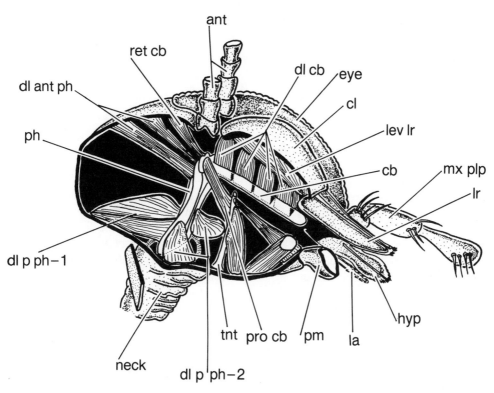

Fig. 17.3 Drawing of a reconstruction of the simuliid head showing cibarium and pharnyx and associated musculature. *Abbreviations:* ant, antennae; cb, cibarium; cl, clypeus; dl ant ph, dilators of the anterior pharynx; dl cb, dilators of the cibarium; dl p ph-1, dilators of the posterior pharynx (group 1); dl p ph-2, dilators of the posterior pharynx (group 2); eye, compound eye; hyp, hypopharynx; la, lacinia; lev lr, levators of the labrum; lr, labrum; mx plp, maxillary palp; neck, neck foramen; ph, pharynx; pm, prementum; pro cb, protractors of the cibarium; ret cb, retractors of the cibarium; tnt, tentorium. (Reproduced from Sutcliffe and McIver 1984 with permission)

Mechanics of Sugar/Nectar-Feeding

The mechanics of nectar-feeding are much simpler than those of blood-feeding. However, the presence of the same sensillar complement on the reduced mouthparts of males and autogenous females as is found on anautogenous females suggests that a number of chemical and physical cues are important in this process. Working with *S. venustum,* Angioy et al. (1982) established that the aboral labellar bristles are salt- and sucrose-sensitive. This was confirmed for *S. decorum* by Crnjar et al. (1983). These may be the first, but certainly not the last, sensilla to contact the nectar source. During nectar-feeding, the labella draw up the nectar into the folded oral labellar cuticle by capillary action. It is then drawn down the food canal by the pumps already described (Sutcliffe and McIver 1984, Sutcliffe 1985).

Simuliids are also capable of feeding from dried sugar deposits. In this mode of feeding, the labellar lobes are everted and applied to the dried deposit. This is then liquefied by saliva pumped into the labellar chamber and then drawn up as described for nectar. This method of sugar-feeding may be more important than presently recognized in Diptera and is discussed most thoroughly for ceratopogonids by Downes (1974).

SUMMARY

The numbers, distribution, and fine structure of the peripheral sensilla of a few species of black flies are reasonably well known, as are the general types of stimuli that elicit most behaviors. A prime area for future investigation is electrophysiological characterization of the spectrum of sensitivities of the various neurons associated with each sensillar type. Structural analyses of, including determination of specific neuronal connections, and electrophysiological recordings from the central nervous system of larvae and adults would provide the bases for understanding integration of sensory information. These crucial types of investigations are dependent upon access to laboratory colonies, as are equally desired critical behavioral studies done under controlled conditions.

The virtual explosion in the past fifteen years of information on the nervous systems of insects has been made possible chiefly through increasingly sophisticated refinements to electron microscopic and electrophysiological techniques. In insects in general the present vanguard is molecular studies on the central nervous system. Compared to some insects, our knowledge of the peripheral nervous system, let alone the central one, of simuliids is elementary.

LITERATURE CITED

Altner, H., and L. Prillinger. 1980. Ultrastructure of invertebrate chemo-, thermo-, and hygroreceptors and its functional significance. *Int. Rev. Cytol.* 67:69–139.

Angioy, A. M., A. Liscia, R. Crnjar, P. Pietra, and J. G. Stoffolano, Jr. 1982. Electrophysiological responses of the labellar, tarsal and palpal chemosensilla of adult female black fly, *Simulium venustum* Say, to NaCl and sucrose stimulation (1). *Boll. Soc. Ital. Biol. Sperimentale* 58:1319–24.

Barr, W. B. 1984. Prolegs and attachment of *Simulium vittatum* (sibling IS–7) (Diptera: Simuliidae) larvae. *Can. J. Zool.* 62:1355–62.

Bassler, U. 1958. Versuche zur Orientierung der Stechmucken: die Schwarmbildung und die Bedeutung des Johnstonschen Organs. *Z. Vgl. Physiol.* 41:300–330.

Boo, K. S., and D. M. Davies. 1980. Johnston's organ of the black fly *Simulium vittatum* Zett. *Can. J. Zool.* 58:1969–79.

Bradbury, W. C., and G. F. Bennett. 1974a. Behavior of adult Simuliidae (Diptera). I. Response to color and shape. *Can. J. Zool.* 52:251–259.

———. 1974b. Behavior of adult Simuliidae (Diptera). II. Vision and olfaction in near-orientation and landing. *Can. J. Zool.* 52:1355–64.

Browne, S. M., and G. F. Bennett. 1980. Color and shape as mediators of host-seeking responses of simuliids and tabanids (Diptera) in the Tantramar marshes, New Brunswick, Canada. *J. Med. Entomol.* 17:58–62.

Carlson, S. D., R. L. Saint Marie, and C. Chi. 1984. The photoreceptor cells. Pp. 397–433 in R. C. King and H. Akai, Eds., *Insect ultrastructure.* Plenum, New York.

Colbo, M. H., R. M. K. W. Lee, D. M. Davies, and Y. J. Yang. 1979. Labro-cibarial sensilla and armature in adult black flies (Diptera: Simuliidae). *J. Med. Entomol.* 15(2):166–175.

Craig, D. A. 1977. Mouthparts and feeding behaviour of Tahitian larval Simuliidae (Diptera: Nematocera). *Quaest. Entomol.* 13:195–218.

Craig, D. A., and A. Borkent. 1980. Intra- and inter-familial homologies of maxillary palpal sensilla of larval Simuliidae (Diptera: Culicomorpha). *Can. J. Zool.* 58:2264–79.

Craig, D. A., and H. Batz. 1982. Innervation and fine structure of antennal sensilla of Simuliidae larvae (Diptera: Culicomorpha). *Can. J. Zool.* 60:696–711.

Crnjar, R., A. Liscia, A. M. Angioy, P. Pietra, and J. G. Stoffolano, Jr. 1983. Observations on the morphology and electrophysiological responses of labellar, tarsal and palpal chemosensilla of the black fly, *Simulium decorum* Walker (Diptera: Simuliidae). *Monitore Zool. Ital.* (n.s.) 17:133–141.

Das, S. C., M. Bhuyan, and N. G. Das. 1984. Attraction of Simuliidae to different colors on humans—field trial. *Mosquito News* 44:79–80.

Davies, D. M. 1972. The landing of blood-seeking female black-flies (Simuliidae: Diptera) on colored materials. *Proc. Entomol. Soc. Ont.* 102:124–155.

———. 1978. Ecology and behaviour of adult black flies (Simuliidae): a review. *Quaest. Entomol.* 14:3–12.

Davies, D. M., and B. V. Peterson. 1956. Observations on the mating, feeding, ovarian development and oviposition of adult black flies (Simuliidae, Diptera). *Can. J. Zool.* 34:615–655.

Downes, J. A. 1974. The feeding habits of adult Chironomidae. *Entomol. Tidskr.* (Suppl.) 95:84–90.

Elizarov, Yu A., and S. Yu Chaika. 1975. An electron-microscopic study of the gustatory and olfactory sensilla of the blackfly *Boophthora erythrocephala* (De Geer) (Simuliidae: Diptera). *Vestnik Moskovskogo Univ. Biol.* 30(5):3–11.

Fallis, A. M., and J. N. Raybould. 1975. Response of two African simuliids to silhouettes and carbon dioxide. *J. Med. Entomol.* 12:349–351.

Fallis, A. M., and S. M. Smith. 1964. Ether extracts from birds and CO_2 as attractants for some ornithophilic simuliids. *Can. J. Zool.* 42:723–730.

Fallis, A. M., G. F. Bennett, G. Griggs, and T. Allen. 1967. Collecting *Simulium venustum* female in fan traps and on silhouettes with the aid of carbon dioxide. *Can. J. Zool.* 45:1011–17.

Faucheux, M. J. 1978. La prise de nourriture chez la larve et l'imago femelle des simulies (Insectes Dipteres Hematophages). *Bull. Soc. Sci. Nat. Ou. Fr.* 76:153–160.

Friend, W. G., and J. J. B. Smith. 1977. Factors affecting feeding by blood-sucking insects. *Ann. Rev. Entomol.* 22:309–331.

Galun, R. 1975. The role of host blood in the feeding behavior of ectoparasites. Pp. 132–162 in A. Zuckerman, Ed., *Dynamic aspects of host-parasite relationships.* Wiley, New York.

Golini, V. I. 1974. Relative response to coloured substrates by ovipositing blackflies (Diptera: Simuliidae). III. Oviposition by *Simulium (Psilozia) vittatum* Zetterstedt. *Proc. Entomol. Soc. Ont.* 105:48–55.

Golini, V. I., and D. M. Davies. 1975. Relative response to coloured substrates by ovipositing black-flies (Diptera: Simuliidae). II. Oviposition by *Simulium (Odagmia) ornatum* Meigen. *Norw. J. Entomol.* 22:89–94.

Grenier, P. 1959. Remarques concernant jonctionnement des mandibles chez les femelles de Dipteres hematophages Nematoceres et Brachyceres. *Ann. Parasitol. Hum. and Comp.* 34:565–585.

Jobling, B. 1976. On the fascicle of blood-sucking Diptera. In addition a description of the maxillary glands in *Phlebotomus papatasi,* together with the musculature of the labium and pulsatory organ of both the latter species and also of some other Diptera. *J. Nat. Hist.* 10:457–461.

Keil, T. A., and R. A. Steinbrecht. 1984. Mechanosensitive and olfactory sensilla of insects. Pp. 477–516 in R. C. King and H. Akai, Eds., *Insect ultrastructure.* Plenum, New York.

Kellogg, F. E. 1970. Water vapor and carbon dioxide receptors in *Aedes aegypti* (L.). *J. Insect Physiol.* 16:99–108.

Kirschfeld, K., and P. Wenk. 1976. The dorsal compound eye of simuliid flies: an eye specialized for the detection of small, rapidly moving objects. *Z. Naturforsch.* 31:764–765.

Lewis, D. J. 1953. *Simulium damnosum* and its relationship to onchocerciasis in the Anglo-Egyptian Sudan. *Bull. Entomol. Res.* 43:597–644.

Marr, J. D. M. 1962. The use of an artificial breeding site and cage in the study of *Simulium damnosum* Theobald. *Bull. WHO* 27:622–629.

McIver, S. B. 1975. Structure of cuticular mechanoreceptors of arthropods. *Ann. Rev. Entomol.* 20:381–397.

———. 1982. Sensilla of mosquitoes (Diptera: Culicidae). *J. Med. Entomol.* 19:489–535.

McIver, S., and R. Siemicki. 1985. Fine structure of antennal putative thermo-/hygrosensilla of adult *Rhodnius prolixus* Stal (Hemiptera: Reduviidae). *J. Morphol.* 183:15–23.

McIver, S., R. Siemicki, and J. Sutcliffe. 1980. Bifurcate sensilla on the tarsi of female black flies, *Simulium venustum* (Diptera: Simuliidae): contact chemosensilla adapted for olfaction? *J. Morphol.* 165:1–11.

Mercer, K. L., and S. B. McIver. 1973a. Studies on the antennal sensilla of selected blackflies (Diptera: Simuliidae). *Can. J. Zool.* 51:729–734.

———. 1973b. Sensilla on the palps of selected blackflies (Diptera: Simuliidae). *J. Med. Entomol.* 10:236–239.

Omer, S. M., and M. T. Gillies. 1971. Loss of response to carbon dioxide in palpectomized female mosquitoes. *Entomol. Exp. Appl.* 14:251–252.

Peterson, B. V. 1959. Notes on the biology of some species of Utah black flies (Diptera: Simuliidae). *Mosquito News* 19:86–90.

Pringle, J. W. S. 1938. Proprioception in insects. II. The action of the campaniform sensilla on the legs. *J. Exp. Biol.* 151:114–131.

Salama, H. S. 1966. The function of mosquito taste receptors. *J. Insect Physiol.* 12:1051–60.

Smith, J. J. B., and W. G. Friend. 1982. Feeding behaviour in response to blood fractions and chemical phagostimulants in the black fly, *Simulium venustum. Physiol. Entomol.* 7:219–226.

Sutcliffe, J. F. 1985. Anatomy of membranous mouthpart cuticles and their roles in feeding in black flies (Diptera: Simuliidae). *J. Morphol.* 186:53–68.

Sutcliffe, J. F. and S. B. McIver. 1975. Artificial feeding of simuliids (*Simulium venustum*): factors associated with probing and gorging. *Experientia* 31:694–695.

———. 1976. External morphology of sensilla on the legs of selected black fly species (Diptera: Simuliidae). *Can. J. Zool.* 54:1779–87.

———. 1979. Experiments on biting and gorging behaviour in the black fly, *Simulium venustum. Physiol. Entomol.* 4(4):393–400.

———. 1982. Innervation and structure of mouthpart sensilla in females of the black fly *Simulium venustum* (Diptera: Simuliidae). *J. Morphol.* 171(3):245–258.

———. 1984. Mechanics of blood-feeding in black flies (Diptera: Simuliidae). *J. Morphol.* 180:125–144.

Thompson, B. H. 1976a. Studies on the attraction of *Simulium damnosum* s.l. (Diptera:

Simuliidae) to its hosts. I. The relative importance of sight, exhaled breath, and smell. *Tropenmed. Parasitol.* 27:455–473.

————. 1976b. Studies on the attraction of *Simulium damnosum* s.l. (Diptera: Simuliidae) to its hosts. II. The nature of substances on the human skin responsible for attractant olfactory stimuli. *Tropenmed. Parasitol.* 27:83–90.

Wenk, P. 1962. Anatomie des Kopfes von *Wilhelmia equina* L. (Simuliidae syn. Melusinidae, Diptera). *Zool. Jahrb. Abt. Anat. Ontog. Tiere* 80:81–134.

————. 1965a. Über die Biologie blutsaugender Simuliiden (Diptera). I. Besamungstrate der ++ beim Blutenbesuch und Anflug auf den Blutwirt. *Z. Morphol. Ökol. Tiere* 55:656–670.

————. 1965b. Über die Biologie blutsaugender Simuliiden (Diptera). II. Schwarmverhalten. Geschlechtserfindung und Kopulation. *Z. Morphol. Ökol. Tiere* 55:671–713.

————. 1981. Bionomics of adult black flies. Pp. 259–279 in M. Laird, Ed., *Blackflies: The future for biological methods of integrated control.* Academic Press, New York and London. 399 pp.

Zacharuk, R. Y. 1980. Ultrastructure and function of insect chemosensilla. *Ann. Rev. Entomol.* 25:27–47.

18 HOST-SEEKING BEHAVIOR AND HOST PREFERENCE OF *SIMULIUM ARCTICUM*

J. A. Shemanchuk

Host-seeking behavior is a complex act that is somewhat difficult to define. Minimally, it should be considered from a physiological as well as a behavioral point of view, since this general act is a composite resulting from the need to acquire a protein source for reproduction and as an extension of a natural circadian rhythm associated with emergence, mating, and nectar-feeding. Also, behavior patterns associated with orientation to a host are directed by responses to stimuli that are distinctly hierarchical (Bradbury and Bennett 1974a,b). Furthermore, it is difficult to distinguish dispersal and migration of adults from host-seeking. With these prefacing remarks, I will describe some observations on adults of *Simulium arcticum* in central Alberta, Canada.

In Canada, black flies, particularly *Simulium arcticum* Malloch, are a serious pest of cattle, causing major losses to producers in areas adjacent to the Athabasca River in central Alberta and the Saskatchewan River in central Saskatchewan. Black flies are considered a limiting factor in the expansion of the livestock industry into northwestern Canada, the last reserve of land suitable for agriculture in Canada. A similar situation is described by Staemm et al. (1980), who identified *Simulium erythrocephalum* De Geer and *Simulium ornatum* (Meigen) as serious pests to cattle and humans in the Federal Republic of Germany. They predict that black fly populations will increase and will be a limiting factor in land utilization along some of the major rivers.

Studies on feeding behavior and host preference generally have been limited to periods of isolated events in the life of adult females. Wenk (1981) provided a general interpretation of the literature concerned with blood- and nectar-feeding as well as host-seeking by black flies. In a more recent study by Porter and Collins (1985) using mark-release-recapture experiments, host-seeking by *Simulium ochraceum,* an anthropophilic species in Guatemala, was shown to be highly regulated by blood-feeding and oviposition, i.e., the length of the gonotrophic cycle. Searching began almost immediately after oviposition, and hosts were quickly located by questing flies. Thus, over a period of approximately 11 days, it was possible for females to enter a host-seeking phase up to four times. Since then, little new information has been added. Until techniques are developed that enable researchers to observe and record the activities of individual or groups of flies in their natural environment, advances in this area will be slow.

Information presented here concerns *S. arcticum* (sibling species IIS–10.11, Procunier 1984), specifically, populations in central Alberta, where descriptions were made under field conditions on behavior that relates host-seeking and blood-feeding. Gaps in our knowledge on host-seeking and feeding behavior are also indicated. My research on host-seeking behavior and host preference of *S. arcticum* is designed to obtain information that can be applied to the identification and development of repellents or management practices that can be recommended to producers to protect cattle from black fly attack.

OBSERVATIONS

Activities at the Breeding Sites

Simulium arcticum develop in large numbers in the Athabasca River, the characteristics of which are described by Haufe and Croome (1980). Many smaller rivers and creeks are present in the area but are not attractive to *S. arcticum* and do not support this species.

Simulium arcticum overwinters in the egg stage on the river bottom. Adults first emerge from the river during the last week in May and the first week in June and emergence continues at varying degrees until about the first week in September (Depner et al. 1980).

Adult black flies rise to the surface of the water inside a bubble of air, and, once through the water surface, they fly to nearby terrestrial resting places. On no occasion was an emerging adult seen to break the water surface and fly directly away in spite of the many hours of observation on various parts of the river. However, many teneral males and females were seen and captured from the moving water surface. Between 5 and 50 adults per square meter of water surface were seen floating past a stationary boat on calm days. From this it was concluded that when the adults break the water surface a fairly high number rest and drift on the water surface while hardening of the cuticle bodies occurs and before they seek terrestrial resting places, plant nectar, or animal hosts. This is the first, albeit passive, transport of adults from their breeding grounds thus facilitating a proliferation of adults over wide areas along the river.

Black fly flight over the Athabasca River, measured by taking samples with standard sweep nets held over the sides of a moving boat, occurred between 0530 and 2330 hours (Shemanchuk and Anderson 1980). Flight activity was most intensive between 1930 and 2230 hours, just before sunset, with smaller activity peaks in the morning between 0830 and 0930 hours and in the afternoon between 1430 and 1530 hours. Black fly populations actively flying over the river were composed of teneral males and females, gravid females, and blood-engorged females (Figs. 18.1 and 18.2). The presence of blood-engorged females indicated that the females had found a host recently and were returning to the river area to rest and develop eggs. This did not indicate where the host was found or the type. The presence of large

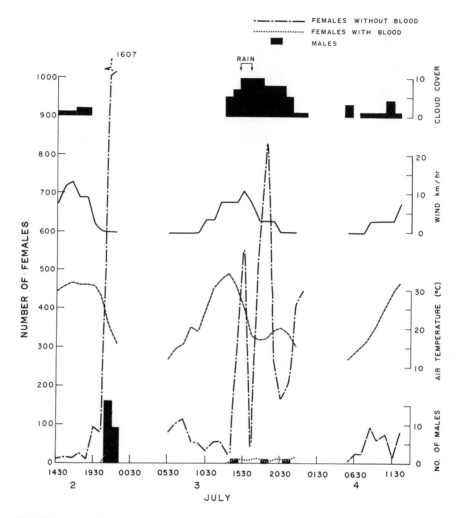

FIG. 18.1 Flight activity of adults of *Simulium arcticum* over the Athabasca River in July 1975.

numbers of gravid females indicated that many females had found hosts, developed eggs, and were depositing eggs into the river at a high rate. The presence of teneral males and females indicated the emergence of new adults. All of these stages occurred simultaneously throughout most of the day.

Mating of *S. arcticum* adults, a prerequisite activity to host-seeking, has not been investigated. However, on four different occasions male swarms, believed to be mating swarms, were observed between 1730 and 1930 hours. One swarm was observed near the bank of the river over the area between the sunny and shaded parts of the water surface. The other three swarms were observed on separate occasions in the shade of an anchored boat near the bank of the river. The temperature at the time of swarming ranged between 19°C and 23°C. The swarms consisted of about 30–100 individuals flying from 30–50 cm above the water surface. No copulation was observed and there were no females captured from the swarm. Further studies

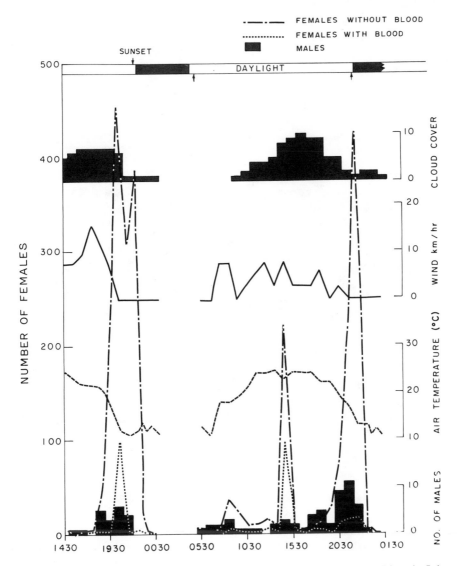

FIG. 18.2 Flight activity of adults of *Simulium arcticum* over the Athabasca River in July 1976.

are required to identify swarming sites, the age of swarming individuals, and the environmental conditions that induce swarming. Such information would be useful for attempting laboratory colonization of the species and for predicting when massive attacks may occur on cattle.

Movement of Adult *S. arcticum* from the River to Cattle

In central Alberta, about two to four days after the first adult emergence from the Athabasca River, nulliparous females, and on rare occasions the odd male, appear around cattle on pastures up to 40 kilometers away from the nearest possible breed-

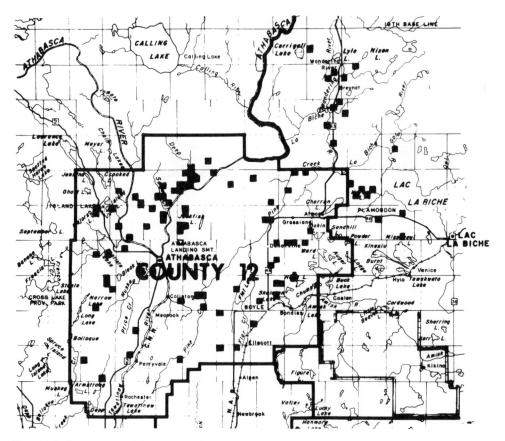

Fig. 18.3 Occurrence of females of *Simulium arcticum* around cattle on farms near the Athabasca River in central Alberta.

ing site (Fig. 18.3). This rapid dispersal of large numbers of adults over wide areas from the breeding site indicates a weather-aided mass transport of adults to areas where potential suitable hosts are present. It is believed that the convection currents above the river surface lift the adults into the upper air currents, which transport the adults away from the river. This type of transport is advantageous to the adults of *S. arcticum* because in the upper currents the adults avoid flight over rugged landscape and through dense forest canopy. Marr (1971) observed *S. damnosum* flying over bushes and trees and suggested that winds associated with squall lines were important in dispersal of adults. This type of weather condition does occur in central Alberta and could be a factor in the transport of adults away from the breeding grounds.

Before cattle were introduced into central Alberta, *S. arcticum* adults probably fed on scattered hosts such as moose, deer, elk, and caribou, whose population concentration was lower than the present confined herds of cattle. Thus rapid dispersion of females over vast areas was an assurance of finding blood meals to produce eggs and perpetuate the species. However, there is also a hazard in dispersing over too large an area, because gravid *S. arcticum* females must then return long distances to their specific oviposition sites. Perhaps the return flight to the breeding grounds by gravid or blood-engorged females is also aided by weather conditions.

An understanding of how female *S. arcticum* move from the breeding grounds to find their blood sources and how they find the oviposition sites after blood-feeding and developing eggs would greatly increase our ability to predict outbreaks, define outbreak areas, and improve protective measures for cattle. This knowledge will only be possible if techniques are developed to tag and follow tagged adults from their breeding sites to hosts and back to oviposition sites. The use of radar and infrared light-detecting techniques is being explored for remote sensing of flight behavior of black flies. Results obtained to date are encouraging.

Black Fly Activity at Farms

At farms in central Alberta, black fly populations are composed of *S. arcticum, Simulium vittatum* Zetterstedt, *Simulium venustum* Say, *Simulium decorum* Walker, and *S. aureum* Fries.; *S. arcticum* is the most abundant.

Simulium arcticum females are not attracted to humans and therefore human bait is not suitable to assess the presence, density, or distribution of *S. arcticum* in an area. Humans walking through the grass in hay fields and pastures or through forests during the daytime hours, when females are active, attract no *S. arcticum*, even though females are known to be present in these areas. However, when cattle are brought into the area, females of *S. arcticum* aggregate in loose swarms around them within two to four minutes of their arrival. Individuals in these swarms fly erratically, usually on the shaded side of the animal, about 30–50 cm above the ground. During periods of light wind, these swarms aggregate on the sheltered (i.e., downwind) side of the animal. Swarms of varying size are present around cattle on most days when the temperature is above 12°C and the wind velocity is below 12 km/hr.

Flight activity of female *S. arcticum* around cattle on a normal summer day occurs between 0600 and 2230 hours with two peaks of activity—one at about 1300 hours and the other at about 1830 hours (Fig. 18.4).

Female *S. arcticum* also are attracted to stationary, dark-colored vehicles. Swarms around a vehicle are similar to those observed around cattle, except that the swarms disappear after 15 to 30 minutes. It is believed that the attraction to stationary vehicles is a response to shape, size, and color that contrast with the landscape, similar to that described by Shipp (1985) when he demonstrated that silhouette traps were effective in trapping *S. arcticum* females.

Not all females swarming around animals attack at the same time. When all females from around an animal in a bait trap are captured, the number of females feeding (blood-engorged) is about equal to the number flying around the animal (non-blood-engorged). Swarming behavior around cattle could be a random search for the chemical landing cues emanating from the animal. From my observations, crowding on the host did not appear to be a feeding deterrent.

Simulium arcticum females bite mostly on the belly and to a lesser degree on the legs, sides of the body, sides of the neck, face, and, when populations are very dense, around the eyes. *Simulium vittatum* bite mainly in the ears, around the eyes,

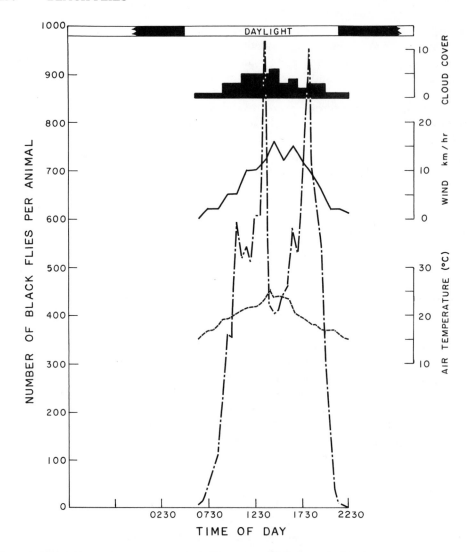

FIG. 18.4 Diel flight activity of females of *Simulium arcticum* around cattle.

and on the sides of the head. *Simulium venustum* and *S. decorum* bite on all parts of the body wherever they can penetrate the hair coat.

Blood from wounds caused by female bites attracts females to the wound areas and stimulates biting activity by other females. A similar behavior was observed in the laboratory when citrinated bovine blood was tested against field-collected females. This indicates that there is some factor in whole blood that stimulates feeding.

The search for a blood meal by *S. arcticum* females begins with the dispersal or displacement of the population over wide areas to occupy potential host habitats. Within the host habitat, I believe that size and shape of the host, in this case quadrupeds large in size contrasting against the background, is the first cue that brings females from their resting sites or patrolling flights into close proximity with the host. Near the host, CO_2, color, movements of the body, and animal body odors

Table 18.1 Number of females collected from bait traps (each containing 40 chickens or 40 rabbits) over a 79-day period in central Alberta

Bait	Simulium				
	arcticum	*venustum*	*vittatum*	*decorum*	*aureum*
Chickens	104(8)*	214(123)	322(58)	89(40)	453(221)
Rabbits	75(0)	53(0)	25(10)	17(0)	0(0)

*Number in brackets is the number of blood-engorged females in the collection.

Table 18.2 Comparison of the number of black flies feeding on horses and steers in bait traps in 13 collections in central Alberta

Bait	Simulium			
	arcticum	*venustum*	*vittatum*	*decorum*
Horse #1	260(185)*	45(9)	49(17)	12(5)
Steer #1	971(704)	48(34)	55(28)	0(1)
Horse #2	278(124)	38(11)	62(17)	1(0)
Steer #2	980(826)	56(20)	49(21)	2(0)
Horse #3	335(270)	109(46)	109(56)	12(7)
Steer #3	565(472)	88(32)	67(35)	5(2)

*Number in brackets is the number of blood-engorged females in the collection.

may keep swarming females in close proximity with the host until landing cues are received. Females may be attracted to parts of the body by stimuli such as light, temperature, humidity, skin and hair texture, color, and odors from whole blood. This is not quite the same hierarchical process described by Wenk (1981).

Host Preference

Studies on host preference of *S. arcticum* were conducted to identify a host other than cattle that could be used to study the seasonal and spatial distribution and abundance of *S. arcticum* females in the rugged environment in central Alberta and to determine if there were differences in tolerance by different breeds of cattle to attack by *S. arcticum* females. Chickens, rabbits, horses, and cattle were exposed in bait traps to natural populations of *S. arcticum* females. Blood-engorged females collected from these traps indicated that feeding had occurred, and this was used as the criterion for comparing host preference.

In one experiment, groups of 40 chickens and 40 rabbits, in a separate bait trap, were exposed to natural populations of *S. arcticum* for 79 days during spring and summer when *S. arcticum* were abundant around cattle. Both rabbits and chickens proved to be poor bait for *S. arcticum* females (Table 18.1). Of the low numbers

Table 18.3 Average number of blood-engorged females of *Simulium arcticum* collected in bait traps from paired steers of the same breed

Breed	Number Engorged Females on Paired Steers		Number of Replicates
Hereford	8,514	7,339	28
Angus	6,014	5,115	10
Galloway	905	739	8
Highland	3,145	2,786	10
Holstein	1,025	896	10
Ayrshire	486	635	10
Charolais	20,666	21,192	10
Highland-Shorthorn cross	2,350	1,870	8

Table 18.4 Comparison of the number of blood-engorged females of *Simulium arcticum* collected in bait traps in 10 different collections from steers of different breeds

	Number of Blood-engorged Black Flies				
	Test Animal	Hereford	Angus	Highland	Ayrshire
Hereford	11,035	—	—	3,586*	—
Hereford	1,494*	—	4,779	—	—
Galloway	134*	673	—	—	—
Galloway	1,888	—	—	376*	—
Galloway	361	—	462	—	—
Highland	3,514*	—	16,456	—	—
Charolais	11,975	—	—	5,981*	—
Charolais	18,000	20,804	—	—	—
Charolais	11,403	—	14,682	—	—
Highland-Shorthorn X	833*	1,497	—	—	—
Highland-Shorthorn X	3,154*	—	9,751	—	—
Highland-Shorthorn X	2,350	—	—	1,791	—
Holstein	387	—	—	—	362

*Significant difference ($p < 0.01$) by Wilcoxon's Signed Rank Test indicating breed tolerance to black fly attack compared to matched animal.

collected, none had fed on rabbits and only 7.7% had fed on chickens. These results indicated that rabbits and chickens are not suitable bait for studies of *S. arcticum*.

In another experiment, steers and horses of comparable weight and hair-coat color were compared to determine if there was a preference for either of these hosts by *S. arcticum* females. It was found that significantly larger numbers of *S. arcticum* females fed on steers (Table 18.2), suggesting that bovines are preferred over equines. However, the numbers of females attracted to horses were sufficient to consider horses as useful bait animals. Horses exhibited more annoyance from the bites than did cattle and in some instances were more difficult to handle.

Yearling Hereford, Angus, Galloway, Highland, Holstein, Ayrshire, Charolais, and Highland-Shorthorn cross steers, paired for uniformity in color, weight, temperament, and texture of hair coat, were compared to detect differences in tolerance to black fly attack between individuals within these breeds. There was no significant difference in tolerance to black fly attack between individuals within the same breed (Table 18.3).

With the use of bait traps, these same breeds, paired for uniformity in size and temperament, were compared to determine tolerance to black fly attack between individuals of different breeds. Results of these observations indicated that Highland, Highland-Shorthorn crosses, and Galloway breeds were significantly more tolerant to black fly attack than Hereford, Angus, Charolais, and Holstein steers. Herefords were more tolerant than Angus and Highland more tolerant than Galloway (Table 18.4). The longer, denser hair on the Highland, Highland-Shorthorn cross, and Galloway cattle is believed to be a deterrent to feeding by black flies on these breeds. If the cattle industry is to expand in black fly infested areas, the use of long-haired breeds of cattle should be considered.

S. arcticum females, as well as other species of black flies, exhibit definite host preferences. An understanding of the factors responsible for these preferences would aid in developing repellents for protection against black flies. This is an area that urgently needs investigation.

LITERATURE CITED

Bradbury, W. C., and C. F. Bennett. 1974a. Behavior of adult Simuliidae (Diptera). 1. Response to color and shape. *Can. J. Zool.* 52:251–259.

———. 1974b. Behavior of adult Simuliidae (Diptera). 1. Vision and olfaction in near-orientation and landing. *Can. J. Zool.* 52:1355–64.

Depner, K. R., W. A. Charnetski, and W. O. Haufe. 1980. Population reduction of the black fly *Simulium arcticum* at breeding sites in the Athabasca River. Pp. 21–37 in W. O. Haufe and G. C. R. Croome, Eds., *Control of black flies in the Athabasca River.* Tech. Rept. Alberta Environment, Edmonton, Alberta.

Haufe, W. O., and G. C. R. Croome. 1980. Control of black flies in the Athabasca River. Tech. Rept., Alberta Environment, Edmonton, Alberta. 241 pp.

Marr, J. D. M. 1971. Observations on resting *Simulium damnosum* (Theobald) at a dam site in northern Ghana. WHO mimeo. doc., WHO/ONCHO/71.85, WHO/VBC/71.298.

Porter, C. H., and R. C. Collins. 1985. The gonotrophic cycle of wild *Simulium ochraceum* and associated development of *Onchocerea volvulus. Am. J. Trop. Med. Hyg.* 34:302–309.

Procunier, W. S. 1984. Cytological identification of pest species of the *Simulium arcticum* complex present in the Athabasca River and associated tributaries. *Farming for the Future Final Report, Agriculture Canada* (82–0101), Lethbridge, Alberta. 44 pp.

Shemanchuk, J. A., and J. R. Anderson. 1980. Bionomics of biting flies in the agricultural area of central Alberta. Pp. 207–214 in W. O. Haufe, and G. C. R. Croome, Eds., *Control of black flies in the Athabasca River.* Tech. Rept., Alberta Environment, Edmonton, Alberta.

Shipp, J. L. 1985. Comparison of silhouette, sticky, and suction traps with and without dry ice bait for sampling black flies (Diptera: Simuliidae) in central Alberta. *Can. Entomol.* 117:113–117.

Staemm, K., H. G. Ziemer, and W. Rühm. 1980. Diseases and fatalities in cattle caused by black flies (Diptera: Simuliidae). *Anz. Schaedlingskd. Pflanzenschutz Umweltschutz* 53:56–64.

Wenk, P. 1981. Bionomics of adult black flies. Pp. 259–279 in M. Laird, Ed., *Blackflies: the future for biological methods in integrated control.* Academic Press, New York and London.

19 OVIPOSITION OF BLACK FLIES

Victor I. Golini and Douglas M. Davies

Female simuliids have evolved various strategies of egg-laying activity that maximize reproduction and the maintenance of species at certain breeding sites. Their oviposition activity is adapted to season and time of day, to weather conditions, type of running-water habitat, and position along the stream, particularly to the presence or absence of suitable substrates on which to lay their eggs. Oviposition is an energy-consuming activity requiring nutrients either transferred from the larvae or imbibed by adult females from nectar of flowers or from blood of vertebrate hosts (Fredeen 1963, Magnarelli and Burger 1984).

In some autogenous species eggs may be partly or fully developed when the female emerges from the pupal stage. Therefore, soon after mating, females of some species, such as *Cnephia dacotensis,* may begin to oviposit a few hours after emergence (Davies and Peterson 1956), or in about two days, as in *Simulium decorum* and *S. vittatum* (Peterson and Wolfe 1958). Females of parthenogenetic species, such as *Prosimulium ursinum,* may oviposit even sooner after ecdysis, and eggs may even hatch from disintegrating pharate adults trapped in the pupal skin, as an adaptation to a short subarctic season (Carlsson 1962). In autogenous species in which newly emerged females have undeveloped eggs, flies may rest on foliage near the breeding site for four or five days, until oogenesis is complete, before ovipositing (Davies 1961). Thus in autogenous species, temporal synchrony of ovipositing simuliids at the breeding site is more likely than in anautogenous species (Fredeen 1963).

In autogenous species for which subsequent gonotrophic cycles require a blood meal, as well as in anautogenous species, dispersal from the breeding site is usually required, unless vertebrate hosts are continually in close proximity, as occurs on some cattle farms or in streams frequented by ducks and shore birds (Bennett 1963, Golini 1975b). In some members of the *S. damnosum* complex in Africa, newly emerged females imbibe nectar, then fly above the canopy and migrate, aided by the wind, before blood-feeding and ovipositing (Garms and Walsh, this volume). Communal or mass oviposition may occur in some anautogenous species if the required oviposition sites are few in number, such as for *S. damnosum* s.l. and *S. verecundum* (Hocking and Pickering 1954, Muirhead-Thompson 1957, Balay 1964). The time from adult female emergence to oviposition in anautogenous species may vary from three days in tropical regions, as in *S. damnosum* s.l. (Lewis et al. 1961), to two to three weeks in temperate regions, as in *S. venustum/verecundum* (Davies 1950, Davies and Peterson 1956), depending on availability of hosts, conditions favorable to search for hosts, and ambient temperature during oogenesis.

Several authors have reviewed the literature on simuliid oviposition (Bequaert 1934, Vargas 1945, Grenier 1949, Rubtzov 1956, Usova 1961, Rühm 1971, Rivosecchi 1978, Wenk 1981). Most simuliid species lay their eggs in or at the edge of running water, with a tendency to select substrates that are lapped or sprayed by vigorous current (Balay 1964). However, some species, such as *S. vittatum, S. decorum,* and *S. vernum,* have been observed to oviposit in almost still water at the edge of streams or on logs in a lake as much as 30 meters from a dam (Wu 1931, Davies et al. 1962, Imhof and Smith 1979). Among the problems that black flies must overcome in remaining within their breeding habitats is the downstream drift and migration of larvae, particularly in large rivers (Rubtsov 1964). Hence, the maintenance of a population within a segment of stream is often compensated for by females flying upstream before laying their eggs (Roos 1957, Adler et al. 1983). Consequently, some species exhibit a behavior of ovipositing at or just below a natural or man-made dam at the head of rapids, as occurs with *S. decorum, S. vittatum, S. longistylatum* (Davies and Peterson 1956, Davies et al. 1962), *S. noelleri* (as *argyreatum*) (Poole 1967, Rühm 1975), *S. arcticum* (Peterson 1959), *S. damnosum* s.l., *S. medusaeforme* (Davies 1962), *P. mixtum* s.l., *Stegopterna mutata, Cn. ornithophilia,* and, in autumn, *S. vittatum* (Colbo 1979).

Females of species in several genera, e.g., *Prosimulium, Cnephia, Eusimulium, Simulium,* and *Austrosimulium,* oviposit, usually while flying upstream, by tapping the water surface with the tip of their abdomen and releasing, usually with each tap, one or more eggs into the water (Wu 1931, Bradley 1935, Fredeen et al. 1951, Davies and Peterson 1956, Peterson 1959, Usova 1961, Wanson and Henrard 1965, Obeng 1967, Moorhouse and Colbo 1973, Mitrokhin 1973, Imhof and Smith 1979, and Colbo, personal communication 1984). In some species this method of oviposition while females are in flight occurs in the middle of the stream, often just above or on the lip of a falls caused by a natural or man-made dam. Females of some species of *Eusimulium* and *Simulium* hover above water pools at the edge of streams or over a solid surface (rock, log, or vegetation) that is continually moist or covered only by a thin, flowing sheet of water; a fly taps the tip of its abdomen briefly through the water, thereby depositing one or more eggs on the substrate or stream bottom (Edwards 1915, Comstock 1925, Gambrell 1933, Bradley 1935, Díaz Nájera in Vargas 1945: 37, Dalmat 1955, Davies and Peterson 1956, Peterson 1959, Obeng 1967, Imhof and Smith 1979). Dalmat (1955) reported that *S. ochraceum* females oviposit by hovering above less turbulent parts of the stream and dropping relatively few eggs in one place on floating, emergent vegetation, as did Grunin (1949) for *P. hirtipes.* Under certain environmental conditions, some, if not all, species that oviposit while flying will also settle at the water's edge and affix eggs to a solid, wet surface (Stone and Jamnback 1955, Dalmat 1955, Peterson 1959, Mitrokhin 1973). However, females of *S. lineatum* (as *salopiense*) lay their eggs into the water while floating on the water surface (Rühm 1971). Recently females of *S. posticatum* in

England were seen laying their eggs not on water but within vertical cracks of moist earth along the river bank (Ladle et al. 1985).

Females of many simuliid species oviposit only when settled on solid objects. The female lands above the water line on a leaf, branch, log, or rock and crawls to the water's edge while palpating the surface with the forelegs and palps (Figs. 19.1 and 19.2). On reaching the water's edge, the fly turns around, thrusts the tip of the abdomen onto the substrate through the water surface, and either taps the substrate or contracts the abdomen, thereby releasing an egg (Davies and Peterson 1956, Imhof and Smith 1979). Several authors have observed that eggs of certain species form compact masses held together by a sticky, gelatinous matrix, as in *S. damnosum* s.l. (Wanson and Henrard 1945, Crisp 1956, Muirhead-Thompson 1957, Davies 1962), *S. cervicornutum* and *S. unicornutum* (Muirhead-Thompson 1956), *S. equinum* (Edwards 1920), *S. ornatum* (Zahar 1951, Obeng 1967, Golini and Davies 1975b), *S. pictipes* (Gambrell 1933), *S. verecundum* (Davies and Peterson 1956, Imhof and Smith 1979), *S. vittatum* (Davies and Peterson 1956), and *S. vernum* (as *latipes* auct.) (Zahar 1951, Rubtsov 1956). Large egg masses usually result from mass egg-laying activity, referred to by Muirhead-Thompson (1956) as "communal oviposition." However, Davies (1962) observed that since oviposition by single flies also occurs at the same sites, mass egg-laying activity is the result of a shortage of available sites rather than a social behavior.

Females of several species crawl below the water surface, up to 15 cm, to oviposit on submerged substrates and may remain under water up to 20 minutes (Newstead 1907). Some of these species include *S. ornatum* (Britten 1922), *S. equinum* (Britten 1915 as *maculatum*, Edwards 1920, Petersen 1924, R. J. Post in litt. 1984), *S. salopiense* (Zivkovic 1949), *S. vernum* (as *latipes* auct.) (Zahar 1951, Ussing 1925, Rubtsov 1956, Wenk 1965), *S. damnosum* s.l. (Barnley 1952, Crisp 1956), *S. hargreavesi* (Meeser 1942, Barnley 1952), *S. elgonensis* (Meeser 1942), *S. adersi* (Marr 1962), *S. mediterraneum* (Rivosecchi 1967), *S. nigritarse* (Chutter 1972), *S. sirbanum*, and *S. schoutedeni* (Walsh 1984). Malloch (1914) stated that laying eggs below the water surface had survival value, especially in streams with fluctuating water levels.

Many species of black flies oviposit preferentially on vegetation, such as leaves of grass, sedge, cattail, reeds, etc., floating on the surface of streams, selecting vegetation that is green, smooth, and shiny. As eggs are laid at the tip and edges, the leaves gradually sink into the water because of the weight of the eggs and the hygroscopic nature of the matrix that binds the eggs together and to the substrate. Some species show a discrete pattern of egg laying: some lay eggs end to end in stringlike fashion, as in *S. vittatum* (Fig. 19.3) (Emery 1913, Wu 1931, Davies and Peterson 1956, Imhof and Smith 1979), *S. decorum* (Davies and Peterson 1956), *S. truncatum* (Usova 1961), *S. monticola*, *S. variegatum*, and *S. reptans* (Obeng 1967), and *S. damnosum* s.l. (Crisp 1956). Others lay eggs side by side in rings, as in *S. pictipes* and *S. longistylatum* (Davies and Peterson 1956), *S. noelleri* (as *argyreatum*), *S. reptans* (Usova 1961), and *S. adersi* (Marr 1962), or side by side in strings, as in *S. decorum* (Imhof and Smith 1979) and *S. damnosum* s.l. (Davies 1962). Females of other species lay their eggs upright on end, as in *S. aureum* (Davies and Peterson 1956, Obeng 1967), *S. sublacustre* (Rühm 1975), *S. equinum* (Welton and Bass 1980), and *S. reptans* (Usova 1961) (Fig. 19.4).

Females of some species, such as *S. verecundum, S. vittatum,* and *S. ornatum,*

FIG. 19.1 Freshly laid eggs of *S. erythrocephalum* on leaves of *Potamogeton* sp. (Photo W. Rühm)

FIG. 19.2 Egg masses of *S. ornatum* laid on tips of grass leaves trailing on the water surface of a stream. (Photo W. Rühm)

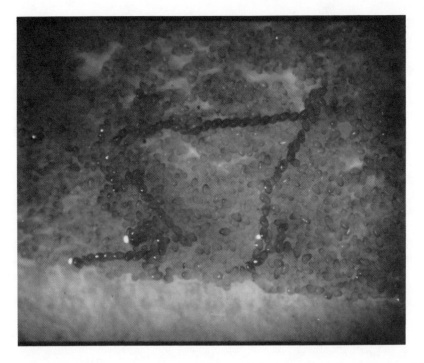

FIG. 19.3 A string of eggs of *S. vittatum* laid over a mass of eggs of *S. verecundum* (Photo Imhof and Smith)

FIG. 19.4 Eggs of *S. equinum* laid upright on end. (Photo W. Rühm)

have been found to lay more eggs selectively on substrates of certain colors, i.e., white, yellow, and light green (Peshken and Thorsteinson 1965, Golini and Davies 1975a,b, Golini 1975a). These preferences were observed for colored oviposition strips floated on the water surface with a natural light-brown stream background. However, eggs were seldom laid on the colored strips floated over a white plastic stream bottom, indicating that the oviposition substrate over a white stream background is less visible or less attractive to ovipositing flies. By contrast, 95% of the eggs of *S. verecundum* were laid on strips floated over a black plastic stream bottom, although there was a shift of color selection, with preferences for light gray, blue, and violet strips approaching those for white, yellow, and light green (Golini and Davies 1975a).

Gravid females of *S. damnosum* s.l. are attracted to shiny metal sheets placed on the bank next to rapids (Bellec 1976, Bellec and Hébrard 1977). Carlsson (1968/1971) suggests that lakes, bogs, and swamps act as "collecting mirrors" for females searching for oviposition sites and hosts. Many gravid females of the *S. damnosum* complex, such as *S. squamosum,* have been taken in UV light traps near oviposition sites (Service 1979), and *S. sirbanum* females have been trapped especially in the first two hours after dark (Marr 1971); gravid females of these flies comprised two-thirds of the catch, while many of the remainder appeared to have already oviposited (Walsh 1978).

The eggs of tropical species, such as those of the *S. damnosum* complex, hatch within four hours of deposition (Wanson and Henrard 1945), whereas those of temperate species, such as those of the *S. venustum/verecundum* complex, may take seven days at 15°C (Davies 1950). The eggs of some temperate univoltine species aestivate from spring until autumn (Davies and Syme 1958, Davies et al. 1962); those of other species laid in the spring hibernate, not hatching until late winter or early spring (Davies and Peterson 1956, Davies et al. 1962), and most eggs of other species, such as *S. arcticum,* laid in early summer to early fall also hibernate (Fredeen et al. 1951). In some temperate multivoltine species, an increasing proportion of eggs laid during the season appears to hibernate or enter diapause through the season, development within the egg stopping at the eye-spot stage. Only exposure of the eggs to cold temperatures of 2°–5°C for about two months will break the diapause (Wood and Davies 1965, 1966).

Delay in egg development may occur as the eggs are dispersed downstream, or as the vegetation on which they are laid decays and sinks to the bottom (Usova 1961). Thus eggs become embedded in the stream bottom as deep as 9 cm (Fredeen et al. 1951), where they remain cool, moist, and at low oxygen tension, even though the stream may become dry. Further development in these eggs is stimulated when floods from rain or melting snow stir the eggs from the bottom (Davies and Peterson 1956). In temporary streams that may flow only once in several years, eggs appear to remain viable buried in moist bottom silt until reactivated when the river is reflooded. Under such droughty conditions *A. pestilens* in Australia was found to persist with up to 20% of its eggs buried in the streambed remaining viable after two years of stream dryness (Colbo and Moorhouse 1974).

Simuliid eggs are unable to withstand prolonged exposure to air, although Ussing (1925) and Edwards (1956) suggested otherwise. Eggs of *S. damnosum* s.l. dried in a shaded beaker may all remain alive for 18 hours, but most are killed after 24 hours (Muirhead-Thompson 1957), and if dried in sunlight, most eggs will not survive more than 40 minutes (Crisp 1956). Few eggs of *S. vittatum* survived exposure to air for 10–14 hours (Wu 1931). Experiments with *S. ornatum* eggs showed that 80 to 90% survived desiccation at 10°C for one day, but survival of those of *S. equinum* was less than 2% (Welton and Bass 1980). In experiments on the tolerance of the various stages of eggs to desiccation, Rühm (1983) showed that eggs of *S. erythrocephalum* and *S. rostratum* cannot survive out of the water at the beginning of the embryonic stage, but they are relatively resistant at the eye-spot stage; this resistance diminishes again toward the end of development. This time-related phenomenon of egg viability may be related to the adaptation of these and other species to oviposit around sunset as a means of reducing the danger of desiccation of eggs at the eye-spot stage (Rühm 1983). Furthermore, Rühm (1975) observed that simuliid eggs of those species that oviposit on vegetation (especially emergent stems) or other solid objects at the water surface are particularly susceptible to desiccation, since sudden decreases in water level leaves the eggs high and dry. This may lead to high mortality of the species at the egg stage, as was observed for *S. erythrocephalum*, and it may be the cause of acyclic seasonal fluctuations in larval and adult populations of these simuliids (Rühm 1969, 1975).

Oviposition activity is affected by weather conditions. Light, lack of wind, high humidity, warm temperature, and shade from direct sunlight provide optimal factors for egg laying (Davies and Peterson 1956, Reuter and Rühm 1976). Such conditions occur most often in the late afternoon or early evening until one hour after sunset (Muirhead-Thompson 1956, Poole 1967, Corbet 1967, Mitrokhin 1973, Reuter and Rühm 1976, Imhof and Smith 1979, Welton and Bass 1980). If temperature is sufficiently high, together with other suitable weather conditions (see above), some oviposition may occur just after sunrise (Corbet 1967). Thunderstorms with rapidly changing atmospheric pressure, cloudiness, and increased humidity often induce egg laying at other times of the day (Davies and Peterson 1956, Reuter and Rühm 1976, Imhof and Smith 1979). In temperate regions oviposition, as for other adult activities, is restricted largely to the warm part of the year, i.e., late spring to late autumn (Davies and Peterson 1956). However, in subtropical and tropical regions egg laying may continue throughout the year. Under adverse environmental conditions, such as when streams become dry, it is possible that some species may delay oviposition by aestivating and resorb all or part of their eggs as a nutrient source, as in *S. damnosum* s.l. (Marr 1962).

Female simuliids are more prone to predation when swarming or landed for oviposition and may be attacked by insects, such as ants, adult odonates, and empidid, ephydrid, and muscid flies (Peterson and Davies 1960, Crosskey and Davies 1962, Balay and Grenier 1964, Elsen 1977) and by speckled trout (Ide 1942). Grunin (1949) observed females of *P. hirtipes* that were infected with mermithid nematodes flying with egg-laying females above a stream, as did Davies (1959) for *P. fuscum/mixtum*. This parasitism appears to have triggered an oviposition behavior in these flies that allows the parasite to return to the water to complete the free-living part of its life cycle (Rubtsov 1966).

In this review we have emphasized patterns in oviposition activity under field conditions as reported by numerous authors for several simuliid species. In summary, various species of black flies exhibit three major methods of oviposition (see Table 19.1): (1) The female flies above the water surface and lays one or more eggs each time she dips her abdomen into the water. (2) The flying female touches the

Table 19.1 Methods of oviposition by species of black flies

Method and Species	References
I. *Freely into the water while flying*	
S. aureum Fries	Davies and Peterson 1956
S. arcticum Malloch	Fredeen et al. 1951; Peterson 1956, 1959
S. canadense Hearle	Peterson 1959
S. canonicolum (Dyar & Shannon)	Peterson 1959
S. corbis Twinn	Wolfe and Peterson 1959
C. dacotensis (Dyar & Shannon)	Davies and Peterson 1956; Davies et al. 1962; Abdelnur 1968
S. decorum Walker	Davies and Peterson 1956
S. emarginatum Davies, Peterson & Wood	Davies et al. 1962
S. euryadminiculum Davies	Davies and Peterson 1956; Davies et al. 1962
P. exigens Dyar & Shannon	Peterson 1959
P. fuscum Syme & Davies	Davies and Peterson 1956; Peterson and Wolfe 1958; Davies et al. 1962
P. hirtipes (Fries)	Grunin 1949; Grenier 1949; Usova 1961
P. irritans Rubtsov	Grunin 1949; Rubtsov 1969
S. jacumbae Dyar & Shannon	Peterson 1959
S. jenningsi Malloch	Bequaert 1934
S. lineatum (Meigen) (as salopiense Edw.)	Rühm 1971, 1975
S. maculatum Meigen	Mitrokhin 1973
P. magnum Dyar & Shannon	Davies and Peterson 1956; Davies et al. 1962
P. mixtum Syme & Davies	Wolfe and Peterson 1959; Davies and Peterson 1956; Davies et al. 1962
St. mutata (Malloch)	Davies and Peterson 1956; Abdelnur 1968
S. ochraceum Walker	Dalmat 1955
C. pecuara (Riley)	Bradley 1935
A. pestilens Mackerras & Mackerras	Moorhouse and Colbo 1973
S. tuberosum (Lundström)	Davies and Peterson 1956; Wolfe and Peterson 1959; Abdelnur 1968
S. venustum Say	Bequaert 1934; Golini and Davies 1975a
S. vernum Macquart (as latipes auct.)	Edwards 1920; Grenier 1949; Obeng 1967; Imhof and Smith 1979
S. virgatum Coquillett	Vargas 1945
S. vittatum Zetterstedt	Wu 1931; Bequaert 1934; Davies and Peterson 1956
S. vulgare Rubtsov	Carlsson 1962
II A. *On trailing vegetation while landed*	
S. adersi Pomeroy	Davies 1962; Marr 1962
S. angustipes Edwards	Rühm and Schlepper 1979
S. aureum Fries	Jobbins-Pomeroy 1916; Zahar 1951; Davies et al. 1962; Obeng 1967
S aokii Takahasi	Ogata et al. 1954
S. noelleri Friederichs (as argyreatum auct.)	Usova 1961; Poole 1967; Rubtsov 1969; Rühm 1975
S. posticatum Meigen (as austeni Edw.)	Usova 1961
S. cholodkovskii (Rubtsov)	Rubtsov 1969
S. damnosum Theobald	Wanson 1950; Crisp 1956; Muirhead-Thompson 1956; Davies 1962; Marr 1971
S. decorum Walker	Abdelnur 1968
S. equinum (Linnaeus)	Zahar 1951
S. erythrocephalum De Geer	Rubtsov 1956; Wenk 1965; Rühm 1971, 1975; Post 1982
S. frigida (Rubtsov)	Usova 1961
S. hargreavesi Gibbins	Davies 1962
S. johannseni Hart	Jobbins-Pomeroy 1916
S. jenningsi Malloch	Jobbins-Pomeroy 1916
S. latigonium (Rubtsov)	Rivosecchi 1967
S. lineatum (Meigen)	Rühm 1975
S. mediterraneum Puri	Rivosecchi 1967; Rubtsov 1969

Table 19.1 (continued)

S. metallicum Bellardi	Dalmat 1955
S. monticola Friederichs	Zahar 1951; Obeng 1967
S. morsitans Edwards	Usova 1961; Mitrokhin 1973
S. noelleri Friederichs	Rühm 1975
S. ochraceum Walker	Dalmat 1955
S. olonicum (Usova)	Usova 1961
S. ornatum Meigen	Britten 1922; Smart 1934; Grenier 1949; Zahar 1951; Usova 1961; Obeng 1967; Rühm 1969, 1971, 1975; Golini and Davies 1975b; Welton and Bass 1980
S. paraequinum Puri	Rubtsov 1969
S. posticatum Meigen	Usova 1961
S. pusillum (Fries)	Mitrokhin 1973
S. reptans (Linnaeus)	Zahar 1951; Usova 1961
S. richteri Enderlein	Usova 1961
S. sublacustre Davies	Rühm 1975
S. turgaica (Rubtsov)	Rubtsov 1969
S. truncatum Lundström	Usova 1961
S. unicornutum Pomeroy	Obeng 1967
S. variegatum Meigen	Zahar 1951
S. venustum Say (= mainly S. verecundum)	Jobbins-Pomeroy 1916; Wu 1931; Davies 1950; Davies and Peterson 1956; Hocking and Pickering 1954; Wolfe and Peterson 1959; Abdelnur 1968
S. vernum Macquart (as latipes auct.)	Britten 1922; Zahar 1951; Usova 1961; Welton and Bass 1980
S. verecundum Stone & Jamnback	Golini and Davies 1975a; Imhof and Smith 1979
S. vittatum Zetterstedt	Jobbins-Pomeroy 1916; Wu 1931; Davies 1950; Davies and Peterson 1956; Wolfe and Peterson 1959; Abdelnur 1968; Golini 1975; Imhof and Smith 1979
S. vulgare Rubtsov	Rubtsov 1969

II B. *On rocks, logs, and twigs while landed*

S. adersi Pomeroy	Marr 1962
S. albella (Rubtsov)	Rubtsov 1969
S. aokii Takahasi	Ogata et al. 1954
S. arcticum Malloch	Cameron 1922; Peterson 1956
S. callidum (Dyar & Shannon)	Dalmat 1955
S. canadense Hearle	Peterson 1959
S. cholodkovskii (Rubtsov)	Rubtsov 1969
S. columbazense Schönbauer	Rubtsov 1969
S. damnosum Theobald	Wanson and Henrard 1945; Wanson 1950; Marr 1962, 1971
S. decorum Walker	Davies and Peterson 1956; Abdelnur 1968; Imhof and Smith 1979
S. hargreavesi Gibbins	Davies 1962
C. lapponica (Enderlein)	Usova 1961
S. longistylatum Shewell	Davies and Peterson 1956; Davies et al. 1962
S. maculatum Meigen	Mitrokhin 1973
S. monticola Friederichs	Obeng 1967
S. noelleri Friederichs (as argyreatum auct.)	Rühm 1975
S. ornatum Meigen	Obeng 1967
S. pictipes Hagen	Jobbins-Pomeroy 1916; Comstock 1925; Gambrell 1933; Davies and Peterson 1956
S. unicornutum Pomeroy	Obeng 1967
S. violens Serban	Rivosecchi 1967
S. vittatum Zetterstedt	Jobbins-Pomeroy 1916; Stone and Jamnback 1955; Davies and Peterson 1956; Peterson and Wolfe 1958; Peschken and Thorsteinson 1965

III. *On submerged substrates while submerged in water*

S. adersi Pomeroy	Gillett and Lebied 1959; Marr 1962; Balay 1964
S. arcticum Malloch	Peterson 1956

Table 19.1 (continued)

S. cholodkovskii (Rubtsov)	Rubtsov 1969
S. damnosum Theobald complex	Barnley 1952; Blanc et al. 1958; Burton and McRae 1965
S. equinum (Linnaeus)	Edwards 1920; Britten 1915 (as maculatum); Petersen 1924; Rubtsov 1969; Post 1984 litt.
S. erythrocephalum De Geer	Wenk 1965
S. elgonensis Gibbins	Meeser 1942
S. hargreavesi Gibbins	Meeser 1942; Barnley 1952; Gillett and Lebied 1959
S. mediterraneum (Puri)	Rivosecchi 1967
S. neavei Roubaud	Wanson and Henrard 1945
S. nili Gibbins	Barnley 1952
S. nigritarse Coquillett	Chutter 1972
S. noelleri Friederichs	Rühm 1975
S. ornatum Meigen	Edwards 1920; Britten 1922
S. pictipes Hagen	Comstock 1925; Gambrell 1933
S. salopiense (Edwards)	Zivkovic 1949
S. schoutedeni Wanson	Walsh 1984
S. sirbanum Vajime & Dunbar	Walsh 1984
S. vernum Macquart (as latipes auct.)	Britten 1922; Ussing 1925; Rubtsov 1956
S. vittatum Zetterstedt	Wu 1931; Davies and Peterson 1956

abdominal tip to or lands on some substrate protruding from the water surface, such as trailing vegetation, rocks, and sticks, and lays eggs on the wet substrate. (3) The female crawls into the water along tree branches, leaves, and rocks and lays eggs on the submerged substrate. How ovipositing females select certain types of habitats is a question with as yet no specific answers. This question may be approached by considering how mosquitoes select their oviposition sites, which for some groups are species-specific. Certain species of black flies are known to respond to visual cues related to substrate color, as do mosquitoes (Golini and Davies 1975a), while tactile stimuli, water chemistry, and other environmental factors, such as weather conditions, may act synergistically in influencing choice of oviposition sites. Some authors (Grenier 1949, Bellec 1976) have suggested that attraction to rapid sections of streams by ovipositing simuliids is influenced by air microcurrents, which stimulate females to fly upwind just above the water surface. As flies age, they may become less selective in their method and site of oviposition, hence ovipositing by other than their usual method. However, we should consider that in certain species observed variations in egg-laying activity may also reflect oviposition preferences of various cytotypes within species complexes.

LITERATURE CITED

Abdelnur, O. M. 1968. The biology of some black flies (Diptera: Simuliidae) of Alberta. *Quaest. Entomol.* 4:113–174.

Adler, P. H., K. C. Kim, and R. W. Light. Flight pattern of the *Simulium vittatum* (Diptera: Simuliidae) complex over a stream. *Environ. Entomol.* 12:232–236.

Balay, G. 1964. Observations sur l'oviposition de *Simulium damnosum* Theobald et *Simulium adersi* Pomeroy (Diptera, Simuliidae) dans l'est de la Haute-Volta. *Bull. Soc. Pathol. Exot.* 57:588–611.

Balay, G., and P. Grenier. 1964. *Lispe nivalis* Wiedemann (Muscidae, Lispinae) et *Ochthera* sp. (Ephydridae), Diptera prédateurs de *Simulium damnosum* Theobald et *S. adersi* Pomeroy en Haute-Volta. *Bull. Soc. Pathol. Exot.* 57:611–619.

Barnley, G. R. 1952. An attempt to eradicate *S. damnosum* Theo. from an area on the Victoria Nile, Uganda. Unpub. rept. (in Crisp 1956).

Bellec, C. 1976. Captures d'adultes de *Simulium damnosum* Theobald, 1903 (Diptera, Simuliidae) à l'aide de plaques d'aluminium, en Afrique de l'Ouest. *Cah. ORSTOM sér. Entomol. Méd. Parasitol.* 14:209–217.

Bellec, C. and G. Hébrard 1977. Captures d'adultes de Simuliidae, en particulier de *Simulium damnosum* Theobald, 1903, à l'aide de pièges d'interception; les pièges vitre. *Cah. ORSTOM sér. Entomol. méd. Parasitol.* 15:41–54.

Bennett, G. F. 1963. Use of P32 in the study of a population of *Simulium rugglesi* (Diptera: Simuliidae) in Algonquin Park, Ontario. *Can. J. Zool.* 41:832–840.

Bequaert, J. C. 1934. Notes on the black flies or Simuliidae, with special reference to those of the *Onchocerca* region of Guatemala. Pt. III. In J. D. Sandground, J. C. Bequaert, and M. M. Ochoa, "Onchocerciasis with special reference to the South American form of the disease." *Contrib. Dept. Trop. Med. and Inst. Trop. Biol. and Med.* (Harvard Univ.) 6:175–224.

Blanc, M. F. d'Aubenton, M. Ovazza, and M. Valade. 1958. Recherche sur la prophylaxie de l'onchocercose en A.O.F.I. Etude hydrobiologique de la Bougouri-Ba et assais de desinsectisation. *Bull. Inst. Fr. Afr. Noire* 20:634–668.

Bradley, G. H. 1935. Notes on the southern buffalo gnat, *Eusimulium pecuarum* (Riley) (Diptera: Simuliidae). *Proc. Entomol. Soc. Wash.* 37:60–64.

Britten, H. 1915. A note on the oviposition of *Simulium maculatum* Mg. *Entomol. Monthly Mag.* 51:170–171.

———. 1922. Notes on the ovipositing of *Simulium ornatum*, Mg. and *S. latipes*, Mg. *Lancashire and Cheshire Natur.* 15:24.

Burton, G. J., and T. M. McRae. 1965. Dam spillway breeding of *Simulium damnosum* Theobald in northern Ghana. *Ann. Trop. Med. Parasitol.* 59:405–412.

Cameron, A. E. 1922. The morphology and biology of a Canadian cattle infesting black fly, *Simulium simile* Mall. (Diptera, Simuliidae). *Can. Dept. Agric. Bull.* (n.s.), *Entomol. Bull.* 20:1–26.

Carlsson, G. 1962. Studies on Scandinavian black flies. *Opusc. Entomol. Suppl.* 21:1–280.

———. 1968 (1971). Comparison between black fly populations in Scandinavian and African watercourses. *Proc. 13th. Int. Congr. Entomol.* 1:121–122.

Chutter, F. M. 1972. Notes on the biology of South African Simuliidae, particularly *Simulium* (*Eusimulium*) *nigritarse* Coquillett. *News Lett. Limnol. Soc. South Afr.* 18:10–18.

Colbo, M. H. 1979. Distribution of winter-developing Simuliidae (Diptera) in eastern Newfoundland. *Can. J. Zool.* 57:2143–52.

Colbo, M. H., and D. E. Moorhouse. 1974. The survival of eggs of *Austrosimulium pestilens* Mack. and Mack. (Diptera: Simuliidae). *Bull. Entomol. Res.* 64:629–632.

Comstock, J. H. 1925. *Introduction to entomology*. Comstock Pub. Associates, Ithaca, New York. p. 821.

Corbet, P. S. 1967. The diel oviposition periodicity of the black fly *Simulium vittatum*. *Can. J. Zool.* 45:583–584.

Crisp, G. 1956. Simulium *and onchocerciasis in the northern territories of the Gold Coast*. Brit. Empire Soc. for the Blind. H. K. Lewis, London. p. 171.

Crosskey, R. W., and J. B. Davies. 1962. *Xenomyia oxycera* Embden, a muscid predator of *Simulium damnosum* Theobald in northern Nigeria. *Proc. R. Entomol. Soc. London* (A) 37:22–26.

Dalmat, H. T. 1955. The black flies (Diptera) of Guatemala and their role as vectors of onchocerciasis. *Smithsonian Misc. Coll.* 125:1–425.

Davies, D. M. 1950. A study of the black fly population of a stream in Algonquin Park, Ontario. *Trans. R. Can. Inst.* 28:121–160.

Davies, D. M. 1959. Some parasites of Canadian black flies (Diptera, Simuliidae). *Proc. 15th Int. Congr. Zool., London:* 660–661.

Davies, D. M., and B. V. Peterson. 1956. Observations on the mating, feeding, ovarian development, and oviposition of adult black flies (Simuliidae, Diptera). *Can. J. Zool.* 34:615–655.

Davies, D. M., B. V. Peterson, and D. M. Wood. 1962. The black flies (Diptera: Simuliidae) of Ontario. Part I. Adult identification and distribution with description of six new species. *Proc. Entomol. Soc. Ont.* (1961) 92:1–154.

Davies, D. M., and P. D. Syme. 1958. Three new Ontario black flies of the genus *Prosimulium* (Diptera, Simuliidae) Part II. Ecological observations and experiments. *Can. Entomol.* 90:744–759.

Davies, J. B. 1962. Egg-laying habits of *Simulium damnosum* Theobald and *Simulium medusaeforme* form *hargrevesi* [sic] Gibbins in northern Nigeria. *Nature* (London) 196:149–150.

Davies, L. 1961. Ecology of two *Prosimulium* species (Diptera) with reference to their ovarian cycles. *Can. Entomol.* 93:1113–40.

Edwards, E. E. 1956. Human onchocerciasis in West Africa with special reference to the Gold Coast. *J. West Afr. Sci. Assoc.* 2:1–35 (p. 23).

Edwards, F. W. 1915. On the British species of *Simulium*. I. Adults. *Bull. Entomol. Res.* 6:23–42.

———. 1920. On the British species of *Simulium*. II. The early stages; with corrections and additions to Part I. *Bull. Entomol. Res.* 11:211–246.

Elsen, P. 1977. Note biologique sur *Xenomyia oxycera* Embden (Muscidae, Limnophorinae) et *Ochthera insularis* Becker (Ephydridae), deux Diptères prédateurs de *Simulium damnosum* Theobald (Diptera: Simuliidae) en Côte d'Ivoire. *Revue Zool. Afr.* 91:732–736.

Emery, W. T. 1913. The morphology and biology of *Simulium vittatum* and its distribution in Kansas. *Kans. Univ. Sci. Bull.* 8:323–362.

Fredeen, F. J. H. 1963. Oviposition in relation to the accumulation of blood thirsty black flies *Simulium* (*Gnus*) *arcticum* Mall. (Diptera) prior to a damaging outbreak. *Nature* (London) 200:1024.

Fredeen, F. J. H., J. G. Rempel, and A. P. Arnason. 1951. Egg-laying habits, overwintering stages, and life-cycle of *Simulium arcticum* Mall. (Diptera: Simuliidae). *Can. Entomol.* 83:73–76.

Gambrell, L. A. 1933. The embryology of the black fly, *Simulium pictipes* Hagen. *Ann. Entomol. Soc. Am.* 26:641–671.

Gillett, J., and B. Lebied. 1959. Observations sur *Simulium medusaeforme* var. *hargreavesi* (Gibbins) et *Simulium adersi* (Pomeroy) faites à Bukavu-Kivu, Congo Belge. *Ann. Soc. Belge Méd. Trop.* 39:823–830.

Golini, V. I. 1975a. Relative response to coloured substrates by ovipositing black flies (Diptera: Simuliidae). III. Oviposition by *Simulium* (*Psilozia*) *vittatum* Zetterstedt. *Proc. Entomol. Soc. Ont.* (1974) 105:48–55.

———. 1975b. Simuliidae (Diptera) of Rendalen, Norway. I. *Eusimulium rendalense* n. sp. and *E. fallisi* n. sp. feeding on ducks. *Entomol. Scand.* 6:229–239.

Golini, V. I., and D. M. Davies. 1975a. Relative response to coloured substrates by ovipositing black flies (Diptera: Simuliidae). I. Oviposition by *Simulium* (*Simulium*) *verecundum* Stone and Jamnback. *Can. J. Zool.* 53:521–535.

———. 1975b. Relative response to coloured substrates by ovipositing black flies (Diptera: Simuliidae). II. Oviposition by *Simulium* (*Odagmia*) *ornatum* Meigen. *Norw. J. Entomol.* 22:88–94.

Grenier, P. 1949. Contribution a l'étude biologique des simuliides de France. *Physiol. Comp. Oecol.* 1:165–330.

Grunin, K. Y. 1949. A mistake in instinct resulting from parasitic castration in *Prosimulium hirtipes* Fries (Diptera: Simuliidae). *Dokl. Akad. Nauk SSR* 66:305–307 (in Russian). (Abstr. in *Rev. Appl. Entomol.* B 39: [1951]: 204).

Hocking, B., and L. R. Pickering. 1954. Observations on the bionomics of some northern species of Simuliidae (Diptera). *Can. J. Zool.* 32:99–119.

Ide, F. P. 1942. Availability of aquatic insects as food of the speckled trout, *Salvelinus fontinalis. Trans. 7th North Amer. Wildlife Conf.:* 442–450.

Imhof, J. E., and S. M. Smith. 1979. Oviposition behaviour, egg masses and hatching response of the eggs of five Nearctic species of *Simulium* (Diptera: Simuliidae). *Bull. Entomol. Res.* 69:405–425.

Jobbins-Pomeroy, A. W. 1916. Notes on five North American buffalo gnats of the genus *Simulium. U.S. Dept. Agric. Bull.* 329:1–48.

Ladle, M., J. A. B. Bass, and L. J. Cannicott. 1985. A unique strategy of blackfly oviposition (Diptera: Simuliidae). *Entomol. Gaz.* 36:147–149.

Lewis, D. J., G. R. L. Lyons, and J. D. M. Marr. 1961. Observations on *Simulium damnosum* from the Red Volta in Ghana. *Ann. Trop. Med. Parasitol.* 55:202–210.

Magnarelli, L. A., and J. F. Burger. 1984. Caloric reserves in natural populations of a black fly, *Simulium decorum* (Diptera: Simuliidae); and a deer fly, *Chrysops ater* (Diptera: Tabanidae). *Can. J. Zool.* 62:2589–93.

Malloch, J. R. 1914. American black flies or buffalo gnats. *U.S. Dept. Agric., Bur. Entomol. Tech. Ser.* 26:1–72.

Marr, J. D. M. 1962. The use of an artificial breeding-site and cage in the study of *Simulium damnosum* Theobald. *Bull. WHO* 27:622–629.

———. 1971. Observations on resting *Simulium damnosum* (Theobald) at a dam site in northern Ghana. WHO mimeo. doc., WHO/ONCHO/71.85, WHO/-VBC/71.298. Pp. 1–12.

Meeser, C. C. V. 1942. Preliminary notes on Simuliidae (Diptera) of South Rhodesia. *Proc. Rhod. Sci. Assoc.* 39:28–38.

Mitrokhin, V. U. 1973. Oviposition of black flies (Fam. Simuliidae) in northern Transural. *Parazitologya* 7:87–88 (trans. from Russian).

Moorhouse, D. E., and M. H. Colbo. 1973. On the swarming of *Austrosimulium pestilens* Mackerras and Mackerras (Diptera, Simuliidae). *J. Austral. Entomol. Soc.* 12:127–130.

Muirhead-Thompson, R. C. 1956. Communal oviposition in *Simulium damnosum* Theobald (Diptera, Simuliidae). *Nature* (London) 178:1297–99.

———. 1957. Effect of desiccation on the eggs of *Simulium damnosum,* Theobald. *Nature* (London) 180:1432–33.

Newstead, R. 1907. Habits and structural characters of the larva of *Simulium. Ann. Trop. Med. Parasitol.* 1:37–41.

Obeng, L. E. 1967. Oviposition and breeding habits of the Simuliidae in relation to control practices. *Proc. Ghana Acad. Sci.* 5:45–64.

Ogata, K., Harada S., and M. Nakamura. 1954. Ecological studies on the black fly, *Simulium aokii* Takahasi, 1941 (Studies on black flies, 4). *Jpn. J. Sanit. Zool.* 5:100–110 (trans. from Japanese).

Peschken, D., and A. J. Thorsteinson. 1965. Visual orientation of black flies (Simuliidae: Diptera) to colour, shape and movement of targets. *Entomol. Exp. Appl.* 8:282–288.

Petersen, A. 1924. Bidrag til de Danske Simuliers Naturhistorie. *D. Kgl. Danske Vidensk. Selsk. Skrifter, Naturvidensk. og Mathem.* Afd. 8 Raekke 5:237–341.

Peterson, B. V. 1956. Observations on the biology of Utah black flies (Diptera: Simuliidae). *Can. Entomol.* 88:496–506.

————. 1959. Observations on mating, feeding and oviposition of some Utah species of black flies (Diptera: Simuliidae). *Can. Entomol.* 91:147–155.

Peterson, B. V., and D. M. Davies. 1960. Observation on some insect predators of black flies (Diptera: Simuliidae) of Algonquin Park, Ontario. *Can. J. Zool.* 38:9–18.

Peterson, D. G., and L. S. Wolfe. 1958. The biology and control of black flies (Diptera: Simuliidae). *Proc. 10th Int. Congr. Entomol.* (Montreal, 1956) 3:551–564.

Poole, A. F. 1967. A note on the oviposition of *Simulium* (*S.*) *argyreatum* Meig. *Entomologist* 100 (1248):1215.

Post, R. J. 1982. Notes on the natural history of *Simulium* (*Boophthora*) *erythrocephalum* De Geer (Diptera: Simuliidae). *Entomol. Monthly Mag.* 118:31–35.

Reuter, U., and W. Rühm. 1976. Über die zeitliche Verteilung der anfliegenden Weibchen von *Boophthora erythrocephala* De Geer und *Simulium sublacustre* Davies bei der Eiablage (Simuliidae, Dipt.). *Z. Ang. Entomol.* 63:385–392.

Rivosecchi, L. 1967. I simulidi degli Appennini. *Parassitologia* 9:129–304.

————. 1978. Simuliidae: Diptera: Nematocera. In *Fauna d'Italia*, vol. 13, E. Calderini and E. Levante, Eds. Bologna. viii+534 pp.

Roos, T. 1957. Studies on upstream migration in adult stream-dwelling insects. I. *Ann. Rep. Inst. Res. Drottningholm, Lund.* 38:167–193.

Rubtsov, I. A. 1956. Fauna of U.S.S.R. Insecta (Diptera). Black flies (Family Simuliidae). *Zool. Inst. Acad. Sci. USSR* (n.s. 64), 6:1–860 (in Russian).

————. 1964. Mode and range of black fly (Diptera: Simuliidae) larval migration. *Entomol. Rev.* 43:27–33.

————. 1966. A new species of parasite from black flies and "errors" of host instinct. *Dokl. Akad. Nauk SSSR* 169:1236–38 (in Russian).

————. 1969. *Short keys to the bloodsucking Simuliidae of the USSR.* IPST Press, Jerusalem. 228 pp.

Rühm, W. 1971. Eiablagen einiger Simuliidenarte. *Z. Ang. Parasitol.* 12:68–78.

————. 1969. Zur populationsdynamik der Kriebelmücken, insbesondere von *Boophthora erythrocephala* de Geer und des *Odagmia ornata*—Komplex. *Z. Ang. Entomol.* 63:212–227.

————. 1975. Freilandbeobachtungen zum Functionkreis der Eiablage verschiedener Simuliidenarten unter besonderer Berücksichtigung von *Simulium argyreatum* Meig. (Dipt. Simuliidae). *Z. Ang. Entomol.* 78:321–334.

————. 1983. Über das Trochenfallen von Simuliiden-Eiern (Dipt., Simuliidae). *Z. Ang. Entomol.* 95:196–205.

Rühm, W., and Schlepper, R. 1979. Versuche zur quantitativen Erfassung der Eiablageintensität von Simuliiden (Dipt.). *Z. Ang. Entomol.* 88:204–216.

Service, M. W. 1979. Light trap collections of ovipositing *Simulium squamosum* in Ghana. *Ann. Trop. Med. Parasitol.* 73:487–490.

Smart, J. 1934. On the biology of the black fly, *Simulium ornatum*, Mg. (Diptera, Simuliidae). *Proc. R. Physical Soc.* (Edinburgh) 22:217–238.

Stone, A., and Jamnback, H. A. 1955. The black flies of New York State. *N.Y. State Mus. Bull.* 349:1–144.

Ussing, H. 1925. Faunistiske og biologiske Bidrag til danske Simuliers Naturhistorie. *Videnskab. Medd. Dansk Naturhist. Foren. Kbh.* 80:517–542.

Usova, Z. V. 1961. Flies of the Karelia and the Murmansk region (Diptera: Simuliidae). Izdatel'stovo Akad. Nauk SSSR. (In Russian; trans. by Israel Prog. for Scient. Transl., 1964).

Vargas, L. 1945. Simulidos del Nuevo Mundo. *Inst. Sal. y Enf. Trop. México Monogr.* 1:1–241.

Walsh, J. F. 1978. Light trap studies on *Simulium damnosum* s.l. in northern Ghana. *Tropenmed. Parasitol.* 29:492–496.

————. 1984. Aspects of the biology and control of *Simulium damnosum* s.l. (Diptera: Simuliidae) in West Africa. Ph.D. Thesis, Salford University England. 432 pp.

Wanson, M. 1950. Contribution a l'étude de l'Onchocercose africaine humaine. *Ann. Soc. Belge Méd. Trop.* 30:667–863.

Wanson, M., and C. Henrard. 1945. Habitat et comportement larvaire de *Simulium damnosum* Theobald. *Rec. Trav. Sci. Méd. Congo Belge* 4:113–122.

Welton, S., and J. A. B. Bass. 1980. Quantitative studies on the eggs of *Simulium (Simulium) ornatum* L. in a chalk stream in southern England. *Ecol. Entomol.* 5:87–96.

Wenk, P. 1965. Über die Biologie blutsaugender Simuliiden (Diptera). III Kopulation, Blutsaugungen und Eiablage von *Boophthora erythrocephala* de Geer im Laboratorium. *Z. Tropenmed. Parasitol.* 16:207–226.

————. 1981. Bionomics of adult black flies. In M. Laird, Ed., *Blackflies: the future for biological methods in integrated control.* Academic Press, New York and London. 399 pp.

Wolfe, L. S., and D. G. Peterson. 1959. Black flies (Diptera: Simuliidae) of the forests of Quebec. *Can. J. Zool.* 37:137–159.

Wood, D. M., and D. M. Davies. 1965. The rearing of simuliids (Diptera). *Proc. 13th Int. Congr. Entomol., London* (1964): 821–823.

————. 1966. Some methods of rearing and collecting black flies (Diptera: Simuliidae). *Proc. Entomol. Soc. Ont.* (1965) 96:81–90.

Wu, Y. F. 1931. A contribution to the biology of *Simulium* (Diptera). *Pap. Mich. Acad. Sci. Arts Lett.* 13:543–599.

Zahar, A. R. 1951. The ecology and distribution of black flies (Simuliidae) in south-east Scotland. *J. Anim. Ecol.* 20:33–62.

Zivkovic, V. 1949. Contribution to the knowledge of *Simulium salopiense* Edw. 1927. *Arh. Biol. nauka Beograd.* 1:5–23 (in Serbian; French summary).

20 REPRODUCTIVE STRATEGIES AND GONOTROPHIC CYCLES OF BLACK FLIES

John R. Anderson

AN OVERVIEW OF REPRODUCTIVE STRATEGIES

Everything an organism does can be said to be linked in some manner to its reproductive strategy, for the most important function of a species' existence is to reproduce itself. During evolution of the species, selection pressures associated with a given habitat will result in the species evolving particular reproductive strategies that result in the production of maximum numbers of reproductive progeny. However, although evolution will proceed toward selection of the individuals best fitted (suited) to reproduce under the environmental conditions existing or encountered, Pianka (1970) pointed out that environmental selective forces change constantly, resulting in constant change among the members of resident populations.

Although such general factors as water temperature and the quality of larval food available will affect reproductive strategies of black flies, in this chapter I primarily consider those factors that impinge most directly on the reproductive strategies of species having bloodsucking females. In accord with many others (e.g., Giesel 1976, Stearns 1976, Bell 1980, Bradshaw and Holzapfel 1983), I have broadly interpreted "reproductive strategy" to encompass all of the different physiological factors and behaviors associated with the successful reproductive efforts of a species in a particular habitat.

Since it was first proposed as a simple measure of r_{max} (the maximum intrinsic rate of increase), the r-K selection theory of MacArthur and Wilson (1967) often has been used to predict the life-history traits associated with populations of r-selected and K-selected species. The possibility of explaining the evolution of several components of fitness with just one variable has made this a popular ecological theory (Stearns 1976), and reproductive strategies have played a major role in the overall analysis of life-history traits.

As interpreted by Stearns (1976), the r- and K-selection theory predicts that a species should possess only r-characters or K-characters; tables of characters postulated to be favored by each type of selection are found in Pianka (1970), Force (1975), and Stearns (1976) and in most ecology texts. Broadly interpreted,

Table 20.1 Certain characteristics of r and K strategists

r strategists	K strategists
Highest population densities in habitats where density-independent factors predominate (variable temperate and arctic climates; disturbed situations); tend to be more tolerant of stressful environmental conditions	Highest population densities in habitats where density-dependent factors predominate (constant tropical climates; undisturbed climax situations); tend to be less tolerant of stressful environmental conditions
Commonly complete oogenesis early and rapidly and then die (semelparous species)	Oogenesis usually requires several days, with multiple gonotrophic cycles being completed during a lifetime of several weeks (iteroparous species)
Usually smaller colonizing or fugitive species	Usually larger, stable species
Associated with nutrient-rich environments where most resources are allocated for reproduction	Associated with environments having marginal food resources and where more resources are allocated to competitive strategies associated with feeding
Opportunistic species that are not good competitors	Specialist species that are good competitors

Source: After Force (1975).

r-selection favors rate of growth in a chancy, temporal environment through rapid sexual maturation, high fecundity, dispersal, and the additional factors identified in Table 20.1. Conversely, *K*-selection favors crowding tolerance within stable populations in stable environments through competitive fitness, longevity, and all of the other factors identified in Table 20.1. In addition to the characteristics in Table 20.1, other authors have noted that *r*-strategists are semelparous (i.e., they reproduce once and then die), that they tend to have population densities usually below carrying capacity, that they frequently recolonize habitats, and that there is less genetic polymorphism determining carrying capacity and niche breadth (e.g., Pianka 1970, Stearns 1976). On the other hand, these authors note that *K*-strategists are iteroparous (i.e., they can reproduce two or more times), that they tend to have population densities usually at or near carrying capacity, that they rarely need to recolonize habitats, and that there is greater genetic polymorphism determining carrying capacity and niche breadth.

Unfortunately, the *r-K* selection theory remains long on theory and short on experimental data. Consequently, it has generated a considerable body of review papers. According to Boyce (1984), much of the controversy associated with the *r-K* selection model has resulted because many authors have overextended the original model by not strictly interpreting the model as one of density-dependent natural selection. Although this may be true, reviews of *r-K* selection have proved useful in stimulating workers in many fields of biology to review life-history and reproductive strategies, to formulate new ideas, and to stimulate original research. Nevertheless, perhaps most authors would now agree with Boyce (1984:441) that "to collapse all environmental variability into a model of *r*- and *K*-selection is naive."

The *r-K* selection model is not the only approach workers have developed for analyzing life-history and reproductive strategies. Examples of other methods of analyzing and predicting reproductive strategies include: Southwood's (1977) reproductive success matrix (designed to predict the number of descendants resulting from each strategy and reflecting the habitat heterogeneity in time and space); and Stearn's (1976) bet-hedging strategy (proposed, in part, to describe the behavior of females that lay eggs in a variety of habitats). Like Southwood's, Giesel's (1976) review considered how the reproductive strategies of organisms were adapted to cope with temporal environmental changes.

Successful adaptations of species to different habitats usually involve a series of strategies that result in the production of maximum numbers of successful progeny. In the case of insects, such strategies may affect any life-history stage, and they may encompass from a few to many types of behavior. In the broadest sense, reproductive strategies include such specialized biological features as speciation, habitat selection, larval and adult feeding, dispersal, gametogenesis, mating, and oviposition. Because most of these aspects of black fly biology are addressed in other chapters, I will focus primarily on the relationship between reproductive strategies and gonotrophic cycles.

REPRODUCTIVE STRATEGIES OF AUTOGENOUS VERSUS ANAUTOGENOUS SPECIES

In relating reproductive strategies to gonotrophic cycles in different species of black flies, it is first necessary to consider separately autogenous and anautogenous species. If one views the ultimate result of reproduction as the production of eggs and progeny, in a narrow sense black flies can be considered to have four basic reproductive strategies: obligate autogeny, facultative autogeny, facultative anautogeny, and obligate anautogeny.

In an earlier, provocative review Downes (1971) concluded that the bloodsucking habit in black flies and other Nematocera was a primitive behavior, and that in all families he studied there had been selection toward a "high effort" into reproduction. It is now commonly recognized that the most primitive bloodsucking members of each taxa are characterized by obligate anautogeny, and females require a vertebrate blood meal to produce their eggs. Conversely, nonbloodsucking species characterized by obligate autogeny either emerge with fully matured eggs (Davies 1954, Davies and Peterson 1956, Rubtsov 1961), or the females mature their eggs exclusively from nutrients carried over from the larva and stored in the copious fat body reserves in the emerged fly (Rubtsov 1956, 1961; Davies and Peterson 1956; Clements 1963; Lea 1970; Downes 1971; Spielman 1971; Davies et al. 1977). Table 20.2 compares the biological features associated with obligate autogeny versus those associated with obligate anautogeny in black flies.

From experimental studies we know that such species as *G. holopticus*, *G. bifistulatus*, *C. dacotensis*, *C. lapponica*, *P. alpestre*, and *P. ursinum* are representative of obligate autogenous species (Davies 1954; Rubtsov 1958, 1961; Davies and Peterson 1956; Downes 1971; Wood 1978), and that *S. ornatum*, *S. venustum*, *S. damnosum*, *S. ochraceum*, *B. erythrocephala*, and *A. pestilens* are representative of obligate anautogenous species (Davies 1957; Davies 1961, 1963; Le Berre 1966; Rühm 1970; Hunter 1978). In facultative species, the richness and quality of the larval diet

Table 20.2 Biological features associated with females of autogenous and anautogenous species of Simuliidae

Obligate Autogenous Species	Facultative Gate	*Obligate Anautogenous Species*
Weakly sclerotized mouthparts incapable of cutting/slashing vertebrate skin	‖‖‖‖‖‖	Thickly sclerotized, strong mouthparts used for cutting/slashing vertebrate skin
All resources for egg development are obtained from nutrients accumulated during larval development[a]		Resources needed for egg development must be supplemented with nutrients derived from vertebrate blood meals[a]
Usually small species and weak fliers/dispersers		Usually larger species capable of moderate to long-range dispersal
Short-lived, semelparous species		Moderate- to long-lived iteroparous species
Mate near larval habitat soon after emerging, or they may be parthenogenetic		Mate one to several days postemergence (near or away from larval habitat)
Usually occur in unpredictive, chancy environments where density-independent factors are a strong force affecting population densities		Usually occur in stable environments where density-dependent factors are the principal mechanism affecting population densities

[a]Some species in both categories may also require a carbohydrate meal before oogenesis is initiated.

determine whether the female imago will be able to develop her eggs autogenously or whether she will need to take and digest a blood meal to obtain the nutrients necessary for egg maturation. When larval food is adequate, the facultative gate opens in the direction of autogeny, but when larval food is scarce, the gate opens in the direction of anautogeny. We know that, depending on which way the facultative gate opens, such species as *S. vittatum, S. decorum, S. hirtipes,* and *O. frigida* can develop their eggs autogenously when developing in richly nourished waters (Wu 1931, Davies and Peterson 1956, Rubtsov 1956, Chutter 1970, Simmons and Edman 1978), or, when emerging from nutrient-poor larval habitats, they can be facultative blood feeders (Rubtsov 1956, Chutter 1970, Lewis and Bennett 1973). Similar examples of facultative autogeny are common among the Nematocera and Brachycera. Even among orthorrhaphous Diptera it has been found that the undernourished larvae of facultative species result in stunted adults that must feed on protein to mature their eggs (Baxter et al. 1973). Another type of facultative autogeny occurs in certain arctic mosquitoes in which carbohydrate-fed females not obtaining a blood meal are capable of utilizing nutrient reserves from degenerating follicles or thoracic muscles to produce 1–5 eggs (Hocking 1954; Corbet 1964, 1967). However, this phenomenon is not known to occur in black flies.

In several species of mosquitoes the expression of autogeny/anautogeny is known to be under genetic control (O'Meara and Craig 1969, Spielman 1971, Trpis 1978), as it also is in different genotypes of the same species (Spielman 1957, Aslamkhan and Laven 1970, O'Meara and Krasnick 1970). Since the earlier reviews by Downes (1971), Rubtsov (1956), and Spielman (1971), autogenous and anautogenous strains of black flies have been reported for several additional species, and it seems likely that, when more thoroughly studied, most bloodsucking species will be found to have an autogenous strain in some part of their geographic range.

Autogeny is a common occurrence among members of the Nematocera and lower Brachycera (Downes 1971). It seems to have evolved as an adaptation associated with successful colonization of unpredictive environments where density-independent factors associated with bad weather are periodically responsible for catastrophic mortalities. Downes (1971) noted that autogeny was the rule in arctic species of black flies, with eight of ten species having atrophied, nonbloodsucking mouthparts. Various authors (Davies and Peterson 1956; Rubtsov 1956, 1961; Downes 1965) have noted that autogenous species adapted for survival in extreme arctic or alpine environments are all semelparous (univoltine) species that undergo only one gonotrophic cycle. The females of several such species (*C. lapponica, C. dacotensis, C. eremites, G. holopticus, P. alpestre*) emerge with fully matured eggs, or eggs nearly matured. They commonly mate at streamside, immediately oviposit, and then die. In the parthenogenetic *P. ursinum* mature eggs are even known to be released from pharate pupae (Carlsson 1962). The females of the autogenous arctic species produce a small number of large eggs (commonly about 20–50/female in most species compared to 250–900/clutch in various anautogenous species). Because these species typically develop in cold, nutrient-poor glacier- or spring-fed creeks, the low fecundity typical of semelparous, autogenous arctic species appears to be an adaptation that contributes to their reproductive success—with a small number of large eggs/female yielding robust first-instar larvae in low population densities that result in reduced intraspecific competition. Conversely, the reproductive success of obligate anautogenous species in warmer ecosystems is largely due to their iteroparous nature, the large number of eggs/gonotrophic cycle, and the fact that some females complete several gonotrophic cycles.

BLOOD VERSUS SUGAR FEEDING

The duality of feeding exhibited by females of many species that feed on both carbohydrate and blood is now a well-recognized behavior (Davies and Peterson 1956; Rubtsov 1956; Downes 1958, 1971; Wenk 1965; Lewis and Domoney 1966; Watanabe 1977; Brenner and Cupp 1980; Walsh and Garms 1980). Because black flies are well-known vectors of pathogens and vicious pests of humans and other animals, many entomologists and other biologists are most familiar with the blood-feeding habit, a primitive behavior associated with species having strongly sclerotized, toothed mandibles capable of biting/slashing (Downes 1958, 1971; McIver and Sutcliff 1987). However, more species feed on carbohydrate than on blood. In fact, carbohydrate feeding appears to be a nearly universal habit for both sexes. Exceptions may be the ephemeral autogenous arctic species that quickly mate, oviposit, and die after eclosion. Some such arctic species (e.g., *C. lapponica* and *P. alpestre*) are known to have a functional diverticulum (Rubtsov 1961), but from what is known of the behavior of these autogenous black flies (Rubtsov 1961, Carlsson 1962, Downes 1971, Wood 1978), it seems highly unlikely that their adults need to feed on plant nectar. Nicholson (1945) and Downes (1958), in fact, noted that the autogenous *C. dacotensis* did not attempt to feed on blood or flowers. In most other species studied, both sexes commonly feed on plant sugars soon after eclosion and prior to mating, as Hunter (1978) reported for *A. pestilens* in Australia and Anderson and Shemanchuk (1987) found for *S. arcticum* in Canada. Since carbohydrate feeding is known to occur in all males studied, and in females of some obligatorily autogenous species, both of which have undeveloped, atrophied mandibles, this feeding behavior obviously is not dependent on having biting/slashing mouthparts.

It commonly has been thought that blood and nectar meals have different functions—carbohydrates being used to provide flight energy and prolong life, and blood meals providing the nutrients needed for egg maturation. This generally is true for black flies, but for certain autogenous species plant nectars are now known also to enhance fecundity. Thus Hunter (1977) found that the autogenous *S. ornatipes* in Australia required carbohydrate nutrient to initiate oogenesis, and Canadian workers found that sucrose-fed females of other autogenous species produced greater numbers of eggs than those fed only water (Chutter 1970, Lewis and Bennett 1973, Mokry 1980b). In mosquitoes as well, sugar feeding is known to enhance egg production in certain species (Nayar and Sauerman 1975) and to be necessary for facultative autogenous egg development in some arctic species (Hocking 1954; Corbet 1964, 1967).

Digestion Rates

Most species of black flies are persistent in their attacks, and once blood feeding has started they are difficult to dislodge. Like other pool feeders, their engorgement proceeds rather slowly, regularly requiring from about 4–6 minutes to twice this long. They usually take an amount of blood equal to or about double their body weight (Bennett 1963, Fallis 1964). Digestion rates are influenced by such factors as prevailing temperatures, the species of fly, and infection with parasites. In temperate species, digestion in Canadian *S. rugglesi* was completed in 4–6 days at 67–70°F, whereas the fastest rate in *S. venustum* was just under 60 hours at the same temperature (Fallis 1964). At laboratory temperatures *B. erythrocephala* completed digestion in 5–6 days (Rühm 1970), as did *S. ornatum* (Davies 1957). *S. damnosum* digested blood in about 72 hours at 23–25°C (Lewis 1953, Le Berre 1966), and Le Berre (1966) noted that blood was digested slower in older *S. damnosum* than in young females. Blood meals are digested by *S. ochraceum* in 3–4 days (Takaoka et al. 1982, Porter and Collins 1985).

Fecundity

The maximum number of eggs that can be produced per gonotrophic cycle shows much variation between species (Davies and Peterson 1956). In other nematocerans studied in laboratory colonies, the largest number of eggs/clutch usually is produced on the first gonotrophic cycle (Lavoipierre 1961, Detinova 1962), and for black flies the number of eggs produced per gonotrophic cycle decreases with the number of cycles completed (Lewis 1958, Le Berre 1966, Abdelnur 1968, Mokry 1980a). In addition to fewer eggs being developed in subsequent gonotrophic cycles, the presence of unlaid, relict eggs in the ovaries of females that have recently oviposited becomes increasingly common in older females having completed two or more gonotrophic cycles. Other factors commonly affecting the number of eggs produced per gonotrophic cycle are size of the fly, host blood source, volume of blood ingested, and the quantity and quality of the diet (Chutter 1970, Mokry 1980b, Colbo and Porter 1981, Cheke et al. 1982, Colbo 1982). In addition, black flies fed on vertebrate hosts infected with filaria produced fewer eggs than females that had fed on noninfected hosts (Cheke et al. 1982, Ham and Banya 1984).

THE GONOTROPHIC CYCLE

As commonly recognized, the gonotrophic cycle is the time required for completion of various physiological events associated with oogenesis, a cycle being completed when a batch of eggs has been matured and laid. The first gonotrophic cycle begins with the development of reproductive tissue and assimilation of nutrient reserves in developing larvae (Rubtsov 1956). Following eclosion, the nutrient reserves in autogenous females are depleted as the eggs develop (Davies and Peterson 1956, Rubtsov 1956, Downes 1971). In some species this physiological process occurs in the pupa and the imago emerges with mature eggs. In anautogenous species the nutrient reserves only partially support development of the primary follicles (see below). Hence, the first gonotrophic cycle in obligate bloodsucking species can be divided into the following phases: (1) search for and feeding on plant nectar (usually soon after eclosion); (2) mating at a unique site (female often receptive at about 24 hours old); (3) search for a blood-meal source and feeding (thought usually to occur soon after mating); (4) digestion of the blood meal and maturation of the eggs (about 3–7 days); and (5) search for oviposition site followed by oviposition. Feeding on plant nectars also may occur at any time after phase two. Subsequent gonotrophic cycles for parous females would of course eliminate phase two. The time required to complete a gonotrophic cycle can vary with the species of fly, type of host blood, the gonotrophic age of the fly, and the temperature. After blood feeding, a cycle may be as short as 3 days or as long as 6–7 days (Le Berre 1966, Duke 1968). The youngest ovipositing females would be about 5 days old.

The sequential morphological changes that occur in the ovarioles during oogenesis appear to be basically similar in both autogenous and anautogenous species. These changes have been described for several species, and the illustrations of Rubtsov (1958), Lewis (1957, 1960), Chutter (1970), and Rühm (1970) represent the typical developmental sequence that occurs in maturing follicles.

Like other nematocerans, the reproductive system of a female black fly (Rubtsov 1958) consists of a pair of ovaries and the associated lateral oviducts, which merge into a common oviduct. The spermathecae and accessory glands join the common oviduct. Each ovary is made up of a series of adjacent ovariole tubes enclosed in a flexible sheath. The number of ovarioles per ovary varies in different species from about 20 to about 500–600 (Davies and Peterson 1956, Downes 1971), although Mokry (1980a) found as many as 900 in nulliparous *S. damnosum*.

Once initiated, the process of oogenesis proceeds through a series of five stages first described for mosquitoes by Christophers (1911) and later modified by Mer (1936). As the process begins the germarium gives rise to the primary follicle containing the oogonium. At stage I the primary follicle contains the oocyte and seven nurse cells. As development of the primary follicle proceeds to stage II and yolk granules appear, the secondary follicle, and often the tertiary one, also buds out of the germarium. During oogenesis the follicles in all activated ovarioles usually develop synchronously. In anautogenous females that have not yet taken a blood meal, development of the primary follicles generally proceeds only to Christophers' stage II; the follicles remain in this stage II "ovarian diapause" until the female takes, and begins to digest, a blood meal. As nutrients are released with digestion of the blood meal, most follicles simultaneously continue developing until each contains a mature egg (stage V). The number of eggs matured may depend on such factors as the size of the blood meal and the species of host fed on. As oogenesis proceeds the secondary follicles remain at developmental stage II, except for some species with autogenous females, which show little or no development of the secondary follicle (Rubtsov 1961, Downes 1971).

The relationship between reproductive strategy and the gonotrophic cycle of obligatorily autogenous species is a simple one; after completing her first and only gonotrophic cycle, the female soon dies (Rubtsov 1961, Downes 1971). These are classical semelparous species that are ecological representatives of "big bang" reproduction (Bell 1980). In species capable of completing more than one gonotrophic cycle, a second blood meal will initiate development of the secondary follicles and the second gonotrophic cycle. As far as is known, anautogenous black flies are characterized by gonotrophic concordance whereby each blood meal gives rise to a separate gonotrophic cycle (Davies and Peterson 1956, Rubtsov 1958, Le Berre 1966, Rühm 1970, Porter and Collins 1985).

Little is known about the hormonal stimuli associated with oogenesis in black flies. However, since the progressive morphological changes seen in the ovarioles of black flies during oogenesis are similar to those in mosquitoes and other Nematocera, it seems likely that the sequence of endocrine-controlled events also may be like that in mosquitoes (Clements 1963, Lea 1970, Hagedorn 1974, Spielman and Wong 1974, Borovsky et al. 1985, Greenplate et al. 1985). Borovsky et al. (1985) postulated that the basic hormones that regulate vitellogenesis are identical in both autogenous and anautogenous mosquitoes, but that the signals governing the release of various hormones were different. In anautogenous mosquitoes ovarian diapause is broken when gonadotropic hormone is released from the brain following a blood meal (Lea 1970). In autogenous species secretion of the egg development neurosecretory hormone (EDNH) from the brain occurs after emergence stimulates oogensis. In bloodsucking species abdominal stretch receptors in the female result in inhibiting engorged individuals from further feeding and host-seeking behavior (Klowden and Lea 1979). Stretch receptors also may trigger the release of a substance from the ovary, which stimulates the release of EDNH from the corpus cardiacum. The action of EDNH on the ovary and the appearance and role of other hormones were recently reviewed by Borovsky et al. (1985) and Greenplate et al. (1985). It now appears that both juvenile hormone and EDNH are released twice during oogenesis. Ultimately, blood-meal proteins (vitellogenin) are incorporated into yolk cells as the primary follicles grow (mature).

LONGEVITY AND GONOTROPHIC CYCLES

The ability to determine the number of gonotrophic cycles a female has experienced and, from that information, to estimate her "physiological age," has provided researchers with a means to determine the age structure of wild populations and to relate directly gonotrophic age (physiological age) to the proportion of the population carrying infective stages of pathogens (Detinova 1962, Gillies 1964). Determination of the age structure of populations has been widely used for mosquitoes and some other nematocerans, but it has not worked for most species of black flies studied. Therefore, instead of using the number of gonotrophic cycles to provide information on daily survival rates, and thus potential infection/transmission rates, as has been the case for anophelines and malaria (Detinova 1962, Gillies 1964, Gillies and Wilkes 1965, Reisen and Aslamkhan 1979), black fly workers have instead had to use data obtained on digestion rates, survival rates, and longevity to determine the number of gonotrophic cycles completed.

Life-table data concerning the age structure of a population are critical to understanding the dynamics of any population, and such data are of particular importance to entomologists who study insect vectors of vertebrate pathogens. In carrying out ecological and epidemiological studies it is particularly important to know as precisely as possible the longevity of the bloodsucking female. In fact, in his thorough review of this subject, Gillies (1964) credited Macdonald (1952) for identifying vector longevity as being one of the most critical factors affecting malaria transmission. Because the epidemiological importance of insect vectors increases with their age and the number of blood meals taken, much past research has been concerned with the search for reliable methods of determining, or estimating, the ages of wild-caught insects.

Methods of Estimating the Age and Parity of Flies

Tyndale-Biscoe (1984) recently published a valuable review of the many methods workers have used to estimate the ages of various adult insects. Among other things, she pointed out (p. 342) that any age-grading technique "should distinguish adults in certain physiological stages," and that the three main functional categories workers have used to age-grade adult insects are: (1) criteria associated with the reproductive system; (2) somatic changes that occur with age; and (3) external changes that occur as a result of wear and tear. As dipterists will know, Tyndale-Biscoe (1984) noted that one criteria for age-grading that has proved highly useful is the Polovodova (1949) technique of identifying follicular relics (follicular dilatations) that have accumulated in the ovariole pedicels. Because the formation of follicular dilatations represents an irreversible functional change, this technique allows workers to distinguish parous females (those that have oviposited at least once) from nulliparous females that have not yet oviposited and completed the first gonotrophic cycle (Polovodova 1949; Lewis 1957, 1958; Rubtsov 1958; Davies 1961, 1963; Detinova 1962; Shipitsina 1962; Gillies 1964; Le Berre 1966; Rühm 1970; Garms 1973; Duke 1975; Anderson and Shemanchuk 1976; Magnarelli and Cupp 1977; Cupp and Collins 1979).

Other characteristics by which workers may distinguish nulliparous from parous black fly females are described in Table 20.3. In addition to characteristics associated with the ovaries, the data in this table include several other useful features associated with age-related somatic changes in different organ systems. Workers who have used all or most of these features when examining dissected flies (Lewis 1957,

Table 20.3 Characteristics of nulliparous and parous black fly females

Item	Nulliparous	Parous
Fat body	Much fat body in haemocoele	Little or no fat body in haemocoele
Ovarioles	Translucent and tightly bunched, with coiled tracheoles making it difficult to separate them	Loosely bunched and easily separated; granular appearance
Ovariole pedicel	Short, narrow, and tubular with no follicular relic present	Varying from long, expanded, and saclike to narrowly contracted tubular pedicels with a distinct follicular relic (dilatation) present
Eggs	No unlaid (relict) eggs retained in ovaries	Unlaid (relict) eggs may be present, especially in older females having completed more than two gonotrophic cycles
Intestines	Midgut sometimes with greenish meconium	Midgut often with old residual blood and remnants of the peritrophic membrane
Rectal papillae	Clear, or containing a white granular material	Tinted light to dark red and often with hematin granules
Spermatophore	Sometimes present on genitalia of recently mated females	Never present on older females

1958; Rühm 1970; Anderson and Shemanchuk 1987) have learned somewhat more about the populations studied than workers who have examined only the ovaries. Most studies of parity and the age composition of black fly populations since Detinova's monograph (1962) have simply assessed the quantity of fat body in the haemocoele and/or the condition of the ovarioles. If some of the other features described in Table 20.3 also had been noted, workers might have been able to obtain information about the age and physiological condition of dispersing flies, or whether a parous fly had been autogenous or anautogenous on its first gonotrophic cycle, for example. Hence, future workers are encouraged to examine routinely more of these features. However, as noted by Lewis (1958), it can be impractical to examine too many features because the examination time required per fly could result in too great a reduction in the number of flies dissected and examined per day. Therefore, workers must set priorities for the number of features to be examined, based on the objectives of the study.

Methods of Determining and Estimating Gonotrophic Cycles

In addition to allowing workers to determine parity, the Polovodova technique has proved useful in allowing workers to determine the number of gonotrophic cycles a female has completed. This has been possible to do because in many Diptera (Detinova 1962, 1968; Hoy and Anderson 1978; Charlwood et al. 1980; Tyndale-Biscoe 1984), the irreversible formation of follicular dilatations is repeated after each batch of eggs has been laid. Consequently, the ovariole pedicels of a biparous female will have two dilatations, those of a triparous female three, and so on. The morphological changes associated with the different phases seen during contraction of the saccate ovariole pedicel following oviposition are illustrated in such publications as Lewis (1960), Detinova (1962), Linley (1965), Hoy and Anderson (1978), Cupp and Collins (1979), and Charlwood et al. (1980).

The formation of the follicular dilatations, therefore, is intimately associated with various physiological changes that occur during the life of the female. Because these events are thought to be closely associated with events occurring during the actual calendar age of the female, it has been common for workers to use the number of gonotrophic cycles completed by a female as an indication of her "physiological age." Hence, if one can determine the duration required for each gonotropic cycle, and the number of cycles completed, it is possible to assess accurately the actual calendar age of the female.

However, as Klowden and Lea (1980) noted for mosquitoes, the term "physiological age" sometimes has been rather loosely and incorrectly applied. In suggesting that the term "gonotrophic age" is more appropriate, they pointed out (p. 1460) that if "physiological age" was equated with the number of gonotrophic cycles "a 1-week-old uniparous mosquito is 'physiologically old', but a 3-week-old nulliparous female is not." Also, an old female could in reality be a gonotrophically young fly. In most instances, however, one would expect a gonotrophically old female to also be a chronologically and physiologically old one, and in any case fly behavior is linked to the physiological state more than it is to chronological age.

In the case of black flies, however, the above semantics may represent a moot point because, except for a few species in Russia (Detinova and Beltyukova 1958; Shipitsina 1962, 1963) and two in the northern United States (Magnarelli and Cupp 1977), researchers in widely different parts of the world have not found it possible to distinguish by the Polovodova technique how many gonotrophic cycles a parous female has completed (Lewis 1960; Davies 1961, 1963; Le Berre 1966; Duke 1968, 1975; Garms 1975; Cupp and Collins 1979).* Because most black fly workers have not been able to determine the number of gonotrophic cycles completed by direct examination of flies, our understanding of the population dynamics of the vectors and the epidemiology of *0. volvulus* and other filarial infections has lagged behind that of anopheline mosquitoes and malaria (Gillies and Wilkes 1965). Therefore, there is a need for more studies to evaluate the use of the Polovodova technique for determining the number of gonotrophic cycles completed by black flies. Since most previous workers seem to have dissected flies soon after they were caught, perhaps more workers should hold flies for a day before dissection to allow the ovariole pedicels to contract fully. There also is a need for black fly workers to evaluate the use of cuticular growth rings on thoracic apodemes to obtain the chronological age of flies, as has been done for some mosquitoes (Schlein 1979,

---

*Rühm (1970) reported seeing two dilatations only rarely, and always in females fed and/or held in the laboratory for oviposition. This did, however, demonstrate that two distinguishable dilatations were formed.

Schlein and Gratz 1972). In various mosquito species daily growth rings are formed for only about a week after eclosion, but this phenomenon appears to have potential for assessing chronological age of young individuals under natural field conditions. This technique could be particularly useful for age determination of males.

As the Polovodova technique presently appears to have serious limitations outside Russia, the recent research by Mokry (1980a) and Porter and Collins (1985) represents useful alternative approaches for estimating the maximum number of gonotrophic cycles that could be completed by the longest surviving females and the length of the gonotrophic cycle under field conditions (Porter and Collins 1985). Mokry (1980a) used the well-known age-related decrease in fecundity reported for various Diptera to estimate the ages of wild-caught *S. damnosum* females caught biting and to estimate how many gonotrophic cycles had been completed. He found that the number of eggs matured/female could be separated into five groups, with nulliparous females having the highest number of eggs. Because Mokry found no correlation between size and fecundity, he speculated that the declining number of eggs in each of his parous groups represented up to four successive gonotrophic cycles associated with advancing age in parous females. However, since it is known that older females produce fewer eggs than young females, and that large flies live longer than small flies (Simmons 1985), a small 1- or 2-parous female would be likely to produce the same number of eggs as a large 4-parous female—a fact that would result in finding no correlation between size and fecundity. Furthermore, in contrast to Mokry's results, Cheke et al. (1982) did find that large *S. damnosum* females had larger numbers of maturing oocytes than small females, and Hawley (1985) found that there was no age-related decrease in fecundity for the mosquito *Aedes sierrensis* Ludlow. Therefore, if others conduct similar studies, they should be aware that the host blood-meal source, vector size and age, volume of blood ingested, and infection with filaria all represent factors known to affect the fecundity of black flies and mosquitoes (Lewis 1958, Clements 1963, Le Berre 1966, Abdelnur 1968, Sutherla and Ewen 1974, Cheke et al. 1982, Ham and Banya 1984). More recently, Mather and DeFoliart (1983) reported that the host blood-meal source also affected the length of the gonotrophic cycle of a mosquito, and Yang and Davies (1977) reported that a microsporidian infection in *P. decemarticulatum* and *S. rugglesi* likewise increased the time required for blood digestion—which also would increase the length of the gonotrophic cycle.

In view of the above limitations, the type of mark-recapture study conducted by Porter and Collins (1985) is the preferable experimental design because it allows researchers to determine the length of the gonotrophic cycles completed, because it permits one to determine the developmental time required for the parasite (*O. volvulus*) under field conditions, and because workers can determine how long an infected female must live to transmit the pathogen. Thus the M-R study by Porter and Collins (1985) additionally permitted them to estimate the daily survival rate and, from this, to estimate the percentage of the vector population that would live long enough to transmit the parasite if females became infected with their first blood meal. Many similar studies have been conducted on mosquitoes and other nematocerans (Gillies 1964, 1974; Reisen and Aslamkhan 1979), and Service (1976) reviewed the literature dealing with use of M-R methodologies for studying mosquito populations.

Applications of Age-Grading Black Fly Populations and Future Needs

As Tyndale-Biscoe (1984) noted, most age-grading studies have concerned insect vectors of medical/veterinary importance. For such diverse insects as mosquitoes, ceratopogonids, black flies, and tsetse flies, age-grading techniques have been used to evaluate sampling methods, to assess the infective vector potential (the epidemiological danger), to detect and evaluate physiological and age-related differences in behavior (e.g., activities like flight and biting times of nulliparous and parous flies), and to obtain survival rates and life-table data.

For black flies, there is a need for additional M-R experiments coupled with parity studies, because, as noted by Gillies (1964) for mosquitoes, there appear to be large differences in the physiological longevity between different species and between populations from different geographical areas. In the case of *S. damnosum,* marked flies could provide much useful information about dispersal and longevity of nulliparous and parous flies and replace past speculation (Johnson et al. 1985; chapter 15) with factual data. With additional research on survival rates and the duration and number of gonotrophic cycles of marked flies, perhaps black fly workers soon will be able to begin comparing the longevity and fecundity of simuliids from different environments and geographical areas, as mosquito researchers have been doing for some time (Gillies, 1964, 1974). Since the vector potentials of different species may depend greatly on their life expectancies and the number of blood meals taken, we must learn more about survival rates and gonotrophic cycles. In the case of *O. volvulus,* for example, there may be considerable mortality of flies that have fed on infective humans (Lewis 1965, DeLeon and Duke 1966, Omar and Garms 1975, Takaoka et al. 1984).

In my view, the above needs can only be obtained by combining M-R studies with dissection and examination of captured and recaptured females. For such studies Bailey's (1952) triple-catch method, in which the population is sampled three different times, will provide the most useful data. However, as the M-R of attacking flies only provides information concerning dispersal and other activities of gonoactive females, it will be essential that future researchers also M-R flies emerging from the principal breeding sites. Finally, for all females dissected it is recommended that, along with examination of the ovaries, workers also record the size and, possibly, the fecundity of all females dissected, as well as most of the features noted in Table 20.3. Considering the time and resources generally invested in capturing females destined to be dissected, it would seem well worthwhile to spend the few extra minutes/fly needed to meet these recommendations. The additional data obtained could prove to be highly useful in elucidating reproductive strategies and population dynamics.

LITERATURE CITED

Abdelnur, O. M. 1968. The biology of some black flies (Diptera: Simuliidae) of Alberta. *Quaest. Entomol.* 4:113–174.

Anderson, J. R., and J. A. Shemanchuk, 1976. Parity and mermithid parasitism of *Simulium arcticum* caught attacking cattle and flying over an Alberta river. *Proc. 1ˢᵗ Inter-Regional Conf. on N. Amer. Blackflies.* pp. 143–145.

————. 1987. The biology of *Simulium arcticum* Malloch in Alberta. Part II. Seasonal parity structure and mermethid parasitism of populations attacking cattle and flying over the Athabasca River. *Can. Entomol.* 119:29–44.

Aslamkhan, M., and H. Laven. 1970. Inheritance of autogeny in the *Culex pipiens* complex. *Pak. J. Zool.* 2:121–147.

Baxter, J. A., A. M. Mjeni, and P. E. Morrison. 1973. Expression of autogeny in relation to larval population density of *Sarcophaga bullata* Parker (Diptera: Sarcophagidae). *Can. J. Zool.* 51:1189–93.

Bell, G. 1980. The costs of reproduction and their consequences. *Am. Nat.* 116:45–76.

Bennett, G. F. 1963. Use of P^{32} in the study of a population of *Simulium rugglesi* (Diptera: Simuliidae) in Algonquin Park, Ontario. *Can. J. Zool.* 41:831–840.

Borovsky, D., B. R. Thomas, D. A. Carlson, L. R. Whisenton, and M. S. Fuchs. 1985. Juvenile hormone and 20-hydroxyecdysone as primary and secondary stimuli of vitellogensis in *Aedes aegypti*. *Arch. Insect Biochem. Physiol.* 2:75–90.

Boyce, M. S. 1984. Restitution of r- and K-selection as a model of density-dependent natural selection. *Ann. Rev. Ecol. Syst.* 15:427–447.

Bradshaw, W. E., and C. M. Holzapfel. 1983. Life cycle stategies in *Wyeomyia smithii*: Seasonal and geographic adaptations. In V. Brown and I. Hodek, Eds., *Diapause and life cycle strategies in insects*. Dr. W. Junk Publishers, The Hague, Boston, and London. 295 pp.

Brenner, R. J., and E. W. Cupp. 1980. Preliminary observations on parity and nectar feeding in the black fly, *Simulium jenningsi*. *Mosquito News* 40:390–393.

Carlsson, G. 1962. Studies on Scandinavian black flies. *Opusc . Entomol. Suppl.* (Lund) 21:1–239.

Charlwood, J. D., J. A. Rafael, and T. J. Wilkes. 1980. Methods to determine the physiological age of Diptera of medical importance. A revision, with special reference to disease vectors in South America. *Acta Amazonica* 10:311–333 (in Portuguese).

Cheke, R. A., R. Garms, and M. Kerner. 1982. The fecundity of *Simulium damnosum* s.l. in northern Togo and infections with *Onchocerca* spp. *Ann. Trop. Med. Parasitol.* 76:561–568.

Christophers, S. R. 1911. Development of the egg follicle in anophelines. *Paludism* 2:73–88.

Chutter, F. M. 1970. A preliminary study of factors influencing the number of oocytes present in newly emerged blackflies (Diptera: Simuliidae) in Ontario. *Can. J. Zool.* 48:1389–1400.

Clements, A. N. 1963. *The physiology of mosquitoes*. Pergamon Press (Int. Ser. Monogr. Pure Appl. Biol. [Zool.], vol. 17. Oxford. 393 pp.

Colbo, M. H. 1982. Size and fecundity of adult Simuliidae (Diptera) as a function of stream habitat, year, and parasitism. *Can. J. Zool.* 60:2507–13.

Colbo, M. H., and G. N. Porter. 1981. The interaction of rearing temperature and food supply on the life history of two species of Simuliidae (Diptera). *Can. J. Zool.* 59:158–163.

Corbet, P. S. 1964. Autogeny and oviposition in arctic mosquitoes. *Nature* 203:668.

————. 1967. Facultative autogeny in arctic mosquitoes. *Nature* (London) 215:662–663.

Cupp, E. W., and R. C. Collins. 1979. The gonotrophic cycle in *Simulium ochraceum*. *Am. J. Trop. Med. Hyg.* 28:422–426.

Davies, D. M., and B. V. Peterson. 1956. Observations on the mating, feeding, ovarian development and oviposition of adult black flies (Simuliidae, Diptera). *Can. J. Zool.* 34:615–655.

Davies, D. M., H. Györkös, and J. E. Raastad. 1977. Simuliidae (Diptera) of Rendalen, Norway. IV. Autogeny and anautogeny. *Norw. J. Entomol.* 24:19–23.

Davies, L. 1954. Observations on *Prosimulium ursinum* Edw. at Holandsfjord, Norway. *Oikos* 5:94–98.

————. 1957. A study of the age of females of *Simulium ornatum* MG. attracted to cattle. *Bull. Entomol. Res.* 48:535–552.

————. 1961. Ecology of two *Prosimulium* species (Diptera) with reference to their ovarian cycles. *Can. Entomol.* 93:1113–40.

————. 1963. Seasonal and diurnal changes in the age-composition of adult *Simulium venustum* Say (Diptera) population near Ottawa. *Can. Entomol.* 95:654–667.

DeLeon, J. R., and B. O. L. Duke. 1966. Experimental studies on the transmission of Guatemalan and West African strains of *Onchocerca volvulus* by *Simulium ochraceum, S. metallicum* and *S. callidum. Trans. R. Soc. Trop. Med. Hyg.* 60:735–752.

Detinova, T. S. 1962. *Age-grouping methods in Diptera of medical importance with special reference to some vectors of malaria.* Monograph Ser. WHO, no. 47. 216 pp.

————. 1968. Age structure of insect populations of medical importance. *Ann. Rev. Entomol.* 13:427–450.

Detinova, T. S., and K. N. Beltyukova. 1958. On the number of gonotrophic cycles in black flies (Simuliidae) near Krasnoyarsk (Siberia). *Med. Parazit.* (Moscow) 27:686–688 (in Russian; English transl.).

Downes, J. A. 1958. The feeding habits of biting flies and their significance in classification. *Ann. Rev. Entomol.* 3:249–266.

————. 1965. Adaptations of insects in the arctic. *Ann. Rev. Entomol.* 10:257–274.

————. 1971. The ecology of blood-sucking Diptera: an evolutionary perspective. Pp. 232–258 in A. M. Fallis, Ed., *Ecology and physiology of parasites: a symposium held at the University of Toronto, 19 and 20 February 1970.* Univ. Toronto Press, Toronto.

Duke, B. O. L. 1968. Studies on factors influencing the transmission of onchocerciasis. IV. The biting-cycles, infective biting density and transmission potential of 'forest' *Simulium damnosum. Ann. Trop. Med. Parasitol.* 62:95–106.

————. 1975. The differential dispersal of nulliparous and parous *Simulium damnosum. Tropenmed. Parasitol.* 26:88–97.

Fallis, A. M. 1964. Feeding and related behavior of female Simuliidae (Diptera). *Exp. Parasitol.* 15:439–470.

Force, D. C. 1975. Succession of r and K strategies in parasitoids. Pp. 112–129 in P. W. Price, Ed., *Evolutionary strategies of parasitic insects and mites.* Plenum, New York. 224 pp.

Garms, R. 1973. Quantitative studies on the transmission of *Onchocerca volvulus* by *Simulium damnosum* in the Bong Range, Liberia. *Z. Tropenmed. Parasitol.* 24:358–372.

————. 1975. Observations on filarial infections and parous rates of anthropophilic blackflies in Guatemala with reference to the transmission of *Onchocerca volvulus. Tropenmed. Parasitol.* 26:169–182.

Giesel, J. T. 1976. Reproductive strategies as adaptations to life in temporally heterogeneous environments. *Ann. Rev. Ecol. Syst.* 7:57–79.

Gillies, M. T. 1964. The study of longevity in biting insects. *Int. Rev. Gen. Exp. Zool.* 1:47–76.

————. 1974. Methods for assessing the density and survival of blood-sucking Diptera. *Ann. Rev. Entomol.* 19:345–362.

Gillies, M. T., and T. J. Wilkes. 1965. A study of the age-composition of populations of *Anopheles gambiae* Giles and *A. funestus* Giles in Northeastern Tanzania. *Bull. Entomol. Res.* 56:237–262.

Greenplate, J. T., R. L. Glaser, and H. H. Hagedorn. 1985. The role of factors from the head in the regulation of egg development in the mosquito *Aedes aegypti. J. Insect Physiol.* 31:323–329.

Hagedorn, H. H. 1974. The control of vitellogenesis in the mosquito, *Aedes aegypti. Am. Zool.* 14:1207–17.

Ham, P. J., and A. J. Banya. 1984. The effect of experimental *Onchocerca* infections on the fecundity and oviposition of laboratory reared *Simulium* sp. (Diptera, Simuliidae). *Tropenmed. Parasitol.* 35:61–66.

Hocking, B. 1954. Flight muscle autolysis in *Aedes communis* (DeGeer). *Mosquito News* 14:121–123.

Hoy, J. B., and J. R. Anderson. 1978. Behavior and reproductive physiology of blood-sucking snipe flies (Diptera: Rhagionidae: *Symphoromyia*) attacking deer in Northern California. *Hilgardia* 46:113–168.

Hunter, D. M. 1977. Sugar-feeding in some Queensland blackflies (Diptera: Simuliidae). *J. Med. Entomol.* 14:229–232.

——. 1978. The sequence of events in outbreaks of *Austrosimulium pestilens* MacKerras and MacKerras (Diptera: Simuliidae). *Bull. Entomol. Res.* 68:307–312.

Johnson, C. G., J. F. Walsh, J. B. Davies, S. J. Clark, and J. N. Perry. 1985. The pattern and speed of displacement of females of *Simulium damnosum* Theobald s.l. (Diptera: Simuliidae) across the Onchocerciasis Control Programme area of West Africa in 1977 and 1978. *Bull. Entomol. Res.* 75:73–92.

Klowden, M. C., and A. O. Lea. 1979. Abdominal distention terminates subsequent host-seeking behavior of *Aedes aegypti* following a blood meal. *J. Insect Physiol.* 25:583–585.

——. 1980. "Physiologically old" mosquitoes are not necessarily old physiologically. *Am. J. Trop. Med. Hyg.* 29:1460–64.

Lavoipierre, M. M. J. 1961. Blood-feeding, fecundity and aging in *Aedes aegypti* var. *queenslandensis. Nature* 191:575–576.

Lea, A. O. 1970. Endocrinology of egg maturation in autogenous and anautogenous *Aedes taeniorhynchus. J. Insect Physiol.* 16:1689–96.

Le Berre, R. 1966. Contribution à l'étude biologique et écologique de *Simulium damnosum* Theobald 1903 (Diptera: Simuliidae). *Mém. ORSTROM,* no. 17. Paris. 204 pp.

Lewis, D. J. 1953. *Simulium damnosum* and its relation to onchocerciasis in the anglo-egyptian Sudan. *Bull. Entomol. Res.* 43:592–644.

——. 1957. Aspects of the structure, biology and study of *Simulium damnosum. Ann. Trop. Med. Parasitol.* 51:340–358.

——. 1958. Observations on *S. damnosum* at Lokoja in Northern Nigeria. *Ann. Trop. Med. Parasitol.* 52:216–231.

——. 1960. Observations on *Simulium damnosum* in the southern Cameroons and Liberia. *Ann. Trop. Med. Parasitol.* 54:208–223.

——. 1965. Features of the *Simulium damnosum* population of the Kumba area in West Cameroon. *Ann. Trop. Med. Parasitol.* 59:365–374.

Lewis, D. J., and G. F. Bennett. 1973. The blackflies (Diptera: Simuliidae) of insular Newfoundland. I. Distribution and bionomics. *Can. J. Zool.* 51:1181–87.

Lewis, D. J., and C. R. Domoney. 1966. Sugar meals in Phlebotominae and Simuliidae (Diptera). *Proc. R. Entomol. Soc. London* (A) 41:175–179.

Linley, J. R. 1965. Changes in the ovaries of certain biting midges (Diptera: Ceratopogonidae) following completion of the gonotrophic cycle. *Mosquito News* 25:306–310.

MacArthur, R. H., and E. O. Wilson. 1967. *The theory of island biogeography.* Princeton Univ. Press, Princeton, N.J. 203 pp.

Macdonald, G. 1952. The analysis of the sporozoite rate. *Trop. Dis. Bull.* 49:569–586.

Magnarelli, L. A., and E. W. Cupp. 1977. Physiological age of *Simulium tuberosum* and *S. venustum* in New York State, U.S.A. *J. Med. Entomol.* 4–5:621–624.

Mather, T. N., and G. R. DeFoliart. 1983. Effect of host blood source on the gonotrophic cycle of *Aedes triseriatus. Am. J. Trop. Med. Hyg.* 32:189–193.

McIver, S. B., and J. F. Sutcliff. 1987. Sensory basis of behavior and structural adaptations for feeding in black flies (this volume).

Mer, G. G. 1936. Experimental study on the development of the ovary in *Anopheles elutus* Edw. (Dipt Culic.). *Bull. Entomol. Res.* 27:351–359.

Mokry, J. E. 1980a. A method for estimating the age of field-collected female *Simulium damnosum* s.l. (Diptera: Simuliidae). *Tropenmed. Parasitol.* 31:128–130.

———. 1980b. Laboratory studies in blood feeding of blackflies (Diptera: Simuliidae). (2) Factors affecting fecundity. *Tropenmed. Parasitol.* 31:374–380.

Nayar, J. K., and D. M. Sauerman, Jr. 1975. The effects of nutrition on survival and fecundity in Florida mosquitoes. III. Utilization of blood and sugar for fecundity. *J. Med. Entomol.* 12:220–225.

Nicholson, H. P. 1945. The morphology of the mouthparts of the non-biting blackfly, *Eusimulium dacotense* D. and S., as compared with those of the biting species, *Simulium venustum* Say. *Ann. Entomol. Soc. Am.* 38:281–297.

Omar, M. S., and R. Garms. 1975. The fate and migration of microfilariae of a Guatemalan strain of *Onchocerca volvulus* in *Simulium ochraceum* and *S. metallicum,* and the role of the buccopharyngeal armature in the destruction and microfilariae. *Tropenmed. Parasitol.* 26:183–190.

O'Meara, G. F., and G. B. Craig. 1969. Monofactorial inheritance of autogeny in *Aedes atropalpus. Mosquito News* 29:14–22.

O'Meara, G. F., and G. J. Krasnick. 1970. Dietary and genetic control of the expression of autogenous reproduction in *Aedes atropalpus* (Coq.) (Diptera: Culicidae). *J. Med. Entomol.* 7:328–334.

Pianka, E. R. 1970. On r- and K-selection. *Am. Nat.* 104:592–597.

Polovodova, J. P. 1949. Determination of the physiological age of female *Anopheles. Medskaya Parazit.* 18:352–355 (in Russian).

Porter, C. H., and R. C. Collins. 1985. The gonotrophic cycle of wild *Simulium ochraceum* and the associated development of *Onchocerca volvulus. Am. J. Trop. Med. Hyg.* 34:302–309.

Reisen, W. K., and M. Aslamkhan. 1979. A release-recapture experiment with the malaria vector, *Anopheles stephensi* Liston, with observations on dispersal, survivorship, population size, gonotrophic rhythm and mating behavior. *Ann. Trop. Med. Parasitol.* 73:251–269.

Rubtsov, I. A. 1956. Nutrition and facultative bloodsucking in blackflies (Diptera, Simuliidae). *Entomol. Obozr.* 35:731–751 (in Russian; English trans.).

———. 1958. The gonotrophic cycle in bloodsucking black-flies. *Parazitol sb. Zool. Inst. AN SSSR* 18:255–282 (in Russian; English trans.).

———. 1961. Gonotrophic cycle in phytophagous species of blackflies (Diptera, Simuliidae). *Entomol. Rev.* (Wash.) 39:392–405.

Rühm, W. 1970. Investigation of the physiological age of the adults of *Boophthora erythrocephala* de Geer and some other species of Simuliidae. *Z. Parasitenkunde* 34:207–225 (in German; English trans.).

Schlein, Y. 1979. Age grouping of anopheline malaria vectors (Diptera: Culicidae) by the cuticular growth lines. *J. Med. Entomol.* 16:502–506.

Schlein, Y., and N. G. Gratz. 1972. Age determination of some flies and mosquitoes by daily growth layers of skeletal apodemes. *Bull. WHO* 47:71–76.

Service, M. W. 1976. *Mosquito ecology field sampling methods.* John Wiley & Sons, New York. 583 pp.

Shipitsina, N. K. 1962. On the gonotrophic cycle and age condition of populations of bloodsucking flies in the vicinity of Krasnoyarsk. I. *Gnus cholodkovskii* and *Simulium reptans* var. *galeratum* near Krasnoyarsk (Siberia). *Med. Parasitol.* (Moscow) 31:18–29 (in Russian; English trans.).

———. 1963. Infestation of simuliids (Diptera) with their parasites and its effect upon ovarian functioning. *Zool. Zh.* (Moscow) 42:291–294 (in Russian).

Simmons, K. R. 1985. Reproductive ecology and host seeking behavior of the black fly

Simulium venustum Say (Diptera: Simuliidae). Ph.D. Diss., University of Massachusetts, Amherst.

Simmons, K. R., and J. D. Edman. 1978. Successful mating, oviposition, and complete generation rearing of the multivoltine black fly *Simulium decorum* (Diptera: Simuliidae) in the laboratory. *Can. J. Zool.* 56:1223–25.

Southwood, T. R. E. 1977. Habitat, the templet for ecological strategies? *J. Anim. Ecol.* 46:337–365.

Spielman, A. 1957. The inheritance of autogeny in the *Culex pipiens* complex of mosquitoes. *Am. J. Hyg.* 65:404–425.

———. 1971. Bionomics of autogenous mosquitoes. *Ann. Rev. Entomol.* 16:231–248.

Spielman, A., and J. Wong. 1974. Dietary factors stimulating oogenesis in *Aedes aegypti*. *Biol. Bull.* 147:433–442.

Stearns, S. C. 1976. Life-history tactics: a review of the ideas. *Q. Rev. Biol.* 51:3–46.

Sutherla, G. B., and A. B. Ewen. 1974. Fecundity decrease in mosquitoes ingesting blood from specifically sensitized mammals. *J. Insect Physiol.* 20:655–660.

Takaoka, H., J. O. Ochoa, E. L. Juarez, and K. M. Hansen. 1982. Effects of temperature on development of *Onchocerca volvulus* in *Simulium ochraceum,* and longevity of the simuliid vector. *J. Parasitol.* 68:478–483.

Takaoka, H., T. Suzuki, S. Noda, I. Tada, M. G. Basáñez, and L. Yarzábal. 1984. Development of *Onchocerca volvulus* larvae in *Simulium pintoi* in the Amazonas region of Venezuela. *Am. J. Trop. Med. Hyg.* 33:414–419.

Trpis, M. 1978. Genetics of hematophagy and autogeny in the *Aedes scutellaris* complex (Diptera: Culicidae). *J. Med. Entomol.* 15:73–80.

Tyndale-Biscoe, M. 1984. Age-grading methods in adult insects: a review. *Bull. Entomol. Res.* 74:341–378.

Walsh, J. F., and R. Garms. 1980. The detection of plant sugars in *Simulium damnosum* s.l. by means of the cold anthrone test. *Trans. R. Soc. Trop. Med. Hyg.* 74:811–813.

Watanabe, M. 1977. Observations on nectar sucking behavior and parous rates of five species of black flies. *Jpn. J. Sanit. Ecol.* 28:401–407.

Wenk, P. 1965. On the biology of bloodsucking simuliids (Diptera). I. Insemination rate of females visiting flowers and attacking blood hosts. *Z. Morphol. Ökol. Tiere.* 55:656–670 (in German; English trans.).

Wood, D. M. 1978. Taxonomy of the Nearctic species in *Twinnia* and *Gymnopais* (Diptera: Simuliidae) and a discussion of the ancestry of the Simuliidae. *Can. Entomol.* 110:1297–1337.

Wu, Y. F. 1931. A contribution to the biology of *Simulium*. *Pap. Mich. Acad. Sci. Arts Lett.* 13:543–599.

Yang, Y. J., and D. M. Davies. 1977. The peritrophic membrane in adult simuliids (Diptera) before and after feeding on blood and blood-sucrose mixtures. *Ent. Exp. Appl.* 22:132–140.

Part V Population Management

21 BLACK FLIES: APPROACHES TO POPULATION MANAGEMENT IN A LARGE TEMPERATE-ZONE RIVER SYSTEM

F. J. H. Fredeen

Black fly management schemes in Saskatchewan developed through three stages, progressing from the homemade remedies of pioneers, to reliance on DDT as a larvicide, and finally to the present-day situation, still in the developmental stages, of use of combinations of selected chemicals to control both larvae and adults. Despite modern advances in black fly management strategies, potential for widespread outbreaks remain.

Stage one, from the beginning of agricultural settlement in the late 19th century until 1948, was an age of relative innocence. Livestock producers were generally unaware of the sources of the erratic and often devastating outbreaks of the black fly *Simulium arcticum* Malloch, that is, the rapids in large mountain-fed rivers that trisected central Saskatchewan. The common names of "sand flies" and "swamp flies" were used, depending upon the latest theories about apparent sources in riverside sandhills or swamps. Those few producers who did appeal for help found that although Cameron (1922) had discovered the sources of outbreaks little real assistance regarding protection was available. Thus producers were forced to accept outbreaks as uncontrollable phenomena, comparable to outbreaks of grasshoppers and epidemics of wheat rust. In years when outbreaks were prolonged, homemade remedies were used—smoke smudges, livestock shelters, and hand-applied lotions such as the one recommended by the Animal Husbandry Department of the University of Saskatchewan ("one tablespoon oil of tar, one teaspoon creolin, and one quart of oil, preferably linseed oil"). Such methods were reasonably effective in those years, when herds were small and located in home pastures with ready access to individual treatments and shelters. Those methods would not be too useful today for the large numbers of animals that are kept in large community pastures, without access either to shelters or close observation. Smudges are sometimes still used, although burning permits are often required.

Stage one came to an end in 1947, the last of four years of devastating outbreaks of *S. arcticum* from the Saskatchewan River. Those outbreaks had resulted in the deaths of more than 1,100 domestic animals, including many purebred herd sires

(Rempel and Arnason 1947, Fredeen 1956). Perhaps in the earliest years of agricultural settlement, improved access to blood meals due to increasing numbers of livestock in central Saskatchewan contributed in part to the increases observed in numbers of black flies, which culminated in the outbreaks of 1944 through 1947. At that time DDT, a remarkably effective, inexpensive insecticide, was identified as a black fly larvicide (Fairchild and Barreda 1945).

Stage two, the age of a simple but naive answer to black fly problems, commenced in 1948, when we performed two tests in the Saskatchewan River with DDT as a larvicide. Tests with DDT at Churchill, Manitoba, the previous year had indicated its potential usefulness as a black fly larvicide in cool Canadian streams (Hocking et al. 1949). In 1948 a 12% solution of DDT in fuel oil and added solvents was sprayed onto the surface of the Saskatchewan River from a DC-3 aircraft. Within 48 hours after a single 36-minute application of an average of 0.13 parts DDT per million parts of river water, no black fly larvae could be found in any rapids as far as the confluence with the North Saskatchewan River, a distance of more than 160 kilometers (Arnason et al. 1949). The river volume was unusually large at that time, flowing at 986 m^3/sec. A second test that year at half the original dosage (0.07 ppm of DDT applied over 34 minutes) on the North Saskatchewan River flowing at 1,790 m^3/sec. was ineffective. However, six additional tests of single 15-minute applications of about 0.1 to 0.4 ppm of DDT in subsequent years showed that those dosages generally could be depended upon to reduce populations of larvae (Fredeen et al. 1953a). Similar dosages of DDT were used until 1968, and during the twenty years that DDT larvicide was used only 115 animals were known to have been killed by black flies. Those outbreaks originated mainly from untreated sections of the rivers. The remarkable efficiency of DDT as a larvicide was attributed in part to its adsorption to silt particles suspended in the turbid river water (Fredeen et al. 1953b). This facilitated long-distance carry of DDT. Also filter-feeding black fly larvae readily ingested those particles and thus were more susceptible to the DDT than non-filter-feeding species. We discovered in the first test in 1948 that whereas only 0.2% of the black fly larvae survived in rapids 27 kilometers downstream from the point of application, 83.5% of the other arthropods survived.

Stage three, the modern, complex stage in the development of black fly management in Saskatchewan, was initiated or accompanied by at least four events in the late 1960s. First was the increasing evidence of the dangers of persistent DDT residues in the global environment. This stimulated initiation of a search for alternative larvicides in 1967, even though at the end of twenty years of use of DDT in the Saskatchewan River residues were relatively low in fish of all trophic levels, both in treated and untreated sections. From treated sections neither DDT, DDD, nor DDE could be detected (< 0.01 ppm combined residues) in the muscle tissues of 17 fish (two to nine years old). Combined residues of only 0.01 ppm were detected in 26 fish, two to six years old, and residues of 0.09 to 0.16 ppm in 34 fish, two to nine years old. In an untreated section separated by a hydroelectric dam, there were no detectable residues in 47 fish two to five years old but residues of 0.06 and 0.11 ppm in two fish one to three years old.

In comparison, mature and seemingly healthy lake trout collected from eight lakes in New York State contained 6.8 to 116.9 ppm DDT plus DDE in their tissues (Burdick et al. 1964). Newly hatched trout from the same lakes contained 0.6 to 14.2

ppm combined residues but suffered 100% mortality when tissue concentrations were 3.7 ppm or higher.

Tests by Travis and Wilton (1965) and Jamnback and Frempong-Boadu (1966) indicated that methoxychlor (and several other chemicals) were also effective black fly larvicides, at least in troughs and streams. Results from our first 15 field tests indicated that methoxychlor also could provide reliable control of black fly larvae in the Saskatchewan River system (Fredeen 1974). Its negative temperature coefficient proved useful in our relatively cool, temperate-zone rivers. On the other hand, temephos, which was so effective in West Africa in recent years, was not effective at 7.0–9.0°C in the Saskatchewan system. Other advantages of methoxychlor were its ability, like DDT, to adsorb to particles suspended in the water (Fredeen et al. 1975), and, unlike DDT, its relatively rapid decomposition into increasingly water-soluble metabolites (Kapoor et al. 1970).

Two other major events ushering in the modern era of black fly management in Saskatchewan were the drastic reductions in summertime river volumes in the entire Saskatchewan River system commencing in the late 1960s and the profound changes in the black fly fauna that followed. Summertime river volumes declined by as much as 90% in the south branch and 50% in the north, due to the combined effects of drought and storage of water in newly constructed hydroelectric reservoirs. In one way those reductions worked to our advantage in that they allowed us to perform larvicide tests with relatively small amounts of chemicals. However, downstream carry of larvicide was drastically reduced, apparently due to losses of injected methoxychlor to the riverbed and to aquatic plants. Transition from deep, turbid water to shallow, clear water with reduced velocities allowed for the first time dense growths of aquatic plants upon previously barren sandbars (Fredeen 1977). Eutrophication was also aided by increasing amounts of nutrients from large cities. Thus distance of effective control achieved by a single injection of methoxychlor eventually was reduced from the maximum of more than 160 kilometers achieved in 1973 in the North Saskatchewan River, when the volume flow was relatively normal (494 m³/sec) (Fredeen 1975), to 20 to 40 kilometers, when the river volume was reduced in the late 1970s to as low as 50 m³/sec.

Reductions in river volumes also ushered in profound changes in the black fly fauna (Fredeen 1977). Larvae of *S. arcticum* became rare, and larvae of *S. luggeri* Nicholson and Mickel, previously restricted to small, weedy prairie rivers, gradually became established. For a few years in the early 1970s it seemed that our black fly problems were vanishing because *S. luggeri*, which had always been considered innocuous, was replacing *S. arcticum*. However in June 1976, about eight years after *S. luggeri* was first discovered breeding in the Saskatchewan River, unexpectedly dense swarms began to emerge and drove cattle out of nearby pastures. That outbreak spread rapidly, and within days livestock and people were being severely harassed in some 23,000 km² of central Saskatchewan. Experimentation with methoxychlor larvicide was accelerated from one test in 1976 to six in 1977, seven in 1978, nineteen in 1979, and five in 1980 (Fredeen 1983). The sudden increase in 1979 was required to prevent reoccurrences of unusually severe outbreaks that occurred in 1978. In that year, chronic outbreaks throughout four months spread at times into some 38,000 km² and resulted in financial losses to beef and dairy producers estimated to have exceeded $2.9 million (Fredeen 1985).

The reasons we were being confronted with such a formidable pest gradually became evident:

1. Adults were produced in immense numbers from the extensive new weed beds growing on previously barren sand and gravel beds. Also, *S. luggeri* was multivoltine, unlike *S. arcticum,* and numbers increased toward midsummer unless larvicide was used, and sometimes even in spite of larviciding when larvae drifted downriver in large numbers from untreated sections. (With exceptions in 1979, the Saskatchewan River was not treated above Prince Albert on the north branch or St. Louis on the south to avoid possible contamination of domestic water supplies.) We also discovered that single larvicide injections were much less effective than under previously weed-free conditions and that large numbers of marginally affected larvae simply released and drifted to reattach in weed beds further downriver. Severe outbreaks arising from the main Saskatchewan River below the confluence of the north and south branches were attributed in part to those recolonizations (Fredeen 1983).

2. Adult black flies were capable of drifting long distances on the wind (in one instance at least 170 kilometers) and also worked their way upwind through tree-sheltered pastures, sometimes for 15 kilometers or more (Fredeen 1985).

3. Adults vigorously attacked domestic animals, especially cattle and horses, and swarmed densely around them, causing hyperactivity and panic. Cattle pushed through fences, and even a barn wall in one instance, in attempting to escape. They ceased grazing and sometimes showed weight losses instead of expected gains. Breeding was interrupted, and the missing of even one estrous cycle meant lost dollars (up to 45 kg less weight per weaned calf) at weaned-calf sales the following year. Stress-related diseases and stampede injuries increased.

4. During outbreaks of *S. luggeri,* people often were prevented from working outdoors, even with the use of repellents. *S. arcticum* seldom attacked people.

These unexpected problems required development of a whole new framework of control strategies. That framework has been under development for the past eight years but still requires considerable refinement.

The fourth event of major importance in the redevelopment of our black fly management program was the 1968 amendment of the Saskatchewan Water Resources Commission Act and Regulations of 1965. For the first time it became mandatory to obtain authorization in writing from the commission before any substance could be added to surface waters for the purpose of poisoning "aquatic nuisances." And before a provincial permit could be obtained, agreement with federal authorities was also required because the Saskatchewan River crossed provincial boundaries. In 1981 federal authorities granted registration for methoxychlor black fly larvicide to be used in single, annual, 15-minute 0.3 ppm injections into each of the Athabasca and North and South Saskatchewan rivers to control larvae of *S. arcticum.* Since then, limited numbers of additional methoxychlor injections have been negotiated annually for experimental control of larvae of *S. luggeri.*

Along with testing the reliability of larviciding as a means of preventing outbreaks, we investigated the environmental impact of methoxychlor larvicide treatments, including a four-year study of six sites in 107 kilometers of the Saskatchewan River

(Fredeen 1974, 1975, 1983). A prerequisite for this was the development of special sampling equipment and methods to allow investigations in rivers of this size despite fluctuating volumes (Fredeen and Spurr 1978). Investigations of the distribution and durability of residues were also required (Fredeen et al. 1975). It was also necessary to develop keys for identification of the fifteen species of black flies now known to inhabit the river (Fredeen 1981a) and descriptions of the seven larval instars of *S. arcticum* (Fredeen 1976) and of *S. luggeri* (Fredeen 1981b). Keys for identification of many nonsimuliid species also were developed: Trichoptera (Smith 1975), Plecoptera (Dosdall and Lehmkuhl 1979), and Chironomidae (Mason, in preparation). Data on economic effects of outbreaks of *S. luggeri* were prepared (Fredeen 1985). By 1981 it was possible to prepare technology transfers that allowed contracting out of monitoring and larviciding for the first time.

In recent years we tested protective effects of permethrin (Ectiban®) sprays and fenvalerate-impregnated ear tags (Bovaid®). Permethrin sprays, costing about two dollars per cow-calf pair, provided six to eight days of complete protection. Although average daily weight-gain advantages over unsprayed animals were scarcely sufficient to pay for the cost of the chemical required, permethrin sprays are useful for short-term emergencies. Bovaid® ear tags, costing about seven dollars per cow-calf pair, appeared to confer six to seven weeks of satisfactory protection when treated herds contained about 30 animals or more. Weight-gain advantages were considered sufficient to pay for the tags several times over. However, unequivocal data are not available because other factors affecting growth rates have not yet been evaluated. The major advantage of using Bovaid® and perhaps other ear tags yet untested is that animals in large pastures apparently are afforded up to six weeks of reasonably good protection without having to be repeatedly rounded up and run through spray chutes. Managers of two of our largest pastures, the 3,230 ha (12.75 mi^2) James Smith pasture and the 1,780 ha (7 mi^2) Garrick pasture, now require that patrons tag all of their animals before being admitted each spring. Past experiences have shown that untagged animals are very disruptive during black fly outbreaks.

Until 1981 the Canadian Department of Agriculture alone was responsible for developing this black fly management program. Since then, the Saskatchewan Department of Agriculture has funded routine monitoring and control projects, and, with assistance from livestock producers, has also funded demonstration projects and some research. The Canada Biting Fly Centre, Winnipeg, funded its own research with *B.t.i.,* and chemical companies assisted with tests of their products. Interestingly enough, two critical decision-making departments, the federal and provincial Departments of the Environment, have been reluctant to assist with research, or even to observe effects of larvicide treatments on river fauna, or effects of outbreaks on human environments resulting from lack of treatments.

A fairly large committee helps us to plan our annual program. Included are livestock producers, extension workers, representatives from regulatory agencies, veterinarian services, fisheries, occasionally politicians from affected areas, and of course entomologists. Long-term commitments for funds are essential. Funding agencies are provided with reviews of progress and problems, reports from contractors, and updates in plans.

Communications are important, and thus we provide extension agents, livestock producers, and other residents, via meetings, news reports, and letters, with information on black fly species, behavior, breeding sites, changes in numbers of larvae, dates and sites of larvicide treatments, and whatever other information may help them make their own decisions about protecting themselves and their livestock.

Development of a black fly management program appropriate for this large river system is ongoing and for some years to come will continue to require careful integration of both practical and research components. These two components are discussed here with suggestions where they may be strengthened:

1. The practical component of black fly management in Saskatchewan consists of government programs for both monitoring populations of larvae and for applying larvicide. These are augmented by on-farm programs administered by many farm owners. Animals can be protected to a large extent with Bovaid® ear tags, especially when treated herds consist of 30 animals or more. But many producers are unwilling to make the investment until an outbreak is upon them, and by then it is too late. *S. luggeri* also attacks people and, when abundant, can prevent them from working outdoors despite use of repellents. For these reasons residents in outbreak areas depend upon larviciding to reduce potential severity of outbreaks at their sources. Until suitable alternatives are available we will have to depend upon methoxychlor for larviciding.

Both monitoring numbers of larvae and chemical larviciding are done by contract using guidelines established by the Research Branch of Canada Agriculture. Numbers of larvae are monitored by anchoring polypropylene ropes in one selected site in each of the North, South, and main Saskatchewan rivers. The rope pieces are exchanged at weekly intervals throughout the spring and summer and the larvae preserved for later identification to species and instars. Weekly collections over the past nine years from those three sites provide benchmark data.

When 1,000 or more larvae accumulate in one week on a one-meter length of rope in one or more of the sites, immediate injections of larvicide are indicated. If larvae are younger than fifth instar, treatment may be delayed for a week to allow time for more eggs to hatch. In most years the first treatments in the spring are often required within four or five weeks after the breakup of winter ice, and the final treatments in early August.

A larvicide treatment consists of a single injection in a site, often repeated two or three times per summer, of sufficient 24% emulsifiable concentrate to provide 0.3 ppm methoxychlor over 15 minutes. The numbers of sites and injections allowed are renegotiated annually with federal and provincial authorities. Generally the larvicide is poured into the water from a ferry making several passes across the river. A boat or helicopter has been used for sites where there were no ferries.

A single injection is expected to reduce numbers of larvae by 75% or more for distances up to 20 kilometers when the river is shallow and weedy, or beyond 120 kilometers when deep and weedless (Fredeen 1974, 1975). However, efficacy relative to various river characteristics has never been accurately determined because of continuous variations in the rivers regarding volume, weediness, siltiness, and other qualities, as well as in the distribution of larvae. Larvae not killed outright will reattach further downriver and have been assumed to contribute to outbreaks in those regions (Fredeen 1983). Also, some outbreaks have arisen from treated sections when the numbers of treatments allowed have not been sufficient to cope with emergencies such as unexpected downriver drift of larvae from untreated sections. Other outbreaks are believed to have arisen directly from those sections left untreated (in order to protect domestic water supplies). It has not been possible to identify origins of outbreaks because of the complex breeding sites situated in adjacent branches of the river.

2. A strong research component is essential: (a) to develop a data base for economic justification of the management scheme; (b) for ongoing field tests of control measures against larvae and adults; (c) to document effectiveness and environmental impact of control measures; (d) to develop and refine monitoring systems for predictions of immediate and long-term outbreak potentials; and (e) to investigate natural control agents.

A study of economic effects of outbreaks cannot be adequately documented in a single season or perhaps even in a dozen seasons. Studies of outbreaks in seven consecutive years, 1976 to 1982, indicated just how much outbreaks could vary from day to day and year to year regarding intensity, durations, and area of country affected (Fredeen 1985). Nevertheless, it is important to eventually publish data that may serve as background for cost-effectiveness studies of alternate management strategies. For example, in 1985, $38,000 was budgeted for monitoring populations of black fly larvae in the Saskatchewan River and for chemical control, i.e., control of black flies at their sources. An alternative scheme would be to protect directly some 40,000 cattle in those districts most likely to be affected if outbreaks occurred. When Bovaid® ear tags were used (a treatment presently registered for control of hornflies), two tags were required for each adult animal and one per sucking calf, for a total cost exceeding $160,000 at today's prices. A third but untenable alternative would be to provide no protection. However, if outbreaks occurred similar in severity to those experienced in 1978, losses could exceed $2.9 million (Fredeen 1985).

One harmful aspect of outbreaks that is generally overlooked regarding economic effects is the unpredictability of those outbreaks in time, in space, and in severity. That unpredictability has been a major part of the problem for producers in chronic outbreak areas in Saskatchewan because the producers are forced to be continually wary throughout the entire black fly season of three or four months. Rather than face uncertainties, some producers have ceased producing livestock and have converted pastures and haylands into less-productive cereal crops or have abandoned the land altogether. Those conversions undoubtedly have reduced economic outputs from some areas, but they have not been investigated.

No data have been accumulated on the disease-vector potential of local black fly species. In Saskatchewan we are concerned about losses from increased incidences of bovine pinkeye, mastitis, and of poultry fatalities during certain black fly outbreaks. Cooperative research projects with veterinarians should be arranged in the event of reoccurrences of severe outbreaks.

Data from field tests with methoxychlor larvicide over a period of thirteen years regarding efficacy, environmental impact, and residues from different environmental conditions have been published (Fredeen 1974, 1975, 1983; Fredeen et al. 1975). Effectiveness and fate of methoxychlor under different conditions of water quality and weediness have not been adequately studied, however. Dr. Galloway has been testing *B.t.i.* Other larvicides such as temephos also require investigation, even though development of tolerance to methoxychlor is not likely to be an issue in the Saskatchewan River because larvae continually drift downriver from long, untreated sections of the river system. Variations in susceptibility between instars should be considered.

Even though larviciding at this time is of prime importance because it allows us to control the black flies in their relatively limited sources rather than waiting for adults to escape into wide areas with unpredictable boundaries, we cannot assume that methoxychlor or any other larvicide will always be environmentally acceptable, cost-effective, or even available.

We need to improve our ability to advise on optimum treatment sites and dates. Possibly phenological data could provide supplementary indicators for initiating treatments in the spring. We depend upon densities and instar frequencies of populations of larvae seen on artificial substrates, but we still have not related those data with actual populations of larvae in the benthos and with subsequent numbers of black flies seen around livestock. Thus we need to determine how many of the drifting larvae entering the control area actually remain to colonize it. Conditions affecting release, drift, and reattachment of larvae, as well as rates of growth and mortality, require investigation. Rates of colonization of artificial substrates vary greatly between rivers, indicating the need to set different actionable levels for initiating larvicide treatments. Sites for larvicide injections may vary with the season depending upon changes in densities of weed growth and distribution of larvae.

Attacking behavior of black flies regarding host preferences, body-site preferences, and potentials for disease transmission, as well as effects of weather conditions on flight initiation, duration, range, and attack behavior, require investigation. A reliable method for obtaining quantitative samples of adults in isolated pastures should be developed.

Behavior of animals under different intensities of attack requires documentation. We suspect that there are variations in attractiveness to black flies among breeds, colors, sexes, physiological conditions, and ages of animals. Possibly also there are differences in reactions to attacks. Data would be useful not only for livestock managers but also for researchers attempting to compare protective values of various chemical treatments.

We need to continue testing pyrethroids and other insecticides against adult black flies. New livestock management strategies are always under consideration, such as comparing breeds for tolerance to black flies, or having cattle bred earlier in the season to avoid interference from black flies.

Our black-fly-management operating plans have never stabilized. Adjustments have been required every year to accommodate changes in ecological conditions in the river system, in species of black flies with new pest potentials, in monitoring and control strategies, in chemicals available for use as larvicides and adulticides, in licensing procedures for larviciding, in livestock management strategies, and in the economics of livestock production. Although past research has provided good foundations for a black fly management program that is reasonably effective and practical for today, we still need to remain alert for early signs of additional changes in black fly populations or other conditions that could require major changes in management strategies.

LITERATURE CITED

Arnason, A. P., A. W. A. Brown, F. J. H. Fredeen, W. W. Hopewell, and J. G. Rempel. 1949. Experiments in the control of *Simulium arcticum* by means of DDT in the Saskatchewan River. *Sci. Agric.* 29:527–537.

Burdick, G. D., E. J. Harris, H. J. Dean, T. M. Walter, J. Skea, and D. Colby. 1964. The accumulation of DDT in lake trout and the effect on reproduction. *Trans. Am. Fish. Soc.* 93:127–136.

Cameron, A. E. 1922. The morphology and biology of a Canadian cattle-infesting black fly, *Simulium simile* Mall. (Diptera: Simuliidae). *Can. Dept. Agric. Tech. Bull.* 5 (n.s.):1–26.

Dosdall, L. M., and D. M. Lehmkuhl. 1979. Stoneflies (Plecoptera) of Saskatchewan. *Quaest. Entomol.* 15:3–16.

Fairchild, G. B., and E. A. Barreda. 1945. DDT as a larvicide against *Simulium*. *J. Econ. Entomol.* 38:694–699.

Fredeen, F. J. H. 1956. Black flies (Diptera: Simuliidae) of the agricultural areas of Manitoba, Saskatchewan and Alberta. *Proc. 10th Int. Congr. Entomol.* 3:819–823.

———. 1974. Tests with single injections of methoxychlor black fly (Diptera: Simuliidae) larvicides in large rivers. *Can. Entomol.* 106:285–305.

———. 1975. Effects of a single injection of methoxychlor black-fly larvicide on insect larvae in a 161-km (100-mile) section of the North Saskatchewan River. *Can. Entomol.* 107:807–817.

———. 1976. The seven larval instars of *Simulium arcticum* (Diptera: Simuliidae). *Can. Entomol.* 108:591–600.

———. 1977. Some recent changes in black-fly populations in the Saskatchewan River system in western Canada coinciding with the development of reservoirs. *Can. Water Res. J.* 2:90–102.

———. 1981a. Keys to the black flies (Simuliidae) of the Saskatchewan River in Saskatchewan. *Quaest. Entomol.* 17:189–210.

———. 1981b. The seven larval instars of *Simulium (Phosterodoros) luggeri* (Diptera: Simuliidae). *Can. Entomol.* 113:161–165.

———. 1983. Trends in numbers of aquatic invertebrates in a large Canadian river during four years of black-fly larviciding with methoxychlor (Diptera: Simuliidae). *Quaest. Entomol.* 19:53–92.

———. 1985. Some economic effects of outbreaks of black flies (*Simulium luggeri* Nicholson and Mickel) in Saskatchewan. *Quaest. Entomol.* (in press).

Fredeen, F. J. H., A. P. Arnason, B. Berck, and J. G. Rempel. 1953. Further experiments with DDT in the control of *Simulium arcticum* Mall. in the North and South Saskatchewan Rivers. *Can. J. Agric. Sci.* 33:379–393.

Fredeen, F. J. H., A. P. Arnason, and B. Berck. 1953. Adsorption of DDT on suspended solids in river water and its role in black fly control. *Nature* (London) 171:700–701.

Fredeen, F. J. H., J. G. Saha, and L. M. Royer. 1971. Residues of DDT, DDE, and DDD in fish in the Saskatchewan River after using DDT as a black fly larvicide for twenty years. *J. Fish. Res. Board Can.* 28:105–109.

Fredeen, F. J. H., J. G. Saha, and M. H. Balba. 1975. Residues of methoxychlor and other chlorinated hydrocarbons in water, sand, and selected fauna following injections of methoxychlor black fly larvicide into the Saskatchewan River, 1972. *Pest. Monit. J.* 8:241–246.

Fredeen, F. J. H., and D. T. Spurr. 1978. Collecting semi-quantitative samples of black fly larvae (Diptera: Simuliidae) and other aquatic insects from large rivers with the aid of artificial substrates. *Quaest. Entomol.* 14:411–431.

Hocking, B., C. R. Twinn, and Wm. C. McDuffie. 1949. A preliminary evaluation of some insecticides against immature stages of black flies (Diptera: Simuliidae). *Sci. Agric.* 29:69–80.

Jamnback, H., and J. Frempong-Boadu. 1966. Testing blackfly larvicides in the laboratory and in streams. *Bull. WHO* 34:405–421.

Kapoor, I. P., R. L. Metcalf, R. F. Nystrom, and G. K. Sangha. 1970. Comparative metabolism of methoxychlor, methiochlor, and DDT in mouse, insects and in a model ecosystem. *J. Agric. Food Chem.* 18:1145–52.

Mason, P. G. Chironomidae (Diptera) of the Saskatchewan River in Saskatchewan. (In preparation).

Rempel, J. G., and A. P. Arnason. 1947. An account of three successive outbreaks of the black fly, *Simulium arcticum,* a serious livestock pest in Saskatchewan. *Sci. Agric.* 27:428–445.

Smith, D. H. 1975. The taxonomy of the Trichoptera (Caddisflies) of the Saskatchewan River system in Saskatchewan. M.Sc. Thesis, University of Saskatchewan. 273 pp.

Travis, B. V., and D. P. Wilton. 1965. A progress report on simulated stream tests of black fly larvicides. *Mosquito News* 25:112–118.

22 MAINTAINING BLACK FLIES IN THE LABORATORY

John D. Edman and Kenneth R. Simmons

Publication of our 1985 review on "Rearing and Colonization of Black Flies" (*J. Med. Entomol.* 22:1–17) dictates a selective approach in this chapter. Other recent reviews (Raybould and Grunewald 1975, Mokry et al. 1981, Raybould 1981) summarize the earlier literature. Larval rearing, perhaps the most important aspect, will be dealt with briefly, since we are unaware of new developments in the past two years. Moreover, major challenges now have been met. Most species probably can be successfully reared if available rearing systems, or some modification, are properly employed. We will emphasize new information for maintaining eggs and adults, and techniques for inducing better survival, mating, blood feeding, and oviposition.

CORRECTIONS AND ADDITIONS TO THE LIST OF REARED AND MATED SPECIES (EDMAN AND SIMMONS 1985)

Two corrections to Table 1A concern the *Lewisellum* group and *Simulium equinum*. Reference to the *Lewisellum* group being reared was given as *Simulium neavei*. Actually, it was two members of the *S. neavei* complex: *Simulium woodi* de Meillon and *Simulium nyasalandicum* de Meillon (tmani form of Lewis 1961) (Raybould and Grunewald 1975). Current name usage favors *Simulium equinum* over *Wilhemia equina*, but these names were incorrectly combined in Table 1B as *Simulium equina*. Four additional Afrotropical species have been reared and should be added to the Table 1A list. Raybould reared *Simulium nigritarse* s.l. Coquillet (unpublished data) and *Simulium unicornutum* Pomeroy (Raybould and Grunewald 1975), and Raybould and Grunewald (unpublished data) independently reared *Simulium hargreavesi* Gibbins and *Simulium ruficorne* Macquart. Twinn (1936) observed *Cnephia lascivum* Twinn (synonym of *C. dacotensis*) mating in the lab; this reference should be added to Table 1B. *Simulium ornatum* Meigen and *Simulium yahense* (V. & D.), additions included at the last minute to the list of colonized species, also should be on the list of mated species.

LARVAL REARING

Edman and Simmons (1985) discussed in detail the three basic systems used to rear black flies. The following practical conclusions can be drawn from this account. Compressed-air systems best support complete development of relatively slow-current species and thus may be more limited in their use. Magnetic stir-bar systems are particularly useful for comparative studies since multiple units can be set up for different treatments or replicates. Recirculating troughs are generally used for large-scale rearing or colonization. Temperature control, filtration, and automatic feeding units provide added flexibility and efficiency to gravity-flow systems. Power failure is a common problem in developing countries; methods for dealing with temporary interruption of flow or for transfer to DC power during AC failure have been designed for some systems. Groud rabbit chow and Tetra fish food are the most common larval foods; diets are summarized in Edman and Simmons (1985).

Rearing larvae to adults with little mortality should not be taken as evidence that larval growth and development needs are fully met. We are relatively ignorant of black fly nutritional requirements, as well as pH and temperature optima. Still, developmental deficiencies can be surmised if emerging adults are smaller than normal. Survival, mating, blood feeding, and fecundity all have been observed to increase with body size (see examples below). Thus the size of reared flies should be monitored as carefully as the number. The upper size range of field populations is a good indicator of successful rearing. A small population of robust adults may lay more fertile eggs than a much larger population of smaller flies.

ADULT MAINTENANCE

Survivorship

Difficulty in maintaining adults for extended periods is common. Female survival for a complete gonotrophic cycle (4–6 days) is critical for colonization. Complete development of parasites such as *Onchocerca* spp. (Lok et al. 1980, 1983; Ham and Bianco 1983; Ham and Gale 1984) demands greater longevity (8–15 days). Rutschke and Grunewald (1984) described a simple apparatus for holding adults in which 50% of female *S. ornatum* survived 10 days and 25% of three temperate species survived 12–21 days. Females always outlived males. In one experiment with a mixed group of *Simulium damnosum* s.l., 20% survived 12 days. High relative humidity (RH) is maintained by forcing pumped air through a column of water in a plastic wash bottle before it passes through the darkened chamber in which flies are held in a series of polystyrene blocks. RH is regulated by the water column in the bottle; fungal growth is avoided by adding methyl-4-hydroxybenzoate (Rutschke and Grunewald 1984).

Ham and Bianco (1983) infected two of these same species with cryopreserved *Onchocerca volvulus* and reported 83% and 93% survival of *S. ornatum* and 52%

and 56% survival of *S. lineatum* held 7 days in constant darkness (19–20°C; 85–90% RH). Cupp (personal communication) obtained 73% survival of *S. yahense* in Liberia over the 7-day period between the infected blood meal and development of L3 filaria (26–28°C; 90–100% RH). Seasonal differences in survival were noted by Rutschke and Grunewald (1984). Simmons (1985) examined different size classes of *Simulium venustum* from field pupae; the number of small females was limited, but their survival was 2–3 days less on average. In blood-feeding studies, Wirtz (in press) noted that about 75% of blood-fed flies survived oogenesis. Together, these data show that acceptable survival of both infected and uninfected flies can be obtained if proper environmental conditions are provided. Darkened chambers with high RH but no surface moisture are ideal.

Mating

Failure of flies to mate has always been considered a major obstacle in colonization. The reason black flies mate so reluctantly in the lab is unknown, but the general consensus relates it to lack of swarming behavior. This hypothesis is not always true since some species known to swarm in nature mate on substrates in the lab. Other factors, particularly the production of vigorous adults, may be equally important. There are now 19 species (or forms) known to mate in captivity, and 11 of these have been maintained for at least one generation (Table 22.1).

Davies and Petersen (1956) observed North American black flies mating in confined tubes in the field. Lewis (1965) described the same phenomenon, which apparently had been observed earlier by Dunbar. Wenk (1965) applied the crowding technique later used to induce many other species to mate when he drew both sexes of *Boophthora erythrocephala* together in an aspirator tube and observed mating. We found aspirators to be the most effective tool for inducing *Simulium decorum* to mate (Simmons and Edman 1978) and subsequently used this technique to induce at least some mating by six additional species. However, for unknown reasons this technique does not work with all species. Other techniques for inducing mating also rely on Wenk's basic principle of spatial concentration. One is phototactic attraction of flies to a small area within their cage. We maintained *S. decorum* by this method for 30 generations after initial selection in aspirator tubes; Wenk and Raybould (1972) used it to induce *S. damnosum* Kibwezi form to mate; Cupp and colleagues

Table 22.1 Black fly species observed mating in the lab

*Cnephia dacotensis**	*Simulium equinum*
Prosimulium fuscum	*Simulium fibrinflatum*
Simulium bovis	*Simulium lineatum**
Simulium damnosum (Kibwezi)	*Simulium maculatum*
Simulium damnosum (Beffa)*	*Simulium ornatum**
Simulium damnosum (West Africa)*	*Simulium pictipes**
*Simulium squamosum**	*Simulium salopiense*
*Simulium yahense**	*Simulium venustum*
*Simulium decorum**	*Simulium vittatum**
*Simulium erythrocephalum**	

*Colonized for one generation or more.

relied on it when maintaining four different species (Brenner and Cupp 1980, Brenner et al. 1980, Cupp et al. 1981, Tarrant et al. 1983), as did Ham and Bianco (1984) in maintaining two temperate species.

When colonies are first established, mating rates may be low and then rise rapidly (Ham and Bianco 1984), or they may remain low for several early generations (Simmons and Edman 1981). When we colonized the Beffa form of *S. soubrense/sanctipauli* from just three egg masses, the sex ratio was distorted and almost no males were produced by F4 (Simmons and Edman 1982). Raybould and Boakye (in press) briefly established two cultures of this same sibling in West Africa, both from single egg batches, without alteration in sex ratios. Their main difficulty was inducing females to blood-feed.

All efforts to induce swarming in the lab have failed. Mokry et al. (1981) attempted to get *S. vittatum* to swarm in a greenhouse; Davies and Petersen (1956) played recordings of the wing beat and rushing water; Simmons (unpublished data) manipulated light levels and encouraged constant flight; Raybould (personal communication) put large numbers of *Simulium adersi* in a 3.7-meter-square outdoor cage containing a tree, chickens, and flowers. More knowledge of mating behavior is obviously needed. Wenk, who with colleagues has provided most information on this subject, provides a summary in Chapter 16. His and Mokry's observations that males may be attracted to the vicinity of hosts to intercept females may be exploited in stimulating lab mating in some species. Also, the temporal and physical (especially visual) aspects of swarms need to be examined carefully with a view toward incorporating commonly found features into the lab whenever feasible.

One reason lab mating of flies has been difficult to achieve in the past may relate to the health of adults produced. Using flies from field pupae may not always alleviate this problem, since they may have developed under suboptimal conditions as well. *Simulium decorum* reared at high density had only half the copulation rate of those reared at low density, and females were less fecund (Simmons and Edman 1981). In another lab experiment, males from high-density rearings were significantly smaller, attempted fewer matings, and inseminated fewer females than those from low-density rearings (Table 22.2).

Refractory sexual behavior is a common feature of both old- and new-world females. We frequently observed what appeared to be physically smaller male *S. decorum* failing to couple with refractory females, while larger males were able to struggle with uncooperative females and eventually make genital contact. When groups of males and females were held together five days and dissected and measured, inseminated females were both significantly larger and more fecund (Simmons 1982, Univ. of Mass., unpublished data). Rearing conditions can influence the reproductive success of both sexes.

Blood Feeding

Wirtz (1983, 1985a,b) studied factors influencing the feeding success of *S. erythrocephalum* and *S. lineatum* on hosts and artificial membranes, and of *S. damnosum* s.l. on membranes. Significant species differences were observed in optimum feeding conditions. Seasonal variation occurred in one case, but not in another (Wirtz 1985a). Similarly, holding wild-caught *S. lineatum* for 4 days reduced feeding, but

Table 22.2 Mating success of male *Simulium decorum* reared under stressed and unstressed conditions (15 replicates; 5 males and 5 females/rep; $N = 75$)

Treatment (larval)	X̄ Subcostal Length (mm) (± S.D.)	X̄ Copulations Attempted/Male (± S.D.)	X̄ No. Females Inseminated/Male (± S.D.)
Low diet	0.87a (±0.05)	1.47a (±1.06)*	1.13a (±1.25)
High diet	0.94b (±0.04)	6.53b (±2.17)	2.67b (±1.11)

*Numbers followed by a different letter are significantly different at $p < 0.01$ (student's *t*-test).

not so for *S. erythrocephalum*. In both, lab-emerged flies fed better than wild ones and 4–6-day-old flies fed better than younger or older ones.

These two species also behaved differently when fed through artificial membranes with an apparatus that kept blood warm and stirred (Wirtz 1985b). For example, maximum feeding by *S. lineatum* through a silicone membrane was at a blood/membrane temperature about 2°C higher than for *S. erythrocephalum*. The author tentatively relates this to the fact that *S. lineatum* feed inside the ears of cattle, where temperatures are higher. Differences in the optimum feeding temperature for the silicone and latex membranes were more difficult to explain. Both species fed better on silicone membranes than on ones of either latex or baudruche. More significantly, 10% stretching of latex or silicone membranes greatly enhanced feeding (Wirtz 1985b). Neither the type and treatment of blood nor the addition of phagostimulant (ATP) were as important as the membrane type, temperature, and stretch. *S. damnosum* s.l. also fed better on silicone than latex but fed best on baudruche; field flies fed better than lab-emerged flies (Wirtz and Raybould, in preparation). This species fed best when one day old, an important fact for those working with African vectors.

Using the feeding apparatus of Rutledge et al. (1964), Ham and Bianco (1985) fed their colonies heparinized fresh or deep-frozen calf blood. Blood temperature was kept at 37°C with a water jacket. Membranes were prepared from the skin of day-old chicks and deep frozen until needed. Whereas 75–99% of *S. erythrocephalum* fed during each generation, 51–63% of *S. lineatum* fed. About 50% of day-old *S. yahense* held on 10% sucrose fed on human volunteers in Liberia (Cupp, personal communication). Simmons (1985) observed that small *S. venustum* females from field pupae had significantly lower blood-feeding rates than larger flies (Table 22.3).

Oviposition

Boakye and Raybould (1985) compared the oviposition success of *S. damnosum* s.l. (mainly *squamosum*) by three techniques. The traditional immersion method was tried both during the day and in the evening under artificial light, along with a modification of the twilight method of Simmons and Edman (1982). Most flies deposited eggs, but nearly twice as many fertile eggs were laid when females were submitted to the twilight method (71% versus 37%). The immersion method may still have advantages for obtaining eggs from individuals; it works with all the *S. damnosum* group attempted, but not with the *S. neavei* group (Raybould, personal

Table 22.3 Relationship between size and blood-feeding rate of female *Simulium venustum* on the same human. Flies emerged from field pupae collected at two ecologically different sites on the Sawmill River, Massachusetts.

Black Fly Population	No. Tested	Feeding Rate* (%)	Subcostal Length[†] (mean ± S.D. in mm)
Lake outlet	137	58.4a[‡]	92.4a (±4.6)
Downstream	100	1.0b	83.5b (±4.8)

*Difference between feeding tested for significance by chi-square test.
[†]Difference between subcostal length tested for significance by student's *t*-test.
[‡]Numbers not followed by the same letter are significantly different at $p < 0.05$.

communication). The latter readily oviposit in tubes provided with a damp substrate (Raybould and Grunewald 1975).

Ham and Bianco (1984) developed a better oviposition method than the Brenner et al. (1980) method they employed initially. It includes covering both ends of a plastic ring with pieces of nylon mesh held by rubber bands. The net-covered ring containing gravid flies is placed into a standard petri dish with wet filter-paper disks in the bottom and lid. Chambers were subjected to daily crepuscular light cycles.

EGG STORAGE (MULTIVOLTINE TEMPERATE SPECIES)

Some investigators successfully store field-collected, nondiapausing eggs for several months. Efficiently done, this method can provide a year-round culture stock. It also allows literally "putting a colony on ice" during slack periods. Eggs normally die when frozen, but they will continue to develop slowly at only 2–3°C. Wet ice is the simplest, reliable medium for maintaining the narrow temperature range suitable for storing temperate fly eggs. Colbo (personal communication) suggests storing eggs inside a crushed-ice machine.

Unfortunately, not all storage attempts on wet ice are successful. We have never obtained the survivorship of *S. decorum* eggs reported by Tarshis (1968) and our Canadian colleagues. Duncan (personal communication) had similar experience with three European species (*S. ornatum, S. equinum,* and *S. erythrocephalum*). He obtained 80–90% hatch when eggs were collected, but no hatch 2–3 months later. Eggs in varying embryonic stages and collected from July through November were compared. Removal from their grass substrate with caustic soda, surface sterilization with Roccal, and exposure to a nitrogen atmosphere did not improve survivorship. We experience good survival of lab-produced *S. decorum* eggs for 1 month and at times for 2–3 months, but rarely longer. We scrape newly deposited eggs from the substrate and tease them apart to form a single layer on wet filter paper in petri dishes on wet ice.

Perhaps only some eggs in multilayered masses are at the proper state of development or insulation to survive cold-induced arrestment, and this is the cohort within field masses that hatches after extended storage. Observations on four temperate species by Imhof and Smith (1979) and on *S. damnosum* s.l. egg masses by Kyorku and Raybould (1982, Akisombo, Ghana, unpublished data) suggest that such could be the case. Marked differences in development rate and survival occurred at various layers within masses. Even when the bottom layer of *S. damnosum* eggs was exposed in flooded petri dishes, only about 30% hatched. Development was 8–10 days longer than for eggs in the top layer of control masses. No unexposed bottom-layer eggs hatched. Hatch rates were somewhat higher and development rates shorter for exposed bottom-layer eggs placed in a rearing trough. The influence of oxygen on egg development was compared using boiled, unboiled, and aerated water. As in the study of Ivashchenko (1977), oxygen seemed important, but even after they were exposed, bottom-layer eggs continued to develop more slowly than top-layer eggs. Raybould (personal communication) suggests that in shipping tropical eggs it may be best to remove the outer layers and thereby avoid in-transit hatching, since the bottom layer will develop more slowly.

Field observations in Ghana (Kyorku and Raybould 1982, unpublished data) indicated that bottom-layer eggs exposed 12 hours after oviposition still took one day longer to develop than top-layer eggs. Also, as they do in the lab, many bottom-layer eggs died. However, such eggs (i.e., with delayed development) may be commonly disrupted and hatch in nature. Scheduling of larviciding should take possible delayed hatching into account. Understanding the factors contributing to egg survival and developmental arrestment would improve storage procedures.

REMAINING PROBLEMS AND FUTURE APPLICATIONS

Some individuals will always have difficulty duplicating the techniques of others. Culturing insects is no exception. A "green thumb" seems to be involved in growing most organisms. Black flies are among the most difficult pest/vector species to culture, but all the major obstacles have now been solved by one group or another. Hence, it should be possible for any serious scientist to combine these successes and maintain colonies. Getting flies both to mate and blood-feed on demand and to survive routinely as long as desired is still difficult. Failure to recognize the importance of the "quality" of adult flies and their natural behavioral rhythms may be the greatest oversight in colonizing flies. More awareness of the age of flies, time of day, light level, and habitat of normal mating behavior could lead to greater copulation success in the lab. The same is true for both blood feeding and oviposition. Better survival rates may be achieved once the natural resting niches of flies are recognized. Black flies are visual-orienting animals, but pheromones and other chemical cues clearly modulate behavior as well. Studies on the sensory aspects of behavior could greatly assist efforts to manipulate behavior. Field studies of adult behavior should have a high priority.

Much time, effort, space, and money are required to establish and maintain colonies. In the end, all that is accomplished is the creation of a ready, albeit rare, supply of standardized experimental animals. The important question is how this new resource can be optimally exploited. If we accept the premise that better understanding should lead to better control prospects, the answer is intuitive. Information gaps on black flies are readily exposed by examining the table of contents in Laird's 1981 book. The chapter on physiology is but seven pages of mostly descriptive information rarely embraced by modern physiology. There are no data on biochemistry, endocrinology, or neuroscience. Genetics is not considered, except as broached in chapters on cytotaxonomy and species complexes. The explosion in genetics research on mosquitoes in the last twenty-five years may never lead to genetic control, but it has contributed immeasurably to our understanding of vector competence, insecticide resistance, host specificity, population interactions, and many other topics with application to contemporary mosquito problems. Recent behavioral studies on black fly feeding have been possible only as reliable methods for maintaining and observing larvae in the lab were developed (see chapters 15, 16, 17, and 18). The usefulness of lab cultures to study biological- and chemical-control agents and for growing the fly stages of human parasites is readily apparent to all. It is here where advances in rearing and colonization have had their most immediate impact.

ACKNOWLEDGMENTS

Several colleagues shared with us in-press or unpublished data; in particular, we thank Drs. John Raybould and Hans-Peter Wirtz.

LITERATURE CITED

Boakye, D. A., and J. N. Raybould. 1985. The effect of different methods of oviposition inducement on egg fertility rates in a *Simulium damnosum* complex species (Diptera: Simuliidae). *J. Am. Mosq. Control Assoc.* 1:535–537.

Brenner, R. J., and E. W. Cupp. 1980. Rearing black flies (Diptera: Simuliidae) in a closed system of water circulation. *Tropenmed. Parasitol.* 31:247–258.

Brenner, R. J., E. W. Cupp, and M. J. Bernardo. 1980. Laboratory colonization and life table statistics for geographic strains of *Simulium decorum* (Diptera: Simuliidae). *Tropenmed. Parasitol.* 31:487–497.

Cupp, E. W., J. B. Lok, M. J. Bernardo, R. J. Brenner, R. J. Pollack, and G. A. Scoles. 1981. Complete generation rearing of *Simulium damnosum* s.l. (Diptera: Simuliidae) in the laboratory. *Tropenmed. Parasitol.* 32:119–122.

Davies, D. M., and B. V. Petersen. 1956. Observations on the mating, feeding, ovarian development and oviposition of adult black flies (Diptera: Simuliidae). *Can. J. Zool.* 34:615–655.

Davies, L. 1965. On spermatophores in Simuliidae (Diptera). *Proc. R. Entomol. Soc. London* (A) 40:30–34.

Edman, J. D., and K. R. Simmons. 1985. Rearing and colonization of black flies (Diptera: Simuliidae): a review. *J. Med. Entomol.* 22:1–17.

Ham, P. J., and A. E. Bianco. 1983. Development of *Onchocerca volvulus* from cryopreserved microfilaria in three temperate species of laboratory-reared blackflies. *Tropenmed. Parasitol.* 34:137–139.

———. 1984. Maintenance of Simulium *Wilhelmia lineatum* Meigen and *Simulium erythro-*

cephalum De Geer through successive generations in the laboratory. *Can. J. Zool.* 62:870–877.

Ham, P. J., and G. I. Gale. 1984. Blood meal enhanced *Onchocerca* development and its correlation with fecundity in laboratory reared blackflies (Diptera: Simuliidae). *Tropenmed. Parasitol.* 35:212–216.

Imhof, J. E., and S. M. Smith. 1979. Oviposition behavior, egg-masses and hatching response of the eggs of five Nearctic species of *Simulium* (Diptera: Simuliidae). *Bull. Entomol. Res.* 69:405–425.

Ivashencko, L. A. 1977. The effect of oxygen and light on embryonic development and time of hatching of simuliid larvae (Diptera: Simuliidae). *Medskaya Paraszit.* 46:37–41.

Laird, M., Ed. 1981. *Blackflies: the future for biological methods in integrated control.* Academic Press. New York and London.

Lok, J. F., E. W. Cupp, and M. J. Bernardo. 1980. The development of *Oncocherca* spp. in *Simulium decorum* Walker and *Simulium pictipes* Hagen. *Tropenmed. Parasitol.* 31:498–506.

Lok, J. F., E. W. Cupp, M. J. Bernardo, and R. J. Pollack. 1983. Further studies on the development of *Onchocerca* spp. (Nematoda: Filarioidea) in Nearctic blackflies (Diptera: Simuliidae). *Am. J. Trop. Med. Hyg.* 32:1298–1305.

Mokry, J. E., M. H. Colbo, and B. H. Thompson. 1981. Laboratory colonization of blackflies. Pp. 299–307 in M. Laird, Ed., *Blackflies: the future of biological methods in integrated control.* Academic Press, New York and London.

Raybould, J. N. 1981. Present progress towards the laboratory colonization of members of the *Simulium damnosum* Complex. Pp. 307–318 in M. Laird, Ed., *Blackflies: the future for biological methods in integrated control.* Academic Press, New York and London.

Raybould, J. N., and D. A. Boakye. 1986. Temporary small-scale colonization of the Beffa form of the *Simulium damnosum* complex (Diptera: Simuliidae) in Africa. *J. Am. Mosq. Control Assoc.* 2 (in press).

Raybould, J. N., and J. Grunewald. 1975. Present progress towards the laboratory colonization of African Simuliidae (Diptera). *Tropenmed. Parasitol.* 27:155–168.

Rutledge, L. C., R. A. Ward, and D. J. Gould. 1964. Studies on the feeding response of mosquitoes to nutritive solutions in a new membrane feeder. *Mosquito News* 24:407–419.

Rutschke, J., and J. Grunewald. 1984. A simple apparatus for maintaining black fly adults (Simuliidae) in the laboratory. *Mosquito News* 44:461–465.

Simmons, K. R., and J. D. Edman. 1978. Successful mating, oviposition and complete generation rearing of the multivoltine black fly *Simulium decorum* (Diptera: Simuliidae) in the laboratory. *Can. J. Zool.* 56:1223–25.

———. 1981. Sustained colonization of the black fly *Simulium decorum* Walker (Diptera: Simuliidae). *Can. J. Zool.* 59:1–7.

———. 1982. Laboratory colonization of the human onchocerciasis vector *Simulium damnosum* complex (Diptera: Simuliidae), using an enclosed, gravity-trough rearing system. *J. Med. Entomol.* 19:117–126.

Simmons, K. R. 1985. Reproductive ecology of *Simulium venustum* Say (Diptera: Simuliidae). Ph.D. Diss., University of Massachusetts, Amherst. 204 pp.

Tarrant, C., S. Moobola, G. Scoles, and E. W. Cupp. 1983. Mating and oviposition of laboratory-reared *Simulium vittatum* (Diptera: Simuliidae). *Can. Entomol.* 115:319–323.

Tarshis, I. B. 1968. Collecting and rearing black flies. *Ann. Entomol. Soc. Am.* 61:1072–83.

Twinn, C. R. 1936. The black flies of Eastern Canada (Simuliidae: Diptera). *Can. J. Res. D.* 1495:95, 150.

Wenk, P. 1965. Über die Biologie blutsaugender Simuliiden. III. Kopulation, Blutsaugen und

Eiablage von *Boophthora erythrocephala* De Geer im Laboratorium. *Z. Tropenmed. Parasitol.* 16:207–226.

Wenk, P. and J. N. Raybould. 1972. Mating, blood feeding and oviposition of *Simulium damnosum* Theobald in the laboratory. *Bull. WHO* 47:627–634.

Wirtz, H. P. 1983. Nahrungsaufnahme und Natalitaet bei palaearktischen und Afrikanischen Simuliiden (Diptera). Ph.D. Diss., University of Tübingen, West Germany.

———. 1985a. Nahrungsaufnahme und Natalitaet bei palaerktischen Simuliiden (Diptera) 1. Blutfuetterung von *Boophthora erythrocephala* De Geer und *Wilhelmia lineata* Meigen am Kaninchen. *Anz. Schaedlk., Pflanzenschutz, Umw. Schutz.* 58:1–10.

———. 1985b. Nahrungsaufnahme und Natalitaet bei palaearktischen Simuliiden (Diptera) 2. Blutfuetterung von *Boophthora erythrocephala* De Geer, 1776 und *Wilhelmia lineata* Meigen, 1804 durch Membranen. *Z. ang. Entomol.* 99:377–393.

23   THE ECOLOGY OF BLACK FLY PARASITES

Daniel P. Molloy

Ecological black fly parasitology is an area of investigation that stems from basic studies of the interrelationships of black flies, their parasites, and the environment. Since relatively few such studies have been conducted, this discipline is only in its early developmental stages. Investigating the ecology of organisms that parasitize black flies, however, is important, since the knowledge gained from such research increases both our understanding of the nature of parasitism and the likelihood of the successful development of biological agents for black fly control.

Black flies, as other animal groups, have a wide variety of parasites, all of which exhibit interesting differences in their approach toward host exploitation. This chapter summarizes information on black fly parasitology and attempts to interpret it in light of some current ecological concepts. How black flies and their parasites interact at both the individual and population levels is discussed, as well as the factors that determine the establishment and size of parasite populations.

Among multicellular organisms that utilize black flies as hosts, endoparasitic mermithid nematodes and ectoparasitic mites have been the most commonly reported. All recorded microbial parasites have been endoparasitic and have included viruses, fungi, and protozoans. Although bacteria have occasionally been isolated from field-collected black flies, none have yet to be identified as primary pathogens. Although the bacterium *Bacillus thuringiensis* var. *israelensis* is the first biological agent commercialized for black fly control (Gaugler and Finney 1982, Guillet 1984), this chapter is limited to naturally-occurring parasites of black flies, and thus discussion of this bacterium is not included here. Also excluded are trichomycete fungi (commensals that attach themselves to gut cuticle; see Moss [1979]), parasitoid Hymenoptera (rarely reported; see Jenkins [1964] and Crosskey [1954]), and parasites of vertebrates for which black flies serve as intermediate hosts (e.g., *Onchocerca* spp. and *Leucocytozoon* spp.). The reader is also referred to a recent review of black fly parasitology (Weiser and Undeen 1981) and several papers focusing on mermithid parasites (Finney 1981, Molloy 1981, Poinar 1981, Gordon 1984).

Lastly, the author wishes to acknowledge a text on the ecology of animal parasites (Kennedy 1975) that, in addition to providing considerable food for thought, provided an excellent overall framework from which to develop the following discussion.

ASPECTS OF THE HOST-PARASITE SYSTEM

Approaches to Invading the Black Fly

The methods used to gain entrance onto or into a black fly are known for just a few parasites. The following few examples, however, are revealing of the variety of strategies employed. *Per os* infection of early through mid-instars with cytoplasmic polyhedrosis virus has been reported (Bailey 1977). Newly hatched preparasites of the mermithid *Mesomermis flumenalis* crawl on the streambed in search of black fly larvae and then enter the hemocoel following penetration of the integument (Molloy 1981). Transovarian transmission of the microsporidian *Tuzetia debaisieux* has recently been demonstrated (Tarrant 1984). Larval mites enter black fly pupal cocoons and attach themselves to emerging adults (Gledhill et al. 1982). Thus, while relatively little data are available, it is evident that a wide variety of strategies are employed by parasites to initiate infection of their black fly hosts.

Commencement of Infection

The successful commencement of infection in a black fly is the result of a variety of factors, including:

1. *Ecological conditions:* The host and parasite must concurrently share a similar microhabitat for infection to commence, and synchronization of parasite and host life cycles increases the probability of this contact. Mermithid life cycles, for example, are synchronized with those of their hosts, with the hatch of infective preparasites occurring during periods when susceptible larvae are present (Ezenwa 1974a, Molloy 1979, Colbo and Porter 1980).

2. *Host defenses:* A parasite might be unsuccessful in penetrating a host's defenses due to the host's behavior or morphology. Larvae being attacked by preparasitic mermithids of *Mesomermis flumenalis* struggled vigorously and at times were capable of mortally wounding attacking nematodes (Molloy 1981). The morphology of the pupa and its case could be an important factor in determining which black fly species are successfully infected by *Sperchon* water-mite larvae. Species whose pupal bodies were tightly appressed to the entrance of their pupal cases had lower infection rates, in theory because this prevented easy access into the pupal chamber (Gledhill et al. 1982).

Maintenance of Stability of Parasite and Black Fly Populations

The concept of stability in a host-parasite system is more applicable at the *population* than at the *individual* level. For example, the effect of a virulent parasite upon an individual black fly might be quite severe and lead rapidly to the fly's death. Thus at the individual level the relationship may be very unstable; however, this does not necessarily mean that the population levels of both host and the parasite could not be quite stable over time. Thus for a host-parasite system to be in equilibrium, stability at the *population* level is the critical element. An indication of the stability of black fly parasite systems is the perennial low-level enzootic infection rates that are so typical of black fly diseases. Very high rates of infection are occasionally reported, but caution must be used in interpreting such "epizootics," since uninfected individuals of the same cohort may well have already emerged. Overinfection of a host population is always a potential danger to a parasite population, and negative feedback controls often operate in host-parasite systems to regulate parasite population levels. Such checks on parasite population growth often operate with increasing severity as the parasite population increases, e.g., increased intraspecific competition and decreased reproductive rate. Mermithid parasites of black flies clearly illustrate these latter two types of density-dependent feedbacks: (1) high densities of preparasitic mermithids cause premature death in early-instar hosts as a result of superparasitism (i.e., high numbers of parasites/ host) (Molloy and Jamnback 1975); (2) high rates of mermithid infection normally coincide with high frequencies of superparasitized black flies, which in turn results predominantly in the production of male mermithids (Ezenwa 1974b, Hominick and Tingley 1984).

Host Specificity

The majority of black fly parasites appear to have a broad host range. Field sampling data indicate that for an individual parasite species a number of black fly species can serve as hosts (Roberts and Strand 1977, Roberts and Castillo 1980, Roberts et al. 1983). However, host-specificity statements, particularly at the species level, must be made cautiously because of systematic problems both among black flies (e.g., prevalence of sibling species) and in most parasite groups. A good example of this is the apparent broad host range of *Coelomycidium simulii*—the most commonly reported and ubiquitous fungal parasite of black flies in the world. These frequent and widespread reports of this fungus in black fly populations have raised the question of whether *C. simulii* may actually be a complex of species. Ultrastructural studies of strains from California (Federici et al. 1977), France (Loubes and Manier 1974), and Czechoslovakia (Weiser and Zizka 1974a,b) have provided some evidence of contrasting morphological features, but they are insufficient to justify taxonomic revision at this time.

When the specificity of both parasites and black flies are examined at the generic level, a broad host range is generally evident (Table 23.1). Among mermithids, fungi, protozoans, and viruses, broad host ranges are particularly evident, respectively, among *Isomermis*, *Coelomycidium*, *Pleistophora*, and cytoplasmic polyhedrosis virus. Conversely, relatively narrow specificity appears among *Hydromermis*, *Tetrahymena*, and iridescent virus. The relatively large numbers of *Simulium* spp. recorded as hosts for all parasite groups is no doubt a reflection not only of the large number of species in the genus but also the research emphasis placed on this genus due to its vector capacity.

Table 23.1 Host range of parasites among black fly genera and species[a]

Parasite	Numbers of Species of Black Flies Recorded as Hosts							
	Austrosimulium	Cnephia	Eusimulium	Gigantodax	Gymnopais	Prosimulium	Simulium	Stegopterna
MERMITHIDS								
Gastromermis	—	3	7	2	—	4	61	3
Hydromermis	—	—	4	—	—	—	20	1
Isomermis	—	—	2	1	—	1	3	—
Limnomermis	—	2	1	—	—	—	18	1
Mesomermis	—	1	—	1	—	3	5	—
FUNGI								
Coelomycidium	—	1	2	1	—	3	15	—
Entomophthora	—	1	—	1	—	1	12	—
Ovarian phycomycete	—	—	1	—	—	1	3	—
Simuliomyces	—	—	1	—	—	1	—	—
PROTOZOANS								
Amblyospora	1	—	4	1	1	5	69	1
Caudospora	—	—	1	1	—	—	6	—
Haplosporidium	—	—	—	—	—	3	2	1
Nosema	—	—	—	—	—	—	1	—
Octosporea	—	—	—	—	—	—	1	—
Pegmatheca	—	—	—	—	—	—	1	—
Pleistophora	1	—	3	—	—	—	23	—
Stempellia	—	—	—	—	—	—	2	—
Tetrahymena	—	—	—	—	—	—	3	—
Thelohania	—	—	—	—	—	1	29	—
Weiseria	—	—	—	—	1	1	—	—
VIRUSES								
Cytoplasmic polyhedrosis	—	—	—	—	—	1	11	1
Densonucleosis (see footnote in text)	—	—	—	—	—	1	5	1
Iridescent	—	—	—	—	—	—	5	—

[a]This table lists the number of species of black flies that have been recorded as hosts for individual genera of parasites. It was produced solely from bibliographic sources covering literature up to 1981 (Roberts and Strand 1977, Roberts and Castillo 1980, Roberts et al. 1983) and should be viewed only as a general indication of parasite specificity. Inclusion of post-1981 literature would certainly broaden this host list. Black fly generic classification follows Crosskey (1981).

Table 23.2 Location of parasites within black flies

PROTOZOANS	
Ciliates	Hemocoel (Lynn et al. 1981, Batson 1983b).
Microsporidia	Primarily fat body, also hemocytes, pigment cells, endocrine glands, corpora alata (Maurand and Manier 1968); nerve cord (Vavra and Undeen 1981); silk glands (Issi 1968); pericardial cells, hypodermis (Maurand 1975); Malpighian tubules (Weiser and Undeen 1981); epithelium of the midgut and hindgut (Mitrokhin 1979); eggs (Tarrant 1984); hemolymph and ovaries (C. Tarrant, personal communication).
FUNGI	
Coelomycidium simulii	Primarily fat body, also integument, hemocytes, pigment cells, gonads, nervous system (Maurand and Manier 1968).
Ovarian phycomycete	Ovaries, possibly also fat body (Yeboah et al. 1984).
Entomophthorales	Earliest stages observed in hemocoel (Kramer 1983); fungus proliferates throughout entire body of cadaver.
VIRUSES	
Cytoplasmic polyhedrosis	Cytoplasm of midgut epithelium and gastric caeca (Bailey et al. 1975, Weiser 1978).
Densonucleosis (see footnote in text)	Nuclei of midgut epithelium and fat body (Federici 1976, Federici and Lacey 1976).
Iridescent	Cytoplasm of oenocytes, fat body, tracheal epithelium, connective tissue covering neural ganglia, muscles, cuticle, hypodermis (Weiser 1968, Batson et al. 1976).
MERMITHIDS	Hemocoel; primarily in abdomen (Molloy 1981, Gordon 1984).
MITES	Engorgement primarily on thorax or neck (Davies 1959, Gledhill et al. 1982).

PHYSIOLOGICAL HOST-PARASITE INTERACTIONS

Location of Infection

Virtually all parasites inhabit precise sites within or on the black fly, to the extent of preferring specific regions or parts of an organ (Table 23.2). Some, like cytoplasmic polyhedrosis virus, have rigid site selection, while others, like iridescent virus and *Coelomycidium simulii,* do not. It is generally unknown why certain sites are chosen and by what mechanism the site is located. The preference of so many intracellular parasites for fat body tissue, however, is understandable, since it is a nutrient storage organ. Even within an organ, there are precise areas that parasites occupy: while the epithelial lining of the midgut is the site of infection for both cytoplasmic polyhedrosis and "densonucleosis"* viruses, they replicate only in the cytoplasm and nucleus, respectively.

---

*Identification of a pathogen found in *Simulium vittatum* as a "densonucleosis virus" (Federici and Lacey 1976) needs to be reconsidered; the pathogen might better have been referred to as a "virus-like" particle (L. Lacey, personal communication).

Table 23.3 Effects of parasitism on black flies

PROTOZOANS

Ciliates

Infection apparently benign in larval and pupal hosts due likely to lower intensity of infection; hosts without overt physical or behavioral abnormalities (Lynn et al. 1981, Batson 1983b); reduced fat body in adults with advanced infection (11,000–19,000 ciliates/fly); dramatic increase of intensity of infection in adults to lethal levels, with death within 2–4 days posteclosion at 15°C (Batson 1983b).

Microsporidia

Lethal in patently infected larvae (Maurand 1975); apparently innocuous in adults, which transmit infection vertically (Tarrant 1984); fat body lobes in larvae considerably hypertrophied, giving abnormal abdominal distortion, with fat body typically opaque white, occasionally red (Vavra and Undeen 1981); lower larval oxygen consumption (Maurand 1975, Boemare and Maurand 1976); retarded development of gonads and histoblasts (Maurand 1975); lengthens duration of larval stage, with infected larvae larger due to additional instars (Maurand 1975); reduces the stamina or responses of the host, resulting in significantly less larval drifting (Adler et al. 1983) [*contrasting finding:* infected larvae had a lowered ability to stay on the substratum in a current and entered the drift more frequently than healthy larvae (Mitrokhin 1979)].

FUNGI

Coelomycidium simulii

Lethal in patently infected larvae (Tarrant 1984); sporangia developing within the integument appear as numerous circles, while those in the body cavity appear as spheres suspended within the hemolymph; sporangia give a white (unpublished personal observation) to pink (Weiser 1978) coloration to abdomen; head capsule size of lab-reared, patently infected larvae not significantly different from uninfected larvae in same cohort (Tarrant 1984); increase in larval size (Rubtsov 1969); growth of thalli destroys fat body and gonads (Rubtsov 1969); usually retardation in development of histoblasts.

Ovarian phycomycete

Nonlethal (Yeboah et al. 1984); no detectable external signs of infection in adults (Yeboah et al. 1984); no effect seen on size of adult female flies (Colbo 1982); results in destruction of the tissues of an infected ovary, with mature eggs rarely found (Yeboah et al. 1984); evidence that infected flies are rendered incapable of a second gonotrophic cycle and do not take a second blood meal, thus eliminating vector potential (Yeboah 1980).

Entomophthorales

Erynia curvispora (Kramer 1983), *Entomophthora culicis* (Shemanchuk and Humber 1978), and *Simuliomyces lairdi* (Nam and Dubitskij 1978) are lethal; larvae infected with *Simuliomyces lairdi* characterized by an enlarged, dull-colored abdomen (Nam and Dubitskij 1978).

VIRUSES

Cytoplasmic polyhedrosis

Apparently innocuous and nonlethal disease (Bailey 1977, Weiser 1978) [*contrasting finding:* potentially lethal (Mokry 1978)]; gastric caeca and the anterior and posterior thirds of the midgut usually have an opaque chalky appearance (rarely the entire midgut) due to the proliferation of virus in the cytoplasm of hypertrophied epithelial cells (Bailey et al. 1975, Weiser 1978); infected last-instar larvae were significantly smaller (Bailey 1977) [*contrasting finding:* Weiser (1978) did not note a reduction in the size of infected larvae].

Densonucleosis
(see footnote in text)

Not highly pathogenic (L. Lacey, personal communication); hypertrophy of the nuclei of midgut epithelium and fat body; localized atrophy of fat body; cuticle translucent, with melanized cells distributed irregularly throughout most larval tissues (Federici 1976, Federici and Lacey 1976).

Table 23.3 (continued)

Iridescent	Patently infected larvae die without pupating (Weiser and Undeen 1981); infected larvae with bluish to bluish-violet opalescence (Weiser 1968, Batson et al. 1976, Avery and Bauer 1984).
MERMITHIDS	Lethal (Gordon 1984); affects of parasitism may include prevention of metamorphosis (Molloy 1979), sterility (Mondet et al. 1976), intersexual development (Rubtsov 1958), reduced muscle tissue (Peterson 1960); decrease in adult size possible, but not always (Colbo 1982); infected adult females lived only half as long as noninfected females (Mondet et al. 1976).
MITES	Affects unknown, except for reduced longevity of parasitized adults noted under laboratory conditions (Semushin 1981).

Effect on the Black Fly by the Parasite

The effects of some parasites upon their hosts may be severe and invariably lead to their deaths (e.g., mermithids), while others appear to be almost benign at times (e.g., cytoplasmic polyhedrosis) (Table 23.3). Infection typically results in atrophied development of a variety of black fly tissues and organs. Parasitism of black fly larvae frequently prevents pupation, and Condon and Gordon (1977) have suggested that this is probably a consequence of severe nutrient depletion rather than an active manipulation of the black fly's hormonal system by the parasite. Deriving its nutrition from the host is of obvious benefit to the parasite, but if parasite nourishment prevents host metamorphosis, then the parasite will be limited to the immature stage of the host, thereby inhibiting its dispersal. Colbo (1982), noting that parasitic development depleted host energies, suggested that poorly nourished simuliid populations may not be capable of supporting certain parasite populations, particularly those that require interstadial passage from larva through adult.

Effect of the Black Fly on the Parasite

Certain parasites appear to be dependent on physiological stimuli from the black fly for their development. This is most apparent with the ovarian phycomycete and ciliates, both of which are carried over into the pupa and adult. Although larvae harbor infection, rapid production of spores of the ovarian phycomycete only occurs when the female fly becomes an adult, suggesting that the fungus is responding to the same stimulus that initiates ovarian development (Yeboah et al. 1984). The ciliate parasite *Tetrahymena dimorpha* remains at unusually low population levels in the larval host, followed by rapid multiplication in the pupa and adult. This has prompted Batson (1983b) to suggest that possibly the reproductive cycle of *T. dimorpha* was controlled by the presence or absence of key nutrients within the flies.

DISPERSAL OF PARASITES

Parasitism of *adult* simuliids is advantageous to parasite populations, since it provides a potential mechanism for dispersal of the parasites to neighboring streams and allows recolonization of upstream areas via ovipositing flies. Dispersal also aids in reducing overcrowding of the parasite population with its resultant mortality. Parasites that typically kill their black fly host prior to its emergence thus limit their potential for dispersal. Examples of parasites that likely benefit significantly from dispersal in their adult hosts include ciliates (Corliss et al. 1979), Entomophthorales (Shemanchuk and Humber 1978, Kramer 1983), mermithids (Colbo and Porter 1980), microsporidia (Tarrant 1984), mites (Gledhill et al. 1982), and the ovarian phycomycete (Yeboah et al. 1984).

Successful dispersal can require morphological adaptations by the parasite. Several species of microsporidia have spores with conspicuous appendages that might possibly assist them in flotation, dispersal, and ingestion (reviewed in Batson 1983a).

It would appear that parasites can modify black fly behavior to facilitate dispersal. Although infected adults are normally sterile, Davies (1958) reported mermithid-infected females with gravid females in oviposition flights. Similarly, Peterson (1960) reported castrated adults (both males and females) over the headwaters of a river flying with mating and ovipositing flies and having worms extruding from their anal orifices. The spores of the ovarian phycomycete are "oviposited" by infected females (Yeboah et al. 1984), which suggests that the fungus may be modifying host behavior.

ALTERNATE HOSTS

The demonstration of obligate alternate hosts in the life cycles of fungal (Whisler et al. 1975) and microsporidian (Sweeney et al. 1985) parasites of mosquitoes has raised some speculation as to whether such heteroecism might occur in the life cycle of black fly parasites. This author believes there is a high likelihood of obligate alternate hosts being involved in the life cycles of a number of parasites of black flies, particularly those parasites that have yet to be successfully transmitted in the laboratory, e.g., *Coelomycidium simulii* and microsporidians. The prior demonstration of the need for alternate hosts in the life cycle of the mosquito parasites is a reflection of the relatively large research effort in mosquito *versus* black fly parasitology. Of course, one does not have to look very far (e.g., *Onchocerca* spp., *Leucocytozoon* spp.) to see that heteroecism can be an essential element in the life cycle of black fly parasites.

CONCLUSIONS

A wide diversity of organisms are parasitic in black flies, and the ecology of these organisms is, at best, only poorly understood. Investigations of black fly diseases are shifting from qualitative, descriptive studies to more quantitative analyses. This is a positive development, since the manipulations of parasites to induce long-term epizootics in black fly populations will require a far better (i.e., quantitative) understanding of the ecology of these parasites than presently exists. The research challenges that lie ahead are formidable, but they may be highly rewarding. Research needs to be continued toward elucidation of parasite life cycles, particularly toward investigating the likelihood of heteroecism.

As researchers, it is of interest to reflect on the fact that we are really just brief spectators in the evolution of relationships between black flies and their parasites. These relationships, like any relationship between two organisms, are not static and unchanging. The behavior, ecology, and physiology of present-day parasites and their black fly hosts do not in any sense represent the culmination of the evolutionary process; instead, they reflect the current status of an ongoing series of host-parasite manipulations and retaliations.

POSTSCRIPT

Recently Moss and Descals (1986) concluded that the parasite commonly referred to as the "ovarian phycomycete" was actually a trichomycete fungus in the order Harpellales. Their finding represents a major breakthrough toward resolving the taxonomy of this fungus. Their identification of this pathogenic fungus as a trichomycete is also significant, since members of this group were previously thought to have only commensal relationships with their black fly hosts (Moss 1979).

ACKNOWLEDGMENTS

Special thanks to Barbara Griffin for assistance in the tabulation of data for this chapter. Continuing financial support from the National Institutes of Health (AI–15605) is gratefully appreciated. Contribution No. 470 of the New York State Science Service.

LITERATURE CITED

Adler, P. H., R. W. Light, and K. C. Kim. 1983. The aquatic drift patterns of black flies (Diptera: Simuliidae). *Hydrobiologia* 107:183–191.

Avery, S. W., and L. Bauer. 1984. Iridescent virus from *Prosimulium* collected in Maine. *J. Invertebr. Pathol.* 43:430–431.

Bailey, C. H. 1977. Field and laboratory observations on a cytoplasmic polyhedrosis virus of blackflies (Diptera: Simuliidae). *J. Invertebr. Pathol.* 29:69–73.

Bailey, C. H., M. Shapiro, and R. R. Granados. 1975. A cytoplasmic polyhedrosis virus from the larval blackflies *Cnephia mutata* and *Prosimulium mixtum* (Diptera: Simuliidae). *J. Invertebr. Pathol.* 25:273–274.

Batson, B. S. 1983a. A light and electron microscopic study of *Hirsutusporos austrosimulii* gen. n., sp. n., (Microspora: Nosematidae), a parasite of *Austrosimulium* sp. (Diptera: Simuliidae) in New Zealand. *Protistologica* 19:263–280.

————. 1983b. *Tetrahymena dimorpha* sp. nov. (Hymenostomatida: Tetrahymenidae), a new ciliate parasite of Simuliidae (Diptera) with potential as a model for the study of ciliate morphogenesis. *Phil. Trans. R. Soc. London (B) Biol. Sci.* 301:345–363.

Batson, B. S., M. R. L. Johnston, M. K. Arnold, and D. C. Kelly. 1976. An iridescent virus from *Simulium* sp. (Diptera: Simuliidae) in Wales. *J. Invertebr. Pathol.* 27:133–135.

Boemare, N., and J. Maurand. 1976. Investigations on the respiratory metabolism of healthy and microsporidian infected *Simulium* larvae. *Bull. Soc. Zool. Fr.* 101:377–385 (in French with French and English summaries).

Colbo, M. H. 1982. Size and fecundity of adult Simuliidae (Diptera) as a function of stream habitat, year and parasitism. *Can. J. Zool.* 60:2507–13.

Colbo, M. H., and G. N. Porter. 1980. Distribution and specificity of Mermithidae (Nematoda) infecting Simuliidae (Diptera) in Newfoundland. *Can. J. Zool.* 58:1483–90.

Condon, W. J., and R. Gordon. 1977. Some effects of mermithid parasitism on the larval blackflies *Prosimulium mixtum fuscum* and *Simulium venustum*. *J. Invertebr. Pathol.* 29:56–62.

Corliss, J. O., D. Berl, and M. Laird. 1979. A note on the occurrence of the ciliate *Tetrahymena,* potential biocontrol agent, in the blackfly vector of onchocerciasis from Ivory Coast. *Trans. Am. Microsc. Soc.* 98:587–591.

Crosskey, R. W. 1954. Infection of *Simulium damnosum* with *Onchocerca volvulus* during the wet season in Northern Nigeria. *Ann. Trop. Med. Parasitol.* 57:152–159.

————. 1981. Simuliid taxonomy—the contemporary scene. Pp. 3–18 in M. Laird, Ed., *Blackflies: the future for biological methods in integrated control.* Academic Press, New York and London.

Davies, D. M. 1958. Some parasites of Canadian black flies (Diptera, Simuliidae). *Proc. Int. Congr. Zool.* 15:660–661.

————. 1959. The parasitism of black flies (Diptera, Simuliidae) by larval water mites mainly of the genus *Sperchon*. *Can. J. Zool.* 37:353–369.

Ezenwa, A. O. 1974a. Ecology of Simuliidae, Mermithidae, and Microsporida in Newfoundland freshwaters. *Can. J. Zool.* 52:557–565.

————. 1974b. Studies on host-parasite relationships of Simuliidae with mermithids and microsporidans. *J. Parasitol.* 60:809–813.

Federici, B. A. 1976. Pathology and histochemistry of a densonucleosis virus in larvae of the blackfly, *Simulium vittatum*. Pp. 341–342 in *Proc. 1st Int. Colloq. on Invertebr. Pathol.* Queen's Univ., Kingston, Ontario.

Federici, B. A., and L. A. Lacey. 1976. Densonucleosis virus and cytoplasmic polyhedrosis virus diseases in larvae of the blackfly, *Simulium vittatum*. *Proc. Pap. Ann. Conf. Calif. Mosq. Control Assoc.* 44:124.

Federici, B. A., L. A. Lacey, and M. S. Mulla. 1977. *Coelomycidium simulii:* a fungal pathogen in larvae of *Simulium vittatum* from the Colorado River. *Proc. Pap. Ann. Conf. Calif. Mosq. Control Assoc.* 45:110–113.

Finney, J. R. 1981. Potential of mermithids for control and *in vitro* culture. Pp. 325–333 in M. Laird, Ed., *Blackflies: the future for biological methods in integrated control.* Academic Press, New York and London.

Gaugler, R., and J. R. Finney. 1982. A review of *Bacillus thuringiensis* var. *israelensis* (serotype 14) as a biological control agent of black flies (Simuliidae). Pp. 1–17 in D. Molloy, Ed., *Biological control of black flies (Diptera: Simuliidae) with* Bacillus thuringiensis var. israelensis *(Serotype 14): a review with recommendations for laboratory and field protocol.* Misc. Publ. Entomol. Soc. Am. 12(4).

Gledhill, T., J. Cowley, and R. J. M. Gunn. 1982. Some aspects of the host:parasite relationships between adult blackflies (Diptera; Simuliidae) and larvae of the water-mite *Sperchon setiger* (Acari; Hydrachnellae) in a small chalk stream in southern England. *Freshwater Biol.* 12:345–357.

Gordon, R. 1984. Nematode parasites of blackflies. Pp. 821–847 in W. R. Nickle, Ed., *Plant and insect nematodes*. Marcel Dekker, New York.

Guillet, P. 1984. The control of human onchocerciasis and the prospects for biological agents. *Entomophaga* 29:121–132 (in French with French and English summaries).

Hominick, W. M., and G. A. Tingley. 1984. Mermithid nematodes and the control of insect vectors of human disease. *Commonw. Inst. Biol. Control Biocontrol News Inf.* 5:7–20.

Issi, I. V. 1968. *Stempellia rubtsovi* sp. n. (Microsporidia, Nosematidae), a microsporidian parasite of *Odagmia caucasica* larvae (Diptera, Simuliidae). *Acta Protozool.* 6:345–352 (in Russian with Russian and English summaries).

Jenkins, D. W. 1964. Pathogens, parasites, and predators of medically important arthropods: annotated list and bibliography. *Bull. WHO* 30 (suppl.). 150 pp.

Kennedy, C. R. 1975. *Ecological animal parasitology*. John Wiley & Sons, New York. 163 pp.

Kramer, J. P. 1983. A mycosis of the black fly *Simulium decorum* (Simuliidae) caused by *Erynia curvispora* (Entomophthoraceae). *Mycopathologia* 82:39–43.

Loubes, C., and J. F. Manier. 1974. Ultrastructural study of *Coelomycidium simulii* Debaisieux, 1920: its systematic position among the Chytridiomycetes. *Protistologica* 10:47–57 (in French with French and English summaries).

Lynn, D. H., D. Molloy, and R. LeBrun. 1981. *Tetrahymena rotunda* n. sp. (Hymenostomatida: Tetrahymenidae), a ciliate parasite of the hemolymph of *Simulium* (Diptera: Simuliidae). *Trans. Am. Microsc. Soc.* 100:134–141.

Maurand, J. 1975. Microsporidia in *Simulium* larvae: systematic, ecological, pathological and cytochemical data. *Ann. Parasitol. Hum. Comp.* 50:371–396 (in French with French and English summaries).

Maurand, J., and J. F. Manier. 1968. Comparative histopathological effects of coelomic parasites (Chytridiales: Microsporides) of simuliid larvae. *Ann. Parasitol. Hum. Comp.* 43:79–85 (in French with French and English summaries).

Mitrokhin, V. U. 1979. The infection of black flies (Simuliidae) with microsporidians in water bodies of the Ob and Irtish Rivers. *Parazitologiya* (Leningrad) 13:245–249 (in Russian with Russian and English summaries).

Mokry, J. E. 1978. Progress towards the colonization of *Cnephia mutata* (Diptera: Simuliidae). *Bull. WHO* 56:455–456.

Molloy, D. 1979. Description and bionomics of *Mesomermis camdenensis* n. sp. (Mermithidae), a parasite of black flies (Simuliidae). *J. Nematol.* 11:321–328.

———. 1981. Mermithid parasitism of black flies (Diptera: Simuliidae). *J. Nematol.* 13:250–256.

Molloy, D., and H. Jamnback. 1975. Laboratory transmission of mermithids parasitic in blackflies. *Mosquito News* 35:337–342.

Mondet, B., B. Pendriez, and J. Bernadou. 1976. Study of the parasitism of simuliids (Diptera) by Mermithidae (Nematoda) in West Africa. 1. Preliminary observations on a temporary savannah water course. *Cah. ORSTOM sér. Entomol. Méd. Parasitol.* 14:141–149 (in French with French and English summaries).

Moss, S. T. 1979. Commensalism of the Trichomycetes. Pp. 175–227 in L. R. Batra, Ed., *Insect-fungus symbiosis: nutrition, mutualism, and commensalism*. Allanheld, Osmun, Montclair, New Jersey.

Moss, S. T., and E. Descals. 1986. A previously undescribed stage in the life cycle of Harpellales (Trichomycetes). *Mycologia* 78:213–222.

Nam, E. A., and A. M. Dubitskij. 1978. A description of a new regulator of the numbers of bloodsucking blackflies, the fungus *Simuliomyces lairdi* g. n. sp. n. (Entomophthorales). *Vestn. Akad. Nauk Kaz. SSR* 0(4):73–75 (in Russian).

Peterson, B. V. 1960. Notes on some natural enemies of Utah blackflies (Diptera: Simuliidae). *Can. Entomol.* 92:266–274.

Poinar, G. O., Jr. 1981. Mermithid nematodes of blackflies. Pp. 159–170 in M. Laird, Ed., *Blackflies: the future for biological methods in integrated control.* Academic Press, New York and London.

Roberts, D. W., and J. M. Castillo, Eds. 1980. Bibliography on pathogens of medically important arthropods: 1980. *Bull. WHO* 58 (suppl.). 197 pp.

Roberts, D. W., R. A. Daoust, and S. P. Wraight, Eds. 1983. *Bibliography on pathogens of medically important arthropods: 1981.* WHO (Geneva)/VBC/83.1. 324 pp.

Roberts, D. W., and M. A. Strand, Eds. 1977. Pathogens of medically important arthropods. *Bull. WHO* 55 (suppl.). 419 pp.

Rubtsov, I. A. 1958. On the gynandromorphs and intersexes in blackflies (Simuliidae: Diptera). *Zool. Zh.* 37:458–461 (in Russian with English summary).

———. 1969. Variability and relationships of coelomycidians with the host. *Zh. Obshch. Biol.* 30:165–173 (in Russian with Russian and English summaries).

Semushin, R. D. 1981. Water mites (Sperchontidae), parasites of black flies (Simuliidae). *Parazitologiya* (Leningrad) 15:27–30 (in Russian with Russian and English summaries).

Shemanchuk, J. A., and R. A. Humber. 1978. *Entomophthora culicis* (Phycomycetes: Entomophthorales) parasitizing black fly adults (Diptera: Simuliidae) in Alberta. *Can. Entomol.* 110:253–256.

Sweeney, A. W., E. I. Hazard, and M. F. Graham. 1985. Intermediate host for an *Amblyospora* sp. infecting the mosquito *Culex annulirostris. J. Invertebr. Pathol.* 46:98–102.

Tarrant, C. A. 1984. The vertical transmission of black fly (Diptera: Simuliidae) parasites. Ph.D. Thesis, Cornell University, Ithaca, New York. 120 pp.

Vavra, J., and A. H. Undeen. 1981. Microsporidia (Microspora: Microsporida) from Newfoundland blackflies (Diptera: Simuliidae). *Can. J. Zool.* 59:1431–46.

Weiser, J. 1968. Iridescent virus from the blackfly *Simulium ornatum* Meigen in Czechoslovakia. *J. Invertebr. Pathol.* 12:36–39.

———. 1978. A new host, *Simulium argyreatum* Meig., for the cytoplasmic polyhedrosis virus of blackflies in Czechoslovakia. *Folia Parasitol.* (Prague) 25:361–365 + 2 plates.

Weiser, J., and A. H. Undeen. 1981. Diseases of blackflies. Pp. 181–196 in M. Laird, Ed., *Blackflies: the future for biological methods in integrated control.* Academic Press, New York and London.

Weiser, J., and Z. Zizka. 1974a. The ultrastructure of the chytrid *Coelomycidium simulii* Deb. I. Ultrastructure of the thalli. *Ceska Mykol.* 28:159–166.

———. 1974b. The ultrastructure of the chytrid *Coelomycidium simulii* Deb. II. Division of the thallus and structures of zoospores. *Ceska Mykol.* 28:227–237.

Whisler, H. C., S. L. Zebold, and J. A. Shemanchuk. 1975. Life history of *Coelomomyces psorophorae. Proc. Nat. Acad. Sci. USA* 72:693–696.

Yeboah, D. O. 1980. A survey of the prevalence and study of the effects of an ovarian phycomycete in some Newfoundland blackflies. M.S. Thesis, Memorial University of Newfoundland, St. John's, Newfoundland. 55 pp.

Yeboah, D. O., A. H. Undeen, and M. H. Colbo. 1984. Phycomycetes parasitizing the ovaries of blackflies (Simuliidae). *J. Invertebr. Pathol.* 43:363–373.

24 THE BIOLOGICAL CONTROL POTENTIAL OF PATHOGENS AND PARASITES OF BLACK FLIES

Lawrence A. Lacey and Albert H. Undeen

The desirability of controlling black flies using biological means has been expressed by a number of authors since the turn of the century (Strickland 1913, Twinn 1939, Jamnback 1973, Laird 1981, Davidson and Sweeney 1983). The environmental impact of conventional insecticides and the development of insecticide resistance make biocontrol agents attractive for black fly suppression. Myriad vertebrate and invertebrate predators feed upon simuliid larvae and adults and sometimes cause a considerable reduction in black fly numbers (Davies 1981). Entomopathogens, however, are usually more specific than predators and certain species are comparable with chemical larvicides in terms of efficacy.

This chapter presents the usefulness or potential of entomopathogens and parasites for the control of the Simuliidae. It is not intended as an exhaustive review of the literature; priority has been given to those organisms with operational control potential.

VIRUS

Several isolations of virus and viruslike pathogens from three virus groups have been reported from black flies (Lacey 1982). Of these, cytoplasmic polyhedrosis virus (CPV) appears to be the most common and most infectious. Although incidence of other viral pathogens of black flies is generally low, Bailey (1977) has reported high levels of infection and a broad host range for a CPV in Newfoundland. He observed that many infections did not become apparent until the larvae were in the last three instars and surmised that larvae with low levels of infection were never detected. Although Bailey (1977) observed pupation and emergence in heavily infected individuals, Mokry (1978) reported a high level of mortality in patently diseased laboratory-reared larvae that were ostensibly infected transovarially with CPV. Bailey (1977) obtained up to 70% and 55% experimental infection of *Simulium venustum* Say and *Stegopterna mutata* (Malloch), respectively, but the results were erratic.

Despite the wide host range and infectivity of the CPV, Bailey (1977) concluded that the virus would be of little value in biological control schemes.

The broad diversity of viruses that has been reported for the Culicidae (Lacey 1982, Federici 1985) has not been observed for the Simuliidae. This is due, at least in part, to greater survey effort in the past for mosquito pathogens. Viruses may offer potential as biological-control agents of simuliids if more virulent isolates are discovered. At present, however, high cost and the small yield of virus associated with *in vivo* virus production methods currently prevents the use of viruses in black fly control programs.

PROTOZOA

Ciliates have occasionally been found in black fly larvae and adults. Those from adult *Simulium damnosum* Theobald (Corliss et al. 1979), collected in the Ivory Coast, were assigned to the genus *Tetrahymena*. *Tetrahymena rotunda* Lynn, Molloy & LeBrun was originally described from very light infections in larvae of *S. tuberosum* and all stages of *S. venustum* (Lynn et al. 1981). Because the mode of transmission of these ciliates is unknown, the biocontrol potential of these organisms also remains unknown.

Microsporidia are common and cosmopolitan in simuliid larvae (Weiser and Undeen 1981), but their potential as biocontrol agents is completely unknown. Because both male and female larvae become heavily infected (Undeen et al. 1984b) and rarely survive to the adult stage, all of the microsporidia found in black flies can be considered pathogenic. To evaluate their biocontrol potential, however, the stages that are infectious to simuliids must be known and some means of producing these infections must be available. So far, attempts to transmit simuliid microsporidia by feeding spores from infected larvae to uninfected ones have all been negative. Therefore, infectivity, spore viability, longevity, host specificity, and potential for mass production all remain unknown.

The known microsporidia of black flies can be assigned to two groups, based upon spores found in the larvae: (1) those microsporidia considered to be dimorphic, which produce groups of uninucleate spores following meiosis, as described for *Amblyospora* sp. in mosquitoes (Hazard and Brookbank 1984); and (2) microsporidia such as the genus *Caudospora* with binucleate spores, also produced in high numbers but without meiosis. Light infections, probably of *Tuzetia debaisieuxi* (Jirovec), have been found in adult simuliids in Newfoundland (Undeen 1981) and in New York (Tarrant 1984), and transovarial transmission of this "group 1" microspordian has recently been demonstrated (Tarrant 1984). A hypothesis of transovarial transmission as a general phenomenon in simuliid microsporidia is consistent with the obvious necessity for upstream transport of the disease. Since none of the spores found in black fly larvae have ever been transmitted *per os* to healthy simuliid larvae, it is also reasonable to postulate an intermediate host as an obligate part of the life cycle.

If the microsporidia in both groups are heterogenetic (have alternating sexual and asexual generations) and heteroxenous (have two or more types of hosts in the life cycle), black fly larvae occupy a different place in the life cycle of each group.

Meiosis is unlikely to precede the production of binucleate spores in *Caudospora* spp. and other "group 2" microsporidians. In such cases the alternate host might harbor the meiotic sequence, producing a uninucleate spore that is infectious to black fly larvae. In this case there is probably some kind of gametic union in young simuliid larvae, without karyogamy. In the life cycles of *T. debaisieuxi* or *Thelohania* spp., where meiosis occurs in the simuliid larvae, the uninucleate spore should infect some other host. Gametogeny and gametic union, again without karyogamy, would be expected in the intermediate host, with the production of binucleate spores to infect simuliid larvae. Alternatively, an asexual generation could occur, producing another uninucleate spore that would infect simuliid larvae, with genetic union occurring there. It is these hypothetical spores, infectious to black fly larvae, that must be studied for suitability as biocontrol agents. Before any biocontrol potential can be evaluated, the entire life cycle of the microsporidian in question must be known. This should be the goal of future research.

FUNGI

A variety of symbiotic relationships exists between fungi and black flies, ranging from commensalism (Manier 1963, Crosby 1974, Nolan and Lewis 1974) to obligate parasitism. Obligately parasitic fungi of black fly larvae and adults are quite common, but their incidence is often low.

The most common parasitic fungus found in larval black flies is the relatively primitive *Coelomycidium simulii* Debaisieux. It is cosmopolitan in distribution, being reported from several species of black flies from the Holarctic region (Strickland 1913, Levchenko et al. 1974, Federici et al. 1977, Takaoka 1982) to the tropics (Henrard 1930; Takaoka 1980, 1981). Infections of *C. simulii* are normally observed only in larvae, but they have also been reported for adult and pupal black flies by Yakushkina and Dubitskii (1980). Patently infected individuals invariably succumb to the disease (Weiser 1964, Federici et al. 1977).

Although the incidence of infection of *C. simulii* is usually less than 5% (Jamnback 1973; Federici et al. 1977; Takaoka 1980, 1981), higher infection rates are reported (Strickland 1913, Weiser 1964, Rubtsov 1969, Levchenko et al. 1974, Takaoka 1982). Attempts to infect experimentally first instars of *Simulium vittatum* Zetterstedt with zoospores of *C. simulii* have been unsuccessful (Jamnback 1973, Tarrant 1984). Studies by Tarrant (1984), however, demonstrated vertical transmission from field-collected adult females to their laboratory-reared progeny. Considering the massive numbers of zoospores produced in infected larvae and their apparent inability to infect other simuliid larvae, it is highly probable that an intermediate host is an obligate stage in the life cycle of *C. simulii*. Until the intermediate host is known, the microbial control potential of *C. simulii* will remain low.

Another fungus or group of related fungi that are both common and exhibit a high incidence of infection are the Phycomycetes found in the ovaries of several black fly species (Undeen 1978, Undeen and Nolan 1977, Yeboah et al. 1984). Infected females produce no or few eggs and they do not seek a blood meal. Unfortunately, attempts to culture isolated spores on artificial media failed (Undeen and Nolan 1977). Despite problems encountered in production, additional research is warranted on the ovarian Phycomycetes. Inundative release of infective stages with subsequent establishment of the fungus may provide long-term partial suppression of target black fly populations.

Other fungi that are less commonly observed but occasionally result in epizootics in adult black flies are species in the Entomophthorales, principally *Entomophthora culicis* Fresenius (Gustafsson 1965, Shemanchuk and Humber 1978), and *Erynia curvispora* (Nowakowski) (=*Entomophthora curvispora*) (Gustafsson 1965, Kramer 1983). Kramer (1983) successfully isolated *E. curvispora,* cultured it on a synthetic medium, and infected adult *S. vittatum* and *Simulium pictipes* Hagen with the resulting conidia. Unfortunately, the ability to sporulate and to grow vegetatively gradually disappeared.

The potential of fungi such as the ovarian Phycomycetes and *E. curvispora* lies not so much in their lethal activity but in their ability to reduce fecundity and perhaps interfere with transmission of vertebrate pathogens. The most notable effect of patent infections of *E. culicis* and *C. simulii* is death of the host, although sublethal inapparent infections may also exist. Studies that could determine the usefulness of these fungi as microbial-control agents are often limited by the lack of sufficient infective inoculum. Basic research on infectious processes, as well as the overall microbial-control potential of obligately parasitic fungi, will be significantly augmented by successful production on synthetic media of infective stages and resting spores.

Sweeney and Roberts (1983) and Gaugler and Jaronski (1983) bioassayed *Culicinomyces clavisporus* Couch, Romney & Rao, a virulent mosquito pathogen cultured on synthetic media, against simuliid larvae under laboratory conditions. Although larvicidal activity was observed for *C. clavisporus* against *S. vittatum* and *S. pictipes* by Sweeney and Roberts (1983), the conclusion of both studies was that *C. clavisporus* was not sufficiently virulent toward black fly larvae to be considered a potential microbial-control agent.

BACTERIA

The natural association of bacteria with black fly larvae has been reported by a number of authors (Fredeen 1964, Burton et al. 1973, Malone and Nolan 1978, Weiser and Undeen 1981). With the exception of fairly rare septicemic infections, the association is usually of little or no consequence to the larvae from which the bacteria are isolated. It is interesting to note that an isolate of *Bacillus sphaericus* Neide from an adult of *S. damnosum* lacked larvicidal activity for black flies but was highly pathogenic to mosquito larvae (Weiser 1984).

Several varieties of *Bacillus thuringiensis* Berliner isolated from sources other than simuliids have been screened against black flies, but most have demonstrated only low to moderate larvicidal activity (Lacey and Mulla 1977, Finney and Harding 1982). However, the discovery and development of *Bacillus thuringiensis* var. *israelensis* de Barjac (serotype H-14) (Goldberg and Margalit 1977, de Barjac 1978) has enabled effective control of black flies (Gaugler and Finney 1982) and mosquitoes (Lacey 1985), with concomitant protection of most nontarget organisms (Dejoux 1979, Colbo and Undeen 1980, Garcia et al. 1981, Molloy and Jamnback 1981, Car and de Moor 1984).

Commercial development of *B. thuringiensis* (H-14) rapidly followed the first demonstrations of larvicidal activity against mosquitoes (Goldberg and Margalit 1977, de Barjac 1978) and black flies (Undeen and Nagel 1978). Currently, it is produced and distributed worldwide. Protocols for the laboratory and field evaluation of *B. thuringiensis* (H-14) formulations against black flies are presented by Lacey et al. (1982b) and Undeen and Lacey (1982), respectively.

Although most formulations contain living spores of the bacterium, larvicidal activity is due to the proteinacious parasporal inclusions that are produced during sporulation. The inclusions must be ingested and subsequently solubilized in the alkaline midgut in order to be active. Particles in the size range of the parasporal inclusions (0.2–0.8 μ) are readily filtered by black fly larvae (Chance 1970, Ross and Craig 1980). After activation the toxic moiety interferes with normal osmotic balance in cells of the gastric ceacae and midgut, resulting in lysis and eventual sloughing of the cells (Lacey and Federici 1979, Federici 1982). Ostensibly larvae die as a result of disruption of the midgut, without septicemia, substantial bacterial multiplication, or amplification of toxin.

Under laboratory conditions several factors were shown to influence larvicidal activity of *B. thuringiensis* against black flies (Lacey et al. 1978, Gaugler and Molloy 1980, Molloy et al. 1981). Most notable were black fly species, larval age, water temperature, formulation, and feeding inhibition. In addition to these factors, duration of application, stream velocity and profile (especially width-to-depth ratio), discharge, and pollution also influence activity and effective carry under natural conditions (Undeen and Colbo 1980, Undeen et al. 1981, Undeen and Lacey 1982, Gaugler et al. 1983, Lacey and Undeen 1984, Car 1984). One of the most striking factors influencing effective carry is stream discharge (Table 24.1). In very small streams (c. 100–160 liters/min) in Guatemala and Mexico, effective control was observed for only 25 to 50 meters downstream from application points after treatment with high concentrations of the Teknar® formulation of *B. thuringiensis* (H-14) (Undeen et al. 1981, Gaugler et al. 1983). By contrast, treatment of large rivers in Ivory Coast (Lacey et al. 1982a) and Arizona (Plantz, unpublished) resulted in extremely good, effective carry when the same formulation was used. In addition to discharge effect, Table 24.1 presents data from field trials conducted with *B. thuringiensis* (H-14) within a fairly narrow temperature range against several black fly species under a variety of stream conditions. Although the relationship between discharge and carry is the most apparent, efficacy is also influenced by the target species' susceptibilities (Molloy et al. 1981). Stream profile can also influence effective carry considerably. When waterways contain slow-moving segments, especially deep pools, where unidirectional flow is negligible, effective carry is drastically reduced due to settling and/or excess dilution of the active moiety. Colbo and O'Brien (1984) cite interruption of stream flow caused by negative relief as the major factor in limiting effective carry of *B. thuringiensis* (H-14) in stream systems in the Canadian Shield. Carry is also curtailed in shallow streams, and this is likely due to filtration of active moiety from the water column via contact with elements of the substratum (Undeen et al. 1984a).

Formulation can influence efficacy and effective carry in a variety of ways, e.g., through the effect of diluents on stability of the toxin and normal black fly feeding or the effect of the formulation process on particle size. Despite excellent larvicidal activity of wettable powders of *B. thuringiensis* (H-14) under laboratory conditions

Table 24.1 Efficacy and carry of the Teknar® formulation of *Bacillus thuringiensis* var. *israelensis* against black flies under various conditions

Species	Discharge (m³/min)	Dosage (mg/l)	Application time (min)	Temperature (°C)	Carry[a] (m)	Reference
Simulium ochraceum, *S. metallicum, S. callidum*	0.1 0.11	45.0 7.5	0.5 1.0	19 19	40 50	(Gaugler et al. 1983), Mexico
S. metallicum, S. ochraceum, *Simulium* spp.	0.16	50.0	10.0	22	25	(Undeen et al. 1981), Guatemala
Austrosimulium spp.	3.4	2.0	15.0	19	544	(Chilcott et al. 1983), New Zealand
S. venustum/verecundum, *S. tuberosum*	6.8 6.8 8.0	20.0 40.0 40.0	1.0 1.0 1.0	20 16 19	750 927 900	(Horosko and Noblet 1983), U.S.A.
S. venustum	13.5	20.0	1.0	16	200+	(Pistrang and Burger 1984), U.S.A.
S. vittatum	25–27	10.0	1.0	22	400	(Lacey and Undeen 1984), U.S.A.
S. damnosum s.l.	27,420	1.5	10.0	27	28,000	(Lacey et al. 1982a), Africa
S. vittatum	54,237	20.0	1.0	17	16,000+	Plantz (personal communication), U.S.A.

[a]75% or greater reduction.

(Molloy et al. 1981, 1984), field use as black fly larvicides has resulted in limited effective downstream carry (Frommer et al. 1981a,b) when compared to flowable concentrate formulations under identical conditions (Lacey and Undeen 1984). Flowable concentrates, especially those made with undried fermentation residues, provide smaller mean suspended-particle size and decreased settling rate (Guillet and Escaffre 1979a, Guillet et al. 1980, Molloy et al. 1984). These characteristics were thought to be responsible for greater downstream carry.

One of the main obstacles to application, especially aerial application in remote or otherwise inaccessible terrain, is the extreme bulk of most *B. thuringiensis* (H-14) formulations in comparison to their chemical counterparts. For example, treatment of the River Marahoué in the Ivory Coast (discharge 457 m^3/sec) required 416 liters of Teknar® (Lacey et al. 1982a), more than 10 times the volume of temephos used. Requirement for additional dilution prior to application further compounds the excess bulk problem (Guillet et al. 1982). Since over 95% of most formulations are carriers, surfactants, and inert fermentation residues, considerable improvement could be made in the further refinement and concentration of the active moiety. Recently developed formulations with higher concentrations of larvicidal toxin and improved miscibility have resulted in increased efficacy without the necessity for prior dilution (Lacey and Heitzman 1985).

Operational, wide-scale application of *B. thuringiensis* (H-14) is being conducted in the Onchocerciasis Control Programme (OCP). Early field and laboratory trials with *B. thuringiensis* (H-14) indicated that it was extremely effective as a larvicide of *S. damnosum* s.l. (Guillet and de Barjac 1979; Guillet and Escaffre 1979a, 1979b; Undeen and Berl 1979). After development of resistance to temephos in *S. damnosum* s.l. (Guillet et al. 1980), and subsequently to chlorphoxim (Kurtak et al. 1982) in 21% of the 764,000 km^2 under OCP operational control, research on the feasibility of routinely using *B. thuringiensis* (H-14) was intensified (Guillet et al. 1982; Lacey et al. 1982a; Kurtak, unpublished data). Currently the *S. damnosum* complex is controlled in the areas where resistance was detected by seasonally alternating the application of *B. thuringiensis* (H-14) (dry season) and chlorphoxim (rainy season) in large rivers, or by using *B. thuringiensis* throughout the year in smaller rivers and streams ($\leq$ 50 m^3/sec) (WHO 1984).

NEMATODA

Mermithid nematodes are commonly found in simuliid larvae and frequently in the adult stages as well (Mokry and Finney 1977, Poinar 1981). They are thought to reduce black fly populations and onchocerciasis transmission by *S. damnosum* s.l. in at least one area in Sierra Leone (Davies et al. 1984). Similarly, Takoaka (1981) observed that mermithids played a chief role in suppressing natural populations of *S. metallicum* and *S. callidum* in the lower segments of perennial streams during the dry season in Guatemala. The mermithid life cycle is well known and preparasitic larvae will infect black fly larvae in the laboratory (Molloy and Jamnback 1975, Mondet et al. 1977). The specificity of nematodes to particular species of simuliids has not been extensively examined.

The only source of infective mermithid preparasites is from adult worms originally obtained directly from field-collected simuliids. Molloy and Jamnback (1977) obtained sufficient *Mesomermis (= Neomesomermis) flumenalis* (Welch) preparasites in this fashion to conduct a field test in a small stream in New York. They obtained an infection rate of 71.4% in a population of *S. venustum* larvae but concluded that the method is not cost-effective. In the Ukraine, *Gastromermis* spp. were obtained from streams and introduced into six other streams in the same region, but in which the mermithids did not naturally occur. Two years later, infected simuliids were found below the introduction sites in three of the six streams. In the same study *Isomermis rossica* Rubtsov from another region was also introduced but did not become established (Likhovoz 1978).

In vivo cultivation of simuliid mermithids has recently been made possible by the development of systems in which the black fly hosts can be maintained in continuous colony (Edman and Simmons 1985). *In vitro* cultivation of mermithids has not yet been achieved but appears to offer promise for eventual production (Finney 1981).

Romanomermis culicivorax Ross and Smith, a readily mass-produced mermithid parasite of mosquitoes, infected and killed first-instar *S. verecundum* under laboratory conditions; however, it was unable to complete its development in this unusual host (Finney and Mokry 1980). Very large numbers of preparasites (50–220/ml) were used to obtain low percentages of infection (6–7%) in moving water. Similar results were obtained against *S. damnosum* s.l. (Hansen and Hansen 1976).

Steinernema feltiae Filipjev (= *Neoaplectana carpocapsae*), an easily cultured nematode parasite of a wide range of terrestrial insects, was found to infect late-instar simuliid larvae (Molloy et al. 1980, Gaugler and Molloy 1981b). In a field test against *S. vittatum* in a small New York stream, over 50% mortality was obtained using a dosage of 34.5 nematodes/ml of stream water (Gaugler and Molloy 1981a). A dosage of 43.8 nematodes/ml was completely ineffective against a simuliid population in Mexico composed predominantly of *S. metallicum* (Gaugler et al. 1983).

Neither *R. culicivorax* nor *S. feltiae* are sufficiently infective to simuliids for biocontrol use. In addition, since running water is an abnormal environment for both species, there is little likelihood that either would have become established. Their use as biological insecticides therefore would be impractical and prohibitively expensive.

CONCLUSION

A wide range of naturally occurring and artificially produced parasites and pathogens are available as potential biological-control agents of simuliids. An agent with high biological-control capacity, however, will not simply be one that is extremely larvicidal or debilitating to the black fly target; it must also be easily mass-produced and remain virulent during storage and application. Agents such as viruses, fungi, protozoans, and nematodes warrant not only additional research on their propagation and feasibility for field use but also increased survey for new candidates. The most efficacious available agent, *B. thuringiensis* (H-14), still requires an augmentation of larvicidal activity and increased ease of handling and application through formulation and/or genetic engineering if it is to compete successfully with chemical larvicides. Public acceptance will be the ultimate limiting factor of any potential microbial-control agent, especially when it is applied to potable water or recreational waterways.

LITERATURE CITED

Bailey, C. H. 1977. Field and laboratory observations on a cytoplasmic polyhedrosis virus of blackflies (Diptera: Simuliidae). *J. Invertebr. Pathol.* 29:69–73

Burton, G. J., I. V. Perkins, and H. S. Sodhi. 1973. Aerobic bacteria in the midgut of *Simulium damnosum* larvae. *Mosquito News* 33:115–17.

Car, M. 1984. Laboratory and field trials with two *Bacillus thuringiensis* var. *israelensis* products for *Simulium* (Diptera: Nematocera) control in a small polluted river in South Africa. *Onderstepoort J. Vet. Res.* 51:141–144.

Car, M., and F. C. de Moor. 1984. The response of Vaal River drift and benthos to *Simulium* (Diptera: Nematocera) control using *Bacillus thuringiensis* var. *israelensis* (H-14). *Onderstepoort J. Vet. Res.* 51:155–160.

Chance, M. M. 1970. The functional morphology of the mouthparts of blackfly larvae (Diptera: Simuliidae). *Quaest. Entomol.* 6:245–84.

Chilcott, C. N., J. S. Pillai, and J. Kalmakoff. 1983. Efficacy of *Bacillus thuringiensis* var. *israelensis* as a biocontrol agent against larvae of Simuliidae (Diptera) in New Zealand. *New Zealand J. Zool.* 10:319–26.

Colbo, M. H., and H. O'Brien. 1984. A pilot black fly (Diptera: Simuliidae) control program using *Bacillus thuringiensis* var. *israelensis* in Newfoundland. *Can. Entomol.* 116:1085–96.

Colbo, M. H., and A. H. Undeen. 1980. Effect of *Bacillus thuringiensis* var. *israelensis* on non-target insects in stream trials for control of Simuliidae. *Mosquito News* 40:368–71.

Corliss, J. O., D. Berl, and M. Laird. 1979. A note on the occurrence of the ciliate *Tetrahymena*, potential biocontrol agent, in the blackfly vector of onchocerciasis from Ivory Coast. *Trans. Amer. Microsc . Soc.* 98:587–91.

Crosby, T. K. 1974. Trichomycetes (Harpellales) of New Zealand *Austrosimulium* larvae (Diptera: Simuliidae). *J. Nat. Hist.* 8:187–92.

Davidson, E. W., and A. W. Sweeney. 1983. Microbial control of vectors: a decade of progress. *J. Med. Entomol.* 20:235–47

Davies, D. M. 1981. Predators upon blackflies. Pp. 139–58 in M. Laird, Ed., *Blackflies: the future for biological methods in integrated control*. Academic Press, New York and London.

Davies, J. B., J. E. McMahon, P. Beech-Garwood, and F. Abdulai. 1984. Does parasitism of *Simulium damnosum* by Mermithidae reduce the transmission of onchocerciasis. *Trans. R. Soc. Trop. Med. Hyg.* 78:424–25.

de Barjac, H. 1978. Une nouvelle variété de *Bacillus thuringiensis* très toxique pour les moustiques: *B. thuringiensis* var. *israelensis* sérotype 14. *C.R. Acad. Sci. sér. D* 286:797–800.

Dejoux, C. 1979. Recherches preliminaires concernant l'action de *Bacillus thuringiensis israelensis* de Barjac sur la faune d'invertebres d'un cours d'eau tropical. *WHO* mimeo. doc. WHO/VBC/79.721. 11 pp.

Edman, J. D., and K. R. Simmons. 1985. Rearing and colonization of black flies (Diptera: Simuliidae). *J. Med. Entomol.* 22:1–17.

Federici, B. A. 1982. Site of action of the delta-endotoxin of *Bacillus thuringiensis* in mosquito and blackfly larvae. Pp. 37–47 in F. Michall, Ed., *Basic biology of microbial larvicides of vectors of human diseases.* UNDP/World Bank/WHO Special Programme for Research and Training in Tropical Diseases. 188 pp.

———. 1985. Viral pathogens of mosquito larvae. In H. C. Chapman, Ed., Biological control of mosquitoes. *Am. Mosq. Cont. Assoc. Bull.* 6:62–74.

Federici, B. A., L. A. Lacey, and M. S. Mulla. 1977. *Coelomycidium simulii:* a fungal pathogen in larvae of *Simulium vittatum* from the Colorado River. *Proc. Calif. Mosq. Cont. Assoc.* 45:110–13.

Finney, J. R. 1981. Mermithid nematodes: in vitro culture attempts. *J. Nematol.* 13:275–80.

Finney, J. R., and J. B. Harding. 1982. The susceptibility of *Simulium verecundum* (Diptera: Simuliidae) to three isolates of *Bacillus thuringiensis* serotype 10 (*darmstadiensis*). *Mosquito News* 42:434–35.

Finney, J. R., and J. E. Mokry. 1980. *Romanomermis culicivorax* and simuliids. *J. Invertebr. Pathol.* 35:211–13.

Fredeen, F. J. H. 1964. Bacteria as food for blackfly larvae (Diptera: Simuliidae) in laboratory cultures and in natural streams. *Can. J. Zool.* 42:527–48.

Frommer, R. L., S. C. Hembree, J. H. Nelson, M. P. Remington, and P. H. Gibbs. 1981a. The evaluation of *Bacillus thuringiensis* var. *israelensis* in reducing *Simulium vittatum* (Diptera: Simuliidae) larvae in their natural habitat with no extensive aquatic vegetative growth. *Mosquito News* 41:339–47.

Frommer, R. L., J. H. Nelson, M. P. Remington, and P. H. Gibbs. 1981b. The influence of extensive aquatic vegetative growth on the larvicidal activity of *Bacillus thuringiensis* var. *israelensis* in reducing *Simulium vittatum* (Diptera: Simuliidae) larvae in their natural habitat. *Mosquito News* 41:707–12.

Garcia, R., B. Des Rochers, and W. Tozer. 1981. Studies on *Bacillus thuringiensis* var. *israelensis* against mosquito larvae and other organisms. *Proc. Calif. Mosq. Vect. Cont. Assoc.* 49:25–29.

Gaugler, R., and J. Finney. 1982. A review of *Bacillus thuringiensis* var. *israelensis* (serotype 14) as a biological control agent of black flies (Simuliidae). Pp. 1–17 in D. Molloy, Ed., *Biological control of black flies (Diptera: Simuliidae) with* Bacillus thuringiensis var. israelensis *(Serotype 14), a review with recommendations for laboratory and field protocol* 1:1–17. Misc. Pub. Entomol. Soc. Am. 12(4). 30 pp.

Gaugler, R., and S. Jaronski. 1983. Assessment of the mosquito-pathogenic fungus *Culicinomyces clavosporus* as a black fly (Diptera: Simuliidae) pathogen. *J. Med. Entomol.* 20:575–76.

Gaugler, R., B. Kaplan, C. Alvarado, J. Montoya, and M. Ortega. 1983. Assessment of *Bacillus thuringiensis* serotype 14 and *Steinernema feltiae* (Nematoda: Steinernematidae) for control of the *Simulium* vectors of onchocerciasis in Mexico. *Entomophaga* 28:309–15.

Gaugler, R., and D. Molloy. 1980. Feeding inhibition in black fly larvae (Diptera: Simuliidae) and its effect on the pathogenicity of *Bacillus thuringiensis* var. *israelensis*. *Environ. Entomol.* 9:704–8.

———. 1981a. Field evaluation of the entomogenous nematode, *Neoaplectana carpocapsae*, as a biological control agent of black flies (Diptera: Simuliidae). *Mosquito News* 41:459–64.

———. 1981b. Instar susceptibility of *Simulium vittatum* (Diptera: Simuliidae) to the entomogenous nematode *Neoaplectana carpocapsae*. *J. Nematol.* 13:1–5.

Goldberg, L. J. and J. Margalit. 1977. A bacterial spore demonstrating rapid larvicidal activity against *Anopheles sergentii, Uranotaenia unguiculata, Culex univittatus, Aedes aegypti* and *Culex pipiens*. *Mosquito News* 37:355–58.

Guillet, P., and H. de Barjac. 1979. Toxicité de *Bacillus thuringiensis* var. *israelensis* pour les larves de simulies vectrices de l'onchocercose. *C.R. Acad. Sci. sér. D* 289:549–52.

Guillet, P., J. Dempah, and J. Cox. 1980. Évaluation de *Bacillus thuringiensis* serotype 14 de

Barjac pour la lutte contre les larves de *Simulium damnosum* s.l. III. Données préliminaires sur la sédimentation de l'endotoxine dans l'eau et sur sa stabilité en zone tropicale. WHO mimeo. doc. WHO/VBC/80.756. 9 pp.

Guillet, P., and H. Escaffre. 1979a. Évaluation de *Bacillus thuringiensis israelensis* de Barjac pour la lutte contre les larves de *Simulium damnosum* s.l. II. Efficacité comparée de trois formulations expérimentales. WHO mimeo. doc., WHO/VBC/79.735. 7 pp.

———. 1979b. Évaluation de *Bacillus thuringiensis israelensis* de Barjac pour la lutte contre les larves de *Simulium damnosum* s.l. I. Résultats des premiers essais réalisés sur le terrain. WHO mimeo. doc., WHO/VBC/79.730. 7 pp.

Guillet, P., H. Escaffre, M. Ouedraogo and D. Quillévéré. 1980. Mise en évidence de'une résistance au téméphos dans le complexe *Simulium damnosum* (*S. sanctipauli* et *S. soubrense*) en Côte d'Ivoire (Zone de Programme de lutte contre l'Onchocercose dans la région du Bassin de la Volta). *Cah. ORSTOM sér. Entomol. Méd. Parasitol.* 18:291–99.

Guillet, P., H. Escaffre, and J.-M. Prud'hom. 1982. L'utilisation d'une formulation à base de *Bacillus thuringiensis* H-14 dans la lutte contre l'onchocercose en Afrique de l'Quest. I. Efficacité et modalités d'application. *Cah. ORSTOM sér. Entomol. Méd. Parasitol.* 20:175–80.

Gustafsson, M. 1965. On species of the genus *Entomophthora* Fres. in Sweden. I. Classification and distribution. *Lantbr. Hogsk. Ann.* 31:103–212.

Hansen, E. L., and J. W. Hansen. 1976. Parasitism of *Simulium damnosum* by *Romanomermis culicivorax*. *IRCS Med. Sci.* 4:508.

Hazard, E. I., and J. W. Brookbank. 1984. Karyogamy and meiosis in an *Amblyospora* sp. (Microspora) in the mosquito, *Culex salinarius* Coquillet. *J. Invertebr. Pathol.* 44:3–11.

Henrard, C. 1930. Quelques protozoaires parasites des larves de *Simulium congolais*. *Rev. Zool. Bot. Afr.* 19:226–31.

Horosko, S., III, and R. Noblet. 1983. Efficacy of *Bacillus thuringiensis* var. *israelensis* for control of black fly larvae in South Carolina. *J. Ga. Entomol. Soc.* 18:531–37.

Jamnback, H. 1973. Recent developments in control of blackflies. *Ann. Rev. Entomol.* 18:281–304.

Kramer, J. P. 1983. A mycosis of the black fly *Simulium decorum* (Simuliidae) caused by *Erynia curvispora* (Entomophthoraceae). *Mycopathologia* 82:39–43.

Kurtak, D., M. Ouedraogo, M. Ocran, B. Télé, and P. Guillet. 1982. Preliminary note on the appearance in Ivory Coast of resistance to chlorphoxim in *Simulium soubrense/sanctipauli* larvae already resistant to temephos (Abate). WHO mimeo. doc., WHO/VBC/82.850. 12 pp.

Lacey, L. A. 1982. Viral pathogens of vector Nematocera and their potential for microbial control. *Proc. 3rd Int. Coll. Invertebr. Pathol.* Pp. 429–436.

———. 1985. *Bacillus thuringiensis* serotype H-14. In H. C. Chapman, Ed., Biological control of mosquitoes. *Am. Mosq. Cont. Assoc. Bull.* 6:132–158.

Lacey, L. A., H. Escaffre, B. Philippon, A. Sékétéli, and P. Guillet. 1982a. Large river treatment with *Bacillus thuringiensis* (H-14) for the control of *Simulium damnosum* s.l. in the Onchoceriasis Control Programme. *Tropenmed. Parasitol* 33:97–101.

Lacey, L. A., and B. A. Federici. 1979. Pathogenesis and midgut histopathology of *Bacillus thuringiensis* in *Simulium vittatum* (Diptera: Simuliidae). *J. Invertebr. Pathol.* 33:171–82.

Lacey, L. A., and C. M. Heitzman. 1985. Efficacy of flowable concentrate formulations of *Bacillus thuringiensis* var. *israelensis* against black flies (Diptera: Simuliidae). *J. Am. Mosq. Cont. Assoc.* 1:493–97.

Lacey, L. A., and M. S. Mulla. 1977. Evaluation of *Bacillus thuringiensis* as a biocide of blackfly larvae (Diptera: Simuliidae). *J. Invertebr. Pathol.* 30:46–49.

Lacey, L. A., M. S. Mulla, and H. T. Dulmage. 1978. Some factors affecting the pathogenicity of *Bacillus thuringiensis* Berliner against blackflies. *Environ. Entomol.* 7:583–88.

Lacey, L. A., and A. H. Undeen. 1984. Effect of formulation, concentration, and application time on the efficacy of *Bacillus thuringiensis* (H-14) against black fly (Diptera: Simuliidae) larvae under natural conditions. *J. Econ. Entomol.* 77:412–18.

Lacey, L. A., A. H. Undeen, and M. M. Chance. 1982b. Laboratory procedures for the bioassay and comparative efficacy evaluation of *Bacillus thuringiensis* var. *israelensis* (serotype 14) against black flies (Simuliidae). Pp. 19–23 in D. Molloy, Ed., *Biological control of black flies (Diptera: Simuliidae) with* Bacillus thuringiensis *var.* israelensis *(serotype 14), a review with recommendations for laboratory and field protocol.* Misc. Pub. Entomol. Soc. Am. 12(4). 30 pp.

Laird, M., Ed. 1981. *Blackflies: the future for biological methods in integrated control.* Academic Press, New York and London. 399 pp.

Levchenko, N. G., A. M. Dubitskii, and V. G. Vakker. 1974. Entomopathogenic blackflies of the genus *Odagmia* (Diptera: Simuliidae) in the Kazakhstan: USSR. *Med. Parazitol. Parazit. Bolezn.* 43:110–12 (in Russian).

Likhovoz, L. K. 1978. Introduction of Mermithids (Nematoda, Mermithidae), parasites of larvae of black flies (Simuliidae, Diptera). *Med. Parazitol. Parazit. Bolezn.* 47:90–94 (in Russian).

Lynn, D. H., D. Molloy, and R. LeBrun. 1981. *Tetrahymena rotunda* n. sp. (Hymenostomatida: Tetrahymenidae), a ciliate parasite of the hemolymph of *Simulium* (Diptera: Simuliidae). *Trans. Am. Microsc. Soc.* 100:134–41.

Malone, K. M., and R. A. Nolan. 1978. Aerobic bacterial flora of the larval gut of the black fly *Prosimulium mixtum* (Diptera: Simuliidae) from Newfoundland, Canada. *J. Med. Entomol.* 14:641–45.

Manier, J.-F. 1963. Trichomycetes de larves de simulies (Harpellales du Proctodeum). *Ann. Sci. Nat. Bot. Biol. Veg. 12 sér.,* 4:737–50.

Mokry, J. E. 1978. Progress towards the colonization of *Cnephia mutata* (Diptera: Simuliidae). *Bull. WHO* 56:455–56.

Mokry, J. E., and J. R. Finney. 1977. Notes on mermithid parasitism of Newfoundland blackflies, with the first record of *Neomesomermis flumenalis* from adult hosts. *Can. J. Zool.* 55:1370–72.

Molloy, D., R. Gaugler, and H. Jamnback. 1980. The pathogenicity of *Neoaplectana carpocapsae* to blackfly larvae. *J. Invertebr. Pathol.* 36:302–6.

———. 1981. Factors influencing efficacy of *Bacillus thuringiensis* var. *israelensis* as a biological control agent of black fly larvae. *J. Econ. Entomol.* 74:61–64.

Molloy, D., and H. Jamnback. 1975. Laboratory transmission of mermithids parasitic in blackflies. *Mosquito News* 35:337–42.

———. 1977. A larval black fly (Diptera: Simuliidae) control field trial using mermithid parasites and its cost implications. *Mosquito News* 37:104–8.

———. 1981. Field evaluation of *Bacillus thuringiensis* var. *israelensis* as a black fly biocontrol agent and its effect on non-target stream insects. *J. Econ. Entomol.* 74:314–18.

Molloy, D., S. P. Wraight, B. Kaplan, J. Gerardi, and P. Peterson. 1984. Laboratory evaluation of commercial formulations of *Bacillus thuringiensis* var. *israelensis* against mosquito and black fly larvae. *J. Agric. Entomol.* 1:161–68.

Mondet, B., D. Berl and J. Bernadou. 1977. Etude du parasitisme des Simulies (Diptera) par des Mermithidae (Nematoda) en Afrique de l'Ouest. III. Elevage de *Isomermis* sp. et infestation on laboratoire de *Simulium damnosum* s.l. *Cah. ORSTOM sér. Entomol. Méd. Parasitol.* 15:265–69.

Nolan, R. A., and D. J. Lewis. 1974. Studies on *Pythiopsis cymosa* from Newfoundland. *Trans. Br. Mycol. Soc.* 62:163–79.

Pistrang, L. A., and J. F. Burger. 1984. Effect of *Bacillus thuringiensis* var. *israelensis* on a genetically-defined population of black flies (Diptera: Simuliidae) and associated insects in a montane New Hampshire stream. *Can. Entomol.* 116:975–81.

Poinar, G. O., Jr. 1981. Mermithid nematodes of blackflies. Pp. 159–170 in M. Laird, Ed., *Blackflies: the future for biological methods in integrated control.* Academic Press, New York and London. 399 pp.

Ross, D. H., and D. A. Craig. 1980. Mechanisms of fine particle capture by larval black flies (Diptera: Simuliidae). *Can. J. Zool.* 58:1186–92.

Rubtsov, I. A. 1969. Variability and relationships of coelomycidians with the host. *Zh. Obshch. Biol.* 30:165–73 (in Russian).

Shemanchuk, J. A., and R. A. Humber. 1978. *Entomophthora culicis* (Phycomycetes: Entomophthorales) parasitizing black fly adults (Diptera: Simuliidae) in Alberta. *Can. Entomol.* 110:253–56.

Strickland, E. H. 1913. Further observations on the parasites of *Simulium* larvae. *J. Morphol.* 24:43–105.

Sweeney, A. W., and D. W. Roberts. 1983. Laboratory evaluation of the fungus *Culicinomyces clavosporus* for control of blackfly (Diptera: Simuliidae) larvae. *Environ. Entomol.* 12:774–778.

Takaoka, H. 1980. Pathogens of blackfly larvae in Guatemala and their influence on natural populations of three species of onchocerciasis vectors. *Am. J. Trop. Med. Hyg.* 29:467–72.

———. 1981. Further studies of pathogens of blackfly larvae in Guatemala: their influence on natural populations of three species of onchocerciasis vectors. Pp. 78–104 in M. Laird, Ed., *Biocontrol of medical and veterinary pests.* Praeger, New York.

———. 1982. Mermithid, microsporidan and fungal parasitism of larval blackflies from Oita, in Japan. *Jpn. J. Sanit. Zool.* 33:149–54.

Tarrant, C. A. 1984. The vertical transmission of black fly (Diptera: Simuliidae) parasites. Ph.D. Diss., Cornell University, Ithaca, New York. 120 pp.

Twinn, C. R. 1939. Notes on some parasites and predators of blackflies (Simuliidae, Diptera). *Can. Entomol.* 71:101–5.

Undeen, A. H. 1979. Observations on the ovarian Phycomycete of Newfoundland blackflies. *Proc. Int. Coll. Invertebr. Pathol.*, pp. 251–55.

———. 1981. Microsporida infections in adult *Simulium vittatum.* *J. Invertebr. Pathol.* 38:426–27.

Undeen, A. H., and D. Berl. 1979. Laboratory studies on the effectiveness of *Bacillus thuringiensis* var. *israelensis* de Barjac against *Simulium damnosum* (Diptera: Simuliidae) larvae. *Mosquito News* 39:742–45.

Undeen, A. H., and M. H. Colbo. 1980. The efficacy of *Bacillus thuringiensis* var. *israelensis* against blackfly larvae (Diptera: Simuliidae) in their natural habitat. *Mosquito News* 40:181–84.

Undeen, A. H., and L. A. Lacey. 1982. Field procedures for the evaluation of *Bacillus thuringiensis* var. *israelensis* (serotype 14) against black flies (Simuliidae) and nontarget organisms in streams. Pp. 25–30 in D. Molloy, Ed., *Biological control of black flies (Diptera: Simuliidae) with* Bacillus thuringiensis *var.* israelensis *(serotype 14), a review with recommendations for laboratory and field protocol.* Misc. Pub. Entomol. Soc. Am. 12(4). 30 pp.

Undeen, A. H., L. A. Lacey, and S. W. Avery. 1984a. A system for recommending dosage of *Bacillus thuringiensis* (H-14) for control of simuliid larvae in small streams based upon stream width. *Mosquito News* 44:553–59.

Undeen, A. H., and W. L. Nagel. 1978. The effect of *Bacillus thuringiensis* ONR-60A strain (Goldberg) on *Simulium* larvae in the laboratory. *Mosquito News* 38:524–27.

Undeen, A. H., and R. A. Nolan. 1977. Ovarian infection and fungal spore oviposition in the blackfly *Prosimulium mixtum.* *J. Invertebr. Pathol.* 30:97–98.

Undeen, A. H., H. Takaoka, and K. Hansen. 1981. A test of *Bacillus thuringiensis* var. *israelensis* de Barjac as a larvicide for *Simulium ochraceum,* the Central American vector of onchocerciasis. *Mosquito News* 41:37–40.

Undeen, A. H., J. Vavra, and K. H. Rothfels. 1984b. The sex of larval simuliids infected with microsporidia. *J. Invertebr. Pathol.* 43:126–27.

Weiser, J. 1964. Parasitology of blackflies. *Bull. WHO* 31:483–85.

———. 1984. A mosquito-virulent *Bacillus sphaericus* in adult *Simulium damnosum* from Northern Nigeria. *Zbl. Mikrobiol.* 139:57–60.

Weiser, J., and A. H. Undeen. 1981. Diseases of blackflies. Pp. 181–96 in M. Laird, Ed., *Blackflies: the future for biological methods in integrated control.* Academic Press, New York and London. 399 pp.

WHO. 1984. Onchocerciasis Control Programme in the Volta River Basin. Long term strategy: Information Document. WHO mimeo. doc., OCP/84.4. 11 pp.

Yakushkina, V. M., and A. M. Dubitskii. 1980. First findings of the fungus *Coelomycidium simulii* in pupae and imagoes of black flies. *Parazitologiya* 14:183–84 (in Russian).

Yeboah, D. O., A. H. Undeen, and M. H. Colbo. 1984. Phycomycetes parasitizing the ovaries of blackflies (Simuliidae). *J. Invertebr. Pathol.* 43:363–73.

25 CONTROL OF BLACK FLY VECTORS OF ONCHOCERCIASIS IN AFRICA

Daniel C. Kurtak, Jorg Grunewald, and D. A. T. Baldry

In Africa, efforts to reduce the numbers of man-biting black flies date back many years (Jamnback 1981). Where the insects posed basically a nuisance problem, the level of control required was not extremely high (reduction from thousands of bites per person per day to several tens or perhaps one hundred bites) and intermittent larviciding was the tactic used (e.g., Adiamah et al. 1986). Where the goal is to interrupt transmission of onchocerciasis, as in the Onchocerciasis Control Programme of the World Health Organization (OCP), a very high level of control is required, leading to virtually no bites (a few hundred per *year*).

Most of the following discussion will concern this aspect of vector versus nuisance control. The vector and its habitat will be briefly introduced, followed by the goals of vector control. Adulticiding and larviciding will be discussed, as well as suitable chemicals. Various alternative tactics in insecticide use will be contrasted and placed in the framework of integrated control. Finally, the resistance problem will be presented.

Since the vector species involved and their bioecology are quite different in East and West Africa, the two situations will be discussed separately.

WEST AFRICA
Simulium damnosum Complex

The only vectors of onchocerciasis in West Africa are members of the *Simulium damnosum* Theobald complex. The biology of this black fly has been amply described in many references (Laird 1981 gives a review).

Briefly, the larvae inhabit swift-flowing portions (0.8 m/sec and above) of medium and large (though not necessarily permanent) rivers. They are most commonly found attached to trailing vegetation. The larval development time (egg hatch to pupation) varies from 4–17 days, and is usually from 8–14 days, increasing with decreasing temperature (Séchan 1980; H. Agoua, personal communication).

The adult flies are fecund (400–600 eggs/female [Bellec and Hébrard 1983], diminishing somewhat with age [Mokry 1980]) and live up to three weeks. The gonotrophic cycle is 3–4 days for nulliparous flies and 4–5 days for parous flies (Le Berre 1966, Wenk 1981). Local dispersal is about 20 kilometers, and migratory flights (wind-assisted) can extend to 400 kilometers (Walsh et al. 1981). Typically, biting densities in an untreated area with productive larval breeding sites are up to several thousand/man/day.

Taxonomically, the species is a complex with six major species in West Africa. These may be separated roughly into "forest" and "savanna" species, with the latter being by far the more dangerous vectors.

Hydrology and Its Relation to Fly Populations

The rivers that contain *S. damnosum* breeding sites are characterized by very large annual variations in discharge. Typically, a river that has a discharge of several hundred m^3/sec in the wet season will be reduced to 1 m^3/sec or 2 m^3/sec in the dry season or may dry up completely. This is most pronounced in the north (sudan savanna and sahel zones), but it is also true in the southern forest, where there is still a distinct dry season lasting several months.

River discharge also follows pluriannual cycles. Since the 1960s there has been a general reduction of rainfall in West Africa, resulting in great distress for the human population of the sahel zone, but benefiting OCP.

The physiography of the OCP area is generally one of low relief, and the average slopes of the streambeds are very gradual, rarely more than 1 m/km. Typically, a river has long stretches of deep, slow-moving water punctuated by rapids as it flows over bedrock ledges. These rapids may be very complex where the river spreads, following fault lines and bedding structure. Figure 25.1 gives a good example.

Water chemistry has been thoroughly studied (review by Grunewald 1981). pH is generally slightly alkaline (7–8), temperature 20°–30°C, and conductivity 50–150 µS/cm. The water is turbid (10–80 JTU) most of the year, with maximum turbidity in the rainy season. Some permanently-flowing rivers have very clear water in the dry season. Water conditons have some influence on the effectiveness of insecticides. Large amounts of planktonic algae, for example, almost completely neutralized the effects of permethrin and considerably reduced the effectiveness of *Bacillus thuringiensis* H-14 (OCP, unpublished data).

Fly populations are generally correlated with water level, but in several different patterns. In the north, in temporary rivers, the relationship is often simple and direct, with maximum numbers occurring when water levels are highest (Fig. 25.2). In permanent rivers in the same zone, the relationship may be inverse, with high numbers in the dry season and low numbers when the rapids are flooded in the wet season. In the south, breeding may be reduced at high water because of flooding of rapids, and also at low water because of the lack of trailing vegetation. Maximum breeding thus occurs twice during the year, at the beginning and end of the wet season (Le Berre 1966). It is thought that optimum nutritive conditions occur at the beginning of the rainy season, when incoming rains flush out stagnant portions of the river that have supported heavy plankton populations during the dry season.

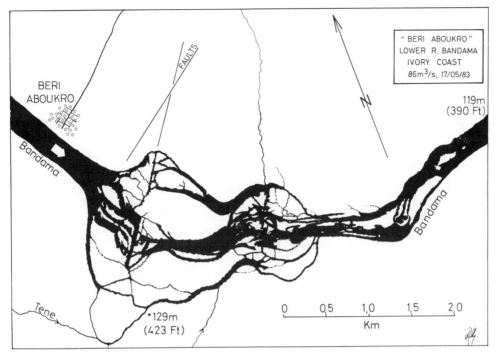

FIG. 25.1 Map of rapids near the village of Beri Aboukro, lower Bandama River, Ivory Coast. River is flowing over Precambrian schists, graywackes, and metavolcanic rocks (Bagarre and Tagini 1965).

Population Dynamics

When adequate larval breeding conditions commence, colonization and population buildup are characterized by several weeks where biting flies are present at the lowest limit of detectability, followed by an almost exponential rise in the daily numbers of flies biting (Davies et al. 1981) (Fig. 25.2). Predicting the beginning of this rise is one of the controller's major problems.

The Goal of Vector-Control Operations

The goal of OCP is to eliminate onchocerciasis as a major public health problem in seven West African countries (Benin, Burkina Faso, Ghana, Ivory Coast, Mali, Niger, and Togo). Extensions are planned to include Guinea, Guinea Bissau, Sierra Leone, and Senegal. In medical terms this means reduction of the disease to a level where its most noxious effect—blindness—has been eliminated. Epidemiologically, this implies reducing incidence of new infections to zero and keeping it at zero until the prevalence of the disease falls to such low levels that the parasite population can no longer maintain itself. Since the parasite is long-lived, this implies a fifteen-year operation.

For the vector-control operation, the study of precontrol data showed that blindness was not found where the Annual Transmission Potential was below 100, al-

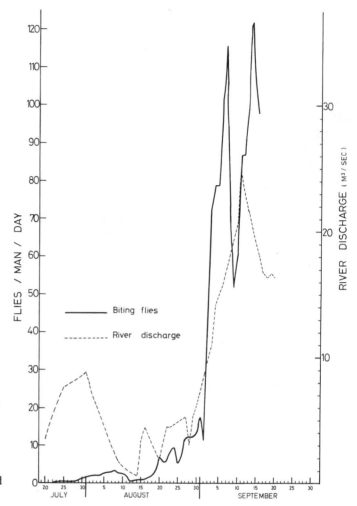

FIG. 25.2 Development of biting population of *Simulium damnosum* (specifically *S. sirbanum*) at Yabo, on the White Volta River, Burkina Faso. River discharge (dashed line) shown for comparison on right-hand scale. (Unpublished OCP data 1979)

though areas with higher ATP did not necessarily have high blindness rates. This figure, calculated from dissecting flies caught biting man (Walsh et al. 1978, 1979), was accepted as the guideline for the operations. Medical evaluation of the results have shown it to be generally correct, and where that level is not exceeded, transmission is indeed completely interrupted and no new cases of the disease are found. The relationship holds in the OCP area for the savanna flies associated with the savanna form of the disease. In the forest zone, little blindness occurs even at very high ATPs as long as only forest flies are present.

Control Methods: Adulticiding

Review.   A review of the early literature (1949–67) on the control of African black fly vectors of onchocerciasis by adulticiding techniques has been provided by Davies et al. (1982). In all cases, fixed-wing or rotary-wing aircraft were used to apply placement or space sprays of insecticides (DDT, HCH, and lindane) to gallery forests adjacent to very productive black-fly breeding sites. The objectives of those operations were to reduce significantly man-biting rates and/or *Onchocerca volvulus* transmission rates resulting from local fly breeding.

The most important potential use of adulticiding techniques for the OCP relates to the control of reinvading savanna cytotypes of *S. damnosum* at arrival sites, where the continued presence of infected flies would have serious epidemiological consequences.

A second possible use of adulticiding techniques could be the containment of an outbreak of resistance to organophosphate larvicides in a population of a savanna cytotype of *S. damnosum*. Adult control measures could complement alternative larviciding operations both at the source of the resistance development and in adjacent areas into which resistant flies had dispersed.

Third, residual adulticiding techniques might have a useful role to play in situations where the cost/benefit ratio of aerial larviciding operations is very poor, e.g., where a single isolated breeding site is distant from other breeding sites, or where a breeding site is productive for a very limited period of the year.

So far, the primary objective of the research program in OCP has been to develop adulticide techniques suitable for reinvasion control. As reinvading flies tend to arrive in a reinvasion zone more or less continuously over periods of several weeks' duration, it is unlikely that fogging/aerosol spraying techniques involving sequential applications of nonpersistant insecticides could ever become cost-effective. Consequently, the attention focused on the application of compounds with good residual properties and good spray coverage should, to some extent, compensate for the factors that inevitably reduce residual efficacy, e.g., extremes of rainfall and relative humidity, and rapid leaf growth. During the wet season, combinations of high rainfall and spate hydrological conditions severely restrict the work and movement of ground-based personnel. Thus more consideration has been given to aerial spraying techniques.

Helicopters, being very maneuverable at low speeds and having the facility for the precise placement of insecticide sprays, with consequent reduced risks of river-water contamination, have been considered better adapted as spray vehicles than fixed-wing aircraft. An additional advantage of a slow-flying helicopter is that the main rotor wake disturbs the gallery forest canopy and facilitates the penetration of spray droplets deep into the understory vegetation, resulting in good spray coverage down to ground level.

Experiments in OCP. In August 1983, some 30.3 hectares of gallery forest along both banks of a 2.1-kilometer stretch of the river La Faya (near Bamako, Mali) were sprayed from the ground up to a height of about 2.5 meters with permethrin at a swath dosage of 315g active ingredient/ha. Wet conditions made the exercise difficult and expensive ($900/km of river).

As a result of the spraying the *S. damnosum* s.l. population was reduced to a very low level and remained so for the ensuing month.

Helicopter spraying techniques being evaluated for riverine tsetse fly control (Baldry et al. 1981) were also studied in early 1978 to determine their potential for the control of populations of *S. damnosum* s.l. in riverine forest in a savanna zone of southwestern Burkina Faso (Davies et al. 1982, 1983; Bellec et al. 1983). Observations were made before and after spraying on populations of aquatic stages, of man-biting females, and of females attracted to sticky aluminum-plaque traps.

Deltamethrin sprayed at a swath dosage of 12.5 g a.i./ha onto a 30-kilometer stretch of the River Comoé gallery forest almost eliminated all female flies for approximately 9 days. Spray that contaminated the river killed all the larvae.

Endosulfan sprayed at a swath dosage of 100 g a.i./ha onto a similar stretch of forest caused a 60% reduction in man-biting females for 11 days. Females caught on sticky aluminum traps were immediately reduced by 30–50%, increasing to 70% after 3 days. Adult population recoveries were complete by the twelfth postspray day. Endosulfan that contaminated the river killed only young *S. damnosum* larvae.

Similarly, in early 1979, helicopter spraying trials for tsetse control (Kuzoe et al. 1981) were studied to evaluate effects of deltamethrin on a riverine population of *S. damnosum* s.l. in the forest/savanna mosaic zone of Ivory Coast (Bellec and Hébrard 1979). Observations were made on all categories of females of *S. damnosum* s.l. collected from sticky aluminum plaques before and after spray applications.

Deltamethrin sprayed at a swath dosage of 12.5 g a.i./ha to a 59-kilometer stretch of the River Marahoué gallery forest in January 1979 had virtually no effect on the *S. damnosum* population. When the spraying was repeated one month later, there was an immediate 70% reduction of *S. damnosum* females (all categories), which reached 85% by the seventh postspray day. Thereafter, the fly population rapidly recovered.

A third helicopter spraying trial was conducted in the Mô Valley reinvasion zone of central Togo during the wet season of 1984 (June). In view of the extensive amount of gallery forest canopy overhanging the River Mô and its tributaries, the spray-swath width was increased in comparison to that used previously (approximately 60 meters instead of 30). This was done by replacing the unilateral technique used in 1978 and 1979 with a bilateral technique (see Fig. 25.3). Unfortunately, this also increased contamination of the river.

The gallery forests along 21.4 kilometers of the Mô and 12.6 kilometers of its tributaries were sprayed with permethrin at a swath dosage of 137.5 g a.i./ha. Immediately after, there was a dramatic reduction in the daily man-biting rate of *S. damnosum* s.l., with a negative catch being recorded in the center of the spray zone the day after spraying. Heavy rain fell over the area on the third postspray day, and by the fifth day daily man-biting rates were returning to their prespray level. Upstream of the spray zone, recovery was less rapid.

Inadvertent permethrin contamination of the riverbed in the center of the spray zone was on the order of 410 g a.i./ha, approximately 50 times greater than the dosage at which this compound is effective as an anti-*Simulium* larvicide under the same conditions. It was thus not surprising that a considerable number of aquatic invertebrates were killed or adversely affected by the spraying. Some mortality of batrachian larvae and fish was also observed. Seven weeks after spraying, populations of aquatic and terrestrial nontarget organisms that had suffered from the spraying were well on the way to recovery.

Conclusions and future work.   The La Faya ground-spraying trial of 1983 clearly demonstrated the impracticability of ground-spraying operations under wet-season conditions. In view of incomplete understanding of the local distributions and behav-

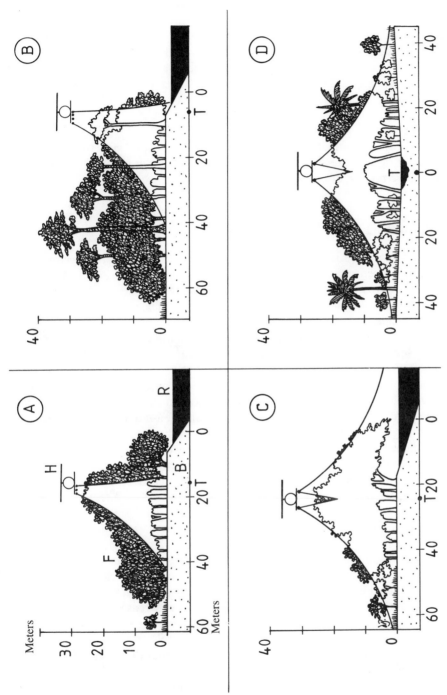

Fig. 25.3 Stylized transverse vegetation profiles of riverine forests and helicopter spray patterns relating to adulticiding trials of: A. River Camoé (unilateral spray technique, 1978), B. River Marahoué (unilateral spray technique, 1979), C. River Mô (bilateral spray technique, 1984), and D. River Samboa-Boa (tributary of Mô) (bilateral spray technique, 1984). *Abbreviations:* R = river, B = riverbank, F = forest, H = helicopter, T = helicopter track

ior of reinvading female *S. damnosum* s.l., none of the helicopter spraying techniques studied had been specifically tailored for adult *Simulium* control.

Encouraging results were obtained when deltamethrin was sprayed under true savanna conditions toward the end of the dry season (River Comoé experiment). Comparatively disappointing results were obtained when that compound was sprayed under humid forest/savanna mosaic conditions and when permethrin was sprayed in the savanna under wet-season conditions. Thus there does not yet exist an operational spraying technique for the control of reinvading flies in savanna areas under wet-season conditions.

It will be necessary to conduct detailed studies of swath widths, overall spray coverages, levels of spray discrimination, and spray droplet sizes with a view to developing spraying techniques that are better adapted for *S. damnosum* s.l. control and less harmful to aquatic nontarget organisms.

Control Methods: Larviciding

Generalities. The great advantage of larviciding is that it attacks the vector at a stage where it is concentrated in a very small area (rapids of large rivers) compared to the much larger area occupied by the adult flies. By the use of aircraft, the larval breeding sites can be located and treated quickly and efficiently using a minimal amount of insecticide.

The major peculiarity of insecticide application for *Simulium* larval control is the fact that the insecticide is carried downstream and diluted by the river current. If the passage of the insecticide slug or wave is measured at various distances below the application point, it is seen that as the wave progresses downstream, exposure to the insecticide becomes much longer but the concentration much less (Fig. 25.4). In the OCP, dosage is arbitrarily calculated on the basis of a ten-minute exposure at the application point. With a ground treatment by drip can, the application time may be literally 10 minutes, but with aerial application (99% of OCP work) the application takes only a few seconds; in this case, the distance above the first rapids is adjusted empirically to allow for some mixing before the wave reaches the rapids. If the treatment is too close, the passage will be too rapid and 100% effect will not be achieved.

The number of applications needed in a given reach of river varies with the density of potential breeding sites and the carry of the insecticide. For OCP purposes, carry is defined as the distance giving 100% mortality. This generally increases with increasing discharge, but the relationship must be determined for each larvicide. The number of potential breeding sites is usually reduced at high water as some rapids are flooded. In some cases, however, the average velocity increases to the point that virtually the entire river is a potential breeding site. In general, low-water treatment is characterized by a large number of precisely placed applications. At high water, there are fewer applications and they may be placed at regular distances. Figure 25.5 illustrates the high and low extremes of applications in the same rapids at high and low water levels. For the entire OCP area, 4,000 kilometers of river are under surveillance and/or treatment in the dry season and 18,000 kilometers in the wet season. At the height of the wet season, this can mean 4,500 applications and 8.5 tons of insecticide per week. Figure 25.6 evokes the magnitude of the task.

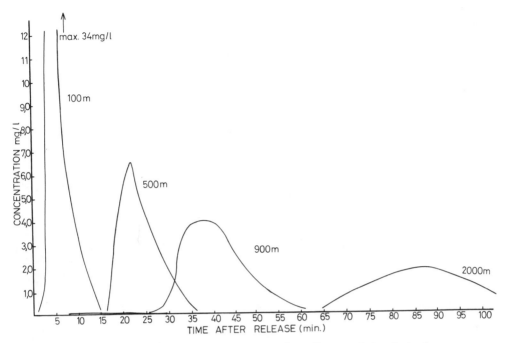

FIG. 25.4 Variation of concentration with time at various distances below instantaneous release of colored *B.t.* H-14 formulation. Target dose 16 mg/l–10 min. Discharge 2.7 m³/sec. Kou River, Burkina Faso, 1984. (Unpublished OCP data, courtesy of R. Meyer)

Almost all applications are done by aircraft. The application equipment is relatively simple, basically a tank, a metering device, and a discharge pipe. For *Bacillus thuringiensis* H-14, however, a boom and nozzle system giving a coarse spray must be used to overcome the poor dispersability of the product.

Obviously, precise dosage relies on a well-calibrated system of stream gauges, read as near to the treatment time as possible. In actual fact, in the rainy season, when discharge may double in a matter of hours, it is not rare for discharge figures to be in error by more than 30%. Satellite-transmitted data are now being used to improve this situation.

Characteristics of suitable larvicides. An ideal *S. damnosum* larvicide must meet a large number of criteria:

1. It must be highly active against all larval instars of *S. damnosum* s.l. Generally the concentration to obtain 100% mortality with a 10-minute exposure should not exceed 0.1 mg/l (equivalent to temephos) and ideally is much lower. Higher dosing rates lead to unacceptably large volumes of product to apply.

2. Since the compound is added to rivers that serve as domestic water supplies, the mammalian toxicity must be low. An oral LD_{50} of 1,000 mg of formulation/kg is considered the minimum. This means moderately toxic compounds could be used as dilute formulations. Danger to the program and aerial contractor staff handling the product must also be limited.

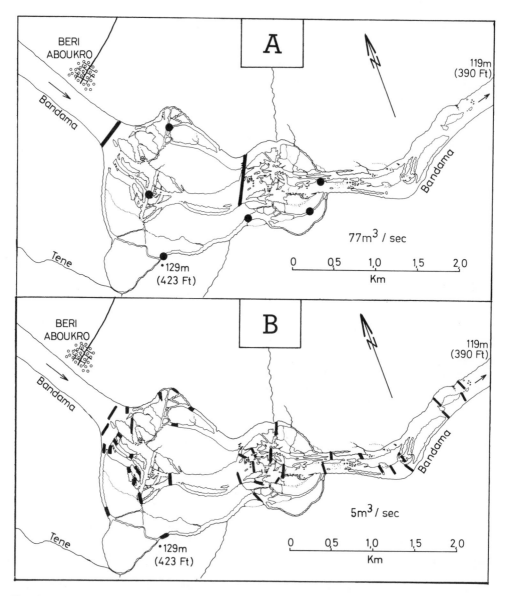

FIG. 25.5 Treatment of the Beri Aboukro Rapids on the Lower Bandama River, Ivory Coast. (Helicopter application of *B.t.* H-14 at a dosing rate of 1.6 mg/1–10 min.) A. (above) wet season (77m³/sec); 2 full doses (black bars) and 6 half doses (black dots). B. (below) dry season (5m³/sec); 42 full doses.

3. The compound should have no acute or long-term effects on fish or crustacea even at considerable overdoses. Toxicity to nontarget invertebrates (other than crustacea) should be minimal, but it is recognized that some reduction will occur. In principle, no important group of invertebrates should be completely eliminated, but shifts in proportions are tolerable.

4. The carry should be 20 kilometers or more under good hydrological conditions.

FIG. 25.6 Bell 204 helicopter treating the Sassandra River in Ivory Coast with *Bacillus thuringiensis* H-14. One of 19 applications of 103 liters of product needed to control 200 km of this river, which represents only a few percent of the total weekly activity of OCP in the wet season.

5. The product should be formulated as an emulsifiable concentrate that is less dense than water and forms a stable emulsion without agitation. Formulation has a very important influence on performance, but the mechanisms of this are not well understood. Wettable powder and flowable formulations are to be avoided because of the need for preparation or dilution in the field.

6. The formulation should not degrade rapidly when stored unprotected in a hot climate (40°C air temperature).

7. As much as possible, solvents corrosive to release equipment and aircraft structure should be avoided.

The insecticides currently used may be discussed by chemical group.

Organophosphates:

Temephos (Abate®) 20% emulsifiable concentrate remains the mainstay of OCP in 75% of the operational zone. It combines excellent carry (up to 50 km) with good selectivity (maximum 25–30% reduction in nontarget invertebrates) (Wallace and Hynes 1981).

Chlorphoxim is more toxic to the nontarget fauna (Gibon and Troubat 1980) but is still acceptable. It is used against strains resistant to temephos.

Bacillus thuringiensis H-14:

Formulations of this product are used against strains resistant to organophosphates. The activity of the current formulation (Teknar® by Sandoz) is rather low (minimum dose, 1.6 mg/l for 10 minutes) and the carry mediocre. Compared with temephos, 3 to 6 times more product must be used at each application point and up to 20 times more for an entire river. Use of the product is therefore limited to discharges below 50m³/sec. Selectivity is excellent, with only some Chironomidae being affected among the nontarget organisms (Gibon et al. 1980, Troubat et al. 1982). Formulations with improved performance are being developed by several manufacturers.

Other Insecticides:

Screening of other compounds is being carried out intensively. To date, one pyrethroid (permethrin) has undergone an operational trial. Its use will be limited to high water because it is somewhat more toxic to nontarget invertebrates than temephos or chlorphoxim. A carbamate (carbosulfan) will begin an operational trial soon. Several IGR compounds of the juvenile hormone type are under small-scale field evaluation. Unfortunately, chitin inhibitors such as diflubenzuron have not shown satisfactory activity against *S. damnosum*.

Evaluation of Treatments

Treatments are evaluated directly by checking the river for immature stages after treatment. The few easily accessible sites on each river are checked weekly by ground-based teams. Checks of the entire river are made by helicopter when needed. An estimation of the potential danger posed by an infested site is based on a rough estimation of the population structure (relative densities of eggs, young larvae, mature larvae, and pupae). The evolution of conditions in the breeding site (rising or falling water, prospects for heavy rain, etc.) is also taken into account. A few larvae in a rapidly declining river at the end of the rainy season are not nearly as dangerous as the same number of larvae in a gradually rising river at the beginning of the season. Density of immature stages is not determined quantitatively, but rather the degree of infestation is estimated qualitatively. The extremely clumped distribution of the larvae makes quantitative estimates difficult (Colbo 1987).

Numbers of adult black flies are monitored by human-bait catches near the river. These catches reveal treatment failures over a wide area by the presence of nulliparous flies and allow calculation of standardized biting rates and transmission potentials (Davies et al. 1978; Walsh et al. 1978, 1979).

An oviposition trap consisting of an aluminum plate is also operational (Bellec 1976; Bellec et al., in press). This allows detection of very low levels of adults and serves as an alarm for beginning treatments.

Table 25.1 Alternatives in treatment tactics

Aspect	"Heavy"	"Light"
Dose rate	several times minimum	minimum for 100% or even slightly less*
Coverage	all breeding sites treated	only major breeding sites treated*
Rhythm	7 days	more than 7 days (adjusted to larval life cycle)
Continuity	52 weeks/yr. as long as river flows	Voluntary suspensions (very low flow, rapids flooded, population "0")

*Some risk of selection of resistance.

Ecological Surveillance

Fish and invertebrate populations are sampled several times a year in treated rivers. To date, no change in fish populations imputable to insecticide use has been found. Invertebrate populations are somewhat modified quantitatively and qualitatively, but the changes are considered to be acceptable and have been demonstrated to be reversible (Dejoux et al. 1980).

Treatment Tactics

The alternatives available to the *S. damnosum* controller are summarized in Table 25.1. A "light" alternative would purport to be less dangerous to the nontarget fauna, possibly less likely to provoke resistance, allow natural biological control to be more effective, and be more economical. Each point will be discussed in detail in view of the OCP experience:

1. *Dosing rate.* Certainly in the opening phases of a treatment the dosing rate should be several times the absolute minimum (if ecological constraints permit). This is to compensate for the complexity of the breeding sites, imprecision of discharge measurements, and baseline variations in susceptibility. When populations are reduced, it would be theoretically possible to reduce the dose. A few larvae escaping to emerge as flies might not result in a population increase, and it has been proposed that a low dose may retard resistance by conserving susceptible genotypes (Tabashnik and Croft 1982).

However, the OCP experience points to constant underdosing as one cause of resistance, and once good control has been achieved it is not acceptable to risk population "escapes" that result in large numbers of bites for several weeks. Therefore, it has seemed wiser to use "high dose" strategy. (Whether this strategy retards resistance by the "functionally recessive" mechanism is questionable.)

2. *Coverage.* Although it is sometimes the case that 90% of the flies in a river basin may come from a few major breeding sites, restricting treatments to these sites is probably only justifiable in nuisance-control situations, or for vector control near the end of OCP activities, when disease prevalence will be low and chemotherapy may be underway.

Operationally, such a tactic is difficult to execute because only detailed aerial prospection (which is expensive) can adequately establish whether the "minor" breeding sites have larvae. A fly-catching point serves as an indicator of breeding over a wide area, but by the time flies are being caught it may be too late to avoid some transmission during the period between the treatments and the decline of the adult population (several weeks). For these reasons, no large-scale experiments of this type have been carried out.

From the standpoint of resistance, limited coverage could theoretically reduce selection pressure by leaving some populations untreated. In practice, however, it is likely that drift of larvicide from the major breeding sites would expose the minor ones to a dangerous underdosing situation.

3. *Treatment rhythm.* Repeating treatments at 7-day intervals ensures that no larvae can pupate in between treatments under most conditions, even allowing for a 24-hour delay due to technical difficulties.

As mentioned above, the larval development time is often longer than 7 or even 8 days and can be predicted to some degree from the water temperature. It is in principle possible to reduce considerably the number of treatment cycles in a year by 25–30% by adjusting the cycle to the larval life cycle.

In practice, a completely open treatment cycle implies a 7-day-per-week evaluation and treatment operation, with extra costs. Other than 7 days, the only cycles that can be maintained in a 5- to 6-day workweek are 8–8–12–8–8–12 days and 9–12–9–12 days (R. Meyer, personal communication). Another problem is that the side streams in a basin may be cool enough to slow down larval development while the main river stays warmer (Ocran et al. 1980). If two separate treatment circuits must be flown, most of the advantage is lost.

Nonetheless, there are some areas in the Western Extension zone of OCP (Guinea, in particular) where water temperatures are cool enough during a sufficiently long part of the year to allow putting an entire basin on a 9–12 cycle. Large-scale experiments in this sense will be carried out before operations begin. In this way, failure will have very little influence on the epidemiological results.

4. *Continuity of treatment.* As OCP progressed, there has been a steady decrease in dry-season treatments as confidence was gained in suspending treatments while a river was still flowing but the biting population reduced to zero. Some high-water suspensions are also carried out routinely. Very few rivers are treated 52 weeks per year. This approach to reducing treatment is by its nature empirical and adjusted to each river and season. It is much aided by careful precontrol studies of the relationship of hydrological conditions and breeding-site productivity.

The principal difficulty in execution is deciding when to start treatment again. *S. damnosum* control in OCP never approaches eradication, even though the population cannot be detected by routine methods. A nontreated breeding site always becomes positive in a matter of weeks or a few months, either from residual population or immigration. A wrong decision on when to start treating again can lead to "explosions" of flies. Given the fact that all sites cannot be checked every week, successful execution will depend on a controller with good knowledge of the river and its "danger points."

Also, the reduction gained by suspension is hard to predict in advance because it depends on rainfall. Therefore, it is difficult to plan to reduce the number of aircraft or flying hours in consequence.

From the standpoint of resistance, changes in treatment rhythm and continuity are neutral or positive (i.e., retard resistance) since survivors are not exposed to insecticide (unless growth rate has a genetic basis, in which case widely spaced treatments might select for rapid growth).

In the background of all attempts to reduce treatment, there remains the question of whether "light" tactics that allow some larvae to escape can result in a constant low level of flies without significant transmission, or whether explosions will result (Birley et al. 1983). OCP hopes to answer this experimentally as the extensions are undertaken.

Interaction with Natural Control

The life table of immature stages of *S. damnosum* is rather poorly known. It is probable that in permanent rivers in the dry season parasites and predators have an influence on populations. Use of a selective insecticide such as *B.t.* H-14 in the dry season may enhance predator effects. In regard to parasites, it is hard to envisage how to enhance their role when the goal of vector control is virtual elimination of the host (Lacey and Undeen 1987).

In the wet season, physical factors probably take over as the main natural control, since predators are highly dispersed (Ross and Merritt 1987). Abrupt fluctuations in water flow undoubtedly wash away or strand many larvae. Experiments are planned to determine if it is necessary to treat during a brief, heavy flood or whether the flood itself may achieve sufficient control.

Interaction with Environmental Control

On some dam spillways it has been possible to achieve good results by alternately drying different parts of the spillways and totally avoiding the use of insecticide.

Resistance

It is obvious that resistance presents a very serious threat to OCP, given the long duration required to achieve the desired results. However, it is not in the scope of this chapter to review the resistance situation exhaustively.

Resistance has occurred to temephos (Guillet et al. 1980) and chlorphoxim (Kurtak et al. 1981) in part of the OCP area (Ivory Coast). It involves for the most part the "forest" members of the *S. damnosum* complex, which are not dangerous vectors in the area concerned. One small population of savanna species in the same area did show signs of development of resistance to temephos, but it was neutralized by a vigorous treatment with *B.t.* H-14.

The resistance in the forest species is much more widespread. The larvae can be controlled by *B.t.* H-14 in the dry season, but the cost of applying the large volumes needed in the rainy season is too high (see Knutti and Beck 1987). Chlorphoxim is still useful in some areas, where the resistance to it reverts when treatments are suspended. The influence of the resistance on the epidemiological results has been slight (see Philippon 1987).

Every effort is being made to find a broad range of larvicides to counteract resistance. Alternation of *B.t.* H-14 with other chemicals will certainly be the primary response to resistance and may be employed from the beginning in new operations in an attempt to retard its onset.

Conclusion

Chemical larviciding will undoubtedly remain the mainstay of vector-control operations directed against *S. damnosum.* The nature of the target species and the level of control required limit the options in the tactics of larvicide use. Some alternatives, such as adjustment of treatment rhythm to larval life cycle, are being tested. Screening of new compounds must continue to ensure that a broad range of replacement compounds is available to counteract resistance. Alternation between *B.t.* H-14 and classical chemicals is an attractive strategy for the future, both in order to retard resistance and to ease pressure on nontarget organisms. A better understanding of the interaction of insecticides with river water and their transport by rivers would help refine formulations and application techniques.

EAST AFRICA

Unlike West Africa, where the epidemiology of onchocerciasis shows relatively consistent distribution over wide areas, the foci in East Africa are highly varied. Most of the disease foci are relatively small and separated from each other, with the exception of the large focus in southern Sudan, which is part of the sub-Saharan belt spreading from Senegal to the east. The largest truly East African focus is that of Ethiopia. The extent of this focus, however, is still not fully determined.

The patchy distribution of onchocerciasis in East Africa is a result of various factors such as topography, climate, and the distribution of man and the various vector species. Most of the foci are restricted to mountainous areas (review by Raybould and White 1979).

Vector Species

In East Africa human onchocerciasis is transmitted by members of the *S. neavei* group and of the *S. damnosum* complex.

S. neavei group. This group, which today consists of about ten species, includes three man-biting species: *S. ethiopiense* Fain & Oomen 1968, a widespread vector in the southwestern highlands of Ethiopia; *S. woodi* de Meillon 1930, a localized vector in mountainous parts of Malawi and Tanzania; and *S. neavei* s.s. Roubaud 1915, an important vector in foci in Uganda and eastern Zaire. It was also an important vector in Kenya until its eradication in the 1950s. None of them occurs in West Africa.

The three species are confined to forest or dense woodland habitats, where they breed in streams that harbor crabs upon which the larvae and pupae attach themselves in a phoretic association. They are very sensitive to ecological changes. Populations decrease when woodland is destroyed. Such a destruction of forests seems to have eliminated the vector and interrupted the transmission of onchocerciasis at a focus in Kenya (Buckley 1951). It also seems to be happening in the eastern Usambara Mountains as an effect of deforestation and agricultural development (Grunewald et al. 1979).

S. damnosum complex. In the *S. damnosum* complex five cytospecies are identified as vectors of onchocerciasis in East Africa. Two of these species, *S. damnosum* s.s. and *S. sirbanum*, are better known as the "savanna" species from West Africa, where they are among the vectors of greatest importance in transmitting the blinding savanna form of onchocerciasis. The other three vectors, *S. kilibanum* and the Jimma form and Nkusi form of the *S. damnosum* complex, are restricted to central and East Africa.

Control Campaigns

S. neavei group. *S. neavei* has been controlled successfully in Kenya and Uganda by employing DDT at dosages between 0.5 and 2.5 ppm/30 min repeated at varying intervals (up to 42 days [Prentice 1974]). The treatments were most effective at the end of the rainy season as the discharge of streams and rivers declined.

The impressive success of McMahon et al. (1958) in eradicating *S. neavei* s.s. from a 40,000 km² focus is well known and has been confirmed by several authors (Nelson and Grounds 1958, McMahon 1967, Roberts et al. 1967). Several other control campaigns failed due to insufficient precontrol survey data and/or to repopulation of breeding sites by reinvading flies.

S. damnosum complex. *S. damnosum* s.l. was controlled in an intensive focus of the Victoria Nile in Uganda in 1952 by employing DDT. A series of 12 treatment cycles at dosages of 0.036 ppm/30 min was necessary to control larval breeding in this part of the river. The onchocerciasis infection rate being 65% in precontrol times (Barnley 1953) dropped to 17% in 1967 and was found to be lower than 0.2% in 1974 (McCrae 1978).

In an earlier attempt, aerial spraying of the riverbanks with DDT at a dosage of 200 g/ha was undertaken to control adult *S. damnosum* s.l. resting on vegetation. However, this method seemed to have more larvicidal than adulticidal effects due to inadvertent spraying of the river (Barnley 1958).

Other control operations against vectors of the *S. damnosum* complex, although carried out successfully, finally failed due to reinvasion of flies and repopulation of the breeding sites.

Conclusions

Several successful operations against the vectors of onchocerciasis in Kenya and Uganda have proved that it is feasible to eliminate the vectors and to interrupt onchocerciasis transmission in certain parts of East Africa. Unlike West Africa, in East Africa control campaigns will benefit from the patchy distribution of the disease foci. Because of their isolation, the risk of reinvasion of flies and of repopulation of breeding sites is rather low and eradication of the vector is possible, especially with *S. neavei*.

In East Africa nearly all control operations against vector species of the *S. neavei* group and the *S. damnosum* complex have employed DDT. Although there is only inadequate information on insecticide-susceptibility levels of vector larvae in East Africa, no resistance to this insecticide among members of both the *S. neavei* group and the *S. damnosum* complex has been reported yet. However, DDT resistance has been observed in various parts of West Africa (Walsh 1970, Guillet et al. 1977).

Insecticide-susceptibility tests have to be carried out and alternative larvicides have to be evaluated against the larvae of vector species. Biodegradable compounds such as temephos and *B.t.* H-14 are of particular interest. However, the employment of temephos against *Simulium* larvae in mountainous areas is hampered by the fact that the efficiency of temephos is reduced by the the low temperatures of mountain streams and rivers. Nevertheless, any control operation against members of the *S. neavei* group will profit from the slow development rate of the aquatic stages (Raybould and Mhiddin 1978), permitting long larvicide application intervals (up to 42 days; Prentice 1974). Efforts, costs, and environmental impact will thus all be reduced (Raybould and White 1979). Temephos has been employed recently in experimental control campaigns in southwestern Sudan (Baker and Abdelnur, in preparation) and in the Tukuyu focus in southern Tanzania, where *B.t.* H-14 has also been tested (Le Berre, personal communication).

By conducting sound onchocerciasis surveys and vector studies, it would be feasible to eliminate vector species and to reduce onchocerciasis transmission in many foci in East Africa. In Ethiopia, Burundi, Cameroon, Congo, Malawi, Tanzania, and Zaire, programs are on the way to collect data on the epidemiology of onchocerciasis, to determine the role of potential vectors on the transmission, to map their distribution and breeding sites, and to evaluate the possibility of control operations.

ACKNOWLEDGMENTS

Much of this chapter is based on the results of the World Health Organization Onchocerciasis Control Programme. In such a program, any published result is the fruit of the work of a large number of personnel at all levels, from the entomologists in charge of treatments and evaluation, the pilots who carry out prospection and treatment missions, to the drivers and vector collectors. We thank them all heartily. Specifically among VCU staff or consultants, we would like to name Dr. H. Agoua, and Messrs. M. Ocran, P. Renaud, B. Cliff, R. Meyer, F. Pleszak, M. Ouedraogo, R. Sawadogo, and B. Télé. Our thanks also to Dr. E. M. Samba, director of OCP, for his continued support and permission to publish this document.

LITERATURE CITED

Adiamah, J. H., J. N. Raybould, D. Kurtak, A. Israel, B. T. A. Maegga, and A. K. Opoku. 1986. The susceptibility of *Simulium damnosum* s.l. larvae from the Volta River in southern Ghana to temephos after nearly eight years of intermittent treatment. *Insect. Science and its Application* 7:27–30.

Bagarre, E., and B. Tageni. 1965. Carte Géographique de la Côte d'Ivoire au 1/1,000,000. Dir. Mines et Géol. Abidjan.

Baker, R. H. A., and O. M. Abdelnur. 1985. Localized onchocerciasis vector control in the Bahr El Ghazal Region of South-Western Sudan. II. Control. (In preparation).

Baldry, D. A. T., J. Everts, B. Roman, G. A. Boon von Ochssee, and C. Laveissière. 1981. The experimental application of insecticides from a helicopter for the control of riverine population of *Glossina tachinoides* in West Africa. Part VIII: The effects of two spray applications of OMS-570 (endosulfan) and of OMS-1998 (decamethrin) on *G. tachinoides* and non-target organisms in Upper Volta. *Trop. Pest Mgmt.* 27:83–110.

Barnley, G. R. 1953. The control of *Simulium damnosum* (Theobald) on the Victoria Nile, Uganda. WHO mimeo. doc. Onchocerciasis 18. 34 pp.

———. 1958. The control of *Simulium* vectors of onchocerciasis in Uganda. *Proc. 10th Int. Congr. Entomol.* (1956) 3:535–537.

Bellec, C. 1976. Captures d'Adultes de *Simulium damnosum* Theobald 1903 (Diptera, Simuliidae) à l'aide de plaques d'aluminium, en Afrique de l'Ouest. *Cah. ORSTOM sér. Entomol. Méd. Parasitol.* 14:209–217.

Bellec, C., and G. Hébrard. 1979. Essais sur le terrain d'adulticide antisimulidien en zone préforestière de Côte d'Ivoire. Unpub. rep. No. 11/ONCHO/rap/79 of Institut Pierre Richet, Bouaké, Ivory Coast. 12 pp.

Bellec, C., G. Hébrard, and A. D'Almeida. 1983. The effects of helicopter-applied adulticides for riverine tsetse control on *Simulium* populations in a West African savanna habitat. II. Effects as estimated by nonbiting stages of *Simulium damnosum* s.l. and other blackfly species caught on aluminium plaque traps. *Trop. Pest Mgmt.* 29:7–12.

Bellec, C., and G. Hébrard. 1983. Fécondité des femelles du complexe *Simulium damnosum* en Afrique de l'Ouest. *Cah. ORSTOM sér Entomol. Méd. Parasitol.* 21:251–260.

Bellec, C., D. G. Zerbo, J. Nion, G. Hébrard, and H. Agoua. Utilisation expérimentale de plaques d'aluminium pour l'évaluation entomologique du Programme de Lutte contre l'Onchocercose dans le Bassin de la Volta. *Cah. ORSTOM sér. Entomol. Méd. Parasitol.* (in press).

Birley, M. H., J. F. Walsh, and J. B. Davies, 1983. Development of a model for *S. damnosum* s.l. recolonization dynamics at a breeding site in the Onchocerciasis Control Programme area when control is interrupted. *J. Appl. Ecol.* 20:507–519.

Buckley, J. J. C. 1951. Studies on human onchocerciasis and *Simulium* in Nyanza Province, Kenya. II. The disappearance of *S. neavei* from bush-cleared focus. *J. Helminth.* 25:213–222.

Colbo, M. H. 1987. Problems in estimating black fly populations in their acquatic stages (this volume).

Davies, J. B., R. Le Berre, J. F. Walsh, and B. Cliff. 1978. Onchocerciasis and *Simulium* control in the Volta River Basin. *Mosquito News* 38:466–472.

Davies, J. B., A. Seketeli, J. F. Walsh, T. Barro, and R. Sawadogo. 1981. Studies on biting *Simulium damnosum* s.l. at a breeding site on the Onchocerciasis Control Programme area during and after an interruption of insecticidal treatments. *Tropenmed. Parasitol.* 32:17–24.

Davies, J. B., C. Gboho, D. A. T. Baldry, C. Bellec, R. Sawadogo, and P. C. Tiao. 1982. The effects of helicopter-applied adulticides for riverine tsetse control on *Simulium* populations in a West African savanna habitat. I. Introduction, methods and the effect on biting adults and aquatic stages of *Simulium damnosum* s.l. *Trop. Pest Mgmt.* 23:284–290.

Davies, J. B., J. F. Walsh, D. A. T. Baldry, and C. Bellec. 1983. The effects of helicopter-applied adulticides for riverine tsetse control on *Simulium* populations in a West African savanna habitat. III. Conclusions: the possible role of adulticiding in onchocerciasis control in West Africa. *Trop. Pest Mgmt.* 29:13–15.

Dejoux, C., J. M. Elouard, J. M. Jesten, F. M. Gibon, and J. J. Troubat. 1980. Action du temephos (Abate®) sur les invertébrés aquatiques. VIII. Mise en évidence d'un impact à long terme après six années de surveillance. Mimeo. rept. No. 36. Laboratoire d'Hydrobiologie de Bouaké, B.P. 1434, Bouaké, Ivory Coast. 14 pp.

Gibon, F. M., J. M. Elouard, and J. J. Troubat. 1980. Action du *Bacillus thuringiensis* var. *israelensis* sur les invertébrés aquatiques. I. Effets d'un traitement expérimental sur la Marahoué. Mimeo. rept. No 38. Laboratoire d'Hydrobiologie de Bouaké. B.P. 1434, Bouaké, Ivory Coast. 11 pp.

Gibon, F. M., and J. J. Troubat. 1980. Effets d'un traitement au chlorphoxime sur la dérive des invertébrés benthoques. Mimeo. rept. No 37. Laboratoire d'Hydrobiologie de Bouaké, B.P. 1434, Bouaké, Ivory Coast. 7 pp.

Grunewald, J. 1981. Hydro-chemical and physical characteristics of the larval sites of species of the *Simulium damnosum* complex. Pp. 227–235 in M. Laird, Ed., *Blackflies: the future for biological methods in integrated control.* Academic Press, New York and London.

Grunewald, J., E. B. Grunewald, and J. N. Raybould. 1979. The hydro-chemical and physical characteristics of the breeding sites of the *Simulium neavei* Roubaud group and their associated crabs in the Eastern Usambara Mountains in Tanzania. *Int. Rev. Gesamt. Hydrobiol.* 64:71–88.

Guillet, P., M. Escaffre, M. Ouedraogo, and D. Quillévéré. 1980. Mise en évidence d'une résistance au téméphos dans le complexe *Simulium damnosum* (*S. sanctipauli* et *S. soubrense*) en Côte d'Ivoire. (Zone du Programme de Lutte contre l'Onchocercose dans la Région du Bassin de la Volta.) *Cah. ORSTOM sér. Entomol. Méd Parasitol.* 18:291–299.

Guillet, P., J. Mouchet, and S. Grebaut. 1977. DDT resistance in *Simulium damnosum* s.l. (Diptera, Simuliidae) in West Africa. WHO mimeo. doc. WHO/VBC/77.678. 7 pp.

Jamnback, H. 1981. The origins of blackfly control programmes. Pp. 71–73 in M. Laird, Ed., *Blackflies: the future for biological methods in integrated control.* Academic Press, New York and London.

Knutti, H. J., and W. R. Beck. 1987. The control of black fly larvae with Teknar® (this volume).

Kurtak, D., M. Ouedraogo, M. Ocran, T. Barro, and P. Guillet. 1982. Preliminary note on the appearance in Ivory Coast of resistance to chlorphoxim in *Simulium soubrense/sanctipauli* larvae already resistant to temephos (Abate®), WHO mimeo. doc. WHO/VBC/82.850.

Kuzoe, F. A. S., D. A. T. Baldry, J. R. Cullen, A. Van der Vloedt, and P. de Raadt. 1981. Experimental application of insecticides by helicopter to control vectors of trypanomiasis in the Ivory Coast. *Rep. 16th Mtg. Int. Sci. Council for Trypanosomiasis Research and Control.* OAU/STRC Publication No. 111. Pp. 427–442.

Lacey, L. A., and A. H. Undeen. 1987. The biological control potential of pathogens and parasites of black flies (this volume).

Laird, M., Ed. 1981. *Blackflies: The future for biological methods in integrated control.* Academic Press, New York and London. 399 pp.

Le Berre, R. 1966. Contribution à l'étude biologique et écologique de *Simulium damnosum* Theobald 1903. (Diptera: Simuliidae). *Mém. ORSTOM* 17:1–204.

McCrae, A. W. R. 1978. Intermittent eradication of *Simulium damnosum* Theo. on the Nile from Jinja, Uganda: 1959–1977. Pp. 133–134 in S. Willmot, Ed., Medical entomology centenary symposium proceedings. *R. Soc. Trop. Med. Hyg.*

McMahon, J. P. 1967. A review of the control of *Simulium* vectors of onchocerciasis. *Bull. WHO* 37:415–426.

McMahon, J. P., R. B. Highton, and H. Goiny. 1958. The eradication of *Simulium neavei* from Kenya. *Bull. WHO* 19:75–107.

Mokry, J. E. 1980. A method for estimating the age of field-collected female *Simulium damnosum* s.l. (Diptera: Simuliidae). *Tropenmed. Parasitol.* 31:121–127.

Nelson, G. S., and J. G. Grounds. 1958. Onchocerciasis at Kodera eleven years after the eradication of the vector. *East Afr. Med. J.* 35:365–368.

Ocran, M. H., J. B. Davies, H. Agoua, C. Gboho, and J. Ouedraogo. (1982). Water temperature in *S. damnosum* breeding rivers of the Onchocerciasis Control Programme area. WHO mimeo. doc., WHO/VBC/82.848. 9 pp.

Philippon, B. 1987. Problems in epidemiology and control of West African onchocerciasis (this volume).

Prentice, M. A. 1974. *Simulium* control programme in Uganda. In *Research and control of onchocerciasis in the western hemisphere. Proc. Int. Symp. Washington, D.C., 1974.* Washington Pan Amer. Health Org. Pp. 87–95.

Prost, A. 1980. Le polymorphisme des onchocercoses humaines ouest-africaines. *Ann. Parasitol. Hum. Comp.* 55(2):239–245.

Prost, A., A. Rougement, and M. S. Omar. 1980. Caractères épidémiologiques, cliniques et biologiques des onchocercoses de savane et de forêt en Afrique Occidentale. Revue critique et éléments nouveaux. *Ann. Parasitol. Hum. Comp.* 55(3):347–355.

Raybould, J. N., and H. K. Mhiddin. 1978. Studies on the immature stages of the *Simulium neavei* Roubaud complex and their associated crabs in the Eastern Usambara Mountains in Tanzania. III. Investigations on development and survival and their relevance to control. *Ann. Trop. Med. Parasitol.* 72:177–187.

Raybould, J. N., and G. B. White. 1979. The distribution, bionomics and control of onchocerciasis vectors (Diptera: Simuliidae) in Eastern Africa and Yemen. *Tropenmed. Parasitol.* 30:505–547.

Roberts, J. M. D., E. Neumann, C. W. Gockel, and R. B. Highton. 1967. Onchocerciasis in Kenya 9, 11 and 18 years after elimination of the vector. *Bull. WHO* 37:195–212.

Ross, D. H., and R. W. Merritt. 1987. Factors affecting larval black fly distributions and population dynamics (this volume).

Séchan, Y. 1980. Durée de développement des stades préimaginaux de *Simulium sirbanum* Vajime et Dunbar, 1975 à la limite nord de son aire de répartition en Afrique occidentale. Note préliminaire. *Cah. ORSTOM sér. Entomol. Méd. Parasitol.* 18:59–60.

Tabashnik, B. E., and B. A. Croft. 1982. Managing pesticide resistance in crop-arthropod complexes: interactions between biological operational factors. *Environ. Entomol.* 11:1137–44.

Troubat, J. J., F. M. Gibon, A. I. Wongbe, and M. Bihoum. 1982. Action du *Bacillus thuringiensis* Berliner H14 sur les invertébrés aquatiques. II. Effets d'un épandage sur le cycle de dérive et les densités d'insectes benthiques. Mimeo. rept. No. 48. Laboratoire d'Hydrobiologie de Bouaké, B.P. 1434, Bouaké, Ivory Coast. 8 pp.

Wallace, R. R., and B. N. Hynes. 1981. The effect of chemical treatments against blackfly larvae on the fauna of running waters. Pp. 237–258 in M. Laird, Ed., *Blackflies: the future for biological methods in integrated control.* Academic Press, New York and London.

Walsh, J. F. 1970. Evidence of reduced susceptibility to DDT in controlling *Simulium damnosum* (Diptera: Simuliidae) on the River Niger. *Bull. WHO* 43:316–318.

Walsh, J. F., J. B. Davies, and R. Le Berre. 1978. Standardization of criteria for assessing the effect of *Simulium* control in onchocerciasis control programmes. *Trans. R. Soc. Trop. Med. Hyg.* 72:675–676.

————.1979. Entomological aspects of the first five years of the Onchocerciasis Control Programme in the Volta River Basin. *Tropenmed. Parasitol.* 30:328–344.

Walsh, J. F., J. B. Davies, and R. Garms. 1981. Further studies on the reinvasion of the Onchocerciasis Control Programme by *Simulium damnosum* s.l.: The effects of an extension of control activities into southern Ivory Coast during 1979. *Tropenmed. Parasitol.* 32:269–273.

Wenk, P. 1981. Bionomics of adult blackflies. Pp. 259–279 in M. Laird, Ed., *Blackflies: the future for biological methods in integrated control.* Academic Press, New York and London.

Part VI Epidemiology and Control of Simuliid-Borne Diseases

26 PROBLEMS IN EPIDEMIOLOGY AND CONTROL OF WEST AFRICAN ONCHOCERCIASIS

Bernard Philippon

The considerations presented in this chapter are based exclusively on the ten-year experience of the Onchocerciasis Control Programme in the Volta River Basin Area in West Africa (OCP).

OCP is at present the largest vector-control program in the world: 764,000 km^2 are currently under control in seven West African countries, and southern and western extensions of control operations covering, respectively, 110,000 and 450,000 km^2 are being prepared (Fig. 26.1); 23,000 kilometers of rivers are under surveillance by more than 800 staff members using 11 aircraft and 250 vehicles distributed in 24 operational bases; the annual budget is about U.S. $20 million. Other main features have been described in program documents (OCP 1973, 1978, and 1984).

Ten years after its inception and halfway through the twenty-year period initially allocated for its completion, OCP now offers a unique opportunity for the evaluation of the problems related to large-scale control programs of vectors of African onchocerciasis.

Despite a number of previous presentations and publications, many questions are still raised concerning the program: Why control exclusively this disease in this particular area, on such a large scale, for such a long period, with strategies and tactics based only on entomological control, and excluding multidisease and/or chemotherapeutical approaches?

ONCHOCERCIASIS IN THE OCP AREA

In spite of several million individuals being infected, human onchocerciasis is neither the most lethal nor the most prevalent vector-borne parasitic disease in West Africa. It is, however, the only disease that generates a high degree of disablement, poverty, and socioeconomic disturbance in heavily affected savanna villages. Onchocerciasis (or "river blindness") is not only a major public health problem but also a disease that presents a serious obstacle to the socioeconomic development of the few irri-

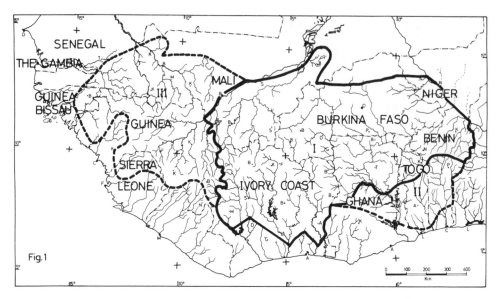

FIG. 26.1 Map of West Africa showing the current OCP area of 764,000 km² (I), the Southern Extension area of 110,000 km² proposed for implementation in 1986 (II), and the Western Extension area of 445,000 km² proposed for implementation in 1986 (III).

gated lands of the arid subregion, the populations of which are among the "poorest of the poor" in the world.

Before the implementation of the OCP, the area concerned was one of the worst foci of African onchocerciasis. Overall, there were 1.5 million people infected out of a total of some 12 million inhabitants, with more than 100,000 blind people being found along the main rivers. In hyperendemic villages onchocerciasis prevalence was over 80% and blindness rates were 25–50% among adults.

It is considered that the life expectancy of blind people in this area is 13 years less than that of people with normal vision, implying that affected communities lose an average of 22 years of productive life per blind man. A rough estimate for Burkina Faso indicates an annual loss of 60,000 man-years of productive life (Prost 1984). Moreover, there is a negative correlation between onchocercal blindness prevalence and population growth for small-size villages and low human population densities (Prost et al. 1979, 1983). The existence of large uninhabited or deserted areas in large river valleys affected by blinding onchocerciasis in the savanna is commonly observed, even if onchocerciasis is obviously not the unique and initial factor causing desertion. An increasing mass of epidemiological data indicates that the situation is very similar in areas adjacent to the present OCP area, and plans are now being formulated for the OCP to deal with them (OCP 1981, 1984).

In West African savanna areas, onchocerciasis control in infected valleys is therefore a prerequisite to any attempts at water-resources management, agricultural production, and socioeconomic development or human resettlement, especially in present contexts of accelerated human population growth and of concentrations of migrants who have been forced to move southward by the persistent and dramatic drought that affects sahelian countries.

OCP OBJECTIVES AND STRATEGY

The final objective of the OCP is to reduce onchocerciasis to a level at which it will no longer constitute a public health problem, or an obstacle to socioeconomic development, thus allowing the repopulation and development of previously infected valleys, without any risk of the inhabitants and/or immigrants losing their sight because of this disease.

Because of the lack of appropriate mass chemotherapy, the OCP's strategy has been, and still is, aimed exclusively at the control of onchocerciasis vectors, species of black flies that belong to the *Simulium damnosum* s.l. complex.

OBJECTIVES, PRINCIPLES, AND TACTICS OF VECTOR CONTROL

In the absence of any feasible method of biological control, chemical control was the only means of vector control selected (OCP 1973); ten years later, it still remains the only operational one.

Taking into account the special biological and distributional characteristics of the members of the *S. damnosum* s.l. complex, the eradication of vector populations would be quite unrealistic. The objective is therefore to reduce vector populations and maintain them below a certain "tolerable" density at which the intensity of transmission is insufficient to enable the development of ocular onchocerciasis. Standardized procedures for catching and dissecting adult female flies have enabled the establishment of thresholds of an Annual Biting Rate (ABR) of 1,000 bites/man/year and an Annual Transmission Potential (ATP) of 100 L_3 *Onchocerca volvulus* larvae/man/year/ (OMS 1977, Walsh et al. 1978).

The control of *S. damnosum* s.l. in the OCP area relies on the weekly aerial application of carefully adjusted dosages of selective and nonpersistent insecticides to rivers containing the larval stages of the vectors (Le Berre et al. 1979, Walsh et al. 1979, Le Berre and Philippon 1982, Philippon et al. 1984, OCP 1984). The standard organophosphate larvicide used in the OCP is temephos, and it is applied at rates of 0.05 to 0.1 mg/l per m^3/s of river discharge for 10 minutes. Other compounds used in special circumstances include the organophosphate chlorphoxim, the biological agent *B.t.* H-14, and the synthetic pyrethroid permethrin.

Entomological assessment of the efficiency of larviciding operations is based mainly on ABR and ATP values calculated from standardized catches and dissections of biting flies performed at some 270 selected sites, distributed all over the OCP area, and monitored weekly or bimonthly. Such large-scale and permanent operations obviously necessitate strong logistic support facilities and organization. It is therefore not surprising that the various activities of the Vector Control Unit, responsible for all entomological operations and research, have represented almost 70% of the overall OCP expenditures during the last decade.

Because of the tremendous flight potential of some species of the *S. damnosum* complex, and, due to a lack of knowledge of vector resting behavior (Bellec and Hébrard 1980), adulticiding techniques of control are impossible to use on a large scale. Larviciding, based on a good knowledge of larval biology and on treatment of clearly defined breeding sites, is therefore the basic control tactic of the OCP.

Prevailing southwesterly winds during the early to mid wet season greatly increase the flight capacity of "savanna" vectors, enabling them to move over long distances (up to 400 km) and thus to invade extensive areas of the OCP treatment zone (Le Berre et al. 1979, Garms et al. 1979, Walsh et al. 1981). It is for this reason that the OCP treats such a large area (764,000 km^2) and is now planning extensions that will involve an additional 550,000 km^2. The great lengths of the rivers requiring weekly surveillance (currently 23,000 km, but soon to expand to 50,000 km) necessitate heavy dependence on the use of aircraft.

The absolute or seasonal limits of the treated areas are also determined by the specific identity of the members of the vector complex and their differential vectorial capacity and role (Philippon 1977, Quillévéré 1979). It is, for example, assumed that in the OCP area blinding and socially intolerable onchocerciasis is associated with *S. damnosum* s.str. and *S. sirbanum*, the so-called savanna species (Prost 1980), which are therefore the primary targets of OCP vector-control activities.

The selection of larvicides for large-scale use in the OCP is based on many chemical and biological considerations. Compounds are screened in relation to mode of action, physicochemical properties (of formulations), ease of application, and toxicity to nontarget organisms. Other factors taken into account are the distribution of larvae in the water, their feeding behavior, their rate of development, and their susceptibility. Because of the strict selection criteria adhered to by the OCP, very few compounds and appropriate formulations are in current use, and the search for new compounds is made very difficult.

OCP RESULTS AFTER TEN YEARS OF VECTOR CONTROL

The most recent OCP results have been reviewed by Ba (1984), Dadzie et al. (1984), Grunewald (1984), Karam et al. (1984), Philippon et al. (1984), Remme (1984), and Zerbo (1984).

S. damnosum s.l. breeding is satisfactorily controlled everywhere in the treated area, even in river basins, where treatments are seasonally suspended, or in the central area, where no larviciding operations have been carried out for several years. Furthermore, onchocerciasis transmission has been reduced to below the accepted limit of tolerability over 90% of the treatment area (Fig. 26.2). However, residual and/or imported transmission continues to be recorded along the western and southeastern borders of the OCP. This situation exists partly because flies enter the OCP area from untreated breeding sites beyond its boundaries (Walsh et al. 1981, Cheke and Garms 1983) and partly because of the development of resistance in two forest species (*S. soubrense* and *S. sanctipauli*) in the southwestern part of the OCP area (Guillet et al. 1980, Kurtak et al. 1982).

After ten years of regular applications of temephos and chlorphoxim, a very careful independent ecological monitoring of the treated rivers revealed no detectable effect of these compounds on fish populations and only a slight, but reversible, impact on the invertebrate fauna (Lévèque, in press). This slight impact is often surpassed by that of direct or indirect application of agricultural pesticides or by natural trauma such as floods and droughts.

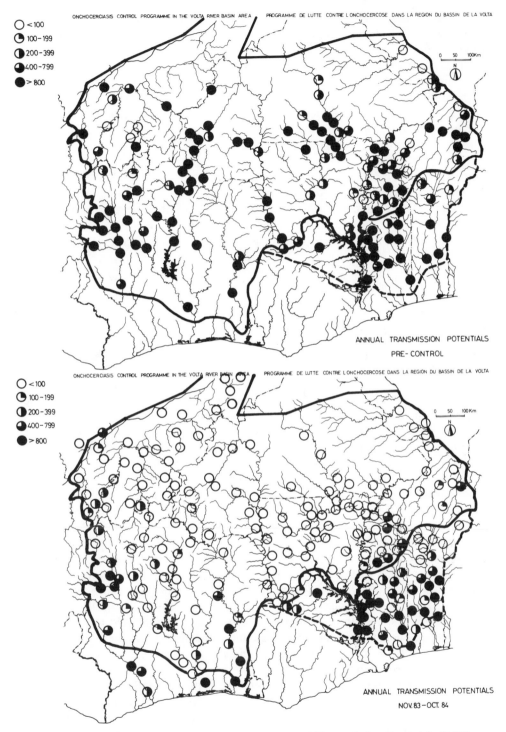

FIG. 26.2 Maps of the current OCP area showing Annual Transmission Potentials (ATP) before the implementation of vector control in 1974 (above) and after ten years of vector control in 1984 (below). The ATP limit of tolerability is 100.

The successful entomological results are confirmed by standardized medical evaluations, which show conspicuous regressions of the prevalence of the infection and of microfilarial loads in man in the well-protected 90% of the treatment area. The virtual interruption of transmission is also confirmed by a 97% reduction in the occurrence of infections among children born since the inception of vector control. At present, about 3 million children are considered to be free from the risk of blinding onchocerciasis. The rapid decrease of the infection indicates an average life span of the adult worms somewhat shorter than initially expected. This trend of decrease of the disease is still more impressive when eye symptoms are considered; ocular parasitism has almost disappeared and no new evolutive eye lesions are being observed.

Medical improvement is confirmed by the magnitude of spontaneous or planned movements of resettlement, which now affect most of the treated and previously uninhabited valleys. For example, in the White and Red Volta valleys in Burkina Faso, the proportion of cultivated land, initially very low, has been multiplied by 2 to 6, while the mileage of unpopulated valleys was reduced by 1.5 to 4 times. In addition, 20% to 32% of the unoccupied arable lands have been put under cultivation (Hervouet et al. 1984).

PROBLEMS IN EPIDEMIOLOGY AND CONTROL

Despite the success of the OCP, a number of entomological and epidemiological problems still remain; others have arisen concerning the future and the consequences of this successful vector-control operation.

The absence of a drug suitable for mass chemotherapy is still a drawback. The development of such a drug, preferably a macrofilaricide, would obviously allow reduction and alleviation of vector control. Even a microfilaricide that was easy to deliver and showed a persistent effect for several months could be an important asset for vector control in areas of seasonal transmission, especially against the aging reservoir of the parasite. Accordingly, the OCP has now developed a chemotherapy research program.

Though the knowledge of the longevity and fertility of adult *O. volvulus* has recently improved considerably, greater precision is still required to predict more exactly the evolution of infection in man after the interruption of transmission.

The follow-up of the trends of reduction of the infection (prevalence and microfilarial loads) and the ophthalmological symptoms of the disease, in both completely and partially protected areas, are also priority studies. They could help to explain the general and comparative epidemiology of onchocerciasis, but they can be carried out only in the OCP in different contexts of vector species and vector-control efficiency, as measured by the ATPs.

However, the main epidemiological unknown facing the OCP is the identity of the pathogenic agent *O. volvulus*. Is this species a complex of forms, of strains, of subspecies, or of siblings? Are each of these forms associated with a particular pattern of the disease or with special species of the vector complex? What are the consequences of these preferential adaptations, if any? Can *O. volvulus* forms be identified, especially at their evolution stages in the vectors (especially L_3 infective-stage larvae) by techniques such as immunology, enzymology, cytology, DNA probe, etc.?

Such identification of infective *O. volvulus* larvae in the vectors might contribute to elucidating the old problem of epidemiological differences between the savanna and forest forms of the disease, which cannot be explained by entomological factors alone (Duke 1968, Philippon 1977) but are undoubtedly related to the action of parasitological factors or different vector-parasite complexes (Duke et al. 1975).

The matter is not purely of academic epidemiological interest. The OCP mandate is the control of a severe, blinding, and socially intolerable form of onchocerciasis, classically associated with savanna biotopes and so-called savanna vector species, namely *S. damnosum* s.str. and *S. sirbanum*. Consequently, the present trend of OCP control policy is to concentrate on those species and to disregard the so-called forest species (*S. soubrense* especially) when they are not associated with savanna-type onchocerciasis, as is usual at low latitudes in forest or forest-like environments of the OCP area.

Unfortunately, the constancy of association between the identity of vectors and the pattern of the disease is not that clear-cut in all situations, and there are cases of overlapping. For example, anthropophilic forest populations with high infection rates are mixed with savanna ones in southern Benin and Togo, and forest populations with similar behavior are associated with savanna species in typical savanna biotopes (western Ivory Coast and Guinea), in both cases in the presence of a very severe savanna-like form of the disease.

Considering the proven high risk of selection of resistant forest populations by extensive applications of organophosphates, the great difficulties and costs of treating these resistant populations in the large rivers in forest areas with existing *B.t.* H-14 formulations, and given that ATP calculations can at best only estimate the relative role of each species pair in overall transmission (without indication of the respective epidemiological impacts), there is an urgent need to determine which form(s) of parasite(s) are prevalent in different geographical and epidemiological areas, and which one(s) are transmitted by the various species of local vectors.

More progress has recently been made in the identification of members of the *S. damnosum* complex in the OCP area (Quillévéré 1979, Meredith et al. 1984), mainly in the field of larval cytotaxonomy. However, the morphological criteria used for adult identification (Garms 1978, Kurtak et al. 1981) show geographical variations and therefore do not apply to individual flies. A special effort is consequently being made in the OCP to identify biting adults by use of micromorphology, morphometry, cytology (especially in adult flies), chemotaxonomy (gas-liquid chromatography of cuticular hydrocarbons), and DNA probes.

This basic need to clarify vector identity is obviously strongly related to research on *O. volvulus* identification, and it is also a prerequisite for other priority studies, such as:

1. *studies of reinvasion.* The importation into the OCP of savanna vectors and parasites constitutes a major threat to the areas under control. It is important that the source breeding sites be precisely detected and treated (by extensions to the OCP control zone).

2. *resistance studies.* Up to now, but with one small exception, resistance has only been detected in two forest species, *S. soubrense* and *S. sanctipauli,* and in relation

to the organophosphates temephos and chlorphoxim. To date, these problems have been overcome by strategies of replacement (temephos replaced by chlorphoxim, which was then replaced by *B.t.* H-14) and of alternation (using chlorphoxim in the wet season and *B.t.* H-14 in the dry season). By the careful implementation of these strategies, there was no recrudescence of transmission, but larviciding costs were markedly increased. Furthermore, it must be stressed that the extension of larviciding operations into vast new savanna areas will considerably increase the risk of resistance to organophosphates emerging in savanna species.

Consequently, the screening of new larvicides and formulations is the top priority and an ongoing research program of the OCP, and the monitoring of the susceptibility of the various vector species to the different compounds in current use, and those of potential use, is a built-in component of entomological surveillance. Furthermore, it is envisaged that the alternation of larvicides belonging to different chemical families will become a systematic procedure.

In relation to the geographical extensions and also in view of future transfer of OCP maintenance activities to the national health authorities of the participating African countries, the program is currently very much concerned with the improvement of its cost-efficiency. Improvement of larviciding efficiency is obviously dependent upon a better knowledge of preimaginal behavior of the different vector species in their various habitats, especially regarding feeding behavior. Besides ongoing alleviations of the entomological evaluation network (including large-scale use of traps; Bellec et al. 1984), efforts are being made to optimize larvicide dosages, treatment frequencies, and treatment interruptions in relation to meteorological and hydrological factors (winds, ITCZ, air and water temperatures, water level, etc.). The use of a predictive mathematical model of larvicide behavior in flowing water and of teletransmission of hydrological information are also being tested.

A relatively new area of research is the introduction of human ecology in the study of the epidemiology of onchocerciasis. In-depth investigations of human activities, space utilization, perception of the disease by the rural communities, and demographic trends related to age, sex, ethnicity, and bioclimatology bring new light to the understanding of the transmission of the disease and can contribute to changing the "epidemio-system" in order to prevent any recrudescence of the disease when the OCP has reached its maintenance phase.

CONCLUSIONS

It is globally considered that the OCP is well on the way to meeting its objectives, i.e., to control the vector populations and reduce the *O. volvulus* transmission enough to allow repopulation and economic development of infected valleys without any risk of onchocercal blindness. From entomological and ophthalmological viewpoints the results are even better than expected, since the transmission of the parasite and the evolution of ocular lesions are virtually interrupted in the center of the treated area.

This success justifies the strategy selected up to the present. Nevertheless, the OCP has now adopted a long-term strategy including several major options, especially the diversification (chemotherapeutical research) and territorial extension of activities, with a more selective and cost-effective approach to vector control in both core areas and zones proposed for extensions. These new approaches include extensive research on parasite and vector identification, vector behavior, man-vector relationships, resistance, insecticides, and vector-control techniques.

All these research activities are directly aimed at the improvement of onchocerciasis control, through control of the members of the *S. damnosum* complex, in the OCP context. They are not necessarily incompatible with more fundamental investigations, as demonstrated several times during the last ten years, and continue to be conducted either by the program's own research teams or in collaboration with outside institutions and/or consultants.

Any expertise or offers of collaboration fitting with the above priorities and that could possibly help the OCP and WHO to reach their final humanitarian objectives within the next ten years would be very much welcomed by the program.

ACKNOWLEDGMENTS

This paper is the result of exchanges of views between the entomologists, epidemiologists, ophthalmologists, parasitologists, socioeconomists, and statisticians of the OCP, to whom the author is deeply grateful. The author is also greatly indebted to Dr. D. A. T. Baldry for his linguistic editing of the manuscript.

POSTSCRIPT

The regularity with which new developments take place to influence significantly the progression of the OCP and the invariability with which challenging new situations arise are two of the most characteristic elements of the program. Accordingly, since the preparation of this chapter, there have been a number of important events that are appropriate to mention here: (1) Territorial extensions of the OCP to the west and to the southeast have been approved and are now entering the implementation phase. (2) As a result of intensive chemotherapeutic research, great progress has been made in the development of a microfilaricide, which holds promise of coming into operational use in the near future. (3) Entomological studies to the west of the OCP have identified most, if not all, of the sources of flies that invade the western flank of the OCP, and experimental larviciding operations in some source areas have amply demonstrated the feasibility of successfully controlling this invasion problem. (4) Resistance to organophosphate larvicides in savanna vectors has spread to a few restricted savanna localities, but it has been effectively kept under control.

LITERATURE CITED

Ba, O. 1984. Infection load in children born since the control operations in OCP. *Proc. 11th Int. Congr. Trop. Med. Malaria,* Calgary, Ontario, 1984.

Bellec, C. and G. Hébrard. 1980. Les lieux de repos des adultes du complexe *Simulium damnosum.* I. Les méthodes d'étude. 2. Etude de la dispersion spatio-temporelle. *Cah. ORSTOM sér. Entomol. Méd. Parasitol.* 18:261–289.

Bellec, C., D. G. Zerbo, J. Nion, G. Hébrard and H. Agoua. 1984. Utilisation expérimentale des plaques d'aluminium pour l'évaluation entomologique du programme de lutte contre l'onchocercose dans la région du bassin de la Volta. *Cah. ORSTOM sér. Entomol. Méd. Parasitol.* 22:191–205.

Cheke, R. A., and R. Garms. Reinfestations of the south-eastern flank of the Onchocerciasis Control Programme by wind borne vectors. *Phil. Trans. R. Soc. London* B 302:471–484.

Dadzie, Y., B. Thylefors, and A. Rolland. 1984. Recent results in ocular onchocerciasis after vector control in the OCP area. *Proc. 11th Int. Congr. Trop. Med. Malaria,* Calgary, 1984.

Duke, B. O. L. 1968. Studies of factors influencing the transmission of onchocerciasis. VI. The infective biting potential of *Simulium damnosum* in different bioclimatic zones and its influence on the transmission potential. *Ann. Trop. Med. Parasitol.* 62:164–170.

Duke, B. O. L., J. Anderson, and H. Fuglsang. 1975. The *Onchocerca volvulus* transmission potentials and associated patterns of onchocerciasis at four Cameroon-Sudan savanna villages. *Tropenmed. Parasitol.* 26:143–154.

Garms, R. 1978. Use of morphological characters in the study of *Simulium damnosum* s.l. populations in West Africa. *Tropenmed. Parasitol.* 29:483–491.

Garms, R., F. J. Walsh, and J. B. Davies. 1979. Studies on the reinvasion of the Onchocerciasis Control Programme in the Volta River Basin by *Simulium damnosum* s.l. with emphasis on the south-western area. *Tropenmed. Parasitol.* 30:345–362.

Grunewald, J. 1984. Advances in the knowledge of the bio-ecology of the *S. damnosum* complex. *Proc. 11th Int. Congr. Trop. Med. Malaria,* Calgary, 1984.

Guillet, P., H. Escaffre, M. M. Ouedraogo, and D. Quillévéré. 1980. Mise en évidence d'une résistance au téméphos dans le complexe *Simulium damnosum* (*S. sanctipauli* et *S. soubrense*) en Côte d'Ivoire, *Cah. ORSTOM sér. Entomol. Méd. Parasitol.* 18:291–298.

Hervouet, J. P., J. C. Clanet, F. Paris, and H. Somé. 1984. Peuplement des vallées protégées de l'onchocercose après 10 ans de lutte antivectorielle au Burkina Faso. Miméo. doc. OMS. OCP/GVA/84.5.

Karam, M. V., H. Schulz-Key, and L. Bullini. 1984. Recent investigations on *Onchocerca volvulus* in West Africa. *Proc. 11th Int. Congr. Trop. Med. Malaria,* Calgary, 1984.

Kurtak, D. C., J. N. Raybould, and C. G. Vajime. 1981. Wing tuft colours in the progeny of single individuals of *Simulium squamosum* (Enderlein). *Trans. R. Soc. Trop. Med. Hyg.* 75:126.

Kurtak, D. C., M. M. Ouedraogo, M. H. Ocran, T. Barro, and P. Guillet. 1982. Preliminary note on the appearance in Ivory Coast of resistance to chlorphoxim in *Simulium sanctipauli/S. soubrense* larvae already resistant to temephos. WHO mimeo. doc., WHO/VBC/82.850.

Le Berre, R., and B. Philippon. 1982. Lutte contre l'onchocercose: stratégie, réalisation, futur. *C.R. Journées Hôpital Claude Bernard,* October 1982.

Le Berre, R., R. Garms, J. B. Davies, J. F. Walsh, and B. Philippon. 1979. Displacements of *Simulium* and strategy of control against onchocerciasis. *Phil. Trans. R. Soc. London* (B) 287:277–288.

Lévèque, C. 1985. The use of insecticides in the Onchocerciasis Control Programme and the aquatic monitoring in West Africa. (In press).

Meredith, S. E. O., R. A. Cheke, and R. Garms. 1984. Variation and distribution of forms of *Simulium soubrense* and *S. sanctipauli* in West Africa. *Ann. Trop. Med. Parasitol.* 77:627–640.

Philippon, B. 1977. Etude de la transmission d'*Onchocerca volvulus* (Leuckart, 1883) per *Simulium damnosum* Theobald, 1903, en Afrique tropicale. *Trav. Doc. ORSTOM* 63. 308 pp.

Philippon, B., D. G. Zerbo, G. B. Cliff, and R. Subra. 1984. General overview on the entomological aspects of OCP after ten years of vector control (objectives, strategies, structures, results, prospects). *Proc. 11th Int. Congr. Trop. Med. Malaria,* Calgary, 1984.

OCP. 1973. Contrôle de l'onchocercose dans la région du bassin de la Volta: *Rapport de la mission d'assistance préparatoire (APG) aux gouvernements de Côte d'Ivoire, Dahomey, Ghana, Haute-Volta, Mali, Niger, Togo.* Geneva, 1973 (PNUD, FAO, BIRD et OMS).

———. 1978. Programme de lutte contre l'onchocercose dans la région du bassin de la Volta. *Rapport d'évaluation 1975–1978.*

———. 1981. Projet Sénégambie. WHO mimeo. doc., VBC/81.2, ICP/MPD/007.

———. 1984. Comité conjoint du Programme de lutte contre l'onchocercose dans la région du bassin de la Volta. *Rapport de la 5e réunion, Niamey,* 1984.

OMS. 1977. Critères biomédicaux pour le repeuplement de l'aire du Programme de lutte contre l'onchocercose dans la région du bassin de la Volta. Mimeo. doc. OMS. OCP/SAP/77.1.

Prost, A. 1980. Le polymorphisme des onchocercoses humaines ouest africaines. *Ann. Parasitol. Hum. Comp.* 55:239–245.

———. 1984. Social, geographical and economic factors of onchocerciasis. *Proc. 11th Int. Congr. Trop. Med. Malaria.* Calgary, 1984.

Prost, A., and F. Paris. 1983. L'incidence de la cécité et ses aspects épidémiologiques dans une région rurale d'Afrique de l'Ouest. *Bull. WHO* 61:491–499.

Prost, A., J. P. Hervouet, and B. Thylefors. 1979. Les niveaux d'endémicité dans l'onchocercose. *Bull. WHO* 57:655–662.

Quillévéré, D. 1979. Contribution à l'étude des caractéristiques taxonomiques, bioécologiques et vectrices des membres du complexe *Simulium damnosum* présents en Côte d'Ivoire. *Trav. Doc. ORSTOM* 109. 296 pp.

Remme, J. H. 1984. Trends of epidemiology of onchocerciasis. *Proc. 11th Int. Congr. Trop. Med. Malaria,* Calgary, 1984.

Walsh, J. F., J. B. Davies, and G. B. Cliff. 1981. WHO Onchocerciasis Control Programme in the River Volta Basin. Pp. 85–103 in M. Laird, Ed., *Blackflies: the future for biological methods in integrated control.* Academic Press, New York and London.

Walsh, J. F., J. B. Davies, and R. Garms. 1981. Further studies on the reinvasion of the Onchocerciasis Control Programme by *Simulium damnosum* s.l. The effects of an extension of control activities into Southern Ivory Coast during 1979. *Tropenmed. Parasitol.* 32:269–273.

Walsh, J. F., J. B. Davies, and R. Le Berre. 1979. Entomological aspects of the first five years of the Onchocerciasis Control Programme in the Volta River Basin. *Tropenmed. Parasitol.* 30:328–344.

Walsh, J. F., J. B. Davies, R. Le Berre, and R. Garms. 1978. Standardization of criteria for assessing the effect of *Simulium* control in the Onchocerciasis Control Programme. *Trans. R. Soc. Trop. Med. Hyg.* 72:675–676.

Zerbo, D. G. 1984. Entomological evaluation strategies and techniques for onchocerciasis vector control in West Africa. *Proc. 11th. Int. Congr. Trop. Med. Malaria,* Calgary, 1984.

27 EPIDEMIOLOGY AND CONTROL OF GUATEMALAN ONCHOCERCIASIS

Hiroyuki Takaoka and Takeshi Suzuki

Human onchocerciasis, a disease caused by the filarial parasite *Onchocerca volvulus*, has been known in Africa, the Arabian peninsula, and Central and South America. In the New World it is sporadically distributed in localized areas of six countries: Mexico, Guatemala, Venezuela, Colombia, Brazil, and Ecuador. In Mesoamerica this disease is also known as "Robles' disease," in honor of Dr. Rodolfo Robles Valverde, who first discovered onchocerciasis in the Western Hemisphere from Guatemala in 1915.

Since the discovery of onchocerciasis in Guatemala, a great deal of work has been carried out on the bionomics and control of the vector black flies, as well as on clinical, epidemiological, pathological, and parasitological aspects of the disease. Excellent reviews of these studies were done by Dalmat (1955), Hamon (1974), and Sasa (1976).

Beginning in the 1970s, more advanced studies have been made through the participation of research workers from foreign countries (e.g., the United States, Germany, and Japan). One such joint project was carried out from 1975 to 1983 by the Guatemala-Japan Cooperative Project on Onchocerciasis Research and Control. Extensive studies on the disease itself and its vector conducted during an early stage of that project were briefly summarized by Ogata (1981). At the end of the project the entire study was thoroughly reviewed by Suzuki (1983).

In the early days, nodule excision, or nodulectomy, which was first recommended by Dr. Robles, was the only countermeasure against onchocerciasis, and it has been carried out as a nationwide campaign from 1935 to the present. A chemical control trial using DDT against black fly larvae was performed in the mid-1950s, with successful suppression of adult density for a short period, but that program was suspended for administrative reasons (Lea and Dalmat 1955a,b).

A major problem in vector control of Guatemalan onchocerciasis is the difficulty in accessing all vector-breeding streams for periodic larviciding, because these numerous, small streams are located mostly in the rugged terrain of mountainous areas. By overcoming these difficulties through basic research on vector bionomics and insecticides, a control trial against larvae of the principal vector, *Simulium ochraceum*, in the San Vicente Pacaya Pilot Area by the Guatemala-Japan Project yielded good results. It has reduced the human biting density of the vector to a very low level, below which transmission may not take place.

In this chapter recent studies on the epidemiology and control of Guatemalan onchocerciasis, chiefly made by the project, are reviewed. First we describe the special epidemiological features of Guatemalan onchocerciasis in relation to vector control. Second, the results of insecticide studies are summarized. And finally, the area vector-control trial is briefly described and discussed.

EPIDEMIOLOGICAL FEATURES OF GUATEMALAN ONCHOCERCIASIS IN RELATION TO VECTOR CONTROL

Distribution of Endemic Areas

The onchocerciasis-endemic areas in Guatemala are distributed in seven departments, which are divided into four zones: North-Western Zone, West-Central Zone, East-Central Zone, and Eastern Zone (Fig. 27.1). Approximately 10% of the 300,000 inhabitants in these endemic areas are supposedly infected (Figueroa 1974). Historically, no sign of enlargement of endemic foci was observed, despite frequent movements of inhabitants, especially by seasonal workers in coffee plantation areas. On the contrary, during the period of the nationwide nodulectomy campaign from 1935 to the present, the nodule rate has been gradually reduced over entire endemic areas (Yamagata et al., unpublished data). In some areas, e.g., the Eastern Zone, the nodule rate has become almost zero. A recent epidemiological survey carried out in the Eastern Zone (i.e., Santa Rosa) showed that out of 2,257 persons examined, 20 (0.9%) were positive for microfilariae and/or nodules (Uchida et al., unpublished data). Among positives, 15 were 30 or more years old, while the youngest was a 10-year-old boy who had recently come from one of the other endemic areas. These data clearly indicate a marked decline or near disappearance of the endemicity in the Eastern Zone. It is, however, still uncertain whether the reduction was due to the direct effect of the nodulectomy campaign or to other factors, such as a change in the socioeconomic condition of the people, or a decrease in the number of suitable streams for vector breeding by deforestation. The gross area endemic for onchocerciasis in Guatemala was calculated as 6,335 km^2 by Figueroa (1974) or as 4,708 km^2 by Garcia-Manzo (1981). These figures were based on an administrative demarcation system and may overestimate the real range of the disease. Further reassessment should be made with regard to the recent analysis of the nodulectomy campaign.

It is well known that the distribution of endemic foci is stable within altitudes from 500 to 1,500 meters above sea level, roughly coinciding with the distribution of *S. ochraceum* breeding sites. Based on experimental infection studies under various temperature conditions, Takaoka et al. (1982) suggested that the distribution of onchocerciasis in this country may have been prevented from extending farther into the lowlands by the intolerance of adult *S. ochraceum* to high temperature, or into

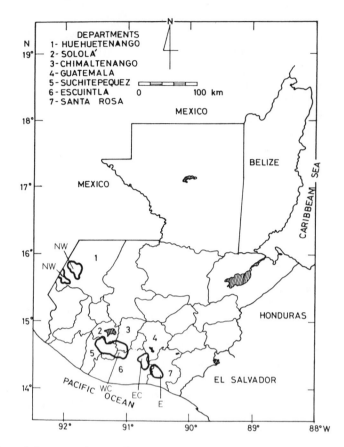

FIG. 27.1 Onchocerciasis endemic zones in Guatemala (after Suzuki 1983).

the uplands by the inability of the parasite to develop in the simuliid vector at low temperature. On the other hand, lateral borders of the disease distribution may be explained by environmental differences, such as topographical and geological features, which influence the availability of larval habitats for *S. ochraceum* (Yamagata et al. 1984).

Disease Manifestations

The most severe symptom of onchocerciasis is an ocular lesion that leads progressively to blindness. In Guatemala the blindness rate seems generally lower than in West Africa. According to Yamada (1978), the blindness rate was 0.5% or less in the San Vicente Pacaya Pilot Area, where of 2,153 inhabitants examined, 30.8% were positive for the infection by the skin-snip method (Tada et al. 1979). In the other Guatemalan endemic areas, the blindness rate was in the range of 1.5% to 4.6% (Brandling-Bennett et al. 1981). It was suggested that the present nodulectomy campaign can be effective in at least suppressing or preventing ocular lesions (Yamada and Oikawa 1980).

Onchocercal nodules are frequently found in the head region of the Guatemalan patients. This characteristic distribution of nodules is probably related to the biting preference of *S. ochraceum* for upper-body regions. However, microfilarial density in skin from the head and arms is usually low (Kawabata et al. 1983). In all age groups, males are more frequently nodule-positive than females, while in either sex the positive rate increases with age. There was a close correlation between nodule rate and microfilarial rate in the San Vicente Pacaya (Tada et al. 1979), and the onchocercal nodule serves as an important index of early infection.

Vector and Transmission

Confirmed and potential vectors.   In Guatemala eight black fly species are captured on human attractants in endemic areas. Among these, *S. ochraceum* is generally regarded as the principal vector because this species (1) often harbors infective larvae of *O. volvulus,* (2) is highly anthropophilic, and (3) exhibits a high human biting density. *S. metallicum* and *S. callidum* are the secondary vectors due to infrequent natural infections and zoophilic biting habit (Dalmat 1955). In addition, recent experimental infection studies indicate that *S. horacioi* (a newly described species belonging to the *S. metallicum* group), *S. colvini* (misidentified as *S. downsi*), and *S. haematopotum* are all capable of supporting the development of *O. volvulus* microfilariae to the third-stage larvae (Ito et al. 1980; Ito, unpublished data; Takaoka et al. 1984). There is a possibility that some of these species might take over the role in transmission if and when *S. ochraceum* density is reduced to an extremely low level by successful vector control. The epidemiological importance of two other species, *S. gonzalezi* (or *S. exiguum*) and *S. veracruzanum,* remains to be studied.

Vector taxonomy.   It is worthwhile to note that *S. ochraceum* is a species complex, comprised of at least three cytoforms (Hirai, unpublished data). Further detailed information on the distribution, biting habit, and susceptibility to *O. volvulus* infection with each form is needed. Dr. Hirai (unpublished data) has also found that *S. metallicum* is divided into two sibling species, which are usually found sympatrically.

Vector biology.   Larvae of *S. ochraceum* usually prefer small permanent streams in rugged mountainous terrain (Dalmat 1955). Cool and minute streams with water temperatures of 16°C to 20°C and a discharge of 0.1 to 1.0 l sec^{-1} are usually colonized by this species. Under such cool water conditions more than two weeks are required for the larvae to develop from hatching to pupation (Suzuki 1983).

It was recently shown that an observed shifting of larval sites of *S. ochraceum* in some localities was related to the pronounced wet and dry seasons in the foothills along the Pacific slope of the Sierra Madre (Takaoka 1981). In the late dry season (February to April), larval sites were restricted to perennial streams in intermediate altitudes, but during the rainy season preimaginal sites of this species extended to the upper reaches of the numerous small, newly emergent, temporary streams that often form subterranean sections along their stretches. Accordingly, seasonal fluctuation of the adult population of *S. ochraceum* varies, depending on the characteristics of the water systems of the localities, although the human biting density of this species generally peaked during the dry season (Takaoka 1981).

Vector efficiency.   *Simulium ochraceum* is characterized by its inefficiency in transmission competence, in terms of the percentage of ingested microfilariae that develop to infective larvae (DeLeon and Duke 1966). This is chiefly because most microfilariae ingested by *S. ochraceum* are destroyed by the cibarial armature before they pass to the stomach, and consequently only a few microfilariae reach the thorax and develop further (Omar and Garms 1975).

Recent natural infection studies also indicate that only a small proportion of wild-caught *S. ochraceum* had infective larvae of *O. volvulus,* ranging from 0.02% to 3% (Garms 1975, Garms and Ochoa 1979, Collins 1979, Ochoa 1982, Takaoka 1982).

Time of transmission.   A year-long collection and dissection of *S. ochraceum* adult females carried out at two localities in endemic areas revealed that the most suitable time for transmission of the disease might be the dry season (November to March), although lower transmission might take place in the rainy season (Ochoa 1982). A similar study (Collins et al. 1981) also showed that the highest infective rates were observed during the period from late February through March.

Critical annual biting rate.   The data accumulated in the Guatemala-Japan Project were theoretically analyzed using Muench's simple catalytic model (Wada 1982). The critical ABR (the number of biting flies per man per year, below which transmission is not maintained) was calculated as 7,665. This tentative value is very close to the value of 8,700 empirically obtained in a village with no cases of eye lesions despite 33% skin biopsy positivity (Collins 1981).

INSECTICIDE STUDIES FOR VECTOR CONTROL

Larvicide Agents

Temephos is well known to be effective against black fly larvae, with comparatively low adverse effects on nontarget organisms, as well as low toxicity to man. Trough tests revealed that this chemical is effective against larvae of *S. ochraceum,* with a minimum concentration of 3 ppm/min for a 95% mortality (Umino et al. 1983b).

A bacterial insecticide, *Bacillus thuringiensis* var. *israelensis,* is also known to be ingested by black fly larvae and to produce mortality at adequately low concentrations, with low toxicity to nontarget organisms. The efficacy of *B.t.i.* against the larvae of *S. ochraceum* was tested (Undeen et al. 1981), and it was shown that a one-minute treatment with initial concentrations of 2×10^5 spores/ml resulted in up to 100% mortality, but that downstream carry was poor.

Larval Susceptibility Level to Insecticides

Insecticide susceptibility tests were carried out with the test kits supplied by WHO (Mizutani, unpublished data). At least in 1983, there existed no sign of temephos resistance in *S. ochraceum* larvae. The baseline susceptibility level of this species in the Rincon area of Guatemala was estimated to be as follows: LC-50 of temephos 0.055 ppm, chlorpyrifos-methyl 0.040 ppm, chlorphoxim 0.0079 ppm, and DDT 0.044 ppm. The possibility of resistance developing in the future cannot be disregarded.

Short Carry of Temephos

A surprising report was made by Umino et al. (1983a) that the carry of temephos was only 25 meters with an application of 2 ppm/10 min in a minute stream, and it could not be increased even with an extremely high dose application of 200 ppm/10 min. Further studies in the laboratory revealed the highly adsorptive nature of temephos (Umino and Suzuki 1984), which was later confirmed in the field by Mizutani (unpublished data).

While Umino et al. (1983b) showed that a dose of more than 3 ppm/min is necessary to expect 95% mortality at a site immediately downstream, some researchers reported that a dose far smaller than 3 ppm/min temephos was effective for a very long distance under field conditions. In the Onchocerciasis Control Programme in West Africa (OCP), application of temephos emulsion at a dose of 0.05–0.1 ppm/10 min (= 0.5–1.0 ppm/min) by aircraft has been the standard control measure, which is reportedly giving excellent control (Davies et al. 1978, Walsh et al. 1981). Helson and West (1978) reported particulated temephos at a dose of 0.1 ppm/15 min (=1.5 ppm/min) was effective 175–960 meters downstream.

Taking into consideration the highly adsorbent nature of temephos, the above discrepancy might be the result of the effect of particulates as carriers of the toxicant in streams, as suggested by Fredeen et al. (1953, 1975) in the cases of DDT and methoxychlor. Once the insecticide is adsorbed, either artificially or naturally, onto particulates of suitable size for ingestion by black fly larvae, the availability of the toxicant could be enhanced and eventually result in a high mortality effect for a long distance downstream.

In Guatemala small target streams are usually distributed in the uppermost part of each channel network, close to the headsprings. Therefore, a short carry of temephos in these streams might be explained by: (1) a high probability of adsorbtion to static soil or substrates on the streambed due to the small size of the stream; or (2) no or only negligible adsorbtion to mobile particulates suspended in the streams due to the clarity of the stream water (Umino and Suzuki 1984). Extensive stream tests revealed that the concentration of temephos had no relationship to its carry, but it was apparent that the larger the water discharge, the longer the carry (Kamimura et al. 1985), which was also reported by Lea and Dalmat (1955b) for DDT.

Formulation of Larvicide and Method of Application

Trough tests failed to find any marked difference in efficacy between emulsifiable concentrate (EC) and water-dispersible powders (wdp) of temephos (Umino et al. 1983b). Furthermore, extensive stream tests of temephos did not indicate any distinct difference in efficacy among four formulations: wdp, EC, oil solution, and solid (Kamimura et al. 1985). In addition, laboratory tests of adsorbtion of temephos to sands did not show any difference between the wdp and EC (Umino and Suzuki 1984). These results all suggest no practical difference in efficacy between the formulations, most likely due to the particular conditions of the Guatemalan streams. However, future studies are badly needed on developing improved larvicide formulations to provide maximum carry in the small streamlets of Guatemala.

No difference was observed in efficacy between the two application methods, i.e., applying during 10 minutes and applying instantaneously, with wdp or EC (Kamimura et al. 1985). The instantaneous application is particularly efficient in Guatemala, where periodic visits to numerous dosing sites located in the mountainous terrain are needed.

Effects of Temephos on Nontarget Organisms

The target streams in Guatemala are rather poor in fish and insect faunas. The temephos application in such streams did not have a serious impact on nontarget organisms, except a slight effect on Chironomidae (Hasegawa et al. 1981). However, the long-term effect of insecticide in downstream areas should be monitored.

AREA VECTOR-CONTROL TRIAL

Following the basic studies on vector bionomics and insecticides, an area vector-control trial for *S. ochraceum* was carried out in the San Vicente Pacaya Pilot Area (236 km^2, in the East-Central Zone; Fig. 27.1) by the Guatemala-Japan Cooperative Project. This consisted of biweekly applications of temephos into breeding streams, and its objective was to suppress the biting-population density to a level low enough to interrupt the transmission of the disease organism (i.e., below the provisional critical ABR of c. 8,000). This control trial began in 1979 in a small valley of Lavaderos, then gradually expanded to other neighboring valleys, with a final coverage of about 90 km^2 in January 1984. An outline of the control operation and the results of entomological evaluations have already been reported (Nakamura et al. 1981, Takaoka et al. 1981). Details of the entire program were reported by Yamagata et al. (1985) and are excerpted below.

Tactics for Larvicide Application

The control operation was divided chronologically into three phases. In phase 1, 10% temephos briquettes were applied with a dose rate of 0.1 ppm/60 min to all the streams with a discharge range of 0.1 to 50 l sec^{-1}. In phase 2, 50% temephos wdp was applied at 2 ppm/10 min into streams of less than 1 l sec^{-1} discharge. In phase 3, a new system of fixed dose application was introduced; 24 grams of 5% temephos wdp in a packet was diluted with stream water and poured into a stream instantaneously every 50 to 100 meters, irrespective of the water discharge at each dosing site. The target streams were those with less than 50 l sec^{-1} discharge. The fixed-dose larviciding system in phase 3 could compensate, at least partially, for the inconsistent carry of temephos.

Under this system, temephos concentration is high in smaller streams and low in larger streams. But from the operational viewpoint, this system had the great advantage that no measurement of water discharge was required at any dosing site or time. This improvement was particularly helpful during the rainy season, when water discharge is extremely variable. The tactics applied in phase 3 of the operation are currently being used.

ABRs Pre- and Postcontrol

Entomological evaluation for this control trial was made every two weeks by collections of adult *S. ochraceum* using human attractants at seven stations (four inside the study area and three outside). The data obtained were summarized using the criterion of the ABR. As a result, the phase 1 and 3 operations, and especially the latter, were effective in suppressing adult density, whereas phase 2 was not satisfactory, presumably because of the neglect of large streams with more than 1 l sec^{-1} discharge. Before the control operation was initiated, the ABRs of *S. ochraceum* were high at any collecting station, ranging from about 50,000 to 300,000 (Table 27.1). In phase 3, the values decreased to the level of 500 to 7,500, which was considered below the provisional permissible value.

Comsumption of Larvicide and Manpower

Consumption of 5% temephos wdp in the phase 3 operation was 488g/km^2 in a biweekly application cycle, and annual consumption of 5% temephos was 12.7kg/km^2, or 634g temephos active ingredient. In phase 3, the mean area covered by one field operator in a biweekly cycle (10 working days) was 4.6 km^2. These figures should be

Table 27.1 Annual Biting Rate (ABR) in the controlled and uncontrolled areas in relation to the control phases (from Suzuki 1983)

Station	Item	1978–1979	1979–1980	1980–1981	1981–1982	1982–1983
Lavaderos	Phase	0	1	1	2	3
	Period	Aug–Mar[a]	June–May	June–May	June–May	June–May
	ABR	315,740	9,315	3,480	3,274	556
Barretal	Phase		1	1	2	3
	Period	—	Aug–July	Aug–July	Aug–July	Aug–May[b]
	ABR		26,852	19,063	47,810	2,263
Peña Blanca	Phase	0	0		2	3
	Period	Oct–Sept	Oct–Sept	—	June–May	June–May
	ABR	84,090	142,371		103,093	7,536
Guachipilín–23	Phase	0	0		2	3
	Period	Oct–Sept	Oct–Sept	—	June–May	June–May
	ABR	120,697	72,720		35,146	865
Rodeo	Phase	0	0	0	0	
	Period	Aug–July	Aug–July	Aug–July	Aug–July	—
	ABR	48,849	48,448	23,068	36,814	
Tarral	Phase	0	0	0		
	Period	Aug–July	Aug–July	Aug–July	—	—
	ABR	21,995	27,796	22,227		
Rincón	Phase	0	0	0	0	
	Period	Sept–Aug	Sept–Aug	Sept–Aug	Sept–Aug	—
	ABR	179,440	103,234	155,011	150,836	

Note: Phase 0: Precontrol phase.
[a]Based on 8 months data.
[b]Based on 10 months data.

valuable from a cost perspective for future programming of a large-scale control operation.

Fly Infiltration

Infiltration of vector species into the treated area from the surrounding untreated areas is one of the most serious problems in many cases of vector control. Gradual expansion of the area under control in this operation made it possible to estimate the extent of infiltration of *S. ochraceum*. Using the relationship of fly densities at each catching station with various distances to the border of the untreated area, it was indicated that infiltration might not occur beyond 3 or 4 kilometers. This distance is much smaller than the flight range (6.3 miles or 10.1 kilometers) estimated by mark-release-recapture experiments (Dalmat and Gibson 1952).

Remarks

Epidemiological evaluation for this vector-control operation is now underway, so its ultimate effect on the human population cannot be assessed at present. The precontrol baseline data for this project were already reported by Yoshimura et al. (1982). However, from the results obtained so far, it is suggested that larval vector control to suppress female density of the vector to a level low enough to stop the transmission of the disease is feasible if realistic planning is made and the staff is devoted in its efforts. Even in a small, limited area a successful vector-control operation might be achieved because of the limited flight range of adult *S. ochraceum*.

In any future vector control of Guatemalan onchocerciasis in which a larvicide is applied, one of the key factors is to cover all the vector-breeding sites without ommission. In order to find all the preimaginal habitats of *S. ochraceum* in the rugged terrain of mountainous areas, the necessity and importance of proper and precise mapping of the target area prior to larviciding cannot be overemphasized. The macrodistribution of *S. ochraceum* larvae may be efficiently delimited by understanding the topographical or geological features of the target areas (Yamagata et al. 1984).

CONCLUSION AND FURTHER RESEARCH NEEDS

Since the mid-1970s, much new information on Guatemalan onchocerciasis has been accumulated. In relation to vector control, some special epidemiological features of the disease were clarified. Furthermore, extensive insecticide studies in the field and laboratory demonstrated that the characteristic situations of Guatemalan streams where *S. ochraceum* breeds require ingenious methods of larviciding. And finally, the feasibility of an area vector control was indicated by the successful control operation in the San Vicente Pacaya Pilot Area, in which a new fixed-dose larviciding method was applied.

Apart from vector control, there remain two other control measures against Guatemalan onchocerciasis. Chemotherapeutic control may be effectively carried out in some low endemic areas with a low vector density. Likewise, it appears that a nodulectomy campaign can be significant in lowering the risk of severe eye lesions caused by invasion of microfilariae, probably from head nodules.

In conclusion, it is emphasized that further research on onchocerciasis and its control in Guatemala should continue in order to improve control measures and its evaluation. As already pointed out by Suzuki (1983), this research should include:

1. Vector biology and control
   (a) Cytotaxonomy of vector species, (b) search for resting black flies, (c) laboratory rearing of *S. ochraceum,* (d) further studies on critical ABR value, (e) role of transmission by minor potential vectors, (f) transmission potential of component cytospecies of *S. ochraceum* complex, (g) effect of reduced microfilarial density in DEC-treated patients on transmission by vector black flies, (h) trial of intermittent vector control, (i) further studies on the time interval between two successive larvicide applications, (j) efficacy of insecticides and formulations against black fly larvae in Guatemala, (k) dispersal range of *S. ochraceum* in large basins.

2. Epidemiology
   (a) Epidemiological evaluation of vector-control operations in the San Vicente Pacaya area, (b) relationship between the prevalence of eye lesions in human population and vector density, (c) human movements between endemic and nonendemic areas, (d) animal distribution and movements in the endemic areas, (e) elucidation of the reasons for sharp decline in endemicity in the Eastern Zone.

3. Parasitology
   (a) Longevity of adult worms of *O. volvulus,* (b) differentiation of *O. volvulus* larvae from other filariae, (c) existence and distribution of impalpable nodules in human body.

4. Immunology
   (a) Improvement of immunodiagnoses.

5. Chemotherapy
   (a) Treatment of patients with DEC and Suramin, (b) trial of chemotherapeutic control by new chemicals, (c) effect of DEC treatments on eye lesions.

ACKNOWLEDGMENTS

We are indebted to Steven Tessler, The Pennsylvania State University, for reading, editing, and retyping the manuscript, and whose efforts helped to clarify many points in our initial draft.

LITERATURE CITED

Brandling-Bennett, A. D., J. Anderson, H. Fuglsang, and R. Collins. (1981). Onchocerciasis in Guatemala: Epidemiology in fincas with various intensities of infection. *Am. J. Trop. Med. Hyg.* 30:970–981.

Collins, R. C. (1979). Onchocerciasis transmission potentials of four species of Guatemalan Simuliidae. *Am. J. Trop. Med. Hyg.* 28:72–75.

————. (1981). Transmission of onchocerciasis in Guatemala: recent studies and their implications for vector control. In *Proc. Guatemala-Japan Joint Conf. on Onchocerciasis Research and Control.* Japan International Cooperation Agency, Tokyo. Pp. 98–101.

Collins, R. C., M. E. Merino, and E. W. Cupp. (1981). Seasonal trends and diurnal patterns of man-biting activity for four species of Guatemalan black flies (Simuliidae). *Am. J. Trop. Med. Hyg.* 30:728–733.

Dalmat, H. T. (1955). The black flies (Diptera, Simuliidae) of Guatemala and their role as vectors of onchocerciasis. *Smithsonian Misc. Coll.* 125:1–425.

Dalmat, H. T., and C. L. Gibson. (1952). A study of flight range and longevity of blackflies (Diptera: Simuliidae) infected with *Onchocerca volvulus*. *Ann. Entomol. Soc. Am.* 45: 605–612.

Davies, J. B., R. Le Berre, J. F. Walsh, and B. Cliff. (1978). Onchocerciasis and *Simulium* control in the Volta River Basin. *Mosquito News* 38:466–472.

DeLeon, J. R., and B. O. L. Duke. 1966. Experimental studies on the transmission of Guatemalan and West African strains of *Onchocerca volvulus* by *Simulium ochraceum, S. metallicum,* and *S. callidum*. *Trans. R. Soc. Trop. Med. Hyg.* 60:735–752.

Figueroa, M. H. (1974). Robles' disease (American onchocerciasis) in Guatemala. In *Pan American Health Organization, Proc. Int. Symp. on Research and Control of Onchocerciasis in the Western Hemisphere.* Washington, D.C., PAHO Sci. Pub. No. 298: 100–104.

Fredeen, F. J. H., A. P. Arnason, and B. Berck. (1953). Adsorption of DDT on suspended solids in river water and its role in black fly control. *Nature* 171:700–701.

Fredeen, F. J. H., J. G. Saha, and M. H. Balba. (1975). Residues of methoxychlor and other chlorinated hydrocarbons in water, sand, and selected fauna following injections of methoxychlor black fly larvicide into the Saskatchewan River, 1972. *Pestic. Monit. J.* 8:241–246.

Garcia-Manzo, G. A. (1981). Geographical distribution of Robles disease in Guatemala. In *Proc. Guatemala-Japan Joint Conf. on Onchocerciasis Research and Control.* Japan International Cooperation Agency, Tokyo. Pp. 52–59.

Garms, R. (1975). Observations on filarial infections and parous rates of anthropophilic blackflies in Guatemala, with reference to the transmission of *Onchocerca volvulus*. *Tropenmed. Parasitol.* 26:169–182.

Garms, R., and J. O. Ochoa A. 1979. Further studies on the relative importance of Guatemalan blackfly species as vectors of *Onchocerca volvulus*. *Tropenmed. Parasitol.* 30:120–128.

Hamon, J. (1974). The onchocerciasis vectors in the Western Hemisphere. Vector biology and vector parasite relationship. In *Pan American Health Organization, Proc. Int. Symp. on Research and Control of Onchocerciasis in the Western Hemisphere,* Washington, D.C., PAHO Sci. Pub. No. 298: 58–68.

Hasegawa, J., M. Yasuno, and M. Sasa. (1981). Effects of insecticide treatment of streams for the control of blackfly larvae on the non-target organisms. In *Proc. Guatemala-Japan Joint Conf. on Onchocerciasis Research and Control.* Japan International Cooperation Agency, Tokyo. Pp. 187–190.

Helson, B. W., and A. S. West. (1978). Particulate formulations of Abate and methoxychlor as blackfly larvicides: their selective effects on stream fauna. *Can. Entomol.* 110:591–602.

Ito, S., I. Tanaka, and J. O. Ochoa A. (1980). Comparative studies on the affinities of two blackflies, *Simulium metallicum* and *S. ochraceum* for the larvae of *Onchocerca volvulus* in Guatemala. *Jpn. J. Sanit. Zool.* 31:261–270.

Kamimura, K., T. Suzuki, T. Okazawa, T. Inaoka, and J. O. Ochoa, A. 1985. Effect of temephos against the blackfly larvae in stream tests in Guatemala. *Jpn. J. Sanit. Zool.* 36:189–195.

Kawabata, M., Y. Hashiguchi, and G. Zea F. (1983). Distribution pattern of microfilariae in relation to sex and age in Guatemalan onchocerciasis. *Trans. R. Soc. Trop. Med. Hyg.* 77:215–216.

Lea, A. O., and H. T. Dalmat. (1955a). A pilot study of area larval control of black flies in Guatemala. *J. Econ. Entomol.* 48:378–383.

———. (1955b). Field studies on larval control of black flies in Guatemala. *J. Econ. Entomol.* 48:274–278.

Nakamura, Y., Y. Yamagata, H. Takaoka, M. Takahashi, J. O. Ochoa A., P. A. Molina, and H. Takahasi. (1981). A control trial of the vector of onchocerciasis, *Simulium ochraceum* (Diptera: Simuliidae) in the Lavaderos River Valley, Guatemala. *Jpn. J. Sanit. Zool.* 32:51–58.

Ochoa A., J. O. (1982). Studies on the anthropophilic blackfly species in Guatemala, with special reference to the transmission of onchocerciasis in the southeastern endemic area. *Jpn. J. Sanit. Zool.* 33:129–138.

Ogata, K. (1981). Preliminary report of Japan-Guatemala onchocerciasis control pilot project. Pp. 105–115. in M. Laird, Ed., *Blackflies: the future for biological methods in integrated control.* Academic Press, New York and London.

Omar, M. S., and Garms, R. (1975). The fate and migration of microfilariae of a Guatemalan strain of *Onchocerca volvulus* in *Simulium ochraceum* and *S. metallicum,* and the role of the buccopharyngeal armature in the destruction of microfilariae. *Tropenmed. Parasitol.* 26:183–190.

Sasa, M. (1976). *Human filariasis.* Univ. Tokyo Press, Tokyo.

Suzuki, R. (1983). *A guidebook for Guatemalan onchocerciasis (Robles disease), with special reference to vector control.* Guatemala-Japan Cooperative Project on Onchocerciasis Research and Control, Guatemala. 155 pp.

Tada, I., Y. Aoki, C. E. Rimola, T. Ikeda, K. Matsuo, J. O. Ochoa A., M. M. Reciones C., S. Sato, H. A. Godoy B., J. O. Castillo J., and H. Takahasi. (1979). Onchocerciasis in San Vicente Pacaya, Guatemala. *Am. J. Trop. Med. Hyg.* 28:67–71.

Takaoka, H. (1981). Seasonal occurrence of *Simulium ochraceum,* the principal vector of *Onchocerca volvulus* in the southeastern endemic area of Guatemala. *Am. J. Trop. Med. Hyg.* 30:1121–32.

———. (1982). Observations on the bionomics of larval and man-biting female populations of *Simulium horacioi,* a new potential vector of *Onchocerca volvulus* in Guatemala. *Jpn. J. Trop. Med. Hyg.* 10:49–62.

Takaoka, H., J. O. Ochoa A., M. Takahashi, and H. Takahasi. (1981). Evaluation of temephos as a larvicide against *Simulium ochraceum* (Diptera: Simuliidae) in Guatemala. *J. Med. Entomol.* 18:145–152.

Takaoka, H., J. O. Ochoa A., E. L. Juarez, and K. Hansen. (1982). Effects of temperature on development of *Onchocerca volvulus* in *Simulium ochraceum* and longevity of the simuliid vector. *J. Parasitol.* 68:478–483.

Takaoka, H., H. Suzuki, S. Noda, J. O. Ochoa A., and I. Tada. (1984). The intake, migration and development of *Onchocerca volvulus* microfilariae in *Simulium haematopotum* in Guatemala. *Jpn. J. Sanit. Zool.* 35:121–127.

Umino, T., T. Suzuki, and J. O. Ochoa A. (1983a). Insecticide studies in vector control of Guatemalan onchocerciasis. 1. Short carry of temephos in minute streamlets. *Jpn. J. Sanit. Zool.* 34:213–219.

Umino, T., T. Suzuki, and E. L. Juarez O. (1983b). Insecticide studies in vector control of Guatemalan onchocerciasis. 2. Efficacy of larvicides assessed by simulated trough tests. *Jpn. J. Sanit. Zool.* 34:269–277.

Umino, T., and T. Suzuki. (1984). Insecticide studies in vector control of Guatemalan oncho-cerciasis. 3. Laboratory tests on adsorption of larvicides to soil. *Jpn. J. Sanit. Zool.* 35:1–6.

Undeen, A. H., H. Takaoka, and K. Hansen. (1981). A test of *Bacillus thuringiensis* var. *israelensis* De Barjac as a larvicide for *Simulium ochraceum,* the Central American vector of onchocerciasis. *Mosquito News* 41:37–40.

Wada, Y. 1982. Theoretical approach to the epidemiology of onchocerciasis in Guatemala. *Jpn. J. Med. Sci. Biol.* 35:183–196.

Walsh, J. F., J. B. Davies, and B. Cliff. (1981). World Health Organization Onchocerciasis Control Programme in the Volta River Basin. Pp. 85–103. In M. Laird, Ed., in *Blackflies: the future for biological methods in integrated control.* Academic Press, New York and London.

Yamada, H. (1978). Onchocerciasis (Robles disease, River blindness) in Guatemala and Ghana. Clinical features and epidemiological research. *Floia Ophthalmol. Jpn.* 29:1817–37.

Yamada, H., and T. Oikawa (1980). Ocular onchocerciasis in heavily endemic focus in Guate-mala. *Floia Ophthalmol. Jpn.* 31:1637–47.

Yamagata, Y., T. Okazawa, and P. A. Molina. (1984). Geologic and geomorphologic studies on distribution of *Simulium ochraceum* (Diptera: Simuliidae) larvae in Guatemala. *Jpn. J. Sanit Zool.* 35:95–102.

Yamagata, Y., J. O. Ochoa A., P. A. Molina, H. Sato, K. Uemoto, and T. Suzuki. (1985). Chemical control of *Simulium ochraceum* (Diptera: Simuliidae) larvae in an oncho-cerciasis endemic area in Guatemala. *Jpn. J. Sanit. Zool.* (In press).

Yoshimura, T., Y. Hashiguchi, M. Kawabata, O. F. Flores C., O. O. Gudiel P., and E. E. C. Mazariegos de L. (1982). Prevalence and incidence of onchocerciasis as baseline data for evaluation of vector control in San Vicente Pacaya, Guatemala. *Trans. R. Soc. Trop. Med. Hyg.* 76:48–53.

28 THE EPIZOOTIOLOGY OF LIVESTOCK AND POULTRY DISEASES ASSOCIATED WITH BLACK FLIES

E. W. Cupp

Black flies cause periodic losses in animal agriculture throughout the world. Their deleterious effects may occur in a variety of habitats and ecological circumstances and involve a moderate number of simuliid species and a limited number of animal pathogens. These unique veterinary problems vary in severity and may include death and morbidity, reduced production of meat, milk, and other animal products, as well as reproductive dysfunction.

Several recent reviews have touched upon this general topic, emphasizing control methods (Jamnback 1973) and economic effects (Watts 1976, Steelman 1976, Fredeen 1985) or summarizing the role of certain species as pests and vectors of disease agents (Fallis 1980). This discussion will briefly expand and comment on certain aspects of the previous reviews and discuss pertinent ecological and epizootiological facets of the major black-fly-associated diseases of livestock and poultry. Where appropriate, preventive and control measures will also be mentioned, as will suggested areas of research. This discussion will first consider the role of certain simuliids as nuisance-pathogenic agents and then focus on the vectorial association between black flies and certain animal pathogens, i.e., *Leucocytozoon* spp., *Onchocerca* spp., and several arboviruses.

Because female black flies are telmophagous, their bites with the accompanying subcutaneous injection of saliva contribute significantly to nuisance and "worry" of both wild and domestic animals. Livestock under severe attack are restless, unproductive, and prone to stampede. Reproduction and lactation in dairy and beef animals are often reduced or curtailed. The udder may become swollen, inflamed, and tender so that nursing is halted, leading to stunted calf crops. Dermatitis, focal hemorrhages, and necrosis of the epidermis, as well as cutaneous and subcutaneous edema, occur as part of a general process of dermal pathogenesis associated with black fly bites (Frese and Thiel 1974).

The saliva is sometimes highly pathogenic, acting directly as a toxic substance or secondarily as a potent allergen. In situations where adults emerge in concentrated, vernal broods, or where certain generations of multivoltine species are extraordinarily large, massive simuliid attack can result in livestock death. Reports of mortality and severe morbidity have been commonplace in North America and central and eastern Europe. Species responsible for "simuliotoxicosis" (Wilhelm et al. 1982) include *Simulium arcticum* in the western provinces of Canada (see Fredeen 1977), *Cnephia pecuarum* in Texas (J. K. Olson, Texas A&M University, personal communication), *S. ornatum* in France, central Europe, and the Balkans (Noirtin and Boiteux 1979, Bock et al. 1982), and *S. erythrocephalum* in Switzerland, central Europe, and Poland (Grafner and Hiepe 1979, Mumcuoglu and Rufli 1980, Niesiolowski 1980). Massive biting by *S. reptans* and *S. lineatum* has also been associated with cattle deaths in Switzerland, Austria (Kutzer et al. 1981), and Italy (Rivosecchi et al. 1981); *S. voilensis* has also been incriminated in Italy.

The ecological patterns leading to outbreaks and the epizootiological picture associated with severe black fly toxicosis in cattle have been described by Rühm (1981, 1982, 1983) for both *S. erythrocephalum* and *S. ornatum* in central Europe. Factors contributing to the large-scale production of blood-seeking females include decreased egg mortality, synchrony of preimaginal development and adult emergence, and the relative amount of swarming and mating prior to appetitive flight. The degree of salivary gland development and concentration of saliva was also an important physiological feature. Key climatic considerations included periods of cool, rainy, and windy weather that tended to suppress swarming and limit foraging behavior, followed by a sudden, rapid rise in temperature that stimulated host-seeking on a mass basis.

The limnological conditions of larval habitats associated with massive outbreaks also appeared to be generally similar. In France and the Federal Republic of Germany, streams and rivers were characteristically polluted with high concentrations of organic matter orginating from dairy farm effluents or the outflows of impounded water. The additions of these materials increased eutrophication and restricted the structural diversity of black fly predators (Noirtin et al. 1981, Bock et al. 1982). In some cases, the prolific growth of certain aquatic plants also provided sheltered microhabitats for larvae and pupae.

Key entomological factors associated with simuliotoxicosis include biting rates by nulliparous females and relative concentration of salivary content per attacking fly. The age, sex, and general sensitivity of each animal within the herd is also an important veterinary consideration. It has been observed by Rühm (1983) and other investigators (Gräfner and Hiepe 1979) that cattle are in particular danger at the beginning of the grazing season when they are put on pasture for the first time. Animals (usually calves) less than 30 months old are particularly at risk (Stamm et al. 1980). However, some immunity can be acquired during the late spring and early summer if simuliid attack is discontinuous and at a low level.

Major outbreaks of *Simulium arcticum* occur between mid-May and the end of June in Saskatchewan and Alberta, Canada. Because of this species' flight capability, infestation of cattle may occur up to 40 kilometers away from the nearest larval habitat (Shemanchuk 1980). *Simulium arcticum* has been responsible for the deaths of thousands of livestock, including the losses of valuable herd sires (Fredeen 1977). The cause of death has been attributed to direct toxemia, with newborn calves and imported animals most susceptible. However, some measures of immunity can be gained if animals are exposed to a moderate number of bites.

Simulium arcticum s. l. is associated with large, silty rivers lacking emergent vegetation. The preimaginal stages are attached to rocks and boulders in massive numbers. This prolific breeding coupled with the female's long-range foraging ability makes this species a dangerous pest. Also, the general pattern of outbreaks, while somewhat typical for subarctic species, is nevertheless unpredictable. Prairie winds may serve to scatter or concentrate females. In the latter case, the sudden aggregation of large numbers of blood-feeding flies may result in the death of livestock recently put on pasture. Indeed it is the rapidity of the attack that often precludes stockmen from responding in time to avoid huge losses.

Early warning of potential outbreaks has been suggested by Rühm (1981) as a means of alleviating black-fly-associated livestock death in central Europe. In the Ruhr region of the Federal Republic of Germany, larval habitats that have proven to be prolific are monitored, with public notices given when populations appear to be dangerously high. Such warnings allow adequate response time to move animals off pasture or to begin some means of protection. In Canada the use of repellents has been tested. Permethrin provided 90% protection for up to seven days against attack by *S. articum* (Shemanchuk 1980). Phosmet, applied as a pour-on, also proved to be effective against this species, as was the use of partially darkened shelters equipped with a back rubber charged with 1% ronnel (Khan 1981).

Source reduction is an ongoing research area, and little needs to be said here as to its importance in preventing or blunting the effects of black fly outbreaks. As possible complementary research areas focused on salivary toxicosis, the pharmacological activity of saliva and the pathological processes associated with acute toxemia should be investigated. Since salivary glands can now be collected in large numbers from female flies that have been mass-reared in the laboratory (Brenner and Cupp 1980), it should be possible to determine if injections with purified gland extracts prior to black fly season could confer partial immunity to valuable animals. The immune mechanisms for resistance should also be investigated.

The role of black flies as biological vectors of agents pathogenic to poultry and livestock is limited to the transmission of protozoan and filarial parasites. In terms of economic importance, Leucocytozoon disease among domestic flocks of ducks, geese, and turkeys can be a very serious problem. Two species, *Leucocytozoon simondi* and *L. smithi,* are noteworthy because of their nearly worldwide distribution (Cook 1971, Fallis et al. 1974).

Leucocytozoon simondi can be particularly pathogenic to domestic ducks and nonimmune geese. The occurrence of this parasite has precluded the production of domestic forms of these anatids in many parts of the northern latitudes (e.g., see Laird and Bennett 1970). Over parts of its range, *L. smithi* is often an impediment to the production of domestic turkeys. High mortality of young birds and reduced rates of reproduction by older, chronically infected turkeys are common occurrences (Barnett 1977).

Several key epizootiological factors that regulate the transmission of these two protozoan parasites are similar. Of primary interest is that both parasites have relatively short development cycles of 3–4 days in their black fly vectors (Fallis et al. 1956, Pinkovsky et al. 1981, Kiszewski and Cupp 1985). This interesting adaptation ensures that nulliparous flies taking an infective blood meal can transmit sporozoites at the beginning of the second gonotrophic cycle. Since survival of the vector population is still relatively high at that time, a large proportion of newly parous flies will therefore be infective. The result is salivary gland infection rates for both parasite species that can often be 30% or higher (Fallis and Bennett 1966, Greiner and Forrester 1979). Therefore, in enzootic situations, prevalence rates in avian hosts can be extremely high, ranging from 27% to 72% (Bennett et al. 1974, Forrester et al. 1974).

The flight range, dispersal pattern, and feeding behavior of ornithophilic black flies are also of great importance in considering potential epizootics of Leucocytozoon disease. *Simulium rugglesi,* a vector of *L. simondi* in Ontario, was shown by Bennett (1963) to move both with and against prevailing winds, sometimes traveling two to six miles from a stream-side, central mark-release site. This species fed most often on hosts at ground level that were positioned next to the shores of lakes and rivers. *Simulium slossonae,* a primary vector of *L. smithi,* in the southeastern United States, commonly traveled up to four miles in search of a host (Moore and Noblet 1974). This species readily attacked penned birds at ground level (Noblet et al. 1975).

Phenological factors are also important in shaping the overall pattern of Leucocytozoon spp. transmission. As noted by Bennett et al. (1974), infection of wild fowl by *L. simondi* may follow a unimodal or bimodal pattern, depending upon the seasonality of the vector, spring recrudescence of the infection in the avian host, and the time of production of nestlings. For example, there is a unimodal pattern in northern Michigan and Ontario associated with such vectors as *S. anatinum,* a late-spring species that overlaps with *S. rugglesi,* an early-summer taxon (Fallis and Bennett 1966). In contrast, in southern Michigan, Pennsylvania, Massachusetts, and Maryland, a bimodal pattern exists due to the occurrence of distinctly vernal ornithophilic species that initiate transmission to adult birds (see Tarshis and Stuht 1970), and other species of the subgenus *Eusimulium,* which transmit the parasite to the young of the year later in the summer.

Transmission patterns for *L. smithi* also differ and are climate-related. *Simulium aureum,* an enzootic vector in New York State, initiates transmission in late June and persists until late September. However, in the mid-Atlantic and southern states, transmission of *L. smithi* can occur throughout the year, with *S. slossonae* serving as a primary vector. *S. congareenarum* and *S. meridionale* are involved on a limited temporal or geographic basis (Noblet et al. 1972, Pinkovsky et al. 1981). A spring relapse also occurs with this parasite (Alverson and Noblet 1977).

The colonization of *Simulium vittatum* (Bernardo et al. 1985), an experimental vector of *Leucocytozoon smithi* (Kiszewski and Cupp 1985), opens the way for continuous laboratory study of the pathogenesis and *in vitro* culture of this and related parasites. Possible areas to be investigated include the search for the mechanism associated with "spring relapse," an important epizootiological factor. With the recent discovery of the hypnozoite, a dormant stage of *Plasmodium vivax* and *P. ovale,* it seems logical that its counterpart would also exist within *Leucocytozoon* spp. *In vitro* culture of both the tissue and blood stages of the parasite could be initiated for drug screening and possible vaccine development.

Another group of black-fly-transmitted parasites of veterinary significance encompasses certain species of *Onchocerca.* These filarial worms are long, thin nematodes that as adults live in the skin, subcutaneous, or deep connective tissues of their hosts (Muller 1979). Two common species that parasitize cattle are *Onchocerca lienalis* in the temperate latitudes and *O. ochengi,* an African species. *Onchocerca gutturosa,* which was believed to be black-fly-transmitted, has recently been shown to be vectored by certain species in the family Ceratopogonidae (Bain 1979). *Onchocerca gibsoni*, also transmitted by certain ceratopogonid species, is an important bovine parasite in Australia, Sri Lanka, and southern Asia. In Australia it is transmitted by *Forcipomyia townsvillensis* (Ottley and Moorhouse 1980).

The pathology associated with *O. lienalis* is not pronounced or overt. It may consist of an intense eosinophilic dermatitis, inflammation of (a) the connective ligament surrounding the adults and (b) the dermis as a result of microfilarial migration (Scholtens et al. 1977). However, there is no ocular disease, nor are subcutaneous nodules formed in response to the adult worms. For these reasons, *O. lienalis* infections frequently go undetected, with evidence of the parasite noted during surveys made at abattoirs.

As a well-adapted parasite, *O. lienalis* tends to be enzootic in ecologically stable foci. In a recent study conducted by Lok et al. (1983) in New York State, *Simulium jenningsi* was shown to transmit the parasite during the warmer months of the year, beginning in early July and continuing through early September. Following collection, identification, and dissections of flies, it was determined that vector infective rates were low, with 1.7% of parous flies harboring third-stage larvae. Filarial infections in the *S. jenningsi* population were usually detected when the parous rate exceeded 50%. Consequently, three peaks of transmission occurred that corresponded roughly to the number of generations of the vector.

Adults of *Onchocera ochengi* (Bwangamoi 1969), a species widely distributed throughout sub-Saharan Africa, are found in nodules located within the reticular layer of the dermis. Such onchocercomata are usually prominent along the posterior-ventral aspects of infected bovids and may occur in the scrotum and udder. *O. ochengi* nodules adversely affect the quality of hides for leather production. Zoophilic members of the *Simulium damnosum* cytospecies complex (e.g., *S. sanctipauli*) serve as vectors (Omar et al. 1979).

Biological vector competence for arboviruses has not been shown conclusively for any simuliid and must still be considered conjectural. However, isolations of some arboviruses from various black fly species collected in nature indicate that during the course of blood-feeding females can become infected and retain certain kinds of viruses for relatively long periods of time. It is worth noting that viruses from the families Bunyaviridae, Togaviridae, and Rhabdoviridae have been isolated from pools of wild-caught black flies during periods of transmission.

Eastern equine encephalomyelitis (EEE) virus was detected in pools of two ornithophilic black flies, *Simulium johannseni* and *S. meridionale*, collected in Wisconsin (Anderson et al. 1961). For the latter species, an isolate was made from a pool of 100 unengorged females collected in a commercial turkey brooder house. However, levels of antibody to this virus in farm turkey flocks were somewhat low, suggesting that the potential for a viral epizootic associated with *S. meridionale* was not significant.

Two arboviruses that have been associated with livestock epizootics during periods of black fly activity include strains of subtype I of the Venezuelan equine encephalomyelitis virus (VEE) groups and the New Jersey serotype of vesicular stomatis (VS) virus, an important pathogen of cattle, horses, and swine. During a major epizootic of VEE in Colombia in 1967, in which thousands of equines died, virus isolates were made from *S. exiguum, S. metallicum, S. callidum, S. mexicanum,* and *S. paynei* (Sanmartin et al. 1973). The sudden appearance of horse cases in isolated montane valleys also suggested the possibility of a strong-flying, migratory vector. However, in a controlled laboratory study, Homan et al. (1985) were unable to infect *S. mexicanum* and *S. metallicum* females with both an enzootic and epizootic strain of VEE virus, leading these investigators to conclude that neither species plays an important role as natural, biological vectors. However, mechanical transmission did occur occasionally.

In a somewhat similar situation, an epizootic of vesicular stomatitis swept through the Rocky Mountain states during the summer and fall of 1982 (Snyder et al. 1983). The rapid spread, seasonality, and association with high levels of insect activity (Buisch 1983) suggested that this epizootic might be vector-associated; interestingly, a similar idea had been considered in 1945 during an outbreak of VS in Colorado (Heiny 1945). Virus isolations from *Simulium vittatum,* a common black fly in the western United States, lends further credence to this possibility (D. B. Francey, Centers for Disease Control, personal communication; Schnitzlein and Reichmann 1985).

Thus there is a continued need to evaluate the vector potential of selected black fly species for arboviruses that, on the basis of epizootiological evidence, appear to be transmitted by simuliids. Given the recent advances made in mass-rearing a number of black fly species (Brenner and Cupp 1980) and holding infected adult *Simulium* spp. for extended periods (Lok et al. 1980), simple experiments concerning virus uptake, replication, and transmission could be conducted to answer fundamental questions concerning the role of black flies as natural vectors.

ACKNOWLEDGMENTS

Some of the information given here was taken from studies by E.W.C. and colleagues that were supported by USDA Specific Cooperative Agreements 1090–20265–013A and 58–32U4–0–245 and Hatch Grant NYC–139417. Some of the findings were also taken from investigations supported by the Filariasis component of the UNDP/World Bank/WHO Special Programme for Research and Training in Tropical Diseases.

LITERATURE CITED

Alverson, D. R., and R. Noblet. 1977. Spring relapse of *Leucocytozoon smithi* (Sporozoa: Leucocytozoidae) in turkeys. *J. Med. Entomol.* 14:132–133.

Anderson, J. R., V. H. Lee, S. Vadlamudi, R. P. Hanson, and G. R. DeFoliart. 1961. Isolation of eastern encephalitis virus from Diptera in Wisconsin. *Mosquito News* 21:244–248.

Bain, O. 1979. Transmission de l'onchocerque bovine, *Onchocerca gutturosa,* par *Culicoides. Ann. Parasitol. Hum. Comp.* 54:483–488.

Barnett, B. D. 1977. *Leucocytozoon* disease of turkeys. *World's Poultry Sci. J.* 33:76–87.

Bennett, G. F. 1963. Use of P^{32} in the study of a population of *Simulium rugglesi* (Diptera: Simuliidae) in Algonquin Park, Ontario. *Can. J. Zool.* 41:831–840.

Bennett, G. F., W. Blandin, H. W. Heusmann, and A. G. Campbell. 1974. Hematozoa of the Anatidae of the Atlantic Flyway. 1 Massachusetts. *J. Wildlife Dis.* 10:442–451.

Bernardo, M. J., E. W. Cupp, and A. E. Kiszewski. 1986. Rearing black flies (Diptera: Simuliidae) in the laboratory: colonization and life table statistics for *Simulium vittatum* Zetterstedt. *Ann. Entomol. Soc. Am.* 79:610–621.

Bock, A., R. Münzhuber, W. Rühm, and R. Schlepper. 1982. Kriebelmücken als Plage- und Schaderreger an der Rur (Simuliidae, Dipt.). *Z. Ang. Zool.* 69:183–217.

Brenner, R. J., and E. W. Cupp. 1980. Rearing black flies (Diptera: Simuliidae) in a closed system of water circulation. *Tropenmed. Parasitol.* 31:247–258.

Buisch, W. W. 1983. Fiscal year 1982–83 vesicular stomatitis outbreak. Pp. 78–84 in *Proc. 87th Ann. Mtg. U.S. Animal Health Assoc.*

Bwangamoi, O. 1969. *Onchocera ochengi* new species, an intradermal parasite of cattle in East Africa. *Bull. Epizoot. Dis. Afr.* 17:321–335.

Cook, R. S. 1971. *Leucocytozoon* Danilewsky, 1890. Pp. 291–299 in J. W. Davis, R. C. Anderson, L. Karstad, and D. O. Trainer, Eds., *Infectious and parasitic diseases of wild birds.* Iowa State Univ. Press, Ames.

Fallis, A. M. 1980. Arthropods as pests and vectors of disease. *Vet. Parasitol.* 6:47–73.

Fallis, A. M., R. C. Anderson, and G. F. Bennett. 1956. Further observations on the transmission and development of *Leucocytozoon simondi. Can. J. Zool.* 34:389–404.

Fallis, A. M., and G. F. Bennett. 1966. On the epizootiology of infections caused by *Leucocytozoon simondi* in Algonquin Park, Canada. *Can. J. Zool.* 44:101–112.

Fallis, A. M., S. S. Desser, and R. A. Khan. 1974. On species of *Leucocytozoon. Adv. Parasitol.* 12:1–67.

Forrester, D. J., L. T. Hon, L. E. Williams, Jr., and D. H. Austin. 1974. Blood protozoa of wild turkeys in Florida. *J. Protozool.* 21:494–497.

Fredeen, F. J. H. 1985. Some economic effects of outbreaks of black flies (*Simulium luggeri* Nicholson and Mickel) in Saskatchewan. *Quaest. Entomol.* 21:175–208.

———. 1977. A review of the economic importance of black flies (Simuliidae) in Canada. *Quaest. Entomol.* 13:219–229.

Frese, K., and W. Thiel. 1974. Zur Pathologie der Hautveränderunger beim kriebelmücken-befull des Rindes. *Zbl. Vet. Med. B,* 21:618–624.

Gräfner, G., and T. Hiepe. 1979. Beitrag zum Krankheitsbild und zur Pathogenese des Kriebelmückenbefalls bei Weidetieren. *Mh. Vet. Med.* 34:538–540.

Greiner, E. C., and D. J. Forrester. 1979. Prevalence of sporozoites of *Leucocytozoon smithi* in Florida blackflies. *J. Parasitol.* 65:324–336.

Heiny, E. 1945. Vesicular stomatitis in cattle and horses in Colorado. *North Am. Vet.* 26:726–730.

Homan, E. J., F. N. Zuluaga, T. M. Yuill, and H. Lorbacher de R. 1985. Studies on the transmission of Venezuelan equine encephalitis virus by Colombian Simuliidae (Diptera). *Am. J. Trop. Med. Hyg.* 34:799–804.

Jamnback, H. 1973. Recent developments in control of blackflies. *Ann. Rev. Entomol.* 18:281–304.

Khan, M. A. 1981. Protection of pastured cattle from black flies (Diptera: Simuliidae): improved weight gains following a dermal application of Phosmet. *Vet. Parasitol.* 8:327–336.

Kiszewski, A. E., and E. W. Cupp. 1986. Transmission of *Leucocytozoon smithi* (Sporozoa: Leucocytozoidae) by black flies (Diptera: Simuliidae) in New York, U.S.A. *J. Med. Entomol.* 23:256–262.

Kurtzer, E., M. Car, and J. Fanta. 1981. Zur Kriebelmückenplage in Österreich. *Wien. tierärztl. Mschr.* 68:22–31.

Laird, M., and G. F. Bennett. 1970. The sub-arctic epizootiology of *Leucocytozoon simondi.* Proc. 2nd Int. Congr. Parasitol. Sect. II. *J. Parasitol.* 56:198.

Lok, J. B., E. W. Cupp, and M. J. Bernardo. 1980. The development of *Onchocerca* spp. in *Simulium decorum* Walker and *Simulium pictipes* Hagen. *Tropenmed. Parasitol.* 31:498–506.

Lok, J. B., E. W. Cupp, M. J. Bernardo, and R. J. Pollack. 1983. Further studies on the development of *Onchocerca* spp. (Nematoda: Filarioidea) in nearctic black flies (Diptera: Simuliidae). *Am. J. Trop. Med. Hyg.* 32:1298–1305.

Moore, IV, H. S., and R. Noblet. 1974. Flight range of *Simulium slossonae,* the primary vector of *Leucocytozoon smithi* of turkeys in South Carolina. *Environ. Entomol.* 3:365–369.

Muller, R. 1979. Identification of *Onchocerca*. Pp. 175–206 in A. E. R. Taylor and R. Muller, Eds., *Problems in the identification of parasites and their vectors. Symp. Br. Soc. Parasitol.,* vol. 17, Blackwell Scientific Publications.

Mumcuoglu, Y., and T. Rufli. 1980. Dermatologische Entomologie. 6. Simuliidae/ Kriebelmücken. *Schweiz. Rund. Med.* (Praxis) 69:245–249.

Niesiolowski, S. 1980. Znaczenie zdrowotne i gospodarcze meszek (Simuliidae, Diptera) z wirzglednieniem aktualnego stanu badán nad tym zagadnieniem w Polsce. *Wiad. parazyt.* 26:663–677.

Noblet, R., T. R. Adkins, and J. B. Kissam. 1972. *Simulium congareenarum* (Diptera: Simuliidae), a new vector of *Leucocytozoon smithi* (Sporozoa: Leucocytozooidae) in domestic turkeys. *J. Med. Entomol.* 9:580.

Noblet, R., J. B. Kissam, and T. R. Adkins, Jr. 1975. *Leucocytozoon smithi:* incidence of transmission by black flies in South Carolina (Diptera: Simuliidae). *J. Med. Entomol.* 12:111–114.

Noirtin, C., and P. Boiteux. 1979. Mort de 25 animaux de ferme (dont 24 bovins) par piqûres de simulies dans les Vosges. *Bull. Men. Soc. Vet. Prat.* 63:41–54.

Noirtin, C., P. Boiteux, P. Guillet, C. Dejoux, F. Beaucournu-Saguez, and J. Mouchet. 1981. Les simulies, nuisance pour le bétail dans les Vosges: les origines de leur pullulation et les méthodes de lutte. *Cah. ORSTOM sér. Entomol. Méd. Parasitol.* 19:101–112.

Omar, M. S., A. M. Denke, and J. N. Raybould. 1979. The development of *Onchocerca ochengi* (Nematoda: Filarioidea) to the infective stage in *Simulium damnosum* s.l. with a note on the histochemical staining of the parasite. *Tropenmed. Parasitol.* 30:157–162.

Ottley, M. L., and D. E. Moorhouse. 1980. Laboratory transmission of *Onchocerca gibsoni* by *Forcipomyia* (*Lasiohelea*) *townsvillensis*. *Aust. Vet. J.* 56:559.

Pinkovsky, D. D., D. J. Forrester, and J. F. Butler. 1981. Investigations on black fly vectors (Diptera: Simuliidae) of *Leucocytozoon smithi* (Sporozoa: Leucocytozoidae) in Florida. *J. Med. Entomol.* 18:153–157.

Rivosecchi, L., E. Zanin, G. Dell'uomo, and C. Cavallini. 1981. Nuove osservazioni su *Simulium reptans* (Diptera, Simuliidae) in provincia di Trento. *Parassitologia* 23:236–239.

Rühm, W. 1981. Ursachen des aperiodischen Schadauftretens blutsaugender Kriebelmückenarten in Mittleuropa (Simuliidae, Diptera). *Mittl. Dtsch. Ges. Allg. Ang. Entomol.* 3:283–286.

———. 1982. Spätes Schaudauftreten von *Boophthora erythrocephala* de Geer (Simuliidae, Diptera). *Anz. Schädlingskde, Pflanzenschutz, Unweltschutz* 55:49–55.

———. 1983. Black-flies (Simuliidae, Diptera), a cause of annoyance and injury to livestock. *Vet. Med. Rev.* (German Federal Republic) 1:38–50.

Sanmartin, C., R. B. Mackenzie, H. Trapido, P. Baneto, C. H. Mullenax, E. Gutierrez, and C. Lesmes. 1973. Encefalitis equina venezolana en Colombia, 1967. *Bol. Of. San. Panam.* 74:108–137.

Schnitzlein, W. M., and M. E. Reichmann. 1985. Characterization of New Jersey vesicular stomatitis virus isolates from horses and black flies during the 1982 outbreak in Colorado. *Virology* 142:426–431.

Scholtens, G., S. R. Adams, and J. R. Broderson. 1977. Evidence of onchocerciasis in Georgia cattle: prevalence at slaughter. *Am. J. Vet. Res.* 38:1093–97.

Shemanchuk, J. A. 1980. Protection of cattle on farms. In W. O. Haufe and G. C. R. Croome, Eds., *Control of black flies in the Athabasca River.* Tech. rept. Lethbridge, Alberta.

Snyder, M. L., E. W. Jenney, F. A. Ericksson, and E. A. Carbrey. 1983. The 1982 resurgence of vesicular stomatitis in the United States: a summary of laboratory diagnostic findings. *Am. Assoc. Vet. Lab. Diag.* 25:221–228.

Stamm, K., H. G. Ziemer, and W. Rühm. 1980. Erkrankungen und Todesfälle bei Rindern durch Kriebelmücken (Simuliidae, Diptera). *Anz. Schädlingskde, Pflanzenschutz, Umweltschutz* 53:56–64.

Steelman, C. D. 1976. Effects of external and internal arthropod parasites on domestic livestock production. *Ann. Rev. Entomol.* 21:155–178.

Tarshis, I. B., and J. N. Stuht. 1970. Two species of Simuliidae (Diptera), *Cnephia ornithophilia* and *Prosimulium vernale,* from Maryland. *Ann. Entomol. Soc. Am.* 73:587–590.

Watts, S. B. 1976. Blackflies (Diptera: Simuliidae): a problem review and evaluation. *Pest Management Papers,* No. 5, Simon Fraser Univ. Burnaby, British Columbia.

Wilhelm, A., P. Betke, and K. Jacob. 1982. Simuliotoxkose beim Ren (*Rangifer tarandus*). Pp. 357–360 in R. Ippen and H. -D. Schräder, Eds., *Erkrankungen der Zootiere. Verhandlungsbericht des XXIV Internationalen Symposium über die Erkrankungen der Zootiere.* Akademie-Verlag, Berlin.

29   MODELS AS AIDS TO UNDERSTANDING ONCHOCERCIASIS

J. B. Davies, D. E. Weidhaas, and D. G. Haile

The general availability and cheapness of the modern microcomputer has brought the use of these machines within the budget of almost any laboratory or scientist. Their ability to perform repetitive complex calculations at high speeds makes them ideal for the construction and running of computer simulations of biological functions, enabling many years of events in real time to be compressed into a few minutes of simulation time.

In the field of onchocerciasis, modeling is not new. Le Berre et al. (1964) and Le Berre (1966) tabulated a simple mathematical description of the dynamics of the transmission of the disease by the vector *Simulium damnosum* s.l. Theobald and used it to predict longevity and survival rates of the fly and the frequency with which transmission might occur. The effect of control measures on the prevalence of onchocerciasis at Abuja, Nigeria, was compared with a hypothetical model by Davies (1963). Mills (1969) published the first attempt to make a mathematical description of the dynamics of the epidemiology of onchocerciasis in which biting and infection rates of *S. damnosum* s.l. were related to the number of infective third-stage larvae (L_3) of *Onchocerca volvulus* Leukhart received by a person per year in each of the three bioclimatic zones of West Africa. He also postulated that the proportion of flies that become infected is a function of the prevalence of the disease in the bitten population.

Other attempts to calculate the dynamics of transmission were made by Duke (1968a,b) and Duke et al. (1972). They proposed the use of the Annual Transmission Potential (ATP) as a measure of transmission (as the daily transmission potential) which was later adopted by the Onchocerciasis Control Programme in the Volta River Basin (Walsh et al. 1978). Somewhat similar calculations were made by Philippon (1977), in which infection rates and transmission levels at a number of sites were compared.

The first computer simulation model was produced by Deitz (1982) and is a complex mathematical model designed to study the progress of the disease in a human population. There are no vector or vector-parasite cycles. Individual persons are not identified and the human population is dealt with as a single entity, although subject to complicated interactions such as differential age survival. The mean microfilarial density is taken as the measure of infection in the population, and the number of infected larvae injected into the human population each year is regarded as a function of the mean microfilarial density and the biting rate. Blindness, worm load, prevalence, etc., are all functions of microfilarial density and human age.

As it is presented, the Deitz model predicts that after twenty years of no transmission there would still be a sufficient reservoir of worms in the human population for the disease to recover to its precontrol level in the ten years following a cessation of control and the return of the vector to precontrol levels. This is alarming, but it is likely that the parameters used in this example overestimated the longevity of *O. volvulus*. If the survival of the adult worm in the host were to be decreased in line with more recent data, a different prediction might be obtained.

The dynamics of the vector were studied by Birley et al. (1983), who used a mathematical model that simulated observed data on the recolonization of a single specific breeding site by *S.damnosum* s.l. after the interruption of control. The model enabled the following parameters to be estimated (p. 512):

Mean generation time	19 days
Adult female offspring per oviposition	1.43
Net reproductive rate	3.76
Female survival per oviposition cycle	0.62

These data have been used for the basis of a model designed to predict the effect of larviciding strategies on *S. damnosum* populations in the field (Birley and Davies 1984). The paper gives a program written in BASIC computer language, which should be applicable to any multivoltine species of *Simulium*.

Whether or not the above models have been successful in simulating the dynamics of onchocerciasis or its vector, they have had an important role in stimulating a detailed examination of the life cycles of the vector and parasite and their interaction with the human host.

CONSTRUCTING AN ONCHOCERCIASIS MODEL

We have been involved in constructing a computer simulation of the interaction between vector, parasite, and host and will use this model to illustrate some of the problems inherent in trying to quantify the dynamics of onchocerciasis.

Once having set up the basic model, the intention is to try to mimic actual field situations by priming the model with field data on prevalence, seasonal biting rates, and ATPs. The model would follow the life cycles of vector (Birley et al. 1983, Mokry 1980), parasite, and host and would thus enable flies to bite people, some become infected, and later transmit infective larvae to other persons, while at the same time laying eggs to perpetuate the fly population. Worms would develop or die in infected persons in whom worm loads may increase or decrease depending on the rates of infection. People are born, age, become infected, and die. Human involvement is expressed in terms of numbers of adult worms per person and by prevalence (Barbiero and Trpis 1984). The fly population is assessed in terms of biting rates and transmission potentials.

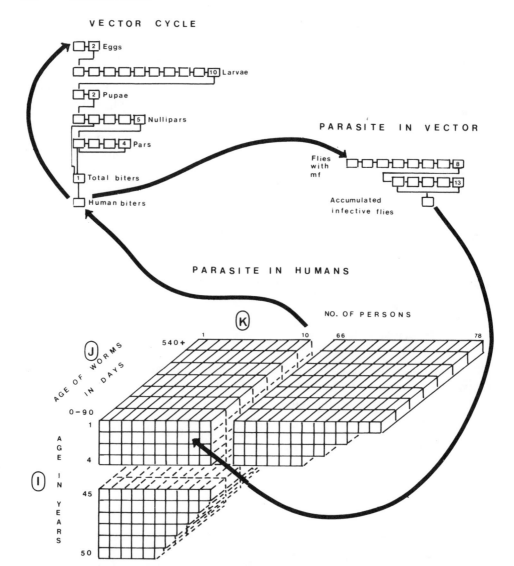

FIG. 29.1 Schematic representation of an onchocerciasis transmission model. For the vector and parasite in vector cycles, each box represents one day. In the parasite in human three-dimensional matrix, each cell of the slice I,K represents one person of age I. Infective *Onchocerca* larvae accumulated over 90 days at the end of the parasite-in-vector cycle are "inoculated" into randomly selected persons in slice J–1 and progressively aged each 90 days over slices J–2 to J–7. Slice J–7 contains the accumulated number of mature female *Onchocerca* in each person.

In order to make a start we accepted that it would not be practical to cover all possible variations in the epidemiology of the disease. We therefore limited the first version to a simple closed system where flies can only bite the designated population and there is no immigration by flies or humans.

We decided to employ a system in which fly and parasite numbers were followed from day to day, and one in which each person in the human population could be identified and the parasite load followed throughout life. This would eventually enable control measures to be applied to specific vector stages on specific days and enable persons to be followed through simulated drug treatments. A scheme of the model is shown in Figure 29.1. It is hoped that a detailed description will be published elsewhere when it is more complete.

BASIC ASSUMPTIONS

To make the model manageable we made the following assumptions. Some are obviously not quite true, but we hoped to be able to make modifications at a later stage as better data became available.

1. Vector
   Flies bite only the defined human population.
   Adult fly survival includes emigrants; there are no immigrant flies.
   Seasonal or slow changes in population can be achieved by changing the adult or immature survival rates.
   Catastrophic changes in population can be made by "killing" a proportion of adults or immatures over a specified time period.

2. Parasite in vector
   Adult fly-biting activity, survival, or fecundity is not influenced by the parasite.
   All flies that bite an infected person take up microfilariae (mf), although not all flies will become infective.

3. Parasite in humans
   No distinction is made between human sex.
   Female worms continue to produce mf for as long as they live.
   The life span of a female worm includes the 9–18 months that mf may survive her death.
   The development time of immature worms covers the time from inoculation of the L_3 to the production of mf by the mature female.
   Risk of infection is related to age.
   Host reaction does not affect the fecundity of the worms.

Parameters

The first computer program was written in FORTRAN IV language for an AMDAHL 470 mainframe computer. More recently, BASIC-language versions have been written for the IBM and ORIC personal computers.

In order to run the model it was necessary to provide numerical values for all the variables in the three cycles. The values chosen are listed in Table 29.1. Data were of two kinds: that which had some experimental or observational basis, and that which was deduced from the first category, estimated or obtained by trial and error.

Table 29.1 Basic parameters

	Observed	Estimated
Vector cycle		
Number eggs per oviposition	400	
Egg development, days	2	
Larvae, days	10	
Pupae, days	2	
Nullipars, days	5	
Gonotrophic cycle, days	4	
Immature daily survival	0.7387	
Adult survival	0.75	
Proportion of females	0.5	
Proportion biting humans		0.95
Parasite in vector		
Proportion becoming infected		Prevalence
Blood to infective bite, days		8
Time to next bite, days		4
Adult survival infective flies	0.75	
O. Volv. larval survival		0.5
L_3 transmitted per bite	2	
Sex ratio $L_3 5$		0.5
Parasite in humans		
Survival per 90 days		
Post L_3 larvae		0.5
Adult worms		0.953
L_3 to mature adult, months	18	
Adult worm life, years	12	
Proportion flies biting age class		
2–5 yrs.		0.05
6–15 yrs.		0.15
16–30 yrs.		0.45
30+ yrs.		0.35
Maximum worm load		40
Minimum number detectable worms		4

Vector Cycle

This is essentially the same as that used by Birley et al. (1983), without the provision for immigrant flies. For parameters we decided to use values applicable to the "savanna" situation because more data were available. Eggs per female was set at 400, being a rough average obtained from Figures 1 and 2 of Cheke et al. (1982) for both uninfected and infected flies. The adult daily survival rate was arbitrarily set at 0.75, being slightly higher than the value of 0.74 estimated by Davies et al. (1981: 33.) at the height of the dry season. To maintain the vector population at a steady level (net reproductive rate = 1), the daily survival rate for immature stages was found by calculation to be 0.7387. It was assumed that the proportion of female flies was 0.5. In the model only females were followed. The proportion of flies biting humans was guessed at 0.95 for the simulations.

Parasite in Vector

It was assumed that the proportion of flies that picked up mf was the same as the prevalence of the mf-positive skin snips in the human population, as suggested by Mills (1969). This prevalence was recalculated every 90 days. For the failure of mf to develop to L_3 in any fly, we adopted a single factor of 0.5, which approximated to the value given by Philippon (1977: 171). The same author (p. 223) gives the mean number of L_3 transmitted per bite by an infective fly as 2.0 in the West African savanna. We have assumed a female sex ratio in L_3s of 0.5; thus in this case one female L_3 is transmitted by each infective bite.

Human Population

The human population structure was based on a hypothetical population approximating to the age pyramid for a West African savanna community given by Gillies et al. (1983). In our model, of a total of 1,655 persons of both sexes, 78 were up to one year old, reducing annually to 5 persons of over 50 years (Fig. 29.1). The difference between the number of persons in any year and the next represents the number of deaths between the years. The birth rate is equal to the overall death rate.

Parasite in Human

This cycle presented the most problems, which were related to the longevity of immature and mature worms and to the age distribution of infective bites. To start, an arbitrary 90-day survival of 0.5 was applied to the immature worms. This had the effect of permitting only 1.5% of L_3s to survive to maturity over the 18 months of development time chosen within the extremes of 7 to 34 months given by Prost (1980). Adult worm survival posed another problem. Since prevalence estimates are based on the presence of one or more mf in one or two skin snips, it was necessary to decide how many adult female worms a person should have in order to be reasonably certain of producing a positive snip. It is a common observation that a few persons exhibiting nodules or clinical symptoms of onchocerciasis may not have a sufficient density of mf in the skin to be detected by one or two snips during a survey. Probably the presence of more than one female worm would be required to assure detection. We arbitrarily set this minimum level for detection at 4 worms. Persons with 1 to 3 worms could be considered subclinical cases.

In the first trial runs it was found that at high biting rates the worm load in some persons exceeded 1,000. The highest reported number of female worms that we could find was 110 in a male from Liberia (Schultz-Key and Albiez 1977). In the same series of patients the mean number of female worms that were digested out of excised nodules was 26.5. As it is not known how many worms lie in undiscovered nodules or free in the body, a maximum of 40 living female worms per person seemed a reasonable estimate. Recently, Albiez et al. (1984) have given data that suggest 34 detectable female worms per person as an average, so our estimate of a maximum number may be on the low side.

For the survival rate for mature worms we adopted a factor of 0.953, which when applied 4 times a year over a 12-year life span (one year longer than the minimum

Table 29.2 Comparison between age prevalences (%) generated by the model and some published examples

Total	Age				
	0–4	5–9	10–14	15–29	30+
Model					
85	36	95	100	100	100
82	28	91	100	100	100
77	10	83	100	100	100
47	0	3	19	88	100
Published					
84	—	29	78	90	96[a]
81	0	62	79	84	90[b]
72	24	36	79	86	91[c]
44	2	4	38	53	70[d]

[a]Picq et al. (1972).
[b]Barbiero and Trpis (1984).
[c]Picq et al. (1974).
[d]Prost (1977).

proposed by Nelson and Grounds [1958]) reduced the maximum of 40 worms to below 4, thus rendering the person negative in the absence of reinfection. In this we have assumed a constant mortality throughout the life of the adult worm regardless of age or total worm load. No doubt in reality some age- or density-dependent mortality operates, but information is lacking.

The next problem centered on the prevalence by age distribution. If the model was run so that all persons had an equal chance of infection, after 10 or more years at high biting rates the prevalence reached 100% over 15 years of age.

The only way that we could find to reproduce prevalence patterns similar to those found in the field was to make the chance of infection dependent on age. When infective bites were distributed through the human population according to the proportions given in Table 29.1, prevalences were generated as shown in Table 29.2, where they are compared with a few examples from the literature. The prevalences generated by the model approximate those found in surveyed villages, except that the model still gives higher prevalences in the lower and higher age groups. A correction could be attempted by reassigning values for risk of infection in Table 29.1.

Examples of Output

The following examples are taken from some trial runs of the model, using the parameters given in Table 29.2.

Figure 29.2 shows the predicted change in prevalence of onchocerciasis in the human population over a period of 20 years when subjected to Annual Biting Rates (ABR) of between 360 and 21,600 applied at a constant rate throughout the year. In contrast, Figure 29.3 shows a similar run, but with the ABR applied over the second half of the year only, simulating a single season of high *Simulium* biting each year. This variable population was achieved by varying the larval survival rate between 0.6042 and 0.8225, as is shown in Figure 29.4.

Comparing Figures 29.2 and 29.3 shows that the model predicts that after starting at 25% the prevalence should decline to zero at ABR 1,800 or less and climb to a stable level depending on ABR at 3,600 or over. The seasonal distribution of biting makes little difference, but it is interesting to note the decline and rise of the prevalence at ABR 3,600, which is more pronounced at the constant biting rate. We suspect that this may be an artifact, but it would be worth investigating further.

Figure 29.5 shows the interaction between prevalence, ABR, and ATP. A human population with 50% prevalence of onchocerciasis benefits from partial control, which reduces the biting rate to about 5 bites per day (ABR 1,825) for 7 years, during which both ATP and prevalence decline. In the last 6 months of year 8 control breaks down, giving rise to an ABR of 10,800 with a corresponding ATP of 420. Renewed control in year 9 reduces the ABR again to 1,825. According to the model, this brief breakdown in control caused the prevalence to jump from 33% to 48% two years later, although the average worm load was only 60% of that in year one.

DISCUSSION

The Birley and Davies (1984) model for investigating larviciding strategies requires the following parameters:

Generation survival rate	Oviposition survival rate
Immigration rate	Presusceptible period
Susceptible period	Postsusceptible period
Treatment survival	Treatment frequency

The estimation of these parameters under field conditions presents the first obstacle to running the model and serves to emphasize the difficulties inherent in obtaining information on population dynamics of the Simuliidae. For example, egg survival and development time should be estimated by collecting new laid eggs in the field and observing hatching in the laboratory. However, hatching may be delayed by nonpredictable factors such as thickness of the egg mass (J. R. Raybould, personal communication). Similarly, observation of marked groups of larvae may be confused by the arrival of others carried by the drift from upstream.

Information is urgently required on the minimum and mean larval development time, as well as the time taken for, say, 90% of larvae to pupate. For adult *S. damnosum* the proportion of anthropophilic females in any given population and adult survival rates are essential data that are almost entirely lacking. The situation is further complicated by the probability that these parameters will differ for each cytospecies, season, and geographic area.

Our knowledge of the parasite in vector cycle is better documented because this cycle can be studied in the laboratory, but we have no idea of the proportion of

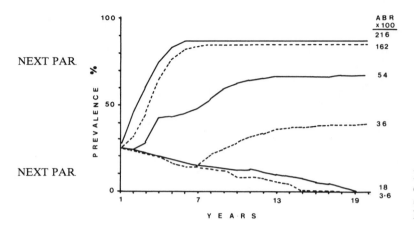

FIG. 29.2 Predicted effect of constant Annual Biting Rate (ABR) on a starting prevalence of 25%.

NEXT PAR.

NEXT PAR.

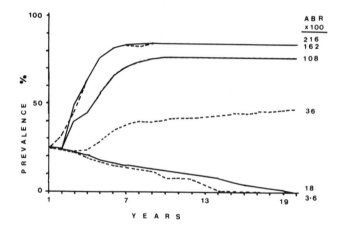

FIG. 29.3 Predicted effect of variable Annual Biting Rate (ABR) on a starting prevalence of 25%.

biting adult *S. damnosum* that become infected in a wild population and no data on the sex ratio of L_3s.

A glance at Table 29.2 will show that of the eight parameters required for the parasite in human cycle, only two have any observational basis, and even these are approximations. All the other parameters, including such vital ones as survival rates and mean and maximum worm load, can at best be described as "guesstimates."

We hope that all the models might be used eventually to help define the unknown parameters by experimenting with different values to see how closely a model can be made to conform to known situations. This kind of sensitivity analysis should show which parameters are most critical, and thereby enable limits to be set.

In this chapter we have attempted to keep the life cycles as simple as possible. There are many aspects that could perhaps be added later, such as the effect of immigration by flies and people. It might be instructive to follow the fate of male *Onchocerca*. Should they prove to have a shorter life span than females, the early death of all male worms could affect the fecundity of the remaining females.

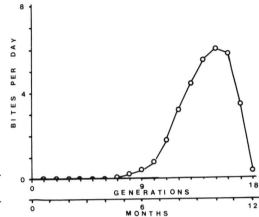

Fig. 29.4 An example of the pattern of biting used with the variable ABR in Figure 29.3. The daily biting rate is plotted for each of 18 consecutive 20-day generations. In this example the ABR was 620.

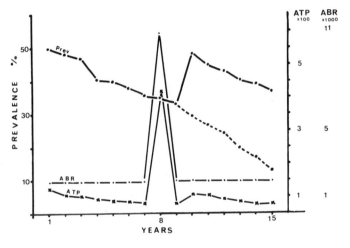

Fig. 29.5 The predicted effect of 7 years of effective vector control, followed by a breakdown of control in year 8, on the ATP and a starting prevalence of 50%. The broken line shows the predicted prevalence if control had been continuously successful.

CONCLUSIONS

The models discussed above show very vividly where the gaps in our knowledge of onchocerciasis lie. More quantitative data are required on the population dynamics of the vector, and especially on the larval and adult stages of *Onchocerca volvulus*. Models now exist that will examine most aspects of the transmission dynamics of onchocerciasis, but they can only be as accurate as the data on which they are based.

LITERATURE CITED

Albiez, E. J., D. W. Buttner, and H. Schultz-Key. 1984. Studies on nodules and adult *Onchocerca volvulus* during a nodulectomy trial in hyperendemic villages in Liberia and Upper Volta. II. Comparison of the macrofilaria population in adult nodule carriers. *Tropenmed. Parasitol.* 35:163–166.

Barbiero, V. K., and M. Trpis. 1984. The prevalence of onchocerciasis on selected divisions of the Firestone Rubber Plantation, Harbel, Liberia. *Am. J. Trop. Med.* 33(3):403–409.

Birley, M. H., J. F. Walsh, and J. B. Davies. 1983. Development of a model for *Simulium damnosum* s.l. recolonisation dynamics at a breeding site in the Onchocerciasis Control Programme Area when control is interrupted. *J. Appl. Ecol.* 20:507–519.

Birley, M. H., and J. B. Davies. 1984. Procedure for investigating *Simulium damnosum* (Diptera: Simuliidae) management strategies in the Onchocerciasis Control Programme Area. *Environ. Entomol.* 13(5):1225–32.

Cheke, R. A., R. Garms, and M. Kerner. 1982. The fecundity of *Simulium damnosum* s.l. in northern Togo and infections with *Onchocerca* spp. *Ann. Trop. Med. Parasitol.* 76(5):561–568.

Davies, J. B. 1963. An assessment of the insecticidal control of *Simulium damnosum* Theobald in Abuja Emirate, Northern Nigeria, from 1955 to 1960. I. The effect on the prevalence of onchocerciasis in the human population. *Ann. Trop. Med. Parasitol.* 57(2):161–181.

Davies, J. B., A. Sékétélé, J. F. Walsh, T. Barro, and R. Sawadogo. 1981. Studies on biting *Simulium damnosum* s.l. at a breeding site in the Onchocerciasis Control Programme Area during and after an interruption of insecticidal treatments. *Tropenmed. Parasitol.* 32:17–24.

Deitz, K. 1982. The population dynamics of onchocerciasis. Pp. 209–241 in R. M. Anderson, Ed., *The population dynamics of infectious diseases—theory and applications.* Chapman & Hall, London.

Duke, B. O. L. 1968a. Studies on factors influencing the transmission of onchocerciasis. IV. The biting cycle, infective biting density and transmission of "forest" *Simulium damnosum. Ann. Trop. Med. Parasitol.* 62:95–106.

———. 1968b. Studies on factors influencing the transmission of onchocerciasis. VI. The infective biting potential of *Simulium damnosum* in different bioclimatic zones and its influence on the transmission potential. *Ann. Trop. Med. Parasitol.* 62:164–170.

Duke, B. O. L., P. J. Moore, and J. Anderson. 1972. Studies on factors influencing the transmission of onchocerciasis. VII. A comparison of the *Onchocerca volvulus* transmission potentials of *Simulium damnosum* populations in four Cameroon rain-forest villages and the pattern of onchocerciasis associated therewith. *Ann. Trop. Med. Parasitol.* 66(2):219–234.

Gillies, H. M., B. M. Greenwood, A. K. Bradley, I. Blakebrough, R. N. H. Pugh, B. Musa, U. Shehu, M. Tayo, and J. Jewsbury. 1983. The Malumfashi Project—an epidemiological, clinical and laboratory study. *Trans. R. Soc. Trop. Med. Hyg.* 77(1):24–31.

Le Berre, R. 1966. Contribution a l'étude biologique et écologique de *Simulium damnosum* Theobald, 1903, (Diptera: Sumuliidae). *Mém. ORSTOM* 17: 204 pp.

Le Berre, R., G. Balay, J. Brengues, and J. Coz. 1964. Biologie et écologie de la femelle de *Simulium damnosum* Theobald, 1903, en fonction des zones bioclimatiques d'Afrique occidentale. *Bull. Org. Mond. Santé* 31:843–845.

Mills, A. R. 1969. A quantitative approach to the epidemiology of onchocerciasis in West Africa. *Trans. R. Soc. Trop. Med. Hyg.* 63(5):591–602.

Mokry, H. F. 1980. A method for estimating the age of field collected female *Simulium damnosum* s.l. (Diptera: Simuliidae). *Tropenmed. Parasitol.* 31:121–127.

Nelson, G. S., and J. G. Grounds. 1958. Onchocerciasis at Kodera eleven years after the eradication of the vector. *East Afr. Med. J.* 35(7):365–368.

Philippon, B. 1977. Etude de la transmission d'*Onchocerca volvulus* (Leuckart, 1893) (Nematoda, Onchocercidae) par *Simulium damnosum* Theobald, 1903 (Diptera, Simuliidae) en Afrique tropicale. *Trav. Doc. ORSTOM.* 63. 308 pp.

Prost, A. 1980. Le polymorphisme des onchocercoses humaines ouest africaines. *Ann. Parasitol. Hum. Comp.* 55:239–245.

Schultz-Key, H., and E. J. Albiez. 1977. Worm burden of *Onchocerca volvulus* in a hyperendemic village in the rain-forest in West Africa. *Tropenmed. Parasitol.* 28:431–438.

Walsh, J. F., J. B. Davies, R. Le Berre, and R. Garms. 1978. Standardization of criteria for assessing the effect of *Simulium* control in onchocerciasis control programmes. *Trans. R. Soc. Trop. Med. Hyg.* 72:675–676.

Part VII Industrial Perspectives

30   THE CONTROL OF BLACK FLY LARVAE WITH TEKNAR®

H. J. Knutti and William R. Beck

This chapter describes the extensive field trials, large-scale demonstrations, and operational-use work with Teknar® (Sandoz Ltd.) by various researchers in the United States and Canada and by WHO and its cooperators in West Africa. Trial results from West Germany and Guatemala are also given. The main findings were:

- The normal fully effective dosage was 1.5–2.25 ppm, calculated per 10-min river discharge (the label rate in the United States is 1.5–2.25 ppm, and the operational-use rate in West Africa is 1.6 ppm). Alterations of dosage periods within the range of 1–15 min did not appear to change the efficacy.

- Carry the furthest distance downstream with 95–100% larval mortality was mainly dependent on river discharge. At the effective rates given above, carry was 25 meters to several hundred meters in creeks, 100 meters to more than 3 kilometers in smaller rivers, and in the larger rivers in West Africa usually 6–10 kilometers in the wet season (little in dry season). Overdosage did not result in much improved carry. The presence of vegetation and pools within creeks and smaller rivers reduced the carry.

- High levels of larval control of all stages was obtained within 24 hours at standard application rates. All black fly species tested were susceptible, and most nontarget organisms were not affected. Extreme temperatures had no adverse effect (range 6°–30°C).

- In West Africa, weekly applications were required, and in other countries application timing varied.

- Adult black fly populations were reduced to almost zero in West Africa. In North America, variable suppression was obtained for various reasons.

- Teknar showed good storage stability even under tropical storage conditions.

As a result of these findings, a more highly concentrated formulation, Teknar HP-D, with much reduced application cost as compared to Teknar, was developed.

GENERAL ASPECTS

Teknar is a biological insecticide that contains delta-endotoxin crystals and spores of *Bacillus thuringiensis* serotype H-14 (*B.t.* H-14). It is selectively toxic to the larvae of mosquito species (Diptera: Culicidae) and black fly species (Diptera: Simuliidae). Teknar was the first commercially available *B.t.* H-14 preparation (registered in 1981).

Teknar provides a unique opportunity for microbial control of mosquito and black fly larvae without harmful effects on humans, domestic animals, wildlife, beneficial insects, aquatic life, and other nontarget organisms. Teknar is registered in the United States for the control of mosquito larvae and black fly larvae (EPA Reg. No. 11273–30). It is exempted from residue tolerance requirements. It was tested and is used operationally by the World Health Organization, Onchocerciasis Control Programme (WHO/OCP), in West Africa against *Simulium damnosum,* the principal vector of onchocerciasis (river blindness). Teknar was tested under code number SAN 402 I SC (= SAN 402 I WDC), with early literature citations reporting results with this code number.

COMMERCIAL FORMULATION

Properties

Teknar is formulated as a suspension concentrate:

insecticidal activity	1500 AAU/mg (IPS 78); AAU = Aedes aegypti units of formulated product
color	light reddish brown
density	1.09 ± 0.05 g/ml at 18°C
flash point	none
water miscibility	freely miscible with water
suspensibility	excellent

Shelf-Life Stability

As Teknar is a biological insecticide containing bacterial spores, it may be impaired by prolonged storage at above 32°C. Nevertheless, it was found that drums stored in the field in the sun for more than 16 months in the Ivory Coast tropical climate (average annual temp. 28°C) showed no loss of activity (Guillet et al. 1982b). This is very important, because there are usually no storage facilities in the shade, and none in air-conditioned rooms in Africa.

QUALITY CONTROL

Sandoz has been engaged since 1974 in the development, manufacturing, and commercialization of biological insecticides, namely Thuricide, which is based on *B.t.* var. *kurstaki,* marketed worldwide for use against lepidopterous pests. Thus, because of Sandoz's thorough fermentation and formulation expertise, the high quality, innocuousness, and uniformity of Teknar can be ensured.

BIOLOGICAL PROPERTIES

Active Ingredient

Teknar is prepared from *B.t.* H-14. The active principle is the delta-endotoxin, contained in the protein crystals (parasporal bodies) of this bacterium. The delta-endotoxin causes destruction of the midgut epithelium after ingestion by the larvae.

Mode of Action

Teknar must be ingested by the larvae to be effective. Within a few hours after ingestion, the paralysis of the midgut takes place and, in most cases, death of mosquito or black fly larvae occurs within 24 hours. There is no direct activity on pupae or adults.

Insect Resistance

Teknar's mode of action, being significantly different from that of most insecticides, such as organophosphates and carbamates, is such that no cross-resistance would be expected to develop. This is confirmed by the fact that Teknar has been applied successfully, on a weekly schedule since late 1981, on some rivers in Ivory Coast.

LARVAL STAGE SUSCEPTIBILITY

At normal rates of application all larval stages (L1–L7) are fully controlled. At subnormal rates, control decreases with increasing larval stage. Table 30.1 lists the results of tests conducted in troughs against larvae of the *Simulium damnosum* complex, revealing this relationship.

SPECTRUM OF ACTIVITY, SCOPE OF TESTING

Molloy (1982) concluded that a wide range of simuliid species are susceptible to various *B.t.* H-14 formulations, although species may vary in their response. Teknar was tested mainly on the following black fly species:

Table 30.1 Mortality of larval stages (L 1–7) of *S. damnosum* complex to various dosages of Teknar (Guillet et al. 1982a)

Dosage in	% Mortality			
mg/l/10 min	L 1–3	L 4–5	L 6–7	All Instars
0.2	46.0	34.9	39.9	40.2 ± 4.2
0.4	94.2	68.3	60.7	72.6 ± 3.2
0.8	97.2	94.6	85.6	91.3 ± 1.8
1.6	100	100	100	100
0	0.9	2.5	1.3	1.6

Note: 1.6 mg of formulation/liter/10 min is the normal operational rate.

- *Simulium verecundum* complex, nuisance spp., in the United States and Canada.
- *Simulium damnosum* complex, an African vector of river blindness.
- *Simulium ochraceum,* the Central American vector of river blindness.
- *Odagmia ornata, Wilhelmia* spp., regionally restricted nuisance species that may cause death of cattle in endemic areas of central Europe.

PERFORMANCE AND USE

United States and Canada

Trials were conducted in Canada and the United States between 1980 and 1983 with Teknar for the control of black fly larvae.

In 1980, three trials conducted by Undeen, Finney, and Colbo (unpublished data) indicated that rates of 10 parts per million (ppm) of Teknar provided high levels of larval control. In these small-stream test sites, 92% to 100% larval mortality was observed 100 to 400 meters downstream of the treatment site. A small-stream trial conducted in New York in 1980 by Molloy (personal communication) provided additional supporting data on this efficacy. In this trial, a 12 ppm dosage for 15 minutes provided 100% larval mortality for one kilometer downstream of the treatment site.

Six trials were conducted in Canada in 1981 in small streams and large river systems. Four of the trials were undertaken by Colbo (1982) in a community-wide adult-suppression program in Bauline, Newfoundland. This suppression program relied on the use of Teknar to control larval populations in the Bauline stream system, thus reducing adult emergence from the principal breeding sites of the area. Monitoring of the six species groups of black flies, along with the other organisms in the streams, was begun in 1980 to determine the pretreatment activity of these aquatic organisms.

Beginning in April 1981, when Teknar was applied at a rate of 10 ppm for one minute to the Bauline stream system, 100% larval control was obtained from the first sampling point at 25 meters to 160 meters, where the stream flowed into a small pond. With the product performing as expected, an area-wide application program involving 28 application dates and 105 application sites was undertaken. Adult populations were also monitored throughout the season. The results of this program provided encouraging information on adult suppression. Adult reductions of 79.6% to 100% were observed for the summer species complex. Variable results from a 77.7% reduction to an adult increase of 66.8% of the winter species complex were observed. This variation was expected, because the main stream was treated with Teknar after most or all of the winter-developing larvae had pupated.

Another Canadian trial was conducted by Galloway (1983) in Saskatchewan. In the large Saskatchewan river, with a flow rate of 150,000 liters per minute, a 3.75 ppm rate of Teknar for 19 minutes gave 100% control of black fly larvae.

An additional eight trials were performed in the northeastern United States. Rates of 0.5 ppm to 5.0 ppm for a 15-minute dosage period were applied to streams with discharges of between 3,333 and 23,000 liters per minute. Larval mortalities of greater than 90% were observed for distances between 100 meters and 2,600 meters below the treatment site. The effective downstream carry appeared to be related to stream discharge in these trials, with the higher discharges providing a greater length of downstream control.

One trial was conducted on a large river system in Pennsylvania in 1981 (Jones 1982). A 45 ppm dose of Teknar, applied in a one-minute dosage, provided greater than 95% control of black fly larvae for at least 3,200 meters downstream of the treatment site. The one-minute dosage time was confirmed as an effective method of application in 1982. In eight trials in the United States, rates were lowered to the recommended label rates of 1.0 to 1.5 ppm/15 min (15 to 22.5 ppm/one min) with acceptable results.

In 1982 three sites were selected in North America to demonstrate the feasibility of reducing adult black fly populations: at Labrador City, Labrador, Newfoundland, Harrisburg, Pennsylvania, and Onchiota, New York. Adult populations were monitored in the nontreatment year of 1982. These data were then compared to populations occurring during the treatment year of 1983.

In 1983 the community-wide adult-suppression programs in Labrador City, Harrisburg, and Onchiota were begun. One trial in Onchiota recorded an 86% adult reduction of black flies at the center of a 12-square-mile area that had a 98% reduction of larval black flies in streams treated with Teknar (Molloy and Struble 1983). This adult suppression was successfully achieved with a total program cost of $800 per square mile. These costs were primarily for labor expenses, with one gallon of Teknar used per square mile of area. This figure is significantly lower than the $5,000-per-square-mile cost of four aerial insecticide applications that is normally paid for black fly suppression programs in the same area.

The two other adult-suppression trials, conducted in Harrisburg and Labrador City, failed to produce acceptable results. While larval control was satisfactory in both trials, various levels of adult suppression were observed. Due to rugged, isolated terrain of the area in Labrador City, access by ground to some major breeding sites was impossible, resulting in the emergence of high numbers of adults (Colbo 1983). This was coupled with an unusually cool, damp season, which provided a longer adult survival period than normal, and a consequently higher migration of adults into the treatment site. These two factors resulted in no significant reduction of adult populations in the Labrador City–Wabush area.

In 1984 the community-wide suppression program in the Labrador City–Wabush area was expanded and continued (Colbo 1984). This program, utilizing Teknar, as well as another formulation of *B.t.* H-14, successfully controlled the black fly larvae in the treated streams. This larval control resulted in a 79% to 82% reduction of the summer adult black fly population in the treatment area.

The trial conducted in Harrisburg, Pennsylvania, demonstrated 50% or less control of adult black fly populations when Teknar was utilized as a larvicide in streams adjacent to the proposed control area. A number of circumstances led to this situation. Applications of Teknar to the first two generations of black flies could not be made because of extremely high water levels in the streams targeted for larvicidal control. A subsequent successful application with good larval control was followed by two unsuccessful applications to control larvae, the first due to high water levels, while the second was made when most larvae had pupated, resulting in poor control.

Additional operational black fly suppression programs were initiated in the Adirondack Mountains in New York, with encouraging reductions in adult black fly populations in the treated areas.

SAN 402 I SC 93, a *B.t.* H-14 formulation containing twice as much active ingredient (3,000 AAU/mg) as Teknar, was also evaluated in field trials in the United States in 1984. Results obtained in Pennsylvania and Tennessee indicated that this formulation was equal to or slightly better than Teknar at equal active-ingredient rates. SAN 402 I SC 93 is now registered in the United States as Teknar HP-D (EPA Reg. No. 11273–53). It was successfully applied undiluted from conventional air and ground equipment, and it can be recommended for undiluted applications through appropriate ultra-low-volume (ULV) application equipment.

The Teknar HP-D formulation was selected for use in 1985 in a year-round black fly larval-control program in the Colorado River near the towns of Bullhead City, Arizona, and Laughlin, Nevada. Applications of Teknar HP-D at concentrations of 10 to 15 ppm in a one-minute dosage time were made from four holding tanks mounted in a dam near the two towns. The river discharge was maintained at 960 cubic meters per second. Greater than 90% larval mortality was observed for 16 kilometers downstream of the treatment site. High levels of adult black fly reductions were observed in the communities involved in the black fly suppression program.

West Africa

Onchocerciasis Control Program (OCP) by WHO.   The objectives, organization, and work of OCP, the river blindness disease, as well as the importance, type of injury, distribution, and life history of the *S. damnosum* complex, have been described in detail by many authors and are covered in other chapters. Thus no review is made here.

In 1980 in Ivory Coast, resistance appeared to temephos in two of the six species of the *S. damnosum* complex (Guillet et al. 1980). Thus an alternative solution to the problem was required, and field-testing of *B.t.* H-14 was intensified.

Development.   The evaluation of the performance of Teknar was conducted in a step-by-step program from the laboratory to small, medium, then to large-scale field trials, and eventually to operational use in the dry and wet seasons. Efficacy in the laboratory was first demonstrated with *B.t.* H-14 ONR6OA strain (Undeen and Nagel 1978).

Teknar samples were first provided to WHO in 1980. At 1.6 ppm of formulation per

10 minutes in river water, 100% mortality of all stages of black fly larvae was obtained within 6–24 hours, while lower concentrations did not give complete mortality (Guillet et al. 1982a). This performance was considered to be the first real success with *B.t.* H-14, due to an acceptable practical rate, and a good formulation that, with some water added, dispersed very well and uniformly in the river water. The formulation's characteristics are very important, when it comes to large-scale use, in view of the fact that the black fly larvae are filter feeders. A product acting only after ingestion must be suspended in an appropriate particle-size range and concentration in order to be taken in with the indigenous food in sufficient toxic amounts.

In typical small-scale trials, Teknar was applied by hand to the rivers, and larval mortality was observed in a trough (minigutter) 20–200 meters downstream. An interesting detail noted was that larvae died and remained attached to the substratum with Teknar, whereas they became detached with chemicals. In large-scale trials, Teknar was applied by boat or helicopter across the river. Evaluation of mortality was usually made by checking larvae on vegetation and/or established larvae on artificial substrates, plastic strips which were hanging in the water, at various locations downstream. In some cases, a trough was used additionally for confirmation of results.

In all types of trials, the amount of Teknar to be applied was calculated on the basis of river discharge per 10 minutes. This period of time was chosen by WHO for all insecticides for various reasons. For example, in order to apply 1.6 ppm/10 min to a river with a discharge of 10 m^3/sec, 9.6 l of Teknar were required.

The main findings with Teknar were (Guillet et al. 1982a and WHO various unpublished documents 1980–82):

- Maximum mortality was usually reached after 6 hours and definitely after 24 hours.
- It was fully effective at 1.6 ppm/10 min. in the dry season, confirming initial results.
- It was fully effective at 1.6 ppm/10 min in the wet season. In a large-scale trial by boat on the River Marahoué, where the river discharge was 457 m^3/sec, a carry of 19 kilometers and partial control for an additional 15 kilometers was obtained (Lacey et al. 1982). In other trials by helicopter, with less ideal conditions, i.e., under normal conditions, the carry was about 6–10 kilometers.
- It had to be diluted with 17% water prior to application with the available equipment in order to get good dispersion in the river (e.g., 2 parts water to 10 parts 1-Teknar).
- Certain dyes, when added to Teknar in order that the pilots could better see the spray hitting the river surface, may have adversely affected the efficacy, demonstrating again the importance of proper formulation.

Operational use of Teknar.   In November 1981, WHO started to use Teknar operationally in the Ivory Coast with applications by helicopter at weekly intervals at 1.6 ppm/10 min to the rivers with active black fly breeding sites. The Teknar was diluted with 17% water to ensure uniform dispersal in the river's water volume.

Teknar was applied by helicopter and was pumped from a 24 1-Teknar container into the helicopter tank. Landing sites and application spots were determined by previous experience with chemicals, with numerous extra spots being added in the rainy season. River discharge was measured prior to each application and the exact amount of Teknar to be applied was calculated for each application location.

Two main types of evaluations of efficacy were made: (1) counts of larval mortality on the vegetation at the edges of rapids, and (2) counts of catches of adult females/day by vector collectors.

When the Teknar operation was started in late 1981, the adult black fly catches/day varied from 500–2,000. These were down to practically zero 2–3 months later, indicating excellent control. In addition, a favorable reaction of the local human population to the black-fly-free environment was noted immediately after the program had begun.

During extensive use since 1982, it was found that, compared to the use of chemicals, the application of Teknar was more demanding on the pilots. Spray equipment on the helicopters also had to be modified to obtain consistently good efficacy, and a larger helicopter (Ligme 173) had to be added to the program for use in larger rivers.

Compared to temephos, the operational cost with the actual Teknar formulation was higher, due to the large spray volume required and the shorter downstream carry in the rainy season. However, where resistance had developed to temephos, this resistance has since remained. Thus Teknar is the product of choice in the rivers of Ivory Coast where such resistance is prevalent or expected. Otherwise, chemicals are used in the OCP.

Future outlook. Sandoz has developed more concentrated formulations of *B.t.* H-14, which can be applied at lower volumes than Teknar and therefore at lower operational costs. As in the United States, encouraging results have been obtained with Teknar HP-D in river trials by WHO/OCP. Applied undiluted at 0.8 ppm/10 min, i.e., half the rate of Teknar, carry was as good or better than with Teknar (unpublished data), and lead to operational use.

DEVELOPMENT IN OTHER COUNTRIES

West Germany

Various tests were conducted with gamma-irradiated Teknar in creeks of varying size against *O. ornata, W. lineata,* and *W. equina* larvae in two regions (Baden Württemberg, Lower Saxony) (Rutschke 1982–84). Applied at 0.7–3.5 ppm/10 min, the carry usually varied from 100–1,000 meters, mainly increasing with reduced presence of vegetation, with increased discharge and increased homogeneous speed of water flow. Applications at temperatures as low as 6°C were also effective, i.e., the critical factor is not the product, but the larvae that must still be feeding. Reapplication may be required after 2–4 weeks. Teknar is considered to be of practical use for black fly larvae control in order to prevent nuisance to humans and animals and to prevent cattle mortality.

Guatemala

Teknar was applied at 1×10^6 spores/ml/10 min to a creek (1.56 m³/10 min) against *S. ochraceum* and other *Simulium* spp. larvae (Undeen et al. 1981). Carry was only about 25 meters, mainly due to the presence of dense vegetation, small pools within the creek, and low discharge. Reference to this research is also made by T. Suzuki and H. Takaoka in Chapter 27.

SAFETY

Various studies were designed and conducted to ascertain the human and environmental safety of *B.t.* H-14. These studies included a comprehensive mammalian toxicity study and a number of studies dealing with nontarget organism hazards. This safety record and the results of the toxicological investigations allow us to consider Teknar safe to humans and the environment. Investigations on the many nontarget organisms associated with Simuliidae showed that the only ones partially affected are certain Chironomidae spp., depending on dosage rates and application conditions.

Dejoux (1979) carried out preliminary field tests with a primary powder in Ivory Coast. He found that at a dosage highly toxic to *S. damnosum* s.l. there was nearly no effect on the associated nontarget fauna. He concluded that it is the safest material among all those used in the past and envisaged for the future.

In a large-scale trial on the River Marahoué in Ivory Coast with Teknar, which was 100% effective (Lacey et al. 1982), the effect on nontarget organisms was also investigated and no apparent effect observed (Gibon et al. 1980). However, the reliability was partially limited due to the small sample size of some nontarget species.

Complete selectivity in creeks in West Germany was found in the trials with Teknar at 0.7–3.5 ppm/10 min, described previously (Rutschke 1982–84).

Rishikesh et al. (1983) concluded that the scientific literature and operational use show that *B.t.* H-14 is an exceptionally safe agent for nontarget organisms, including man and other vertebrates, as well as insects of economic importance, such as silkworms.

ACKNOWLEDGMENTS

Sandoz acknowledges the contributions of WHO and its cooperators and of the many other researchers in the laboratory and in the field evaluations of Teknar and in the basic work of *B.t.* H-14.

LITERATURE CITED

Colbo, M. H. 1982. Development of *Bacillus thuringiensis* var. *israelensis* for the biocontrol of Simuliidae. Canada Dep. of Supply and Services report. File No. 05–SU–1800–0–0073; 15 July 1982.

———. 1983. Development of a field protocol for the ground application of *Bacillus thuringiensis* var. *israelensis* as a black fly larvicide in northern Canada. Canada Dept. of Supply and Services report. DSS File No. 14–SU.CD.3252006.

————. 1984. Development of a field protocol for general application of *Bacillus thuringiensis* var. *israelensis* as a black fly larvicide in northern Canada. Canada Dept. of Supply and Services report. DSS Contract 8–SU82–00283.

Dejoux, C. 1979. Recherches préliminaires concernant l'action de *Bacillus thuringiensis israelensis* de Barjac sur la faune d'invertèbres d'un cours d'eau tropical. WHO mimeo. doc., WHO/VBC/79.721. 11 pp.

Galloway, M. 1983. *Evaluation of Bacillus thuringiensis H-14 (B.t.i) as a black fly larvicide.* Canada Biting Fly Centre. Winnipeg, Manitoba. (In press).

Gibon F. M., J. M. Elouard, and J. J. Troubat. 1980. Action du *Bacillus thuringiensis* var. *israelensis* sur les invertébrés aquatiques. *Rap. ORSTOM*, No. 38. 16 pp.

Guillet P., H. Escaffre, M. Quedraogo, and D. Quillévéré. 1980. Mise en évidence d'une résistance au témephos dans le complexe *Simulium damnosum* (*S. sanctipauli* et *S. soubrense*) en Côte d'Ivoire (zone du programme de lutte contre l'onchocercose dans la région du bassin de la Volta). *Cah. ORSTOM Sér. Entomol. Méd. Parasitol.* 18:291–299.

Guillet, P., H. Escaffre, and J. M. Prud'hom. 1982a. L'utilisation d'une formulation à base de *Bacillus thuringiensis* H-14 dans la lutte contre l'onchocercose en Afrique de l'Ouest. I. Efficacité et modalités d'application. *Cah. ORSTOM sér Entomol. Méd. Parasitol.* 20:175–180.

————. 1982b. L'utilisation d'une formulation à base de *Bacillus thuringiensis* H-14 dans la lutte contre l'onchocercose en Afrique de l'Ouest. II. Stabilité dans les conditions de stockage en milieu tropical. *Cah. ORSTOM sér. Entomol. Méd. Parasitol.* 20:181–185.

Jones, Gary E. 1982. Black fly project progress report. April 1982. Pennsylvania Dept. of Environmental Resources.

Lacey, L. A., H. Escaffre, B. Philippon, A. Sékétéli, and P. Guillet. 1982. Large river treatment with *Bacillus thuringiensis* (H-14) for the control of *Simulium damnosum* s.l. in the Onchocerciasis Control Programme: preliminary trials with the Sandoz 402 formulation. *Tropenmed. Parasitol.* 33:97–101.

Molloy, D. 1982. Biological control of black flies (*Diptera: Simuliidae*) with *Bacillus thuringiensis* var. *israelensis* (serotype 14): a review with recommendations for laboratory and field protocol. *Misc. Pub. Entomol. Soc. Am.* 12(4). 30 pp.

Molloy and Struble. 1983. Unpublished data.

Rishikesh et al. 1983. Operational use of *Bacillus thuringiensis* serotype H-14 and environmental safety. WHO unpub. doc., WHO/VBC/83.871. 9 pp.

Rutschke, J. 1982–84. Personal communication.

Undeen, A. H., and W. L. Nagel. 1978. The effect of *Bacillus thuringiensis* ONR-60A strain (Goldberg) on *Simulium* larvae in the laboratory. *Mosquito News* 38:524–527.

Undeen, A. H., H. Takaoka, and K. Hansen. 1981. A test of *Bacillus thuringiensis* var. *israelensis* de Barjac as a larvicide for *Simulium ochraceum*, the Central American vector of onchocerciasis. *Mosquito News* 41:37–40.

WHO/OCP. 1980–82. Application de *Bacillus thuringiensis* H-14 contre *S. damnosum*. Unpublished data.

31 RECENT EXPERIENCES WITH VECTOBAC FOR BLACK FLY CONTROL: AN INDUSTRIAL PERSPECTIVE ON FUTURE DEVELOPMENTS

Robert J. Cibulsky and Robert A. Fusco

The use of *Bacillus thuringiensis* var. *israeliensis* (serotype H-14) (*B.t.i.* H-14) to control mosquito and black fly larvae has been extensively investigated since the late 1970s. During the same period, there has been a growing concern for human and environmental protection from the undesirable effects of toxic chemicals introduced into water resources. Therefore, we have witnessed a resurgence of interest in biological-control agents that are more environmentally compatible than their chemical counterparts. Microbial pesticide development for human-nuisance pest control is directly related to sociological pressures emanating from the general public. Only in specific situations, such as the WHO onchocerciasis program, has a medically important target been involved.

As a result of the intensified effort on the part of both public and private sectors of our economy, advances have been made for the application of *B.t.i.* as an effective and economical control agent for black fly and mosquito control. But what has pushed *B.t.i.* into the forefront for black fly control? First, safety. *B.t.i.* is a nontoxic organism. Second, efficacy. The efficacy record for *B.t.i.* for black fly control has been nothing short of superlative. Similar efficacy can be obtained with *B.t.i.* as with the best chemical alternatives. Third, selectivity. *B.t.i.* has exhibited a selective activity not previously available with any chemical, although it has shown effective control of mosquito and black fly species. Fourth, immediate mode of action. *B.t.i.* produces a quick response in both mosquito and black fly species. In some cases, control can be evaluated within 2–4 hours following application. This is advantageous when making an assessment of whether or not further treatment in a particular area is justified. This has made *B.t.i.* more acceptable to operational program managers. Fifth, production in existing equipment. A significant amount of capital expenditure was not required to modify existing fermentation equipment to accommodate *B.t.i.* production on a large scale. Sixth, standardized, quick bioassay system. The organism's rapid action and the existing mosquito-rearing technology provided the means for an accurate, simple, and quick bioassay to determine product potency.

HISTORICAL BACKGROUND

Abbott entered the *B.t.i.* business with a wettable powder (WP) formulation during the late 1970s. The primary reason for selection of this formulation was the exceptional stability exhibited by agricultural *B.t.i.* formulations. The obvious drawbacks were the difficulty in mixing WP formulations on a large scale and the poor suspendability characteristics exhibited by most WPs. Further, the WP did not fit all the various habitats occupied by mosquito and black fly species. In spite of these drawbacks, the preliminary results developed by a number of cooperators indicated excellent control of mosquitoes and black flies with the WP formulation.

For densely vegetated mosquito habitats, Abbott developed a granular (G) product form that could penetrate most vegetation and have an impact on the water surface. Dense canopy over breeding areas necessitated the development of a large particle size to penetrate the canopy, as well as a floating characteristic that would keep the *B.t.i.* in the upper surface layers of the water and available for consumption by the target species.

The application of *B.t.i.* via ultra-low-volume (ULV) application equipment required the development of a liquid formulation with a very small particle size. After screening a number of formulation candidates, Abbott selected the current aqueous formulations with product potencies of 600 and 1,200 ITU/mg. These product formulations have produced excellent control of both mosquito and black fly species in a variety of habitats. The major drawback of aqueous microbial formulations is lower stability compared to WP or G product forms. A number of product modifications were made from 1983–86 in order to improve upon product stability. Further advances were made in final particle size to improve upon dispersion in the water target area. The Vectobac AS and 12HS marketed today are produced from a continuous fermentation process that guarantees uniform particle size.

Vectobac 12AS is recommmended for black fly control applied either undiluted or diluted with water in a rate range of 1–25 ppm for 1–15 minutes duration. This broad rate range provides for a program to fit the variety of stream conditions that are encountered in any black fly control program. *B.t.i.* carry is directly related to the stream-flow rate or discharge. The greater the discharge, the greater the ultimate carry downstream for the *B.t.i.* This can vary with local rainfall, water-management practices, or a variety of other reasons. Smaller streams with a lesser discharge generally may require a higher rate and a longer application period than larger rivers with greater discharge.

BLACK FLY DATA

In 1983 Molloy, in New York, evaluated Vectobac AS for black fly control in small streams for several years and obtained excellent control at a rate range of 10–30 ppm. During the same year, Jones, in Pennsylvania, conducted trials with Vectobac AS in the Susquehanna River during 1983–84 via both ground and aerial applications and produced 95–100% control from a 20–30 ppm application. Carry in the latter program ranged from 1,000–3,000 meters. Ground applications by Colbo in Newfoundland during 1983–84 produced 91–95% control at 5–10 ppm for a distance of 3,000 meters downstream.

Table 31.1 Efficacy of Vectobac AS for control of black flies, 1985

Black fly Species	Location	Investigator	Method of Application	Rate ppm	Control %
S. jenningsi	Susquehanna River	G. Jones, PA DER	air	10–23	95–100 2–4 miles
S. venustum P. mixtum S. vittatum	Carrabassett River	K. Gibbs, U. of Maine	ground	10	90+
P. fuscum P. mixtum S. venustum S. decorum S. vittatum	Dixville Notch, NH	J. Burger, U. of NH	ground	10–20	95
S. vittatum	Kingsport, TN	L. Lacey, USDA	ground	10	90
Simulium spp.	Labrador City	M. Colbo, Memorial U.	ground, air	10	90

Note: S. = Simulium; P. = Prosimulium.

Table 31.2 Efficacy of Vectobac 12AS for control of black flies, 1986

Black fly Species	Location	Investigator	Method of Application	Rate ppm	Control %
S. Jenningsi	Susquehanna, Allegheny R.	V. McElhattan, PA DER	air	22–24	92–100 2–5 miles
P. fuscum P. mixtum S. venustum S. decorum S. vittatum	Dixville Notch, NH	J. Burger, U. of NH	ground	5– 10	65–100
S. tuberosum S. vittatum S. venustum S. verecundum	South Carolina	R. Noblet, Clemson U.	ground	1	97
S. vittatum	Kingsport, TN	L. Lacey, USDA	ground	10	92
S. tuberosum S. vittatum S. venustum S. verecundum P. mixtum	Walsh River, Newfoundland	M. Colbo, Memorial U.	ground	5	94–100

Note: S. = Simulium; P. = Prosimulium.

In 1985 Vectobac AS and in 1986 Vectobac 12AS were used exclusively for control of black flies in the Pennsylvania DER state program conducted in the Susquehanna River in the Harrisburg area. The results were 95–100% control of larvae and 80+% reduction of adults with these formulations applied undiluted via a helicopter application system.

We have demonstrated that we possess adequate technology to apply the organism and obtain consistent, excellent control of black fly larvae with these Vectobac formulations.

NONTARGET SPECIES

We have amply demonstrated that *B.t.i.* will produce effective mosquito and black fly control without affecting nontarget species occupying similar aquatic habitats. Information on this subject is available in a number of publications as well as in our product technical literature. During 1984 we investigated nontarget activity in a study conducted in the Yukon, which was probably our most complete effort to date. This study was designed to satisfy safety questions raised by Canadian regulatory agencies. *B.t.i.* activity was limited to simuliid and culicid species, with some slight activity noted in chironomid species.

We cannot guarantee that *B.t.i.* is totally safe to every member of an aquatic community. However, based on testing information, we can make a reliable estimate that it poses the least threat to nontarget aquatic organisms of any material yet discovered for mosquito and black fly control.

FUTURE DEVELOPMENTS

Where are we going within the next five years?

The first area is formulation improvement. We have not yet optimized formulation dispersability. Refinement of particle size and utilization of dispersing agents may improve black fly control by improving downstream carry.

The second area is higher product potency. The more concentrated the product form, the greater the area that can be treated with a given volume of product. This has particular importance in aerial application programs, which are limited by the total volume of product that can be distributed via an aircraft with a limited lift capability.

If we can accomplish these two goals, we will improve efficacy and lower the final user cost. However, we want to accomplish these goals without affecting the safety profile we have developed with Vectobac during the last six years. We have no intention of introducing any components into the formulation that may be more deleterious to human or other nontarget populations than the active ingredient itself.

To meet these goals, during 1986 we tested in the field a new product formulation, Vectobac 24AS. This formulation, the result of new fermentation technology, has the potency of 2,400 ITU/mg, twice the potency of the current 12AS formulation. It exhibits excellent stability properties, small particle size, and has a viscosity of less than 600 CPS at 25C. These properties provide excellent efficacy in cold rivers or streams with high silt loads and allow for a reduction in handling and application costs.

CONCLUSION

In summary, certain factors can impede or eliminate the development of a microbial control. Some of the more important obstacles to commercial development of a selective microbial pesticide are cost, efficacy, method of production, and overall market potential. These obstacles appear to have been successfully overcome with *B.t.i.* If further improvements are achieved in the next 1–5 years, it would appear that *B.t.i.* will not only be competitive with current chemical-control programs for mosquito and black fly control, but it may be the pesticide of choice for these markets.

Part VIII Black Fly Species of the World

32 AN ANNOTATED CHECKLIST OF THE WORLD BLACK FLIES (DIPTERA: SIMULIIDAE)

Roger W. Crosskey

CONTENTS

SYNOPSIS

This work provides a complete checklist of all formally described black flies (Simuliidae) known in the world fauna up to mid-1985. It is the first such list since 1945, and it includes just over 2,000 specific/subspecific names and 122 generic/subgeneric names. A total of 1,461 species are listed as valid on the available evidence. The geographical distribution of each valid species is given in brief. Explanatory notes are provided when necessary to call attention to taxonomic or nomenclatural points concerning some names. The type species of all nominal genera or subgenera are shown in an alphabetical index of genus-group names. The checklist is a practical tabulation in which taxa considered valid are cited alphabetically in their next higher taxon; nevertheless, it reflects my viewpoint on the extent and ranking of supraspecific taxa considered most appropriate and useful at present in the light of a world perspective on classification. In accord with this, *Simulium* is treated as a broad genus containing subgenera and species groups.

INTRODUCTION

It is forty years since the last world checklist of Simuliidae was published (Smart 1945). That work includes 860 names applied to 617 extant species then considered valid, but it is now of no more than historical interest. These four decades have been years of unprecedented faunal and taxonomic activity on black flies in every zoogeographical region, and we now have a totally new global perspective on the Simuliidae. It is one that has not as yet found much expression in the black fly literature because so few workers are in the privileged position of having worldwide collections and sufficiently complete libraries at their fingertips. It is now time to distill from the primary literature a new checklist aimed at helping those working on simuliids— whether taxonomist, aquatic biologist, parasitologist, cytologist—to find their way around the multiplicity of black fly names that nowadays features in the fast-expanding taxonomic, ecological, epidemiological, and control literature.

The checklist presented here collates the basic data needed for an up-to-date perspective on the formally described simuliid species now known in the world fauna, including their names, assignments to subgenera and genera, and (in brief) their geographical distributions. The work contains just over 2,000 specific names, of which 1,461 are listed as valid for extant species; the remainder are junior synonyms, except for a few that are *nomina dubia* and unplaceable *nomina nuda*.

Concerning validity, it must be stressed that few groups of simuliids have been revised to the best modern taxonomic standards, and many species have had to be entered as valid in the checklist merely because there is no contrary published evidence. Some names accepted as valid may well prove to be synonyms, but future revision is equally likely to restore to validity some names that have long been in synonymy—particularly when more cytologically recognized sibling species are brought into formal zoological nomenclature. The future establishment of new synonyms and the exhumation of old ones are, broadly speaking, likely to counterbalance one another, and for this reason I regard the round-figure number of 1,500 as a fair estimate of the actual number of existing black fly morphospecies that have been described and named. (To this number can be added perhaps 150 cytologically recognized sibling species that at present are subsumed nomenclaturally under their relevant morphospecies.)

Many cytologically-based sibling species have a vernacular terminology such as letter references, number, or locality names, or have "handles" based on particular inversion sequence numbers on certain chromosome arms; such terminology does not enter zoological nomenclature, and it has been found impracticable to attempt its inclusion in the checklist. Misidentifications are also excluded.

Checklist Arrangement

An alphabetical arrangement of valid taxa within their next higher taxon has been adopted throughout the checklist, in accordance with its main purpose of providing quick access to information. Names treated as synonyms are indented and listed chronologically under the valid names in order to show their relative priorities. A question mark precedes a few of the listed synonyms to indicate that the synonymy is considered almost certainly correct, but that it awaits formal publication; most such query markings apply to Enderlein names for European nominal species that are expected to be definitely synonymized in a forthcoming publication by Dr. Heide Zwick. The few fossil nominal species described from Baltic amber (Oligocene age) are included in the short list of *nomina dubia* given at the end of the checklist; other fossils are nonsimuliid (see note concluding the Introduction).

The subspecies is a little-used category in Simuliidae, but it presents a problem for checklisting because when used it is not always related to the geographically-based definition of a subspecies that most taxonomists accept (e.g., Lincoln et al. 1982). I have considered it best to list the names of subspecies in their relevant chronological positions in the synonymy under valid names and to give them the suffix marking "ssp". This has been done when the name marked is applied to a subspecies considered valid by one or some authors in a current classification; no marking is given when a name that once stood for a subspecies no longer does so in modern literature.

Members of sibling species complexes are listed in the same manner as other species when they have been formally described and named (e.g., several members of the *Simulium damnosum* complex). To indicate that a listed species is now known to represent a complex of siblings, but these have not yet been formally named, the word "complex" is suffixed to the species name; this indicates that the cytotaxonomic literature contains evidence for such a complex. (I have not searched the cytological literature exhaustively, and there could be more proven complexes than I have indicated.)

South America has given the most difficulty for the catalogue arrangement because of the scarcity of overview taxonomic works, and I am grateful to Dr. A. J. Shelley for his help in deciding some questions of validity and subgeneric assignment. Nevertheless, many South American species of *Simulium* s.l. have had to remain unassigned to subgenera because of inadequate taxonomic knowledge.

Nomenclature

Although some of the niceties of nomenclature are regarded as arcane and futile by many nontaxonomists (and a great many taxonomists), I have made special efforts to ensure that all nomenclatural matters governed by mandatory requirements of the *International Code of Zoological Nomenclature* (new edition, February 1985) are properly attended in the checklist. My view is that the checklist entries should be as reliable as possible on matters regulated by Code provisions, viz. orthography, authorship, and publication dates of names, their availability in the technical meaning of the Code, and their validity according to the principles of priority and coordination.

In conformity with this view I have paid special attention to two mandatory Code articles that, wittingly or unwittingly, are frequently unobserved by simuliid taxonomists; namely, that gender orthography of each adjectival specific name must agree with the gender of the genus to which it is currently assigned (Article 31 [b]), and that describers' names for species no longer placed in their original genera must be cited in parentheses (Article 51 [c]). Both articles have been carefully observed in the checklist for valid names and synonyms, but it remains possible that a few specific names that are adjectives have been missed. It should be noted that *Simulium,* and all generic names with a "*-simulium*" suffix, are neuter and that adjectival specific names associated with them must take neuter endings, e.g., the suffix "*-ense*" not "*-ensis*", "*-oide*" not "*-oides*", "*-tarse*" not "*-tarsis*". (While mandatory gender agreement seems pedantic, it is difficult for technical nomenclatural reasons to find a fully satisfactory alternative, and the rule is retained in the new edition of the Code; parenthesizing of authors' names for generically transferred species, on the other hand, is valueless ritual that could have been eliminated from the new Code without loss or difficulty.)

Routine nomenclatural matters such as the existence of homonymy and the establishment of new synonymy are annotated appropriately in the checklist text, but more complex nomenclatural annotations when needed for certain names are given in the section entitled Explanatory Notes on Checklist Entries. An asterisk (*) with a text entry refers the checklist user to that section.

The type-species and the gender for all generic or subgeneric names in Simuliidae (i.e., "genus-group" names in Code terminology) are given in the section entitled Index Catalogue of Nominal Genus-Group Taxa and Their Type-Species. The list contains 122 genus-group names and supersedes the list of Stone (1963), which contained 75 such names; four additional names in Stone (viz. *Atractocera* Meigen, *Melusina* Meigen, *Pseudosimulium* Handlirsch, and *Simulidium* Westwood) no longer apply to Simuliidae and are omitted from this Appendix.

The publications have been seen that contain the original proposals of all included names to confirm their orthographical accuracy and their availability status. Publication-year dates have been determined with maximum accuracy by scrutinizing the periodical parts or the books containing the original descriptions to find exact issue dates (or printing dates if necessary). Many discrepancies exist in simuliid taxonomic literature between the nominal year dates cited on title pages or reprints and the actual issue dates; discrepancies usually involve actual issue in the year after the nominal year, and it is then the actual year that is cited for the name. If a discrepancy is suspected but cannot be proved (e.g., December journal part reaching libraries the following autumn), the year-date stipulated on the title page is accepted as correct (Article 21[b]).

The few completely unplaceable *nomina dubia* and *nomina nuda* are listed at the end of the checklist. *Nomina nuda* for which the specific assignment is known are listed in the synonymy of the appropriate species.

All names that have been proposed for family-group taxa in Simuliidae (i.e., suprageneric names) and are based on different type-genera are included in the checklist. A detailed account of such names and nomenclatural matters concerning them is given in another work (Crosskey 1985).

Authors' Names

Reference to original descriptions sometimes shows that authors have published under slightly variant versions of their names. I have then standardized the spelling that is the predominant or latest usage, e.g., Baranov (not Baranoff), Ramírez-Pérez (not Ramírez Pérez). The spelling "Rubtsov" has been used in accordance with the British system of transliteration from the Cyrillic alphabet, but there are four versions of Dr. I. A. Rubtsov's name in his Roman-alphabet publications (Rubtsov, Rubtzov, Rubzov, Rubzow).

Classification

While there is a substantial measure of agreement between specialists on the phylogenetic relationships of black fly groups, this is not reflected in an agreed classification. Taxonomists differ in the levels at which they rank supraspecific groups and in the degree to which they restrict the scope of such groups. This is reflected in the two main systems of classification existing at present. That of Rubtsov (1974) splits named supraspecific taxa very finely and elevates them to relatively high rank in the hierarchy, whereas mine (Crosskey 1969, 1981) recognizes fewer named taxa and places the majority of black flies in a broadly conceived genus *Simulium* containing subgenera.

The question of classification needs comment here only insofar as the checklist has at all points required decisions to be made on the scope and ranking of the taxa to which species are assigned. For this purpose I have adopted the same approach to classification as recently advocated (Crosskey 1981) and have rejected Rubtsov's system, which I consider unnecessarily complex to express the phylogeny of such a homogeneous family and inconvenient from the practical viewpoint. The rank to be accorded to a taxon, however, is entirely subjective and a matter of taste, and it should be stressed that my system and that of Rubtsov coincide to a large extent on the scope of supraspecific taxa to be recognized even if they differ in hierarchical ranking.

A few classificatory points should be noted. I continue to recognize two subfamilies—Parasimuliinae for *Parasimulium* and Simuliinae (all other black flies)—but the recent discovery of the long-unknown early stages of *Parasimulium* could necessitate a reconsideration of this system (Courtney 1986). The subdivision of the Simuliinae into two tribes Prosimuliini and Simuliini I maintain as useful while recognizing that not all black flies can unambiguously be assigned to one tribe or the other (the genera *Metacnephia* and *Sulcicnephia* could be placed in either according to how their characters are evaluated). Several genera and subgenera that are known to me only from the literature have been accepted as valid for the checklist, but with considerable doubts: the genus *Levitinia* seems hardly distinct from *Gymnopais* (perhaps subgeneric or species-group rank within *Gymnopais* would be more appropriate), *Rubzovia* should perhaps be subsumed in *Nevermannia,* and the subgenera *Cerqueirellum, Coscaroniellum,* and *Inaequalium* might be better merged with *Psaroniocompsa* (from which their distinctions appear very intangible).

Taxonomic comments on some genera, subgenera, or species-groups have been given in the section Explanatory Notes on Checklist Entries, and (as for nomenclatural comments) the names concerned are marked with an asterisk in the checklist text. For most of the taxa ranked as species-groups in the checklist there exist names of the genus group that apply to them if and when they are ranked as subgenera or genera; the name that is applicable as the valid subgeneric/generic name for any such promoted species-group is noted in the comments.

Geographical Information

As this work is not a detailed catalogue, it has been necessary to package the geographical data very tightly. The information given, however, should enable anyone to extract, if desired, a species list for any zoogeographical region or a likely list for a particular country. If a species is known from only one or very few countries, these are named, but wider distributions are indicated by regional or continental entries; limited distributions within the area of a very large country (Canada, USSR) are indicated by suitable parenthetical entries, e.g., "USSR (n European)" shows the known range to be in the northern part of European Russia. Distributional data for the USSR, which has a very large and scattered simuliid faunal literature, have been checked against the recent work on Palaearctic Simuliidae by Rubtsov and Yankovsky (1984).

Note on Fossil Taxa

Several fossil Simuliidae have been described, but only those from Baltic amber are acceptable as belonging to this family. The others are omitted from the checklist but are mentioned here because their existence precludes the use of the same specific names for any other species of *Simulium* s.l. (under the Code rules relating to primary homonymy). The names are: *Simulium humidum* Westwood 1845 (type-species of *Pseudosimulium* Handlirsch 1908, ? Ceratopogonidae), *Simulia pasithea* von Heyden 1870 (? Ceratopogonidae); and *Simulia terribilis* Förster 1891 (? Ceratopogonidae). In addition, there is *Simulidium priscum* Westwood 1854 (type-species of *Simulidium* Westwood and now in Protopleciidae).

Acknowledgments

I am indebted to Dr. P. H. Adler, Dr. D. C. Currie, Dr. B. V. Peterson, Dr. A. J. Shelley, Dr. H. Takaoka, Dr. D. M. Wood, and Dr. H. Zwick for guidance on the placement of some problematical names that would have been less appropriately assigned without their help, and to my wife, Margaret E. Crosskey, for preparing the index and helping to verify the checklist for publication.

ABBREVIATIONS

c	central	NY	New York
e	eastern	preocc.	preoccupied
ec	east-central	publ.	published
f.	form	Qd	Queensland
FE	Soviet Far East (Dalny Vostok)	reg.	region
		repl.	replacement
incl.	including	s	southern
Is.	islands	SA	South Australia
n	northern	sc	south-central
ne	northeastern	se	southeastern
nom. nud.	*nomen nudum*	s.l.	sensu lato
NSW	New South Wales	ssp.	subspecies
NT	Northern Territory	s.str.	sensu stricto
nw	northwestern	**stat. n.**	new status

Subg.	Subgenus	w	western
sw	southwestern	WA	Western Australia
syn. n.	new synonym	wc	west-central
unav.	unavailable		

EPITOME OF THE SUPRASPECIFIC ARRANGEMENT

The following epitome is for rapid orientation into the checklist arrangement and lists the supraspecific taxa only by their valid names; synonyms can be found in the checklist text. The order of species-groups, subgenera, and genera is alphabetical within the next higher category.

Family SIMULIIDAE Newman, 1834

Subfamily PARASIMULIINAE Smart, 1945

    Parasimulium Malloch, 1914

        Subg. Astoneomyia Peterson, 1977
        Subg. Parasimulium *s.str.*

Subfamily SIMULIINAE Newman, 1834

Tribe PROSIMULIINI Enderlein, 1921

    Araucnephia Wygodzinsky & Coscarón, 1973
    Araucnephioides Wygodzinsky & Coscarón, 1973
    Cnephia Enderlein, 1921
    Cnesia Enderlein, 1934
    Cnesiamima Wygodzinsky & Coscarón, 1973
    Crozetia Davies, 1965
    Ectemnia Enderlein, 1930
    Gigantodax Enderlein, 1925
    Greniera Doby & David, 1959
    Gymnopais Stone, 1949
    Levitinia Chubareva & Petrova, 1981
    Lutzsimulium d'Andretta & d'Andretta, 1947

        Subg. Kempfsimulium Py-Daniel & Nunes de Mello, 1982
        Subg. Lutzsimulium *s.str.*

    Mayacnephia Wygodzinsky & Coscarón, 1973
    Metacnephia Crosskey, 1969
    Paraustrosimulium Wygodzinsky & Coscarón, 1962
    Prosimulium Roubaud, 1906

        Subg. Distosimulium Peterson, 1970
        Subg. Helodon Enderlein, 1921
        Subg. Paracnephia Rubtsov, 1962
        Subg. Parahelodon Peterson, 1970
        Subg. Procnephia Crosskey, 1969
        Subg. Prosimulium *s.str.*

           Group 1: *aculeatum* species-group
           Group 2: *hirtipes/mixtum* species-group
           Group 3: *macropyga* species-group

Stegopterna Enderlein, 1930
Sulcicnephia Rubtsov, 1971
Tlalocomyia Wygodzinsky & Díaz Nájera, 1970
Twinnia Stone & Jamnback, 1955

Tribe SIMULIINI Newman, 1834

Austrosimulium Tonnoir, 1925

Subg. Austrosimulium *s.str.*
Subg. Novaustrosimulium Dumbleton, 1973

Simulium Latreille, 1802

Subg. Afrosimulium Crosskey, 1969
Subg. Anasolen Enderlein, 1930
Subg. Boophthora Enderlein, 1925
Subg. Byssodon Enderlein, 1925

Group 1: *griseicolle* species-group
Group 2: *meridionale* species-group

Subg. Cerqueirellum Py-Daniel, 1983
Subg. Chirostilbia Enderlein, 1921
Subg. Coscaroniellum Py-Daniel, 1983
Subg. Crosskeyellum Grenier & Bailly-Choumara, 1970
Subg. Dexomyia Crosskey, 1969
Subg. Ectemnaspis Enderlein, 1934
Subg. Edwardsellum Enderlein, 1921
Subg. Eusimulium Roubaud, 1906
Subg. Freemanellum Crosskey, 1969
Subg. Gomphostilbia Enderlein, 1921
Subg. Hearlea Vargas, Martínez Palacios & Díaz Nájera, 1946
Subg. Hebridosimulium Grenier & Rageau, 1961
Subg. Hellichiella Rivosecchi & Cardinali, 1975

Group 1: *annulum* species-group
Group 2: *subexcisum* species-group

Subg. Hemicnetha Enderlein, 1934
Subg. Himalayum Lewis, 1973
Subg. Inaequalium Coscarón & Wygodzinsky, 1984
Subg. Inseliellum Rubtsov, 1974
Subg. Lewisellum Crosskey, 1969
Subg. Meilloniellum Rubtsov, 1962
Subg. Metomphalus Enderlein, 1935
Subg. Montisimulium Rubtsov, 1974
Subg. Morops Enderlein, 1930
Subg. Nevermannia Enderlein, 1921

Group 1: *feuerborni* species-group
Group 2: *loutetense* species-group
Group 3: *ruficorne* species-group
Group 4: *vernum* species-group

Subg. Notolepria Enderlein, 1930
Subg. Obuchovia Rubtsov, 1947
Subg. Parabyssodon Rubtsov, 1964
Subg. Phoretomyia Crosskey, 1969
Subg. Pomeroyellum Rubtsov, 1962

Subg. Psaroniocompsa Enderlein, 1934
Subg. Psilopelmia Enderlein, 1934
Subg. Psilozia Enderlein, 1936
Subg. Pternaspatha Enderlein, 1930
Subg. Rubzovia Petrova, 1983
Subg. Schoenbaueria Enderlein, 1921
Subg. Shewellomyia Peterson, 1975
Subg. Simulium *s.str.*

 Group 1: *argenteostriatum* species-group
 Group 2: *bimaculatum* species-group
 Group 3: *bukovskii* species-group
 Group 4: *crassifilum* species-group
 Group 5: *ephemerophilum* species-group
 Group 6: *hunteri* species-group
 Group 7: *jenningsi* species-group
 Group 8: *malyschevi* species-group
 Group 9: *melanopus* species-group
 Group 10: *metallicum* species-group
 Group 11: *multistriatum* species-group
 Group 12: *nobile* species-group
 Group 13: *noelleri* species-group
 Group 14: *ornatum* species-group
 Group 15: *reptans* species-group
 Group 16: *tuberosum* species-group
 Group 17: *variegatum* species-group
 Group 18: *venustum* species-group
 Ungrouped species of *Simulium s.str.*

Subg. Tetisimulium Rubtsov, 1963
Subg. Trichodagmia Enderlein, 1934
Subg. Wallacellum Takoaka, 1983
Subg. Wilhelmia Enderlein, 1921
Subg. Xenosimulium Crosskey, 1969

Subgenerically unassigned species
Nomina dubia (*Simulium* s.l.)
Nomina nuda (unplaceable)

THE CHECKLIST TEXT

Family SIMULIIDAE Newman, 1834

Subfamily PARASIMULIINAE Smart, 1945

PARASIMULIUM Malloch, 1914

 Subg. ASTONEOMYIA Peterson, 1977
  melanderi Stone, 1963 .... USA (Washington)

 Subg. PARASIMULIUM s.str.
  crosskeyi Peterson, 1977 .... USA (Oregon)
  furcatum Malloch, 1914 .... USA (California)
  stonei Peterson, 1977 .... USA (California, Oregon)

Subfamily SIMULIINAE Newman, 1834

Tribe PROSIMULIINI Enderlein, 1921
    HELLICHIINI Enderlein, 1925
    ECTEMNIINAE Enderlein, 1930
    STEGOPTERNINAE Enderlein, 1930
    CNESIINAE Enderlein, 1934
    GYMNOPAIDINAE Rubtsov, 1955
    CNEPHIINI Grenier & Rageau, 1960
    HELODOINI [*sic*] Ono, 1982

ARAUCNEPHIA Wygodzinsky & Coscarón, 1973
    montana (Philippi, 1865) .... Chile

ARAUCNEPHIOIDES Wygodzinsky &
Coscarón, 1973
    schlingeri Wygodzinsky & Coscarón,
    1973 .... Chile

CNEPHIA Enderlein, 1921
    ASTEGA Enderlein, 1930
        alticola (Dyar & Shannon, 1927) .... Mexico
        angarensis Rubtsov, 1956 .... USSR (Siberia)
        arborescens Rubtsov, 1971 .... USSR (e Siberia, FE)
        dacotensis (Dyar & Shannon, 1927) .... Canada, USA
            lasciva (Twinn, 1936)
        eremites Shewell, 1952 .... Alaska, Canada
        intermedia Rubtsov, 1956 .... USSR (Siberia)
        lapponica (Enderlein, 1921) .... Scandinavia, nw USSR
        lyra (Lundström, 1911) .... Scandinavia, nw USSR
        ornithophilia Davies, Peterson &
        Wood, 1962 .... e Canada, ne USA
        pecuarum (Riley, 1887) .... s & c USA

CNESIA Enderlein, 1934
        dissimilis (Edwards, 1931) .... Argentina, Chile
            gynandrum (Edwards, 1931)
        ornata Wygodzinsky & Coscarón, 1973 . Argentina
        pusilla Wygodzinsky & Coscarón, 1973 . Argentina

CNESIAMIMA Wygodzinsky & Coscarón, 1973
        atroparva (Edwards, 1931) .... Argentina, Chile

CROZETIA Davies, 1965
        crozetensis (Womersley, 1937) .... Crozet Islands

ECTEMNIA Enderlein, 1930
        invenusta (Walker, 1848) .... Canada, USA
            loisae (Stone & Jamnback, 1955)
        taeniatifrons (Enderlein, 1925) .... Canada, USA

GIGANTODAX Enderlein, 1925

    ARCHINESIA Enderlein, 1934

abalosi Wygodzinsky, 1958	Peru
antarcticus (Bigot, 1888)	Argentina, Chile
aquamarensis (de Leon, 1945)	Guatemala
araucanius (Edwards, 1931)	Argentina, Chile
bettyae Wygodzinsky, 1974	Venezuela
bolivianus Enderlein, 1925	Bolivia, Peru
bonorinorus Coscarón & Wygodzinsky, 1962	Tierra del Fuego
brophyi (Edwards, 1931)	Argentina
cervicornis Wygodzinsky, 1974	nw South America
chilensis (Philippi, 1865)	Argentina, Chile
conviti Ramírez-Pérez, 1980	Venezuela
corniculatus Wygodzinsky, 1974	Venezuela
femineus (Edwards, 1931)	Argentina, Chile
fulvescens (Blanchard, 1852)	Argentina, Chile
horcotiani Wygodzinsky, 1949	Argentina
igniculus Coscarón & Wygodzinsky, 1962	Tierra del Fuego
impossibilis Wygodzinsky, 1974	Venezuela
kuscheli Wygodzinsky, 1952	Juan Fernandez Is.
marginalis (Edwards, 1931)	Argentina, Chile
nigrescens (Edwards, 1931)	Argentina
ortizi Wygodzinsky, 1974	Venezuela
pennipunctus Enderlein, 1934	Peru
rufescens (Edwards, 1931)	Argentina, Chile
rufinotum (Edwards, 1931)	Argentina, Chile
shannoni (Edwards, 1931)	Argentina
viannamartinsi Ramírez-Pérez, 1980 ...	Venezuela
wittmeri Wygodzinsky, 1951	Argentina
wrighti (Vargas, Martínez Palacios & Díaz Nájera, 1944) .... *vargasi* (de Leon, 1945)	Guatemala, Mexico
wygodzinskyi Moncada, Muñoz de Hoyos & Bueno, 1981	Colombia

GRENIERA Doby & David, 1959

abdita (Peterson, 1962)	Canada, ne USA
abditoides (Wood, 1963)	Canada, ne USA
brachiata (Rubtsov, 1961)	USSR (n European)
denaria (Davies, Peterson & Wood, 1962)	Canada, ne USA
dobyi Beaucournu-Saguez & Braverman, 1987	Israel/Syria
fabri Doby & David, 1959	w Europe
ivanovae (Ivashchenko, 1970)	USSR (European)
nairica Terteryan, 1972	USSR (Transcaucasia)
poljakovae (Patrusheva, 1977)	USSR (w Siberia)
rivi (Ivashchenko, 1970)	USSR (European)
sedecimfistulata Rubtsov, 1963	Poland, Romania
zverevae Rubtsov, 1964	USSR (n European)

GYMNOPAIS Stone, 1949

andrei Vorobets, 1984	USSR (Yakutia)
bifistulatus Rubtsov, 1955	USSR (e Siberia, FE)
dichopticoides Wood, 1978	Alaska, nw Canada
dichopticus Stone, 1949	Alaska, nw Canada
fimbriatus Wood, 1978	nw Canada
frontatus Yankovsky, 1982	USSR (Kamchatka)
holopticoides Wood, 1978	Alaska, n Canada
holopticus Stone, 1949	Alaska, n Canada
lindneri Rubtsov, 1963	USSR (Tuva)
rubzovi Bobrova, 1967	USSR (e Siberia)
sexcornutus Bodrova, 1975	USSR (Primorye)
trifistulatus Rubtsov, 1955	USSR (Siberia)

LEVITINIA Chubareva & Petrova, 1981

freidbergi Beaucournu-Saguez	
& Braverman, 1987	Israel/Syria
tacobi Chubareva & Petrova, 1981	USSR (Tadzhikistan)

LUTZSIMULIUM d'Andretta & d'Andretta, 1947

Subg. KEMPFSIMULIUM Py-Daniel &
Nunes de Mello, 1982 **stat. n.**

simplicicolor (Lutz, 1910)	Brazil
hebeticolor (Lutz, 1910)	
rondonense Py-Daniel, 1982 (*nom. nud.*)	

Subg. LUTZSIMULIUM s.str.

flavopubescens (Lutz, 1910)	Brazil
hirticosta (Lutz, 1909)	Argentina, Brazil
cruzi d'Andretta & d'Andretta, 1947	
pernigrum (Lutz, 1910)	Brazil

MAYACNEPHIA Wygodzinsky & Coscarón, 1973

aguirrei (Dalmat, 1949)	Guatemala
atzompensis (Díaz Nájera, 1962)	Mexico
fortunensis Petersen, 1984	Panama
grenieri (Vargas & Díaz Nájera, 1948) .	Mexico
mixensis (Díaz Nájera, 1962)	Mexico
muzquicensis (Díaz Nájera, 1971)	Mexico
osborni (Stains & Knowlton, 1943)	w Canada, w USA
pachecolunai (de Leon, 1945)	Guatemala, Mexico
roblesi (de Leon, 1943)	Guatemala
stewarti (Coleman, 1953)	w Canada, w USA

METACNEPHIA Crosskey, 1969

aldanica Vorobets, 1984	USSR (Yakutia)
amphora Ladle & Bass, 1975	England
aspinosa Rubtsov, 1973	USSR (FE)
bilineata (Rubtsov, 1940)	USSR (n Urals)
blanci (Grenier & Theodorides, 1953) .	sw Palaearctic reg.

borealis (Malloch, 1919) .... n Canada
breevi (Rubtsov, 1956) .... USSR (n European)
crassifistula (Rubtsov, 1956) .... USSR (Siberia, FE)
danubica (Rubtsov, 1956) .... ec Europe
edwardsiana (Rubtsov, 1940) .... USSR (Siberia, FE)
   ? lanata (Takahasi, 1940) .... China (Manchuria)
freytagi (DeFoliart & Peterson, 1960) . w North America
fuscipes (Fries, 1824) .... n Europe
gorodkovi (Rubtsov, 1964) .... USSR (Tadzhikistan)
hajotsdzorensis (Terteryan, 1962) ...... USSR (Transcaucasia)
hirta (Rubtsov & Terteryan, 1954) .... USSR (Transcaucasia)
jeanae (DeFoliart & Peterson, 1960) .. w North America
kirjanovae (Rubtsov, 1956) .... USSR (central Asia)
korsakovi (Rubtsov, 1956) .... USSR (European)
lesnei (Séguy, 1925) .... France
lyrata (Rubtsov, 1956) .... USSR (Siberia)
multifilum (Rubtsov, 1947) .... USSR (central Asia)
nigra (Rubtsov, 1940) .... Romania, USSR
   saxicola (Rubtsov, 1956) (ssp.)   (Caucasus, Turkmenistan)
nuragica Rivosecchi, Raastad &
   Contini, 1975 .... sw Palaearctic reg.
pallipes (Fries, 1824) (complex) .... n Holarctic reg.
   heymonsi (Enderlein, 1921)
pamiriensis Petrova, 1977 .... USSR (Pamir)
parapallipes Bobrova, 1980 .... USSR (Siberia)
pectinata Patrusheva, 1976 .... USSR (Siberia)
pedipupalis (Rubtsov, 1947) .... USSR (Kazakhstan)
persica (Rubtsov, 1940) .... Iran, sw & sc USSR
ramificata (Rubtsov, 1956) .... Mongolia, USSR (FE)
saileri (Stone, 1952) .... n North America
sardoa (Rivosecchi & Contini, 1965) .. Italy (Sardinia)
saskatchewana (Shewell & Fredeen,
   1958) .... c Canada
sedecimfistulata Rubtsov, 1976 .... USSR (Kazakhstan)
slepjani (Rubtsov, 1967) .... USSR (Turkmenistan)
sommermanae (Stone, 1952) .... Alaska, nw Canada
sorkulensis Rubtsov, 1971 .... Afghanistan, USSR
     (Pamir)
subalpina (Rubtsov, 1956) .... Turkey, USSR
     (Transcaucasia)
tabescentifrons (Enderlein, 1929) .... Scandinavia, USSR (n
     European, w Siberia)
   brevis (Rubtsov, 1956)
taimyrica Patrusheva, 1976 .... USSR (Siberia)
terterjani (Rubtsov, 1955) .... USSR (Transcaucasia)
tetraginata (Rubtsov, 1951) .... USSR (central Asia)
tredecimata (Edwards, 1920) .... n Eurasia
trigonia (Lundström, 1911) .... Scandinavia, USSR (n
     European, Siberia)
trispina Rubtsov, 1973 .... USSR (Primorye)
uzunovi Kovachev, 1985 .... Bulgaria

variafilis Rubtsov, 1976 .... USSR (Tadzhikistan)
vestita (Enderlein, 1929) .... Scandinavia
villosa (DeFoliart & Peterson, 1960) .. w Canada, w USA

PARAUSTROSIMULIUM Wygodzinsky &
Coscarón, 1962

anthracinum (Bigot, 1888) .... s Chile, Tierra del Fuego
moorei (Silva Figueroa, 1917)

PROSIMULIUM Roubaud, 1906

Subg. DISTOSIMULIUM Peterson, 1970

daisetsense Uemoto, Okazawa &
Onishi, 1976 .... Japan
pleurale Malloch, 1914 .... Alaska, n Canada
tenuicalx Enderlein, 1925
pancerastes Dyar & Shannon, 1927

Subg. HELODON Enderlein, 1921

HAIMOPHAGA Rubtsov, 1977*
AHAIMOPHAGA Chubareva &
Rubtsov, 1978*

albense Rivosecchi, 1961 .... Italy
silana Rivosecchi, 1967 (unav.)
albertense Peterson & Depner, 1972 ... w Canada
alpestre Dorogostaisky, Rubtsov &
Vlasenko, 1935 .... Siberia (incl. Commander
altaicum Rubtsov, 1956 (ssp.)   Is.) to Canada
relense Rubtsov, 1956 (ssp.)
komandorense Rubtsov, 1971 (ssp.)
apoina Ono, 1977 .... Japan
aridum Rubtsov, 1971 .... Mongolia
arshanense Rubtsov, 1956 .... USSR (e Siberia)
buturlini Rubtsov, 1956 .... USSR (FE)
candicans Rubtsov, 1956 .... USSR (Siberia)
chechciri Popov, 1977 .... USSR (Siberia)
clavatum Peterson, 1970 .... nw Canada
czenkanowskii Rubtsov, 1956 .... USSR (Siberia)
intercalare Rubtsov, 1956 .... USSR (Siberia)
irkutense Rubtsov, 1956 .... USSR (e Siberia, FE)
kamtshaticum Rubtsov, 1940 .... USSR (Kamchatka)
kamui Uemoto & Okazawa, 1980 ...... Japan
karibaense Ono, 1980 .... Japan
martini Peterson, 1970 .... ne Canada
mesenevi Patrusheva, 1975 .... USSR (Siberia)
multicaulis Popov, 1968 .... USSR (Siberia, Primorye)
oligoaristatum Rubtsov, 1971 .... USSR (Tadzhikistan)
onychodactylum Dyar & Shannon, 1927
(complex) .... nw North America
pamiricum Chubareva & Petrova, 1983 . USSR (Pamir)
pecticrassum Rubtsov, 1956 .... USSR (e Siberia)

perspicuum Sommerman, 1958 .... Alaska, nw Canada
phytofagum Rubtsov, 1976 .... USSR (Kazakhstan)
rubicundum (Rubtsov, 1956) .... USSR (e Siberia, FE)
rufum (Meigen, 1838) .... Scandinavia, nw USSR
    boreale (Zetterstedt, 1842)
    ferrugineum (Wahlberg, 1844)
sarurense Ono, 1976 .... Japan
susanae Peterson, 1970 .... w Canada
yezoense Shiraki, 1935 .... Japan
    alpium Ogata, 1956 (unav.)

Subg. PARACNEPHIA Rubtsov, 1962*

barnardi (Gibbins, 1938) .... South Africa
brincki (de Meillon, 1955) .... South Africa
harrisoni (Freeman & de Meillon,
    1953) .... South Africa
herero (Enderlein, 1935) .... Namibia
muspratti (Freeman & de Meillon,
    1953) .... South Africa
thornei (de Meillon, 1955) .... South Africa
turneri (Gibbins, 1938) .... Botswana, South Africa

Subg. PARAHELODON Peterson, 1970

decemarticulatum (Twinn, 1936) .... Alaska, Canada, ne USA
gibsoni (Twinn, 1936) .... s Canada, n USA
vernale Shewell, 1952 .... e Canada

Subg. PROCNEPHIA Crosskey, 1969

damarense (de Meillon & Hardy, 1951) . Namibia
morotoense (McCrae & Prentice, 1965) . Uganda
rhodesianum Crosskey, 1968 .... Zimbabwe

Subg. PROSIMULIUM s.str.

    HELLICHIA Enderlein, 1925
    TAENIOPTERNA Enderlein, 1925
    MALLOCHELLA Enderlein, 1930
    MALLOCHIANELLA Vargas &
      Díaz Nájera, 1948
    UROSIMULIUM Contini, 1963

Group 1: ACULEATUM
species-group*

aculeatum Rivosecchi, 1963 .... Italy (Sardinia, Sicily)
    stefanii (Contini, 1963)
juccii (Contini, 1966) .... Italy (Sardinia)

Group 2: HIRTIPES-MIXTUM
species-group s.l.*

approximatum Peterson, 1970 .... e Canada, ne USA
arvum Adler & Kim, 1985 .... ne USA
calabrum Rivosecchi, 1966 .... Italy

caudatum Shewell, 1959 .... w Canada, nw USA
constrictistylum Peterson, 1970 .... w Canada
daviesi Peterson & DeFoliart, 1960 .... w USA
dicentum Dyar & Shannon, 1927 .... w USA
dicum Dyar & Shannon, 1927 .... w North America
diminutum Rubtsov, 1956 .... USSR (e Siberia, FE)
doveri Sommerman, 1962 (complex) ... Alaska
esselbaughi Sommerman, 1964 .... nw North America
exigens Dyar & Shannon, 1927 .... w Canada, w USA
    hardyi (Stains & Knowlton, 1940)
faurei Bertrand, Grenier &
    Bailly-Choumara, 1972 .... Morocco
flaviantennus (Stains & Knowlton,
    1940) .... w USA
fontanum Syme & Davies, 1958 .... e Canada, ne USA
formosum Shewell, 1959 .... w Canada
frohnei Sommerman, 1958 .... Alaska, w Canada
frontatum Terteryan, 1956 .... USSR (Transcaucasia)
    stenopalpe Rubtsov, 1956
fulvipes (Edwards, 1921) .... s Europe
fulvithorax Shewell, 1959 .... w Canada
fulvum (Coquillett, 1902) .... nw North America
fuscum Syme & Davies, 1958 .... Canada, ne USA
gigas Rubtsov, 1956 .... USSR (Ciscaucasia)
hirtipes (Fries, 1824) (complex) .... Europe, USSR (Siberia)
    sibiricum (Enderlein, 1930)
impostor Peterson, 1970 .... w Canada
irritans Rubtsov, 1940 .... n China, USSR (FE)
isos Rubtsov, 1956 .... USSR (FE)
italicum Rivosecchi, 1967 .... Italy
jacuticum Rubtsov, 1973 .... USSR (e Siberia)
jezonicum (Matsumura, 1931) .... Japan
    sapporoense (Shiraki, 1935)
kanii Uemoto, Onishi & Orii, 1973 .... Japan
kiotoense Shiraki, 1935 .... Japan
laamii Beaucournu-Saguez &
    Bailly-Choumara, 1981* .... Morocco
latimucro (Enderlein, 1925) .... Europe
    inflatum Davies, 1957
    goidanichi Rubtsov, 1964
longilobum Peterson & DeFoliart, 1960 . w USA
luganicum Rubtsov, 1956 .... c & e Europe
magnum Dyar & Shannon, 1927 .... e Canada, c & e USA
    frisoni (Dyar & Shannon, 1927)
    albionense Rothfels, 1956
maruashvili Machavariani, 1966 .... USSR (Transcaucasia)
mixtum Syme & Davies, 1958
    (complex) .... e Canada, ne USA
multidentatum (Twinn, 1936) .... e Canada, ne USA
mysticum Peterson, 1970 .... e Canada, ne USA
petrosum Rubtsov, 1955 .... sw USSR, ? Lebanon
    nigritum Rubtsov, 1956 (ssp.)

pronevitschae Rubtsov, 1955 ....   USSR (Transcaucasia)
  rachiliense Dzhafarov, 1954
rhizomorphus Rubtsov, 1971 ....   USSR (FE)
rhizophorum Stone & Jamnback, 1955 .   ne USA
rufipes (Meigen, 1830) ....   c & s Europe
  gallii (Edwards, 1921)
  conistylum Rubtsov, 1956
  aestivale Knoz, 1963 (unav.)
saltus Stone & Jamnback, 1955 ....   ne USA
shewelli Peterson & DeFoliart, 1960 ...   w USA
subrufipes Knoz, 1980 ....   c Europe
tomosvaryi (Enderlein, 1921) ....   Europe
  picipes (Stephens, 1829) (*nom.*
    nud.)
  fuscipes (von Roser, 1840)
  nigripes Enderlein, 1925
  pexifrons Enderlein, 1925
  balcanicum Enderlein, 1925
  canbalicum (Smart, 1944)
  pseudohirtipes (Smart, 1944)
  arvernense Grenier, 1947
  duodecimfiliatum Rubtsov, 1955
transbrachium Adler & Kim, 1985 .....   ne USA
travisi Stone, 1952 ....   nw North America
tridentatum Rubtsov, 1940 ....   USSR (e Siberia, FE)
uinta Peterson & DeFoliart, 1960 ......   w USA
unicum (Twinn, 1938) ....   w USA
unispina Rubtsov, 1967 ....   USSR (Buryat)
woodorum Peterson, 1970 ....   w Canada

Group 3: MACROPYGA
species-group*

erythronotum Rubtsov, 1956 ....   USSR (FE)
kolymense Patrusheva, 1975 ....   USSR (Siberia)
macropyga (Lundström, 1911) ....   n Scandinavia, n USSR
  latifrons (Enderlein, 1925)
  ventosum Rubtsov, 1956 (ssp.)
  zaitzevi Rubtsov, 1956 (ssp.)
  arcticum Rubtsov & Carlsson, 1965
    (ssp.)
  korshunovi Patrusheva, 1975 (ssp.)
neomacropyga Peterson, 1970 ....   Alaska, nw Canada
tredecimfistulatum Rubtsov, 1956 ......   USSR (Siberia)
ursinum (Edwards, 1935) (complex) ...   Alaska, n Canada,
  browni (Twinn, 1936)   Greenland, Iceland, n
                                                 Scandinavia, Bear I.

STEGOPTERNA Enderlein, 1930

asema Rubtsov, 1956 ....   USSR (e Siberia, FE)
decafilis Rubtsov, 1971 ....   USSR (e Siberia, FE)
duodecimata (Rubtsov, 1940) ....   USSR (Siberia, FE)
emergens (Stone, 1952) ....   nw North America

freyi (Enderlein, 1929) .... Scandinavia, n USSR
    richteri Enderlein, 1930
    majalis Rubtsov & Carlsson, 1965 (ssp.)
    dentata Rubtsov & Carlsson, 1965 (ssp.)
    haematophaga Rubtsov &
      Carlsson, 1965 (ssp.)
    longicoxa Rubtsov, 1971 (ssp.)
hamuligera Yankovsky, 1977 .... USSR (FE)
mutata (Malloch, 1914) (complex) ..... n & c North America
    permutata (Dyar & Shannon, 1927)
    (ssp.)
nukabirana Ono, 1977 .... Japan
tschukotensis Rubtsov, 1971 .... USSR (Siberia)

SULCICNEPHIA Rubtsov, 1971

alichurensis (Rubtsov, 1967) .... USSR (Tadzhikistan)
argylacea (Rubtsov, 1947) .... USSR (Tadzhikistan)
derzhavini (Rubtsov, 1940) .... USSR (Kamchatka)
filidistans (Rubtsov, 1947) .... USSR (Tadzhikistan)
flavipes (Chen, 1984) **comb.n.** .... China (Inner Mongolia)
jankovskiae (Rubtsov, 1956) .... USSR (Kirgiziya)
jeholensis (Takahasi, 1942) .... China (Manchuria)
jingpengensis (Chen, 1984) **comb.n.** ... China (Inner Mongolia)
lobashovi Rubtsov, 1976 .... USSR (Tadzhikistan)
octodecimfiliata (Rubtsov & Violovich,
    1965) .... USSR (Tuva)
ovtshinnikovi (Rubtsov, 1940) .... USSR (central Asia,
    undecimfilum (Rubstov, 1947)   Siberia)
pandjensis (Rubtsov, 1967) .... USSR (Tadzhikistan)
petrovae Rubtsov, 1976 .... USSR (Tadzhikistan)
stegostyla (Rubtsov, 1961) .... USSR (Kirgiziya, Tuva)
sulcata (Rubtsov, 1956) .... USSR (Tadzhikistan)
syrdarjensis Rubtsov, 1978 .... USSR (Kazakhstan)
tungus (Rubtsov, 1956) .... Mongolia, USSR (Siberia)
undecimata (Rubtsov, 1951) .... USSR (central Asia)
vitalii (Rubtsov, 1967) .... USSR (central Asia)
znojkoi (Rubtsov, 1940) .... USSR (Transcaucasus)

TLALOCOMYIA Wygodzinsky & Díaz Nájera, 1970

revelata Wygodzinsky & Díaz Nájera,
    1970 .... Mexico

TWINNIA Stone & Jamnback, 1955

cannibora Ono, 1977 .... Japan
hirticornis Wood, 1978 .... w Canada
hydroides (Novák, 1956) .... w & c Europe
japonensis Rubtsov, 1960 .... Japan
magadensis Rubtsov, 1973 .... USSR (Siberia)
nova (Dyar & Shannon, 1927) .... w Canada, nw USA
    biclavata Shewell, 1959

sedecimfistulata (Rubtsov, 1955) .... USSR (e Siberia, FE)
subtibbelesi [*sic*] Ono, 1980 .... Japan
tatrensis Novák, 1959 .... c & s Europe
tibblesi Stone & Jamnback 1955 .... e Canada, ne USA

UNDETERMINED GENUS ("*Cnephia*" of authors)

aurantiacum Tonnoir, 1925 .... e Australia, Tasmania
fergusoni Tonnoir, 1925 .... Australia (NSW, SA)
fuscoflava Mackerras & Mackerras,
    1948 .... Australia (Qd)
orientalis Mackerras & Mackerras, 1950 . e Australia, Tasmania
strenua Mackerras & Mackerras, 1950 . Australia (Qd)
terebrans Tonnoir, 1925 .... se Australia
tonnoiri Drummond, 1931 .... Western Australia
umbratorum Tonnoir, 1925 .... se Australia

Tribe SIMULIINI Newman, 1834
    NEVERMANNIINI Enderlein, 1921
    WILHELMIINI Baranov, 1926
    FRIESIINI Enderlein, 1936 (unav.)
    ODAGMIINI Enderlein, 1936 (unav.)
    AUSTROSIMULIINI Smart, 1945
    EUSIMULIINI Rubtsov, 1974

AUSTROSIMULIUM Tonnoir, 1925

Subg. AUSTROSIMULIUM s.str.*

albovelatum Dumbleton, 1973 .... New Zealand
australense (Schiner, 1868) .... New Zealand
    caecutiens (Walker, 1848) (*nom. nud.*)
    tillyardi (Tonnoir, 1923)
bicorne Dumbleton, 1973 .... New Zealand
campbellense Dumbleton, 1973 .... Campbell Island
cornutum Tonnoir, 1925 .... e Australia, Tasmania
crassipes Tonnoir, 1925 .... e Australia
dumbletoni Crosby, 1976 .... New Zealand
fulvicorne Mackerras & Mackerras,
    1950 .... Australia (Qd)
laticorne Tonnoir, 1925 .... New Zealand
    alveolatum Dumbleton, 1973 (ssp.)
longicorne Tonnoir, 1925 .... New Zealand
mirabile Mackerras & Mackerras, 1948 . Australia (Qd)
montanum Mackerras & Mackerras,
    1952 .... se Australia
multicorne Tonnoir, 1925 .... New Zealand
    fiordense Dumbleton, 1977 (ssp.)
stewartense Dumbleton, 1973 .... New Zealand
tillyardianum Dumbleton, 1973 .... New Zealand
    tillyardi Tonnoir, 1925 (preocc.)
ungulatum Tonnoir, 1925 .... New Zealand

unicorne Dumbleton, 1973 .... New Zealand
vexans (Mik, 1881) .... Auckland Island,
Campbell Island

Subg. NOVAUSTROSIMULIUM
Dumbleton, 1973*

bancrofti Taylor, 1918 .... Australia, Tasmania
furiosum (Skuse, 1889) .... Australia, Tasmania
  weindorferi Tonnoir, 1925
  simile Tonnoir, 1925
  austrosimile (Smart, 1944)
magnum Mackerras & Mackerras, 1955 . Australia (Qd)
pestilens Mackerras & Mackerras, 1948 . n & e Australia
torrentium Tonnoir, 1925 .... e Australia, Tasmania
  hilli Mackerras & Mackerras, 1949
  (ssp.)
victoriae (Roubaud, 1906) .... e Australia, Tasmania
  tasmaniense Tonnoir, 1925

SIMULIUM Latreille, 1802

Subg. AFROSIMULIUM Crosskey, 1969

gariepense de Meillon, 1953 .... Botswana, South Africa

Subg. ANASOLEN Enderlein, 1930

bisnovem Gibbins, 1938 .... Uganda, Zaire
  edwardsi Gibbins, 1937 (*nom.
  nud.*)
dentulosum Roubaud, 1915 .... Afrotropical reg.
  gilvipes Pomeroy, 1920
  adolffriedericianum Enderlein, 1930
  ruwenzoriense Gibbins, 1934
  emfulae de Meillon, 1937
  britannicum Davies, 1966
  altissimum Fain, Bafort &
    Silberstein, 1977 (ssp.)
  bambusicola Fain, Bafort &
    Silberstein, 1977 (ssp.)
  trifurcatum Fain, Bafort &
    Silberstein, 1976 (ssp.)
heptaspicae Gouteux, 1977 .... Zaire
kauntzeum Gibbins, 1938 .... Uganda, Zaire
masabae Gibbins, 1934 .... Uganda
ngabogei Fain, 1950 .... Rwanda
nili Gibbins, 1934 .... Arabian peninsula,
Uganda
octospicae Gibbins, 1937 .... Uganda
rhodesiense de Meillon, 1942 .... Zimbabwe
shoae Grenier & Ovazza, 1956 .... Ethiopia
voltae Grenier, Ovazza & Valade, 1960 . West Africa

Subg. BOOPHTHORA Enderlein, 1925

> *PSEUDOSIMULIUM* Baranov,
> 1926 (preocc.)

bujakovi Rubtsov, 1940 .... USSR (Siberia)
chelevini (Ivashchenko, 1968 [? date]) . USSR (European)
erythrocephalum (De Geer, 1776) ..... Europe, Asiatic USSR
> *sericatum* Meigen, 1830
> *tenuifrons* Enderlein, 1921
> *mihalyii* (Rubtsov, 1967) (ssp.)
sinense (Enderlein, 1934) .... n China, Mongolia
yonagoense Okamoto, 1958 .... Japan
> *makunbei* (Ono, 1977) (ssp.)

Subg. BYSSODON Enderlein, 1925

> *PSILOCNETHA* Enderlein, 1935
> *TITANOPTERYX* Enderlein, 1935
> *ECHINOSIMULIUM* Baranov,
> 1938
> *GIBBINSIELLUM* Rubtsov, 1962

Group 1: GRISEICOLLE
species-group*

bifila Freeman & de Meillon, 1953 ..... Sudan
griseicolle Becker, 1903 .... tropical Africa, Egypt
> *scapulatum* (Enderlein, 1935)
> *dentulatum* Wanson & Henrard,
> 1944
tridens Freeman & de Meillon, 1953 .. tropical Africa
trisphaerae Wanson & Henrard, 1944 . Zaire

Group 2: MERIDIONALE
species-group*

buxtoni Austen, 1923 .... Iraq, Jordan
> *bipunctatum* Austen, 1923
>   (preocc.)
> *irakae* Smart, 1944
gutsevitshi (Yankovsky, 1978) .... e USSR, Mongolia
heptapotamicum Rubtsov, 1940 .... Iran, USSR (central Asia,
      Transcaucasia)
koidzumii (Takahasi, 1940) .... n China, Mongolia
maculatum (Meigen, 1804) .... c Palaearctic reg.
> *pungens* (Meigen, 1806)
> *subfasciatum* Meigen, 1838
> *vigintiquaterni* (Enderlein, 1929)
> *echinatum* (Baranov, 1938) (ssp.)
> *ussurianum* Rubtsov, 1940 (ssp.)
> *danubense* (Rubtsov, 1956)
> *uralense* (Rubtsov, 1956) (ssp.)
> *lenae* (Rubstov, 1956) (ssp.)

meridionale Riley, 1887 .... w & c North America
    occidentale Townsend, 1891
    tamaulipense Townsend, 1897
    forbesi Malloch, 1914
pseudonearcticum Rubtsov, 1940 .... USSR (Kamchatka)

Subg. CERQUEIRELLUM Py-Daniel, 1983*

amazonicum Goeldi, 1905 .... nw South America
argentiscutum Shelley & Luna Dias,
    1980 .... Brazil, Colombia
chaquense Coscarón, 1971 .... Argentina
cuasisanguineum Ramírez-Pérez,
    Yarzábal & Peterson, 1982 .... Venezuela
cuneatum (Enderlein, 1936) .... Paraguay
delponteianum Wygodzinsky, 1961 ..... Argentina
minusculum Lutz, 1910 .... Argentina, Brazil
nahimi Py-Daniel, 1984 .... Brazil
oyapockense Floch & Abonnenc, 1946 . n South America
    pseudosanguineum Ramírez-Pérez
      & Peterson, 1981
    sanchezi Ramírez-Pérez, Yarzábal
      & Peterson, 1982
pseudoamazonicum Ramírez-Pérez &
    Peterson, 1981 .... Venezuela
roraimense Nunes de Mello, 1974 ...... Brazil, Venezuela
sanguineum Knab, 1915 .... Colombia, Panama
venezuelense Ramírez-Pérez &
    Peterson, 1981 .... Brazil, Venezuela

Subg. CHIROSTILBIA Enderlein, 1921

dekeyseri Shelley & Py-Daniel, 1981 .. Brazil
distinctum Lutz, 1910 .... Brazil
    prumirimense Coscarón, 1981
laneportoi Vargas, 1941 .... Brazil
    pilosum Lane & Porto, 1940
      (preocc.)
pertinax Kollar, 1832 .... c & s South America
    inexorabile Schrottky, 1909
    infuscatum Lutz, 1909
    flavifemur (Enderlein, 1921)
    lutzianum (Enderlein, 1921)
      (preocc.)
    septentrionale Cerqueira & Barbosa
      de Almeida, 1970 (preocc.)
    cerqueirai Nunes de Mello &
      Barbosa de Almeida, 1974
serranus Coscarón, 1981 .... Brazil
spinibranchium Lutz, 1910 .... Brazil, Venezuela

Subg. COSCARONIELLUM Py-Daniel, 1983*

cauchense Floch & Abennenc, 1946 ... n South America
  sextobecium Nunes de Mello, 1974
  rangeli Ramírez-Pérez, Rassi &
    Ramírez, 1977
quadrifidum Lutz, 1917 .... Brazil, Venezuela
  torrealbai Ramírez-Pérez, 1980
  rassii Ramírez-Pérez, 1980

Subg. CROSSKEYELLUM Grenier &
  Bailly-Choumara, 1970*

gracilipes Edwards, 1921 .... Morocco

Subg. DEXOMYIA Crosskey, 1969*

atlanticum Crosskey, 1969 .... St. Helena Island

Subg. ECTEMNASPIS Enderlein, 1934

adolfolutzi Wygodzinsky, 1951 .... Argentina
antonii Wygodzinsky, 1953 .... Bolivia
bicoloratum Malloch, 1912 .... n South America, USA
  gaudeatum Knab, 1914   (NY)
  macca (Enderlein, 1934) (preocc.)
  molli Vargas, 1943
bicornutum Wygodzinsky & Coscarón,
  1982 .... Colombia
cormonsi Wygodzinsky, 1971 .... Venezuela
furcillatum Wygodzinsky & Coscarón,
  1982 .... Colombia
ignescens Roubaud, 1906 .... nw South America
jaimeramirezi Wygodzinsky, 1971 ...... Ecuador, Venezuela
pifanoi Ramírez-Pérez, 1971 .... Venezuela
romanai Wygodzinsky, 1951 .... Argentina
roquemayu Coscarón, 1985 .... Bolivia
rubiginosum (Enderlein, 1934) .... Argentina to Peru
sicuani Smart, 1944 .... Peru
  limbatum (Enderlein, 1934)
    (preocc.)
  incaicum Vargas, 1945
tolimaense Coscarón, 1985 .... Colombia
  simplex Wygodzinsky & Coscarón,
    1982 (preocc.)

Subg. EDWARDSELLUM Enderlein, 1921*

buisseti Fain & Elsen, 1980 .... Zaire
damnosum Theobald, 1903 (complex) . tropical Africa
  cingulatum (Enderlein, 1921)
dieguerense Vajime & Dunbar, 1975 .. Mali
juxtadamnosum Gouteux, 1978 .... Zaire
kilibanum Gouteux, 1977 .... Zaire

latipollex (Enderlein, 1936) ....   South Africa
luadiense Elsen, Fain, Henry & de
    Boeck, 1983 ....   Zaire
machadoi Luna de Carvalho, 1962 ....   Angola
maertensi Elsen, Fain, Henry & de
    Boeck, 1983 ....   Zaire
mengense Vajime & Dunbar, 1979 ....   Cameroon, Tanzania
microlepidum Elsen, Fain, Henry & de
    Boeck, 1983 ....   Zaire
nganganum Elsen, Fain, Henry & de
    Boeck, 1983 ....   Zaire
repertum Elsen, Fain, Henry & de
    Boeck 1983 ....   Zaire
sanctipauli Vajime & Dunbar, 1975 ...   West Africa
sirbanum Vajime & Dunbar, 1975 .....   West Africa to Sudan
    sudanense Vajime & Dunbar,
    1975*
soubrense Vajime & Dunbar, 1975 ....   West Africa
squamosum (Enderlein, 1921) ....   West Africa to Zaire
vilhenai Luna de Carvalho, 1962 ....   Angola
wambanum Elsen, Fain, Henry & de
    Boeck, 1983 ....   Zaire
yahense Vajime & Dunbar, 1975 ....   West Africa

Subg. EUSIMULIUM Roubaud, 1906

angustipes Edwards, 1915 ....   Europe
    securiforme (Rubtsov, 1956)
    latizonum (Rubtsov, 1956)
    paludicolum (Rivosecchi, 1963)
annae (Rubtsov, 1956) ....   USSR (European)
argentipile (Rubtsov, 1962) ....   USSR (European)
armeniacum (Rubtsov, 1955) ....   USSR (Transcaucasia)
aureum Fries, 1824 ....   n Eurasia, Iceland
    flavipes Stephens, 1829 (*nom.*
    nud.)
azerbaidzhanicum (Dzhafarov, 1953) ..   USSR (Transcaucasia)
azorense (Carlsson, 1963) ....   Azores
baatori (Rubtsov, 1967) ....   Mongolia
bonninense (Shiraki, 1935) ....   Bonin Is.
brachyantherum Rubtsov, 1947 ....   Iran, sw & sc USSR
bracteatum Coquillett, 1898* ....   USA, ? Canada
donovani Vargas, 1943* ....   Guatemala, Mexico
    diazi de Leon, 1945
erimoense (Ono, 1980) ....   Japan
guimari Becker, 1908 ....   Canary Is.
    submorsitans Séguy, 1921 **syn. n.**
horvathi (Enderlein, 1922) ....   c Europe
kaszabi (Rubtsov, 1969) ....   Mongolia
kazahstanicum (Rubtsov, 1976) ....   USSR (Kazakhstan)
krymense (Rubtsov, 1956) ....   e Europe, Caucasus
kuandianense (Chen & Cao, 1983) .....   China

longitarse (Rubtsov & Violovich, 1965) . USSR (Tuva)
maritimum (Rubtsov, 1956) .... USSR (Caucasus), ? China
nigrofusipes Rubtsov, 1947 .... USSR (central Asia,
                                            Transcaucasia)
paucicuspis Rubtsov, 1947 .... USSR (central Asia,
                                            Transcaucasia)
petricolum (Rivosecchi, 1963) .... sw Palaearctic reg.
pilosum Knowlton & Rowe, 1934* ..... w USA
   utahense Knowlton & Rowe, 1934
reginae Terteryan, 1949 .... USSR (Transcaucasia)
salinum (Rubtsov, 1956) .... USSR (e Siberia)
satsumense Takaoka, 1976 .... Japan
silvaticum (Rubtsov, 1962) .... s Europe, USSR
                                            (European)
taipei (Shiraki, 1935) .... Taiwan
velutinum (Santos Abreu, 1922)* .... w Palaearctic reg.
   nigripes (Santos Abreu, 1922)
      syn. n.
   pseudolatipes (Santos Abreu, 1922)
      syn. n.
   serbicum Baranov, 1925 (preocc.)
      syn. n.
   primum (Baranov, 1926) (preocc.)
      syn. n.
   secundum (Baranov, 1926)
      (preocc.) **syn. n.**
   rubzovianum (Sherban, 1961)
      syn. n.
   latinum (Rubtsov, 1962) **syn. n.**

Subg. FREEMANELLUM Crosskey, 1969

   berghei Fain, 1949 .... tropical Africa
   debegene de Meillon, 1934 .... s Africa
   empopomae de Meillon, 1937 .... South Africa
   hessei Gibbins, 1941 .... South Africa
   hirsutilateris de Meillon, 1937 .... South Africa
   manense Elsen & Escaffre, 1976 .... West Africa, ec Africa
   spinulicorne Fain & Elsen, 1980 .... Zaire

Subg. GOMPHOSTILBIA Enderlein, 1921*

   NIPPONOSIMULIUM Shogaki,
      1956 (unav.)

   ambigens Delfinado, 1969 .... Philippines
   apoense Takaoka, 1983 .... Philippines
   atratum de Meijere, 1913 .... Java
   baisasae Delfinado, 1962 .... Philippines
   barretti Smart & Clifford, 1965 .... New Guinea
   batoense Edwards, 1934 .... Java, Ryukyu Is.
   bicolense Takaoka, 1983 .... Philippines
   bucolicum Datta, 1975 .... India
   catleyi Smart & Clifford, 1965 .... New Guinea, New Britain

centrale Smart & Clifford, 1965 .... New Guinea
ceylonicum (Enderlein, 1921) .... Sri Lanka
chomustachi (Vorobets, 1977) .... USSR (Yakutskaya)
darjeelingense Datta, 1973 .... India
davaoense Takaoka, 1983 .... Philippines
epistum Delfinado, 1971 .... Philippines
fidum Datta, 1975 .... India
flavocinctum Edwards, 1934 .... Sumatra
friederichsi Edwards, 1934 .... Java
heldsbachense Smart & Clifford, 1965 . New Guinea
hemicyclium Smart & Clifford, 1965 ... New Guinea, New Britain
inthanonense Takaoka & Suzuki, 1984 . Thailand
keravatense Smart & Clifford, 1965 .... New Guinea, New Britain
kuingingiense Smart & Clifford, 1965 . New Guinea
lagunaense Takaoka, 1983 .... Philippines
lepnevae (Rubtsov, 1956) .... USSR (Tadzhikistan)
litoreum Datta, 1975 .... India
luzonicum Takaoka, 1983 .... Philippines
mangasepi Takaoka, 1983 .... Philippines
metatarsale Brunetti, 1911 .... Oriental reg.
miblosi Takaoka, 1983 .... Philippines
mindanaoense Takaoka, 1983 .... Philippines
montiblense Takaoka, 1983 .... Philippines
munumense Smart & Clifford, 1965 .... New Guinea, New Britain
nami Smart & Clifford, 1965 .... New Guinea
nepalense Lewis, 1964 .... Nepal
ogatai (Rubtsov, 1962) .... Japan
okinawaense Takaoka, 1976 .... Okinawa
omutaense Ogata & Sasa, 1954 .... Japan
pattoni Senior-White, 1922 .... India
pegalanense Smart & Clifford, 1969 .... Sabah
peregrinum Mackerras & Mackerras,
  1950 .... Australia (Qd)
rayohense Smart & Clifford, 1969 ...... Sabah
shogakii (Rubtsov, 1962) .... China, Japan
siamense Takaoka & Suzuki, 1984 ..... Thailand
sundaicum Edwards, 1934 .... Java, Malaya, Sumatra
synanceium (Chen & Cao, 1983) .... China
tenuistylum Datta, 1973 .... India, Sikkim
tokarense Takaoka, 1973 .... Japan (Tokara Is.)
tuenense Takaoka, 1979 .... Taiwan
unum Datta, 1975 .... India
varicorne Edwards, 1925 .... Malaya, Sumatra
visayaense Takaoka, 1983 .... Philippines
zonatum Edwards, 1934 .... Malaya, Sumatra

Subg. HEARLEA Vargas, Martínez
  Palacios & Díaz Nájera, 1946

ayrozai Vargas, 1945 .... Mexico
burchi Dalmat, 1951 .... Guatemala
canadense Hearle, 1932 .... w Canada to Mexico
  fraternum Twinn, 1938

capricorne de Leon, 1945	Guatemala, Mexico
carolinae de Leon, 1945	Guatemala, Mexico
chiriquiense Field, 1967	Costa Rica, Panama
contrerense Díaz Nájera & Vulcano, 1962	Mexico
dalmati Vargas & Díaz Nájera, 1948 ..	Mexico
delatorrei Dalmat, 1950	Guatemala
deleoni Vargas, 1945	Mexico
estevezi Vargas, 1945	Mexico
ethelae Dalmat, 1950	Guatemala
gorirossiae Vargas & Díaz Nájera, 1957 .	Mexico
johnsoni Vargas & Díaz Nájera, 1957 .	Mexico
juarezi Vargas & Díaz Nájera, 1957 ...	Mexico
larvispinosum de Leon, 1948	Guatemala, Mexico
menchacai Vargas & Díaz Nájera, 1957 .	Mexico
microbranchium Dalmat, 1949	Guatemala
nigricorne Dalmat, 1950	Guatemala
temascalense Díaz Nájera & Vulcano, 1962	Mexico

Subg. HEBRIDOSIMULIUM Grenier & Rageau, 1961

jolyi Roubaud, 1906	Vanuatu
laciniatum Edwards, 1924	Fiji

Subg. HELLICHIELLA Rivosecchi & Cardinali, 1975

BOREOSIMULIUM Rubtsov & Yankovsky, 1982 **syn. n.**

Group 1: ANNULUM species-group*

annuliforme (Rubtsov, 1962)	USSR (n European)
annulum (Lundström, 1911)	Scandinavia, n USSR
arctium (Rubtsov, 1956)	nw USSR
canonicolum (Dyar & Shannon, 1927) .	nw North America
quadratum (Stains & Knowlton, 1943)	
emarginatum Davies, Peterson & Wood, 1962	e Canada, ne USA
euryadminiculum Davies, 1949	s Canada, ne USA
kariyai (Takahasi, 1940)	China (Manchuria)
olonicum Usova, 1961	USSR (n European)
tsheburovae (Rubtsov, 1956)	USSR (n European)

Group 2: SUBEXCISUM species-group*

acutum (Patrusheva, 1971)	USSR (nw Siberia)
anatinum Wood, 1963	Canada, ne USA
baffinense Twinn, 1936	n Holarctic
pallens Twinn, 1936	
barabense (Rubtsov, 1973)	USSR (Siberia)

congareenarum (Dyar & Shannon, 1927) (complex) .... e USA
crassum (Rubtsov, 1956) .... n Scandinavia & nw USSR
dogieli (Rubtsov, 1956) .... USSR (n European, w Siberia)

excisum Davies, Peterson & Wood, 1962 .... Canada, ne USA
fallisi (Golini, 1975) .... Norway
innocens (Shewell, 1952) .... e Canada, ne USA
latipes (Meigen, 1804) .... n Europe
    subexcisum Edwards, 1915
    yerburyi Edwards, 1920
minus (Dyar & Shannon, 1927) .... w USA
nebulosum Currie & Adler, 1986 .... w Canada
rendalense (Golini, 1975) .... Norway
rivuli Twinn, 1936 .... e Canada, ne USA
saccai (Rivosecchi, 1967) .... Italy
usovae (Golini, 1987) .... Norway

Subg. HEMICNETHA Enderlein, 1934

    DYARELLA Vargas, Martínez Palacios & Díaz Nájera, 1946

brachycladum Lutz & Pinto, 1932 ...... Brazil
    brevibranchium Lutz & Machado, 1915 (*nom. nud.*)
bricenoi Vargas, Martínez Palacios & Díaz Nájera, 1946 .... Mexico
dehnei Field, 1969 .... Panama
earlei Vargas, Martínez Palacios & Díaz Nájera, 1946 .... Mexico to Panama
freemani Vargas & Díaz Nájera, 1949 . Mexico
giganteum (Rubtsov, 1940)* .... USSR (n European, w Siberia), nc Canada

guerrerense Vargas & Díaz Nájera, 1956 .... Mexico
hinmani Vargas, Martínez Palacios & Díaz Nájera, 1946 .... Mexico
keenani Field, 1949 .... Panama
mexicanum Bellardi, 1862 .... Mexico to n South America
    aureopunctatum Malloch, 1914
    placidum Knab, 1915
    turgidum (Hoffmann, 1930)
    lugubre Lutz & Nunes Tovar, 1928
muiscorum Bueno, Moncada & Muñoz de Hoyos, 1979 .... Colombia
paynei Vargas, 1942 .... Mexico to n South America
    mexicanum (Enderlein, 1934) (*preocc.*)
    mathesoni Vargas, 1943
    bilimekae Smart, 1944
    acatenangoense Dalmat, 1951

conviti Ramírez-Pérez & Vulcano,
   1973
pulverulentum Knab, 1915 .... Belize, Venezuela
rubicundulum Knab, 1915 .... Mexico to El Salvador
rubrithorax Lutz, 1909 .... Brazil
scutistriatum Lutz, 1909 .... Brazil
seriatum Knab, 1914 .... Peru
smarti Vargas, 1946 .... Guatemala, Mexico
solarii Stone, 1948 .... s USA, Mexico
tsharae Yankovsky, 1982* .... USSR (Siberia)
virgatum Coquillett, 1902 .... nc & s USA to Central
   cinereum Bellardi, 1859 (preocc.)   America
   tephrodes Speiser, 1904
   hippovorum Malloch, 1914
   chiapanense Hoffmann, 1930
yepocapense Dalmat, 1949 .... Guatemala
   ardeni Dalmat, 1953

Subg. HIMALAYUM Lewis, 1973

indicum Becher, 1885 .... Afghanistan to n Burma
   kashmiricum Edwards, 1927
nigrogilvum Summers, 1911* .... Thailand

Subg. INAEQUALIUM Coscarón &
Wygodzinsky, 1984

baiense Pinto, 1932 .... Brazil
beaupertuyi Ramírez-Pérez, Rassi &
   Ramírez, 1977 .... Venezuela
clavibranchium Lutz, 1910 .... Brazil
diversibranchium Lutz, 1910 .... Argentina, Brazil
   missionum Coscarón, 1976
inaequale Paterson & Shannon, 1927 .. c South America
   manicatum Enderlein, 1934
   jundiaiense d'Andretta & Dolores
      Gonzalez, 1964
mariavulcanoae Coscarón &
   Wygodzinsky, 1984. .... Brazil
pseudoexiguum Nunes de Mello &
   Barbosa de Almeida, 1974
subclavibranchium Lutz, 1910 .... Brazil
subnigrum Lutz, 1910 .... ec South America
   diversifurcatum Lutz, 1910
   mbarigui Coscarón &
      Wygodzinsky, 1973
travassosi d'Andretta & d'Andretta,
   1947 .... Argentina, Brazil

Subg. INSELIELLUM Rubtsov, 1974*

adamsoni Edwards, 1932 .... Marquesas Is.
buissoni Roubaud, 1906 .... Marquesas Is.
cheesmanae Edwards, 1927 .... Tahiti

gallinum Edwards, 1932 .... Marquesas Is.
guamense Stone, 1964 .... Micronesia (Guam)
hukaense Séchan, 1983 .... Marquesas Is.
mataverense Craig & Craig, 1986 .... Cook Is. (Rarotonga)
mumfordi Edwards, 1932 .... Marquesas Is.
oviceps Edwards, 1933 (complex) ...... Tahiti
palauense Stone, 1964 .... Micronesia (Palau Is.)
tahitiense Edwards, 1927 (complex) .... Tahiti
teruamanga Craig & Craig, 1986 .... Cook Is. (Rarotonga)
trukense Stone, 1964 .... Micronesia (Truk Is.)
uaense Séchan, 1983 .... Marquesas Is.

Subg. LEWISELLUM Crosskey, 1969

atyophilum Lewis & Disney, 1969 ...... Cameroon
ethiopiense Fain & Oomen, 1968 .... Ethiopia
goinyi Lewis & Hanney, 1965 .... Kenya, Uganda
hightoni Lewis, 1961 .... Kenya, Uganda
kivuense Gouteux, 1978 .... Zaire
neavei Roubaud, 1915 .... Kenya, Uganda, Zaire
    renauxi Wanson & Lebied, 1950
nyasalandicum de Meillon, 1930 .... Kenya, Malawi, Tanzania
ovazzae Grenier & Mouchet, 1959 ..... Congo, Uganda, West
    ivoriense Gouteux, 1979 (ssp.)   Africa
woodi de Meillon, 1930 .... Malawi, Tanzania

Subg. MEILLONIELLUM Rubtsov, 1962

adersi Pomeroy, 1922 .... tropical & s Africa
hirsutum Pomeroy, 1922 .... tropical & s Africa
    dubium Pomeroy, 1922
sexiens de Meillon, 1944 .... e Africa, Ethiopia
urundiense Fain, 1950 .... Burundi
yemenense Crosskey & Garms, 1982 ... Saudi Arabia, Yemen

Subg. METOMPHALUS Enderlein, 1935*

africanum Gibbins, 1934 .... Kenya, Uganda
    trimicrosphaerae Fain, Bafort &
      Silberstein, 1976 (ssp.)
akouense Fain & Elsen, 1973 .... Cameroon
albivirgulatum Wanson & Henrard,
  1944 .... Congo & Zaire to s Africa
arnoldi Gibbins, 1937 .... Sudan to Zimbabwe
bovis de Meillon, 1930 .... tropical & s Africa
    faini Wanson, 1947
    ulangae Lewis & Raybould, 1974 (ssp.)
cavum Gibbins, 1938 .... Uganda
    obscurum Gibbins, 1937 (preocc.)
chutteri Lewis, 1965 .... South Africa
colasbelcouri Grenier & Ovazza, 1951 . tropical Africa
    tchabalense Fain & Elsen, 1973 (ssp.)
crosskeyi Lewis & Disney, 1970 .... Cameroon
danense Gouteux, 1979 .... Ivory Coast

dawaense Uemoto, Ogata & Mebrahtu, 1977 .... Ethiopia
eouzani Germain & Grenier, 1970 ..... Cameroon
fragai Abreu, 1960 .... Angola
futaense Garms & Post, 1966 .... West Africa
gibense Uemoto, Ogata & Mebrahtu, 1977 .... Ethiopia
gyas de Meillon, 1951 .... Madagascar
hargreavesi Gibbins, 1934 .... Afrotropical reg.
    elgonense Gibbins, 1934
    tisiphone de Meillon, 1936
    loangolense Roubaud & Grenier, 1943
janzi Abreu, 1961 .... Angola
jimmaense Uemoto, Ogata & Mebrahtu, 1977 .... Ethiopia
kingundense Fain & Elsen, 1974 .... Zaire
kwangoense Fain & Elsen, 1974 .... Zaire
letabum de Meillon, 1935 .... South Africa
medusaeforme Pomeroy, 1920 .... tropical & s Africa
    ugandae Gibbins, 1934
    capense (Enderlein, 1935)
    caffrum (Enderlein, 1935)
    pseudomedusaeforme de Meillon, 1936
    angolense Abreu, 1961 (unav.)
natalense de Meillon, 1950 .... South Africa
ngouense Fain & Elsen, 1973 .... Cameroon, Nigeria
pentaceros Grenier & Brunhes, 1972 .. Madagascar
ruandae Fain, 1950 .... Rwanda
taylori Gibbins, 1938 .... Uganda
tondewandouense Fain & Elsen, 1973 . Cameroon
touffeum Gibbins, 1937 .... Kenya, Uganda
vorax Pomeroy, 1922 .... tropical & s Africa
    limbatum Enderlein, 1921 (preocc.)
    lepidum de Meillon, 1935
    tangae Smart, 1944
wellmanni Roubaud, 1906 .... tropical & s Africa
    magoebae de Meillon, 1935
zombaense Freeman & de Meillon, 1953 . Malawi

Subg. MONTISIMULIUM Rubtsov, 1974

alpinum Rubtsov, 1947 .... USSR (Kirgiziya)
arpiense (Terteryan & Kachvoryan, 1982) .... USSR (Transcaucasia)
assadovi (Dzhafarov, 1956) .... USSR (Transcaucasia)
asulcatum (Rubtsov, 1956) .... USSR (Uzbekistan)
brachystylum (Rubtsov, 1976) .... USSR (Tadzhikistan)
brevicorne (Rubtsov, 1964) .... USSR (Tadzhikistan)
bulbosum Lewis, 1973 .... Pakistan
chowi Takaoka, 1979 .... Taiwan

decafile (Rubtsov, 1976) .... USSR (Kazakhstan)
decimfiliatum (Rubtsov, 1956) .... USSR (central Asia)
djebaglense (Rubtsov, 1956) .... USSR (Kirgiziya)
duodecimcornutum (Rubtsov, 1956) ... USSR (Tadzhikistan)
    duodecimfilum (Rubtsov, 1947)
      (*nom. nud.*)
    duodecimatum (Rubtsov, 1951)
      (preocc.)
ghoomense Datta, 1975 .... n India
gviletense (Rubtsov, 1956) .... USSR (Caucasus)
    alizadei (Dzhafarov, 1954) (ssp.)
    lachense (Rubtsov, 1962)
      (ssp.)
    megrichaense (Rubtsov, 1962)
      (ssp.)
inflatum (Rubtsov, 1951) .... USSR (Tadzhikistan)
kerzhneri (Rubtsov, 1975) .... Mongolia
kirgisorum (Rubtsov, 1956) .... USSR (Kirgiziya)
kobayashii Okamoto, Yoshida, Sato &
  Shogaki, 1958 .... Japan
kurganense (Rubtsov, 1956) .... USSR (Kirgiziya)
litshkense (Rubtsov, 1956) .... Iran, USSR
                        (Transcaucasia)
longifiliatum (Rubtsov, 1976) .... USSR (Kazakhstan)
montium Rubtsov, 1947 .... USSR (Caucasus, central
                        Asia)
nemorivagum Datta, 1973 .... n India
ocreastylum (Rubtsov, 1956) .... USSR (central Asia,
                        Transcaucasia)
octofiliatum (Rubtsov, 1956) .... USSR (central Asia)
    batifile (Rubtsov & Shakirzyanova,
      1976) (ssp.)
    breviatum (Rubtsov &
      Shakirzyanova, 1976) (ssp.)
odontostylum Rubtsov, 1947 .... USSR (Tadzhikistan)
quattuordecimfiliatum (Rubtsov, 1976) . USSR (central Asia)
quattuordecimfilum Rubtsov, 1947 ..... USSR (Tadzhikistan)
    vallesense (Rubstov, 1962) (ssp.)
sakhalinum (Rubtsov, 1962) .... Japan, USSR (Sakhalin)
saradzhoense (Rubstov, 1956) .... USSR (Tadzhikistan)
schevyakovi Dorogostaisky, Rubtsov &
  Vlasenko, 1935 .... USSR (Kazakhstan, s
    comosum (Rubtsov, 1956) (ssp.) Siberia, FE)
shadini (Rubtsov, 1956) .... USSR (Tadzhikistan)
sheveligiense (Rubtsov & Violovich,
  1965) .... USSR (Tuva)
stackelbergi (Rubtsov, 1956) .... USSR (Tadzhikistan)
sytshevskiae (Rubtsov, 1967) .... USSR (Tadzhikistan)
tatianae (Bodrova, 1981) .... USSR (Primorye)
violovitshi (Rubtsov, 1962) .... USSR (Sakhalin)

Subg. MOROPS Enderlein, 1930*

alienigenum Takaoka, 1983	Philippines
aureonigrum Mackerras & Mackerras, 1950	Australia (Qd)
avilae Smart & Clifford, 1965	New Guinea
banauense Takaoka, 1983	Philippines
bansonae Takaoka, 1983	Philippines
botulus Smart & Clifford, 1965	New Guinea
brandti Smart & Clifford, 1965	New Guinea
cervus Smart & Clifford, 1965	New Guinea
clathrinum Mackerras & Mackerras, 1948	Australia (NSW, Qd)
clavum Smart & Clifford, 1965	New Guinea
cristatum Smart & Clifford, 1965	New Guinea
dycei Colbo, 1976	Australia (NT, Qd)
evelynae Smart & Clifford, 1965	New Guinea
faheyi Taylor, 1927	Australia (NT, Qd)
farciminis Smart & Clifford, 1965	New Guinea
fimbriatum Smart & Clifford, 1965	New Guinea
gagiduense Smart & Clifford, 1965	New Guinea
gorokae Smart & Clifford, 1965	New Guinea
ifugaoense Takaoka, 1983	Philippines
inornatum Mackerras & Mackerras, 1950	e Australia
inuitkiense Smart & Clifford, 1965	New Britain
josephi Smart & Clifford, 1965	New Guinea
kainantuense Smart & Clifford, 1965 ..	New Guinea
kaiti Smart & Clifford, 1965	New Ireland
kokodae Smart & Clifford, 1965	New Guinea
lalokiense Smart & Clifford, 1965	New Guinea
lawnhillense Colbo, 1976	Australia (NT, Qd)
liliwense Takaoka, 1983	Philippines
longirostre Smart, 1972	New Guinea
rostratum Smart & Clifford, 1965 (preocc.)	
mackerrasorum Colbo, 1976	Australia (NT, Qd, WA)
mafuluense Smart & Clifford, 1965	New Guinea
manbucalense Takaoka, 1983	Philippines
matokoense Smart & Clifford, 1965	New Guinea
melatum Wharton, 1949	e Australia
mendiense Smart & Clifford, 1965	New Guinea
minji Smart & Clifford, 1965	New Guinea
mussauense Delfinado, 1971	New Guinea (Mussau Island)
nicholsoni Mackerras & Mackerras, 1948	e Australia
oculatum (Enderlein, 1936)	New Guinea
papuense Wharton, 1948	New Guinea
purosae Smart & Clifford, 1965	New Guinea
raunsimnae Smart & Clifford, 1965	New Guinea, New Britain

riverai Takaoka, 1983 .... Philippines
rounae Smart & Clifford, 1965 .... New Guinea
saihoense Smart & Clifford, 1965 .... New Guinea
salazarae Takaoka, 1983 .... Philippines
sherwoodi Stone & Maffi, 1971 .... Solomon Is. (Guadalcanal)
standfasti Colbo, 1976 .... Australia (Qd)
tafae Smart & Clifford, 1965 .... New Guinea
torresianum Mackerras & Mackerras,
1955 .... Australia (Qd)
wamenae Smart & Clifford, 1965 .... New Guinea
wantoatense Smart & Clifford, 1965 ... New Guinea
wilhelmlandae Smart, 1944 .... New Guinea
    pygmaeum (Enderlein, 1922)
    (preocc.)

Subg. NEVERMANNIA Enderlein, 1921

    CNETHA Enderlein, 1921
    STILBOPLAX Enderlein, 1921
    PSEUDONEVERMANNIA
      Baranov, 1926
    CRYPTECTEMNIA Enderlein,
      1936
    CHELOCNETHA Enderlein, 1936

Group 1: FEUERBORNI
species-group*

bryopodium Delfinado, 1971 .... Philippines
chitoense Takaoka, 1979 .... Taiwan
feuerborni Edwards, 1934 .... Bali, Java
fuscinervis Edwards, 1933 .... Sabah
mie Ogata & Sasa, 1954 .... Japan
morisonoi Takaoka, 1973 .... Japan
perlucidulum Takaoka, 1983 .... Philippines
praelargum Datta, 1973 .... n India
rufithorax Brunetti, 1911 .... India
sasai (Rubtsov, 1962) .... Japan
senile Brunetti, 1911 .... n India

Group 2: LOUTETENSE species-group

loutetense Grenier & Ovazza, 1951 .... tropical & s Africa
narcaeum de Meillon, 1950 .... South Africa
rutherfoordi de Meillon, 1937 .... South Africa, Zimbabwe,
? Yemen

Group 3: RUFICORNE species-group*

alatum Fain & Dujardin, 1983 .... Kenya
angustitarse (Lundström, 1911) .... Europe, USSR
    melanobrachium (Enderlein, 1924)
    mazedonicum (Baranov, 1926)
    knochi (Enderlein, 1929)
    ? *flavicorne* (Enderlein, 1929)

    equitarse (Rubtsov, 1962) (ssp.)
    dispinum (Rubtsov & Carlsson,
      1965)
    marrucinum (Rivosecchi, 1966)
    celticum Davies, 1966 (preocc.)
    brevipes (Rubtsov, 1967) (ssp.)
    hungaricum (Rubtsov, 1967) (ssp.)
    cambriense Davies, 1967

antibrachium Fain & Dujardin, 1983 ..   Cameroon, Kenya
arabicum Crosskey, 1982 ....   Arabia, tropical Africa
aspericorne Fain, Bafort & Silberstein,
    1976 ....   Kenya
aureohirtum Brunetti, 1911 ....   Oriental region
    geniculare Shiraki, 1935
    philippinense Delfinado, 1962
    tuaranense Smart & Clifford, 1969
aureosimile Pomeroy, 1920 ....   Cameroon, Kenya, Nigeria
baforti Fain & Dujardin, 1983 ....   Kenya
brachium Gibbins, 1936 ....   e Africa to South Africa
brevitarse (Rubtsov, 1976) ....   USSR (Transcaucasia)
brunneum (Yankovsky, 1977) ....   USSR (FE)
buckleyi de Meillon, 1944 ....   Kenya, Rwanda
    vulcani Fain, 1950
bulbiferum Fain & Dujardin, 1983 .....   Rwanda, Zaire
candelabrum Fain & Dujardin, 1983 ..   Tanzania
crassicaulum (Rubtsov, 1955) ....   USSR (central Asia)
delizhanense (Rubtsov, 1955) ....   USSR (Transcaucasia)
duboisi Fain, 1950 ....   Kenya, Rwanda
falcoe (Shiraki, 1935) ....   Taiwan
flavinotatum Fain & Dujardin, 1983 ...   Rwanda
flavipes Austen, 1921 ....   Israel/Jordan
    jerichoense Smart, 1944*
fuscicorne Fain, 1950 ....   Rwanda
ibleum (Rivosecchi, 1966) ....   circum-Mediterranean
katangae Fain, 1951 ....   tropical & s Africa
latigonium (Rubtsov, 1956) ....   n & c Europe
longipes (Rubtsov, 1956) ....   USSR (Kazakhstan)
loveridgei Crosskey, 1965 ....   St. Helena Island
lundstromi (Enderlein, 1921) ....   n & c Europe
    kerteszi (Enderlein, 1922)
milloti Grenier & Doucet, 1949 ....   Madagascar
montshadskii (Rubtsov, 1956) ....   USSR (central Asia)
neornatipes Dumbleton, 1969 ....   New Caledonia
nigritarse Coquillett, 1902 ....   tropical & s Africa
    caffraricum (Enderlein, 1935)
norfolkense Dumbleton, 1969 ....   Norfolk Island
nyanzense Fain & Dujardin, 1983 ......   Kenya
ornatipes Skuse, 1890 (complex) ....   Australia, New Guinea
    biroi (Enderlein, 1936)
perforatum Fain & Dujardin, 1983 ....   Burundi, Rwanda, Zaire
politum Crosskey, 1977 ....   St. Helena Island
raybouldi Fain & Dujardin, 1983 ....   Tanzania

rubescens Fain & Dujardin, 1983 .... Rwanda, Zaire
ruficorne Macquart, 1838 .... Africa, Arabia, Middle
  beckeri Roubaud, 1906   East, Malagasia, s Iberia,
  annulipes Becker, 1908   Cape Verde Is., Canary
  divergens Pomeroy, 1922   Is.
  diversipes Edwards, 1923
sacculiferum Fain & Dujardin, 1983 ... Burundi, Rwanda
simplex Gibbins, 1936 .... Kenya, Uganda
  elgonicum Séguy, 1938
sirimonense Fain & Dujardin, 1983 .... Kenya
speculiventre Enderlein, 1914 .... Seychelles
starmuhlneri Grenier & Grjebine, 1964 . Madagascar
subgriseum Rubtsov, 1940 .... n China, USSR (central
                                             Asia, Transcaucasia)

tenuitarsus (Rubtsov, 1969) (preocc.,
  no publ. repl. name) .... Mongolia
tolongoinae Grenier & Brunhes, 1972 . Madagascar
vitile (Rubtsov, 1955) .... USSR (Transcaucasia)

Group 4: VERNUM species-group*
aberrans Delfinado, 1969 .... Philippines
acmeria (Ono, 1978) .... Japan
aestivum Davies, Peterson & Wood,
  1962 .... e Canada, ne USA
ammosovi (Vorobets, 1984) .... USSR (Yakutia)
amurense (Rubtsov, 1956) .... USSR (Amur)
angustatum (Rubtsov, 1956) .... e Europe
angusticorne (Rubtsov, 1956) .... USSR (Primorye)
angustifrons (Enderlein, 1921) .... France
armoricanum Doby & David, 1961 .... w Europe
australe (Rubtsov, 1955) .... USSR (Transcaucasia)
beltukovae (Rubtsov, 1956) .... USSR (European, w
                                             Siberia)

bertrandi Grenier & Dorier, 1959 ...... c & s Europe
biancoi (Rubtsov, 1964) .... Italy
bicorne Dorogostaisky, Rubtsov &
  Vlasenko, 1935 .... USSR (e Siberia), Alaska,
                                             nw Canada
boldstemta (Ono, 1978) .... Japan
brevidens (Rubtsov, 1956) .... sw Europe to USSR
                                             (Transcaucasia)

caledonense Adler & Currie, 1986 ...... w Canada
carpathicum (Knoz, 1961) .... c Europe
carthusiense Grenier & Dorier, 1959 .. c & sw Europe
chubarevae (Kachvoryan & Terteryan,
  1981) .... USSR (Armenia)
clarkei Stone & Snoddy, 1969 .... ec USA
codreanui (Sherban, 1958) .... se Europe
corniferum (Yankovsky, 1979) .... USSR (European, Siberia)
costatum Friederichs, 1920 .... Europe
  incornutum (Enderlein, 1929)
  barbativentre (Enderlein, 1929)

couverti (Rubtsov, 1964) .... Italy
craigi Adler & Currie, 1986 .... w Canada
crenobium (Knoz, 1961) .... c & s Europe
croxtoni Nicholson & Mickel, 1950 .... s & c Canada, n USA
cryophilum (Rubtsov, 1959) .... Europe
    brevicaulis Dorier & Grenier, 1961
curvans (Rubtsov & Carlsson, 1965) .. n Europe, n & e USSR
decolletum Adler & Currie, 1986 .... w Canada
dentatura (Vorobets, 1984) .... USSR (Yakutia)
djafarovi (Rubtsov, 1962) .... USSR (Transcaucasus)
    subcostatum (Dzhafarov, 1953) (preocc.)
dolomitense (Rivosecchi, 1971) .... Italy
dunfellense Davies, 1966 .... British Isles
duplex Shewell & Fredeen, 1958 .... wc Canada
elatum (Rubtsov, 1955) .... USSR (Transcaucasia)
elburnum (Rubtsov & Carlsson, 1965) . Scandinavia, n USSR
erectum (Rubtsov, 1959) .... USSR (European, Siberia)
florae (Dzhafarov, 1954) .... USSR (Transcaucasia)
fluviatile Radzivilovskaya, 1948 .... USSR (FE)
fontinale Radzivilovskaya, 1948 .... USSR (FE)
fontium (Rubtsov, 1955) .... USSR (Caucasus)
fucense (Rivosecchi, 1962) .... Italy
garniense (Rubtsov, 1955) .... USSR (Transcaucasia)
gejgelense (Dzhafarov, 1954) .... USSR (Transcaucasia)
gomphocorne (Rubtsov, 1964) .... USSR (Caucasus)
gouldingi Stone, 1952 .... n North America
gracile Datta, 1973 .... n India
impar Davies, Peterson & Wood, 1962 . ne North America
jilinense Chen & Cao, 1983 .... China
johannseni Hart, 1912 .... wc Canada, n USA
karzhantavicum (Rubtsov, 1956) .... USSR (central Asia)
keiseri (Rubtsov, 1955) .... USSR (central Asia, Transcaucasia)

kugartsuense (Rubtsov, 1956) .... USSR (Kirgiziya)
kuznetzovi Rubtsov, 1940 .... USSR (n European)
larvipilosum Okazawa, 1984 .... Japan
latifile (Rubtsov, 1956) .... USSR (e Siberia, FE)
lidiae Semushin & Usova, 1983 .... USSR (Yakutia)
lilotense (Rubtsov, 1971) .... USSR (e Siberia)
luppovae (Rubtsov, 1956) .... USSR (Tadzhikistan)
marsicanum (Rivosecchi, 1962) .... s Europe
meigeni (Rubtsov & Carlsson, 1965) ... USSR (European)
minutum (Rubtsov, 1959) (preocc., no
    publ. repl. name) .... s & e Europe
murvanidzei (Rubtsov, 1955) .... USSR (Transcaucasia)
naturale Davies, 1966 .... British Isles, nc & w Europe
oligotuberculatum (Knoz, 1965) .... c Europe
orsovae Smart, 1944 .... Romania
    laticalx (Enderlein, 1936) (preocc.)
paracorniferum (Yankovsky, 1979) .... USSR (FE)
pathrushevae (Boldarueva, 1979) .... USSR (Siberia)

planipuparium Rubtsov, 1947 .... USSR (Tadzhikistan)
pugetense (Dyar & Shannon, 1927) .... Alaska, Canada, n & c
   ? longipile (Rubtsov, 1956)   USA, ? e USSR
purii Datta, 1973 .... n India
quasidecolletum Crosskey **n. name** ..... s Europe
   truncatum (Rivosecchi & Cardinali,
   1975) (preocc.)
quebecense Twinn, 1936 .... e Canada, ne USA
rebunense (Ono, 1979) .... Japan
rivosecchii (Contini, 1965) (preocc., no
   publ. repl. name) .... Italy (Sardinia)
saliceti (Rubtsov, 1971) .... USSR (Siberia)
silvestre (Rubtsov, 1956) .... USSR (n European to FE)
strelkovi (Rubtsov, 1956) .... USSR (Sakhalin)
subcostatum (Takahasi, 1950) .... China, Japan, Korea
   chejuense Takaoka, 1974 (ssp.)
   koshikiense Takaoka, 1976 (ssp.)
taulingense Takaoka, 1979 .... Taiwan
tauricum (Rubtsov, 1956) .... USSR (Crimea)
timondavidi Giudicelli, 1961 .... France (Corsica)
tjibodense Edwards, 1934 .... Indonesia (Java)
tosariense Edwards, 1934 .... Indonesia (Java)
toubkal Bouzidi & Giudicelli, 1986 .... Morocco
tricrenum (Rubtsov & Carlsson, 1965) . Scandinavia
uchidai (Takahasi, 1950) .... China, Japan
urbanum Davies, 1966 .... British Isles
vernum Macquart, 1826 (complex) ..... n Holarctic reg.
   pubiventre Zetterstedt, 1838
   trabeatum (Enderlein, 1921)
   pritzkowi (Enderlein, 1926)
   albipileatum (Enderlein, 1926)
   schielei (Enderlein, 1926)
   wigandi (Enderlein, 1928)
   fluminale (Rubtsov, 1956) (ssp.)
   hatangense (Rubtsov, 1956) (ssp.)
   shutovae (Rubtsov, 1956) (ssp.)
   aestivale (Rubtsov, 1962) (ssp.)
   meridionale (Rivosecchi &
     Lipparoni, 1965) (preocc.)
vidanoi (Rubtsov, 1964) .... Italy
wyomingense Stone & DeFoliart, 1959 . nw USA
xinbinense Chen & Cao, 1983 .... China
yushangense Takaoka, 1979 .... Taiwan
zakhariense (Rubtsov, 1955) .... USSR (Transcaucasia)
zhiltzovae (Rubtsov, 1976) .... USSR (Transcaucasia)

Ungrouped Species of
NEVERMANNIA

dasguptai Datta, 1974 .... n India
konoi (Takahasi, 1950) .... Japan
yamayaense Ogata & Sasa, 1954 .... Japan

Subg. NOTOLEPRIA Enderlein, 1930

blantoni Field, 1967 .... Panama
exiguum Roubaud, 1906 (complex) .... Central America to n
   glaucophthalmum Knab, 1914   Argentina
   delpontei Paterson & Shannon,
   1927
gonzalezi Vargas & Díaz Nájera, 1953 . Central America
paraguayense Schrottky, 1909 .... Paraguay
subexiguum Field, 1967 .... Panama

Subg. OBUCHOVIA Rubtsov, 1947*

adornatum (Rubtsov, 1956) .... USSR (Caucasus)
albellum Rubtsov, 1947 .... Afghanistan, USSR
   (central Asia)
auricoma Meigen, 1818 .... c & s Europe
   djerdapense Baranov, 1937 **syn. n.***
biseriatum Rubtsov, 1940 .... China (Tibet)
brevifile (Rubtsov, 1956) .... s Europe to Crimea
continii (Rivosecchi & Cardinali, 1975) . Italy (Sardinia)
emiliae (Rubtsov, 1976) .... USSR (Tadzhikistan)
galloprovinciale Giudicelli, 1963 .... sw Europe
ibericum Crosskey & Santos Grácio,
   1985 .... Portugal & Spain
margaritae (Rubtsov, 1956) .... USSR (Transcaucasia)
popowae Rubtsov, 1940 .... USSR (Transcaucasia)
   terminasjanae Terteryan, 1952
   atrofuscum (Rubtsov, 1956) (ssp.)
segusina (Couvert, 1968) .... Italy
syriacum Roubaud, 1909* .... Syria
transcaspicum Enderlein, 1921 .... Iran, USSR (central Asia)
versicolor (Rubtsov, 1956) .... USSR (Kazakhstan)

Subg. PARABYSSODON Rubtsov, 1964

rugglesi Nicholson & Mickel, 1950* ... North America
slossonae Dyar & Shannon, 1927* ...... c & e USA
transiens Rubtsov, 1940 .... n China, Mongolia, across
   USSR, wc Canada

Subg. PHORETOMYIA Crosskey, 1969*

afronuri Lewis & Disney, 1970 .... Cameroon
baetiphilum Lewis & Disney, 1972 ..... Cameroon
berneri Freeman, 1954 .... tropical Africa
copleyi Gibbins, 1941 .... Kenya, Uganda
diceros Freeman & de Meillon, 1953 .. Zaire
dukei Lewis, Disney & Crosskey, 1969 . Cameroon
kumboense Grenier, Germain &
   Mouchet, 1966 .... Cameroon
lumbwanum de Meillon, 1944 .... tropical Africa
   lerabanum Gouteux, 1979 (ssp.)
marlieri Grenier, 1950 .... Zaire

melanocephalum Gouteux, 1978 .... Zaire
moucheti Gouteux, 1977 .... Zaire
rickenbachi Germain, Grenier &
    Mouchet, 1966 .... Cameroon
zairense Gouteux, 1977 .... Zaire

Subg. POMEROYELLUM Rubtsov, 1962*

alcocki Pomeroy, 1922 .... tropical & s Africa
    kenyanum Séguy, 1938
    henrardi Gibbins, 1941
allaeri Wanson, 1947 .... Zaire
audreyae Garms & Disney, 1974 .... Cameroon
aureliani Fain, 1950 .... Rwanda
awashense Uemoto, Ogata &
    Mebrahtu, 1977 .... Ethiopia
bayakorum Fain & Elsen, 1974 .... Zaire
bequaerti Gibbins, 1936 .... e & s Africa
    phoroniforme de Meillon, 1937
blacklocki de Meillon, 1930 .... Liberia, Sierra Leone
cervicornutum Pomeroy, 1920 .... tropical & s Africa
coalitum Pomeroy, 1922 .... West Africa
djallonense Roubaud & Grenier, 1943 . West Africa
duodecimum Gibbins, 1936 .... tropical Africa
ekomei Lewis & Disney, 1972 .... Cameroon
evillense Fain, Hallot & Bafort, 1966 .. tropical & s Africa
garmsi Crosskey, 1969 .... West Africa
    violaceum Pomeroy, 1922 (preocc.)
    occidentale Freeman & de Meillon,
      1953 (preocc.)
geigyi Garms & Häusermann, 1968 .... Tanzania
gilleti Fain & Hallot, 1964 .... Zaire
harrisoni Freeman & de Meillon, 1953 . s Africa
hissetteum Gibbins, 1936 .... tropical Africa
    vargasi Grenier & Rageau, 1949
impukane de Meillon, 1936 .... tropical & s Africa
ituriense Fain, 1951 .... Zaire
johannae Wanson, 1947 .... tropical & s Africa
    roubaudi Grenier & Rageau, 1949
    jadini Fain, 1950
    akanyaruense Fain, 1950
    novemcornutum Fain & Elsen,
      1980 (ssp.)
kenyae de Meillon, 1940 .... tropical Africa
leberrei Grenier, Germain & Mouchet,
    1966 .... Cameroon
liberiense Garms, 1973 .... Liberia
mayumbense Fain & Elsen, 1973 .... Zaire
mcmahoni de Meillon, 1940 .... tropical & s Africa
    altipartitum Roubaud & Grenier,
      1943
merops de Meillon, 1950 .... e & s Africa

nyaense Gouteux, 1977 .... Zaire
oguamai Lewis & Disney, 1972 .... Cameroon
palmeri Pomeroy, 1922 .... West Africa
pauliani Grenier & Doucet, 1949 .... Madagascar
rodhaini Fain, 1950 .... Rwanda
rotundum Gibbins, 1936 .... tropical & s Africa
schoutedeni Wanson, 1947 .... tropical Africa
schwetzi Wanson, 1947 .... Zaire
sextumdecimum Luna de Carvalho,
    1962 (unav.)* .... Angola
tentaculum Gibbins, 1936 .... c, e, & s Africa
unicornutum Pomeroy, 1920 .... tropical & s Africa
    monoceros Roubaud & Grenier,
        1943
    wolfsi Wanson & Henrard, 1944
    bertrandi Luna de Carvalho, 1962
        (unav.)
vangilsi Wanson, 1947 .... Zaire
weyeri Garms & Häusermann, 1968 ... Tanzania

Subg. PSARONIOCOMPSA Enderlein,
1934

  PLIODASINA Enderlein, 1936

aequifurcatum Lutz, 1910 .... Brazil
anamariae Vulcano, 1962 .... Brazil
angrense Pinto, 1932 .... Brazil
auripellitum Enderlein, 1934 .... Argentina, Brazil,
                                            Paraguay, Uruguay

auristriatum Lutz, 1910 .... Brazil
    infuscatum Lutz, 1910
bonaerense Coscarón & Wygodzinsky,
    1984 .... Argentina
brevifurcatum Lutz, 1910 .... Argentina, Brazil
catarinense Pinto, 1932 .... Brazil
fuliginis Field, 1969 .... Panama
guttatum (Enderlein, 1936) .... Paraguay
incrustatum Lutz, 1910 .... ec South America
    opalinifrons (Enderlein, 1934)
jujuyense Paterson & Shannon, 1927 .. Argentina
    mendozanum (Enderlein, 1936)
limbatum Knab, 1915 .... n South America
    machadoi Ramírez-Pérez, 1971
        (preocc.)
    meruoca Nunes de Mello, Barbosa
        de Almeida & Dellome, 1973
    machadoallisoni Vulcano, 1981
    ? *yarzabali* Ramírez-Pérez, 1980
marathrumi Fairchild, 1940 .... Panama
schmidtmummi Wygodzinsky, 1973 .... Colombia

Subg. PSILOPELMIA Enderlein, 1934

LANEA Vargas, Martínez Palacios
& Díaz Nájera, 1946

alirioi Ramírez-Pérez & Vulcano, 1973 .   Venezuela
antenusi Lane & Porto, 1940 ....   Brazil
antillarum Jennings, 1915 ....   n Neotropical reg.
    wolcotti Fox, 1953
bivittatum Malloch, 1914 ....   wc Canada to n Mexico
    clarum (Dyar & Shannon, 1927)
    idahoense Twinn, 1938
callidum (Dyar & Shannon, 1927) .....   Mexico to Venezuela
    mooseri (Dampf, 1927)
dandrettai Vargas, Martínez Palacios &
    Díaz Nájera, 1946 ....   Mexico
dinellii (Joan, 1912) ....   Guatemala to Argentina
    bipunctatum Malloch, 1912
    miniatum (Enderlein, 1934) (1)
    miniatum (Enderlein, 1934) (2)
      (preocc.)
    martinezi Vargas, 1943
downsi Vargas, Martínez Palacios &
    Díaz Nájera, 1946 ....   Mexico to Venezuela
dugesi Vargas, Martínez Palacios &
    Díaz Nájera, 1946 ....   Guatemala, Mexico
escomeli Roubaud, 1909 ....   Chile to Ecuador
    rufidorsum (Enderlein, 1934)
gabaldoni Ramírez-Pérez, 1971 ....   Venezuela
gonzalezherrejoni Díaz Nájera, 1969 ...   Mexico
griseum Coquillett, 1898 ....   wc Canada & w USA
haematopotum Malloch, 1914 ....   Cuba, Mexico to n South
    pseudohaematopotum Hoffmann,   America
      1930
    boydi de Leon, 1945
iracouboense Floch & Abonnenc, 1946 .   French Guiana
jacobsi Dalmat, 1953 ....   Guatemala
jerezense Díaz Nájera, 1969 ....   Mexico
kabanayense Ramírez-Pérez & Vulcano,
    1973 ....   Venezuela
letrasense Díaz Nájera, 1969 ....   Mexico
lewisi Ramírez-Pérez, 1971 ....   Venezuela
longithallum Díaz Nájera & Vulcano,
    1962 ....   Mexico
lutzianum Pinto, 1932 ....   w & n South America
mangabeirai Vargas, 1945 ....   Mexico
mauense Nunes de Mello, 1974 ....   Brazil
mazzottii Díaz Nájera, 1981 ....   Mexico
mediovittatum Knab, 1915 ....   n Mexico, sc USA
netteli Díaz Nájera, 1969 ....   Mexico
nilesi Rambajan, 1979 ....   Guyana
notatum Adams, 1904 ....   sw USA

nuneztovari Ramírez-Pérez, Rassi &
    Ramírez, 1977 .... Venezuela
ochoai Vargas, Martínez Palacios &
    Díaz Nájera, 1946 .... Mexico
ochraceum Walker, 1861 (complex) .... s Mexico to n South
    America

olimpicum Díaz Nájera, 1969 .... Mexico
panamense Fairchild, 1940 .... Central America
perflavum Roubaud, 1906 .... Argentina to Venezuela
pseudoantillarum Ramírez-Pérez &
    Vulcano, 1973 .... Venezuela
pseudocallidum Díaz Nájera, 1965 ..... Mexico
quadrivittatum Loew, 1862 .... Cuba, Central & n South
    mallochi (Enderlein, 1925)   America
    fairchildi Vargas, 1942
rorotaense Floch & Abonnenc,
    1946 .... n South America
    marionense Floch & Abonnenc,
      1946
    wuayaraka Ortiz, 1957
    fulvinotum Cerqueira & Nunes de
      Mello, 1967
    ignacioi Ramírez-Pérez & Vulcano,
      1973
samboni Jennings, 1915 .... Central America
    colvini Dalmat, 1952
shewellianum Coscarón, 1985 .... Colombia, Ecuador
spinifer Knab, 1914 .... Ecuador, Peru
suarezi Ramírez-Pérez, Rassi &
    Ramírez, 1977 .... Venezuela
sucamense Nunes de Mello, 1974 .... Brazil, Venezuela
    santaelenae Ramírez-Pérez &
      Peterson, 1981
trivittatum Malloch, 1914 .... n Mexico, sw USA
    distinctum Malloch, 1913 (preocc.)
venator Dyar & Shannon, 1927 .... sw USA
    beameri Stains & Knowlton, 1943
veracruzanum Vargas, Martínez
    Palacios & Díaz Nájera, 1946 .... Central America
vulcanoae Díaz Nájera, 1969 .... Mexico
wolffhuegeli (Enderlein, 1922) .... Argentina, Bolivia
    haarupianum (Enderlein, 1936)
zempoalense Vargas, Martínez Palacios
    & Díaz Nájera, 1946 .... Mexico

Subg. PSILOZIA Enderlein, 1936
        NEOSIMULIUM Vargas, Martínez
        Palacios & Díaz Nájera, 1946

argus Williston, 1893 .... sw Canada, w USA
    obtusum (Dyar & Shannon, 1927)

kamloopsi Hearle, 1932
hearlei Twinn, 1938
encisoi Vargas & Díaz Nájera, 1949 ...   Mexico, w USA
vittatum Zetterstedt, 1838 (complex) ..   Nearctic reg. (incl.
nasale Gistel, 1848 (*nom. nud.*)   Greenland), Iceland,
tribulatum Lugger, 1897   Faeroe Is.
glaucum Coquillett, 1902
venustoide Hart, 1912
groenlandicum Enderlein, 1936
  (preocc.)
asakakae Smart, 1944

Subg. PTERNASPATHA Enderlein, 1930*

DASYPELMOZA Enderlein, 1934
ACROPOGON Enderlein, 1934

albicinctum (Enderlein, 1934) ....   Peru
albilineatum (Enderlein, 1936) ....   Peru
annulatum Philippi, 1865 ....   Argentina, Chile
varipes Philippi, 1865
bachmanni Wygodzinsky & Coscarón,
1967 ....   Argentina
barbatipes Enderlein, 1934 ....   w South America
bordai Coscarón & Wygodzinsky, 1972 .   Bolivia
caprii Wygodzinsky & Coscarón, 1967 .   Argentina
cotopaxi Wygodzinsky & Coscarón,
1979 ....   Ecuador
deagostinii Coscarón & Wygodzinsky,
1962 ....   Tierra del Fuego
dureti Wygodzinsky & Coscarón, 1967 .   Argentina
edwardsi (Enderlein, 1934) ....   Argentina, Chile
hectorvargasi Coscarón &
Wygodzinsky, 1972 ....   Chile
herreri Wygodzinsky & Coscarón, 1967 .   Peru
horocochuspi Coscarón & Wygodzinsky,
1972 ....   Argentina
huemul Wygodzinsky & Coscarón, 1967 .   Argentina
limay Wygodzinsky, 1958 ....   Argentina
llutense Coscarón & Matta, 1982 ....   Chile
luchoi Coscarón & Wygodzinsky, 1972 .   Chile
nemorale Edwards, 1931 ....   Argentina, Chile
nigristrigatum (Enderlein, 1930) ....   Argentina
philippii Coscarón, 1976 ....   Chile
pichi Wygodzinsky & Coscarón, 1967 .   Argentina
prodexargenteum (Enderlein, 1936) ....   Argentina to Peru
pulchrum Philippi, 1865 ....   Chile
quechuanum Coscarón & Wygodzinsky,
1972 ....   Argentina, Chile
schoenemanni (Enderlein, 1934) ....   Chile
simile Silva Figueroa, 1917 ....   Argentina, Chile
punctativentre (Enderlein, 1936)
figueroa Smart, 1944*

illiesi Wygodzinsky & Coscarón,
1967
stelliferum Coscarón & Wygodzinsky,
1972 .... Chile
strigidorsum (Enderlein, 1934) .... Argentina, Peru
walterwittmeri Wygodzinsky, 1958 ..... Argentina
yacuchuspi Wygodzinsky & Coscarón,
1967 .... Peru

Subg. RUBZOVIA Petrova, 1983 **stat. n.**

CRENOSIMULIUM Giudicelli &
Thiery, 1985 **syn. n.**

knidirii Giudicelli & Thiery, 1985 ...... Morocco
lamachi Doby & David, 1960 .... France, Morocco
vantshi Petrova, 1983 .... USSR (Tadzhikistan)

Subg. SCHOENBAUERIA Enderlein, 1921

MIODASIA Enderlein, 1936

annulitarse Zetterstedt, 1838 .... Scandinavia
minutissimum Zetterstedt, 1850
brachyarthrum (Rubtsov, 1956) .... USSR (Siberia, FE)
chelevini (Ivashchenko, 1978) .... USSR (European)
dendrofilum (Patrusheva, 1962) .... USSR (Siberia, FE)
flavoantennatum Rubtsov, 1940 .... China (nw Tibet)
furculatum Shewell, 1952* .... Alaska, Canada, n USA
nigrum (Meigen, 1804) .... n Europe
mathiesseni (Enderlein, 1921)
? peetsi (Enderlein, 1921)
? behningi Enderlein, 1926
? opalinipenne (Enderlein, 1936)
parapusillum (Rubtsov, 1956) .... USSR (e Siberia)
patrushevae (Ivashchenko, 1978) .... USSR (European)
pseudopusillum (Rubtsov, 1956) .... USSR (Kazakhstan)
pusillum Fries, 1824 .... n Europe, USSR (Siberia,
pygmaeum Zetterstedt, 1838   FE), ? n Canada
arcticum (Enderlein, 1936)
(preocc.)
fridolini Rubtsov, 1940
roevdeae Smart, 1944
rangiferinum (Rubtsov, 1956) .... USSR (European, Siberia,
                                            FE)
rubzovium (Ivashchenko, 1978) .... USSR (European)
subpusillum Rubtsov, 1940 .... Scandinavia, n USSR
transbaikalicum Rubtsov, 1940 .... USSR (Siberia)
tshernovskii (Rubtsov, 1956) .... USSR (Siberia)

Subg. SHEWELLOMYIA Peterson, 1975

HAGENOMYIA Shewell, 1959
(preocc.)

longistylatum Shewell, 1959 .... Canada, n USA

pictipes Hagen, 1880 (complex) ....   Canada, USA
   innoxium Comstock & Comstock,
   1895
   aldrichianum (Enderlein, 1936)

Subg. SIMULIUM Latreille s.str.
   ODAGMIA Enderlein, 1921
   DISCOSPHYRIA Enderlein, 1922
   GYNONYCHODON Enderlein,
   1925
   PSEUDODAGMIA Baranov, 1926
   DANUBIOSIMULIUM Baranov,
   1935
   CLEITOSIMULIUM Séguy &
   Dorier, 1936
   GNUS Rubtsov, 1940
   PHOSTERODOROS Stone &
   Snoddy, 1969
   PHORETODAGMIA Rubtsov,
   1972
   PARAGNUS Rubtsov &
   Yankovsky, 1982
   ARCHESIMULIUM Rubtsov &
   Yankovsky, 1982
   ARGENTISIMULIUM Rubtsov &
   Yankovsky, 1982
   STRIATOSIMULIUM Rubtsov &
   Yankovsky, 1982

Group 1: ARGENTEOSTRIATUM
species-group*

argenteostriatum Strobl, 1898 ....   c & s Europe, USSR
   schoenbaueri Enderlein, 1921   (Transcaucasia)
   ? *alternans* Enderlein, 1921
   rupicolum Séguy & Dorier, 1936
   simici Zivkovic, 1959
aureofulgens Terteryan, 1949 ....   USSR (Transcaucasia)
hispaniola Grenier & Bertrand, 1954 ..   s Europe
   parvifrons (Rivosecchi & Cardinali,
   1975) (ssp.)
tjanschanicum Rubtsov, 1963 ....   USSR (Kirgiziya)

Group 2: BIMACULATUM
species-group

bimaculatum (Rubtsov, 1956) ....   China, s USSR
platytarse (Yankovsky, 1977) ....   USSR (Siberia)
sexafile (Rubtsov, 1976) ....   USSR (Kazakhstan)
trilineatum (Rubtsov, 1956) ....   USSR (central Asia)

Group 3: BUKOVSKII species-group*

bukovskii Rubtsov, 1940 ....   c Europe to Caucasus
degrangei Dorier & Grenier, 1960 .....   sw Europe

sastshcheri Machavariani, 1966 ....   USSR (Transcaucasia)
vigintifile (Dinulescu, 1966) ....   Romania

Group 4: CRASSIFILUM
species-group
crassifilum Rubtsov, 1947 ....   USSR (Tadzhikistan)

Group 5: EPHEMEROPHILUM
species-group*
alajense (Rubtsov, 1972) (preocc., no
    publ. repl. name) ....   USSR (Kirgiziya)
ephemerophilum Rubtsov, 1947 ....   n Pakistan, USSR (central
                                Asia)
jani Lewis, 1973 ....   n Pakistan
obikumbense (Rubtsov, 1972) ....   USSR (Tadzhikistan)
rashidi Lewis, 1973 ....   n Pakistan
rithrogenophilum (Konurbaev, 1984) ..   USSR (Kirgiziya)

Group 6: HUNTERI species-group*
anduzei Vargas & Díaz Nájera, 1948 ..   Mexico
bustosi Vargas, Martínez Palacios &
    Díaz Nájera, 1946 ....   Mexico
costalimai Vargas, Martínez Palacios &
    Díaz Nájera, 1946 ....   Mexico
covagarciai Ramírez-Pérez, Yarzábal,
    Takaoka, Tada & Ramírez, 1984 ....   Venezuela
hechti Vargas, Martínez Palacios &
    Díaz Nájera, 1946 ....   Mexico
hunteri Malloch, 1914 ....   Alaska to wc & sw USA
iriartei Vargas, Martínez Palacios &
    Díaz Nájera, 1946 ....   Mexico, USA (Arizona)
jacumbae Dyar & Shannon, 1927 ......   wc USA to Guatemala
    guatemalense de Leon, 1945
kompi Dalmat, 1951 ....   Guatemala
lassmanni Vargas, Martínez Palacios &
    Díaz Nájera, 1946 ....   Mexico, USA (Arizona)
marquezi Vargas & Díaz Nájera, 1957 .   Mexico
matteabranchium Anduze, 1947 ....   Venezuela
parrai Vargas, Martínez Palacios &
    Díaz Nájera, 1946 ....   Guatemala, Mexico
patzicianense Takaoka & Takahasi,
    1982 ....   Guatemala
piperi Dyar & Shannon, 1927 ....   w Canada, w USA
    sayi Dyar & Shannon, 1927
    knowltoni Twinn, 1938
    stonei Stains & Knowlton, 1943
ruizi Vargas & Díaz Nájera, 1948 ......   Mexico
tricorne de Leon, 1945 ....   Guatemala

Group 7: JENNINGSI species-group*
aranti Stone & Snoddy, 1969 ....   se USA
dixiense Stone & Snoddy, 1969 ....   se USA

fibrinflatum Twinn, 1936 .... e Canada, e USA
haysi Stone & Snoddy, 1969 .... se USA
jenningsi Malloch, 1914 (complex) ..... e Canada, c & e USA
    nigroparvum Twinn, 1936
jonesi Stone & Snoddy, 1969 .... se USA
lakei Snoddy, 1976 .... e USA
luggeri Nicholson & Mickel, 1950 ...... c Canada, c & e USA
notiale Stone & Snoddy, 1969 .... e USA
nyssa Stone & Snoddy, 1969 .... c & e USA
penobscotense Snoddy & Bauer, 1978 . ne USA
podostemi Snoddy, 1971 .... se USA
snowi Stone & Snoddy, 1969 .... se USA
taxodium Snoddy & Beshear, 1968 .... se USA
underhilli Stone & Snoddy, 1969 .... e USA

Group 8: MALYSCHEVI
species-group*

acrotrichum Rubtsov, 1956 .... USSR (central Asia,
                               Siberia)
arcticum Malloch, 1914 (complex) ..... w Canada, w USA
    nigresceum Knowlton & Rowe,
      1934
    brevicercum Knowlton & Rowe,
      1934
bidentatum (Shiraki, 1935) .... Japan
cholodkovskii Rubtsov, 1940 .... Mongolia, n & e USSR
corbis Twinn, 1936 .... n Holarctic reg.
    ? *murmanum* Enderlein, 1935
    relictum Rubtsov, 1940 **syn. n.**
    forsi (Carlsson, 1961) **syn. n.**
daisense (Takahasi, 1950) .... Japan
decimatum Dorogostaisky, Rubtsov &
    Vlasenko, 1935 .... Mongolia, nc to e USSR
    wagneri Rubtsov, 1940
    xerophilum (Rubtsov, 1969) (ssp.)
defoliarti Stone & Peterson, 1958 ...... w Canada, w USA
fulvipes (Ono, 1978) .... Japan
gabovae (Rubtsov, 1966) .... USSR (Komi)
hirtipannus Puri, 1932 .... ne India
howletti Puri, 1932 .... India
ibariense Zivkovic & Grenier, 1959 .... c & se Europe
    novaki Knoz, 1960
jacuticum Rubtsov, 1940 .... China (Manchuria), USSR
    halonense (Takahasi, 1940)   (e Siberia, FE)
kisoense Uemoto, Onishi & Orii, 1974 . Japan
kyushuense Takaoka, 1978 .... Japan
malyschevi Dorogostaisky, Rubtsov &
    Vlasenko, 1935 .... Alaska, w & c Canada,
    albipes (Rubtsov, 1956) (ssp.)   USSR (e Siberia, FE), n
    lucidum (Rubtsov, 1956) (ssp.)   China, Japan

nacojapi Smart, 1944 .... Japan, Korea, USSR (e
                                            Siberia)

japonicum (Shiraki, 1935) (preocc.)
nigricoxum Stone, 1952 .... Alaska, nw Canada
  simile Malloch, 1919 (preocc.)
omorii (Takahasi, 1942) .... China (Manchuria)
pavlovskii Rubtsov, 1940 .... n China, USSR (e Siberia,
                                            FE)

ishikawai Takahasi, 1940
rubroflavifemur Rubtsov, 1940 .... nw China
saccatum (Rubtsov, 1956) .... n China
subvariegatum Rubtsov, 1940 .... Mongolia, USSR (e
                                            Siberia, FE)

Group 9: MELANOPUS species-group

abatanense Takaoka, 1983 .... Philippines
acostai Takaoka, 1983 .... Philippines
aeneifacies Edwards, 1933 .... Sabah
argentipes Edwards, 1928 .... Malaya
atrum Delfinado, 1969 .... Philippines
crassimanum Edwards, 1933 .... Sabah
discrepans Delfinado, 1969 .... Philippines
fuscopilosum Edwards, 1928 .... Malaya
gatchaliani Takaoka, 1983 .... Philippines
iwahigense Takaoka, 1983 .... Philippines
laterale Edwards, 1933 .... Sabah
melanopus Edwards, 1929 .... Philippines
nigripilosum Edwards, 1933 .... Sabah
palawanense Delfinado, 1971 .... Philippines
retusum Delfinado, 1971 .... Philippines
salebrosum Takaoka, 1983 .... Philippines
simulacrum Delfinado, 1969 .... Philippines
subatrum Takaoka, 1983 .... Philippines
suplidoi Takaoka, 1983 .... Philippines
taalense Takaoka, 1983 .... Philippines
tomentosum Delfinado, 1969 .... Philippines

Group 10: METALLICUM
species-group

horacioi Okazawa & Onishi, 1980 ...... Guatemala
jobbinsi Vargas, Martínez Palacios &
  Díaz Nájera, 1946 .... Guatemala, Mexico
metallicum Bellardi, 1859 (complex) ... Mexico to n South
  riveti Roubaud, 1906   America, Trinidad
  nitidum Malloch, 1912
  avidum Hoffmann, 1930
morae Ramírez-Pérez, Rassi &
  Ramírez, 1977 .... Venezuela
puigi Vargas, Martínez Palacios & Díaz
  Nájera, 1945 .... Mexico

racenisi Ramírez-Pérez, 1971 .... Venezuela
spilmani Stone, 1969 .... Dominica
tescorum Stone & Boreham, 1965 ...... sw USA

Group 11: MULTISTRIATUM
species-group*

ambiguum Shiraki, 1935 .... Japan
argyrocinctum de Meijere, 1913 .... Java, Sumatra
barraudi Puri, 1932 .... n India
chiangmaiense Takaoka & Suzuki, 1984 . Thailand
consimile Puri, 1932 .... n India, Pakistan
dentatum Puri, 1932 .... n India
digitatum Puri, 1932 .... n India
eximium de Meijere, 1913 .... Java
fenestratum Edwards, 1934 .... Sumatra
griseifrons Brunetti, 1911 .... India, Malaya, Thailand
    digrammicum Edwards, 1928
grisescens Brunetti, 1911 .... India, Japan, Korea,
    longiunguis (Enderlein, 1936)   Thailand
hirtinervis Edwards, 1928 .... Malaya
horokaense Ono, 1980 .... Japan
japonicum Matsumura, 1931 .... Japan
    annulipes Shiraki, 1935 (preocc.)
kapuri Datta, 1975 .... ne India
katoi Shiraki, 1935 .... Taiwan
kawamurae Matsumura, 1921 .... Japan
konakovi Rubtsov, 1956 .... USSR (Kurile Is.)
kurilense Rubtsov, 1956 .... Japan, USSR (Kurile Is.,
    Sakhalin)
lineothorax Puri, 1932 .... India
multistriatum Rubtsov, 1947 .... USSR (central Asia)
nakhonense Takaoka & Suzuki, 1984 .. Thailand
novolineatum Puri, 1933 .... India
    lineatum Puri, 1932 (preocc.)
oshimanum Shiraki, 1935 .... Ryukyu Is.
pallidum Puri, 1932 .... n India
palmatum Puri, 1932 .... India
quinquestriatum (Shiraki, 1935) .... Japan, Korea, Thailand
sakishimaense Takaoka, 1977 .... Japan, Taiwan, Thailand
striatum Brunetti, 1912 .... India, Sri Lanka
    latistriatum Senior-White, 1922
subornatoide Rubtsov, 1947 .... USSR (central Asia)
thailandicum Takaoka & Suzuki, 1984 . Thailand
thienemanni Edwards, 1934 .... Java
ufengense Takaoka, 1979 .... Taiwan
xanthogastrum Rubtsov, 1951 .... USSR (central Asia)

Group 12: NOBILE species-group*

baltazarae Delfinado, 1962 .... Philippines
benquetense Takaoka, 1983 .... Philippines
cotabatoense Takaoka, 1983 .... Philippines
delfinadoae Takaoka, 1983 .... Philippines

iridescens de Meijere, 1913 .... Java, Sumatra
latistylum Takaoka, 1983 .... Philippines
leytense Takaoka, 1983 .... Philippines
nebulicola Edwards, 1934 .... Java
nobile de Meijere, 1907 .... Indonesia, Malaysia,
    kiuliense Smart & Clifford, 1969   Philippines
nodosum Puri, 1933 .... India, Thailand
shirakii Kono & Takahasi, 1940 .... Taiwan
    minutum Shiraki, 1935 (preocc.)

Group 13: NOELLERI species-group*

decorum Walker, 1848 (complex) ...... North America
    piscicidium Riley, 1870
    katmai Dyar & Shannon, 1927
    ottawaense Twinn, 1936
nikkoense Shiraki, 1935 .... Japan
noelleri Friederichs, 1920 .... n & c Eurasia
    subornatum Edwards, 1920
    tenuimanus Enderlein, 1921
    septentrionale Enderlein, 1935
    lindneri (Enderlein, 1943)*
    avidum Rubtsov, 1963 (unav. &
      preocc.)
    triangulare (Rubtsov, 1963) (ssp.)
    bonomii Rubtsov, 1964 (unav.)
palustre Rubtsov, 1956 .... USSR (Siberia, FE)
parargyreatum Rubtsov, 1979 .... USSR (Tadzhikistan)
vershininae Yankovsky, 1979 .... USSR (Siberia)
yokotense Shiraki, 1935 .... Japan

Group 14: ORNATUM species-group*

adventicium Datta, 1985 .... n India
baracorne Smart, 1944 .... e Europe
    ruficorne (Baranov, 1926) (preocc.)
    primum (Baranov, 1926) (preocc.)
    secundum (Baranov, 1926)
      (preocc.)
    ponticum (Rubtsov, 1956)
    acutiphallus (Rubtsov, 1963)
bronchiale (Rubtsov, 1962) .... USSR (European)
caucasicum Rubtsov, 1940 .... Iran, sw USSR, Turkey
    sevanense Rubtsov & Terteryan,
      1952 (ssp.)
    cisalpinum (Rubtsov, 1956) (ssp.)
    longicaulis (Rubtsov, 1956) (ssp.)
    abacum (Rubtsov, 1963) (unav.)
    minutistyli (Rubtsov, 1963) (unav.)
    maculitibia (Rubtsov, 1963) (unav.)
croaticum (Baranov, 1937) .... Yugoslavia
    decoloratum (Baranov, 1937)
    nigrinum (Baranov, 1937)

deserticola Rubtsov, 1940 .... Mongolia, USSR (central Asia)

egregium Séguy, 1930* .... Morocco

ferganicum Rubtsov, 1940 .... USSR (central Asia)

flaveolum Rubtsov, 1940 .... USSR (central Asia, Altay)

fontanum Terteryan, 1952 .... e Europe

frigidum Rubtsov, 1940 .... USSR (central Asia)

fuscum (Rubtsov, 1963) .... USSR (European)

intermedium Roubaud, 1906* .... w Palaearctic reg.
  nitidifrons Edwards, 1920 **syn. n.**
  ? specularifrons (Enderlein, 1921)
  h-nigrum (Santos Abreu, 1922)*
    syn. n.
  insolitum (Santos Abreu, 1922)
    syn. n.
  maderense (Carlsson, 1963) **syn. n.**
  flavitibia (Rivosecchi, 1966) (ssp.)

iwatense (Shiraki, 1935) .... Japan

kanchaveli (Machavariani, 1966) .... USSR (Transcaucasia)

kiritshenkoi Rubtsov, 1940 .... n Iran, USSR (Transcaucasia)

mesasiaticum Rubtsov, 1947 .... USSR (central Asia)

ornatum Meigen, 1818 (complex) ...... Europe, n Asia
  fasciatum Meigen, 1830
  crassitarse Macquart, 1834
  tibiale Macquart, 1834
  ? pratorum Friederichs, 1920
  konsuloffi (Enderlein, 1924)
  simoffi (Enderlein, 1924)
  primum (Baranov, 1926) (preocc.)
  secundum (Baranov, 1926)
    (preocc.)
  babici (Baranov, 1937)
  borcici (Baranov, 1937)
  bartulici (Baranov, 1937)
  guelminoi (Baranov, 1937)
  nikolici (Baranov, 1937)
  anderliceki (Baranov, 1937)
  zagrebiense (Baranov, 1937)
  barense (Baranov, 1939)
  arensae Rubtsov, 1940
  oblimatum (Odintsov, 1961)
  amnis (Rubtsov, 1962) (ssp.)
  albatum (Rubtsov, 1962) (ssp.)
  hibernale (Rubtsov, 1962) (unav.)
  brevicorne (Rubtsov, 1962) (unav.)
  curvifila (Rivosecchi, 1963) (unav.)
  albifrons (Rubtsov, 1964) (unav.)
  apenninicum (Rivosecchi, 1966)
    (ssp.)

pontinum Rivosecchi, 1960 .... Italy
rotundatum (Rubtsov, 1956) .... e Europe
savici (Baranov, 1937)* .... Yugoslavia
    tenuitarsus (Baranov, 1937)
      (preocc.) **syn. n.**
    baranovi Smart, 1944
septentrionale (Tan & Chow, 1976)
    (preocc., no publ. repl. name) ...... China
trifasciatum Curtis, 1839* .... Europe
    ? angustimanus (Enderlein, 1921)
    ? wilhelmianum (Enderlein, 1921)
    ? nigriperna (Enderlein, 1922)
    ? odagmiina (Enderlein, 1922)
    spinosum Doby & Deblock, 1957
      syn. n.

Group 15: REPTANS species-group*

banaticum Dinulescu, 1966 .... Romania
colombaschense (Fabricius, 1787) .... se Europe
    ? lanio (Linnaeus, 1771)
    columbaczense (Schoenbauer,
      1795)
    flaviventre Strobl, 1898
    violaceum Enderlein, 1922
    profundale Baranov, 1937
    litorale Baranov, 1937
    intermedium (Baranov, 1939)
      (preocc.)
flavicans Rubtsov, 1956 .... USSR (central Asia)
flavidum Rubtsov, 1947 .... USSR (central Asia,
                       Tuva)

flavigaster Rubtsov, 1969 .... Mongolia
kurense Rubtsov & Dzhafarov, 1951 .. USSR (Transcaucasia)
    shachbuzicum Dzhafarov, 1960
latitarsus Rubtsov, 1971 .... Mongolia
liriense Rivosecchi, 1961 .... Italy
nanum Zetterstedt, 1838 .... Scandinavia
parvum Enderlein, 1921 .... "Europe"
pulchripes Austen, 1925 .... European Turkey
remotum Rubtsov, 1956 .... n China
reptans (Linnaeus, 1758) .... Europe
    niger (Linnaeus, 1746) (no status,
      pre-1758)
    argyropeza (Meigen, 1804)
    varipes (Meigen, 1818) (unav.)
    elegans Meigen, 1818
    cinctum Meigen, 1830
    pictum Meigen, 1838
    galeratum Edwards, 1920
    ? latimanus Enderlein, 1921
    heidenreichi Enderlein, 1921

? heringi Enderlein, 1925
ornatoide Baranov, 1926
calopum Baranov, 1926
pseudocolumbaczense Baranov,
    1937
tumanicum Baranov, 1937
vardaricum Baranov, 1937
pukovacense Baranov, 1937
glumovoense Baranov, 1937
agnatum Baranov, 1937 **syn. n.***
reptantoide Carlsson, 1962
? knechteli Dinulescu, 1966
rheophilum Tan & Chow, 1976
    (preocc., no publ. repl. name) .... China
tarnogradskii Rubtsov, 1940 .... USSR (Caucasus)
voilense Sherban, 1960 .... Balkans, Italy
zetterstedti Carlsson, 1962 .... Scandinavia

Group 16: TUBEROSUM
species-group*

angustifilum Rubtsov, 1947 .... USSR (Tadzhikistan)
arisanum Shiraki, 1935 .... Taiwan
corpulentum Rubtsov, 1956 .... USSR (European)
gusevi Rubtsov, 1976 .... USSR (European)
jugatum Boldarueva, 1979 .... USSR (e Siberia)
nigrifacies Datta, 1974 .... n India
nitidithorax Puri, 1932 .... n India, Thailand
parnassum Malloch, 1914 .... e Canada, e USA
    hydationis Dyar & Shannon, 1927
petersoni Stone & DeFoliart, 1959 ..... w USA
polare Rubtsov, 1940 .... USSR (European, Siberia)
puliense Takaoka, 1979 .... Taiwan
pullus Rubtsov, 1956 .... USSR (central Asia, s
    Siberia)
quasifrenum Delfinado, 1971 .... Philippines
ramosum Puri, 1932 .... n India
rufibasis Brunetti, 1911 .... Pakistan, Oriental reg.
    fasciatum Puri, 1932 (preocc.)
sabahense Smart & Clifford, 1969 ...... Sabah, Sarawak
splendidum Rubtsov, 1940 .... n & e USSR
subtile Rubtsov, 1956 .... e Europe, Transcaucasia
suzukii Rubtsov, 1963 .... Japan, Korea, Ryukyu Is.,
    ryukyuense Ogata, 1966   Taiwan
tuberosum (Lundström, 1911)
    (complex) .... n Holarctic reg.
        ? janzeni Enderlein, 1922
        perissum Dyar & Shannon, 1927
        vandalicum Dyar & Shannon,
            1927
        turmale Twinn, 1938
        twinni Stains & Knowlton, 1940

tumulosum Rubtsov, 1956 .... USSR (Siberia, FE)
vulgare Dorogostaisky, Rubtsov &
    Vlasenko, 1935 .... USSR (European to FE)

Group 17: VARIEGATUM
species-group*

aokii (Takahasi, 1941) .... Japan
argyreatum Meigen, 1838 .... Europe
    obreptans Edwards, 1920
    ? montanum Enderlein, 1921
      (preocc.)
    ? mehelyi Enderlein, 1926
    polae Smart, 1944
    celticum Doby & Rault, 1960
    rheophilum (Knoz, 1961)
    daviesi (Rubtsov, 1964) (unav.)
    petrophilum (Rubtsov, 1964)
      (unav.)
    edwardsi (Rubtsov, 1964) (unav.)
    stenostylum (Rubtsov & Carlsson,
      1965)
barnesi Takaoka & Suzuki, 1984 .... Thailand
chamlongi Takaoka & Suzuki, 1984 .... Thailand
christophersi Puri, 1932 .... n India
debacli Terteryan, 1952 .... USSR (Transcaucasia)
exile (Rubtsov, 1956) .... e Europe
gribae (Rubtsov, 1956) .... USSR (Tadzhikistan)
gurneyae Senior-White, 1922 .... c & s India
hackeri Edwards, 1929 .... Malaya, Thailand
himalayense Puri, 1932 .... n India
humerosum Rubtsov, 1947 .... USSR (Tadzhikistan)
maximum (Knoz, 1961) .... c & se Europe
monticola Friederichs, 1920 .... c & s Europe
    dorieri Doby & David, 1960
    sicanum (Rivosecchi, 1963) (ssp.)
monticoloide (Rubtsov, 1956) .... USSR (Caucasus)
niha Giudicelli & Dia, 1986 .... Lebanon
nilgiricum Puri, 1932 .... India, Sri Lanka
oitanum (Shiraki, 1935) .... Japan
schamili (Rubtsov, 1964) .... USSR (s European)
stenophallum Terteryan, 1952 .... USSR (Transcaucasia)
taiwanicum Takaoka, 1979 .... Taiwan
variegatum Meigen, 1818 .... Europe, Transcaucasia
    varium Meigen, 1818
    luteicorne Stephens, 1829 (*nom.*
      nud.)
    affine Stephens, 1829 (*nom. nud.*)
    rivulare Planchon, 1844
    veneficum Friederichs, 1920
    ? bulgaricum (Enderlein, 1921)
    vernale (Rubtsov, 1956) (ssp.)

autumnale (Rubtsov, 1956) (ssp.)
padanum (Rubtsov, 1964) (unav.)
slovakense (Rubtsov, 1964) (unav.)
pseudovernale (Rubtsov, 1964)
　　(unav.)
xanthinum Edwards, 1933 ....　sw Palaearctic reg.
　? *gaudi* Grenier & Faure, 1957*

Group 18: VENUSTUM species-group

abbreviatum Rubtsov, 1957 ....　"Europe" (? c Asia)
aemulum Rubtsov, 1940 ....　USSR (Siberia, FE)
　submorsitans Rubtsov, 1940
　　(preocc.)
arakawae Matsumura, 1921 ....　Japan
　nipponense Shiraki, 1935
bergi Rubtsov, 1956 ....　USSR (Transcaucasia)
curvistylus Rubtsov, 1957 ....　ne Europe
curvitarse Rubtsov, 1940 ....　ne China, USSR (FE)
hibernale Rubtsov, 1967 ....　USSR (European)
kamtshaticum Rubtsov, 1940 ....　USSR (Kamchatka)
latilobus Rubtsov, 1973 ....　USSR (e Siberia)
longipalpe Beltyukova, 1955 ....　USSR (w Siberia, FE)
morsitans Edwards, 1915 ....　Europe
　? *wilhelmii* Enderlein, 1922
　? *gerstaeckeri* Enderlein, 1936
paramorsitans Rubtsov, 1956 ....　Europe, n USSR
　paelignum Rivosecchi, 1966 (ssp.)
pitense Carlsson, 1962 ....　Scandinavia
posticatum Meigen, 1838 ....　nw Europe
　austeni Edwards, 1915
　? *pseudoreptans* Enderlein, 1935
promorsitans Rubtsov, 1956 ....　nc USSR
rezvoi Rubtsov, 1956 ....　USSR (Kazakhstan)
rivosecchii Rubtsov, 1964 ....　Italy
rostratum (Lundström, 1911) ....　n Europe & n North
　　　　　　　　　　　　　　　　　　　　America, Greenland

　groenlandicum Enderlein, 1935
　　syn. n.
　sublacustre Davies, 1966
rubtzovi Smart, 1945 ....　Alaska, USSR (n
　simile Rubtsov, 1940 (preocc.)　　　　European, Siberia)
shevtshenkovae Rubtsov, 1965 ....　USSR (European)
　venustoide Rubtsov, 1963 (preocc.)
simulans Rubtsov, 1956 ....　USSR (European,
　　　　　　　　　　　　　　　　　　　　Kazakhstan)
tobetsuense Ono, 1977 ....　Japan
truncatum (Lundström, 1911) ....　n Europe, n & e USSR,
　　　　　　　　　　　　　　　　　　　　Canada, ne USA

venustum Say, 1823 (complex) ....　North America, USSR
　molestum Harris, 1841　　　　　　　　(FE), ? Japan
　minutum Lugger, 1897

irritatum Lugger, 1897
rileyanum (Enderlein, 1922)
verecundum Stone & Jamnback, 1955* .   North America

Ungrouped species of *SIMULIUM*
s.str.

biforaminiferum Datta, 1974	n India
canlaonense Delfinado, 1969	Philippines
forcipatum Delfinado, 1969	Philippines
gravelyi Puri, 1933	s India
karenkoense (Shiraki, 1935)	Taiwan
kinabaluense Smart & Clifford, 1969	Sabah
mongolicum (Rubtsov, 1969)	Mongolia
nishijimai (Ono, 1978)	Japan
palniense Puri, 1933	s India
singtamense Datta & Pal, 1975	n India
tarbagataicum (Rubtsov, 1967)	USSR (Buryatskaya)
tenuitarsus Puri, 1933	n India

Subg. TETISIMULIUM Rubtsov, 1963*

FRIESIA Enderlein, 1922 (preocc.)

alajense Rubtsov, 1938   USSR (central Asia,
   sbergi Rubtsov, 1940   Transcaucasia)
   hiemale (Rubtsov, 1956) (ssp.)
bezzii (Corti, 1914)   s Palaearctic reg.
   delphinense Villeneuve, 1918
   tristrigatum (Enderlein, 1921)
   ? obscurum (Enderlein, 1924)
   kondici (Baranov, 1926)
   atlas Séguy, 1930
   crinitum (Rubtsov, 1956)
   ? gorjense (Dinulescu, 1966)
   ? graium (Couvert, 1967)
coarctatum Rubtsov, 1940   n China, USSR (central
                       Asia)
desertorum Rubtsov, 1938   China, USSR (central
                       Asia)
kerisorum (Rubtsov, 1956)   USSR (Transcaucasia)
kozlovi Rubtsov, 1940   "Tibet" (?), sw USSR
latimentum (Rubtsov, 1956)   USSR (central Asia, w
                       Siberia)
stevensoni Edwards, 1927   n Pakistan

Subg. TRICHODAGMIA Enderlein, 1934

THYRSOPELMA Enderlein, 1934
GRENIERELLA Vargas & Díaz
   Nájera, 1951*

chalcocoma Knab, 1914   Bolivia, Peru
   latitarse (Enderlein, 1934)
guianense Wise, 1911   n South America
huairayacu Wygodzinsky, 1953   Argentina

itaunense d'Andretta & Dolores
  Gonzalez, 1964 .... Brazil
lahillei (Paterson & Shannon, 1927) ... Argentina
nigrimanum Macquart, 1838 .... Brazil, Paraguay
  pruinosum Lutz, 1910
orbitale Lutz, 1910 .... South America
  brasiliense (Enderlein, 1934)
pintoi d'Andretta & d'Andretta, 1945 . n South America
  ortizi Ramírez-Pérez, 1971

Subg. WALLACELLUM Takaoka, 1983

cabrerai Takaoka, 1983 .... Philippines
carinatum Delfinado, 1969 .... Philippines
makilingense Takaoka, 1983 .... Philippines
ogonukii Takaoka, 1983 .... Philippines
recurvum Takaoka, 1983 .... Philippines
resimum Takaoka, 1983 .... Philippines
spinosibranchium Takaoka, 1983 .... Philippines
tuyense Takaoka, 1983 .... Philippines
yonakuniense Takaoka, 1972 .... Ryukyu Is., Taiwan

Subg. WILHELMIA Enderlein, 1921*

angustifurca (Rubtsov, 1956) .... USSR (Ciscaucasia)
balcanicum (Enderlein, 1924) .... se Europe
  secundum (Baranov, 1926)
  danubiense Zivkovic, 1955
  severinense (Dinulescu, 1966) (ssp.)
bravermani Beaucournu-Saguez,
  1986 .... Israel
dahestanicum (Rubtsov, 1962) .... USSR (Dagestan,
                                            Transcaucasia)
equinum (Linnaeus, 1758) .... Palaearctic reg.
  ater (Linnaeus, 1746) (no status,
    pre-1758)
  marginatum Meigen, 1818
  cinereum Macquart, 1834
  pubescens Macquart, 1834
  canum Meigen, 1838
  dahlgrueni (Enderlein, 1921)
  orichalcea (Enderlein, 1922)
  begbunaricum Baranov, 1924
  secundum (Baranov, 1926) (preocc.)
  tertium (Baranov, 1926)
  brunettii (Enderlein, 1934)
  ivashentzovi Rubtsov, 1940 (ssp.)
  bianchii Rubtsov, 1940
  avetjanae (Rubtsov & Terteryan, 1952)
  zetlandense Davies, 1966 **syn. n.**
golani Beaucournu-Saguez, Braverman
  & Tsafrir, 1977 .... Syria
lama Rubtsov, 1940 .... China, Mongolia

lineatum (Meigen, 1804) ....   Europe, USSR
   falcula (Enderlein, 1921)   (Transcaucasia,
   ? annulitibia (Enderlein, 1922)   central Asia)
   salopiense Edwards, 1927
   nigrifacies (Rivosecchi, 1964)
     (*nom. nud.*)
paraequinum Puri, 1933 ....   se Europe, sw Asia
   transcaucasicum (Rubtsov, 1956)
pseudequinum Séguy, 1921 ....   s Palaearctic reg.
   canariense Séguy, 1921
   brnizense Baranov, 1924
   mediterraneum Puri, 1925
   stylatum (Baranov, 1926)
   primum (Baranov, 1926) (*equinum*
     f.)
   primum (Baranov, 1926) (*stylatum*
     f., preocc.)
   quartum (Baranov, 1926)
   barbaricum Séguy, 1930
   sulfuricola (Rivosecchi, 1972) (ssp.)
   fluminicola (Rivosecchi, 1972)
     (ssp.)
   cineirifacies (Rivosecchi, 1964)
     (*nom. nud.*)
quadrifila Grenier, Faure & Laurent,
   1957 ....   Iberia, North Africa
sangrense (Rivosecchi, 1967) ....   Italy
sergenti Edwards, 1923 ....   Iberia, North Africa
   ariasi Séguy, 1925 **syn. n.**
takahasii (Rubtsov, 1962) ....   Japan
talassicum (Yankovsky, 1984) ....   USSR (Kirgiziya)
turgaicum Rubtsov, 1940 ....   sc Asia (Transcaucasia,
     Iran to n China)

veltistshevi Rubstov, 1940 ....   e Europe to central Asia

Subg. XENOSIMULIUM Crosskey, 1969

   ambositrae Grenier & Grjebine, 1959 .   Madagascar
   griveaudi Ovazza & Ovazza, 1970 ......   Madagascar
   imerinae Roubaud, 1905 ....   Comoro Is., Madagascar
   iphias de Meillon, 1951 ....   Madagascar
   neireti Roubaud, 1905 ....   Madagascar

Subgenerically Unassigned Species

   acarayense Coscarón & Wygodzinsky,
     1972* ....   Argentina, Paraguay
   albopictum Lane & Porto, 1940 ....   Brazil
   argentatum (Enderlein, 1936) ....   Peru
   benjamini Dalmat, 1952 ....   Guatemala
   blancasi Wygodzinsky & Coscarón,
     1970* ....   Peru
   botulibranchium Lutz, 1910 ....   Argentina, Brazil

chilianum Rondani, 1863 .... Chile
clarki Fairchild, 1940 .... Panama, Venezuela
costaricense Smart, 1944 .... n Neotropical reg.
    rufidorsum (Enderlein, 1936)
      (preocc.)
    costarricense Vargas, 1945
diaznajerai Vargas, 1943 .... Mexico
    tenuifrons (Enderlein, 1936)
      (preocc.)
ecuadoriense (Enderlein, 1934) .... Ecuador
falculatum (Enderlein, 1929) .... Mexico
    coffeae Vargas, 1945
flavipictum Knab, 1914 .... Peru
ganalesense Vargas, Martínez Palacios
    & Díaz Nájera, 1946 .... Mexico
goeldii Cerqueira & Nunes de Mello,
    1967 .... Brazil, Venezuela
    scorzai Ramírez-Pérez, 1980
guerreroi Ramírez-Pérez, 1971 .... Venezuela
hirtipupa Lutz, 1910 .... Brazil
hoffmanni Vargas, 1943 .... Peru
    angustitarse (Enderlein, 1934)
      (preocc.)
iguazuense Coscarón, 1976 .... Argentina
incertum Lutz, 1910 .... Brazil
laticalx (Enderlein, 1934) .... Peru
latidigitus (Enderlein, 1936) .... Colombia
lurybayae Smart, 1944 .... Bolivia
    angustifrons (Enderlein, 1934)
      (preocc.)
lutzi Knab, 1913 .... Brazil
    exiguum Lutz, 1909 (preocc.)
    minutum Surcouf &
      Gonzalez-Rincones, 1911
      (preocc.)
    lutzi Malloch, 1914
macca (Enderlein, 1934) .... Peru, Venezuela
magnum Lane & Porto, 1940 .... Brazil
mutucuna Nunes de Mello & Vieira da
    Silva, 1974 .... Brazil
nigrifemur (Enderlein, 1936) .... Chile
noguerai d'Andretta & Dolores
    Gonzalez, 1964 .... Brazil
obesum Vulcano, 1959 .... Brazil
oviedoi Ramírez-Pérez, 1971 .... Venezuela
papaveroi Coscarón, 1982* .... Brazil
paranense Schrottky, 1909 .... Paraguay
penai Wygodzinsky & Coscarón, 1970* . Chile
petropoliense Cocarón, 1981 .... Brazil
philippianum Pinto, 1932 .... Chile
    tarsatum Philippi, 1865 (preocc.)

putre Coscarón & Matta, 1982 .... Chile
quadristrigatum Enderlein, 1934 .... Brazil
rappae Py-Daniel & Coscarón, 1982 ... Brazil
rivasi Ramírez-Pérez, 1971 (*ribai, rivai*) . Venezuela
scutellatum Lane & Porto, 1940 .... South America
souzalopesi Coscarón, 1981 .... Brazil
spadicidorsum (Enderlein, 1934) .... Brazil
strigatum (Enderlein, 1934) .... Peru
striginotum (Enderlein, 1934) .... Bolivia
subpallidum Lutz, 1910* .... Argentina, Brazil
    subviride Lutz & Machado, 1915
      (*nom. nud.*)
    guarani Coscarón & Wygodzinsky,
      1972
tallaferroae Ramírez-Pérez, 1971 .... Venezuela
tarsale Williston, 1896 .... West Indies
    clavipes Malloch, 1914
tarsatum Macquart, 1846 .... Colombia
tenuipes Knab, 1914* .... Chile
townsendi Malloch, 1912 .... Peru
urubambanum Enderlein, 1934 .... Peru
varians Lutz, 1909 .... Brazil
versicolor Lutz & Nunes Tovar, 1928 . Venezuela
violacescens Enderlein, 1934 .... Colombia, Mexico,
      Venezuela

Nomina Dubia (*SIMULIUM* s.l.)

    [**affine** Meunier, 1907] .... [Baltic amber]
      [*meunieri* Smart, 1944]
    canescens Brème, 1842 .... Switzerland
    [**cerberus** (Enderlein, 1921)] .... [Baltic amber]
    hematophilum Laboulbène, 1882 .... Canada (Newfoundland)
    humerale Zetterstedt, 1855 .... Sweden
    [**importunum** Meunier, 1907] .... [Baltic amber]
    incanum Loew, 1840 .... Poland
    lividum (Schellenberg, 1803) .... Switzerland
    ochrescentipes Enderlein, 1921 .... USSR (Turkmenistan)
    [**oligocenicum** Rubtsov, 1936] .... [Baltic amber]
    [**pulchellum** Meunier, 1907] .... [Baltic amber]
    sanguinarium (Pallas, 1771) .... USSR (Volga)
    sericeum (Linnaeus, 1767) .... Sweden
    varicolor Séguy, 1925 .... France

Nomina Nuda (unplaceable)

    anomalum Eversmann, 1834
    calceatum Harris, 1835

EXPLANATORY NOTES ON CHECKLIST ENTRIES

Entries in the following list of annotations relate to those names marked by asterisks in the foregoing checklist. Names are listed alphabetically, but they are numbered to facilitate reference to them by later authors; they are printed uniformly in italic type, irrespective of any availability or validity considerations that may apply to them. Titles of articles are omitted from cited literature to condense the text. The *International Code of Zoological Nomenclature* (1985 edition) is abbreviated to Code.

1. *acarayense* Coscarón & Wygodzinsky. Coscarón (1982, Revista de la Sociedad Entomológica Argentina 41:65–67) associates this species, *papaveroi* Coscarón, and *subpallidum* Lutz to form the *subpallidum* species group but does not assign the group to a subgenus.

2. *aculeatum*-group. The name *Urosimulium* Contini validly applies to this group when it is ranked as a subgenus or genus. Rothfels (1979, Annual Review of Entomology 24:515) thinks it possible that *Urosimulium stefanii* Contini (synonymous with *aculeatum*) belongs cytologically in the *hirtipes* group.

3. *agnatum* Baranov. The female holotype (only specimen apart from a female paratype) has been examined. Preparation of the terminalia confirms the position of *agnatum* in the *reptans*-group: I see no difference from *reptans* and synonymize *agnatum* therewith.

4. *Ahaimophaga* Chubareva & Rubtsov. This nominal genus-group taxon is subsumed in *Helodon*, in accord with the opinion of Rothfels (1979, Annual Review of Entomology 24:513–514) that its species do not warrant their exclusion from *Helodon* on cytological grounds.

5. *annulum*-group. The name *Boreosimulium* Rubtsov & Yankovsky validly applies to this group when it is ranked as a subgenus or genus.

6. *argenteostriatum*-group. The name *Cleitosimulium* Séguy & Dorier validly applies to this group when it is ranked as a subgenus or genus.

7. *Austrosimulium* Tonnoir s.str. Dumbleton (1973, New Zealand Journal of Science 15 [1972]:494) recognized three species groups in this subgenus; they are not used for checklist purposes.

8. *blancasi* Wygodzinsky & Coscarón. Wygodzinsky & Coscarón (1970, American Museum Novitates 2433:2–4) associate this species, *penai* Wygodzinsky & Coscarón, and *tenuipes* Knab to form the *blancasi* species group but do not assign the group to a subgenus.

9. *bracteatum* Coquillett. This North American name has been in synonymy with *aureum* Fries, but the latter is misidentified from the New World; the name *bracteatum* is recalled from synonymy, as it is certainly applicable to one of the Nearctic *aureum*-group siblings (probably to sibling "A").

10. *bukovskii*-group. The name *Paragnus* Rubtsov & Yankovsky validly applies to this group when it is ranked as a subgenus or genus.

11. *buxtoni* Austen. This is the correct name, although originally applied to a variety, for the species *bipunctatum* Austen and comes into use for this species because *Simulium bipunctatum* Austen is a junior primary homonym of *bipunctatum* Malloch. The name *irakae,* proposed by Smart (1944, Proceedings of the Royal Entomological Society of London [B] 13:134), is an unnecessary replacement name and is invalid.

12. *Cerqueirellum* Py-Daniel. This recently described subgenus is accepted as valid for checklist purposes but closely resembles *Psaroniocompsa* and may not be fully warranted.

13. *corbis* Twinn. This North American nominal species occurs widely in northern Eurasia, where it has been misidentified as *S. rostratum.*

14. *Coscaroniellum* Py-Daniel. Comment as for *Cerqueirellum* q.v.

15. *Crosskeyellum* Grenier & Bailly-Choumara. The paper of Grenier & Bailly-Choumara (1970, Cahiers ORSTOM, Entomologie médicale et Parasitologie 8:95–105), in which *Crosskeyellum* was proposed as a subgenus for *Simulium gracilipes* Edwards, has been overlooked by Rubtsov & Yankovsky (1984, Opredeliteli po Faune SSSR 142:1–175) and is omitted from their bibliography. They assign *gracilipes* to *Schoenbaueria* in error.

16. *Dexomyia* Crosskey. This subgenus is retained as valid for checklist purposes but is only doubtfully warranted from a phyletic viewpoint. Its one aberrant species (from Saint Helena) appears to have a *ruficorne*-group ancestry, and *Dexomyia* might better be merged with *Nevermannia*.

17. *djerdapense* Baranov. Crosskey & Peterson (1972, Bulletin of the British Museum [Natural History] [Entomology] 27:205) placed this nominal species in the *ornatum*-group (*Odagmia*) because the only specimen (holotype female) has the pleural membrane haired and the *ornatum* kind of scutal pattern. My examination of the holotype while preparing this work shows that *djerdapense* belongs to subgenus *Obuchovia* (some species of which share *ornatum*-like features); it shows no detectable difference (female terminalia examined) from *auricoma* Meigen, with which the name is synonymized in the checklist.

18. *donovani* Vargas. This Mexican name has been in synonymy with *aureum* Fries, but the latter is misidentified from the Nearctic/Neotropical region; the name *donovani* is recalled from synonymy, as it applies to one of the New World *aureum*-group siblings (almost certainly sibling "G" from Mexico/southern USA).

19. *Edwardsellum* Enderlein. Elsen (1983, Revue de Zoologie Africaine 97:633) proposes three species groups in this subgenus; they are not recognized for checklist purposes. *Edwardsellum* is not, as usually supposed, exactly equivalent to the *Simulium damnosum* complex, as species morphologically quite distinct from those of this complex also belong to the subgenus.

20. *egregium* Séguy. The female holotype has been examined during checklist preparation. It has the pale ashy-gray pollinose frons of most *ornatum*-group species (i.e., it is not *intermedium*), but *egregium* is not synonymous with *ornatum* as expected (the fore tarsi are of the slender kind and not the dilated kind found in *ornatum*).

21. *ephemerophilum*-group. The name *Phoretodagmia* Rubtsov validly applies to this group when it is ranked as a subgenus or genus.

22. *feuerborni*-group. This group has been proposed by Datta (1973, Oriental insects 7:368) and is here adopted for a group of species not assignable satisfactorily to any other group.

23. *figueroa* Smart. This is an unjustified replacement name for *S. simile* Silva Figueroa 1917, mistakenly supposed by Smart (1944, Proceedings of the Royal Entomological Society of London [B] 13:133) to be preoccupied by *simile* Malloch. The latter was not described until 1919 (cited inadvertently as 1914 by Smart). The name *simile* Silva Figueroa is valid for the *Pternaspatha* species concerned (Wygodzinsky & Coscarón 1967, Bulletin of the American Museum of Natural History 136:79).

24. *furculatum* Shewell. The relationships of this species are uncertain. It is here assigned to the subgenus *Schoenbaueria* Enderlein on the advice of the Canadian specialist D. M. Wood (personal communication). Some of its characters resemble those of *Montisimulium* and the *feuerborni* and *loutetense* groups of *Nevermannia*. The phyletic affinities of *Schoenbaueria*, *Nevermannia*, and *Montisimulium* need clarification.

25. *gaudi* Grenier & Faure. This name is almost certainly a junior synonym of *xanthinum* Edwards, but further study of recently obtained material is needed to confirm this. In both nominal species the adult body color is orange-yellow, unlike other Palaearctic simuliids.

26. *giganteum* Rubtsov. This and the closely related Russian species *tsharae* Yankovsky have been placed by Rubtsov & Yankovsky (1984, Opredeliteli po Faune SSSR 142:113) in *Hemicnetha* Enderlein. Their assignments for these species are accepted for checklist purposes but appear to be inappropriate. *Hemicnetha* is a New World taxon best developed in the Neotropical region, and the descriptions and figures that have been published for *giganteum* and *tsharae* do not suggest strong affinity with it.

27. *Gomphostilbia* Enderlein. Takaoka (1983, Blackflies of the Philippines, 58–59) recognizes three species groups in this subgenus, as represented in the Philippines fauna; they are not used for checklist purposes.

28. *Grenierella* Vargas & Díaz Nájera. This subgenus of doubtful status (type species *lahillei*) is subsumed in *Trichodagmia* for checklist purposes until these understudied South American subgenera are clarified. *Grenierella* may, however, have closer affinity to *Hemicnetha* than to *Trichodagmia*.

29. *griseicolle*-group. The name *Psilocnetha* Enderlein validly applies to this group when it is ranked as a subgenus or genus distinct from *Byssodon*.

30. *groenlandicum* Enderlein. It has been known for some years that the species of *Simulium* s.str. occurring in western Greenland is *Simulium groenlandicum* Enderlein 1935, and that it is not morphologically distinct from *S. verecundum* Stone & Jamnback 1955 of North America (e.g., specimens from Greenland stand in the Canadian National Collection named as *verecundum*); it is a member of the *verecundum* sibling complex. Sibling "ACD" (e.g., Rothfels et al. 1978, Canadian Journal of Zoology 56:1110) of this complex is the only one known from Greenland, and the name *groenlandicum* is accordingly here restricted for taxonomic and nomenclatural purposes to this sibling. The same sibling "ACD" occurs widely in North America and also in northwestern Europe (including Britain); in the latter area sibling "ACD" has been known by the name *sublacustre* Davies, but both this name and *groenlandicum*, as proved by cytology and the morphology of their types, are junior synonyms of *rostratum* Lundström (*venustum*-group).

31. *h-nigrum* Santos Abreu. The one circumstance in which the Code permits a hyphen in a specific name is when the first element of the name is a single Latin letter (Article 31 [d] [iii]). The Code cites "c-album" as an example. Under Article 28 every specific name must have a lower case initial letter, and the original published orthography (with capital H) has to be altered to read *h-nigrum* and not *H-nigrum*.

This is an unusually absurd result from otherwise sensible requirements because the "H" refers to a color-pattern feature that cannot sensibly be rendered as "h".

32. *Haimophaga* Rubtsov. This nominal genus-group taxon is subsumed in *Helodon* in accord with the opinion of Chubareva (1978, Parazitologiya 12:42) and Rothfels (1979, Annual Review of Entomology 24:513–514) that the included species (*multicaulis* Popov) does not warrant its exclusion from *Helodon* on cytological grounds.

33. *hirtipes/mixtum*-group. There is no agreed classification into species groups of all the *Prosimulium* s.str. species described both from the Nearctic and the Palaearctic areas. The Holarctic species variously assigned to the *hirtipes*, *magnum*, or *mixtum* groups in the literature are combined for checklist purposes into the *hirtipes/mixtum* group.

34. *hunteri*-group. The name *Aspathia* Enderlein will apply to this group if it is ranked as a valid genus-group taxon. (*Aspathia* is not treated as valid in any current classification.)

35. *Inseliellum* Rubtsov. The three Micronesian species *guamense* Stone, *palauense* Stone, and *trukense* Stone are known only from adults and from such evidence do not clearly fit any particular group within "*Eusimulium*" s.l. They are provisionally assigned to *Inseliellum* alongside the Polynesian species, pending data from early stages and chromosomes.

36. *intermedium* Roubaud. After examination of material from a wide geographical range, I can find no convincing evidence that there is more than one morphospecies in the *ornatum*-group in which the frons of the female is shining black or brownish black (instead of being pale gray pollinose). I therefore bring together as new synonyms of *intermedium* Roubaud those *ornatum*-group names that are based on female types possessing the shiny frons character, viz. *nitidifrons* Edwards (name alluding to the shiny frons), *h-nigrum* Santos Abreu, *insolitum* Santos Abreu, and *maderense* Carlsson (types of all examined). The name *specularifrons* Enderlein (also alluding to the shiny frons) is presumed to be another synonym and is being treated by Zwick (in preparation). The proposed synonymy is not contraindicated chromosomally, at least on evidence to date, and *intermedium* is sibling "D" of the *ornatum*-group reported by Rothfels (1979, Annual Review of Entomology 24:526–527) as having been cytologically examined from Germany, Majorca, and Norway; also sibling "D" is present in Madeira (Rothfels, personal communication in litt. 24 February 1981), type locality of the synonymic name *maderense* Carlsson.

37. *jenningsi*-group. On present evidence, the name *Phosterodoros* Stone & Snoddy validly applies to this group when it is ranked as a subgenus or genus. However, it is not clear how this taxon can be satisfactorily differentiated from the *nobile*-group (q.v.).

38. *jerichoense* Smart. This is an unjustified replacement name, published (as *jerichoensis*) by Smart (1944, Proceedings of the Royal Entomological Society of London [B] 13:133) on the assumption that *flavipes* Austen 1921 is preoccupied by *flavipes* Stephens 1829. Under the present Code, the latter is an unavailable *nomen nudum* and therefore does not preoccupy *flavipes* Austen.

39. *laamii* Beaucournu-Saguez & Bailly-Choumara. This species is intermediate in its morphological characters (chromosomes unstudied) between *Helodon* and *Prosimulium* s.str. Its describers preferred not to recognize *Helodon* as a valid taxon; the species is listed in *Prosimulium* s.str. in preference to *Helodon* for checklist purposes, pending cytological assessment of the relationships.

40. *lindneri* Enderlein. This is listed as a valid species of *Argentisimulium* by Rubtsov & Yankovsky (1984, Opredeliteli po Faune SSSR 142:149), but the holotype was seen by Rubtsov and bears his identification label as "Simulium noelleri Fried." I agree with the label opinion and place *lindneri* as a synonym of *noelleri* in accordance with the earlier opinion of Rubtsov & Carlsson (1965, Acta Universitatis Lundensis [II] 18:35). (The male holotype of *lindneri* from the Naturkundemuseum, Stuttgart, was examined for the present work: it consists only of a wing and Rubtsov's mount of the dissected genitalia, but the latter confirms the identity as *noelleri*.)

41. *macropyga*-group. The name *Hellichia* Enderlein will validly apply to this group if it is at some time ranked as a subgenus or genus (*Hellichia* is not treated as valid in any current classification). Peterson (1970, Memoirs of the Entomological Society of Canada 69:1–216) refers to the same group as the "*ursinum*-group," but "*macropyga*-group" is preferred because is has more extensive usage.

42. *malyschevi*-group. The name *Gnus* Rubtsov validly applies to this group when it is ranked as a subgenus or genus. The group as here recognized subsumes the *decimatum*, *pavlovskii*, and *subvariegatum* groups of Rubstov (1962, Fliegen der palaearktischen Region 14:442–447).

43. *meridionale*-group. The name *Byssodon* Enderlein validly applies to this group when it is ranked as a subgenus or genus, and the *griseicolle*-group (q.v.) is excluded as the separate genus-group taxon *Psilocnetha*.

44. *Metomphalus* Enderlein. Crosskey (1969, Bulletin of the British Museum [Natural History] [Entomology] Supplement 14:118–119) recognized three species-groups in this subgenus; they are not used for checklist purposes.

45. *Morops* Enderlein. Crosskey (1967, Journal of Natural History 1:48–49) recognized six species groups in this subgenus; they are not used for checklist purposes.

46. *multistriatum*-group. The name *Striatosimulium* Rubtsov & Yankovsky validly applies to this group when it is ranked as a subgenus or genus. As used here, the group subsumes the *subornatoide*-group of Rubtsov (1963, Fliegen der palaearktischen Region 14:538).

47. *nigrogilvum* Summers. Takaoka & Suzuki (1984, Japanese Journal of Sanitary Zoology 35:22) consider this a valid species and have recovered the name from its old synonymy with *indicum* Becher first established by Edwards (1928, Journal of the Federated Malay States Museum 14:59). This is accepted for the checklist, but further work is needed to confirm their conclusion.

48. *nobile*-group. The name *Gynonychodon* Enderlein will apply to this group if it is ranked as a valid genus-group taxon. (*Gynonychodon* is not treated as valid in any current classification.)

49. *noelleri*-group. The name *Argentisimulium* Rubtsov & Yankovsky validly applies to this group when it is ranked as a subgenus or genus.

50. *Novaustrosimulium* Dumbleton. Dumbleton (1973, New Zealand Journal of Science 15 [1972]:494) recognized two species groups in this subgenus; these are not recognized for checklist purposes.

51. *Obuchovia* Rubtsov. Crosskey (1967, Transactions of the Royal Entomological Society of London 119:31) and Crosskey & Santos Grácio (1985, Aquatic Insects 7:155) recognize two species groups in this subgenus; they are not used for checklist purposes.

52. *ornatum*-group. The name *Odagmia* Enderlein validly applies to this group when it is ranked as a subgenus or genus. This is the most confused and difficult taxon in the European simuliid fauna, and many of the listed species have only very dubious validity. The group has been particularly confused by Baranov's lavish provision of many names proposed for "forms" that remain technically available in nomenclature and theoretically should at some time be tied to recognized sibling or semisibling species.

53. *papaveroi* Coscarón. See entry for *acarayense*.

54. *Paracnephia* Rubtsov. Crosskey (1969, Bulletin of the British Museum [Natural History] [Entomology] Supplement 14:116) recognized three species groups in this subgenus; they are not recognized for checklist purposes.

55. *penai* Wygodzinsky & Coscarón. See entry for *blancasi*.

56. *Phoretomyia* Crosskey. Crosskey (1969, Bulletin of the British Museum [Natural History] [Entomology] Supplement 14:118) recognized three species groups in this subgenus, and others have been characterized by later authors; they are not recognized for checklist purposes.

57. *pilosum* Knowlton & Rowe. This North American name has been in synonymy with *aureum* Fries, but the latter is misidentified from the Nearctic region; the name *pilosum* is recalled from synonymy, as it applies to one of the Nearctic *aureum*-group siblings (probably sibling "B" from Utah).

58. *Pomeroyellum* Rubtsov. Crosskey (1969, Bulletin of the British Museum [Natural History] [Entomology] Supplement 14:117–118) recognized five species groups in this subgenus; these are not recognized for checklist purposes.

59. *Pternaspatha* Enderlein. Wygodzinsky & Coscarón (1967, Bulletin of the American Museum of Natural History 136:53) recognized four species groups in this subgenus; they are not recognized for checklist purposes.

60. *reptans*-group. This group includes the type-species of *Simulium* (viz. *colombaschense* Fabricius of the Danube) and is the nominotypical group to which the name *Simulium* applies.

61. *ruficorne*-group. The name *Nevermannia* Enderlein validly applies to this group when it is ranked as a subgenus or genus. Rubtsov & Yankovsky (1984, Opredeliteli po Faune SSSR 142:104) wrongly use *Chelocnetha* Enderlein for the group, but this name (1935) is a junior synonym of *Nevermannia* (1921). The *ruficorne*-group has been known in Palaearctic literature as the *angustitarse*-group, but *ruficorne*-group is preferred as it has been in use longer and is based on the type-species of *Nevermannia*.

62. *rugglesi* Nicholson & Mickel. This species and *slossonae* Dyar & Shannon appear to be closely related and assignable to the same supraspecific taxon, but their affinities to other *Simulium* s.l. are

uncertain. I agree with the opinion of B. V. Peterson and D. M. Wood (personal communications) that they are provisionally best assigned to the subgenus *Parabyssodon* Rubtsov as the classification stands at present. Taxonomic revision is needed to determine how *Parabyssodon* should best be redefined following the inclusion of *rugglesi* and *slossonae*.

63. *savici* Baranov. Type examination shows that this name should not continue to be placed in synonymy with *ornatum*, as the female fore tarsi are of the very slender form instead of the conspicuously dilated form of *ornatum*. The name *tenuitarsus* Baranov (female holotype also examined while preparing this work) appears to apply to the same species but cannot be the valid name, as it is preoccupied in *Simulium*. Provisionally, and pending thorough revision of the European entities in the group, I recall *savici* from synonymy and hold it as valid with *tenuitarsus* (*baranovi* Smart, replacement name) as synonyms. The relationship to *trifasciatum* will need to be determined.

64. *sextumdecimum* Luna de Carvalho. This name was expressly proposed by Luna de Carvalho (1962, Publicações Culturais de Companhia de Diamantes de Angola 60:19) for a "form" of *Simulium alcocki* Pomeroy, but as it was published after 1960 it is infrasubspecific and unavailable under Code Article 16. The taxon to which the name *sextumdecimum* was applied (characterized by a pupal gill with 16 filaments arising from a long stalk) appears to warrant recognition as a valid species, but at present there is no available name for it. It will require description as a new species whenever the group concerned is taxonomically revised.

65. *slossonae* Dyar & Shannon. See entry for *rugglesi*.

66. *subexcisum*-group. The name *Hellichiella* Rivosecchi & Cardinali validly applies to this group when it is ranked as a subgenus or genus, and the *annulum*-group (q.v.) is excluded as the separate genus-group taxon *Boreosimulium*. Although *subexcisum* is now a junior synonym of *latipes* Meigen, the name *subexcisum*-group (Davies 1966, Transactions of the Royal Entomological Society of London 118:451) is used as the valid name in the checklist to avoid confusion with former use of "latipes"-group for what is now the *vernum*-group (q.v.), and as recommended by Crosskey & Davies (1972, Entomologist's Gazette 23:254). Code priority provisions do not apply to names of species groups and as such can be based when convenient on synonymic names.

67. *subpallidum* Lutz. See entry for *acarayense*.

68. *sudanense* Vajime & Dunbar. The validity of this name vis-à-vis *sirbanum* Vajime & Dunbar depends on critical evaluation of complex chromosomal criteria. Vajime (1984, XI International Congress of Tropical Medicine and Malaria, Calgary, Abstract Volume: 159) states that "both subsiblings [i.e., *sudanense* and *sirbanum*] are cytologically variable populations of a single taxon, *S. sirbanum*." This statement from the senior describer of *sudanense*, that *sudanense* has no specific validity distinct from *sirbanum*, is taken to imply the new synonymy of the name *sudanense* with *sirbanum* even though not explicitly so marked.

69. *syriacum* Roubaud. This name was omitted from the catalogue of Smart (1945, Transactions of the Royal Entomological Society of London 95:463–532), but it is an available name and has a type specimen (located and examined for this work). The name was published by Bezzi (1909, Broteria, Zoologica 8:38) with the heading "Simulium reptans L., var. syriacum Roub. in litt." and with a short Latin description written by Roubaud and exactly quoted by Bezzi. The name is nomenclaturally available and takes Roubaud as author (in Bezzi) under Code Article 50. (The words "other than publication" occur in the new 1985 Code version of Article 50 and were not present in the predecessor 1961 version of the Code: Roubaud therefore becomes author of *syriacum*, not Bezzi, as I stated earlier [1967, Transactions of the Royal Entomological Society of London 119:2].) One of the two female specimens mentioned by Bezzi has been found (Milan Museum) and examined: it belongs to the subgenus *Obuchovia*, to which the name *syriacum* is assigned as valid. (It might prove to be synonymous with *auricoma*, the only older name in *Obuchovia*, but this cannot be determined in the absence of other material from Syria-Lebanon and with the prevailing poor knowledge for *auricoma*.)

70. *tenuipes* Knab. See entry for *blancasi*.

71. *Tetisimulium* Rubtsov. This subgenus contains species closely allied to *Simulium* s.str., and its recognition as valid is only doubtfully warranted; it is treated as such for checklist purposes but should probably be downgraded to a species group (the *bezzii*-group) within *Simulium* s.str. for a better-balanced classification.

72. *trifasciatum* Curtis. Crosskey (1982, Entomologist's Gazette 33:208) concluded that this name is almost certainly a senior synonym of *spinosum* Doby & Deblock, but the *trifasciatum* female holotype from the National Museum of Victoria was not then available. Examination of the holotype, received on loan from Australia while preparing this work, however, fully confirms the previously suspected synonymy, and *spinosum* is treated as a new synonym of *trifasciatum*. The fore tarsus is of the slender kind

characteristic of *spinosum* and not the more strongly dilated kind occurring in *ornatum* (comparative data will be given in a later work). Hitherto the name *trifasciatum* has stood in synonymy with *ornatum* Meigen since Edwards (1915, Bulletin of Entomological Research 6:30) first placed it there, but it is restored to validity in this checklist after examination of Curtis's type-specimen; the latter bears its original, now faded but clearly legible ink label reading "Sallow June Niton," conforming exactly to the statement of Curtis (1839, British Entomology 16:765) that his description was based on a specimen caught in June on sallow at Niton (on the Isle of Wight). Both *Simulium trifasciatum* and *S. ornatum* are common on the Isle of Wight; *trifasciatum* is more closely associated with breeding sites near the chalk formations than is *ornatum* (see Crosskey 1982, Entomologists's Gazette 33:199–212), and this accords with the type local- ity, as Niton is a chalk-edge village.

73. *tsharae* Yankovsky. See entry for *giganteum*.

74. *tuberosum*-group. The name *Archesimulium* Rubtsov & Yankovsky validly applies to this group when it is ranked as a subgenus or genus.

75. *variegatum*-group. The name *Pseudodagmia* Baranov will apply to this group if it is ranked as a valid genus-group taxon. (*Pseudodagmia* is not treated as valid in any current classification.)

76. *velutinum* Santos Abreu. My revisionary studies on western Palaearctic *Eusimulium*, based on a wide geographical range of material (including many of the types), have shown that several names apply to the species that is specially common in the Mediterranean subregion (but present in northern Europe) and is characterized by lacking the sclerotized "neck" extension to the spermatheca. This species has recently been known as *latinum* Rubtsov, but the oldest available names for it are the three (see checklist) of Santos Abreu (1922, Memorias de la Real Academia de Ciencias y Artes de Barcelona 17:317, 322, 326) for which the types have been studied. As first reviser, I select *velutinum* to be the valid name of the three simultaneously published synonymic names. Detailed taxonomic findings on western Palaearctic *Eusimulium* will be presented in future papers (in preparation).

77. *verecundum* Stone & Jamnback. Cytological studies have confirmed that the morphospecies known by this name is a sibling-species complex (Rothfels et al. 1978, Canadian Journal of Zoology 56:1110). The most widespread member is sibling "ACD," to which the name *rostratum* Lundström correctly applies (see entry 30 above), but this particular sibling has never been found among extensive cytotyped collections of *verecundum* complex made throughout Pennsylvania, including Monroe County (type locality of *verecundum* as nearly as it is known). On the other hand, *verecundum* complex sibling "AA" is the most common sibling throughout Pennsylvania (P. H. Adler, personal communication). It is reasonable to infer that true *verecundum,* as represented by its adult male holotype, is most likely to be sibling "AA" and very unlikely to be sibling "ACD." The name *verecundum* is therefore not treated as a synonym of *rostratum* (sibling "ACD") in the checklist, but is listed as a valid species name applying *sensu stricto* to sibling "AA". This interpretation ensures that the well-established name *verecundum* can continue to be used as a valid name in a refined sense for a recognized sibling. See also entry for *groenlandicum.*

78. *vernum*-group. The name *Cnetha* Enderlein validly applies to this group when it is ranked as a subgenus or genus. This group has in the past been known as the *latipes*-group because of the misidentifi- cation of Meigen's *latipes* (which correctly interpreted from the holotype is a species of subgenus *Hellichi- ella*).

79. *Wilhelmia* Enderlein. Rubtsov (1962, Fliegen der palaearktischen Region 14:397–414) recognizes three species groups in this subgenus (genus *sensu* Rubtsov); they are not used for checklist purposes.

INDEX CATALOGUE OF NOMINAL GENUS-GROUP TAXA AND THEIR TYPE SPECIES

All genus-group names are listed alphabetically irrespective of whether they were originally proposed for a genus or a subgenus; original status is indicated in paren- theses after each reference to the original description. Where the original journal reference for a type species is the same as that for the proposal of the genus-group name, this is indicated by use of "ibid." in the type-species reference. Names of type species are always cited in their original binomials or (occasionally as necessary) trinomials; when the name of the type species is now a junior synonym, this is indicated by giving the oldest-known senior synonym in square brackets (in its own original combination and with its own original reference). The mode of designation or fixation cited for each type species conforms strictly to the provisions of Chapter XV (Types in the Genus Group) of the new (1985) edition of the *International Code of Zoological Nomenclature* (abbreviated as Code in the text). The International Commission on Zoological Nomenclature is abbreviated ICZN.

The gender of each genus-group name is given to help ensure that any adjectival specific name combined in a valid binomen with a particular generic name can be given its correct terminal orthography in accordance with Article 31 (b) of the Code. Anomalies concerning publication dates, availability of names, or misidentificatis of type species are mentioned in *Notes*.

The names *Atractocera* Meigen, *Melusina* Meigen, *Pseudosimulium* Handlirsch (fossil), and *Simulidium* Westwood (fossil) are omitted because they no longer apply in Simuliidae.

Acropogon Enderlein 1934, Deutsche Entomologische Zeitschrift 1933: 276 (as genus). Type species: *Acropogon barbatipes* Enderlein 1934 (ibid.: 277), by original designation. Gender: masculine.

Afrosimulium Crosskey 1969, Bulletin of the British Museum (Natural History) (Entomology) Supplement 14:30 (as genus). Type species: *Simulium gariepense* de Meillon 1953 (Journal of the Entomological Society of Southern Africa 16:227), by original designation. Gender: neuter.

Ahaimophaga Chubareva & Rubtsov in Chubareva 1978, Parazitologiya 12:42 (as genus). Type species: *Prosimulium alpestre* Dorogostaisky, Rubtsov & Vlasenko 1935 (Parazitologicheskii Sbornik 5:136), by original designation. Gender: feminine.

Notes: Rubtsov & Yankovsky (1984) cite the name *Ahaimophaga* as attributable to Rubtsov & Chubareva in Rubtsov 1977 (New and little-known species of insects of the European part of the USSR: 47), but there is no designation of a type species in that work from among six included species and the name is therefore unavailable; it takes authorship Chubareva & Rubtsov (not Rubtsov & Chubareva) and availability from the 1978 paper of Chubareva (reference above).

Anasolen Enderlein 1930, Archiv für klassifikatorische und phylogenetische Entomologie 1:94 (as genus). Type species: *Anasolen adolffriedericianus* Enderlein 1930 (ibid.: 94) [= *Simulium dentulosum* Roubaud 1915 (Bulletin de la Société Entomologique de France 1915: 294)], by original designation. Gender: masculine.

Araucnephia Wygodzinsky & Coscarón 1973, Bulletin of the American Museum of Natural History 151:165 (as genus). Type species: *Simulium montanum* Philippi 1865 (Verhandlungen der kaiserlich-königlichen zoologisch-botanischen Gesellschaft in Wien 15:633), by original designation. Gender: feminine.

Araucnephioides Wygodzinsky & Coscarón 1973, Bulletin of the American Museum of Natural History 151:179 (as genus). Type species: *Araucnephioides schlingeri* Wygodzinsky & Coscarón 1973 (ibid.: 181), by original designation. Gender: masculine.

Archesimulium Rubtsov & Yankovsky 1982, Entomologicheskoe Obozrenie 61:185 (as subgenus of *Simulium*). Type species: *Melusina tuberosa* Lundström 1911 (Acta Societatis pro Fauna et Flora Fennica 34 [12]:14), by original designation. Gender: neuter.

Archinesia Enderlein 1934, Deutsche Entomologische Zeitschrift 1933: 273 (as genus). Type species: *Simulium* (*Gigantodax*) *femineum* Edwards 1931 (Diptera of Patagonia and South Chile II [4]:135), by original designation.
Gender: feminine.

Aspathia Enderlein 1935, Sitzungsberichte der Gesellschaft naturforschender Freunde 1935: 359 (as genus). Type species: *Simulium hunteri* Malloch 1914 (Technical Series, Bureau of Entomology, U.S. Department of Agriculture 26:59), by original designation.
Gender: feminine.

Astega Enderlein 1930, Archiv für klassifikatorische und phylogenetische Entomologie 1:88 (as genus). Type species: *Cnetha lapponica* Enderlein 1921 (Sitzungsberichte der Gesellschaft naturforschender Freunde 1920: 213), by original designation.
Gender: feminine.

Astoneomyia Peterson 1977, Proceedings of the Entomological Society of Washington 79:105 (as subgenus of *Parasimulium*). Type species: *Parasimulium melanderi* Stone 1963 (Bulletin of the Brooklyn Entomological Society 58:127), by original designation.
Gender: feminine.

Austrosimulium Tonnoir 1925, Bulletin of Entomological Research 15:230 (as genus). Type species: *Simulia australensis* Schiner 1868 (Reise der österreichischen Fregatte Novara 2,1 [B]:15), by original designation.
Gender: neuter.

Boophthora Enderlein 1921, Deutsche Tierärztliche Wochenschrift 29:199 (as genus). Type species: *Simulia argyreata* Meigen sensu Enderlein [= *Tipula erythrocephala* De Geer 1776 (Mémoires pour servir à l'Histoire des Insectes 6:431)], by original designation.
Gender: feminine.
Notes: The type species was misidentified by Enderlein, and since *Boophthora* is currently treated as a valid generic or subgeneric name the type species should strictly be determined (Code Article 70 [b]) by application to ICZN. The same applies to *Pseudosimulium* Baranov (q.v.), which is a junior objective synonym of *Boophthora*.

Boreosimulium Rubtsov & Yankovsky 1982, Entomologicheskoe Obozrenie 61:183 (as genus). Type species: *Melusina annulus* Lundström 1911 (Acta Societatis pro Fauna et Flora Fennica 34 [12]:17), by original designation.
Gender: neuter.

Byssodon Enderlein 1925, Zoologischer Anzeiger 62:209 (as genus). Type species: *Simulium forbesi* Malloch 1914 (Technical Series, Bureau of Entomology, U.S. Department of Agriculture 26:63 [= *Simulium meridionale* Riley 1887 (Report U.S. Department of Agriculture 1886: 513)], by original designation.
Gender: masculine.

Cerqueirellum Py-Daniel 1983, Amazoniana 8:165 (as subgenus of *Simulium*). Type species: *Simulium amazonicum* Goeldi 1905 (Memorias du Museu Goeldi de Historia Natural e Ethnographia 4:134), by original designation.
Gender: neuter.

Chelocnetha Enderlein 1936, Sitzungsberichte der Gesellschaft naturforschender Freunde 1936: 117 (as genus). Type species: *Chelocnetha biroi* Enderlein 1936 (ibid.: 117) [= *Simulium ornatipes* Skuse 1890 (Proceedings of the Linnean Society of New South Wales (2)5:632)], by original designation.
Gender: feminine.

Chirostilbia Enderlein 1921 (April), Deutsche Tierärztliche Wochenschrift 29:199 (as genus). Type species: *Chirostilbia flavifemur* Enderlein 1921 (ibid.: 199) [= *Simulium pertinax* Kollar 1832 (Reise im Innern von Brasilien 1:117; Brasiliens vorzüglich lästige Insecten: 19)], by original designation.

Gender: feminine.

Notes: The key characters cited by Enderlein (above reference) confer availability both on the new generic name and the new specific name (*flavifemur*) not previously published, under Code Article 12 (b) (6). Enderlein's intended original description of *flavifemur* appeared later (December) the same year (Sitzungsberichte der Gesellschaft naturforschender Freunde 1921: 79).

Cleitosimulium Séguy & Dorier 1936, Annales de l'Université de Grenoble (n.s.) (Sciences-Médecine) 13:141 (as subgenus of *Simulium*). Type species: *Simulium rupicolum* Séguy & Dorier 1936 (ibid.: 133) [= *Simulia argenteostriata* Strobl 1898 (Glasnik Zemaljskog Museja u Bosni i Hercegovini 10:594)], by original designation.
Gender: neuter.

Notes: Séguy & Dorier's original descriptions of *Cleitosimulium* and *rupicolum* have almost always been erroneously cited as in Travaux du Laboratoire d'Hydrobiologie et de Pisciculture de l'Université de Grenoble 27–29:183–197. In fact, the "Travaux" contains only a subsequently (1939) printed version of the original 1936 paper; to complicate the position, the reprint of the "Travaux" version bears the nominal year "1936", not the actual 1939 distribution date. Although Grenier (1953) correctly cited the original description, current specialists continue mistakenly to cite the "Travaux" as the original reference (e.g., Rubtsov & Yankovsky 1984, Opredeliteli po Faune SSSR 142:140, 171).

Cnephia Enderlein 1921, Deutsche Tierärztliche Wochenschrift 29:199 (as genus). Type species: *Simulium pecuarum* Riley 1887 (Report U.S. Department of Agriculture 1886: 512), by original designation.
Gender: feminine.

Cnesia Enderlein 1934, Deutsche Entomologische Zeitschrift 1933: 273 (as genus). Type species: *Simulium* (*Cnephia*) *gynandrum* Edwards 1931 (Diptera of Patagonia and South Chile II[4]:147) [= *Simulium* (*Cnephia*) *dissimile* Edwards 1931, ibid.: 145)], by original designation.
Gender: feminine.

Cnesiamima Wygodzinsky & Coscarón 1973, Bulletin of the American Museum of Natural History 151:184 (as genus). Type species: *Simulium* (*Cnephia*) *atroparvum* Edwards 1931 (Diptera of Patagonia and South Chile II [4]:148), by original designation.
Gender: feminine.

Cnetha Enderlein 1921, Deutsche Tierärztliche Wochenschrift 29:199 (as genus). Type species: *Simulium vernum* Macquart 1826 (Recueil des Travaux de la Société des Sciences, de l'Agriculture et des Arts de Lille 1823/1824:79), by designation of ICZN (1986, Bull. Zool. Nomencl. 43:264) in Opinion 1416.
Gender: feminine.

Notes: Cnetha is a senior objective synonym of *Pseudonevermannia* Baranov (q.v.) and is on the ICZN Official List of Generic Names in Zoology.

Coscaroniellum Py-Daniel 1983, Amazoniana 8:183 (as subgenus of *Simulium*). Type species: *Simulium quadrifidum* Lutz 1917 (Memorias do Instituto Oswaldo Cruz 9:66), by original designation.
Gender: neuter.

Crenosimulium Giudicelli & Thiery 1985, Bulletin Zoologisch Museum Universiteit van Amsterdam 10:118 (as subgenus of *Simulium*). Type species: *Simulium lamachi* Doby & David 1960 (Vie et Milieu 11:106), by original designation.
Gender: neuter.

Notes: Crenosimulium is a junior objective synonym of *Rubzovia* Petrova, q.v.

Crosskeyellum Grenier & Bailly-Choumara 1970, Cahiers ORSTOM, Entomologie Médicale et Parasitologie 8:96 (as subgenus of *Simulium*). Type species: *Simulium gracilipes*

Edwards 1921 (Annals and Magazine of Natural History [7]9:143), by original designation.

Gender: neuter.

Crozetia Davies 1965, Proceedings of the Linnean Society of London 176:167 (as genus). Type species: *Simulium* (*Cnephia*) *crozetense* Womersley 1937 (British, Australian, and New Zealand Antarctic Research Expedition 1929–1931 Reports [B]4:66), by original designation.

Gender: feminine.

Cryptectemnia Enderlein 1936, Sitzungsberichte der Gesellschaft naturforschender Freunde 1936: 114 (as genus). Type species: *Cryptectemnia laticalx* Enderlein 1936 (ibid.: 114) [junior secondary homonym in *Simulium*, = *Simulium orsovae* Smart 1944 (Proceedings of the Royal Entomological Society of London (B) 13:131, replacement name)], by original designation.

Gender: feminine.

Danubiosimulium Baranov 1935, Arbeiten über morphologische und taxonomische Entomologie 2:158 (as subgenus of *Simulium*). Type species: *Culex columbaczensis* Schönbauer 1795 (Geschichte der Schädlichen Kolumbatczer Mücken im Bannat: 24) [= *Rhagio colombaschensis* Fabricius 1787 (Mantissa insectorum . . . 2:333)], by monotypy.

Gender: neuter.

Dasypelmoza Enderlein 1934, Deutsche Entomologische Zeitschrift 1933: 274 (as genus). Type species: *Simulium varipes* Philippi 1865 (Verhandlungen der kaiserlich-königlichen zoologisch-botanischen Gesellschaft in Wien 15:634) [= *Simulium annulatum* Philippi 1865 (ibid.: 634)], by original designation.

Gender: feminine

Dexomyia Crosskey 1969, Bulletin of the British Museum (Natural History) (Entomology) Supplement 14:49 (as subgenus of *Simulium*). Type species: *Simulium* (*Dexomyia*) *atlanticum* Crosskey 1969 (ibid.: 52), by original designation.

Gender: feminine.

Discosphyria Enderlein 1922, Konowia 1:72 (as genus). Type species: *Discosphyria odagmiina* Enderlein 1922 (ibid.: 72) [? = *Simulium trifasciatum* Curtis 1839 (British Entomology 16:765)], by original designation.

Gender: feminine.

Notes: The holotype (and only original specimen) of *odagmiina* is an intersex specimen not recognized as such by Enderlein.

Distosimulium Peterson 1970, Memoirs of the Entomological Society of Canada 69:30 (as subgenus of *Prosimulium*). Type species: *Prosimulium pleurale* Malloch 1914 (Technical Series, Bureau of Entomology, U.S. Department of Agriculture 26:17), by original designation.

Gender: neuter.

Dyarella Vargas, Martínez Palacios & Díaz Nájera 1946, Revista del Instituto de Salubridad y Enfermedades Tropicales 7:105 (as subgenus of *Simulium*). Type species: *Simulium mexicanum* Bellardi 1862 (Saggio di ditterología messicana [2] appendice: 6), by original designation.

Gender: feminine.

Echinosimulium Baranov 1938, Veterinarski Arhiv 8:317, 322 (as genus). Type species: *Echinosimulium echinatum* Baranov 1938 (ibid.: 313, 323) [= *Atractocera maculata* Meigen 1804 (Klassifikazion und Beschreibung der europäischen Zweiflügeligen Insekten 1:95)], by original designation.

Gender: neuter.

Ectemnaspis Enderlein 1934, Deutsche Entomologische Zeitschrift 1933: 281 (as genus). Type species: *Ectemnaspis macca* Enderlein 1934 (ibid.: 281) [junior secondary homonym in *Simulium,* = *Simulium molli* Vargas 1943 (Revista de la Sociedad Mexicana de Historia Natural 4:142, replacement name) and = *Simulium bicoloratum* Malloch 1912 (Proceedings of the U.S. National Museum 43:649)], by orginal designation. Gender: feminine.

Ectemnia Enderlein 1930, Archiv für klassifikatorische und phylogenetische Entomologie 1:88 (as genus). Type species: *Cnetha taeniatifrons* Enderlein 1925 (Zoologischer Anzeiger 62:206), by original designation. Gender: feminine.

Edwardsellum Enderlein 1921, Deutsche Tierärztliche Wochenschrift 29:199 (as genus). Type species: *Simulium damnosum* Theobald 1903 (Report of the Sleeping Sickness Commission of the Royal Society 3:40), by original designation. Gender: neuter.

Eusimulium Roubaud 1906, Compte Rendu Hebdomadaire des Séances de l'Académie des Sciences, Paris 143:521 (as subgenus of *Simulium*). Type species: *Simulia aurea* Fries 1824 (Observationes entomologicae 1:16), by monotypy. Gender: neuter.

Freemanellum Crosskey 1969, Bulletin of the British Museum (Natural History) (Entomology) Supplement 14:92 (as subgenus of *Simulium*). Type species: *Simulium berghei* Fain 1949 (Revue de Zoologie et de Botanique Africaines 42:296), by original designation. Gender: neuter.

Friesia Enderlein 1922, Konowia 1:69 (as genus). Type species: *Nevermannia tristrigata* Enderlein 1921 (Sitzungsberichte der Gesellschaft naturforschender Freunde 1921: 213 [= *Melusina bezzii* Corti 1914, Atti della Società Italiana di Scienze Naturali e del Museo Civico di Storia Naturale in Milano 53:197, 198)], by original designation. Gender: feminine.

Notes: Friesia Enderlein is a junior homonym, preoccupied by *Friesia* Barnes & McDunnough 1912 (Lepidoptera), and is an isogenotypic synonym of *Tetisimulium* Rubtsov, q.v.

Gibbinsiellum Rubtsov 1962, Zoologicheskii Zhurnal 41:1494 (as genus). Type species: *Simulium griseicollis* Becker 1903 (Mitteilungen aus dem Zoologischen Museum in Berlin 2:78), by original designation. Gender: neuter.

Notes: Gibbinsiellum is a junior isogenotypic synonym of *Psilocnetha* Enderlein, q.v.

Gigantodax Enderlein 1925, Zoologischer Anzeiger 62:205 (as genus). Type species: *Gigantodax bolivianus* Enderlein 1925 (ibid.: 205), by original designation.

Gender: masculine; termination *-odax* or *-dax* is an arbitrary combination of letters not classically derived and masculine gender attributed in original description by ending given to the adjectival name of the only included species (*bolivianus*).

Gnus Rubtsov 1940, Fauna of USSR, Insecta 6(6):363 (as subgenus of *Simulium*). Type species: *Simulium decimatum* Dorogostaisky, Rubtsov & Vlasenko 1935 (Parazitologicheskii Sbornik 5:145, 201), by original designation. Gender: masculine.

Gomphostilbia Enderlein 1921 (April), Deutsche Tierärztliche Wochenschrift 29:199 (as genus). Type species: *Gomphostilbia ceylonica* Enderlein 1921 (ibid.: 199), by original designation. Gender: feminine.

Notes: The key characters cited by Enderlein (above reference) confer availability both on the new generic name and the new specific name (*ceylonica*) not previously published, under Code Article 12(b)(6). Enderlein's intended original description of *ceylonica* appeared later (December) the same year (Sitzungsberichte der Gesellschaft naturforschender Freunde 1921: 77).

Greniera Doby & David 1959, Compte Rendu Hebdomadaire des Séances de l'Académie des Sciences, Paris 249:763 (as genus). Type species: *Greniera fabri* Doby & David 1959 (ibid.: 763), by original designation.

Gender: feminine.

Notes: Both generic and specific names of *Greniera fabri* are available from their first publication by Doby & David 1959 (reference above, issued August 1959) and take the 1959 date. A complete specific description appeared in January 1960 (Doby & David 1960, Bulletin de la Société de Pathologie exotique 52 [1959]: 669) and is usually cited (erroneously) as the original description.

Grenierella Vargas & Díaz Nájera 1951, Revista de la Sociedad Mexicana de Historia Natural 12:141 (as subgenus of *Simulium*). Type species: *Eusimulium lahillei* Paterson & Shannon 1927 (Revista del Instituto Bacteriológico, Buenos Aires 4:740), by original designation.

Gender: feminine.

Gymnopais Stone 1949, Proceedings of the Entomological Society of Washington 51:260 (as genus). Type species: *Gymnopais dichopticus* Stone 1949 (ibid.: 261), by original designation.

Gender: masculine.

Gynonychodon Enderlein 1925, Zoologischer Anzeiger 62:208 (as genus). Type species: *Simulium nobile* de Meijere 1907 (Tijdschrift voor Entomologie 50:206), by original designation.

Gender: masculine.

Hagenomyia Shewell 1959, Canadian Entomologist 91:83 (as subgenus of *Simulium*). Type species: *Simulium pictipes* Hagen 1880 (Proceedings of the Boston Society of Natural History 20:306), by original designation.

Gender: feminine.

Notes: Hagenomyia Shewell is a junior homonym, preoccupied by *Hagenomyia* Banks 1911 (Neuroptera). See *Shewellomyia.*

Haimophaga Rubtsov 1977, New and little-known species of insects in the European part of the USSR: 49 (as subgenus of *Ahaimophaga*). Type species: *Prosimulium multicaulis* Popov 1968 (Parazitologiya 2:444), by original designation.

Gender: feminine.

Notes: The nominal taxon *Haimophaga* was proposed as a subgenus of *Ahaimophaga* monotypic for *multicaulis* Popov, but the simultaneously proposed new generic name *Ahaimophaga* is not available because no type species was designated (see entry for *Ahaimophaga*). The availability of *Haimophaga* from the Rubtsov 1977 work is questionable because, although a type species is designated, there is no description or definition for the new nominal genus-group taxon—only a statement that *multicaulis* differs from the other *Ahaimophaga* species by the bloodsucking structure of the mouthparts. Although extremely borderline for availability under the Code, *Haimophaga* is here accepted as available from the 1977 Rubtsov work, in accordance with Rubtsov & Yankovsky (1984, Opredeliteli po Faune SSSR 142:37); if not so treated, then it becomes available from that 1984 work (which contains an extensive diagnosis) and takes Rubtsov & Yankovsky joint authorship.

Hearlea Vargas, Martínez Palacios & Díaz Nájera 1946, Revista del Instituto de Salubridad y Enfermedades Tropicales 7:104, 106, 159 (as subgenus of *Simulium*). Type species: *Simulium virgatum canadensis* Hearle 1932 (Proceedings of the Entomological Society of British Columbia 29:14), by original designation.

Gender: feminine.

Notes: Hearlea Rubtsov 1940 (Fauna of USSR, Insecta 6 [6]:116, 126) is an unavailable name, for although accompanied by designation of a type species there is no description or definition of the taxon. *Hearlea* takes availability and authorship from Vargas et al. (reference above).

Hebridosimulium Grenier & Rageau 1961, Bulletin de la Société de Pathologie exotique 54:96 (as genus). Type species: *Simulium jolyi* Roubaud 1906 (Bulletin du Muséum d'Histoire Naturelle, Paris 12:142), by original designation.
Gender: neuter.

Hellichia Enderlein 1925, Zoologischer Anzeiger 62:203 (as genus). Type species: *Hellichia latifrons* Enderlein 1925 (ibid.: 204) [= *Melusina macropyga* Lundström 1911 (Acta Societatis pro Fauna et Flora Fennica 34 (12):20)], by original designation.
Gender: feminine.
Notes: Hellichia Enderlein and *Taeniopterna* Enderlein (q.v.) are simultaneously published isogenotypic synonyms.

Hellichiella Rivosecchi & Cardinali 1975, Rivista di Parassitologia 36:69 (as genus). Type species: *Eusimulium saccai* Rivosecchi 1967 (Rivista di Parassitologia 28:63), by original designation.
Gender: feminine.

Helodon Enderlein 1921, Deutsche Tierärztliche Wochenschrift 29:199 (as genus). Type species: *Simulia ferruginea* Wahlberg 1844 (Öfversigt af Kongl. Vetenskaps-Akademiens Forhandligar, Stockholm 1:110) [= *Simulia rufa* Meigen 1838, Systematische Beschreibung der bekannten europäischen zweiflügeligen Insekten 7:54)], by original designation.
Gender: masculine.

Hemicnetha Enderlein 1934, Sitzungsberichte der Gesellschaft naturforschender Freunde 1934: 190 (as genus). Type species: *Hemicnetha mexicana* Enderlein 1934 (ibid.: 190) [junior secondary homonym in *Simulium*, = *Simulium* (*Eusimulium*) *paynei* Vargas 1942 (Revista del Instituto de Salubridad y Enfermedades Tropicales 3:245, replacement name)], by original designation.
Gender: feminine.

Himalayum Lewis 1973, Bulletin of Entomological Research 62:460 (as subgenus of *Simulium*). Type species: *Simulium indicum* Becher 1885 (Journal of the Asiatic Society of Bengal 53 [1884]: 199), by original designation.
Gender: neuter.

Inaequalium Coscarón & Wygodzinsky 1984, Arquivos de Zoología, São Paulo 31:78 (as subgenus of *Simulium*). Type species: *Eusimulium inaequalis* Paterson & Shannon 1927 (Revista del Instituto Bacteriológico, Buenos Aires 4:739), by original designation.
Gender: neuter.
Notes: The name was first published by Coscarón (1981, Revista de la Sociedad Entomológica Argentina 39[1980]:293, 301) as *Simulium* (*Inaequalium*) without named included species and without a definition or description of the subgeneric taxon; *Inaequalium* Coscarón is therefore unavailable (*nomen nudum*).

Inseliellum Rubtsov 1974, Trudy Zoologicheskogo Instituta, Leningrad 53:275 (as genus). Type species: *Simulium oviceps* Edwards 1933 (Pacific Entomological Survey Publication 6[7]:37), by original designation (and monotypy; see Notes).
Gender: neuter.
Notes: No description or definition of *Inseliellum* was given by Rubtsov when he proposed the name and none has been given subsequently. Availability of the name rests upon his inclusion of only one species (*oviceps*), his citation of this as the type species, and his back-reference to the work of Grenier & Rageau (1960, Bulletin de la Société de Pathologie exotique 53:727–742), in which *oviceps* is described and figured. Since *Inseliellum,* as proposed, was monotypic, the characters cited for

oviceps by Grenier & Rageau also constitute defining criteria for *Inseliellum* Rubtsov and accord this name availability under Article 13(a)(ii) of the Code, even though Grenier & Rageau did not base any group as such on *oviceps*.

Kempfsimulium Py-Daniel & Nunes de Mello in Py-Daniel 1982, Amazoniana 7:294 (as genus). Type species: *Simulium simplicicolor* Lutz 1910 (Memorias do Instituto Oswaldo Cruz 2:251), by original designation.

Gender: neuter.

Lanea Vargas, Martínez Palacios & Díaz Nájera 1946, Revista del Instituto de Salubridad y Enfermedades Tropicales 7:103, 107 (as subgenus of *Simulium*). Type species: *Simulium haematopotum* Malloch 1914 (Technical Series, Bureau of Entomology, U.S. Department of Agriculture 26:62), by original designation.

Gender: feminine.

Levitinia Chubareva & Petrova 1981, Entomologicheskoe Obozrenie 60:898 (as genus). Type species: *Levitinia tacobi* Chubareva & Petrova 1981 (ibid.: 899), by original designation.

Gender: feminine.

Lewisellum Crosskey 1969, Bulletin of the British Museum (Natural History) (Entomology) Supplement 14:76 (as subgenus of *Simulium*). Type species: *Simulium neavei* Roubaud 1915 (Bulletin de la Société Entomologique de France 1915: 293), by original designation.

Gender: neuter.

Lutzsimulium d'Andretta & d'Andretta 1947, Memorias do Instituto Oswaldo Cruz 44 (1946): 402 (as genus). Type species: *Lutzsimulium cruzi* d'Andretta & d'Andretta 1947 (ibid.: 402) [= *Simulium hirticosta* Lutz 1909 (Memorias do Instituto Oswaldo Cruz 1:135)], by original designation.

Gender: neuter.

Notes: Because of typographical errors, including the misarrangement of paragraphs, the paper containing the original description of *Lutzsimulium* and its type species was reprinted the next year in the same journal; see d'Andretta & d'Andretta (1948, Memorias do Instituto Oswaldo Cruz 45 [1947]: 667–677). The authors' names are misspelled: "d'Andreta" in the first (1947) version, but corrected to "d'Andretta" in the 1948 version.

Mallochella Enderlein 1930, Archiv für klassifikatorische und phylogenetische Entomologie 1:91 (as genus). Type species: *Mallochella sibirica* Enderlein 1930 (ibid.: 91) [= *Simulia hirtipes* Fries 1824 (Observationes entomologicae 1:17)], by original designation.

Gender: neuter.

Notes: Mallochella Enderlein is a junior homonym, preoccupied by *Mallochella* Duda 1925 (Diptera Sphaeroceridae). See *Mallochianella.*

Mallochianella Vargas & Díaz Nájera 1948, Revista del Instituto de Salubridad y Enfermedades Tropicales 9:67. Replacement name for *Mallochella* Enderlein (preoccupied) and same type species.

Gender: feminine.

Mayacnephia Wygodzinsky & Coscarón 1973, Bulletin of the American Museum of Natural History 151:144 (as genus). Type species: *Simulium pachecolunai* de Leon 1945 (Boletín Sanitario, Guatemala 52:67), by original designation.

Gender: feminine.

Meilloniellum Rubtsov 1962, Zoologicheskii Zhurnal 41:1496 (as genus). Type species: *Simulium hirsutum* Pomeroy 1922 (Bulletin of Entomological Research 12:458), by original designation.

Gender: neuter.

Metacnephia Crosskey 1969, Bulletin of the British Museum (Natural History) (Entomology)

Supplement 14:26 (as genus). Type species: *Cnephia saileri* Stone 1952 (Proceedings of the Entomological Society of Washington 54:82), by original designation.

Gender: feminine.

Notes: The year 1962 given for *saileri* at the head of the original description of *Metacnephia* is an error for 1952.

Metomphalus Enderlein 1935, Sitzungsberichte der Gesellschaft naturforschender Freunde 1935:361 (as genus). Type species: *Metomphalus caffer* Enderlein 1935 (ibid.: 362) [= *Simulium medusaeformis* Pomeroy 1920 (Annals and Magazine of Natural History (9) 6:76)], by original designation.

Gender: masculine.

Miodasia Enderlein 1936, Tierwelt Mitteleuropas 6(2) (Insecta 3):39 (as genus). Type species: *Miodasia opalinipennis* Enderlein 1936 (ibid.: 39) [? = *Atractocera nigra* Meigen 1804 (Klassifikazion und Beschreibung der europäischen Zweiflügeligen Insekten 1:96)], by original designation.

Gender: feminine.

Notes: The nominal type species *opalinipennis* is expected to be synonymized shortly with *nigra* Meigen. When that synonymy has been formally established, *Miodasia* will become a junior isogenotypic synonym of *Schoenbaueria* Enderlein, q.v.

Montisimulium Rubtsov 1974, Trudy Zoologicheskogo Instituta, Leningrad 53:275 (as genus). Type species: *Simulium schevyakovi* Dorogostaisky, Rubtsov & Vlasenko 1935 (Parazitologicheskii Sbornik 5:173), by original designation.

Gender: neuter.

Notes: The proposal of *Montisimulium* is not associated with a description or definition of the taxon, but as the name is accompanied by back-reference to the prior description of the *montium*-group by Rubtsov (1956, Fauna of USSR [Ed.2] 6[6]:392), and by designation of a species included in that group, it is available under Article 13(a)(ii) of the Code.

Morops Enderlein 1930, Archiv für klassifikatorische und phylogenetische Entomologie 1:93 (as genus). Type species: *Wilhelmia pygmaea* Enderlein 1922 (Konowia 1:70) [junior secondary homonym in *Simulium*, = *Simulium wilhelmlandae* Smart 1944 (Proceedings of the Royal Entomological Society of London (B) 13:132, replacement name)], by original designation.

Gender: masculine.

Neosimulium Vargas, Martínez Palacios & Díaz Nájera 1946, Revista del Instituto de Salubridad y Enfermedades Tropicales 7:103, 108, 160 (as subgenus of *Simulium*). Type species: *Simulia vittata* Zetterstedt 1838 (Insecta lapponica: 803), by original designation.

Gender: neuter.

Notes: Vargas et al. attributed the name *Neosimulium* to Rubtsov (1940, Fauna of USSR, Insecta 6[6]:116, 124), but the name in Rubtsov's work is not accompanied by a description or definition of the taxon and is an unavailable *nomen nudum*. The genus-group name *Neosimulium* therefore takes availability from Vargas et al. (reference above).

Nevermannia Enderlein 1921, Deutsche Tierärztliche Wochenschrift 29:199 (as genus). Type species: *Simulium annulipes* Becker 1908 (Mitteilungen aus dem Zoologischen Museum in Berlin 4:72) [= *Simulium ruficorne* Macquart 1838 (Mémoires de la Société Royal des Sciences, de l'Agriculture et des Arts de Lille 1838(2):88)], by original designation.

Gender: feminine.

Nipponosimulium Shogaki 1956, Zoological Magazine, Tokyo 65:276 (as subgenus of *Simulium*). Unavailable name.

Gender: neuter.

Notes: Shogaki proposed the subgenus *Nipponosimulium,* with some descriptive matter and figures, for one Japanese species given the vernacular terminology "sp. J-4" by Bentinck (1955, Black Flies of Japan and Korea: 7). As it is a post-1930 proposal not based on a nominal species eligible to be its type, the name *Nipponosimulium* is unavailable. There is no later use of *Nipponosimulium* that confers availability on this name, but it should be noted that *Eusimulium shogakii* Rubtsov (1962, Fliegen der palaearktischen Region 14:305) is a formal description of "sp. J-4".

Notolepria Enderlein 1930, Archiv für klassifikatorische und phylogenetische Entomologie 1:95 (as genus). Type species: *Simulium exiguum* Roubaud 1906 (Bulletin du Muséum d'Histoire Naturelle, Paris 12:108), by original designation.

Gender: feminine.

Novaustrosimulium Dumbleton 1973, New Zealand Journal of Science 15 (1972): 484 (as subgenus of *Austrosimulium*). Type species: *Simulium bancrofti* Taylor 1918 (Australian Zoologist 1:168), by original designation.

Gender: neuter.

Obuchovia Rubtsov 1947, Izvestiya Akademii Nauk SSSR (Biol.) 1947 (1):90, 105 (as subgenus of *Simulium*). Type species: *Simulium* (*Obuchovia*) *albellum* Rubtsov 1947 (ibid.: 116), by monotypy.

Gender: feminine.

Odagmia Enderlein 1921, Deutsche Tierärztliche Wochenschrift 29:199 (as genus). Type species: *Simulia ornata* Meigen 1818 (Systematische Beschreibung der bekannten Europäischen zweiflügeligen Insekten 1:290), by original designation.

Gender: feminine.

Parabyssodon Rubtsov 1964, Fliegen der palaearktischen Region 14:623 (as genus). Type species: *Simulium* (*Byssodon*) *transiens* Rubtsov 1940 (Fauna of USSR, Insecta 6[6]:361), by original designation.

Gender: masculine.

Notes: There is no formal definition or description with the original publication of this name, but it is available because some characters are cited that compare *transiens* (the only included species and the designated type species) with the preexisting genus *Byssodon* Enderlein.

Paracnephia Rubtsov 1962, Zoologicheskii Zhurnal 41:1491 (as genus). Type species: *Cnephia muspratti* Freeman & de Meillon, 1953 (Simuliidae of the Ethiopian Region: 30), by original designation.

Gender: feminine.

Paragnus Rubtsov & Yankovsky 1982, Entomologicheskoe Obozrenie 61:184 (as genus). Type species: *Simulium bukovskii* Rubtsov 1940 (Fauna of USSR, Insecta 6[6]:418), by original designation.

Gender: masculine.

Parahelodon Peterson 1970, Memoirs of the Entomological Society of Canada 69:36 (as subgenus of *Prosimulium*). Type species: *Simulium* (*Prosimulium*) *decemarticulatum* Twinn 1936 (Canadian Journal of Research [D] 14:110), by original designation.

Gender: masculine.

Parasimulium Malloch 1914, Technical Series, Bureau of Entomology, U.S. Department of Agriculture 26:24 (as genus). Type species: *Parasimulium furcatum* Malloch 1914 (ibid.: 24), by original designation.

Gender: neuter.

Paraustrosimulium Wygodzinsky & Coscarón 1962, Pacific Insects 4:241 (as subgenus of *Austrosimulium*). Type species: *Simulium anthracinum* Bigot 1888 (Mission scientifique du Cap Horn 1882–1883 6[2] Diptères: 15), by monotypy.

Gender: neuter.

Phoretodagmia Rubtsov 1972, Entomologicheskoe Obozrenie 51:406 (as genus). Type species: *Simulium* (*Odagmia*) *ephemerophilum* Rubtsov 1947 (Izvestiya Akademii Nauk [Biol.] 1:90, 115), by original designation.
Gender: feminine.

Phoretomyia Crosskey 1969, Bulletin of the British Museum (Natural History) (Entomology) Supplement 14:79 (as subgenus of *Simulium*). Type species: *Simulium copleyi* Gibbins 1941 (East African Medical Journal 18:210), by original designation.
Gender: feminine.

Phosterodoros Stone & Snoddy 1969, Bulletin of the Alabama Agricultural Experiment Station 390:32 (as subgenus of *Simulium*). Type species: *Simulium jenningsi* Malloch 1914 (Technical Series, Bureau of Entomology, U.S. Department of Agriculture 26:41), by original designation.
Gender: masculine.

Pliodasina Enderlein 1936, Sitzungsberichte der Gesellschaft naturforschender Freunde 1936: 124 (as genus). Type species: *Pliodasina guttata* Enderlein 1936 (ibid.: 124), by original designation.
Gender: feminine.

Pomeroyellum Rubtsov 1962, Zoologicheskii Zhurnal 41:1492 (as genus). Type species: *Simulium cervicornutum* Pomeroy 1920 (Annals and Magazine of Natural History [9]6:73), by original designation.
Gender: neuter.

Procnephia Crosskey 1969, Bulletin of the British Museum (Natural History) (Entomology) Supplement 14:21 (as subgenus of *Prosimulium*). Type species: *Prosimulium rhodesianum* Crosskey 1968 (Journal of Natural History 2:488), by original designation.
Gender: feminine.

Prosimulium Roubaud 1906, Compte Rendu Hebdomadaire des Séances de l'Académie des Sciences, Paris 143:521 (as subgenus of *Simulium*). Type species: *Simulia hirtipes* Fries 1824 (Observationes entomologicae 1:17), by subsequent designation of Malloch 1914 (Technical Series, Bureau of Entomology, U.S. Department of Agriculture 26:16).
Gender: neuter.

Psaroniocompsa Enderlein 1934, Sitzungsberichte der Gesellschaft naturforschender Freunde 1934: 192 (as genus). Type species: *Psaroniocompsa opalinifrons* Enderlein 1934 (ibid.: 192) [= *Simulium incrustatum* Lutz 1910 (Memorias do Instituto Oswaldo Cruz 2:243)], by original designation.
Gender: feminine.

Pselaphochir Enderlein 1936, Sitzungsberichte der Gesellschaft naturforschender Freunde 1936: 120 (as genus). Type species: *Pselaphochir oculata* Enderlein 1936 (ibid.: 121), by original designation.
Gender: feminine.

Pseudodagmia Baranov 1926, Neue Beiträge zur systematischen Insektenkunde 3:164 (as subgenus of *Odagmia*). Type species: *Simulia variegata* Meigen 1818 (Systematische Beschreibung der Europäischen zweiflügeligen Insekten 1:292), by original designation.
Gender: feminine.

Pseudonevermannia Baranov 1926, Neue Beiträge zur systematische Insektenkunde 3:164 (as subgenus of *Nevermannia*). Type species: *Simulium vernum* Macquart 1826 (Recueil des Travaux de la Société des Sciences, de l'Agriculture et des Arts de Lille 1823/1824: 79), by original designation of ICZN (1986), Bull. Zool. Nomencl. 43:264) in Opinion 1416.
Gender: feminine.

Notes: Pseudonevermannia is a junior objective synonym of *Cnetha* Enderlein, q.v., and is on the ICZN Official Index of Rejected and Invalid Names in Zoology.

Pseudosimulium Baranov 1926, Neue Beiträge zur systematische Insektenkunde 3:164 (as subgenus of *Simulium*). Type species: *Simulia argyreata* Meigen sensu Baranov [= *Tipula erythrocephala* De Geer 1776 (Mémoires pour servir à l'Histoire des Insectes 6:431)], by original designation.

Gender: neuter.

Notes: Pseudosimulium Baranov is a junior homonym, preoccupied by *Pseudosimulium* Handlirsch 1908 (nonsimuliid fossil genus); no replacement name is required as it is a junior objective synonym of *Boophthora* Enderlein. The generic name is based on a misidentified type species, the actual species concerned being *erythrocephala* De Geer, as for *Boophthora* (q.v.).

Psilocnetha Enderlein 1935, Sitzungsberichte der Gesellschaft naturforschender Freunde 1935: 359 (as genus). Type species: *Psilocnetha scapulata* Enderlein 1935 (ibid.: 359) [= *Simulium griseicollis* Becker 1903 (Mitteilungen aus dem Zoologischen Museum in Berlin 2:78)], by original designation.

Gender: feminine.

Notes: Psilocnetha is a senior isogenotypic synonym of *Gibbinsiellum* Enderlein (q.v.).

Psilopelmia Enderlein 1934, Deutsche Entomologische Zeitschrift 1933: 283 (as genus). Type species: *Psilopelmia rufidorsum* Enderlein 1934 (ibid.: 283) [= *Simulium escomeli* Roubaud 1909 (Bulletin de la Société de Pathologie exotique 2:428)], by original designation.

Gender: neuter.

Psilozia Enderlein 1936, Sitzungsberichte der Gesellschaft naturforschender Freunde 1936: 113 (as genus). Type species: *Psilozia groenlandica* Enderlein 1936 (ibid.: 114) [junior secondary homonym in *Simulium*, = *Simulium asakakae* Smart, 1944 (Proceedings of the Royal Entomological Society of London (B) 13:131), replacement name, and = *Simulia vittata* Zetterstedt 1838 (Insecta lapponica: 803)], by original designation.

Gender: feminine.

Notes: Psilozia is a senior isogenotypic synonym of *Neosimulium* Vargas, Martínez Palacios & Díaz Nájera (q.v.).

Pternaspatha Enderlein 1930, Archiv für klassifikatorische und phylogenetische Entomologie 1:88 (as genus). Type species: *Pternaspatha nigristrigata* Enderlein 1930 (ibid.: 88), by original designation.

Gender: feminine.

Rubzovia Petrova 1983, Zoologicheskii Zhurnal 62:1912 (as genus). Type species: *Simulium (Simulium) lamachi* Doby & David 1960 (Vie et Milieu 11:106), by original designation.

Gender: feminine.

Schoenbaueria Enderlein 1921 (April), Deutsche Tierärztliche Wochenschrift 29:199 (as genus). Type species: *Schoenbaueria mathiesseni* Enderlein 1921 (ibid.: 199) [= *Atractocera nigra* Meigen 1804 (Klassifikazion und Beschreibung der europäischen Zweiflügeligen Insekten 1:96)], original designation.

Gender: feminine.

Notes: The key characters cited by Enderlein (above reference) confer availability both on the new generic name and the new specific name (*mathiesseni*) not previously published, under Code Article 12(b) (6). Enderlein's intended original description of *mathiesseni* appeared later (June) the same year (Sitzungsberichte der Gesellschaft naturforschender Freunde 1921: 214).

Shewellomyia Peterson 1975, Canadian Entomologist 107:111. Replacement name for *Hagenomyia* Shewell (preoccupied) and same type species.
Gender: feminine.

Simulium Latreille [1802], Histoire naturelle, générale et particulière, des Crustacés et Insectes 3:426 (as genus). Type species: *Rhagio colombaschensis* Fabricius 1787 (Mantissa insectorum . . . 2:333) [? = *Culex lanio* Linnaeus 1771 (Mantissa plantarum altera: 541)], by monotypy.
Gender: neuter.

Notes: It is nearly certain that the oldest name for the type species of *Simulium* is *lanio* Linnaeus. The original Linnaean description refers to a species clearly simuliid (compared by Linnaeus to *equinum*) from the province of Banat (i.e., Danube basin area, where the Golubatz fly was widely known in the 18th century as a severe biting pest). The description fits *colombaschense* Fabricius well. Types do not exist for either name and *colombaschense* is maintained as the valid name in the interests of continuity.

The title page of Latreille's work in which *Simulium* was first described bears the year "an X" (= year 10), but this is incorrect. It was actually published in an XI (= year 11) of the Revolutionary Calendar (i.e., 22 September 1802 to 21 September 1803) and is accepted as published in 1802: see Griffin (1938, Journal of the Society for the Bibliography of Natural History 1:157).

Stegopterna Enderlein 1930, Archiv für klassifikatorische und phylogenetische Entomologie 1:89 (as genus). Type species: *Stegopterna richteri* Enderlein 1930 (ibid.: 90), by original designation.
Gender: feminine.

Stilboplax Enderlein 1921, Deutsche Tierärztliche Wochenschrift 29:199 (as genus). Type species: *Simulium speculiventre* Enderlein 1914 (Transactions of the Linnean Society of London [2]16:374), by original designation.
Gender: feminine.

Striatosimulium Rubtsov & Yankovsky 1982, Entomologicheskoe Obozrenie 61:186 (as subgenus of *Simulium*). Type species: *Simulium japonicum* Matsumura 1931 (6000 Illustrated Insects of the Japanese Empire: 407), by original designation.
Gender: neuter.

Notes: Rubtsov & Yankovsky in the original description of *Striatosimulium*, and in their re-diagnosis (1984, Opredeliteli po Faune SSSR 142:149) cite *japonicum*, as described by Matsumura on page 62 of his work entitled "Erster Beiträg zur Insekten-Fauna von Sachalin" (Journal of the College of Agriculture, Tohoku Imperial University 4:1–145). The page citation is correct for the only mention of Simuliidae, but Matsumura there refers to "Simulium columbatczensis Schin. Faun. Austr. [= Fauna Austriaca] p.367 (1864)"; there is no mention of the name "*japonicum*", either for a species, a subspecies of "*columbatczensis*" (= *colombaschense* Fabricius), or even as a *nomen nudum*. The citation by Rubtsov & Yankovsky (1984, p. 152) of *japonicum* as originally described by Matsumura in 1911 (as a subspecies of *colombaschense*) is an error. Matsumura did not describe *japonicum* until the 1931 work (reference above). Rubtsov (1963, Fliegen der palaearktischen Region 14:540) correctly attributed *japonicum* Matsumura to the 1931 work.

Sulcicnephia Rubtsov 1971, Annales Historico-naturales Musei Nationalis Hungarici (Zoologica) 63:263 (as genus). Type species: *Simulium (Astega) ovtshinnikovi* Rubtsov 1940 (Fauna of USSR, Insecta 6[6]:323), by original designation.
Gender: feminine.

Taeniopterna Enderlein 1925, Zoologischer Anzeiger 62:203 (as genus). Type species: *Melusina macropyga* Lundström 1911 (Acta Societatis pro Fauna et Flora Fennica 34[12]:20), by original designation.

Gender: feminine.

Notes: Taeniopterna is a simultaneously published isogenotypic synonym of *Hellichia* Enderlein (q.v.)

Tetisimulium Rubtsov 1963, Fliegen der palaearktischen Region 14:497 (as genus). Type species: *Melusina bezzii* Corti 1914 (Atti della Società Italiana di Scienze Naturali e del Museo Civico di Storia Naturali in Milano 53:197, 198), by original designation.

Gender: neuter.

Notes: The name *Tetisimulium* was first published by Rubtsov in 1960 (above-cited work, 117–122), who gave it a "nom. n." marking and (by inference) intended it to be a replacement name for *Friesia* Enderlein (preoccupied) (q.v.); it is not available, however, from the 1960 work because it was not expressly proposed as a replacement for a stipulated available name (Code Article 13[a][iii]). The name takes availability from its subsequent proposal (reference above) in 1963 for a new nominal genus.

Thyrsopelma Enderlein 1934, Deutsche Entomologische Zeitschrift 1933:284 (as genus). Type species: *Thyrsopelma brasiliense* Enderlein 1934 (ibid.: 284) [= *Simulium orbitale* Lutz 1910 (Memorias do Instituto Oswaldo Cruz 2:231)], by original designation.

Gender: neuter.

Titanopteryx Enderlein 1935, Sitzungsberichte der Gesellschaft naturforschender Freunde 1935: 360 (as genus). Type species: *Atractocera maculata* Meigen 1804 (Klassifikazion und Beschreibung der europäischen Zweiflügeligen Insekten 1:95), by original designation.

Gender: feminine.

Notes: Titanopteryx is a senior isogenotypic synonym of *Echinosimulium* Baranov (q.v.).

Tlalocomyia Wygodzinsky & Díaz Nájera 1970, Revista de Investigación en Salud Pública 30:83 (as genus). Type species: *Tlalocomyia revelata* Wygodzinsky & Díaz Nájera 1970 (ibid.: 88), by original designation.

Gender: feminine.

Trichodagmia Enderlein 1934, Deutsche Entomologische Zeitschrift 1933: 288 (as genus). Type species: *Trichodagmia latitarsis* Enderlein 1934 (ibid.: 289) [= *Simulium chalcocoma* Knab 1914 (Proceedings of the Biological Society of Washington 27:85)], by original designation.

Gender: feminine.

Twinnia Stone & Jamnback 1955, Bulletin of the New York State Museum 349:18 (as genus). Type species: *Twinnia tibblesi* Stone & Jamnback 1955 (ibid.: 19), by original designation.

Gender: feminine.

Urosimulium Contini 1963, Memorie della Società Entomologica Italiana 42:89 (as genus). Type species: *Urosimulium stefanii* Contini 1963 (ibid.: 89) [= *Prosimulium aculeatum* Rivosecchi 1963 (Parassitologia 5:119)], by original designation.

Gender: feminine.

Notes: The name *aculeatum* dates from July 1963 and *stefanii* from October 1963; the former is the senior synonym.

Wallacellum Takaoka 1983, Blackflies of the Philippines: 20 (as subgenus of *Simulium*). Type species: *Simulium (Eusimulium) carinatum* Delfinado 1969 (Journal of Medical Entomology 6:206), by original designation.

Gender: neuter.

Wilhelmia Enderlein 1921, Deutsche Tierärztliche Wochenschrift 29:199 (as genus). Type species: *Atractocera lineata* Meigen 1804 (Klassifikazion und Beschreibung der europäischen Zweiflügeligen Insekten 1:95), by original designation.

Gender: feminine.

Xenosimulium Crosskey 1969, Bulletin of the British Museum (Natural History) (Entomology) Supplement 14:86 (as subgenus of *Simulium*). Type species: *Simulium imerinae* Roubaud 1905 (Bulletin du Muséum d'Histoire Naturelle, Paris 11:426), by original designation.

Gender: neuter.

REFERENCES

Courtney, G. W. 1986. Discovery of the immature stages of *Parasimulium crosskeyi* Peterson (Diptera: Simuliidae), with a discussion of a unique black fly habitat. *Proc. Entomol. Soc. Wash.* 88:280–286.

Crosskey, R. W. 1969. A re-classification of the Simuliidae (Diptera) of Africa and its islands. *Bull. Br. Mus. (Nat. Hist.) (Entomol.) Suppl.* 14:1–195.

———. 1981. Simuliid taxonomy—the contemporary scene. Pp. 3–18 in M. Laird, Ed., *Blackflies: the future for biological methods in integrated control.* Academic Press, New York and London. xii + 399 pp.

———. 1985. The authorship, dating, and application of suprageneric names in the Simuliidae (Diptera). *Entomol. Monthly Mag.* 121:167–178.

Lincoln, R. J., G. A. Boxshall, and P. F. Clark. 1982. *A dictionary of ecology, evolution and systematics.* Cambridge Univ. Press. Cambridge. [viii] + 298 pp.

Rubtsov, I. A. 1974. On the evolution, phylogeny and classification of blackflies (Simuliidae: Diptera). *Trudy Zoologicheskogo Instituta, Leningrad* 53:230–281 (in Russian).

Rubtsov, I. A., and A. V. Yankovsky. 1984. Key to the genera of Palaearctic blackflies. *Opredeliteli po Faune SSSR* 142:1–175 (in Russian).

Smart, J. 1945. The classification of the Simuliidae (Diptera). *Trans. R. Entomol. Soc. London* 95:463–532.

Stone, A. 1963. An annotated list of genus-group names in the family Simuliidae (Diptera). *U.S. Dept. Agric. Tech. Bull.* 1284:1–28.

INDEX TO THE CHECKLIST

The index is confined to the page entry for each name given in the main checklist text. The valid names for genera and subgenera are shown in bold type. Multiple uses of the same specific name by the same author are differentiated by the addition of the appropriate generic or subgeneric names. Names now known not to belong in the Simuliidae, although once thought to apply to black flies (see the Introduction), are included in order that they can still be traced.

INDEX

This index contains subject entries and scientific names of genera and species complexes. Scientific names are in italic and species complexes are indexed under each generic name.